I0592139

Wilhelm Busch

England Under the Tudors

Wilhelm Busch

England Under the Tudors

ISBN/EAN: 9783744713689

Printed in Europe, USA, Canada, Australia, Japan

Cover: Foto ©ninafisch / pixelio.de

More available books at **www.hansebooks.com**

BURT FRANKLIN RESEARCH & SOURCE WORKS SERIES 80

ENGLAND UNDER THE TUDORS.

ENGLAND
UNDER THE TUDORS

KING HENRY VII
(1485–1509).

BY

DR. WILHELM BUSCH

TRANSLATED

BY

ALICE M. TODD

WITH AN INTRODUCTION AND SOME COMMENTS BY
JAMES GAIRDNER

BURT FRANKLIN RESEARCH & SOURCE WORKS SERIES 80

BURT FRANKLIN
NEW YORK

PUBLISHED BY
BURT FRANKLIN
235 EAST 44TH ST.
NEW YORK, N. Y. 10017

FIRST PUBLISHED

LONDON

1895

PRINTED IN U.S.A.

INTRODUCTION.

ALTHOUGH English history has been his principal study, the name of Dr. Wilhelm Busch is not yet so well known in this country as in his own, where, after being eagerly sought for as a teacher by one university after another, he now fills a professorship of history at Freiburg, in Baden. Yet his writings on sixteenth-century diplomacy, and especially on the foreign policy of Cardinal Wolsey, have attracted the attention of scholars, not only in this country and in Germany, but in France; and it is already evident that whoever hereafter intends to make himself thoroughly acquainted with the beginnings of our modern European system must devote a certain amount of study to Dr. Busch's writings. But, if we may judge of the future by the past, the student's debt to him will certainly be much more considerable when he has finished the work of which the first volume, published in German three years ago at Stuttgart, is here presented to the English reader in his own language.

As I have special reason for taking an interest in this first volume, and some notes of mine are actually appended to it, I may perhaps be allowed here to say a few words, not only for Dr. Busch, but for myself. It is very many years now since my attention was first devoted to the reign of Henry VII., and I collected in one of the earlier volumes of the Rolls Series of Chronicles certain "Memorials" of that reign, which I heartily wish had been edited with better knowledge and training on my part. The contents of that volume, however, being original documents of the period, had a value independent of the editing; and it was shortly afterwards followed up by two other volumes of papers relating to the same period. In these three volumes I really exhausted all the more readable and significant of the then unprinted documents of the reign that were to be found in our English archives, either in the Record Office, the British Museum, or, so far as I knew, in other repositories at home. The extreme scantiness of this sort of material was the more to be regretted as the period was one in which there were no more monastic chronicles, and for anything like a full account of its history from a contemporary pen we were indebted only to the Italian, Polydore Vergil, who is the main source of the information given by Bacon, Hume, Lingard, and all our English historians in treating of Henry VII.'s time.

Since that day, however, the archives of Simancas and of Venice and Northern Italy have been explored by students employed by the British Government, and a flood of light has been thrown on many matters that were before obscure. Much occupied with other things, it was always a source of regret to me that I have never been able to follow up the advantages thus gained by a fuller and more systematic study both of the new evidences and of the old; and even when Mr. John Morley did me the honour to ask me to contribute a volume on Henry VII. to his series of "Twelve English Statesmen," although I felt unable to decline, I could not help feeling a slight misgiving about putting forth another imperfect study on a subject on which I had already written with inadequate information without being able even yet to do it serious justice. No one, however, had as yet popularized the new material, and it seemed right that the results of so much investigation should be combined and made more generally known. So I trust that my volume supplied a real want, even though it was quite impossible for me to devote very elaborate study to its production.

The day will doubtless come when the documentary evidences at home for the reign of the first Tudor will be more comprehensively treated than they can possibly be even yet for some time to come. But I can certify from personal knowledge that Professor Busch has made the best use of those now available, even in MS., in his researches at the Record Office and the British Museum. The reader will also see that he has made a very careful study of printed evidences like the Rolls of Parliament. These studies, however, taken by themselves, would not have enabled him to perform such a service to English history as he has done in the present volume. Just as we are indebted to two foreigners—Polydore Vergil and Bernard André (for even the latter tells us something)—for the only contemporary histories of Henry VII., so also the most significant contemporary documents connected with the reign are to be found in foreign archives. And though a rich harvest of these has been already gathered in for the English student by the researches of Bergenroth and Rawdon Brown, there is certainly more to be found in the archives of German duchies and the commercial records of the Hanseatic League. The latter, indeed, have been already published; but Dr. Busch has been the first to utilise their contents specially in connection with English history. And the same may be said of his use of Ulmann's important labours on the reign of Maximilian in Germany, and of a number of foreign publications most helpful to the general student of the period, which in England we should be in danger of treating with too much neglect. For the foreign policy of Henry VII. was really the mainstay of his government; and it is obvious that a foreign policy in any age can only be appreciated when we have before us a clear view of the international relations of all foreign countries.

It is not, therefore, altogether a surprising thing that a learned German has been able to throw a number of sidelights upon this particular epoch of our own history, which an Englishman, after many years of study, would not easily have discovered. That which an English reader might be less prepared to expect is a very careful analysis of such original evidences as we possess at home, whether published or unpublished, and, at the same time, a very clear-sighted examination of the working of our English Constitution at a particularly interesting stage of its development. It is true, of course, that the British Constitution is a never-ending study to foreigners, and not least to Germans; but it is not always historically treated even by them, and still more rarely, I fear it must be said, among ourselves. Perhaps the very liberty which we enjoy at the present day disables us to a large extent from realizing the "enlightened despotism" out of which it may really be said to have been gradually evolved.

With these general remarks I leave Dr. Busch's work to find its own way among English readers of English history.

JAMES GAIRDNER.

KING HENRY VII.

(1485–1509).

BY

DR. WILHELM BUSCH.

TO

WILHELM MAURENBRECHER,

JULY 30, 1892.

AUTHOR'S PREFACE.

To my kind and fatherly friend and teacher I dedicate this opening volume of my work, as a humble offering, on the twenty-fifth anniversary of the day on which he entered upon his first regular duties as Professor of history. What I here present is the outcome and expansion of the studies begun under his guidance.

I purpose writing the history of the Tudor period, in a series of six volumes, down to the death of Elizabeth; and though in the titles I cannot conveniently indicate this, I propose that every two volumes shall definitely comprise one of the following principal epochs in the development of this period:—First, the establishment and building up of the new Tudor Absolutism by Henry VII. and Cardinal Wolsey; secondly, the struggle over the Church begun by this absolute monarchy with the schism under Henry VIII.; finally, the completion of the whole work of the century in the age of Elizabeth.

My first intention was to treat of the time of Henry VII. briefly as a mere introduction to the rest, but as I went on, the fundamental importance of this reign, from every point of view, became more clear to me, and I saw the necessity of investigating it in all its aspects, and treating them in

connection with each other. For my desire is to take as
comprehensive and many-sided a view as possible of the
development of England in the sixteenth century. How I
propose to carry this out, this first volume will show. Much
must, of course, be reserved to be dealt with later on. Thus,
the history of intellectual development cannot be detached
from the story of the next epoch, and will therefore be discussed in its true connection in the following volume.

I must in my history of necessity tread upon much
ground where I am not, nor can be, at home ; and although
I have been fortunate enough to obtain much advice from
friends, I feel I must still beg for indulgence. I can only
hope that, with those advantages which naturally belong to
the historian who treats his subject as a connected whole,
I may be able to contribute something to further the general
appreciation of such subjects as trade, industry, agriculture,
and the administration of justice, which have hitherto always
been separately dealt with.

I give in Appendix II. full particulars as to the materials
which form the basis of my work. In order to avoid the
danger of too great length in the narrative portion, all
discussion is relegated to the notes in Appendix I. ; in
which, also, to shorten the footnotes, I have placed the
references whenever they could be collected in larger paragraphs. Of satisfactory previous investigations there is a
great dearth. In fact, the only exceptions are, for single
points, Mr. Gairdner's prefaces to his various publications,
and especially his monograph on Perkin Warbeck, on which
subject Madden had preceded him. Otherwise, this minute
research into details had still to be gone through, and especially that thorough examination into the original sources,
according to the principles of comparative historical criticism,

which had not as yet been attempted. Thus a dispro-
portionate increase of the critical appendix was not to be
avoided, and I can only hope that it will increase the value
of the previous narrative.

To compress the references into as small a space as possible, I have abbreviated all the titles of books mentioned,
and in Appendix III. subjoin a list of these in alphabetical
order, under the leading words by which they are cited,
with their full title and description. Owing to State Papers
having been repeatedly published, and often without knowledge of the earlier editions, I have considered it necessary to
mention all the publications I have come across which contain them. A general alphabetical index will follow shortly
with the second volume; the materials for this volume have
already for the most part been collected, and I hope before
very long to announce its appearance.

I have received much assistance in many ways in the
prosecution of my work. To Mr. James Gairdner, of the
London Public Record Office, I acknowledge not only that
debt of gratitude which every historical inquirer owes to the
predecessor of whose work he makes use and in whose foot-
steps he treads, but also a further obligation for the ready
personal help of all kinds which he bestowed on me when
I was in London. Every facility and convenience for my
studies were also given me by the authorities at the British
Museum, especially by my kind friend Mr. Fortescue. I
gladly acknowledge, with special thanks, the friendly
assistance afforded me for various sections of my work
by my friends Professor Richard Schmidt, at Freiburg
in Baden; Professor Brockhaus, Dr. Gess, and Professor
Stein, in Leipzig; and my brother-in-law, Professor Sering,
in Berlin.

CONTENTS.

ENGLAND UNDER THE TUDORS.

INTRODUCTION.

THE whole development of the English State throughout the last six centuries has been indissolubly bound up with the growth of its Parliamentary Constitution: Development both advanced together. Like an island in the of the English midst of this stream of steady and uninterrupted nation. progress, stands out the epoch of personal government under the House of Tudor. The Parliament had but a small share in the great onward movement and mighty revolutions of that remarkable century; rather it lost much of the position which it had won for itself in the English State before the close of the Middle Ages.

Her Parliamentary Constitution had been England's chief creation during the Middle Ages, and was peculiar to herself. Her isolated position, surrounded by the sea, had afforded a possibility of development, undisturbed by outside influences, such as had been granted to no other country. The sea, however, had not served always as a bulwark to England, for, in the first centuries of historic times, one foreign race after another poured as conquerors into the country, and a long struggle ensued between various nations for the lordship and possession of the land. These struggles became the more wild and bloody, because it was difficult, if not impossible, for the vanquished to be dislodged, or for the invaders to draw back from the island.

The Keltic Britons, whom Cæsar encountered as the aboriginal inhabitants of the country, did not exercise any

B

appreciable influence on its future development, and even of
the Roman rule, which gave to the Britons culture, political
order, and Christianity, only fragmentary relics remain. The
history of the English nation begins, in fact, in the fifth
century, with the occupation of the country by the North
German tribes, who, under the collective name of the Anglo-
Saxons, after a war of conquest lasting for two hundred years,
made themselves masters of the land. But the political
institutions, which they originated, were not destined to
endure. In the year 1066, the Anglo-Saxon kingdom, already
falling to pieces under a degenerate monarchy, was overthrown
by a new conqueror, the Norman duke, William.

With this powerful founder of a kingdom the history of
the English State begins. The long war of races was drawing
Norman and to a close. The vanquished Anglo-Saxons still,
Angevin indeed, confronted the Franco-Norman invaders,
kings. but, instead of one race seeking to supplant and
destroy the other, a period of national fusion set in. The
result was that the conquered race remained almost intact
in its national peculiarities, and absorbed the more pliable
conqueror, whilst, on the other hand, the Anglo-Norman
State became a perfectly new creation, into which were
engrafted only those institutions of the ruined Anglo-Saxon
polity, that were suitable to it.

Over these nationalities, standing side by side, but at first
in hostility, arose the autocratic monarchy of William and his
successors, dominating and holding them together. It was
the beginning of a united State under a monarchy, without
a homogeneous people, and without a national king. And
whilst, favoured by the ruler, national unity soon began, the
hope that the monarchy itself might become a national one
seemed to recede still further into the background. When
Henry II., in 1154, began the glorious line of princes of the
House of Anjou-Plantagenet, England formed only one part
of the great Angevin kingdom on both sides of the Channel,
the continental possessions of which comprised more than
half of France. England was threatened with the fate of
being compelled to expend her powers on a task contrary to
her national interests, that of supporting the imperial policy
of her kings against the not unreasonable claims of the

French Crown. But this dangerous imperialism lasted only a short time; the rule of such a miserable monarch as Henry's younger son John was destined to confer upon the country a blessing which cannot be too highly valued. Under him the greater part of these continental possessions fell into the hands of France, and the kingdom, till then half French, confined more and more to England alone, began to become entirely English.

The short period during which the Angevin kingdom lasted was also of the highest importance from another point of view: to it belongs the internal development of the Constitution, which throughout the whole Middle Ages was being defined by the struggle between two powers in the State— the monarchy and the aristocracy. In the place of the Germanic monarchy of the Anglo-Saxons, ruling in conjunction with a national assembly, the Norman conquerors, with their own peculiar form of the feudal system, had substituted a completely autocratic feudal monarchy, which made every effort to keep in check ambitious vassals. We are reminded of the struggle of the German sovereigns with the aristocratic constitutional party in the Empire. It was to the quarrel which had broken out between the Crown and the Hierarchy that the English magnates also owed the great change which took place in their own position. In the struggle between Henry IV. and Gregory VII. the German monarchy received its death blow; a century later King Henry II. of England called his vassals to his assistance in his struggle with the Church, and in return found himself obliged to give them a joint participation in the government.

In Germany the success of the nobility had involved an increase of power for individual territorial lords, and at the same time the inevitable disruption of the empire as a whole; whereas it was the incomparable good fortune of England that, from the very beginning of the new movement, the increase of power benefited not the individual, but the whole body of vassals together. In the old Anglo-Saxon kingdom, whenever the monarchy was weak, disruption and disintegration were at once imminent—never more so than on the eve of the Conquest; now, after the amalgamation of the two races had been accomplished, the new aristocratic revolution, which began in England, offered in conjunction with the monarchy, not disruption, but a fresh guarantee for the unity of the kingdom; the destructive power of individualism was here no longer known.

Again, John's unhappy reign was rendered memorable by that confirmation of their new position, which the vassals, **The Great** in coalition with the ecclesiastical lords, wrested **Charter.** from their tyrannical ruler in the Great Charter of 1215. This important document marks the first stage in the early development of the English Constitution.

No peace, however, was brought about by this means; the great struggle went on without interruption, and occupied the whole reign of John's weak son, Henry III. The contending parties endeavoured to enlist allies, and sought them far and wide in the various ranks of the nation. After some imperfect assemblies had already been called, it was Simon de Montfort, the leader of the nobles, who, in 1264, formed a precedent by summoning, together with the barons, knights from each shire and burgesses from various towns, an example which later was followed by Edward I. in 1295.

The reign of this monarch marks a memorable epoch. In it the legal system of the England of to-day and England's present Constitution had their origin. His distinguished predecessors, the Norman William I., the Frenchman, Henry II., were foreigners; Edward was the first great English king. Henry II. had led the way to the conquest of Ireland; but far more important were the new advances made by Edward, in subduing Wales and establishing England's feudal supremacy over Scotland. The unity of Great Britain could not be accomplished without a struggle of many centuries; the same also was needed for completing the structure, and establishing the constitutional position of the Parliament founded under Edward I.

Henceforth it was recognised that the Estates of the realm assembled in Parliament—the prelates and barons as a body, **The Parlia-** the borough and county constituencies through **ment.** representatives drawn from the propertied classes —should, by their constitutional rights to a share in the government, limit the power of the Crown. The union of the lower vassals, the knights of the shire. to the burgesses representing the towns, and the fact that, to enable any Act of Parliament to pass, the concurrence of all three Estates was necessary, prevented the separation of those Estates, which might otherwise easily have taken place. Though the Lords and Commons sat in two separate Houses, the common voice of the State was nowhere so clearly heard as in the Parliament representing the nation.

Parliament still continued to be the representative of the national interests, when the Crown once more indulged in the imperialistic ideas of the Angevins, when Edward III. put forward his claim to the French throne, and that unhappy hundred years' war against France began. No doubt in this war of conquest was displayed the power of the kingdom, which, under a national monarchy, had been gathering strength and unity both in constitution and nationality. No doubt it was a time of outward splendour and warlike glory for the Crown, but the enduring benefits remained with the Parliament ; the sacrifices made by the country for this policy of war, which only served the personal ambition of the king, had to be paid for ; royal prerogatives were given up one by one to the Parliament in exchange for grants of money.

When, in 1399, the usurper Henry IV., belonging to the collateral branch of Lancaster, had, with the assent of Parliament, succeeded in deposing the elder Plantagenet, Richard II., the period of a purely parliamentary rule began. The conflicts with Scotland, Wales, and France, the arduous task of preserving his usurped throne against serious revolts of the nobles, consumed the power of this gifted monarch, and at the same time kept him in dependence upon the assistance of the Parliaments he was forced to summon. Thus they were enabled to make conditions as to the employment of the money granted, and with regard to the appointments of the great offices of State. Henry found himself compelled to yield with prudent submissiveness to the demands of the Estates ; to the Church, which had also helped him to gain his throne, he was obliged to surrender the heretic Lollards, and under his rule blazed the first fires at Smithfield.

His son, Henry V., preserved the same attitude towards Parliament and Church. He had not, like his father, to defend a usurped throne ; but he needed the generous support

of his subjects when he carried on to its fullest development
that policy of imperialism which Edward III. had revived,
and obtained the formal recognition of his right of succession
to the French throne. The utter collapse under John of the
empire Henry II. had created, and the failure of the policy of
conquest of Edward III. during the last years of that prince
and under Richard II., were evidences of the fate which
always attends such efforts after imperialism. How would
it have affected England's future if Henry V. had reached the
very summit of his ambition? For his kingdom's sake, his early
death (in 1422) was perhaps not too much to be lamented.

But at once disruption set in under his young son, Henry
VI., who, even after he had reached manhood, never laid aside
the helplessness of the child. The result, so disastrous for
kingdom and throne, was, not that the untenable continental
possessions were lost, but that a period of fearful anarchy in
England began.

That England could be great without a great monarch was
not yet conceivable; the decay of the monarchy would
inevitably involve the ruin of the State. But what in this
fifteenth century had become of the monarchy, which William
the Conqueror had grounded so firmly, and with which the
glorious times of Henry II., Edward I., Edward III., and
Henry V. were so closely bound up? The usurpation of the
Lancastrian prince, and the deposition of the lawful king, had
set an ominous precedent; the murder of Richard II. was to
be avenged in blood on Henry VI. and his son. With the
security of the throne, respect for its dignity also vanished.
Each man, who was conscious that some drops of royal blood
were in his veins, could aspire to possess the throne, if only he
had strength enough to struggle for it and to keep it.
England was then to learn to her cost that a crown which
sinks into a mere prize for personal ambition, is no longer
a blessing to the country, but a curse.

With Richard II. the old line of the Plantagenets had
come to an end; with the House of Lancaster a younger
branch ascended the throne, sprung from John of Gaunt, the
fourth son of Edward III. But Duke Richard of York, the
grandson of Gaunt's next youngest brother Edmund, had,
through his mother, inherited also the rights of the third

branch of Edward's children. As the Lancastrian prince had raised the claims of the younger branch to the throne against the Plantagenet Richard II., so now this Duke of York raised the claims of the elder branch against the House of Lancaster.

Scarcely more than a quarter of a century after the death of Henry V. nothing was left of the great continental conquests except one poor remnant, the town of Calais. Personal squabbles among the leading The period of the Civil War. men were occupying the reign of the feeble Henry VI., when the ambition of Richard of York let loose civil war upon the country : the thirty years' war of the Two Roses—the white rose of York and the red rose of Lancaster. The war devoured its originator, and it was Richard's son, who, having succeeded to his father's claims, assumed the crown as Edward IV. But the throne thus usurped stood on shaky foundations. Edward had temporarily to give way before his rival, and it was not till 1471 that he definitely made his power secure by the victories of Barnet and Tewkesbury. Henry VI., whose son had already fallen, came to a mysterious end in the Tower.

But where was the Parliament all this time? Might it not have been expected that the Commons, who under Edward III. and Henry IV. had stepped forward so firmly, would now offer their support to the State, when the Crown no longer performed its duty, when the party conflicts of the nobles, and the struggle of the powerful for the throne had brought disorder and confusion into the country? Yet nothing of the kind happened. The outward structure of the Parliamentary Constitution was indeed completed, but its powers had not yet gathered strength enough for independent action. However contradictory it may sound, it was the great epochs of the monarchy that had also been the chief epochs for the development of the Constitution, especially of the House of Commons. The powerful nobility, once the old rival of the Crown, became also the most dangerous opponent of the Commons. Only when the monarchy was victorious in its great conflict with the aristocracy did the Commons step forward, and succeed in making use of the king's need of money to augment their own power. But no sooner, under a weak monarch, had the nobility gained the upper hand, than

the Commons relapsed into silence; and this had been especially the case in the unhappy times of the Wars of the Roses.
If the party in the ascendant called a Parliament, the Upper
House, with the assembled peers, represented the party itself;
the Commons always bent before the storm, for the Lower
House, which in its composition had already been subject to
the strongest possible influences, followed obediently almost
every command, recognised each successful competitor as
king, proscribed each vanquished foe, and was ready to
reverse every previous attainder just as the victor desired.

Neither the constitutional government of the realm, nor
the courts of justice asserted themselves in this time of
personal feuds; law and justice alike became instruments in
the hand of the powerful.   Possibly because the Constitution
showed itself so pliant to every one, no one at such a time
thought of threatening its existence; it was enough merely
to suppress its independent utterances.   One thing the years
of disorder showed very plainly; that in spite of all that had
been achieved in the construction of the English constitutional
system, nowhere, and least of all in the Constitution itself, did
a force exist, which could take the place of a strong monarchy.
The monarchy had brought ruin; on it alone depended the
hope of a revival.

It seemed as if this hope were about to be fulfilled in
Edward IV.   For a while England was able to breathe again

Edward IV.   under the leadership of this strong and masterful
king; some accordingly see in Edward the founder
of the new despotic form of monarchy in the English State,
but have thereby attributed to him an achievement which
does not properly belong to him.[1]   We find in his reign,
felicitous and promising ideas and new departures; the first
Tudor in after years in many of his laws and in many a
feature of his financial and parliamentary policy could do
no better than revert to measures of Edward, but Edward
did not understand how to construct; he was able to bring
about a truce in the struggles, but not a lasting peace.

---

[1] This has been done for general history by Green, Short History of the English People ; for the legislation, by Finlason in his edition of Reeves' Hist. of the
Eng. Law, iii., 121, note. Hallam also, Const. Hist. i. 10, overrates Edward IV.
and considerably underrates Henry VII., when he says the latter did not carry
the authority of the Crown beyond the point at which Edward IV. had left it.

The cause lay in the existing circumstances, it lay also, however, in Edward's own character, for in spite of his ability, he was not the man to create a new and stable condition of society out of the chaos in England. He possessed, no doubt, the power to will and to do, but work was always to him a distasteful interruption to the enjoyments of life ; excesses and pleasures occupied his thoughts more than all else, and brought him to an early grave. He was able to win the love of his subjects by his handsome person and attractive manners ; but all the sharper is the contrast presented by that cruelty with which he climbed through streams of blood to the throne, and ruthlessly destroyed everything which might be to him a danger, sparing none, not even his own brother.

How can Edward be regarded as the founder of the new monarchy, when he was not even able to make his dynasty endure ? Even after his coronation, a ten years' struggle was necessary to establish his throne, and then he only made it firm for his own lifetime ; the boy whom he left behind him was not able to carry on a sovereignty thus won. Edward's youthful sons fell victims to the same cruel selfishness which had been his own guiding motive. As if the evil deeds of this wicked century were finally to be summed up in one person, the monster Richard III. appears on the scene at its close.

In his choice of a wife Edward IV. had acted, as he often did, from sudden caprice. In September, 1464, the world learnt that the king had married Elizabeth, the youthful widow of Sir John Grey, and daughter of the Earl Rivers, one of the Woodville family. The rise of this family was viewed with disfavour, and when after Edward IV.'s death on April 9, 1483, Elizabeth and her partisans, in opposition to the views of the Privy Council, laid claim to the guardianship of Edward V., a boy of twelve, the dispute became publicly known. Richard, Duke of Gloucester, the younger brother of the late king, and one of his ablest and most successful supporters, was then on the Scottish border. He came south, and in conjunction with the Duke of Buckingham, by a clever stroke snatched his nephew from the hands of Earl Rivers, and took prisoner the Earl and his principal adherents. Queen Elizabeth fled for protection into a sanctuary.

Richard did not stop here; one hideous crime after another paved for him the way from a Protectorate over the young king to the fulfilment of his own designs on the throne. Lord Hastings, who had opposed him, was seized after a sitting of the Council and beheaded without trial ; the Archbishop of Canterbury and John Morton, Bishop of Ely, were thrown into prison ; Lord Rivers and three adherents perished on the scaffold. On the 25th of June, 1483, Parliament met, without a very exact observance of forms, and on the 26th of June, Richard accepted the crown offered him by the Lords and Commons,[1] the youthful Edward and Duke Richard of York were declared bastards, the pretext of a previous betrothal of their father serving to make his union with Elizabeth appear invalid ; and on the 6th of July followed the coronation.

Richard III.

The blackest stain which indelibly clings to Richard's memory is the murder of his two nephews, who stood between him and the throne. He had induced Elizabeth to give Prince Richard also into his hands, and kept both brothers in the Tower, where they eventually disappeared. At the time, and also subsequently, attempts were made to dissipate the horrible suspicion which was at once cast upon the king, a pretender even rose up against Henry VII. in the character of Richard of York, but all attempts to clear Richard III. have been in vain.[2]

A formidable danger soon threatened the usurper. Already a movement had been set on foot in the south, in favour of the captive princes, and the wide-spread rumour of their murder gave special vigour to a great insurrection which broke out in October, 1483, at the head of which was none other than Richard's former colleague and abettor, the Duke of Buckingham. The duke, in spite of the rich reward he had received, is said to have been bitterly annoyed that all his demands were not satisfied. It is clear that his assistance had never been given in loyal earnest, but that he had sought thereby to acquire power and riches for himself, and for the same end was quite ready to abandon the cause he

---

[1] See Gairdner, Lett. and Pap. i. 12 ; Pref. 17, f., and Gairdnér, Rich. III., p. 110, ff.

[2] See in Appendix I., p. 319. Note 1.

had once espoused. Though, as being nearly allied to the House of Lancaster, he may possibly for a time have entertained an idea of putting in a claim for the Crown, he soon perceived that another descendant of the Lancastrian branch stood nearer to the throne than he did ; and the ample reward which he might expect in return for participation in his enterprise seemed a more sure gain than the doubtful prospect of acquiring the throne for himself. This other descendant was Henry Tudor, Earl of Richmond.

CHAPTER I.

EARLY HISTORY OF HENRY VII.

JOHN OF GAUNT, the ancestor of the House of Lancaster, had a son, John Beaufort, born out of wedlock ; his mother was Katharine Swynford. As Katharine was afterwards raised to the position of lawful wife, a later Act of Parliament, under Richard II., recognised the legitimacy of the Beaufort family ; but Henry IV., with obvious intention, caused to be inserted into this Act a clause, not legally valid, excluding the Beauforts from any claim on the throne.[1] The daughter of the younger son of John Beaufort was Buckingham's mother, while the daughter of the elder was Margaret, the mother of Henry Tudor.

Henry was at this time living as a fugitive in Brittany. He was born on the 28th of January, 1457, in Wales, the native land of the Tudors, at Pembroke Castle, the property of Jasper, Earl of Pembroke, his uncle on the father's side. His father, Edmund, whom Henry VI. had created Earl of Richmond, had died three months before. The uncle provided for Henry's education. Andreas Scotus, and Haseley, Dean of Warwick, are mentioned as his tutors, and Scotus is said to have spoken in high terms of his pupil. Jasper also introduced the boy to Henry VI. To escape the persecutions of Edward IV., he fled with him to France ; but, being driven on shore in Brittany, they were hospitably received by Duke Francis II. The duke, after some hesitation, refused Edward's summons to give Henry up, as well as a like demand on the part of Louis XI. of France, who was anxious to hold in his own hands a valuable hostage against

Henry in Brittany.

---

[1] See Gairdner, Rich. III., p. 137. Pauli, Eng. Gesch., v. 521, and especially the older accounts, as Hallam, Con. Hist., i. 8, accept the interpolation as valid.

England. He kept, however, his *protégés* under strict supervision till Edward's death.[1]

Buckingham entered into communications with Henry. Evidently Henry had no knowledge of the formal legitimation of his House, and Buckingham, who knew of it, kept his knowledge to himself, not wishing to play out for Richmond's benefit all the trumps he held in his hand, when about to start the conspiracy in his favour. It was quite overlooked that, not Henry himself, but his mother Margaret, who had married as her third husband Thomas, Lord Stanley, was the nearest heir to the throne.

Buckingham's rebellion.

The whole scheme, especially the idea of bringing over Richmond, was due, not to Buckingham, but to John Morton, Bishop of Ely, then under his patronage. Before this, Henry's mother had applied to the duke to intercede for her with the king, and, as a means of drawing closer to the House of York, had proposed Henry's marriage with a daughter of King Edward. Buckingham now took up this idea in his interviews with John Morton, in order to strengthen Henry's claims as opposed to Richard, by a union of the rival royal Houses. Meanwhile Margaret, on her own account, had, through her physician, communicated the proposed marriage to Queen Elizabeth, then in sanctuary at Westminster. On gaining Elizabeth's consent, she was about to send word to her son in Brittany, by Christopher Urswick, when her servant, Reginald Bray, summoned by Morton, brought her news of Buckingham's intentions. Provided with money, Hugh Conway now went to Richmond, in order to arrange a simultaneous move. Other messengers followed. On the 24th of September, 1483, Buckingham wrote himself to the earl that on the 18th of October operations should begin.

At that time the exile enjoyed greater liberty, and while Duke Francis of Brittany sought to stand well with Richard, who had made overtures to him, he yet gave support to Henry. There were even rumours of a plan for the marriage of Henry with Anne, the duke's eldest daughter and heiress. Thus the undertaking

Failure of the project.

[1] On the birth and early career of Henry, see Note 2, p. 319.

seemed to be in good train, when Fortune again showed herself on Richard III.'s side. In Kent the rising broke out too early. The king soon learnt who was the leader of the conspiracy, and a proclamation of October 23, 1483, placed a high price on the head of Buckingham and of his supporters. Strange to say, Richmond's name was not mentioned. The elements, too, came to Richard's assistance; a violent thunderstorm prevented Buckingham from advancing at the right moment. He turned to fly, but was captured and beheaded on the 2nd of November, on the market-place at Salisbury.

Henry's fleet, which on the 12th of October had put to sea with fifteen vessels and five thousand men, was dispersed by the storm, and when he arrived off the English coast, near Plymouth, in Devonshire, he had only two vessels with him. In vain the royal troops tried to entice him to land. When no friendly ship was to be seen, he put about, and landed in Normandy. Thence, with the permission of the French Government, he betook himself, before October was over, through France into Brittany.[1]

There he learnt the fate of the whole conspiracy. Many of the participators had happily escaped, Bishop Morton was in Flanders, and now a considerable number of fugitives gathered round Henry, on whom Duke Francis bestowed a new mark of favour in the shape of a subsidy of ten thousand crowns.[2] The idea of a matrimonial alliance, however, was dropped, and on Christmas Day, 1483, Henry took a solemn oath in church, in the presence of his confederates, to marry King Edward's daughter Elizabeth as soon as he had attained to the throne, whereupon they tendered him an oath of faithful allegiance. Henry led them to Duke Francis, who renewed his promise of helping him to return to his native land.[3]

After his victory Richard acted without delay. The Parliament, which met in January, 1484, pronounced sentence

---

[1] On Buckingham's insurrection, see Note 3, p. 320.
[2] Henry's receipt is dated as early as Oct. 29, 1483. See Brit. Mus. MS. Add., 19,398, No. 16, fol. 33; also Lett. and Pap., i. 54, f.
[3] Gairdner, Rich. III., 194, f., follows Hall, 396, f.; I prefer the simpler account in P. V., 702, f., which serves as a basis for Hall's and is only embellished by him: cf. Cont. Croyl., 571.

of outlawry on Henry and a great number of his adherents. Margaret also was attainted, but, out of consideration for Thomas, Lord Stanley, she was not hardly treated; her property was adjudged to her husband, who was also ordered to keep a strict watch over her.[1] These sentences were followed by many striking acts of clemency, such as the pardon of Bishop Morton.

Richard III.'s measures in England.

Above all, the king tried to upset his opponent's matrimonial designs. The Princess Elizabeth was with her mother safe in the Sanctuary of Westminster. Richard swore by his royal word, and on the sacred Gospels, before the Lords spiritual and temporal, before the mayor and aldermen of London to protect the Queen and her daughters.[2] Elizabeth trusted the murderer of her sons, deserted Henry's cause, after the failure of his first attempt, and, to escape from an unbearable position in which she was little better than a captive, gave herself up to the king, who was plotting nothing less against Richmond than to win his chosen bride for himself. The only obstacle to this was removed by the sudden death of Richard's consort, Anne.[3] Nevertheless Richard hesitated to carry out this well-considered plan, and meantime the end of his reign was approaching.

Henry's anxieties, however, still continued, and new difficulties were also pressing on him. Richard, after his first unsuccessful overtures to Duke Francis, in the summer of 1483, had not relaxed his endeavours to induce him to deliver up the rebels.[4] The duke himself continued friendly to Henry ; but he was in failing health, and often lapsed for a time into a state of complete mental incapacity, while in his favourite, the Treasurer Peter Landois, Richard's emissaries found a more willing listener. Fortunately for Henry, Morton heard from England of these intrigues, and was able to give him, through Christopher Urswick, timely warning of the new danger.

A new place of refuge had already been found, and a new

---

[1] This last reported only by P. V., 703; for the rest, see the Act of Parl., Rot. Parl., vi. 244-251, especially 250, f.

[2] Ellis, Orig. Lett., ii. 1, p. 149, f.

[3] " Sive dolore seu veneno confecta," P. V., 707.

[4] P. V., 703; cf. Lett. and Pap., ii. 4 and 48, f. for the rest, especially P. V. 703-706. On the earlier negotiations, see Rym., xii. 194; Morice, iii. 430, f.

friend, who promised the exile more lasting assistance than the Duke of Brittany. This powerful ally was France. The Pretender became thus mixed up in the quarrels of these two countries, a circumstance which was hereafter to involve him, as king, in the first serious foreign complications of his reign. Ever since the time of Louis XI., French policy had striven to break down the independence of this last great feudatory province, which stood in the way of a homogeneous state under the crown of France. If Duke Francis and his advisers had assisted Henry and Buckingham, it was in the hope that, should they be successful, the new king of England would prove a grateful friend, and aid Brittany in frustrating such designs. With a similar motive Landois turned to Richard III. again, when the latter had been successful in maintaining his power. A truce was even brought about, and as early as June, 1484, a detachment of English troops was sent to oppose possible French attacks.[1]

It was therefore quite intelligible that France should willingly extend a hand to Henry when he was deserted by the rulers of Brittany. The relations of France with the royal House of York had been somewhat strained, even as far back as under Louis XI., and so they had remained after his death in 1483, under the regency, during the minority of Charles VIII. Henry therefore was allowed to travel unmolested through France in October, 1483 ; indeed, at that time Duke Francis even received a promise of help against any powerful enemies, an evident allusion to a possible act of revenge on the part of Richard.[2] The French Government, however, kept its hand free, and a general proposition of alliance from Richard in March, 1484, was answered in August by an offer of sending envoys to negociate peace and friendship. In spite of this the regency still kept in touch with the English exile in Brittany,[3] and all thought of an alliance with Richard fell to the ground when the change in

---

[1] See Gairdner, Rich. III., 217, f.

[2] See the later reference in a Report of the Council of April 5, 1484, in Pélicier, Essai sur le Gouvern. de la Dame de Beaujeu. Pièces just., p. 227.

[3] Rym., xii. 221–223 ; see Gairdner, Rich. III., p. 219 ; Letter to Richard in the Report of the Council, Aug. 12, 1484, in Procès-verbaux des séances, etc., ed. Bernier, 45, f. This shows, in opposition to Mr. Gairdner's view (Rich. III., p. 219), that the French Government formally agreed to Richard's offer. Cf. further the orders to the admiral in Normandy : Rep. Counc., Aug. 16, 1484. Proc.-verb., 53, f.

Brittany's policy drove Henry entirely over to the side of France.

Henry, who had received through Christopher Urswick the assurance of French support, together with more detailed instructions, made preparations secretly to escape from Brittany. But few friends were taken into **Flight from Brittany.** his confidence, so that the others were greatly surprised when they heard that he had secretly fled in disguise to France. It is related that he only escaped with the greatest difficulty from the troopers sent in pursuit by Peter Landois. This took place towards the end of September, 1484.[1]

The French regency had given orders that he should be hospitably received, and conducted to Chartres ; Duke Francis too, who was again recovering, did not approve of Landois' proceedings against Henry. He sent after him his friends who had remained behind, well provided with money, and in France also, Henry received for them a considerable sum and materials for their equipment.[2] New fugitives joined them ; the Earl of Oxford, one of the most faithful adherents of the House of Lancaster, who had been detained by Edward IV. at Hammes, near Calais, gained over the commander of the castle ; they made the fortress capable of defence and hastened to join Henry, who at once sent Oxford back again with reinforcements. They failed, indeed, to hold Hammes, against the attacks of the Calais garrison, but were allowed to pass out free.

In spite of the increase in his adherents, and in spite of French protection, Henry's condition was a precarious one, as his fate was affected by the difficulties which beset the Regent's government in France. The **Henry in France.** Regency was in the hands of the still youthful but clever and energetic Anne, elder sister of King Charles VIII., who had been given in marriage by her father Louis XI. to Peter of Beaujeu, brother and heir-presumptive to the powerful Duke of Bourbon. The leaders of the opposition

---

[1] On the preceding overtures, see the allusion in the orders of the Government, October 11, 1484. Proc.-verb., 128. An earlier view of Gairdner's, that the flight had already taken place in the spring, was founded on Proc.-verb., 178, already corrected by Pélicier, p. 86, note 2. Cf. on the subject André, Vita, p. 24.

[2] Report, 4, 17, Nov. 19, 1484, Proc.-verb., pp. 148, 164, 168.

were the queen-mother, and more particularly Duke Louis
of Orleans, the husband of Anne's younger sister, who
himself stood near to the throne, which he ascended subsequently, as Louis XII. These rivalries at home became
mixed up with complications abroad ; if the Regent helped
the Tudor leader, the Orleans party took part with Richard,
and the possibility of an English attack on France was even
contemplated ;[1] if the Orleans party allied with the rulers
of Brittany, Anne granted protection to Breton nobles.
These, under the command of the Marshal de Rieux, sought
her assistance after an unsuccessful attempt against Landois,
but the high price they had to pay for this was the formal
recognition, at Montargis, October, 1484, of Charles VIII.
as successor to their duke, should the latter die without heirs
male.   Finally, to the negotiations of Orleans with the Archduke Maximilian, Anne retorted by an alliance with the
Flemish towns, then in revolt against the Hapsburger.

In spite of the remarkable skill with which Anne managed
to keep in power, Henry's future remained uncertain, and
before long he had to cope with the open desertion of many
of his friends.   Queen Elizabeth, faithless herself, induced
the Marquis of Dorset, her son by her first marriage, then
in company with Henry, to take flight secretly, and Cheney,
who hastened after him, had some difficulty in persuading
him to return.[2] Such incidents as this, together with the
general position of affairs, urged the conspirators to prompt
action ; it was better to risk something by boldness, rather
than to spoil all by hesitation.   It was then probably that
a notification was sent by Henry to his friends in England,
to the effect that his action would depend on their readiness
to support him.[3] A small subsidy was supplied by the
French Government, and in return for this advance, Henry
had to leave behind as hostages, John Bourchier and the still
wavering Dorset. Whilst he remained at Rouen, a squadron
was assembling in the mouth of the Seine, far smaller than
the fleet with which he had set out the year before.

---

[1] Report, Council, Dec. 22, 1484, Proc.-verb., 226, and later royal letter of
June 25, 1485, Pélicier, Pièces just., p. 256 ; also Pélicier, p. 87, and André,
Vita in Memor., p. 25.

[2] With P. V., 708, f., whom I principally follow here, cf. André, 24.

[3] Undated in Halliwell, Lett. of the Kings of Engl. i., 161, f.

His eyes were now turned to Wales, the home of his race. When the disquieting intelligence reached him that Richard had definitely resolved on marrying Elizabeth of York himself, Henry made use of the freedom this seemed to give him to offer his hand to a sister of Walter Herbert, a Welshman of good position.[1] By this offer he hoped to gain the Welsh, whose attitude throughout had caused him some anxiety, and continued to do so after he had landed. But as his messengers did not even succeed in getting into the country, no more thought was given to this plan, which could hardly ever have been seriously contemplated. With about two thousand men, amongst whom was a company of Frenchmen, Henry put to sea from Harfleur on August 1, 1485, and after a seven days' voyage, landed without opposition at Milford Haven, near the place of his birth.

Richard had long been prepared for a forward movement on the part of his adversary. Whilst safe in France with "the king's old enemy" Charles, Henry was beyond the reach of his power, and Richard had to content himself with an angry proclamation, in which he appealed to the national pride of England to oppose a pretender who had bought the help of the hereditary foe against his native country.[2] But this appeal fell flat. Henry landed on English soil and marched forwards. Serious resistance he met with nowhere; he even received some not inconsiderable reinforcements. Still, as was natural, the attitude of most men was doubtful and hesitating; they were anxious before they joined him to have some security as to the turn affairs were likely to take. This was obvious at once in a certain section of the Welsh ; one of the most powerful of them, however, Rice ap Thomas, about whom at first disquieting rumours had been received, joined Henry in Shrewsbury with a considerable number of men ;[3] thither too came good news from the messengers sent to his mother, the Stanleys, and other friends.

Above all, the attitude assumed at that time by his stepfather, Thomas, Lord Stanley, with his brother, Sir

---

[1] P. V., 709 ; I cannot otherwise explain this offer of Henry's, for that here a serious resolve was in question is inconceivable.

[2] June 23, 1485, Past. Lett., ed. Gairdner, iii., 316-320.

[3] On Rice ap Thomas, see Note 4, p. 321.

William, was of importance. Lord Stanley had always been a favourite with Richard ; now, however, on account of the family connection between Stanley and Henry, he considered it prudent to keep in his hands a surety in the person of George, Lord Strange, Stanley's son. While Sir William Stanley had a short conference in Stafford with Henry, who had advanced thither by way of Newport, Lord Stanley, who had remained at Lichfield with a considerable body of troops, withdrew as soon as he heard of Richmond's approach to Atherstone. There, apparently, Richmond had a secret interview with the brothers, which is said to have been very friendly, though it remains uncertain how far he secured their support. He was reassured, however, in some degree by other more numerous accessions. Gilbert Talbot joined him in Newport, Walter Hungerford and Thomas Bourchier on the march to Tamworth ; many others followed.

With every mile that Henry advanced, Richard's partisans fell away. This was a circumstance which, with all his anxiety, Richard had not foreseen. It must have filled him with rage to see men whom he had specially trusted open a free passage to his rival. As soon as he had collected sufficient troops, he started for Leicester, and prepared to do battle with Henry, then in the neighbourhood, at Tamworth. The moment for a decisive engagement had arrived.

Near the market town of Bosworth Richard fixed his camp, a stream separating him from Henry. On the 22nd of **Bosworth,** August, a Monday, the king led his troops to battle. **August 22,** In numbers he was far superior to his adversary, **1485.** whose fighting force was estimated at about five thousand men. To the last the Stanleys maintained a suspiciously neutral attitude. Lord Stanley, when called upon by both parties, responded to neither, and even his brother William, who had been outlawed by Richard, re-mained with his men in a state of inaction, in the rear of the king's position to the north. Not till the battle was raging furiously, and when Henry himself was in danger and his troops were losing courage, did William Stanley rush in with his three thousand men. His onslaught was successful, and this decided the fortune of the day. Despairing of victory, Richard plunged into the *mêlée*, and was slain, fighting heroically.[1] Of his faithful followers, the Duke of Norfolk, leader of the advanced guard, Walter, Lord Ferrers, Sir Robert Brackenbury, Sir Richard Ratcliff, had fallen with him ;. Norfolk's son, the Earl of Surrey, and the Earl of Northumberland, were taken prisoners. Lord Lovell and the two Staffords sought refuge in a sanctuary. They met their fate soon afterwards in a rising against the new monarch.

The regal circlet of gold which Richard had worn on his helmet, was found in the midst of the slain, and placed by Lord Stanley on Henry's head, while the bystanders joyfully hailed him as king. Men saw the body of his fallen rival thrown naked by a trooper across the back of his horse, with head and legs hanging down on either side, and borne away. Thus carried to Leicester, it was exposed to view for two days in the church of the Franciscans, and then buried by the friars.[2] The Tudor prince was now king of England.

Henry was in his twenty-ninth year when he gained for himself throne and kingdom at Bosworth. A task awaited him, which might well have daunted a more ex- perienced man ; but from the first he showed **Henry's claim to the throne.** himself equal to it ; from the first he displayed a faculty for seizing with clear judgment and firm grasp on that which lay nearest to his hand, and never made the mistake of taking what should be the second step before the first. After what England had but just passed through, everything depended on whether Henry would succeed in fixing firmly on his head the crown he had gained, in preparing the ground for a new dynasty, and thus securing for the still tottering throne a position of power and dignity in the State.

Henry's ideas and those of his partisans did not now quite coincide. The latter wished to conciliate and gain over the House of York by uniting the claims of both parties through Henry's marriage with Elizabeth of York. This, too, had once been Henry's idea ; but the oath to marry the princess, which he had taken long before in Brittany, had been a

---

[1] "Inter pugnandum, et non in fuga dictus Rex Richardus multis letalibus vulneribus ictus, quasi princeps animosus et audentissimus in campo occubuit." Contin. Croyl., 574.

[2] On the battle, see Note 5, p. 322.

concession wrung from him by necessity; for, before all
things, he desired to acquire and retain his kingdom by
his own right alone.

Definite constitutional views on the order of the succession to the crown did not then exist in England. An atten-
tive Italian observer says that an hereditary monarchy was
indeed recognised in England, but if no immediate offspring
were forthcoming, or the succession to the throne happened
to be controverted, then the question was settled by force
of arms, and "who lost the day lost the kingdom." [1] It was
the destructive war waged by Edward IV. and Richard III.
against other members of their royal House which really
prepared the way for the Tudor king. The flourishing race
of the Plantagenets had been almost exterminated. In spite
of this, Henry's claim was certainly doubtful; especially
must it have appeared so to himself, as he probably was still
unaware of the legitimation of the Beaufort family. In fact,
were succession in the female line once admitted, the younger
branch of York would come before the older Lancastrian
branch as heir to the line from John of Gaunt's elder brother,
Lionel, the male issue in which had early become extinct. One
male representative of the male line of York was still living—
Edward, Earl of Warwick, son of George, Duke of Clarence,
who had fallen a victim to his brother, Edward IV. Richard
III. had provisionally chosen the earl as heir, after the death
of his son, but subsequently had set him aside for a sister's
son, John de la Pole, Earl of Lincoln. Warwick, too, belonged to a branch of the family, which had lost its rights by
attainder.

It was only in this prevailing uncertainty as to what constituted a right to succession, that Henry was able to come
forward with his independent hereditary claim in the face of
other existing claims, and for his still doubtful partisans,
his union with a daughter of Edward IV. sufficed as a com-
promise for setting aside Warwick's right. But to carry out
his personal claim as the real Lancastrian heir was only made
possible for Henry by the recognised right of war. So, even
at Bosworth, he regarded himself as rightful king, and at
once exercised his royal prerogative by knighting eleven of

[1] Italian Relation, about 1500, published by the Camden Society, p. 46.

his faithful followers on the battle-field.   He passed over the Earl of Warwick, as Richard had done, caused the young prince, a boy of fifteen, to be brought from Sheriff Hutton, where he had been kept in confinement, to London, and shut up in the Tower.   The Princess Elizabeth, too, was removed from Sheriff Hutton to London, and there handed over to her mother.   Of the promised marriage, there was for the present no mention.

Henry himself proceeded from Bosworth to the capital. On the 27th of August, five days after his victory, he was received in London with great pomp, escorted by the Lord Mayor and aldermen, and joyfully greeted by a closely packed crowd of citizens.[1]   He rode through the town to St. Paul's Church, where he hung up the three banners under which he had gained his victory, and for several days processions were formed to the various churches in the town to offer up thanksgiving.

On the 15th of September, 1485, he summoned a Parliament for the 7th of November, "to discuss pressing and weighty measures for the government and defence First admini-of the kingdom and Church of England."[2]   He strative rewarded his partisans—amongst them the Stan-measures. leys, Rice ap Thomas, Sir Richard Edgecombe, Hugh Conway, Christopher Urswick, and especially the Earl of Oxford—with dignities, offices, and pensions.   The revenues of the "rebels," Richard's adherents, were handed over by Henry to his own friends; important offices, such as those of the judges, and the attorney-general, were filled with new men, and a number of enactments were made.[3]   In order to give a feeling of security after the recent revolution, a general, and, with but few exceptions, unlimited pardon was issued on the 24th of September, 1485, and was widely circulated through the counties.[4]

At this moment a grievous misfortune befell England, full of gloomy foreboding for the new ruler.   Towards the end of September a hitherto unknown disease broke out

---

[1] See Note 6, p. 322.   [2] Campbell, Materials, i. 6.
[3] Royal decrees issued before the opening of Parliament, Campbell, i. 6–110.
[4] A part printed from the York City Archives in the *Gentleman's Magazine*, New Ser. xxxv. (1851), p. 165.   In consequence of the incorrect arrangement in P. V., 719, it has hitherto been wrongly stated.

in London, spread through and ravaged the country, scattering fear and horror far and wide. Over the bodies of those attacked by this disease, there broke out a copious sweat, emitting an unpleasant odour; tortured by fever, most of them threw off their clothes and swallowed cold drinks, but they succumbed to the malady just as soon as those who by warmer covering increased heat and perspiration; not till a later return of the epidemic was it discovered that to let it run its course without interference was the wisest treatment. Being extremely infectious, it spread rapidly, to disappear again after a short but virulent career.

The sweating sickness.

On this its first appearance, according to one account, doubtless exaggerated, but nevertheless significant, only one in a hundred of those attacked recovered. Further, it was remarkable that the disease at that time was entirely confined to England, and spared even Ireland and Scotland; hence it received the name of the " English sweating sickness." [1] Towards the middle of October the disease died out in London; two mayors and many aldermen had fallen victims to it; in the country it lasted on into the next month.

Meanwhile, before Parliament had even assembled, Henry made arrangements for his coronation—the solemn act by which he should be publicly recognised as king. It was fixed for the 30th of October. On the three preceding days, the king dined at Lambeth as the guest of the Archbishop of Canterbury; then rode with a splendid escort over London Bridge to the Tower, and was welcomed again by the Lord Mayor with the aldermen and city guilds. On this occasion it was remarked that his escort rode, after the French fashion, two together on one horse. The next day he distributed some fresh honours to his followers; his uncle Pembroke was raised to the rank of Duke of Bedford, Lord Stanley was made Earl of Derby, and Sir Edward Courtenay, Earl of Devonshire. The king summoned to his Council, amongst others, his uncle, Bedford, the Earls of Oxford and Derby, and his principal political counsellors throughout his reign, Bishop John Morton, Reginald Bray, and Richard Fox.[2]

---

[1] See Note 7, p. 323.

[2] See, on the main point, P. V., 719, who, however, is chronologically inexact, and in this, as in details, is supplemented by Stow (p. 860), founded on Fabian,

Special attention was excited by a measure, which was quite in opposition to all English tradition and bore witness early to Henry's views on the position of the monarch : for the greater exclusiveness and dignity of his royal person, he surrounded himself with a small body-guard, the model of which he had seen in France.[1]

On the 7th day of November, after the king's coronation had taken place with great pomp and ceremony,[2] the Estates of the realm assembled round him. Parliament was opened at Westminster in presence of the king, who, sitting on the royal throne, listened to an ornate speech from the Lord Chancellor Thomas Alcock, Bishop of Worcester. Two days afterwards the Commons presented as their speaker, Thomas Lovell, a member of the King's Privy Council. He was accepted by Henry, who then expounded in a few words the views he held and had long since made known by his deeds, that his right to the crown rested on hereditary succession, and the decision of God by the sword. He once again announced to all his subjects, excepting for those who had " offended his sovereign majesty," protection for their possessions and rights.

The Parliament.

The Commons responded to this promise of protection on the part of the king by a very important grant : the duties comprised under the name of tonnage and poundage were promised to the king at fixed rates " during his lifetime, for the defence of the realm and especially the safeguard and keeping of the sea." To these first really important words of the Commons to the king, after the presentation of the speaker, the following equally important supplementary clause was added, " that these be not taken in ensample to the kings of England in time to come." Parliament also enacts that the revenues of the Crown

Tonnage and poundage.

and by Campbell, pp. 11. 131, 241. The composition of the Privy Council probably did not take place till between the coronation and the opening of Parliament.

[1] P. V., 720 ; Stow, 884 ; the latter, probably after Fabian, also gives the name " Yeomen of the Guard ;" Hall 425, here puts together the accounts of P. V. and Fabian. The Italian Relation already cited mentions (p. 47) among the persons living in the king's pay the " Soldati cortigiani, che sono da 150 fino in 200 per la sua guardia."

[2] Date in P.V., 718 ; Fabian's Abridgment, pp. 681, 683 ; Grey Friars Chronicle, p. 24 ; preparatory royal orders, Campb., i. 92, 97, f., cf. 206, f. ; detailed plan for the ceremonial in Rutland Papers, pp. 2-24, cf. Ives, Select Pap., 93-119.

should be brought into the same condition in which they were in 1455, and, as the property of the outlawed enemies of Henry now fell in to the Crown, the king had been so generously treated by his first Parliament that no need remained for further demands for money.

These last-named enactments had been preceded by the important decision by which Parliament took up its position **Recognition as king.** with regard to the rights of the dynasty. In this confirmatory Act of Parliament no mention was made of the legal rehabilitation of the Beauforts, nor yet of any proof or grounds of Henry's claims, the existing state of things was simply accepted and recognised : " To the pleasure of Almighty God, the wealth, prosperity, and surety of this realm of England, to the singular comfort of all the king's subjects of the same, and in avoiding of all ambiguities and questions, be it ordained, stablished and enacted, by the authority of this present Parliament, that the inheritance of the crowns of the realms of England and of France, . . . be, rest, remain and abide in the most royal person of our now sovereign lord King Harry the VII., and in the heirs of his body lawfully coming, perpetually with the grace of God so to endure, and in none other." This declaration was made with the following formalities : the Commons brought forward the motion, to which the Lords gave their assent, then followed the declaration : " Le Roy le voet en toutz pointz."

Those sentences of outlawry which had been pronounced under Richard III., "in fact but not of right King of England," were revoked with the proviso that the persons concerned, amongst whom were Henry's mother Margaret, the son of the Duke of Buckingham who had been executed, and the Duke of Bedford, should not enter upon the enjoyment of their reacquired rights until after the expiration of the parliamentary session. The difficulty had already arisen that many of the persons summoned to Parliament, even Henry himself, were under sentence of outlawry ; so it was decided by the judges that the proscribed persons should not take part in the sittings till after the sentence of the outlawry had been annulled ; the king alone was at once to be considered as freed "by reason of the fact that he has taken upon him the supreme authority, and is king."[1]

By the side of conciliatory mercy stood revengeful retribution upon those nearest adherents of his fallen opponent, who had already been excepted from the general pardon. In order to be able with legal formality to pass sentence on these, Henry's reign was supposed to begin on the 21st of August, so that all who on the 22nd had borne arms against him at Bosworth, had offended against the king's majesty, and were found guilty of high treason ; their property naturally fell to the Crown. Besides Richard himself, the following were attainted : the Duke of Norfolk, his son Thomas, Earl of Surrey, the Lords Lovell, Ferrers, and Zouche, and some twenty knights and squires. Henry only succeeded in passing this penal Act in the face of much opposition ; "there was many gentlemen against it, but it would not be, for it was the king's pleasure."

Attainders.

But having promised peace and security to his subjects, he exacted a like promise to keep the peace from the Estates of his realm. Every man on his part was to put a stop to those causes which were likely to bring back the lawless condition of recent times ; no one should keep followers wearing the special badge of their master, nor, as a rule, take any man into his service by indenture or oath ; no one should favour unlawful assemblies, nor interfere by bribery or force with the regular course of justice, nor hinder those charged with the office from carrying out the king's command, nor grant protection to fugitive criminals. On the 19th of November the knights and esquires of the Royal Household and of the Lower House had to swear to these articles ; after they had been dismissed, the assembled lords—thirty spiritual and eighteen temporal—took the same oath, after a solemn address from the Chancellor. It was certain that all this was not directed against the Commons, but against the great lords, who favoured illegal conduct, exercised club law with their armed followers, oppressed the weak, and impeded the action of law and justice. They had to swear to respect the despised law before a higher power, that is, the king, and no doubt

Oath of Lords and Commons to preserve peace.

Laws against Maintenance and Livery.

---

[1] Year Book, 1 Henry VII., fol. 4b, cf. Rot. Parl., 275.

they acquiesced none too willingly in the changed order of things which this implied. We find in a private letter, written shortly before the prorogation of Parliament: "There is much runyng (murmuring) amongst the Lords, but no man wot what it is; it is said it is not well amongst them." It was the beginning of the destruction of the splendour of the nobility under the Tudor monarchy.

Many other important laws, dealing with trade, foreign commerce, and navigation, were passed in the course of a two-months' session by this first Parliament of Henry's; above all, the ratification of his right to the throne had been clearly and definitely pronounced. It was now simply an act of prudence on the part of the king not to lay aside altogether the question of his promised marriage with the Yorkist heiress. When, on the 10th of December, 1485, both Houses met together for a solemn final sitting in the presence of the king, the Commons of England appealed "to his royal highness in a humble petition by their Speaker," that, whereas by the resolve of Parliament the crowns of England and France were settled on Henry and his heirs, he would now take to wife Elizabeth of York. The Lords joined in this desire of the Commons, but there was no reference to Henry's original promise. Henry answered shortly, that he was already prepared to act according to their wish. With a caution to remember their oath, and to preserve peace and quietness, the Lord Chancellor announced the prorogation of Parliament till the 23rd of January, 1486.[1]

Prorogation of Parliament.

When the new year began, the tendency of the king's policy became clearly evident; the opinion of Parliament had indeed been asked on all important measures, and these, being issued as Acts of Parliament, carried with them the weight of its consent; but the new dynasty was to stand in its own strength, and the preservation of peace, of justice, and of law had been announced as its supreme aim and object. For this very reason, murmurs and discontent were rife in the ranks of the Lords, but we possess an opposite and trustworthy opinion from a more impartial quarter. John de Giglis, collector of the Papal dues, called "Peter's

---

[1] On the Parliament, see Note 8, p. 323.

pence," wrote, a few days before the prorogation of Parliament, to the Pope Innocent VIII.[1] : " The king shows himself very prudent and clement ; all things appear disposed towards peace, if only the minds of men would remain constant. Nothing has done this realm so much harm as ambition and covetous desire, and if God will only deliver us from these, then the kingdom will be at peace."

One thing still was expected of Henry, and had not been carried out—his marriage with Elizabeth. No reason for further delay existed, and perhaps it was to meet the last wish expressed by Parliament that, before it reassembled, he hurried on the matter, and did not even wait for the dispensation from the Pope necessary for this marriage between two persons, who were relatives, though certainly somewhat distant. A dispensation from the papal legate, James, Bishop of Imola, was made to suffice for the time being. On the 18th of January, 1486, the wedding took place with great pomp, and, according to the report of Bernard André, Henry's historiographer royal, amid general rejoicing. The papal bull was dated the 6th of March ; in it, at Henry's express desire, the previous action of the legate in granting the dispensation was specially commended. Soon afterwards, Innocent also gave the formal papal recognition of Henry's sovereign rights. The bull of the 27th of March, 1486, which threatened with excommunication any who should rebel against Henry, asserts it was issued by the Pope spontaneously and without prompting from the king ; but it is at once obvious from its wording who must have suggested it to the Pope. It also reflects clearly the king's own point of view—that in order to set aside any still-existing scruples as to the rights of his dynasty, the acknowledgment by the people through Parliament had been added to the right of war, and to an undoubted hereditary claim ; nevertheless, with a view to settling the old dispute between York and Lancaster, Henry had resolved on a marriage with Elizabeth, with the proviso that, on Elizabeth's death, his children from any other marriage should still possess unrestricted hereditary right to the crown. It is just these points, so essential for Henry, which were specially emphasized in that English

(marginal note: Marriage with Elizabeth of York.*)*

----

[1] Dec. 6, 1485, Campbell, i. 198, f.; Brown, i., No. 506.

version of the bull which was distributed throughout the country. The great importance of this marriage for the security of his throne was no secret to Henry, and he never contemplated abandoning it ; but in the manner of its final settlement he kept most unmistakably to his own point of view.[1]

No one could expect that with the new reign peace and order would at once be restored all over England. Already in the autumn the king had been threatened with an attack from Scotland, the old border enemy in the north, and this danger was not to be underrated, because the enemy from without was able to unite himself with foes within. But as a prompt summons to arms from Henry showed him to be prepared for defence, the Scottish king, James III., desisted from his undertaking, and after a few negotiations a suspension of hostilities was agreed to on the 30th of January, 1486, and peace soon followed. It was in the north especially that the feeling of the population was unsafe, and full of menace for Henry. An evidence of this was given him by the conduct of York, the northern capital of England, which, in the case of official elections, acted expressly in direct contradiction to the king's wishes.[2] Henry was anxious, therefore, after the close of the parliamentary session, to look into the matter himself ; a loan from the city of London, which, however, did not reach the amount of his demands, had to furnish him the means of appearing with an armed escort.[3]

It was soon evident that cause for apprehension existed. In Lincoln, at Easter, Henry learnt that some fugitive

First rising against Henry: Lovell and the Staffords.

partisans of King Richard—Francis, Viscount Lovell, with the brothers Thomas and Humphrey Stafford, had left the sanctuary at Colchester, and that no one knew where they were in hiding. It was not till he had proceeded further that the news

---

[1] See Note 9, p. 324.

[2] See the two papers and published correspondence in the *Gentleman's Magazine*, New Ser., vol. xxxv. (1851).

[3] On the loan : City Chronicle, fol. 114b ; Fabian's Abridgment, 683 ; Stow, 861 ; on the king's journey and the insurrection : Herald's account in Leland, Collectanea, iv. 185, ff. ; P. V., 721, f., partly supplemented by Hall, 426-428 ; Plumpton Corres., 50, f. ; Paston Letters, iii. 327, f.; Year Book, 1 Henry VII., fol. 22b-24a, 25a-26b ; *Gentleman's Magazine*, New Ser., 35, pp. 481-483. P. V., 722, is wrong in his assertion that Henry had come to York before his victory.

came that Lovell was waylaying him with a body of armed
men, and that the Staffords were trying to incite the population of Worcester to insurrection.   Whilst Henry's uncle,
Bedford, with a few thousand men, who had been hastily
collected, advanced to meet the rebels, the king devised the
clever plan of promising, in a public proclamation, exemption
from punishment to those who should at once tender their
submission.   These two things worked together; the confederates of the insurgents gave themselves up to the
king, the leaders fled.   Lovell remained in hiding in Lancashire.   In May he turned towards Ely, either with the idea
of escaping to the sea, or of seeking safety in a sanctuary.
What he exactly did we do not know ; anyhow, he succeeded
in joining a fresh conspiracy against Henry in England, before
he fled from the country in January, 1487.   The Stafford
brothers had again sought a sanctuary at Abingdon, but were
taken out and brought to the Tower.   When Humphrey,
before the Court of King's Bench, appealed to the ancient
right of asylum granted to the place by a king of Mercia,
this right itself, and especially its validity in such a case of
high treason, was disputed by the judges.   Humphrey died
the death by torture of a traitor ; the younger brother Thomas
was pardoned, because he was considered to have been led
astray by the elder.

The threatening cloud had been quickly dispersed.   Again
a victor, Henry entered York on the 22nd of April, 1486,
where a triumphal welcome had this time been prepared for
him.   After staying there some weeks, he returned through
Worcester, Hereford, Gloucester, and Bristol, to London,
where he arrived in June.   This year, which had
threatened to be so unquiet, was now to be a   Birth of
joyful one to the king.   Eight months after her   Prince Arthur.
marriage, Elizabeth gave birth at Winchester to a son, who
received the name of Arthur, after the hero of tradition.[1]
The first offspring of the united houses of York and Lancaster !   The blind poet André celebrated the happy event
in verse and prose, and tells us he sang of it in a hundred
poems.   In truth, the birth of an heir was the greatest happi-
ness which could befall the founder of a rising dynasty.   But

[1] See Note 10, p. 324.

at the same time a new danger, more threatening than the last, was gathering over Henry's head.

The year 1486 had not closed before sinister rumours were afloat. In a private letter written towards the end of November, it is stated that people had not been saying much about the imprisoned Earl of Warwick, but that there would be more talk of him presently;[1] and towards the beginning of 1487 Henry heard that in Ireland a rival had risen up against him, who gave himself out to be Warwick. At the same time the king knew that the impulse to this new movement came from two centres, Ireland and the Flemish Court of Margaret, widow of Charles the Bold of Burgundy, and sister of Edward IV. This lady of the house of York was destined to cause the Tudor king many an anxious hour. Every Yorkist rising found in her a devoted ally. Her widow's court afforded a safe place of refuge for fugitive insurgents from England.

The soul of the new conspiracy was her sister's son, John de La Pole, Earl of Lincoln, the same who had been chosen as heir to the throne by Richard III. He, as well as his father, the Duke of Suffolk, who was still living, had experienced no ill-treatment from Henry, but rather, had been entrusted with posts of confidence. It is possible that the prospect he had once had of the crown may have kept alive the ambition of the earl. About the end of the year 1486 he devised with friends in England some treasonable plans, in which his chief confederate was Francis, Viscount Lovell, who had been fortunate enough to escape the snares prepared for him. Made wiser by the failure of the last enterprise, they resolved not to take England itself as their centre of action, but to carry on their preparations for the attempt in safe quarters outside the country. Lincoln still considered himself secure, but Lovell fled away to Margaret in January, 1487. Though the plans were laid in England and the preparations made in Flanders, the decisive attack was to be carried out from another quarter, and by special means—by setting up a Yorkist pretender in Ireland.

In Henry's time the English kings had for three hundred

The Earl of Lincoln.

[1] The first allusion in a letter of Nov. 29, 1486; Plumpton Corr., p. 54.

years borne the title of "Lord of Ireland." But since the
first attempt at a conquest of Ireland under   Ireland.
Henry II., this lordship had been not much more
than a name. It comprehended still in the reign of Henry VII.
only the so-called Pale, the English boundary—the counties
of Louth, Meath, Kildare, and Dublin—not really much more
than the strip of coast from Dublin to Dundalk, stretching
thirty English miles inland. Within this territory, which was
protected by fortresses against "wild Ireland," a miniature
copy of English political institutions had been created ; outside
this, the Anglo-Irish barons, descendants of the Norman
invaders, who in name and character had become Irishmen,
continued to live among the Keltic aborigines, a rough
undisciplined life of robbery and strife. Here the great
chiefs were the veritable lords of the land, and the most
important quarrel among them, the race enmity between
the Butlers and Geraldines, had in these latter times been
associated with the quarrel between the Yorkists and
Lancastrians in England. The Yorkists had, on account
of their landed property, some influence in Ireland ; the
head of the Geraldines, the Earl of Kildare, held, under
Edward IV., the office of Lord Deputy, and on his death
it was handed down to his son, who retained it also under
Richard III.[1] The titular dignity of Lord Lieutenant proper
was borne under Edward and Richard by the Duke of
Clarence and the Earl of Lincoln, but the power remained
in the hands of the chieftain of the most prominent Irish
party, with the title of Lord Deputy, and he was a partisan
of the Yorkists.

Henry, who had come forward as a Lancastrian, had a
difficult position with regard to him. If at the beginning of
his reign he had attempted to change the existing condition
of things by force, he might have destroyed the slender hold
which the English rule at that time kept in Ireland. So he
wisely remained in the background, and only, as was reasonable, restored to their rights the outlawed Butlers, who had
been loyal to the Lancastrian cause. He also appointed
their chief, Thomas, Earl of Ormond, then living in England,
to be chamberlain to the queen, with a fixed yearly salary,

[1] Lett. and Pap., i. 44, 74, f.

D

and received him into his Privy Council.[1]   At the same time
he left Kildare unmolested ; setting up his uncle Bedford as
lord-lieutenant, he confirmed the earl in his dignities, and
wisely waited a few years before interfering in the affairs of
Ireland.[2]   This the Irish themselves made necessary, when
they took part as confederates and allies in the new Yorkist
conspiracy.

About the turn of the year 1486–87 there appeared amongst
them a young priest of eight and twenty, named Richard
Appearance Simons, who brought with him a handsome youth
of Lambert of humble origin, Lambert Simnel, the son of an
Simnel. organ-builder.   This boy was to undertake the
part of the Yorkist pretender, only who he should impersonate
was not yet decided.   Rumour, ever ready, hinted that the
unhappy sons of Edward IV. had not been murdered, and so
Lambert was at first chosen for one of them.   Then, however,
reports were spread about young Warwick ; finally, it was
said that he had been killed, or that his murder had been
planned.   Possibly, for this reason, the leaders of the undertaking were induced to give out that Simnel was the imprisoned
earl.   But as Lincoln must have been accurately informed of
the real circumstances, this plan appears almost incredible in
its folly ; for Henry could at any moment bring forward the
true Warwick and unmask the deception ; unless, indeed, the
conspirators meditated using Simnel merely as a puppet, and
substituting the true Yorkist prince for him, if things turned
out successful.   There is no hint as to how far such an
intention could fall in with Lincoln's private ambitious
designs.   Ireland, the scene of action, was sufficiently remote
from London, and it was thought something might be expected from the credulity of the warm-blooded Kelts.   The
project succeeded.   How Simons acted with regard to
individual leaders we do not know ; the Geraldines were
gained over, Thomas Fitzgerald, Chancellor of Ireland,
brother of the Earl of Kildare, and the earl himself, joined

---

[1] On Ormond : P. V., 720, Campb., i. 130, 295, 528, Carew Pap., p. 354,
Ware, Rer. Hibern. Ann., p. 4.   Among the unpublished papers of the English
Record Office, is found an undated draft of an order for the complete restitution of
Ormond, with corrections, apparently in Henry's own hand ; Bedford's appoint-
ment for two years, March 11, 1486, Camph., i. 384 ; its renewal, the same, ii.
351 ; Kildare : Ware, p. 2.

[2] See Note 11, p. 324.

the conspiracy, and easily drew after them the credulous populace. Simnel was acknowledged as the true heir to the throne. Though some important towns, such as Waterford, kept aloof, in spite of all Kildare's threats, still this affair of the pretender grew in a short time into a popular rising among the Irish, which was full of danger for Henry.

The king continued to bide his time; he is said indeed to have been informed of Lovell and his new intrigues, even while he was still in England. Towards the beginning of February single rebels were pro- claimed,[1] but not till Candlemas (February 2nd) did the Privy Council meet at Sheen, the modern Richmond, in order to decide what definite steps to take. The Earl of Lincoln was present at these sittings. Again a timely proclamation of pardon, as in the last insurrection, was to lead back to the king those who repented at once. It was ordered that the captive Warwick should be publicly shown to the people. But what excited the most attention were the sharp measures taken against Henry's mother-in-law, the widowed Queen Elizabeth. Her widow's jointure was withdrawn from her "for various considerations," and she herself was removed to the convent at Bermondsey, and a yearly income of 400 marks (£266 13s. 4d.) assigned to her, which was subsequently raised.

There must have been some well-grounded reason for these harsh and severe measures, and although none is mentioned, we are naturally led to seek one in the Yorkist rising, concerning which, especially, the council had met together. Once already had Elizabeth changed sides, when she gave Henry up for the murderer of her sons. Why should not the new prospect for her husband's House fill her with new hopes, though she would thereby be working for her nephew and not for her own daughter? Elizabeth had never shown herself a woman of firm and clear resolve. It is peculiar, certainly, that nowhere should there be any explanation as to the reason for this sentence; the mistaken idea that it was a case of mere arbitrary harshness against an innocent member of the House of York was contradicted by Henry, when he handed over the whole property to her

Margin note: Meeting of the Council at Sheen.

---

[1] Lett. and Pap., ii. 369, previously i. 234, and Past. Lett., iii. 329.

daughter, his wife. Nor could it be a deep-seated grudge on account of that first desertion to Richard, for Henry had before expressly reinstated the queen in all her rights by an Act of Parliament, and had endowed her with an ample income. The cause was a repetition of her former defection. All the threads were not yet in Henry's hand, otherwise the head of the conspiracy, the Earl of Lincoln, could hardly have taken part as a spy in the sittings of the council and remained to the end, before he followed his friend Lovell to Flanders.

The king betook himself to London, and caused the true Warwick to be shown through the streets of the city, without, however, any effect penetrating to Ireland. The conspirators were arming in the Low Countries—mainly with the money granted by Margaret—two thousand German mercenaries under an experienced captain, Martin Schwarz, with whom they landed in Ireland on the 5th of May, 1487. On the 24th Lambert was borne through the streets of Dublin, **Simnel's coronation.** amidst great general rejoicing, and crowned king of Ireland with a crown taken from an image of the Virgin. Then he started to take possession of his own special kingdom of England, accompanied, besides the mercenaries, by crowds of poorly clothed and badly armed Irish, under Thomas Fitzgerald.

In consequence of Lincoln's escape, Henry ordered the east coast to be closely watched, since a descent would surely be made on that side from the Netherlands. At the end of March he left Sheen, went by way of Colchester to Norwich, where he kept the Easter festival, and made a pilgrimage to Walsingham. Through Lord Howth he received news of the events in Ireland ; and at the end of April he moved westwards from Cambridge to Coventry, and marched, apparently undecidedly, hither and thither, till he fixed his head-quarters, on the 8th of May, at Kenilworth. The nobles from the neighbouring counties assembled at his summons in great numbers, with their dependents ; the Duke of Bedford and the Earl of Oxford were given the chief command. When the troops of horse sent out to reconnoitre announced that the enemy had landed on the 4th of June on the coast of Lancashire, Henry set out. More reinforcements fell in on the way. Both parties seemed disposed to vie with each other in trying to gain the favour of the people, for when Henry issued severe regulations for the protection of the inhabitants, Lincoln sought on his side to prevent all plundering.   Hoping for reinforcements, Lincoln advanced slowly ; but his hopes were in vain ; still he did not lose courage, but marched southwards on Newark, and encountered the troops of the king at Stoke on the 16th of June, 1487.

The Germans and the half-naked Irish fought with infuriated bravery, but after three hours, the victory declared for Henry.   The leaders, Lincoln, Schwarz, Fitz- **Henry's** gerald, were slain ; Lord Lovell disappeared after **victory at** the battle ; Simnel and his teacher, Simons, were **Stoke.** taken prisoners, and the latter, whom rumour designated as the real originator of the insurrection, was condemned to imprisonment for life, whilst Simnel was treated with great indulgence.   Henry considered his whole participation in the affair as a joke, and assigned to the mock king a place in his kitchen as scullion.   When he showed himself skilful, he was promoted and given a post among the king's falconers. Henry abode for awhile in Kenilworth, then travelled slowly through the northern part of his kingdom, where many suspected persons suffered punishment.   The citizens in the loyal town of Waterford received in the autumn authority to seize Kildare and his companions where they could, and to confiscate their property.   The Pope, too, again lent his aid to Henry ; a bull limited the much-abused right of asylum in England, especially in the case of those guilty of high treason.   Those who had been excommunicated on account of the insurrection might be absolved by the Archbishop of Canterbury ; a special inquiry was instituted against many Irish bishops by the Pope, and he insisted especially that even ecclesiastics should conform to the obligation of loyalty to the king.   Alexander VI. renewed, later on, the power of absolution for the Primate, and extended it to all bishops, adding, as a condition, that they should act in the matter exclusively according to the king's wish.[1]

Henry did not return to London till the 4th of November, where a rumour of his defeat had been maliciously circulated.[2]

[1] On the insurrection, see Note 12, p. 326.
[2] Harl. MS., 541 fol. 218*b*.   On the rumour in London, see Lett. and Pap., i. 94, Brown, No. 519 ; City Chronicle, fol. 142*a* ; cf. Leland, Collect., iv. 213.

It was just at this time, after the youthful Tudor monarchy had held out firmly against two Yorkist insurrections, that
Henry conceded to his Yorkist wife the supreme dignity which till then had been withheld from her. On the 25th of November, 1487, her solemn coronation took place.[1]

Elizabeth's coronation.

The Estates of the realm had already been called together on the 9th of November for the second Parliament under Henry VII.[2] They had to ratify the Bill of Attainder against those who had taken part in the last conspiracy, by which twenty-eight persons were affected; strange to say, Lovell was not mentioned.[3] For another reason also this Parliament was an important one for Henry's reign. At the opening of it John Morton appears for the first time as Lord Chancellor, the principal official in the kingdom; he had already been promoted to this new dignity, and to be Archbishop of Canterbury in Bourchier's place the year before, whilst Ely had been given to Alcock, who had to resign the Chancellorship in Morton's favour.[4] Morton was thus raised to the public position which befitted his importance for Henry's reign, and he remained till his death the first counsellor of the king.

Second Parliament, 1487.

It was this Parliament which placed in Henry's hand a most effective weapon for his struggle with the aristocracy, and, at the same time, one of the most important means of furthering his monarchical policy. This was the institution of the Star Chamber, whereby the judicial powers of the King's Privy Council were legally confirmed, and a court of justice established, which was immediately under the control of the Crown, and always at its disposal.[5]

Institution of the Star Chamber.

---

[1] Detailed account in Ives, p. 120–156, f.; also City Chronicle, fol. 142*b*; Fabian's Abridgment, p. 683; Hall, 438; Arnold, p. 38; and Grey Friars Chron., p. 24, in the wrong year; Wriothesley, p. 1; Ricart, 47.

[2] Writ of summons of the 1st of September, 1487; Campb., ii. 189.

[3] Rot. Parl., vi. 397–400. On Lovell, see Note 12, p. 326.

[4] There is no special notice of Morton's appointment as Chancellor, but when the temporalities of Canterbury were delivered to him, July 13, 1486 (Rym., xii. 302, f.), he is already called Chancellor. On his and Alcock's ecclesiastical elevation, see also Rym., p. 317, 318; Brown, No. 513, f.; P. V., 730. On Morton, cf. Gigli's account, Oct. 5, 1488; Brown, No. 535.

[5] On this and the rest of the laws of this Parliament, see the concluding chapter.

Henry now made a demand of his second Parliament, to which it consented, and thereby signified its acquiescence in a new departure in the royal policy—Henry's first appearance in the conflict between the foreign Powers on the Continent. At the very beginning of the session, Parliament granted two fifteenths and tenths of the movable property of the lay population of the kingdom, and a graduated poll-tax on foreign traders in England " for the immediate and necessary defence of the realm." [1] Scarcely had the new king conquered his position and maintained it against repeated hostile attacks within his kingdom, when the further necessity was laid upon him of defending himself outside it. Henry was drawn into that struggle which had already affected him when a refugee —the struggle for the independence of Brittany.

[1] Rot. Parl., vi. 400–402, cf. Campb., ii. 228. Gairdner, Henry VII., p. 58, is mistaken in supposing that each " native artificer " paid 6s. 8d. In the grant is expressly stated : " Every person Artificer not borne within this youre said Realme, not made Denyzen."

CHAPTER II.

FOREIGN COMPLICATIONS: FRANCE, BRITTANY, AND SPAIN.

WHEN Henry VII. ascended the throne, England had lost that magnificent position in Europe which had been acquired for her by Henry V. As piece by piece the continental conquests fell back again to France, England's prestige disappeared, and the long and destructive civil war caused the influence of the kingdom to lie completely fallow, so far as foreign affairs were concerned. To dream of regaining the former powerful position was out of the question; the new ruler had to be content, if he could regain for England that measure of respect which she could not dispense with in her intercourse with her neighbours.

It was in France that Henry had last found shelter and help to enable him to come home; therefore, on his return from exile, a definite connection existed between him and France, not at all in keeping with the national tradition, founded on a century of enmity. Thus he appeared from the first destined to put an end to the old quarrel between the two countries; as early as the 12th of October, 1485, even before his coronation, he announced a one year's truce with France, which promised for his subjects safe commercial intercourse, and this after some negotiations was extended to two years, and again on the 17th of January, 1486, replaced by a new three years' treaty.[1]

Besides the French ambassador, others also had soon

---

[1] Engl. Proclam. of first truce, in Rym., xii. 277; French Proclam. of the second, Du Mont, iii. 2, p. 149, f.; Godefroy, Hist. de Charles VIII., p. 501, f.; Negotiations: Campb., i. 199; Brown, i. No. 506; power for conclusion of treaty: Rym., 278, f.; Treaty, ib., 281, f., Du Mont, 150, f.; cf. Campb., i. 192, f., 602.

appeared, from the Archduke Maximilian of Austria and the Duke of Brittany; all, it was believed, with peaceful intentions. But to keep up such friendly relations on all sides for any length of time was obviously impossible; for Anne de Beaujeu still continued to strive with ever-increasing energy for the final incorporation of the duchy.[1] The neighbouring States, such as Burgundy, Spain, and England, had an interest in its preservation; they could not fail to regard the extension of the power of France with dislike; England, especially, after the disappearance of an independent Brittany, would find herself exposed to a long line of unbroken French coast. It remained to be seen whether this interest would so far outweigh the desire for peace and internal stability for England and his new monarchy, that Henry would, for the sake of it, risk the danger of difficult foreign entanglements, and the rupture of relations lately established with France.

In Brittany the enemies of Landois had contrived in July, 1485, to get the hated favourite into their power, and to have him executed, whereupon De Rieux and his companions again returned from France. The victory of her friends was also a gain for Anne de Beaujeu, especially as in France itself the overthrow of the Duke of Orleans took place at the same time, and an advance of Maximilian's into Artois was checked. Of no less importance for Anne was Henry's victory over Richard, which would withdraw England from the ranks of her enemies; she intended now to spend all her energies on Brittany.

How could Duke Francis resist such a foe without allies? As a reward for help, he offered the hand of his eldest daughter Anne, still a child, whom the Breton Estates had acknowledged by an oath of fealty to be his heiress and successor.[2]

The indefatigable Maximilian was the first in the field. Since the death of his wife, Mary (March 26, 1482), he had laid claim to the government of her greatly diminished Burgundian inheritance, in the place of his son Philip, still a minor; but it was not till the summer of 1485, after a long dispute, that he was recognised as

---

[1] See Note I, p. 328.   [2] Feb. 8, 1486, Morice, iii. 499-504.

guardian by the Flemish Estates, who were constantly being stirred up and helped against him by France. On the 16th of February, 1486, took place at Frankfort his election as king of the Romans and successor to his father, the old Emperor Frederick III.   Eager to requite his enemies for the support afforded to his Flemish foes, he concluded on the 15th of March, 1486, a treaty which was to secure independence to Brittany, and which promised to him the hand of the Princess Anne, and to his son Philip that of her younger sister Isabeau.

This did not prevent Duke Francis from making the same offer of his daughter's hand to the powerful Lord d'Albret in the south of France, in order to gain his support for Brittany.   France, however, arrived more quickly on the scene of action, and made the attack with three armies at once. Meanwhile a sharp contention was going on in the Breton Government between the native nobles and the fugitive French, amongst whom was Louis of Orleans. A series of fortified places fell, and D'Albret, who was advancing with a few thousand men, was driven back.   But the siege of the strongly fortified town of Nantes had to be raised in August, 1487, and thus the campaign, which had begun successfully for the French, ended with a disaster ; and still more serious was Rieux's defection from the treaty concluded with Anne de Beaujeu. Maximilian's offer to send forces for the purpose of protecting Brittany caused her less anxiety, for he was soon entirely taken up with his quarrel with the rebellious Flemish towns.

Notwithstanding the conclusion of a treaty of peace, Anne de Beaujeu deemed it advisable, in consequence of recent events, to secure for herself the neutrality of Henry. Perhaps she was not very sorry that Simnel's insurrection should keep a check on the king, but the victory at Stoke, in June, 1487, had quickly brought it to an end. When, after a long stay in the north of England, Henry was returning slowly to London, there met him in Leicester,[1] at the beginning of September, a French embassage which was to justify the action of France, and, if possible, to beg for

---

[1] P. V., 730, f. ; the date according to the decrees dated from Leicester, Sept. 8-10, 1487, Campb., ii. 190, f.

Henry's aid. No one had more cause to draw back from foreign complications than Henry, who had but just passed through dangers at home ; still, prudence bade him assume, at least outwardly, an independent attitude, that he might thereby not appear indifferent in an affair which concerned English interests. He seized on the convenient *England's* plan of offering to both parties his mediation, *attitude as* through Christopher Urswick, in May, 1488, and *mediator.* the French Government, hoping thus to gain time, agreed. But in Brittany, where Louis of Orleans was the ruling spirit, Urswick was dismissed, and a demand made for help from England, whilst France made use of the delay thus given to again beleaguer Nantes.[1]

Henry had reserved for himself a free hand : Brittany had not been mentioned in the French treaty, nor indeed had France, in a similar commercial treaty with Duke Francis.[2] He endeavoured to inspire a certain amount of respect for his office of mediator by equipping a fleet, for which Parliament had granted the necessary funds, but much to his annoyance, and against his express command, his wife's uncle, Edward, Lord Woodville, sailed over secretly from Southampton in a Breton ship, with two hundred warlike adventurers, to take part in the war against France. On the way too they captured a French vessel, and so arrived in Brittany with war booty.[3] Henry immediately made his apologies to France, where the occurrence had caused such bitterness of feeling that the English ambassador, Urswick, was even exposed to personal danger. Henry's best apology was the renewal, at Windsor, on the 14th of July, 1488, of the treaty which would have expired in the coming January, and was now extended for a year longer, to January, 1490.[4]

Breton affairs entered shortly afterwards upon a new phase. On the 28th of July, 1488, at St. Aubin du Cormier, a decisive battle was fought between the victoriously advancing French, under the youthful La Tremouille, and the Bretons,

---

[1] On the negotiations ; P. V., 731, f. ; Brown, i. No. 529.
[2] July 22, 1486 ; Rym., xii. 303-312 ; Du Mont, iii. 2, p. 159-164 ; Campb., i. 515, f.
[3] On the equipment of the fleet in February and May, 1488, Campb., ii. 240, 249, 251, 300 ; Past. Lett., iii. 344, of May 13, 1488. Ibid. and P. V., 733, on Woodville's expedition.
[4] Rym., xii. 344, f. ; Campb., ii. 334.

on whose side were fighting Orleans, D'Albret, and Wood-ville. It ended in a complete victory for the French. Orleans was taken prisoner, Woodville fell, and with him nearly all the Englishmen.[1] After some further small engagements, Duke Francis was forced to beg for peace in a humble epistle to his "sovereign lord," Charles VIII., and to promise, in the treaty of Sablé (August 20, 1488), to send the enemies of France out of his country, and, above all, not to marry his daughter without the permission of the French

Death of Francis II. of Brittany. king. On the 31st of August he signed the treaty, and on the 9th of September he died, to be suc-ceeded by his daughter Anne, a child of twelve.

Anne de Beaujeu, whose husband had, at the beginning of 1488, inherited the power and dignity of the Dukes of Bourbon, now at once raised a claim for the wardship, in opposition to the Marshal de Rieux. She disputed the right of the youthful Anne to bear the ducal title, and the consequence was that the war of devastation in Brittany went on. The young duchess Anne could expect but little help in this juncture from her suitor Maximilian, for he had been taken prisoner at Bruges in February, 1488, by the rebellious Flemings, and although, at the price of certain concessions, he had regained his freedom in May, he subsequently took part in the war of retaliation undertaken by his father against the Netherlands. The most important places remained in the hands of the French, who had marched to the assistance of the Flemings. In the following year Maximilian betook himself to the Empire to beg for help against the French, and was there for a time detained. On the other hand, Henry of England had made good his peaceful intentions by renewing the treaty with France, and, in spite of some scruples, he would certainly rather have seen Brittany become French than throw himself between France and the duchy, while he was not yet firmly established in England. But now a change began.

In the autumn of 1488 Henry again entered into friendly relations with the government of the regency in Brittany. He offered his help, even to come himself, and proposed

---

[1] Hall, p. 441, gives the 27th as the day of the battle. This date also in Pélicier, p. 144; Dupuy, ii. 139, gives the 28th, both without authorities. The last date is correct according to La Tremouille's letter written the day after the battle (Morice, iii. 594).

that Anne should be united in marriage with the son of his
cousin, the Duke of Buckingham who had been executed.
Not long after, in December, embassies were de- Warlike
spatched to the various powers—to France, Brittany, preparations
Spain, Portugal, to Maximilian, Philip, and the in England.
Flemish Estates, all with instructions to conclude friendly
treaties of peace. The great almoner, Urswick, was to renew
in France Henry's offer of mediation for peace, whilst Edgecombe, on the other hand, in Brittany was to make an offer
of English help for the war, and demand portions of the land
as security, and also the pledge that the marriage of the
Duchess Anne should be made to depend on Henry's consent.
Thus the offers in Brittany and France stood in marked
opposition the one to the other. The proposal of mediation
in France appears to be only a first attempt to secure for
himself in case of necessity, as dignified a retreat as possible
from the existing covenant. Henry said also to the Pope's
collector, De Giglis, that he was plotting nothing against the
French king. The gratitude he owed to the late Duke Francis
obliged him to protect the interests of Brittany, which, owing
to the close connection between the two countries, were also
those of England ; for, should the duchy be broken up, his own
kingdom would be in danger. If he succeeded in his efforts
at mediation, all would then be well ;. if not, he would defend
Brittany and her duchess with all his might.

As early as December, 1488, orders to muster had been
sent out to the counties, as the king, "with the agreement of
his council, wished to send an armed force to the assistance
of Brittany." Six hundred men were to be raised at once,
and embarked ; fresh orders followed in January, and the
manufacture of war material was proceeded with. On the 13th
of January, 1489, a new Parliament met, from which Henry
demanded £100,000 for the maintenance of ten thousand
archers for the war. After a long discussion an agreement
was entered into with the convocations of Canterbury and
York, then also sitting, that the clergy should undertake one
quarter, and the lay population raise the remaining £75,000
by the levy of a tenth on all incomes. On the 23rd of February the consent of the Commons was given by the mouth of
the Speaker, and Parliament, which besides this had prepared

no noteworthy measure, was prorogued till the 14th of October.[1]

At the same time, the emissaries sent out in December had concluded treaties, which were really the very opposite of peaceful. In Portugal there had simply been a resumption of friendly relations by the conferring of the Order of the Garter, and the renewal of an old friendly treaty concluded under Richard II., in 1387. The treaty made by the plenipotentiaries of Maximilian and Philip was of greater importance.

Henry's relations with Burgundy had been shortly before rather strained. The first overtures were of a more friendly nature ; the treaty with Burgundy, concluded by Edward IV. in 1478, was first of all renewed for a year on the 2nd of January, 1487, and Henry declared himself ready for further negotiations, but at the same time made complaints about the annoyance caused to Englishmen by Flemish pirates. He was especially vexed because Margaret's dower court in Burgundy had become the centre of Yorkist intrigues. We find accordingly, in the beginning of 1488, a partial restriction of trade placed on the dominions of the King of the Romans, whilst Henry met fresh piracies with special counter measures. He expressed himself, in July, 1488, with much irritation, before the Spanish ambassador Puebla, on the subject of Maximilian, with whom he refused to enter into any alliance. Treaties with Nevertheless even in this we find him subsequently Maximilian turning round again, for in December an embassage and Brittany. of peace was sent to Maximilian as well as to the other monarchs, and on the 14th of February, 1489, a friendly alliance for mutual defence was concluded.

But far closer than this alliance was the covenant with the Breton Government. The ambassador, Edgecombe, who, on his landing, had scarcely escaped imprisonment, concluded, on the 10th of February, a treaty which completely fulfilled the wishes of England. Henry promised to the duchess protection for her dominions at his own cost, but against securities in Brittany until repayment of the same ; Anne's marriage and every treaty of alliance, except with Maximilian or the Spaniards, were to be subject to his approval.[2]

---

[1] See Note 2, p. 328.
[2] Portugal : Memor., p. 193 ; Rym., xii. 378, f. 380, f. ; Campb., ii. 474. First

Only the direst necessity could force the Bretons to such concessions ; Henry had gained the consent of Parliament for war expenses, and besides had stipulated for compensation and securities from Brittany.   The most important thing, however, was this, that England was drifting fast into open war with France.

What could induce Henry to make such a venture ?   We feel from his behaviour that he was only driven against his will to take such decided steps.   His rule in England, still by no means secure, ran great danger thereby ; there was no sign, either, of any warlike disposition in the nation.   That Woodville should have been able so soon after the long civil war to get together a few hundred adventurous spirits means nothing ; the length of the discussion in Parliament, before consent was at last given, points rather to disapproval and opposition, and, worst of all, the levy of a war contribution called forth a fresh and serious rebellion.   The **Revolt in the north of** England was not yet pacified; in **north of** February, 1489, there were disturbances in York **England.** at the time of the election of a mayor.   But far worse was to follow.   The royal tax-collectors encountered opposition in York and Durham.   The Earl of Northumberland, Richard's companion at Bosworth, but raised by Henry to be Warden-General of the East and Middle Marches against Scotland, and later, Sheriff of Northumberland, tried in person to quell the threatening storm, but he was slain on the 28th of April, 1489, by the rebels who had collected at Topcliff under a certain John a Chambre.   The signal thus given, John Egremond, a restless knight, took the lead.   The town of York even was attacked, but Henry at once went to the rescue.   Again a former partisan of Richard's, the Earl of Surrey, who had lately been released from captivity, was given the chief command ; the king himself followed him to meet the insurgents, who were repulsed.   John a Chambre was executed at York, and Egremont fled to that refuge for all the Tudor's enemies, Margaret of Burgundy.   Surrey's reward was his

relations with Maximilian: Rym., 318, 321 ; L. and P., ii. 52–54 ; Campb., ii. 232–234 ; Berg., 1, 10, f.   Treaty of Feb. 14, 1489 : Rym., 359–362 ; in a divergent French form in Du Mont, iii. 2, p. 191, f. ; cf. Molinet, iii. 474–476.   Treaty with Brittany : Rym., 362–372 ; Du Mont, 224–230 ; cf. D'Argentré, L'hist. de Bret., 984, f., and Morice, iii. 617–627 ; Edgecombe's arrival : Past. Lett., iii. 349, f.

appointment, soon afterwards, as the successor of Northumberland.[1]

The consequences of a war policy in England being so bad, why was it pursued ? Various views are possible, but this at least is certain—public opinion did not incline to war.[2] Nor is the motive for this change of policy to be sought in Henry's relations with France, to which country he was bound by a heavy debt of gratitude, nor in Brittany, nor in England itself, least of all in Henry's personal inclination ; this change was really the first important result of a new alliance, now just beginning, between England and Spain and their royal Houses, the maintenance of which was to be the central point of Henry's whole policy throughout a decade and a half.

One thing was especially needful for Henry, as a means of consolidating his power—to get his youthful dynasty recognised as of equal standing by the older ruling *Overtures to Spain.* Houses of Europe. For this it was not enough to conclude a political alliance binding the States together ; a connection by marriage was also necessary, which should mark the recognition by the kings themselves of his perfect right to be held their equal. Therefore a future wife should be chosen as early as possible for his first-born, Arthur, still an infant in the cradle ; and this was specially in Henry's thoughts when he turned his eyes towards Spain. Friendly relations had indeed existed between England and the Spanish kingdoms, but of late they had relaxed somewhat, and the existing commercial intercourse had but little effect in drawing the two countries together. Was it accident, or was it the far-sightedness of the English king, which led him to seek a union with those prominent rulers, who had raised Spain to the important position she was destined to hold in Europe throughout the following century ?

Spain, too, was then at the beginning of a new and important development ; a certain likeness prevailed between the constitutional problems set before the two kings, Ferdinand and Henry, in their respective countries. The tendency towards disruption, which had long since disappeared in England, was especially strong in Spain. No united Spanish kingdom really yet existed, and it was only through the union by marriage of their rulers that the kingdoms of Castile and Aragon held together. King Ferdinand of Aragon owed it to a long struggle between his father, Henry II., and the insurgent Catalonians, that the undivided authority of the Aragonese throne, to which Sardinia and Sicily belonged, had passed to him. His wife, Isabella of Castile, found herself, after the death of the king, her brother, face to face with a strong party wishing to raise to the throne his daughter, whose legitimacy was much called in question. As this princess was betrothed to Alfonso V. of Portugal, the triumph of Isabella and her husband decided the great question of the future—whether the dominating kingdom in the Pyrenean peninsula should be formed into a homogeneous State with Portugal or with Aragon. In a hard but successful struggle, this royal couple had maintained the dignity of their throne as representatives of the State in the face of an independent and turbulent nobility, and their new centralising monarchy was now to exercise complete authority over the separative forces of the old feudal State. By raising the government and the administration of justice, by a prudent if un-scrupulous financial policy, by the use in politics of the Inquisition and of the authority of the Church, combined with a firm and unrelenting consistency of purpose, but also by harsh and even foul means, Ferdinand and Isabella advanced step by step towards their goal. Though com-pletely separate in their internal government, the two king-doms appeared in their external action as one, far outweighing those kingdoms which still remained independent in the peninsula—Portugal in the west, the little kingdom of Navarre in the north, and Granada, the last remnant of Moorish power, in the south.

The leading mind in this joint rule was Ferdinand's, and it is an evidence of Henry's insight, that he spared no pains and no sacrifice to secure as an ally this prince, the greatest statesman of his day. These two sovereigns were somewhat kindred spirits, not so much in the outwardly prominent hardness and the darker side of their nature, as in the lofty aims of their monarchical policy.

It was an important moment for England's future, when

E

Henry made the first step towards an understanding with Spain by issuing powers for an embassage on the 10th of **Henry's over-** March, 1488. He proposed a treaty of mutual **tures to Spain.** peace and commerce, but the main point in the English demands was the matrimonial alliance between Arthur, Prince of Wales, and Katharine, the youngest child of the Spanish monarch, born on the 5th of December, 1485. The powers in reply from the Spaniards are dated the 30th of April, and were brought to England by a special envoy called Sepulveda. In them they agreed to all Henry's proposals for a friendly and matrimonial alliance. The plenipotentiaries in London were able to meet at once for the first preliminaries, and on the 7th of July, 1488, a provisional settlement was prepared. Agreed as to first principles, they reserved the more detailed conditions for future arrangement. Henry had received with unaffected pleasure the intelligence of the favourable reception of his proposals by the Spaniards, whose ambassador, Puebla, reports that he showed his satisfaction by the joyful exclamation, " Te Deum laudamus ! " [1]

There was a good reason for this prompt agreement. When Henry made his overtures to Ferdinand and Isabella, they were in the midst of that ten years' war, which they had been carrying on since 1482, to the complete destruction of the Moorish power, a war which gave to the Spaniards their great military school, fanned the last flicker of crusading enthusiasm, and called together combatants from foreign lands, from Germany, France, and England,[2] which was the chief object at that time of the whole Spanish policy, and in which all their strength was employed. Even before the struggle for Brittany began, the Spaniards had achieved a brilliant success by the capture and fearful punishment of Malaga in the summer of 1487, a foretaste of what would be the fate of Granada. In the middle of this great struggle they were but little inclined to split up their strength over the affairs of Brittany. On the other hand, this complication aroused their own not unimportant claims against France. Ferdinand's father had been obliged to give in pledge to Louis XI. the two border countries — Cerdagne and the

[1] See Note 5, p. 329.
[2] Cf. for this Campb., i. 343, f. ; Berg., i. Nos. 5 and 67.

county of Roussillon—in return for his powerful aid against
the Catalonians (1462). During the ten years between 1470
and 1480, the French monarchy had held out victoriously
against a revolt of the inhabitants, supported by Aragon.
Spanish policy, however, continued to aim at regaining the
lost provinces, and for this purpose the Breton complication
afforded the most favourable opportunity, exciting as it did
enmity from all sides against the greed of France.

In no case should this opportunity be allowed to pass
unused ; the Moorish war, however, obliged them to reduce
as much as possible the forces for this additional task, and
the English offer of friendship came to them as the most
welcome solution of the dilemma. The price which Henry
had to pay for the matrimonial alliance was fixed by them at
the outset. Roussillon and Cerdagne were to be conquered
for Spain, in Brittany.

This reason for their prompt acquiescence came out undis-
guisedly in the stipulation that Henry, if Spain declared war
on France, should immediately join in the war, and Spain's inten-
that without Spain he must not conclude any peace tions in the
or truce with France. Ferdinand and Isabella treaty with
only promised to include England in any peace of England.
their own with France. The English plenipotentiaries naturally refused thus to sacrifice England to Spanish interests ; it
was "against right, against God and their conscience." They
were then reminded of the painful truth, that Spain's powerful
alliance was valuable to Henry "in order to make that impossible which has so often happened to English kings, and
still happens." The hollow show of an equality of conditions
was given by the subsequent proposal that Henry should
have the right to retreat alone from the war, if France
gave him back the English possessions, Guienne and
Normandy ; Spain retaining the same right in the event
of the two counties, Roussillon and Cerdagne, being ceded.
One glance at the map will make us perceive the cleverness of the tactics which made England's withdrawal from
the war depend upon a price such as France would never
pay until she was at the last extremity, whilst for Spain it
was merely a question of a corner of territory, and that a
possession held only in forfeit by France. In return for this,

Henry received very doubtful promises that in the event of an English attack the Spaniards would also support Brittany, while all the time they were even raising objections against his project of a marriage between the Duchess Anne and young Buckingham.

The aim of Spanish policy was expressed in the treaty of alliance in such plain words, that to mistake that aim was altogether impossible; nevertheless, to Henry, the Spanish alliance seemed worth such a heavy price. How resigned his words sounded—that he felt himself in duty bound to Charles of France, that to break with him would cost him many friends, but that he was ready to give them up in order to come to an understanding with Spain.[1] Ferdinand and Isabella not only demanded the breaking up of this old friendship, but Henry was also obliged, simply that he might please them, to forget his grudge against Maximilian. In accordance with their wishes, in December, 1488, he prepared the draft on which the subsequent treaty with Maximilian, directed solely against France, was based.[2] *v. p. 46.*

On the same day, as we know, on the 11th of December, 1488, he despatched an embassy to Spain. It was conducted by Thomas Savage and Richard Nanfan, and its duty was to conclude a treaty of friendship, commerce, and marriage, on the lines laid down, and agreed upon in London. The same ambassadors had then to take the Order of the Garter to Portugal; Puebla and Sepulveda accompanied the Englishmen. The outward course of the journey is described in detail to us by Richmond herald, who was of the party; of the negotiations themselves we learn next to nothing. On the 19th of January, 1489, the ambassadors took ship, but contrary winds drove them back, and detained them in England for a month. On the 16th of February they landed in Laredo, on the north coast of Spain. They passed through all sorts of petty travelling adventures during their journey through the country. One scene was amusing, when the Englishmen, trying to make themselves agreeable, were almost turned out of doors by a rough and cross-grained hostess. On the 12th of March they entered the royal camp

---

[1] Correspondence on these negotiations in Berg., i. Nos. 21–32.
[2] Cf. ibid., pp. 14 and 20.

at Medina del Campo, to the south of Valladolid.   Two days after, they were received in solemn audience; the Bishop of Ciudad Rodrigo answered Savage's speech of greeting, " but the good bishop was very old, and had lost all his teeth, so that only with great trouble could we understand what he said."   Receptions and tournaments alternated for the next few days.   Not till the 26th of March, as the herald relates, were the envoys sent for "in order to bring to an end the settlement of that business which they had to perform ; " on one article alone they could not agree until the following day, when the Spanish king swore to the treaty, the ratification of which bears the date of the 28th of March.

The work had indeed been quickly accomplished.   This treaty of the 27th of March, 1489, marks the first important alliance which the Tudor monarch concluded with   Treaty of a foreign power.   Friendship and alliance, mutual   alliance and protection for their present and future possessions,   marriage. free intercourse between their subjects—these were   Medina del the leading provisions ; each one promised, and   Campo. this was the principal point for Henry, neither to harbour nor support any rebels against the other, and the war with France was determined on, according to the Spanish demand.   It was indeed settled that neither party should make peace without the other; but then, either was bound to begin the war against France at the wish of the other.   The Spaniards were indeed safe against such a wish on the part of Henry. They even saw how to turn the affair sophistically, in such wise that, with a show of regard for the Anglo-French truce, which was still to last till the 17th of January, 1490, they might leave the conduct of the war in 1489 to the English king, and wait till the next year to take part in it themselves. And so accordingly they did.   The fact that owing to circumstances one clause, contrary, no doubt, to the intentions of the Spaniards, still put into Henry's hands a right by treaty to decide for himself when to begin the war, could be of no practical use to him, under the actual relations which existed between them.   Of course there remained as a condition for breaking off the war, the acquisition of Guienne and Normandy on the one part, or Cerdagne and Roussillon on the other.   As the price for this very one-sided preservation

of Spanish interests, Henry was granted his marriage treaty :
the marriage was to be concluded as soon as the royal children
were of suitable age, the dowry was to amount to two hundred
thousand scudi, at the rate of four shillings and twopence, the
half of it payable on Katharine's arrival in England, the other
half two years later; the right of succession to the thrones
of Castile and Aragon was to remain to Katharine.[1]

Thus in one year—a time certainly not very long when
we remember the pace at which business matters were carried
on in those days—the close alliance had been concluded, the
Tudor dynasty acknowledged as of equal standing by its
family connection with the royal Houses of Spain, and a
certain guarantee thus secured for their assistance, in
particular against the hostility of Yorkist rivals and their
friends from abroad. But the sacrifice Henry had to pay
was great, it was the breach with his old ally, the French
Government. Henry had given a proof of the honesty of his
intentions, for even while negotiations were still in progress,
he began arming for war, and at once made the first advance.
It was a kind of payment beforehand, to make the settlement
still more secure for him.

Hostilities had already begun. France regarded with
some uneasiness the threatening preparations of her former
friend ; an English attack on St. Omer was
expected there, while in England, in the autumn
of 1488, there was talk of an unsuccessful attempt
by the French on Calais.[2] Once again the French made an
effort to send envoys to negotiate peace, but just as these
were returning home without success, the English troops
crossed over, and on landing in April, 1489, took Guingamp,
which had shortly before been vacated by their adversaries ;
otherwise they did not do much harm. It was only on
Flemish soil that any English passage of arms worthy of
mention took place : there the covenant with Maximilian
really led to some action in common.

War in Flanders and Brittany.

The rebellious Flemings still continued to hold out, with
the help of France, whose troops, under D'Esquerdes, were
besieging Dixmuiden, a little fortress not far from the border.

[1] On negotiations and treaty, see Note 6, p. 330, and comments by Mr.
Gairdner, p. 435.
[2] Lett. and Pap., ii. 288, f. ; Brown, i. No. 535.

A company under Lord Morley, reinforced by the English garrison of the Calais district under Lord Daubeney and by a few hundred Germans, first relieved the place—where in the struggle Lord Morley fell—and afterwards brought assistance to hard-pressed Nieuport.[1]

This was indeed a slight success ; but as a whole the deeds of arms by no means fulfilled the expectations which had been called forth by the preparations, and were quite inadequate, if it was really desired to give Brittany the aid that had been promised. Another cause of hindrance was the divided condition of the Breton Government, and the English plenipotentiary Edgecombe had much trouble, owing to the personal quarrels between the leading men. Henry, however, was not at all in earnest with his help, he did only what was necessary in order to carry out his desire for a treaty with Spain, besides seeking to keep some advantage for himself by the rich grants from Parliament, and the money for Breton fortresses held in pledge. His position with regard to France was strange enough ; war was not even declared, and yet English and French troops were fighting in various places in Flanders and Brittany.

Henry became soon enough aware of the faithlessness of his allies, and the first who disregarded the covenant was the friend imposed on him by Spain, Maximilian, king of the Romans. The idea of the Spanish *Secession of Maximilian.* monarchs had been to put pressure on France by annoyance from all sides, but none of her adversaries had shown themselves very formidable. It was not till the beginning of 1490 that the Spaniards themselves sent a thousand men into Brittany, who besieged Redon,[2] and with inconsiderable forces undertook an advance on Roussillon. Still France, hemmed in by a circle of hostile alliances, was obliged to look about for a way of escape, and tried to do so by gaining over Maximilian, to whom she promised her help as arbitrator in his dispute with the Flemings. In the Frankfort treaty of the 22nd of July, 1489, they wisely postponed a decision on questions of territory to a later

---

[1] On the events of the war, see Past. Lett., iii. 357, f. ; shortly in P. V., 734 ; confirmed independently by Hall, 444-447 ; cf. the herald's report, Leland Coll., iv. 247, f. ; City Chronicle, fol. 143 ; Fabian's Abridgment, 683.

[2] Zurita, v. fol. 3*a*.

time; the French Government promised, besides their help in Flanders, to give up the places they held in Brittany to the duchess, if she would have all Englishmen sent out of the country and pledge herself not to allow them to settle in it again.[1]

Treaties at that time were seldom concluded on a basis of really common interests, which would have guaranteed joint action. The art of diplomacy consisted solely in the endeavour of each power, in its own interests, to overreach the other, and it was considered quite justifiable to pass over to the enemy at any moment, for more favourable offers. The bewildering number and variety of the treaties entered into by each State are the sign of their complete untrustworthiness; the standard of political morality was very low, and that this lack of principle should have been so universal is the excuse for individual monarchs. So France and Maximilian combined together, without hesitation, abandoning their former allies, the Flemish towns and Henry of England.

With Spain, too, France sought, in the summer of 1489, an independent alliance. A meeting between Anne of Beaujeu and Isabella was already spoken of for the next year, to settle the question of Roussillon.[2] The Spanish monarchs, upon the whole, had the same ends in view. For them the Frankfort treaty was naturally inopportune,[3] and the hopes they had entertained from the alliance with England seemed likely to be realised. In all the difficulties that beset the French government there was no talk of the Spaniards, so that after the Frankfort treaty Henry seemed the only remaining obstacle to a settlement.

Henry's situation had thus become anything but pleasant. Once entangled in this business, so disagreeable to himself, *Henry's diffi- cult position.* he could not well draw back again without having achieved some success, and without recouping himself for the expense he had incurred. The Spanish and English troops in the duchy did not pull very well together; there were disagreements too between the English captains and the Breton Government. The French

[1] Du Mont, iii. 2, pp. 237–239; Molinet, iv. 54–60.
[2] See on this Brown, No. 586.
[3] Berg., p. 29.

Orleanist party, which had the control of the duchess, suspected the Englishmen of treating with Marshal de Rieux,
who was again working vigorously for an agreement with
the French government.[1]   However, there was less danger
for the English king in the prosecution of this war, which
was simply devastating unhappy Brittany, than there would
have been to his authority and to the position of his dynasty
in England, if he had broken it off without accomplishing
anything.   His negotiations with France, however, did not
cease.   Whilst the troops, without indeed doing each other
much injury, were standing face to face in Brittany, the
diplomatists were discussing a renewal of the armistice, which
would expire in January, 1490.   Henry, with   Fresh
much astuteness, made his envoys give the Par-   parliamentary
liament, which had just met together for a new   grants.
session on the 14th of October, 1489, some insight into these
negotiations.   He would thus be able to meet the demands
of the French by a reference to the adverse attitude of his
Parliament.   Then he prorogued Parliament, from the 4th of
December to the 24th of January, 1490, and when the negotiations still did not advance one step, the Estates had to
agree to a new grant for the war on the 27th of February, the
last day of this third session.   This grant was at the same
time to indemnify the king, because the last had been almost
two-thirds below the estimate.   The usual form of taxation
of a fifteenth and tenth was now again chosen, amounting,
with the expenses deducted, to about £32,000, which were
distributed over two years.[2]

Thus Henry had secured for himself the means of carrying on the war, the sole aim of which was to keep hold on the
Breton towns pledged to him, until they were redeemed.
In the spring of 1490, Pope Innocent VIII. had, very much
to Spain's annoyance, sent a message of peace to Henry's
court by Lionel Chieregato, Bishop of Concordia.   This had
failed, indeed, but the bishop renewed his efforts in the
summer of 1490, at a peace congress at Boulogne and Calais,
where, besides the English and French plenipotentiaries,

---

[1] Breton ambassadors' instructions, Aug. 10, 1489; Morice, iii. 649–654 ; cf.
Berg., p. 29.
[2] Rot. Parl., vi. 424, 426, 437–439 ; cf. City Chronicle, fol. 143a.

envoys had also come from the Emperor Frederick, from
Maximilian, and Brittany.   But as England demanded compensation for her expenses even from France, and France the
evacuation of the fortresses, and the Bretons at least a respite,
the negotiations were broken off in August, and French,
Spaniards, and English remained in the country.[1]

Whilst these unsuccessful attempts at making peace were
going on, Henry, with greater success, had negotiated again
on his own account with the Breton Government.   He fitted
out new forces by land and sea, and managed to obtain, as a
further security, the seaport of Morlaix, the revenues of which
were to bring him in six thousand crowns a year.   During
the progress of these settlements, the English garrison
quartered in the town had to suppress an insurrection of
Breton peasants, who, driven to despair by the never-ending
misery of war, revolted against their own government.   Elsewhere, too, similar outbreaks took place among the unhappy
inhabitants.[2]

Henry himself tried to gain new confederates for the war,
and to retain his old ones.   It was just then, on the 27th of
New treaties. July, 1490, that a treaty of peace and commerce,
which had already been mooted, was concluded
with Ludovico Sforza, Duke of Milan ;[3] even a matrimonial
alliance between their Houses was thought of.   Besides this,
Henry made a league again with his faithless ally of the
year before, the King of the Romans.   As the English would
not give up the places they held, and the French, on that
account, would not vacate the duchy, one condition of the
Frankfort treaty remained unfulfilled.   Maximilian had
attained his principal end in this treaty, when, by means
of French help, he accomplished the subjection of the Flemings, on the 30th of October, 1489, and was recognised as

[1] On these negotiations, see the accounts of Chieregato, and especially his
companion Flores, in Brown, i. Nos. 556, 558, 560, 563, f., 566, f., 571, 574, f., 579,
f., 585, 587, 589-593 ; also the English powers for negotiations with France,
June 19, 1490, Rym., xii. 453, f. ; Spanish opinion : Berg., No. 45.

[2] Negotiations and powers of Feb. 15 and April 12: Rym., xii. 387-389,
451, f.; Morice, iii. 658-660, 665, f. ; in Morice the last power is incorrectly
called a "treaty," Mem., 200-222.   Treaty of July 26th, the greater part in
Rym., printed twice over by mistake, 394-397 and 456-458, also 458, f. ; appointment of the English commander, July 16th, Rym., 455, f.   Pay to the troops, July
1st, in manuscript, in the Record Office.   Peasants' revolt : Mem., 208, 217.

[3] See De Maulde, Louis XII., ii. 289-291.

guardian of his son. He therefore made use of the continued presence in Brittany of the French troops as a pretext to declare the Frankfort treaty, now become useless to him, broken off, and to make friends again with England. On the 11th of September, 1490, a treaty for mutual defence was drawn up, the special intention of which was the joint protection of Brittany against France. As a special mark of friendship, Henry sent to the King of the Romans the Order of the Garter. On the 17th of September the treaty was publicly announced in England, and with it the treaty of alliance long before concluded with Spain.

The latter had had a peculiar history. Henry had striven for it with all the means in his power, but when his envoys came home after the treaty of Medina del Campo, with the Spanish ratification, Henry hesitated to confirm it. He took advantage of the Spanish project of a marriage between Anne of Brittany and the Infant Don Juan to make his consent depend upon the condition that the treaty should be altered, that Katharine should be sent to him earlier and the dowry paid sooner. Perhaps he thought, on the whole, that he would wait to see whether the fortune of war would put him in a favourable position for altering the treaty according to his wishes; but all these expectations were disappointed, and on the 23rd of September, 1490, Henry himself also signed the treaty on the terms settled at Medina del Campo. Still he held to his proposal of alterations; certain undefined points in the marriage treaty were to be settled. The manner and time of mutual help in war were to be fixed more definitely, and according to a second proposal, the articles favouring Spain alone about the war with France were to be set aside. He had both proposals drafted in the form of supplementary treaties already ratified by him.[1]

The situation had changed; Henry appears as the one who wished to keep to the great coalition against France, and he was rightly anxious lest his unreliable allies should leave him in the lurch. He had good cause for these fears, for Maximilian, as well as the Spaniards, were withdrawn from Brittany by more important tasks. Henry could hope

---

[1] On Henry's negotiations with Maximilian and the Spaniards, see Note 7, p. 330, and comments by Mr. Gairdner, p. 438.

for but little advantage from a covenant with Maximilian, who had undertaken to fight with France, whilst in the summer of 1490, he was really engaged in driving out the Hungarians from Lower Austria, and pursuing after them as far as Stuhlweissenburg. His prospects with Ferdinand and Isabella were not much better; in the eighth year of the Moorish war, 1489, they made unusual efforts, and conquered Baza, after an unfortunate campaign, whereupon Almeria and the whole district of El Zagals in the east of Granada fell into their hands. They then armed themselves for a great and decisive attack on the town of Granada in the year 1491.

Maximilian had special reasons for an alliance with England. It did not suit him to give up a project so easily; the prospect of the once-promised hand of Anne of Brittany had disappeared, as long as her counsellors inclined to France, but when France refused Rieux's attempt at an agreement in the summer of 1490, and prepared a new attack, Maximilian could hope again. Accordingly, believing England to be occupied in Brittany, he urged on the arrangements for the marriage, and in December, 1490, his marriage with the duchess, then scarcely fourteen years of age, took place by proxy, and with the usual ceremonial. Anne assumed the title of "Queen of the Romans."[1]

Maximilian's marriage with the Duchess Anne.

Nobody could expect that France would remain silent after this, and that this fresh provocation should be given her must have been very unwelcome to Henry. Maximilian, who could not hope to defend alone the claims raised by his marriage, looked to Brittany and her other allies to do his work for him. But the Spaniards, who were just now gathering all their forces for a decisive struggle with Granada, behaved as might have been expected; they agreed with France upon an armistice for half a year, and, at the beginning of the winter, withdrew their troops from Brittany on account, as they afterwards said, of the insurmountable difficulties of their maintenance; only in Redon, which they held in pledge, did they leave a small garrison. In the spring the troops were to return, but instead of them, came a summons from Isabella to Henry that he should send sufficient troops to

[1] See Note 8, p. 332.

Brittany while hers were occupied in the south of Spain. Thus, whilst they themselves, contrary to the precise terms of the treaty, suspended hostilities against France, they required from their ally that he should conform to it exactly.[1]

In spite therefore of the ratification of the Spanish treaty, in spite of the new covenant with Maximilian, Henry stood alone, exposed to the danger of a war with France. For France, at the same time, the position had become particularly favourable. Rieux's defection and the reunion of the two parties in the Breton Government was indeed painful to her, but in return she succeeded The advance in gaining that old suitor for Anne's hand, the of France. Lord of Albret, till then protected by Rieux. For the sake of money and other advantages he delivered up Nantes, which still held out, to the enemy, and on the 4th of April, 1491, Charles VIII. made his entry. In France itself, the unfortunate quarrel between the two parties had been made up, and Louis of Orleans was set free from captivity by the king who just now came of age. On the 4th of September the formal reconciliation with the Bourbons took place. By this means, the Orleanist party, which before had been working against them in Brittany, was won over.

The Duchess Anne was now in the most difficult position. Her contract of marriage with Maximilian only hastened the advance of France, whilst her still unknown husband was vacillating between the duties which called him imperatively alike to the east and to the west. He had contemplated seriously a war with France,[2] but at last the fighting in Hungary became as much more important to him than Brittany, as the struggle in Granada was to the Spanish monarchs. Henry remained Anne's last hope. Whilst he was only thinking of the damages he could claim, a new appeal for help came to him in May, 1491, from Anne in her own and her husband's name ; but could Henry venture on a great war with France, the burden of which would fall on him alone? This almost seemed to be his inten- Preparations tion, for he made exceptionally great war prepa- for war. rations. In order to get more substantial assistance, he followed an example set by Edward IV., and

---

[1] See Note 9, p. 322.   [2] Ulmann, i. 129, f.

turned to private individuals of property with demands for
money. On a resolution of the Council, commissioners were
sent out in July, 1491, to appeal to his faithful subjects "to
support him according to their means, and to grant him aid
either personally or in any other way as seemed best," against
the danger that was threatening him from France; the
commissioners treated with private individuals,
who then, "willingly or no," had to contribute
considerable sums. This not very popular way of
exacting money was called a "benevolence."[1]

The Benevo-
lence.

But this was not enough. Even before the expiration of
the second term of payment for the grant of the preceding
year, the fourth Parliament met on the 14th of October, 1491,
and Morton, in his opening speech, drew out the points of
similarity between the Jugurthian campaign of Sallust, and
the English one now before them. Two fifteenths and tenths
were granted to the king, who wished to take the field in
person, and, if the war should last eight months, the half again
of that sum. On the 4th of November the sittings were
prorogued till the following January.[2]

Henry displayed remarkable ardour in this cause, which
he had espoused only under pressure from Spain, and it was
he who now urged on his loitering allies. The proposals he
had made in September, 1490, for the alteration of the treaty
of Medina del Campo appear to have met with opposition
in Spain. On the 22nd of November, 1491, he had two new
propositions drawn up on the model of the old ones, and the
warlike energy he at the same time displayed was the best
advocate for his wishes. This time he divided the treaty of
marriage and the treaty of alliance into two separate documents, and, with remarkable moderation, he only demanded
that the necessary supplements to the old treaty of marriage
should be made on those points which had remained either
not clearly defined or open to question; the war with France
he proposed they should both declare on the 15th of April,
1492, and begin it at any time before the 15th of June. In

[1] Order to the commissioners, July 7, 1491: Rym., xii. 446–448; cf. ibid.,
464, f.; Lett. and Pap., ii. 372; P. V., 739; City Chronicle, fol. 144*a*; Fabian's
Abridgment, 684; Ricart, p. 48. On the costs of the collection there is a carefully
kept account in the manuscripts of the Record Office.
[2] Opening, Rot. Parl., vi. 440; Grant, ibid., 442–444; Stat., ii. 555, f.

everything else, and we know what that meant for Henry, those clauses of the treaty of Medina del Campo, which were advantageous to Spain, remained unchanged.[1]

Henry showed great earnestness in his demands for money from his subjects ; he went to the very limit of their capacity for giving, although he, whose crown was anything but secure, had to risk all by so doing.

Even if his allies had been able at once to respond to his appeal, it was already too late. France seized her opportunity when Maximilian was detained in the East, and the Spaniards in the South, and gave the king of the Romans the answer that was to be expected. Nantes was in Charles's hand ; his troops, who had marched in during the summer, took from the Spaniards Redon, from the English Concarneau, and besieged Anne in Rennes; only in Morlaix did the English garrison hold out. Even though Henry was making great preparations for war, his mere written assurances of aid from Maximilian and his own promise not to fail her, could no longer help the duchess in her extremity. She yielded to the strongest. After a preliminary treaty of the 15th of November, there followed at Langeais in Touraine, on the 6th of December, 1491, the final agreement which united Anne with Charles VIII., and her duchy with the kingdom of France.[2]

Brittany
united to
France.

It was a grand success, this that the policy of Anne of Beaujeu had so long striven to obtain, and a humiliating defeat for the three kings leagued together to defend Brittany. Henry, with all his preparations for war, was the least interested of the three. He was neither concerned in Spanish designs on Roussillon and Cerdagne, nor in Maximilian's desire to win Anne, who had been betrothed to him. It was Maximilian who suffered the most. By the earlier treaty of Arras (December 23, 1482), he had bestowed on Louis XI. the Duchy of Burgundy, together with the hand of his little daughter Margaret, for Charles, the heir to the throne. King Charles VIII., however, by his treaty at Langeais, contemptuously set aside the daughter of the king of the Romans,

---

[1] Rym., xii. 460–463 ; Du Mont, iii. 2, p. 271 ; Berg., No. 63. The latter only gives the war clauses.

[2] Letter from Henry to Anne, Oct. 19, 1491 ; D'Argentré, p. 1003 ; the treaties, Du Mont, iii. 2, p. 269, f., 271, ff. ; D'Argentré, 1006–1009.

who had been brought up in France, but kept the duchy, and at the same time robbed Maximilian of his affianced wife.

But though exasperated at this twofold humiliation, Maximilian and his father could do nothing. Maximilian, indeed, towards the end of 1491, spoke of marching once more into " Britani or Burgundi,"[1] when he should have finished his work in the east of Europe; but he could not bring matters to a close there, and all his efforts to obtain help from the Empire were in vain. If power was wanting to him, so was good will to the Spaniards. The news that Granada had fallen at last, in January, 1492, was hailed with befitting ceremony in England, and, in the following April, Ferdinand and Isabella appointed plenipotentiaries in order to discuss the changes in the treaty, which had been proposed by Henry; otherwise a profound silence was observed on the affair of the league; just once a hint of war was given, but no more.[2]

Henry was thus thrown back on his own resources. He tried to make other alliances, appealed to the Pope, warned his newly won friend of Milan, Ludovico Sforza, of the danger that threatened him from Charles VIII., and summoned him to take part in the war, but without success. In January, 1492, he made a plan for getting Brest into his hands by combining with treacherous Bretons, and at the same time negotiated with the disaffected nobles in the country. During the new session (from January 24 to March 5, 1492), Parliament issued regulations for war, for the levying and payment of troops; and the convocation of the clergy added a tenth to the grants made by the laymen. Ships and war material were provided, contracts for levying soldiers were concluded with the great lords. The troops were to assemble at Portsmouth in June, and the king had three great breweries erected there, in order to provide them with beer. The fleet then actually crossed the Channel, but without accomplishing much. The French Government also discovered the Breton conspiracy, and entertained the idea of anticipating Henry

---

[1] Max. to Prüschenk, Sept. 21, 1491, in Kraus, Max's correspondence, p. 80; cf. also Ulmann, I, 155, ff.

[2] The festivities in London : Hall, pp. 453-455 ; the Spanish powers, April 26th : Berg., i. No. 72, cf. No. 77.

by an attack on England. An order was accordingly issued at the beginning of August to the inhabitants of the south-eastern counties of Kent and Sussex to hold themselves in readiness to respond at any time to a hasty summons.[1]

Winter, spring, and summer passed away in these pre-parations; a really great war seemed in prospect. Henry himself announced as his aim the reconquest of his French possessions—of "his kingdom of France." It remained, however, inexplicable, that he did not make use of the fine season of the year, that autumn came, and a fresh winter was at the doors, before he made ready to cross the Channel. Meanwhile a few skirmishes by land and sea took place; the small forces which Maximilian had left behind in the Low Countries under Albert of Saxony took Sluys, supported from the sea by the English under Sir Edward Poynings. A partisan of the rebellious towns, the Lord of Ravenstein, had, with the help of France, held Sluys, and made it a centre from whence he carried on a privateering war,[2] causing damage even to the trade of England. Arras also was taken by German troops, but the bulk of the English army remained quietly in their own land.

Henry's more serious threats of war.

The king hoped by noisy threats of war to avoid war himself, and to exercise some effect on the peace negotiations which were being carried on without interruption from the end of spring right through the summer, at first by two pleni-potentiaries, and later by a regular congress of ambassadors at Calais and Etaples. The result was unsatisfactory; sorely against his will and with a heavy heart, Henry had to pass from threats to deeds. He requisitioned Venetian merchant galleys for the transport of his troops, and after he had formally invested the young Prince of Wales at Sandwich on the 2nd of October, 1492, with the dignity of viceroy during his absence, he crossed over to France on the same day in the *Swan*. Minstrels played before him during the passage, and his Spanish fool entertained him with jokes, till he landed at Calais at eleven o'clock. There he lingered for nearly two weeks. At last, on the

Siege of Boulogne.

[1] See Note 10, p. 332.
[2] Hall, 452; cf. Rym., xii. 492; Poynings' appointment, Lett. and Pap., ii. 373.

F

18th of October, he appeared before Boulogne and besieged the town.[1]

Now at last Henry achieved his end ; on the 27th of October, he was able to lay before his counsellors and chief officers the scheme of a treaty sent by him to Etaples. In high-sounding words he had summoned his people to war, and now that all hopes of glory and of great conquests were frustrated, he managed matters so cleverly that he made it appear as if his chief captains had forced him to this inglorious peace. He himself had never thought of conquest, for him the war was, after all, only a money affair, which he was anxious to finish without loss. It was also a clever idea on his part to point to the similar treaty of Picquigny, between Edward IV. and Louis XI. (August 29, 1475) as the model to which he had closely adhered. The opinion of his generals naturally agreed with his own, they put forward the difficulty of the season, the strength of Boulogne, the success at Sluys, the disloyal conduct of the allies, the rich offer of money from France. On the 30th of October, Henry sent a new power to his representatives, who, at Etaples, on the 3rd of November, 1492, agreed upon a treaty of peace, which they sent to the kings to be ratified.

Peace, friendship, and liberty of trading, the same as the former treaties had determined, were to exist between the two kings and their people ; each side promised not to support the enemies of the other, Henry, especially, was not to help Maximilian, should the latter continue the war with France. Charles undertook to pay 745,000 gold crowns in half-yearly instalments of 25,000 francs, he promised also in a special document, that he would not harbour any rebels against Henry. The Estates of both realms were to agree to the treaty.

Peace of Etaples, 1492.

On the 4th of November the peace was announced before Boulogne; at once the camp was broken up and the troops began to make their way back by Calais. On the 9th of November the Lord Mayor of London read out at Guildhall the royal message of peace, and the Chancellor ordered a " Te Deum " to be sung in St. Paul's.

On the 22nd of December, Henry visited the capital ; the

[1] See Note 11, p. 333.

Lord Mayor, aldermen, and citizens went to greet him on Blackheath, and accompanied him through the city to West-minster. The announcement of peace must have sounded pleasanter in the ears of the commercial and tax-paying citizens than it did to the war-loving barons, whose hopes of fame and booty were dashed to pieces by this mercenary peace.[1]

Henry himself had gained by it all he could wish for. The Spanish alliance, to him the first prize of the war, was not indeed regarded as such in the eyes of the world ; but he had brought the war, which had been forced upon him, to a conclusion with some considerable gain, and this meant so much the more for him, since he had to aim at establishing a well-ordered and prosperous system of finance. Henry had, on the whole, nothing to demand from France, for he no longer held to the medieval policy of conquest, and what he had let fall on the subject in public was uttered with a purpose. It was just on the preservation of her isolated position as an island that, for the future, England's greatness depended, and this insular policy, clearly pronounced before the world in the peace of Etaples, was pursued by Henry throughout the rest of his reign.

In fact, there was no reason for him to be vexed that his allies, without the same effort, had outwardly arrived at greater results than he. Spain gained by the treaty of Barcelona (January 19, 1493), the two border countries without having to give anything in return ; Ferdinand and Isabella did not hesitate to promise Charles that they would lend him their help, especially against his "old enemies" the English, and against the king of the Romans, and that they would not marry their own children with them or with their children.[2] Thus the king of the Romans was left in the lurch by both his allies ; still he did not lay down his arms ; his commander-in-chief, Kappeller, gained on the 19th of January a decisive victory at Dournon in Franche Comté, and in spite of his unfortunate position, Maximilian kept his hold on that country as well as on Artois. Both were confirmed to him in the peace of Senlis on the 23rd of May,

France's treaties with Spain and Maximilian.

---

[1] See Note 12, p. 333.   [2] Du Mont, iii. 2, pp. 297-301.

1493,[1] and his daughter, who had been brought up in France, was conducted home to him with much ceremony.

What had especially contributed to the advantageous terms that Maximilian as well as the Spaniards and Henry had secured, was the ambitious policy of the French king, who with each sacrifice purchased for himself freedom of action, that he might be able to hasten on towards his great aim, the conquest of Naples ; thus sacrificing a secure possession on his border for a phantom. But Maximilian still pursued the English king with bitter hatred for his defection, without reflecting that Henry at Etaples had only been retaliating on him for his conduct at Frankfort. The dislike these two monarchs had early conceived for each other, though vigorously combated by Spain, was now stronger than ever ; after the peace of Etaples, Henry could not help seeing in Maximilian an embittered enemy, who was soon to have an opportunity of wreaking his vengeance.

THE BEGINNINGS OF COMMERCIAL POLICY; THE HANSA AND VENICE.

The treaty of Etaples had enabled Henry again to relapse into that inaction out of which he had only allowed himself to be forced by weighty considerations, and which he was henceforth to observe in all questions of general policy. Nowhere else but in the British isles did he again take up arms. The liberty and accumulation of strength which he gained from this inaction, he spent by entering boldly and energetically on a fresh field in politics, that of trade, in which he was to promote to a remarkable degree the future development of England. The commercial efforts of the English, and the guiding, enterprising, or else restrictive commercial policy of the king, stood not only in the closest connection with his State policy in general—the one acting upon the other—but more particularly with the relations he endeavoured to establish with foreign powers.[2]

English trade.

[1] Du Mont, 303-310; cf. for the rest, Ulmann, i. 165-171, 174, Note 1. After the account of Henry's expedition and treaty of peace follows in Weinreich's Dantzig Chronicle (Script. Rer. Pruss., iv. 791), "Der zoch in sein heimot in Engellandt und liesz den Romischen Konig zwischen 2 stole dael siczen ;" cf. Pauli, 563, note 3.

[2] I here take the opportunity of making a general reference to the thorough, and in spite of a few shortcomings, excellent work of Schanz, Englische Handels politik gegen Ende des Mittelalters. We shall often refer to it.

Commerce was the pulse of the whole economic life of the nation; on it depended the breeding of sheep, which supplied foreign countries with wool; on it the prosperity of the youthful industry, seeking a foreign market; it threw, as it were, a bridge across the sea, and connected the island of England with the states of the Continent. Already in the Middle Ages, English trade had reached a flourishing condition; afterwards, in consequence of the civil wars and of reverses on the Continent, it had lost both in vigour within the country, and in the area of its predominance abroad. Ever since the thirteenth century, England had been working towards her future destiny, that of a mercantile nation; the reigns of the great Edwards, the first and third, were periods of progressive development. Under Edward III., who had induced Flemish weavers to settle in England, the English cloth industry made rapid progress, and was able gradually to enter into competition with that of the Low Countries, which till then had been far superior. The cloth industry now became the petted child of royal care, the object of which was to enable English wool to be made up in the country itself, so that manufactured goods might gradually take the place of the raw material as an export.

Still, however, raw material predominated among the exports; it formed the connecting link between England and the Netherlands, which were through it inseparably united in their economic relations; the Netherlands, though the most advanced in industry, were really the most dependent, for if the English wool export stopped, the looms there would stand still. As befitted its importance, the Anglo-Flemish commerce was the first to assume definite forms; English merchants met together in companies in the Staple, which, after some changes, took as its fixed abode the English continental seaport of Calais. The Staple of Calais represented the conservative tendency in commerce, and was based on the privileges granted by monarchs to that rich and secure monopoly, the export trade in raw material with the neighbouring continent. To support this Staple was extremely important to the Government, from financial considerations, because of the heavy export duties on wool, and also from the ease with which a compact might be made with such a firmly united and exclusive association.

But the power of making further progress was taken away from the Staple. The pioneers of the expanding commerce *The Staplers* were the Merchant Adventurers, who, since the *and Merchant* beginning of the fifteenth century, had entered *Adventurers.* into more decided competition with the Staplers. They formed at first no close body, but included all who were not men of the Staple ; being far more free in their movements than these, who were kept bound down to Calais, they attracted to themselves the trade with the Low Countries, and with other places over sea, and as the basis of the Staple was wool, which was confined more closely to its local markets, so the basis of the trade of the merchant adventurers was English cloth, for which new outlets were required. The Flemings knew how to protect themselves from this competition in their own country, but in the interior of Germany it had already become serious for them. Vexatious friction ensued, and the consequent transference of the English mart in the Low Countries from Bruges to Antwerp. The charter of Henry IV. (February 5, 1407) bestowed on the merchant adventurers rights of corporation and self-government ; Englishmen on the Continent were by this means to be given a local centre, and an organised governing body. Henry VII. very soon felt how great the power of these merchant princes was, when they raised objections to the levying of tonnage and poundage before the parliamentary grant; and the king had to make an abatement for them.[1] They had been favoured also from another quarter, when their position with regard to native traders was fixed by the charter of Duke Philip of Burgundy (August 6, 1446). The trade of the English with Antwerp increased extraordinarily, they brought there almost all their cloth goods, also skins and hides, mineral products, and other articles, for which they exchanged the numerous commodities flowing in to that great market of the world.

Next in importance to the Netherlands for English commerce were the German Hansa towns in the north, and

---

[1] Campb., i. 273; Henry IV.'s Charter in Rym., viii. 464, f., and in Henry VII.'s ratification in Schanz., ii. Urk. Beil., 545, f.

Italy, especially Venice, in the south of Europe. The competition of the trade carried on by the league of the Hansa
and the Venetians with England, was more directly
felt, as the enterprising foreigner, still far superior The German Hansa.
to the Englishmen in cleverness and mer-
cantile experience, appeared in their own land, where, however, they could more easily protect themselves against him.
Men had not yet abandoned the view held throughout
antiquity and the Middle Ages, that the foreigner was simply
an enemy ; nations did not yet stand in close enough relation
to one another; and the more limited their knowledge of
foreigners was, the narrower was their view, and the more
rude and prejudiced their self-satisfied arrogance.   Each one
who went abroad was conscious of this fault in others, without
being aware of it in himself.   English ambassadors wrote in
the year 1505 from Spain to their king : " Many noblemen
and gentlemen of this country have no knowledge of your
grace nor of your kingdoms, they imagine there is no other
country but Spain."   Such an opinion, however, is much more
true about the English themselves, of whom an observant
Italian spoke in almost the same words : " They have great
affection for themselves and for all that they have.   They
fancy there are no other men but themselves, and no other
world but England ; " their highest praise for a stranger is
that he looks like an Englishman.   " They have a dislike to
foreigners, who they imagine only come into the country
to take possession of it, and to appropriate their goods." [1]

This innate hatred for strangers was increased in the case
of the merchants of the German Hanseatic League, by reason
of their extraordinary privileges, which, after all sorts of
persecutions, they had managed cleverly to revive, by taking
advantage of the internal condition of England during the
wars of the Roses.   It was at that time that they drove the
English out of their old commercial position in the Scandi-
navian kingdoms ; only in Iceland, which belonged to the
Crown of Norway, did the English keep their hold, by a
flourishing contraband trade, which almost degenerated into

---

[1] English account : Mem., p. 255 ; Ital. Relation, p. 20, f., 23, f. ; on the
English feeling against foreigners, even in Henry VIII.'s time, cf. polite remark
in Thomas, the Pilgrim, p. 6, f.

piracy; otherwise the Hansa enjoyed almost exclusive monopoly.[1] By way of thanks for their generous support against Henry VI., Edward IV. gave them a quite exceptional commercial position in England, by the Utrecht treaty of the 28th of February, 1474. By this they were granted less heavy taxes than the English themselves had to pay, besides full liberty of trade, even in jealous London itself, and the right of judgment by special judges. Their home in London, the renowned Steelyard, on the left bank of the Thames, not far above London Bridge, was recognised as their free property, as well as the house in Boston; and at Lynn they received permission to acquire land. Further, the damages suffered by them in recent times were to be compensated for by £10,000, which they were allowed to deduct from the dues to be paid in the course of the following year.

These privileges were very one-sided, for the security granted in return to Englishmen in the territory of the Hansa was so vague, that they were exposed to much arbitrary treatment. The Prussian trade was not unimportant, in consequence of the export of cloth, and the commodities brought in exchange from thence to England; and in the chief town, Dantzic, the English had formerly possessed privileges of forming a guild, and a house of their own. This last had been taken from them in 1414, and their trade— especially the direct interchange with merchants coming from the East to Dantzic—had been impeded. The only concession to them in the covenant of Utrecht consisted in renewed permission to stay in the Hanse towns, and "to buy and sell with anybody." In spite of this arrangement, the English found themselves pushed out from the markets of the Baltic, whilst the men of the Hansa played a not unimportant part in England's own foreign trade.[2]

This was the state of things Henry found, and he did not dare at once to irritate the powerful league of the towns, who

---

[1] See the complaint of the English in : Hanserecesse, edited by Schäfer, ii. No. 31 ; later complaints about the English in Iceland, Past. Lett., iii. 367, f.

[2] Treaty of Utrecht in Rym., xi. 793–803; the date given by Schäfer in Hanserec., i., Introd., p. vii., Feb. 18, is a printer's error for the 28th ; the king's ratification is of the 20th July, not of February, as Schanz says (i. 177); cf. also ibid., 178, f., on the treaty, and p. 182, on the extent of the Hanseatic trade in England.

might support his enemies, as before they had supported the
Yorkist prince, Edward IV. In the grant of tonnage and
poundage by his first Parliament, "the Merchaunts of the
Hanze in Almayne, haveing a house in the citte of London,"
were exempted from the higher rates fixed for foreigners. A
royal charter of the 9th of March, 1486, confirmed the Utrecht
treaty, a second, of the 29th of June, specially ratified the grant
of compensation to be deducted from the dues up to £10,000.[1]

Placed in a difficult position between the two parties,
Henry had been obliged to grant these privileges, but how
could he seriously hope that they would be exactly carried
out, when in England these advantages to foreigners were
most unpopular, where the complaint was that their trade,
"an intolerable burden," was driving out Englishmen in
every place, and where towns like London, Hull, York, and
Lynn took the matter into their own hands, and in opposition
to the treaty, resorted to all sorts of vexatious
measures against the Hanse merchants. It seemed
as if Henry were only waiting for an opportunity
and a pretext to act contrary to his promise. As
early as the spring of 1486 he began with complaints of Hanseatic piracies, the following year it was stated
more plainly that the rights of the Hanse merchants would
be observed if they would do the same. A restrictive export
law of Richard III. was also made use of against them. The
Hanse traders complained of annoyances, that they were
only allowed to export cloth which was completely finished,
in order that the benefit from shearing to finish might fall to
the English operative. With much craftiness the privilege of
the Hanse trader with regard to "his own commodities" was
restricted to the products of the Hanseatic towns alone.
Henry seized with pleasure on the proposal of the Hanse
merchants established in London to adjust grievances at a
commercial diet, but Cologne, and, later on, the Diet of the
Hansa at Lubeck (February, 1488) refused it ; for it was clear

*Vexatious
measures
against the
Hanse
merchants.*

[1] Act of Parl. : Rot. Parl., 270; Campb., i. 115, the same restriction in favour
of the Hanse in the second Parl. : Rot. Parl., 407 ; charter, Mar. 9th, Hanserec.,
ii. No. 30, of June 29th, ibid., No. 33. Also, Lappenberg, Geschichte des
Stahlhofes, p. 161, f. ; Campb., i. 476–478 ; Schanz, p. 183, gives by mistake
the date of the increased privilege as that of the ratification of the treaty of
Utrecht in general.

that the English would only make use of such a diet to gain
for themselves fresh privileges, whilst for the Hanse merchants
it was simply a question of securing the recognition and
observance of their declared rights. They complained that
they were made to bear the burden of Danish piracies, and
that the whole body of traders in general was held responsible
for the offences of individuals.[1]

His first victories in England itself, and his success in
Spain, had encouraged Henry to more decisive measures ;
accordingly, while the Breton complication and the preparations for the French war were going on, he opened an attack,
though certainly with other weapons, on the mercantile
supremacy of the Hanseatic league.   Instead of abandoning
his original views, he caused the new regulations to be carried
out with greater severity than ever, and if before, in a complaint, the English merchants had said it would be better
to change such a state of things for open war, cost what
it might, now they were not far from a state of actual
warfare.

The Hanse merchants were attacked quite openly on the
sea. A Dantzic trading-vessel was captured by the royal
guard-ships and taken off to Calais ; the Hanse merchants
were advised not to send ships to Hull, where there might be
fighting and murder; the German merchant was no longer
sure of his life in the London streets. Henry was trying to
force on the diet; he hinted that it was no longer possible
for him to shut his ears to the complaints of his subjects,
and the Hanse merchants were even threatened with ex-
pulsion.[2]

Meanwhile the king had been preparing for more vigorous
action. On the 6th of August, 1489, he sent off Dr. James
Hutton, accompanied by several others, charged to
Treaty with Denmark. conclude a treaty with Denmark, with whom at
that time England was engaged in a regular
privateering warfare, and he gave his ambassador, as was his

---

[1] On these negotiations and complaints : Hanserec., ii. No. 26, § 17, f., Nos.
31, f., 103–109, 161 (pp. 176–180, cf. No. 160, § 178), 188, 189 (by this Schanz's
statement, i. 187, can be corrected), 191–193, 217, § 28 (cf. 18–20), 218, 220, f.,
226 (cf. 220, 223, f.).

[2] Ibid., Nos. 223, 301–311, 313, 315, f., 339 ; Weinreich's Dantzic Chronicle,
as above, p. 780, for 1490.

custom in the first years of his reign, the instrument of a
treaty already fully executed on his part.

But the subsequent agreement entered into in Denmark
on the 20th of January, 1490, far exceeded these proposals.
King John of Denmark caught joyfully at the proffered
alliance as a means of resisting the powers of the Hanseatic
league. He gave to the English most favourable terms,
conceding to them all the rights which they had ever enjoyed
in Denmark : fullest liberty of trading in Iceland, rights of
corporation, a court of justice of their own, permission to
purchase land in various places. Whilst Henry in England
was oppressing the men of the Hansa, he was trying by this
treaty to gain a footing in the very region where they had a
monopoly of trade. It was, however, no fresh conquest, but
only the reclaiming of an old possession, from which the
English had been obliged to retreat, as also from Bergen and
Iceland, in the periods of their own weakness.[1]

A herald brought the complaints and demands of the
English king to the Hanseatic Diet, then sitting at Lubeck.
The pressure from him, possibly also the danger that might
accrue from an Anglo-Danish combination, took effect, and
the towns gave in. They declared themselves willing to
have the diet, and after a few further negotiations, Antwerp
was selected as the place of meeting. Thither went, in the
first days of May, 1491, the burgomasters of the leading towns,
accompanied by capable assistants.

But the English envoys, who had already received their
power on the 20th of April, did not appear. Henry had
wished to humble the league less by an open
breach of privilege than by petty vexations. He   **Diet at Antwerp.**
continued this policy by the contempt he openly displayed for the town republics, and he made it even worse by his
utterances and by the scant apologies of his plenipotentiaries,
who arrived on the scene a whole month too late. Besides,
at the instigation of King John, Henry had entered upon
fresh negotiations with Denmark, with an idea of a combined

---

[1] Powers and Treaty, Rym., xii. 373-377, 381-387 ; Du Mont, iii. 2,
pp. 244-247 ; cf. Schanz, i. 256-258 ; Anderson, Origin of Comm., i. 527. Hellwald's Theory (Sebast. Cabot, p. 8), that for Henry it had been a question in
Iceland of a staple for further expeditions to the north-west, is a purely unfounded
supposition.

movement against the towns, and the towns' deputies, hearing of this, suspected that the cause of the delay was Henry's desire to wait first for an answer from Denmark.

The diet now had to hear claim against claim, complaint against complaint. In point of fact, right was on the side of the men of the Hansa, although they had paid but little heed to the limited trade privileges allowed to the English ; but it was not possible that a great State could long be content to waive for itself claims which it had been obliged to grant to others. Henry was really only claiming for his sub-jects in the Hanseatic territory a part of the privileges allowed to Hanseatic traders in England. First of all the ancient position of Englishmen in Dantzic had to be regained, but Dantzic held out firmly, even against the pressure put on her by her fellow towns. Only a few concessions, and these restricted, were wrung from her—permission to frequent the Dantzic "Artushof," and for the English to traffic with other foreign merchants without the intermediary of the Dantzic citizens, during the Dominikus fair in August. The Utrecht treaty, if correctly carried out, would have conceded this last right without any limitation as to time. The agreement, signed at Antwerp on the 28th of June, 1491, gave to the Hanse merchants a confirmation of their established rights, whilst Henry had made one opening, though that a small one, in the exclusive system of Prussian trade ; a modest gain, certainly, but one which in connection with his new relations with Denmark was of some value, as representing the first definite success of his commercial policy towards the north. All this took place at the same time that con-tinental affairs seemed to be entirely engaging his attention, and this no doubt accounts for his desire to keep his hands free a little longer, and the consequent postponement of negotiations with the Hanse towns till May, 1493.[1]

The conflict about privileges with the Hanseatic league was only one portion of a scheme of commercial policy em-

Venice.   bracing the whole north and south of Europe. As the Hanse towns had the ascendancy in the north, so had Venice in the south. The Italian who traded in England was, however, far less advantageously

[1] See Note 13, p. 333.

situated than the Hanse merchant, for he had to pay the
heavy customs levied on foreigners, and was especially
affected by the laws against aliens passed under Henry VI.
and Richard III. It was not, therefore, any privileged position which was the cause of the unpopularity of the Italian,
but rather his superior acuteness in commercial matters, and
that greater unscrupulousness which usually accompanies it.
Richard tried to gain favour with his people by a hostile
attitude towards these strangers, and their position at that
time became so trying that the Venetians began to talk
of reviving an ancient regulation, and giving up trade with
England altogether.

But England would not allow matters to go as far as that.
Was it not the Venetians who brought her the commodities
of the East, as well as those of their own country—fine stuffs,
glass wares, books, the wood that was indispensable for the
bows of the English archers, and, above all, the wines of the
South, for a country so unproductive of vines, and yet so
in want of wine as England?[1] In exchange they exported
English cloth, and, like the Low Countries, were dependent
on England for her excellent wool, which commanded the
market. They made use at once of the change of dynasty to
effect an improvement in their position. Cautiously modest
in their demands, they did not beg that the legal restrictions
on them should be set aside, but only that the heavy penalties
should be removed, and even agreed that the king should
be free to reimpose them at will. Henry complied with
this reasonable request.[2] Yet the.Venetians could no more
found expectations on this favourable policy of the new
king with regard to strangers, than could the Hanse merchants on the ratification of their privileges. The heavy
customs levied on foreigners remained as before, and when
many tried to evade them by becoming naturalised English
citizens, Henry's first Parliament enacted that such naturalised
Englishmen must pay the foreigner's dues, in spite of the
exemption already granted to them by Edward IV., while
English-born subjects of the king were alone considered as

---

[1] At that time England was not quite without vines. We read in the Ital.
Relat., p. 9, "Non sono senza viti; et io hò gustato dell' una matura, et in le
parti australi fariano del vino, ma saria forse austero."

[2] Stat., ii. 507, f.; Rot. Parl., vi. 289, f.

natives by the tax-collectors.   Naturalised foreigners were
also accused of having been the means of smuggling in at
cheaper rates the merchandise of strangers.[1]

England was still only looked upon by the Venetians as a
kind of midway station for Flemish trade.   The ships going
to the East bore the name of the Flanders galleys.   These
galleys were let out to merchant speculators, but belonged to
the State, shipping in general being a government monopoly
in Venice.   In August, 1485, French pirates captured the
four Flanders galleys, and the consequences were at once felt
in Venice, from the non-arrival of the return cargo of English
wool.   The weavers appeared before the Senate, and begged
that something might be done, as their trade was at a stand-
still, and the operatives would starve.   The government
decreed a diminution in customs duties, in order to attract
importation from other parts.[2]

This state of affairs was evidently not unfavourable to
England, and Henry hastened to make use of it.   In the
case of the Hanse merchants, it had been a question of oust-
ing them from their privileged position in England herself,
and opening up the hitherto closed North to foreign trade.
In the case of Venice, things were more simple, the republic
being itself dependent on English exports ; so here the move
was made exclusively for the advantage of the new navigation
policy now inaugurated by Henry.

If the carrying trade of England still remained in the
hands of foreigners, the main reason lay in the fact that the
English merchant shipping was by no means adequate to the demands made upon it.   The fleet,
like everything else in England, was at the conclusion of the Middle Ages, in a complete state of decay.
An attempt made by Edward IV. to direct English merchants
as much as possible to use English ships had been abandoned.
Henry followed on the same lines, but more cautiously.   His
first Parliament resolved that, on account of "the grete
mynishyng and decaye that hathe ben now of late tyme of
the navie within this Realme of England and ydelnesse of
the Mariners within the same, by the whiche this noble

Navigation Act.

---

[1] 1 Hen. VII., c. 2 ; Stat., ii. 501, f. ; cf. Campb., ii. 246.
[2] On this Brown, i. Nos. 498-500, 502-505, 507, f., 510-512, 515, 517,
esp. 503.

Realme within short processe of tyme withoute reformacion be had therein shall not be of habilite and power to defend itself," wines from Guienne and Gascony were to be imported into England only in English, Irish, or Welsh bottoms, manned by sailors of the same countries.[1] This law was to hold good till the next Parliament. The king reserved for himself the right of granting exemptions ; but, excepting for the limitations in time, wares, and place, the same legislative idea is expressed in it, in a small way, which, nearly two centuries later, was expressed in a more comprehensive way in the great Navigation Act of the Commonwealth.

The same desire—to make the shipping of his country able to compete with that of others, and to make this competition easier—animated the king with regard to Venice. Under the name of malmsey — a wine much in demand in England — was understood, not only the growth of the Venetian Malvasia, but southern wines in general, and especially that from Candia, likewise belonging to Venice. The Flanders galleys exported it ; but they were much interfered with by the English, who far underbid their rate of freight by charging four ducats the butt, instead of seven. The Venetian Senate, by a resolution, on the 18th of November, 1488, tried to regulate this by imposing an additional duty of four ducats the butt on every foreign ship.[2] By this the English wine trade would have been made well nigh impossible. Henry resolved on countermeasures, and endeavoured to frighten Venice, as he had the Hansa when he made the league with Denmark, by opening a trade with the Florentine seaport town of Pisa, where an English consul already resided. There, as at Calais for the neighbouring continent, a wool staple was to be established for the countries of the Mediterranean. By this the king sought to bully Venice, English wool being a necessity to her.

In vain Venice essayed to avert the blow, by entreaties and threats. On the 15th of April, 1490, in London, a treaty was concluded with Florence, which conceded to the English every advantage, even that wool should be conveyed exclusively in English ships, only obliging them to deliver the amount required by Italy.

Struggle for the wine trade.

Treaty with Florence.

---

[1] Stat., ii. 502.   [2] Brown, No. 544.

Venice alone was excepted. With regard to her, Henry reserved for himself freedom of action. This and the limitation of the treaty to the 15th of April, 1496, show that its purpose was hostile, that it was not intended to last, and that Henry scarcely believed in its being carried out. But for Florence, the hoped-for gain from an alliance with England was sufficient to make her accede to all the conditions, so that in this treaty also England came off with the lion's share.[1]

It is remarkable that the Navigation Act, which had not been renewed in the second Parliament, was, during the parliamentary session of January to February, 1490, again decreed to come into operation as a permanent law from the following 24th of June ; that it was extended to the Toulouse woad-dye, and further enlarged by the regulation that Englishmen should only freight foreign ships when no English ones lay in the harbour. This extension of the Act with increased severity, shows us that the king now felt himself secure in the line of navigation policy on which he at first ventured so cautiously.[2]

He held firmly and obstinately to his plan regarding Venice. When his demands for a diminution in the duties were refused, and when the Florentine treaty did not exercise the desired pressure, Parliament, at the beginning of the war year, 1492, resolved on a like high additional duty on every butt of malmsey wine imported into England by foreigners, and, in order to provide against an increase in the price of wine, fixed the rather low figure of £4 as the maximum price, and the rather high quantity of 126 gallons as the minimum measure of the butt. The Venetians, in alarm, threatened to stop the supply of wine. As, however, the continuance of the English duty was bound up with that of the Venetian duty, and the English were even then in a more favourable position than the Venetians, Henry let the republic do as it liked, and the duty was not taken off.[3]   For

[1] The treaty in Rym., xii. 389–393 ; Du Mont, iii. 2, pp. 247–249 ; abstract in Anderson, i. 529, f. ; cf. Schanz., i. 134, ff. ; to the English consul in Pisa, Rym., 270, f., 314, f., 553, f. ; Venetian counter-measures, Brown, Nos. 561, f., 569 ; cf. 572, 603.
[2] 4 Hen. VII., c. 10 ; Stat., ii. 534, f.
[3] Customs Law, 7 Hen. VII., c. 7 ; Stat., ii. 553 ; Schanz., i. 140, note, gives the opening day of Parliament, Oct. 17, 1491, as the date of the Act ;

years this uncomfortable war of tariffs went on, with its constant friction; but at last the Venetians gave in, and justified the calculations of the king.

Thus Henry's enterprising commercial policy soon embraced all Europe. In it were brought into play those powers of the State which had been fostered by a cautious home policy. Even in his intercourse with other powers, Henry always kept commercial interests in view: the first treaties with France were essentially commercial, his Navigation Act did not seem to be regarded there as a serious annoyance, until the war at last dissolved all connection between the two countries. The strained relations with Maximilian appeared doubly serious on account of the close mercantile connection with the Netherlands, and the damage to English commerce had been the principal reason for the first quarrel which was settled through the intervention of Spain.

Trade rela- tions with France and Spain.

Henry forgot his anxiety to be circumspect even with Spain, when it was a question of commercial interests. The treaty of Medina del Campo had arranged that for the future the duties which had been customary thirty years before should be paid, but in this matter the Spaniards did not remember that since then their merchants in England had been granted peculiar privileges. Hence the unforeseen consequence was a rise in duties. Ferdinand and Isabella at first demanded that the treaty should be carried out according to the spirit of the treaty, not according to the letter of the unsatisfactory clause, and finally that the clause should be altered. Owing to the unsafe condition of affairs, the Spanish merchants begged for royal licences in greater numbers, though in truth these had now become superfluous, in consequence of the treaty. Henry, however, troubled himself but little about such wishes on the part of his allies, he allowed the situation which suited him to remain the same for years; for it was to his advantage financially, and afforded at the same time a useful diplomatic weapon.[1]

---

according to Rot. Parl., vi. 457, the statute probably was passed in the session Jan. 27 to Mar. 3, 1492; also see Brown, Nos. 606, 609, 627.
[1] On this article: Rym., xii. 421; Du Mont, iii. 2, p. 221; Berg., p. 21; also Berg., pp. 25, 28, f., 37; the licences in Campb., ii. 516; Berg., Nos. 39, 42–44, 47, 50, 61, f., 65, f., 69, 74–76, 86–88.

A monarch with clear insight and firm will stood at the head of the English Government. The first years of his reign show us his political character; temperate, disinclined to a policy of adventure, and with a remarkably clear comprehension of the special interests of his island kingdom. The new dynasty had consolidated itself, and was already inaugurating a new state of things for England. In July, 1490, the Milanese ambassador wrote that he had little to report on the condition of the kingdom, it being good. Henry, however, was not long to enjoy any rest; when he concluded the treaty of Etaples, a storm was brewing which would soon vent its fury on his head.

CHAPTER III.

PERKIN WARBECK.

MUCH against his will Henry's attention had been directed to Ireland at the time when the false Warwick rebelled against him there. But nothing could prevail upon the king to abandon his prudent and watchful attitude with regard to this, the most insecure part of his dominions. After the victory of Stoke, he left it to the Pope to proceed against the prelates, who were implicated in the affair; while he himself made no move till after his spiritual ally had done so, and then with every precaution. Not till May, 1488, a **Measures in Ireland.** year after, did he send Sir Richard Edgecombe to Ireland, in order to receive into the king's favour those Irishmen who were ready to make submission, and to administer a new oath of allegiance; at the same time he was to proceed against rebels and traitors, as Maurice Earl of Desmond had already been commissioned to do in the southern counties. Edgecombe first visited the loyal town of Waterford; in Kinsale, Dublin, Drogheda, and Trim, the authorities took the required oath; but it was only after long negotiations, and after having been obliged to consent to a modification of the form of oath, that he induced the Earl of Kildare with his confederates to take it on the 21st of June, 1488. Henry's special desire to persuade the Earl to come to England, by the promise of a safe conduct, remained unfulfilled; the king was compelled to be satisfied with what he had already achieved.[1]

Not till July, 1490, two years later, was this attempt with

---

[1] Desmond's and Edgecombe's powers: Campb., ii. 291, 315; general pardon: ibid., 315-317; Edgecombe's detailed report in Harris, Hibernica, pp. 29-38, given again, abridged by Ware, pp. 17-24.

Kildare repeated.   John Estrete, the receiver of taxes in Dublin, was told to promise him the same favour which he had received from King Edward, and to offer him the dignity of Deputy for another ten years, if he would come to England in the course of the following year, to discuss the affairs of Ireland ; he was also promised a safe conduct and pardon for any possible offence.   The earl's reply was silence ; not till just before the expiration of the given time did he condescend to make excuses for his non-appearance.   Many lords, spiritual and temporal, wrote with the same intention, saying that as Kildare's presence was indispensable, they also had persuaded him not to go ; and they assured the king of the earl's loyalty.[1]   Time was shortly to throw light on the questionable nature of this assurance.

The victory at Stoke had certainly put an end to an attempted Yorkist rising, but not to the Yorkist party, which still continued to work unremittingly against the Tudor usurper.   In December, 1489, was discovered a new plot to set the Earl of Warwick free by force, in which two of Lincoln's companions, who had been fortunate enough to escape, the Abbot of Abingdon, and a certain John Maine, took part ; they died on the gallows at Tyburn.   In the spring of 1491, there were troubles again in Yorkshire, always more or less disturbed, and the Earl of Surrey had to put down the insurgents by force at Ackworth, near Pontefract.[2]

We find in the same year, 1491, the first indication of a new and wide-spreading conspiracy, which also inscribed the name of Warwick on its banner.   Faithful adherents of the House of York, both English and Irish, met together and entered into league with the French Government, then on the eve of war.   A certain John Taylor, formerly a merchant in Exeter, had been a court official and surveyor of the customs in many of the seaport towns under Edward IV. and Richard III.,

The new Yorkist conspiracy.

---

[1] See Note 11 to the first chapter ; not long after Edgecombe had been sent, a very serious complaint was lodged with Henry against Kildare by one of the writers of the letter, the Archbishop of Armagh : Lett. and Pap., ii. 383, f.

[2] The conspiracy of the Abbot of Abingdon : Rot. Parl., vi. 436, f. ; Plumpt. Corres., 87, see also note. Pauli., p. 595, places the event wrongly in 1487, because he does not notice that the Act speaks of two insurrections, of participation in that of Lincoln of 1487, and in a fresh one of 1489 ; on the rising in Yorkshire : Plumpt. Corres., 95–97, note.

and had received a pardon from Henry only in June, 1489. This man was residing in France. It was necessary, for the plan of an attack on England, to gain over persons of standing in the southern ports, and Taylor therefore addressed himself by letter, from Rouen, on the 15th of September, 1491, to an acquaintance of his, and a former servant of Warwick's father Clarence, John Hayes, to whom Henry had assigned many influential posts of confidence in the seaport towns of Exeter and Dartmouth. Taylor spoke of the help they expected from the French and from other confederates ; they would find support, he said, in "three different places outside the kingdom." Hayes was to speak to his friends, and he gave as the object for which they were to contend in England, with the connivance of France, the elevation to the throne of the " son of your lord." This, again, was none other than the Earl of Warwick. Unfortunately we are able but slightly to raise the veil which covers these preliminary intrigues. It is clear, however, that the name of the Earl of Warwick was once more used as a pretext for the undertaking, and this second plan seems in its earlier development to have been a mere repetition of the former ; a false Warwick was again to be set up in Ireland against Henry. The year was one of famine in the island, so much the more, therefore, was there hope of stirring up the people to sedition and war. Chance put into the hands of the ringleaders a suitable pretender, just at the outset of the conspiracy. It was, perhaps, at the time when Taylor despatched his letter, or perhaps rather later, that there landed in the town of Cork, in the south of Ireland, a Breton merchant named Pregent Meno. He had in his service a handsome youth of seventeen, who flaunted through the streets of the town attired in

Warbeck in Ireland.

silken garments, the property of his master, probably with the idea of advertising them in this way, as a specimen of the stock-in-trade, and he attracted thereby the attention of the Yorkist partisans, who were staying in Cork. They tried to persuade him to personate Warwick, but he is said to have refused in the most decided manner, and to have sworn on the gospels, before the mayor of the town, that he was neither the son of the Duke of Clarence, nor one of his race. The plan was therefore allowed to drop, but still the conspiracy was held to,

and so was the person of the now chosen pretender. John
Walter, a well-known citizen of Cork, who had often held the
post of mayor, and Stephen Poytron, an Englishman, tried to
persuade him to come forward as a bastard son of Richard III. ;
at last they agreed he should personate the second son of
Edward, Richard of York, who had been murdered in the
Tower, and whom Simnel at first was to have represented.
John Taylor, who had returned from France, and a Hubert
Burgh were selected as leaders, the help of the Earls of Kildare
and of Desmond was counted upon, in spite of the recent
assurances given to Henry of Kildare's loyalty. "And so,
against my will," as the pretender afterwards said, "they
made me to learne English, and taught me what I should
do and saye."

In this way was set up the new opposition king, Perkin
Warbeck, who was to cause Henry more trouble and danger
than any other, and whose career was wrapped in all the
charm of romance.

This Warbeck was born in 1474 or 1475 in the Flemish
town of Tournay, where his father John Werbeque or
Warbeck lived as a boatman on the Scheldt, and at the
same time was a surveyor of customs. His real Christian
name was Peter, Perkin being a diminutive pet name meaning
" little Peter,"—" Peterkin." From his very childhood he lived
a life of constant change and adventure ; at Antwerp and
Tournay, again at Antwerp, at Middelburg and Lisbon, he
had already served under five different masters, when, still
scarcely seventeen, he entered the service of Pregent Meno
and went with him to Ireland, where his historical career
began.[1]

The chief distinction between the new and the earlier
rising, was that this time no man of note appears at the
head. John Walter and John Taylor came forward as leaders,
Perkin Warbeck was only an instrument in their hands, but
soon he stood in the foreground as head of the whole movement. The undertaking was to be placed on a broader basis
than the earlier one led by Lincoln ; a league had already
been made with English malcontents and with France.
Perkin himself applied to the Earls of Kildare and Desmond,

[1] On Perkin Warbeck's previous history, see Note 1, p. 335.

and with the latter, to England's border enemy, the Scottish king, as early as the beginning of 1492.

Charles VIII. of France had jumped at the welcome proposals against England ; he invited the pretender to France, where Perkin appeared and was received with honour. It is evident from Taylor's letter that serious plans were entertained for an attack, in conjunction with the anticipated insurrection of the Yorkists, but, in consequence of the peace negotiations, which occupied the whole of the year 1492, and of the treaty of Etaples, which followed after a short warlike demonstration, no further move was made by Perkin. Henry was already on his guard ; the intrigues between Taylor and Hayes were discovered, and Charles VIII. was obliged to undertake, in a special agreement made at the same time as the great treaty of peace, not to entertain or to support any rebels or traitors against Henry. Perkin was dismissed from France and took refuge with Margaret of York.

The danger which he had hitherto caused Henry in Ireland and France had vanished as it came ; now, received by Margaret as her nephew, he came forward more openly with his claims. We cannot discover whether the Dowager Duchess, who was so much to the front throughout the whole of this business, acted in the service of Maximilian, or whether it was she who won over the King of the Romans to make his policy serve the interests of her house. In any case, his dislike to the Tudor monarch was nothing new ; their transient alliance gave place, after the peace of Etaples, to the most bitter hatred on the part of Maximilian, so that he scarcely needed any incentive to receive as a friend an opponent of Henry. Neither Maximilian nor Margaret had any special interest in the person of the pretender. Perkin asserted later on, on oath, that Margaret had known as well as himself that he was not king Edward's son. For them, as before for the Yorkist partisans, he was only the instrument of their policy against Henry.

As soon as the king had received information as to Perkin's whereabouts and conduct, he began to take active measures. In July, 1493, Sir Edward Poynings and William Warham went with a power to Maximilian, who had not

been in the Netherlands since 1489, and also to his son the
Archduke Philip ; at the same time Henry issued orders to
his subjects to be ready for war, in order to protect England
against surprises.   He was already accurately informed of
the personality and former history of his rival.   When the
council of the young archduke put the ambassadors off with
the excuse that Margaret could not be interfered with, as
she was sole mistress in her dower lands, Henry set to work
in right earnest.   However much he had till now shown
himself anxious to promote the interests of commerce, the
interests of the dynasty were of paramount importance to him,
and for these he demanded sacrifices even from commerce
itself. He knew how seriously it would affect the Netherlands

Stoppage of
trade.

when he forbade traffic with Philip's subjects, and
when he removed the mart kept by the merchant
adventurers in Antwerp to Calais on the 21st of
September, 1493.   Flemings were ordered out of England and
their goods were seized.   Not till half a year later (April 8,
1494), did the retaliation come, forbidding the importation of
English cloths, their purchase, sale, and shipment, and closing
the Low Countries to the English merchant.

It was a cheap war for the lord of the land, which was
carried on only with the purse of his subjects.   As in the case
of Venice, Henry reckoned on the dependence of the Netherlands upon English wool, and on the stoppage to trade, which
the absence of the English must produce at Antwerp.   We
hear, also, that this prohibition was evaded in various ways
in the Netherlands, and it had to be renewed with emphatic
severity in January, 1495.

But in England, too, the consequences were being felt ;
here it came at last to a wild outburst of the long smouldering
hatred for strangers, which was directed against the Hanse
merchants, who were getting some advantage from the
situation, by attracting to themselves the whole of the trade
now forbidden between the English and the Flemings.
As yet the effect of the prohibition could scarcely have
been felt to any great extent, nor had the counter-measure
of the Netherlanders yet been carried out, when that bitter
feeling against more fortunate rivals, which had only been
waiting for a favourable occasion, burst forth.   The members

of the Mercers' Guild took the lead, the others followed, and
the citizens of the metropolis were ready. On the 15th of
October, 1493, took place a regular storming of the Hanseatic
Steelyard in London, and it was only with difficulty that the
inmates could defend themselves till the Lord Mayor brought
an armed force to their assistance.[1]

Nothing could have been more foolish than such discord
between two countries so naturally connected as England and
the Burgundian Netherlands. No adequate motives are to
be found for the Burgundian policy in bringing about this
rupture on the occasion of the Yorkist rising; the only
explanation lies in Maximilian's personal influence, and in his
newly awakened grudge against Henry after the treaty of
Etaples. As the alliance with Henry had not quite answered
his expectations with regard to France, he possibly cherished
the hope that a Yorkist king at the head of English affairs,
supported by himself, would be more likely to fall in with his
wishes.[2] It was imprudent enough on his part to break with
England for the sake of such extravagant plans, and from
personal irritation, but this antagonistic attitude appears still
more serious in view of the political situation in general.

Charles VIII. of France made good use of the liberty he
had bought so dearly by the treaties of Etaples, Barcelona,
and Senlis. He represented in Naples the right
of succession of the house of Anjou to the throne   The situation
of that kingdom, in opposition to the illegitimate   in Europe.
collateral branch of the house of Aragon, which had worn the
crown since the middle of the century. In September, 1494,
he crossed the Alps with a splendid army, advanced to
Florence without encountering any resistance, and from there
to Rome ; King Alfonso II. abdicated the throne in favour of
his son, Ferdinand II., but on the 22nd of February, 1495,
Charles was master of Naples, and Ferdinand was obliged
to fly. Seldom has conqueror found his work so easy ; the
question now simply was, whether Charles had ability and

---

[1] On the beginnings of Warbeck's political career and the events connected
with it, see Note 2, p. 339.
[2] Cf. the words of Maximilian's ambassador, Brown, No. 648 ; the Venetian
reports, ibid., Nos. 650, 677 ; and Henry's own view in an instruction to the
ambassadors of Aug. 10, 1494, in Archæol., xxvii. pp. 201-204 ; Lett. and Pap.,
ii. 293-297.

power enough to keep hold of the prize he had won. This would have implied an overwhelming position for France ; therefore the common interest of the other powers was aroused against such a preponderance of one single nation. For Italy it was ominous that the prize of the long ten years' war, now about to begin, should be a portion of Italian territory, and above all that Italy herself must be the battle-field.

It was Spain, the ally of France in the league of Barcelona, who now took the lead against her threatening ascendancy. Ferdinand forthwith raised objections, not from any special affection for his illegitimate cousins, but in the interests of his whole House, and also because he might be annoyed in Sicily by the proximity of the French. The protection of the Pope, Alexander VI., a Borgia, elected August, 1492, served as a pretext for this proceeding on the part of the Spaniards; they even managed to find out a justification for it from a clause in the treaty of Barcelona itself, and when Charles, already standing on the soil of Naples, repudiated these objections, the ambassador Fonseca, in a pre-arranged theatrical manner, tore up the original document of the treaty before the eyes of the French king. Venice first had taken the side of Spain in her policy against France; at Venice took place in March, 1495, the final negotiations, which led to the conclusion of the "Holy League" on the 31st of March. The Pope, Spain, the King of the Romans, Milan, and Venice bound themselves together for the mutual defence of their countries, and if no names were mentioned, the obvious wording of the first article of the treaty could only point to the French conqueror.

With such enmity on all sides, the danger was far greater for Charles than at the time of the Breton war. Spain especially, no longer withheld by other enterprises, threatened him with the full force of her great power. Charles would not wait to be attacked ; he had himself crowned solemnly at Naples on the 12th of May, 1495, and then began to turn homewards, to fight his way through the troops of the league at Fornuovo. The fugitive king, Ferdinand II., returned with some Spanish troops under Gonsalvo de Cordova; unsuccessful at first, they became in the summer of 1496 masters of the French garrisons, who had been shamefully left in the lurch by their country.

But as there was always a fear that the French might repeat their invasion, the League was compelled to keep together and to increase its strength. Ferdinand therefore desired, before all things, to draw England into the coalition, especially as the vacillating Duke of Milan had passed over to Charles VIII., and made with him the separate peace of Novara in August, 1495. The manner in which Henry's Spanish friend tried to force him into the new league against France did not show much respect for him. What Henry had to expect from Spanish good faith with regard to treaties was already evident from the article in the treaty of Barcelona, in which the Spaniards had promised the French king that they would help him against England, and avoid an Anglo-Spanish alliance by marriage. It almost seemed as if this last arrangement was to be literally fulfilled.

Henry and the Holy League.

Ferdinand and Isabella had agreed in principle to a definite drafting of the marriage treaty, which had been urged upon them, and Henry now proposed a form, in March, 1493, which left the old treaty intact, but with the addition of the supplements already demanded, and with the alterations naturally required by the changes brought about by time, and especially by the treaty with France. The answer was a long time coming, external circumstances contributed to cause delay, and it did not appear till the end of 1494 and beginning of 1495.[1] In clearness it left nothing to be desired. The treaty of Medina del Campo had lost its interest for the Spaniards, after they had acquired Roussillon and Cerdagne. We can hardly understand how they could inform Henry that they had been justified in making peace with France because Henry had neither sworn to their treaties nor sent them back, whilst all the time they themselves had previously spoken of "the concluded treaties."[2] With this audacious assertion, they had but one end in view, to declare the treaty null and

The attitude of Spain.

[1] English proposal and Spanish answer : Rym., xii. 517–523 (the extract in Berg., No. 81, is incomplete) ; 523, f. ; Berg., No. 90.
[2] For instance, Berg., No. 72 ; cf. No. 91.

void. They showed themselves, however, ready, if Henry wished it, to conclude a new covenant.

No easier way could they have found of throwing aside a treaty now unnecessary and perhaps burdensome to them, and at the same time of making English policy useful to themselves by the offer of a new treaty. They could not also have shown the English king in a more insulting manner the inequality of their positions, especially now when a new Yorkist rival had just arisen. Henry, however, controlled his feelings, he again gave way to the pressure of the stronger. On the agreement to this demand we have only one report, that of the Spanish ambassador Puebla, who says that Henry spoke of the marriage of Arthur and Katharine, and acknowledged that the earlier treaties were no longer valid, but that nothing more was said on the subject.[1] Nevertheless Henry kept in mind the treatment he had received, and waited only a convenient season for retaliation.

While endeavouring to draw Henry into the League in a way to him so offensive, the Spaniards were especially annoyed by his increasingly amicable relations with France, and his new quarrel with the King of the Romans, a member of the League. After the peace of Etaples, he had returned to his original policy of friendship with France. He was met in a friendly spirit, the conditional payments were made punctually, Charles gave information about Perkin's doings in the Netherlands, he offered Henry, in spite of his Italian campaign, the help of his fleet in the event of war, and all support of the pretender was forbidden in France under heavy penalty.[2] The Spanish ambassador drew the attention of his sovereigns to the effect such friendly overtures would have in England, and Ferdinand and Isabella therefore earnestly warned Henry against French untrustworthiness, which they declared themselves to have experienced.[3]

But the quarrel with Maximilian caused them even greater anxiety, especially as they themselves were planning

[1] Berg., No. 94.
[2] Archæol., xxvii. 201-204. Lett. and Pap., ii. 293, f., 296, f.; Receipts of payment, 1493-1496: Rym., xii. 526, f., 550, f., 569, 575, 623, f., 630.
[3] Berg., Nos. 98-101.

the closest union with him by the double marriage of their children—their eldest son, Don Juan, who, however, died early, with Margaret, formerly the affianced bride of Charles VIII., and their second daughter, Joanna, with the young Archduke Philip. They had, there- **Maximilian and Warbeck.** fore, every reason to smooth down the quarrel between two princes, who were in the future to be closely allied to them. They paid no heed to an appeal for aid from Perkin, supported by the Duchess Dowager; they even offered to Henry their mediation with Maximilian, and acknowledged the justness of his point of view; they promised him their assistance against Perkin, and declared that they were fully resolved to conclude the marriage treaty on the basis of the old terms, but that Henry's reconciliation with Maximilian must absolutely first take place.[1]

It lay completely in Maximilian's hands to make this reconciliation, but if the Spaniards insisted that he was ready to do so, and declared he would not support the pretender, it was clear that he had no such intentions himself. When Perkin found he could obtain no satisfactory help from Flanders, he had applied to Maximilian himself, and was presented to the King of the Romans by Albert of Saxony in the autumn of 1493 at Vienna, where he took part in the funeral ceremony of the Emperor Frederick III.[2] When Maximilian, after an absence of five years, again entered the Netherlands, in August, 1494, Perkin was among his followers. He appeared at Antwerp with much pomp, surrounded himself with a suite, and bore the white rose on his coat of arms, which he also displayed on the house where he was residing. One day, however, it was torn down and thrown into the mud of the street by a mob of angry Englishmen; the perpetrators made their escape.[3] Maximilian was still try- ing to make inquiries about his *protégé*. It was asserted that he firmly believed in Perkin; at any rate he acted as if he did.[4] Scotch ambassadors, too, appeared at his court in June, 1495,

---

[1] Berg., Nos. 92, 97–99, 103, 107; Perkin's letter, ibid., No. 85; cf. 99.
[2] Archæol., xxvii. 207, f.; Lett. and Pap., ii. 321. Unrest, Chron. Austr. in Hahn, Collect Monum., i. 784; cf. 785; Lichnowsky, Gesch. des Hauses Habsb., viii. p. 724, No. 2000; cf. Ulmann, i. 262.
[3] Molinet, v. 15, f.
[4] Venetian report, Brown, No. 665; cf. Zurita, v. fol. 170*a*.

to discuss a simultaneous movement. It is uncertain, however, whether the Scottish king had any share in the equipment of Perkin,[1] which was principally undertaken by Maximilian. The King of the Romans tried at the same time to place his own demands on a more secure footing. Perkin had not only to promise large money payments and other benefits to the Duchess Margaret, as soon as he should have conquered his kingdom, but he had first and foremost to acknowledge Maximilian as his heir in all his dominions, in the event of his dying without children.[2] Nothing could show more clearly than this condition that the participation of the king in the undertaking was a mere senseless political adventure, and on this the most vital interests of the Netherlands were with careless indifference to be staked.

In May the Duchess Margaret again applied to Pope Alexander VI. to take the side of the rightful heir of York against the usurper Henry.[3] She said it was mere talk when the Spaniards maintained that Perkin had left Flanders because Maximilian wanted to be quit of him, for Maximilian himself declared it had been at his instigation that Perkin, in June, 1495, had put to sea with a fleet of fourteen vessels and some thousand men.[4]

It was of great importance for the pretender that he should get hold of a party in England ready for action. In February, 1493, he had already from Flanders entered into relations with confederates at Westminster, and there seems to have been some suspicion that on this occasion the Hanse merchants were prepared to act the part of a go-between. Henry made another move against Perkin when, on the 1st of November, 1494, he conferred on his second son Henry, born at Greenwich on the 22nd of June, 1491, the title of Duke of York, which the pretender had assumed. More important still was the

Warbeck's adherents in England.

---

[1] Brown, Nos. 642, 644, 647, f.

[2] See details and authorities in Ulmann, i. 264, by which Gairdner's statements, Perkin Warbeck, 355–357, are to be corrected; cf. Brown, No. 693.

[3] Mem., 393–399.

[4] Berg., pp. 63, 67, 95; Brown, No. 677. On number and equipment of Perkin's fleet: City Chronicle, fol. 154a. Cf. the account in Gairdner, Perkin Warbeck, 363; also Ware, p. 52; the statements of the Venetian ambassador, Brown, No. 644, rest upon intentionally exaggerated information from Maximilian; cf. for contrary rumours, ibid., No. 641.

work which his spies did for him on both sides of the Channel. In November, 1494, and January, 1495, a number of men, both in high and low positions, amongst them some ecclesiastics of note, as the Dean of St. Paul's and the Provincial of the Dominicans, were brought up for trial. The churchmen were protected by their Order; among the others, Sir Simon Montford, Robert Ratcliff, and William Daubeney were beheaded on Tower Hill on the 27th of January, 1495. Two others concerned, Cressyner and Astwood, were pardoned at the place of execution, "which gladded moche people, for they were both yong men."

On the 29th and 30th of January other executions followed at Tyburn. John Ratcliff, Lord Fitzwater, was kept in prison at Calais, where in November of the following year he paid with his life for an attempt to escape. We find from a confession, made later on, that many other guilty persons, especially from among the ranks of the higher clergy, had escaped discovery. The king no doubt owed the accurate knowledge he possessed of these intrigues to the circumstance that he found an informer among the conspirators themselves. A certain Sir Robert Clifford had been induced, by the promise of free pardon and high reward, to return from Flanders at the end of 1494, and it was his revelation that led, shortly before Christmas, to the much-talked-of arrest of Sir William Stanley.

Unfortunately we have no record that enables us to see exactly the connection between these events. Stanley had been given the post of chamberlain to the king; Sir William he was regarded as a man to whom Henry was Stanley. under special obligations for his opportune assistance at Bosworth. But we must remember that Stanley had remained in a most uncertain state up to the very last moment in the battle; he could scarcely ever have been a reliable partisan, and Henry had been watching him for a long time, without showing outwardly any mistrust, till Clifford's revelation enabled him to set Stanley on his trial. On the 30th and 31st of January the trial took place before the Court of King's Bench in Westminster Hall, and Stanley was beheaded on Tower Hill, the 16th of February, 1495, but without the extreme cruelty of the judicial sentence.

His very valuable property in land and money was confiscated, and his body buried at the king's expense.[1]

Every dangerous movement inside the country was suppressed with energy, and yet it is strange that Henry in December should have sent word to France[2] that he was better obeyed than any English king before him. Anyhow he had taken good care, by preparing his small fleet to defend the coast, that Perkin should not succeed in England, as he had himself on his landing in Wales. On the 3rd of July, 1495, Perkin appeared with his squadron before Deal in Kent, some six hundred of his men landed, but a rising of the neighbourhood soon drove them back. About a hundred and seventy men were captured alive and brought to London, where they were kept in the Tower and in Newgate, and before July was over, all, Englishmen as well as foreigners, were sentenced and hanged at various places on the coast of Kent, Essex, Sussex, and Norfolk. At the beginning of September the leaders, amongst whom were a Spaniard and a Frenchman, were executed in London, and their heads set up on London Bridge. Some more sentences of death completed the work of vengeance, which was carried out with more unsparing cruelty than Henry ever exercised before or after.[3]

Possibly the whole attack was against the will of Perkin, who could not yet reckon in the least on success in England, and had himself remained in his ship. He had suffered heavy losses; his squadron had been dispersed, one ship ran on to the coast of Normandy; but he himself made his way to Ireland, the country which, at the outset, had been chosen as the basis of his enterprise.

In Ireland things had altered much. Two aspirants for the throne had first come forward there, and it was absolutely

Changed attitude with regard to Ireland. necessary for Henry to take energetic measures against this centre of Yorkist animosity. What had availed him his clemency to Kildare, who had at once taken the side of Perkin? Henry's patience was at an end; on the 11th of June, 1492, he

---

[1] On Warbeck's connection with English malcontents, see Note 3, p. 340.
[2] Dec. 30, 1494; Brit. Mus. Mss., Cott. Cal., D, vi. fol. 206, f.
[3] See Note 4, p. 341.

appointed the Archbishop of Dublin, Walter Fitzsimons, to be Lord Deputy ; Alexander Plunket to be chancellor ; and Sir James Ormond, a half-brother of the earl, to be lord treasurer in the place of Kildare's father-in-law, who had held that office for thirty-eight years.   Kildare tried to exculpate himself, but his envoys were dismissed by the angry king, and the earl even begged his old rival Ormond to intercede on his behalf.[1]

The family feud between the Butlers and Geraldines lay dormant for a while ; Kildare had not only at that time asked for help from the chief of the hostile race, but he had even given his daughter Margaret in marriage to Piers Butler, a member of that family.   In a quarrel between Piers Butler and that Sir James Ormond who had been singled out for Henry's confidence, Kildare espoused the cause of his brother-in-law, and it came to a regular faction-fight in the streets of Dublin.[2]

These events and the impression they created in England, and the promise of pardon if he would give up his son as a hostage for his good faith, induced Kildare at length, in May or June, 1493, to seek in person his pardon from the king. Henry invited him, and the other Irish nobles staying in London, to a banquet, and after he had mockingly assured them that next time they would let an ape be crowned, he caused them to be waited upon at table by their former king, Lambert Simnel.   Lambert pledged them in a cup of wine, but, overcome by shame, none responded, and the wish was uttered that the devil had taken him before ever they saw his face.   Only the jovial Lord Howth cried out to him : " Bring me the cup if the wine be good, and I shall drink it off for the wine's sake and mine own sake also ; and for thee, as thou art, so I leave thee—a poor innocent."

The visit ended with the full pardon of the earl, on the 22nd of June, 1493, without, however, his being reinstated in his old office.   This was given in September to Robert Preston, Viscount Gormanston, who had also been in London.   The Archbishop of Dublin had been summoned to give more

---

[1] The appointments : Rym., xii. 481 ; Lett. and Pap., ii. 372, f. ; Ware, 35, f. ; Kildare to Ormond, Feb. 11, 1493 : Lett. and Pap., ii. 55, f.
[2] Book of Howth, Car. Pap., 176 ; cf. Lett. and Pap., ii. 56.

H

exact information to the king, and possibly in consequence of this, Kildare considered it prudent to take a fresh journey with a view to his justification, but he met with no further success, either for himself or for the cause he represented.[1]

Henry did not consider a mere change in individuals sufficient, he resolved also on trying a change of system. The rule in Ireland by natives under English control should be set aside, and in its place should be adopted rule by Englishmen in closest union with the English Government; at the same time the boundary of authority should be extended beyond the Pale to the wild portions of Ireland. On the 11th of September, 1494, the title of Lord-Lieutenant, which had been resigned by the Duke of Bedford, was bestowed on Henry, the second son of the king, while the trusty Sir Edward Poynings received the post of deputy, with ample powers bound only by the laws of England; Henry Dean, the bishop-elect of Bangor, became chancellor; Sir Hugh Conway, treasurer.

On the 13th of October, Poynings landed at Howth with about a thousand men. The Earl of Kildare, who till then had been detained in England, was among his followers. From Dublin Poynings advanced against Warbeck's adherents in Ulster, and passed through the O'Hanlon's country, laying waste as he went. Then it was that Kildare, embittered, perhaps, by the disappointment of his hopes, entered into treasonable relations with O'Hanlon and other chieftains against the deputy, and, together with the Earl of Desmond, proposed to the Scottish king a joint attack on the English power in Ireland. It was also ascribed to his instigation that his brother, James Fitzgerald, seized the castle of Carlow, and planted there the banner of the Geraldines, till Poynings compelled him to surrender, after a protracted siege. As winter was at hand, Poynings resolved to put an end to this campaign, which consisted of constant skirmishes in an inhospitable country, and in which the success his troops achieved was not at all commensurate with the money expended. For the future he adopted the more successful plan of making terms with the chieftains, by means of money payments.

Poynings.

[1] See Note 5, p. 341.

On the 1st of December, 1494, he opened, in Drogheda, an Irish Parliament, which was to frame and legally establish the new system of government. The most important measures—the Statutes of Drogheda, or, Poynings' Law—ordained that no Irish Parliament should be summoned and no Act passed without the previous approval of the English king, which was to be procured by the lieutenant or his council, and given under the great seal ; further, they extended to Ireland the operation of all laws already enacted in England. Other measures granted the power to dismiss the officials and judges hitherto appointed for life ; the authority of the Viceroy, which had been reduced as regarded the Crown, was strengthened still further in Ireland ; liveried and paid retinues were forbidden, as also the battle-cry of the hostile families, the " Crom-abo " and " Butler-abo," and the right of coining enjoyed by the great nobles. Kildare, too, in consequence of his last act of high treason, was attainted by the Parliament, and when he appeared in Dublin, Poynings had him apprehended and brought to England.

The Statutes of Drogheda.

It is remarkable that Poynings by this legislation placed the government of Ireland on an entirely fresh basis, which retained its validity as long as any Irish parliament was in existence ; while only just before, he had been compelled to acknowledge, in his advance on Ulster, the insufficiency of his military powers to control the country by force of arms. For that, however, the power of the king, of which so much had been heard in France, sufficed, when Warbeck appeared again in the country. In vain Henry had sought to win over the Earl of Desmond with his followers, by offering him his pardon, and various customs dues. Desmond forthwith joined Warbeck, and assaulted the town of Waterford from the land, while the latter's fleet was attacking it from the sea. Poynings was supported by money and troops from England, ships had been fitted out, and as Dublin also gave assistance, he was able to relieve the garrison ; the siege had to be raised after going on for eleven days, and Perkin was forced to sail away again with the loss of three ships.

Thus this danger, which was certainly not small, had been happily averted ; still there was no relaxation in the work of providing for the future security of the country. In England itself Henry took active measures to this end, and, in September, 1495, caused a strict inquiry to be made concerning all the Irish, with their wives and children, living in the kingdom. As for Ireland itself, although its dependence had been in other ways increased, it was his special desire to make the island as independent of England, in matters of finance, as possible, so that the expenses of government should be met by the revenues of the country itself. Accordingly, the under-treasurer, Hattcliffe, had to send in an exact report on the extent and produce of the crown lands, on the average amount of receipts from tolls, fines, and other dues ; he had to verify the accounts of officials, call in arrears, and ascertain the cause why the returns were delayed. Hattcliffe kept most exact accounts, but the first financial year showed, that Ireland could not produce even the cost of troops for the garrison, and Henry had to send over large sums for that purpose, and especially for Poynings' compacts with the chieftains.

Even for so capable a man as Poynings, it was not possible really to carry out the new system of government. In January, 1496, he was recalled, the duties of his office were handed over to the chancellor ; it may be that his own report led Henry to make fresh projects. Kildare too succeeded in regaining Henry's confidence, which had been severely shaken, and, ignorant of all court ways, the Irishman brought his cause himself in somewhat rude fashion before the king. **Kildare restored to favour.** When the Bishop of Meath, who appeared as his accuser, cried out that all Ireland could not rule this man, Henry aptly rejoined, he then should rule all Ireland. The English parliament removed the ban from the Earl, he received a present of money, and was reinstated in his dignity as deputy on the 6th of August, 1496, which he continued to hold into the reign of Henry VIII. Thus, though Henry kept to the laws which had been proclaimed, he returned, so far as the question of persons was concerned, to the old form of self-government, and from that time the Earl of Kildare remained faithful.[1] If Ireland did not quite become what the Statute of Drogheda required of her, she did not, at least, offer any further refuge and

[1] On the events after Poynings' appointment, see Note 6, p. 342.

assistance to the Tudor's enemies.   That she should cease to
play her former part against Henry was enough for him.

Wherever Perkin Warbeck had appeared, in Ireland, in
France, or with Maximilian, he had called forth old and new
animosities against Henry, and he constituted a   Scotland.
danger wherever his wandering life led him.
When driven from Ireland, he had taken refuge in Scotland,
and his presence there at once caused the semblance of peace,
which till then existed between England and her northern
neighbour, to give way to open strife.   In spite of truces
and treaties of peace constantly renewed, the predatory war
on the English and Scotch Border went on.   A special subject
of dispute was the Border fortress of Berwick, which had been
mostly in English hands since the times of Edward I. and
III.   King James III. had it in view when he began to take
arms shortly after Henry's accession, but a three years' peace,
from the 3rd of July, 1486, averted the danger ; a matrimonial
alliance was even in contemplation between the two royal
Houses.   The treaty of peace required that the disputed
question of Berwick should be settled within a year ; and as
this was not done, the treaty fell to the ground in July, 1487 ;
new settlements were made to take its place, but they led to
nothing beyond the consoling prospect of a possible final
agreement.[1]
The old state of things continued.   The victory over
Simnel had protected England from immediate danger
from the north ; yet subsequently Henry considered it
necessary to be always ready armed in case of attack.   In
spite of a provisional treaty of the 28th of November, 1487,
the Scotch parliament urged more strongly in the following
January its claims on Berwick, demanding that at least the
fortifications should be demolished.[2]   Preparations were
again being made for fresh negotiations, when the decisive
catastrophe approached in Scotland itself.   A party of rebel
lords had managed to attract to their side the young heir to
the throne.   James III. was declared deposed, and James IV.

---

[1] On the treaties between Henry VII. and James III., see Note 7, p. 343.
[2] War preparations: Brown, No. 520 ; Bain, Cal. relat. to Scot., iv. No. 1528;
Parliamentary resolution : Acts of Parl. of Scot., ii. 182.

was to be placed on the throne in his stead.   Henry kept up
relations with both sides, he negotiated at the same time
with the king and with the rebels, before whom he even called
the young prince by the name of king.[1]   For the moment a
settlement seemed possible in Scotland, but soon the two
armies stood again face to face, and in June, 1488, James III.
perished at Sauchieburn, not far from the renowned battle-
field of Bannockburn ; he was murdered in a peasant's hut,
while trying to make his escape.   Over the body of his
father, James IV. ascended the throne.   He was only sixteen
years of age.

Henry was on his guard against surprises,[2] for the feeling
in Scotland, even after the change of ruler, was anything but
friendly.   When the Scotch parliament resolved
in October, 1488, that a wife should be sought for
the young king in one of the courts of Europe,
France, Brittany, and Spain, were named, but not England,
in spite of the previous agreement on the subject ; indeed,
just at that time, when a war between England and France
was imminent, Scotland renewed her "holy league and
covenant" with England's enemy.   It was only a project,
however, and the rumour which spoke of a treaty as already
concluded was an error.[3]   On the 5th of October, 1488, a
three years' truce was once more agreed to, but mistrust and
strife did not cease ; from the Scotch side energetic measures
on the border were insisted upon, while Henry, in May, 1490,
ordered that all Scots, who were at all to be suspected, should
be sent out of England.[4]

Whilst James IV. remained on good terms with Henry's
old enemy, Margaret of Burgundy, Henry on his side tried
to take advantage of the perpetual quarrels between parties
in Scotland.   In January, 1489, the Master of Huntly
addressed himself to Henry in the name of those who had
formed the party of James III., to request his support and the

Marginal note: Henry and James IV.

---

[1] For the negotiations with the king, Dec., 1487, Jan., Feb., May, 1488 :
Rot. Scot., ii. 482, 485 : Rym., xii. 334 ; Past. Lett., iii. 344 ; with the Lords,
May, 1488 : Rym., xii. 340, f. ; Rot. Scot., ii. 485, f. ; Bain, iv. No. 1539.

[2] Orders for equipment of the 16th and 19th July, 1488 : Rot. Scot., ii. 486 ;
Bain, iv. No. 1542.

[3] Acts of the Parl., ii. 207, 214 ; Berg., No. 26.

[4] Truce : Rot. Scot., ii. 488–490 ; Bain, iv. No. 1545 ; also Rot. Scot., 491,
493, 496 ; Bain, No. 1559 ; Acts of the Parl., ii. 220.

punishment of the king's murderers, and on the 17th of
April, 1491, Henry even made a compact with John Ramsay,
Lord Bothwell, and his friend Thomas Todd—who since the
murder had been living in England—that they, in league
with Earl Buchan, should get possession of the person of
James IV., and also, if possible, of his brother the Duke of
Ross, and deliver them up in England.   This intrigue came
to nothing; it serves only to illustrate the mutual relations
of the two countries, for in spite of it and in spite of the
simultaneous resumption of a projected covenant of the Scots
with France, both sides, in the same month of April, resolved
to treat for an extension of the armistice which was drawing
to its close in October, 1491.   Thus matters went on; the
relations of Scotland and France became still more intimate
towards the end of 1491 and beginning of 1492; Perkin
Warbeck had no sooner appeared in the political world, in
March, 1492, than he was at once regarded at the Scotch court
as the son of King Edward IV., whilst, on the 16th of November,
1491, Henry made a similar but more important treaty than
that with Lord Bothwell, with Archibald Douglas, the powerful
Earl of Angus and his son George; both promised to promote
a peace policy in Scotland and to combat those who were
against it.   The Earl of Angus belonged to the party that had
overthrown James III., but the young king had withdrawn his
confidence from his abettors in the insurrection.   This compact of the earl with Henry shows how they retaliated.
Apparently it was discovered in Scotland, for a part of his
property was taken away from Angus and bestowed on
Patrick, Lord Hailes, who had already been given the lands of
the attainted lord of Bothwell, with the title Earl of Bothwell.
Angus, however, was soon received into favour again by the king.

In spite of these hostile covenants, a treaty was again
made on the 21st of December, 1491, which Henry, but not
James, confirmed; almost exactly the same settlement was
then come to on the 3rd of November, 1492, and on the 25th
of June, 1493, the peace was extended to seven years.   Henry
even acknowledged that the last treaty had been violated
more seriously by the English than by the Scotch; he
promised to pay £1000 in compensation.[1]   Nothing testifies

[1] On the negotiations and agreements subsequent to the treaty of Oct. 5, 1488,
see Note 8, p. 344.

more forcibly to the weakness and unreliability of these treaties of peace than the great number of them, the necessary negotiations which accompanied them, and the constant complaints of violation. It was not to be imagined that the promised peace would really last till the year 1501 : some crisis only was needed to expose to the light of day the real condition of affairs. This was supplied by Perkin Warbeck.

How far an agreement had existed between James and Perkin since the first overtures in March, 1492, is not known ; but in June, 1495, we find Scotch ambassadors **Warbeck in Scotland.** taking part in the preparations for the expedition from the Netherlands. Henry was kept fully informed of the plans of the king of Scots in connection with Perkin, either through Clifford from the Netherlands, or more probably through his Scotch friend Bothwell, who, why or how we know not, had received permission to return home, but still continued to draw his English allowance. Orders were issued in the northern counties [1] to arm and be ready ; once again, indeed, an attempt was made at a peaceful settlement, but without any hope of success.

In England, at first, no one knew where the adventurer, when driven out of Ireland, had taken refuge.[2] James, however, who had demanded contributions from his subjects for the support of Perkin, was making preparations at Stirling to give him a suitable reception, where, on the 27th of November, 1495, he appeared with his English followers. An attack on England was shortly afterwards arranged ; Perkin wrote to the Earl of Desmond for aid ; in Scotland preparations for war were begun, but in spite of the hopeful reports circulated abroad, nothing at first was done. James showed himself now and then in company with his guest, whom he entertained like a prince, and to whom he even gave in marriage a kinswoman of his own, Katherine Gordon, the daughter of the Earl of Huntley. In words of admiration, full of poetic enthusiasm, Perkin Warbeck writes to the lady of his heart ; " whose face, bright and serene, gives splendour to the cloudy sky, whose eyes, brilliant as the stars, make all pain to be forgotten, and turn despair into delight ; whosoever sees her

---

[1] Rym., xii. 568, 569–571 ; Bain, No. 1608.
[2] Berg., pp. 85, 89.

cannot choose but admire her, admiring, cannot choose but love her, loving, cannot choose but obey her." Yet the beauty of the adored fair lady did not make Perkin forget her riches and her rank, she seems to him "not born in our days, but descended from heaven." Such wooing found a hearing. The fair Scotch lady remained the faithful companion of his wanderings, till he was captured and his imposture completely unmasked.[1]

Henry meant to attack James with the same weapons, when he tried to get into his hands John Stuart, Duke of Albany, the king's cousin, then living in France.[2] It was, of course, far more important for him to get possession of the pretender himself; he turned therefore to his old friends the Lords of Bothwell and Buchan; but in spite of their encouraging words, nothing came of it, and the king could only console himself with the news of the strong resistance which James' projects were encountering from the Scotch nobles and people. Perkin also had some reinforcements from England, besides a small company which came to him from Flanders in two ships, so that in September, 1496, he had gathered about fourteen hundred men around him. James, however, would not give his help for nothing, and after some debate, they agreed together that if Perkin were victorious, Berwick should be surrendered and a payment of £50,000 be made.[3]

With an unscrupulousness that was almost naïve, Bothwell reported to Henry all that went on, the strength of the troops, the amount of artillery, and tried to stir him up to an energetic assault on his own sovereign. He was not misrepresenting matters when he said that the Scotch were setting about the enterprise with quite inadequate means; moreover, amongst the men who on this occasion were giving their counsel were to be found the very keenest partisans of the enemy, as Bothwell's own example proves.

King James kept to his plans, in spite of all the attempts to dissuade him. Herein it was especially to the interest of

---

[1] See Note 9, p. 345.

[2] Brit. Mus. MS., Cott., Cal., D, vi. fol. 26a.

[3] See Bothwell's undated letter, Pinkerton, Hist. of Scot., ii. 442, f.; Ellis, i. 23, f. (on the same, Tytler, iv. 326; Gairdner, Perk. Warb., 368), and that of Sept. 8, 1496; Pink, 438–441; Ellis, 25–32; cf. also Gairdner, as above, 368, ff.

Spain, as in the case of Maximilian, to ward off complications which should delay Henry's joining the League. In 1488, James IV. had already wished to make terms with the Spanish king and queen, and the year following they offered him a not very honourable alliance, with a natural daughter of Ferdinand, but in 1495, another marriage was talked of, when Scotch ambassadors sued for the hand of an Infanta for their master. Ferdinand and Isabella pretended to agree to this, but they required in return that Scotland should join the League, should give up the pretender, and make peace with England. Pope Alexander exhorted James to comply. All they gained was at the most promises of peace, which were not kept.

Attempts at mediation.

A genuine but somewhat feeble attempt at mediation, made at the last moment by France, through the Lord of Concressault, had no better success. The envoy, in accordance with Charles VIII.'s promise to Henry, declined to pledge his master to any actual interference, for he did not mean to irritate Henry and drive him into the arms of the League. Instead, however—and this was an idea the Spaniards at that time entertained for themselves—Concressault tried to bring about the surrender of Perkin to France, and offered 100,000 crowns. Henry knew of these plans. Bothwell, indeed, did not quite trust the French ambassador, who was often in secret company with Perkin, perhaps in the hope of inducing the latter to escape to Charles of his own accord.

If Henry reminded the French king of the help promised to him, he was not thinking of the literal fulfilment of this promise, he was only hoping that such threats might frighten James; Concressault's mission was to satisfy his demands outwardly at least. However, the Frenchman had as little success with the Scotch king as had the Spaniards.[1]

But Henry did not rely upon the ever-doubtful help of his good friends, he took care of himself. On the 14th of October, 1495, a new parliament met, after an interval of three

---

[1] On the Spanish and Scotch relations: Acts of the Parl., ii. 207, 214; Berg., pp. 26, 69, 71, 72, 91, 96, f., 98, 99, 105, 115, f.; on Concressault's mission, see besides Bothwell's letter of Sept. 8, Henry's instructions to France: Brit. Mus. MS., Cott., Cal., D, vi. fol. 28*a*, f., and Archæol., xxvii. p. 203; Lett. and Pap., ii. 296.

years, and its very first measure promised protection to all who, in the event of a rebellion, remained firm to their duty and supported the king *de facto*. Henry's adherents might very well say to each other that, in spite of this seeming security, a victorious Yorkist prince *Preparations for war.* would repeal the law, and thus the measure proved to be in fact chiefly a conciliatory one to original Yorkist partisans ; for from the benefit of the statute only such were excluded who should afterwards desert the king.   Further, Parliament assigned by law a fixed income for keeping up the fortifications of the border towns of Berwick and Carlisle.   Henry did not claim any special grant this time, it seemed to satisfy him that his parliament gave him power to collect like taxes such contributions towards the last benevolence as had remained unpaid, and that alienated crown lands, and above all, the property of the numerous outlawed rebels, should be adjudged to him ; besides these, he received a tenth from the convocation of the clergy.[1]

If Henry really considered the danger which was threatening him from Scotland so trifling as he gave Charles of France to understand,[2] the sequel proved him right, for the long-planned enterprise was after all but an ordinary raid, such as the border *Scottish inroad.* counties had often had to endure.   In the middle of September, 1496, the incursion took place, announced by a wordy proclamation from Perkin, full of promises of good government and full of hatred for Henry, for whose head he offered as a reward £1000 and a large income from land.   He even promised that his companions, the Scots, would do no harm to his future subjects ; but these companions did not trouble themselves much about this, they burnt and laid waste to their heart's content.   If he and James were reckoning on a rising for the Yorkist cause in the uncertain north of England, this mode of warfare did not tend to attract men to their party.   The enterprise was badly prepared and badly conducted.   The Scots ventured on no encounter, and quite four days before the English forces

---

[1] On the Parliament and its resolutions : Rot. Parl., vi. 458–508 ; Stat., ii. 568–635.   The convocations : Wilkins, Concilia, iii. 644.
[2] Cott., Cal., D, vi. fol. 26.

actually started from Carlisle, the mere intelligence of their approach made the Scots retreat in the greatest haste. On the 21st of September, Perkin stood again on Scottish ground at Coldstream ; and thus all ended in most pitiable failure.[1]

Still James did not give up his *protégé ;* just as before he had rejected the enticing offers of France, now also he kept true to Warbeck, when the hopes founded upon him had been so bitterly disappointed. We cannot help thinking that James really believed in the impostor,[2] in any case Perkin Warbeck's personality charmed him. Judging from the astonishing impression which Warbeck seems to have made on the people with whom he came in contact, he must have possessed, besides his attractive outward appearance, a particularly winning manner ; that letter to his lady-love, if it was really his own, is a composition which bears no bad testimony to the gifts of a wandering youth of humble origin. His fearless, romantic, and adventurous audacity charmed the Stuart king, and touched a responsive chord in him. The youthful monarch was himself imbued with a chivalrous spirit, bold and straightforward, of a character that won the highest esteem from Ayala, the Spanish ambassador, but, like almost all the men of his house, he was deficient in the gifts of statesmanship and forethought. The pretender's adventure attracted him, though the utter hopelessness of it was clear as day ; he remained firmly and honourably true to his *protégé,* and was even bound to him by ties of personal affection. Thus Perkin and his followers remained in Scotland, and lived at the king's expense till the summer of the next year.[3]

At this time a danger arose for Henry in England, Preparations threatening to shake his very throne, and well cal-for war of culated to inspire the two friends with the most retaliation. exultant hope. The English king had issued a proclamation declaring James had broken the peace, and

[1] Perkin's proclamation quoted in Bacon, Works, ed. Spedding, vi. 252–255, undated, but issued after crossing the border. "We . . . be now . . . entered into this our realm ;" on the invasion : P. V., 757, City Chronicle, 160a, Fab. Abridgment, 685, f. ; notice in Lett. and Pap., ii. 330 ; cf. Rot. Parl., 513, and the inexact accounts in Brown, Nos. 727, 735.

[2] Cf. Gairdner, Lett. and Pap., ii. Pref., 57 ; Tytler, iv. 323, f., 361, f.

[3] See Rot. Scacc., x. 555, 576, xi. 4, 15, 39, 49.

that henceforth war would prevail between their two king-doms.[1] He prepared for the struggle in the most energetic manner. In order to secure the money required, he did not summon a formal Parliament, but, according to an ancient custom, a "great council," to which he invited, besides the Lords, "certain burgesses and merchants from all towns and parishes in England." They sat from the 24th of October till the 5th of November, 1496, and voted the king a grant of £120,000 for the war.

This was not a legal grant, but rather the guarantee of one from a kind of preliminary Parliament, intended to give Henry the credit necessary for a loan, which he forthwith solicited throughout the country, and which finally brought him in £58,000. The arming by land and sea had begun in December, then on the 16th of January, 1497, the Estates assembled at Westminster. The chancellor, Morton, at the opening ceremony, quoted examples from the history of Rome of mustering subjects for the defence of the kingdom, and warning them against rebellion and civil war. It was only, he said, on account of the Scots' breach of the peace that writs for a fresh election had been so soon issued.

This Parliament did really pass a few measures, but its main object was the confirmation of that grant, for which the very same men who were now assembled in Parliament had given their voice. The Commons enlarged both on the breach of the peace and on *Grant of taxes.* the violation of the allegiance of the Scottish vassal—an antiquated claim which had been enforced in former days; and they granted to the king two whole fifteenths and tenths payable on the ensuing 31st of May and 8th of November, and, for the further prosecution of the war, a second tax of like severity, without even the abatements made. from the first; but no one was to be assessed who possessed less than twenty shillings rent from land, or less than twenty marks in personal property; the clergy also voted specially heavy taxes. On the 13th of March Parliament was dissolved.[2]

---

[1] Bain, iv. App. i. No. 35; here placed in the foll. year, 1497, whilst from its contents, and from the date of the month occurring in it (Sept. 25), it is unquestionably connected with the attack of 1496.

[2] On the "great council" and the loan, see City Chron., fol. 161*a*, f. 162*b*,

A heavy demand had been made upon the country, and though the poor had been exempted from it as much as possible, the tax-collectors probably did not always act with the prescribed moderation. When they came to Cornwall, they were met with open resistance. The rough inhabitants of this extreme south-west portion of the kingdom lived far from the Scottish Border and the dangers in the north; they were only conscious of the burden laid upon them for a cause that was indifferent to them. Clever agitators at once made use of the first indication of disturbance, and gave it a definite aim. They asserted they were not drawing the sword against the king, that their whole hatred was directed against his counsellors. A lawyer, Thomas Flammock, and a blacksmith, Michael Joseph, put themselves at the head, and led the mob to London. At Wells they found a new captain, in the person of a nobleman, James Touchet, Lord Audley, who, having lost his patrimony, turned rebel from vexation. The town of Bristol refusing to grant them admission, the insurgents passed on through Winchester and Salisbury to Kent. The men of Kent stood in bad repute in consequence of the earlier popular risings under Wat Tyler and Cade, but quite lately they had shown themselves loyal, and held out against Perkin Warbeck's followers. Now a body of men was quickly collected together under the Earl of Kent and other nobles to oppose the Cornishmen. The first reverse discouraged many of the insurgents; a portion of them were already beginning to run away, when the ringleaders pressed on to the capital for the decisive encounter.

Here the king was expecting them. The startling news of the rising had reached him at the beginning of June, just as he was busily arming against the Scots, when great sums for pay had been despatched to the north, and Lord Daubeney was already on his way thither with the troops that had been collected. He at once received the order to return, the whole fighting force was brought to bear on the enemy at home, and the muster from the border counties was to suffice

The Cornish insurrection.

172*b*; the preparations for war in Dec.: Exc. Hist., p. 110; on the Parliament: Rot. Parl., vi. 513–519; Stat., ii. 642–647; City Chron., 162*a*, f.; Convocations: Wilkins, iii. 645, f.; cf. City Chron., 162*a*.

against any possible attack from Scotland. The nobility
from the neighbourhood of London came with their followers
into the capital. Daubeney's arrival on the 13th of June
relieved the citizens from great anxiety. On the following
day a division of his troops encountered in a skirmish the
rebels who were approaching from the south-west by Guildford.
A secret message from some one among their ranks betrayed
a distrust of their leaders. Daubeney had been drawn up in
St. George's Fields since the 15th, a Thursday. On the
Friday he pushed forward to reconnoitre as far as Kingston,
and joined the king on his return, so that about twenty-five
thousand men were massed together against fifteen thousand
rebels.

On the Friday afternoon the Cornishmen appeared, and
encamped on Blackheath, lying under the dark shadow of its
elms to the south-east of London, a spot where formerly
rebel armies had also pitched their tents. It was with difficulty
that the leaders kept up the failing courage of their men ;
they prepared to hold the bridge, which led westward from
the foot of the hill over the Deptford brook. On the morning
of the Saturday, the 17th of June, 1497, Henry ordered his
troopers and archers, under the command of the Earl of
Oxford, to surround the enemy's position on the right flank
and the rear, in order to cut off his retreat. Daubeney, with
the bulk of the troops, attacked the bridge ; the king brought
up the rear-guard. The rebels fought with desperate bravery.
Even Daubeney was for the moment made prisoner ; but
when they saw themselves taken in the rear and in flank they
held out no longer. About a thousand were left on the field ;
the rest, among them the three leaders, surrendered.

After the battle, at about two o'clock in the afternoon,
the king rode into the town, where the mayor, John Tate,
and the aldermen, attired in scarlet, awaited him ; after
thanking them for the maintenance of the troops, which had
been undertaken by the town, Henry knighted on the spot
the mayor, one sheriff, and the recorder. He then betook
himself to St. Paul's to offer up thanks, and from thence to
the Tower, where on the Monday the three rebel leaders
were brought before the king and council.

Only these three suffered the penalty of the law ; all the

rest received the king's pardon. On Monday, the 26th, the blacksmith and Flammock were sentenced, and on the day following hanged at Tyburn, their bodies quartered, and their heads cut off; on the Wednesday, Lord Audley, attired in a paper coat, on which his arms were painted, was led through the streets in a mock procession from Newgate to Tower Hill, and there beheaded. The heads of the victims were stuck up on London Bridge, and over the four gates of the city, the quarters of Flammock's body; the blacksmith's remains were sent to Cornwall and Devonshire.[1]

The sedition had now been completely quelled, but the effect it produced outside the country was bad. Henry felt conscious of this, and did his best to counteract it. **Defeat of the insurrection.** All thought of revenge on Scotland was forgotten, in view of these serious disturbances in his own kingdom; he was even prepared to make sacrifices to ensure peace. He had already, in the year 1493, offered the Scotch king marriage with a distant kinswoman of his mother, but had treated the matter with indifference, when the offer was passed over in silence. In June, 1495, he took a more decided step, by making the first proposition of a marriage which was to be of great importance for Great Britain's future—the marriage of his daughter Margaret with King James; several times, in May, June, and again on the 2nd of September, 1496, he issued powers for these marriage negotiations, but they seem to have come to nothing.[2]

James held back; his own proposals were such as Henry could not accept. After the treaty of peace had been broken in September, 1496, Henry was thinking seriously of **Negotiations with Scotland.** a war of retaliation, when his mind was diverted by the Cornish rising. Notwithstanding his victory, he dreaded another war, and above all the necessity of renewed taxation, after his recent experience. On the 4th of July, 1497, he sent Richard Fox, Bishop of Durham, accompanied by William Warham and John Cartington, as plenipotentiary, to Scotland. At the same time he assumed

---

[1] On hist. of the Cornish rising, see Note 10, p. 345.
[2] First proposal of marriage from England of May 28, 1493; Rym., xii. 529–531, 538, 540; power for Margaret's marriage, June 23, 1495: ibid., 572, f.; Bain, iv. No. 1612, later powers: Rot. Scot., ii. 520, 521, f.; Bain, No. 1622; Rym., 635, f.

a threatening attitude, and issued the order that all the Scots
living in his kingdom should be expelled or pay a heavy fine;
and £12,000 out of the last subsidy went towards arming for
war in the north.[1]   Meanwhile Fox was to arrange that
Perkin should be given up and an embassage of peace despatched from Scotland, for it was necessary that England, as
the stronger, should keep up appearances, and not make the
first formal overtures of peace ; a personal meeting between
the monarchs was also proposed.   Henry was ready indeed
to forego the surrender of Warbeck, and to make still greater
concessions ; only peace there must be now at any price—all
other matters might be settled later on.   The motives, however, which urged Henry to peace, tempted James to war.
Possibly the danger created by the rebel host marching to the
very gates of London seemed greater than it really was ; in
any case the opportunity was favourable.   The expense of
Warbeck's maintenance also, and the constant opposition of
his own nobles, may have urged the king to venture on a
decisive move.   So Henry's efforts for peace, as well as those
of the Spaniards, who tried to mediate between the parties,
were in vain.

In the summer of 1496, Ferdinand and Isabella had again
despatched Don Pedro de Ayala on a special mission to
Scotland, but their ambassador arrived too late   Spanish
to be able to prevent the invasion.   They tried   intrigues in
to attract James by the pretended offer of a   Scotland.
marriage, and in order again to free themselves from this
promise with a good grace, they proposed to Henry that he
should give his daughter to James, probably without knowing
of the king's own plan.   They offered Ayala's services as
mediator.   They were honestly anxious for peace, and when
they heard of the warlike preparations of the English, they
warned them of the uncertain fortunes of war ; still they had
in the background their own selfish ends, and their primary
aim, as it had been before with the French king, was to get
Warbeck into their own hands.

Henry had already felt some suspicion of his Spanish

---

[1] Power, July 4, 1497 : Rym., xii. 676, f. ; Instruct., July 5, Lett. and Pap.,
i. 104-111 ; Bain, iv. No. 1635, esp. Lett. and Pap., p. 110 ; Decree of July 1st :
Bain, No. 1614.   Payment of the £12,000 : Exc. Hist., p. 117.

friends, on account of their relations with Warbeck, and events proved he was not altogether mistaken. Their London ambassador, Puebla, had first suggested the design with regard to the impostor, but in order to keep Henry in the dark if possible, any intention of the kind was disclaimed even to Puebla himself. In October, 1496, Warbeck begged a Yorkist partisan in Spain to do something for him, especially to let him know the sentiments of the king and queen. The answer was brought by Ayala, who was then anxious to prevail upon James to give Warbeck up, and who offered him compensation for all the expense he had incurred. Above all, he tried to gain Perkin himself; he put before him the inevitable reconciliation between the English and Scotch, the fate which would then await him, and offered him a safe refuge in Spain. He brought with him a carefully prepared plan, that Perkin should sail to Ireland, where Spanish fishing-boats would take him aboard; time and place were fixed upon.

But James would not be led astray, he held firmly to his friend; Warbeck, however, acted less honourably, hoping to get help from both sides and ready to deceive both when the time came. The King of Scots, who was already sending the links of his gold chain to the mint to be turned into coin to supply his failing funds, was arming for a double assault, —he was to attack by land, Perkin by sea. As they might reckon on the insurgent Cornishmen aiding Perkin, and as money was scarce, they only made ready one ship for him, at Ayr, in the Firth of Clyde; but the two boldest pirates of that time, Andrew and Robert Barton, joined him there in their own vessel, and the captain of a Breton merchant ship was induced, either willingly or by force, to take part in the expedition.

At the beginning of July, 1497, Warbeck set sail; James waited for some weeks, and then in August, when he might hope that Perkin was on the march, advanced on **A new Border war.** the Border fortress, Norham on Tweed, devastating the plain with his scouring parties as he went.

Henry was better prepared than before. Whilst Norham made a successful resistance, the Earl of Surrey advanced from Yorkshire with nearly twenty thousand men to its relief, and a

fleet under Lord Broke put to sea. James had scarcely expected
this, and as nothing was heard of Perkin's advance, he turned
back again. Before August was over, Surrey, crossing the
Scotch Border in pursuit, took various strongholds, amongst
them, after a sharp bombardment, Ayton, lying to the north
of Berwick. James did not venture to relieve it ; in chivalrous
fashion, he offered to fight the earl in single combat for the
possession of Berwick, but the earl, as the servant of his king,
refused this form of decision ; bad weather, and difficulties in
provisioning his forces, obliged Surrey to turn homewards
at the end of a week, and to discharge his troops in
Berwick.

The warlike King of Scots had received a sharp lesson ;
and as Henry's friendly overtures still went on, and Warbeck
had shamefully disappointed all the hopes set on him,
negotiations were at once begun. Ayala fulfilled his office of
mediator ; the Spanish marriage still remained his bait for
James, and so at last, on the 30th of September, 1497, at
Ayton, the place lately so fiercely contested, they agreed to
a seven years' treaty, which, however, was framed exactly
on the model of the usual temporary English and Scotch
treaties, and in no way met the special wishes of the English.
To Ayala, who had been expressly appointed mediator, was
entrusted the further settlement of various disputed points, and he managed to arrange, in   Peace with
London, on the 5th of December, an extension   Scotland.
of the peace for the lifetime of the two sovereigns ; the
public announcement was at once made in London.[1]

The fate of the faithless Warbeck was also sealed. When
he reckoned on making use of both Scots and Spaniards for
his own advantage, he was completely mistaken. As Ayala
had planned, Perkin, accompanied by his courageous wife,
sailed for Ireland ; but against Ayala's wish, who could hardly
have countenanced hostilities against England, he allowed himself to be led astray by Sir James Ormond, then an enemy to
Henry, and set up his claim again in Ireland. A Spanish
knight, Don Pedro de Guevara, who with his two brothers had
been in the service of Maximilian and of the Archduke Philip,
joined him. A simultaneous movement had been frustrated

---

[1] On this second attack and the attitude of Spain, see Note 11, p. 346.

by delay; for James began hostilities while Warbeck was still loitering in Ireland.

But there could be no longer any hope of success in that country; for Kildare now held to the king, and Desmond, who two years before had refused Perkin's request for help, had also made his peace with Henry, a fact of which Perkin must have been aware. On the 25th of July, 1497, he landed at Cork, the same place where he had made his first appearance. There he was received by his old friend, John Walter; even men of good position in Cornwall, and also in Devonshire, now entered into communication with him, for in spite of the victory at Blackheath and the leniency then shown, seditious feeling in these counties was not yet subdued, and a prospect was held out to him of a favourable reception and willing support.

Warbeck's landing in Ireland and England.

For more than a month, Warbeck remained in Ireland. Towards the end of July, the citizens of Waterford, getting news of his presence and of his intentions with regard to Cornwall, sent word to the king; yet, it was only after some hesitation that they endeavoured to obey his command to get possession of Perkin. Whilst Kildare and Desmond were trying to catch the pretender, the men of Waterford despatched four ships after him; Walter, aware of the peril to his friend, conveyed him secretly in a boat to Kinsale, where three Spanish merchant vessels, possibly those provided by Ayala, awaited him. Warbeck induced the captain, a Spaniard from San Sebastian, to take him over to Cornwall. His ship was seized by the king's men, but the crew hid Perkin in a cask in the ship's hold, and in spite of the high reward offered, denied that he was there. On the 7th of September, 1497, Warbeck landed safely in Whitsand Bay, in the extreme south-west of Cornwall.[1]

The king, meanwhile, had had sufficient time to prepare. Lord Daubeney was sent to the west by land, Lord Broke by sea. The pretender quickly gathered a following among the disturbed population of Cornwall and Devon; on the 17th of September, a Sunday, he appeared before Exeter at the head of a force of six to eight thousand men. Refused admission, he began to storm the town; he was

[1] For Perkin's journey to Ireland and Cornwall, see Note 12, p. 347.

repulsed, and failed in a renewed attack on the following day.
He turned towards Taunton, but hearing that Daubeney's
forces were drawn up only a few miles to the north, near
Glastonbury, his courage failed him ; he stole away secretly
at midnight on the 21st of September, with a few companions, and finally, finding the coast guarded, he fled to the
sanctuary of the convent church of Beaulieu, near Southampton.   A thousand marks were set upon his head.   The
pursuers, who had followed him on horseback, tracked him
thither, where, since there was no chance of escape   Warbeck's
and he was assured of pardon from the king, after   capture.
a short parley he surrendered with his companions,
Heron, Skelton, and Ashley.

On the 4th of October, Henry had come to Taunton ; on
the 5th, Perkin was brought before him, and made a full
confession.   He followed the king to Exeter, whither his
wife, whom he had left behind when he made his way to the
coast, was brought.   She was treated in the most lenient
manner ; Henry received her graciously, ordered £20 to be
at once paid to her, and sent her under safe escort to the
queen at Sheen.

The betrayed Cornish people had dispersed after the
flight of their leader, and when the repentant inhabitants of
Devon appeared before the king, begging for mercy, he only
reserved the ringleaders for punishment, and allowed the
bulk of the insurgents to go their way ; his commissioners
did the same in Cornwall.   But the guilty did not escape scot-
free ; many of them had, the next year, to purchase their
pardon with a large sum of money ; and even in the year
1500, many were sued for arrears, and some thousands of
pounds thus swept into the king's coffers.   The citizens of
Waterford were graciously rewarded by the grant of special
privileges.

Henry did not honour the captive impostor with further
attention.   Now at last, in his extremity, the pretended
king's son remembered his old parents in Tournay, and wrote
a melancholy letter to his mother, full of anxiety as to his
approaching fate.   He did not, however, forget to beg for
money wherewith to dispose his gaolers more favourably
towards him.

Journeying slowly homewards, Henry arrived at West-minster on the 27th of November. Along the way the people ran together to stare at Perkin ; at Westminster he had again to repeat his confession before the town authorities, then he was led through the city to the Tower. Behind him followed a man in fetters, a servant of the king, who, having deserted with another companion, was executed as a traitor at Tyburn on the 4th of December. Meanwhile for Warbeck, as a foreigner, and not guilty of treason to his own lord, a mild captivity was reserved. Attendants were appointed to keep constant guard over him. The following month a dwelling was even assigned to him in the king's palace, and a horse kept for him at Henry's expense.

His wife, the companion of his last adventurous voyage, remained separated from him. Possibly the love of the high-born Scotchwoman had received a severe shock, when she learnt that her husband was an ordinary impostor of humble origin, who, besides, at the decisive moment had fled, like a coward. She was honourably entertained at court ; Henry often paid small sums for her wardrobe. She subsequently married a Welshman, Sir Matthew Cradock; and from her only daughter are descended the Earls of Pembroke. After her death Lady Katharine was buried by the side of her second husband in the church at Swansea on the south coast of Wales.[1]

But the leniency that had been shown him did not tame Warbeck's restless spirit. On the 9th of June, 1498, he made
Warbeck's attempt at escape. He deceived his
attempt at guards, and fled at midnight. The very next day
escape. the king's order came to watch the seaports, and a hundred pounds were offered for his arrest. Warbeck, finding his escape was cut off on all sides, took refuge from his pursuers in the monastery at Sheen, and begged the prior to intercede for him with the king. Here also his personal charm must have had its effect, for the prior complied, and the king again granted Warbeck his life. The morning after the 15th of June he was publicly set in the stocks at Westminster, exposed to the jeers of the populace. At the same time he had to read out his confession, as he had made it at Taunton

---

[1] See Note 13, p. 348, and comments by Mr. Gairdner, p. 440.

before Henry, and at Westminster before the town authorities. Three days subsequently he had to repeat this in London itself, in Cheapside. He was then kept in the Tower, " so that he sees neither sun nor moon, in such fashion that he will never, with God's help, be able to play such another trick again." Those who saw him in this close confinement were struck by the alteration in his appearance.

Severity, however, restrained him as little as kindness. In the Tower he managed to get into communication with other prisoners, among them some of his former companions. But what was more important, they got hold of the Earl of Warwick, who was still shut up there. It was with his name that Warbeck was to have begun his imposture, now the name and person of the royal prisoner were to give new stability to the shaky credit of the adventurer. Warwick, whose mind had no doubt been weakened by long confinement, was only a tool in the hands of the others ; with no suspicion of the importance of what he was doing, he said " Yes " to everything.

The plans of the conspirators, when discovered, seemed but little dangerous to king and State ; the only real danger for Henry lay in Warwick, the most innocent of the party. He, the last male descendant of the house of York, had seen his name made use of in nearly all the intrigues against the Tudor ; in his name Simnel's rising took place, and the scheme of the Abbot of Abingdon ; with his name the plot was concocted in which Warbeck took part ; and now, to his misfortune, after Warbeck's second capture, a fresh impostor tried to misuse his name in the same way as Simnel had done. Under the guidance of Patrick, an Augustinian friar, a young man named Ralph Wilford began, in Kent, to confide to various individuals that he was the Earl of Warwick ; but before definite action could be taken, teacher and pupil were caught, and the latter executed on the 12th of February, 1499, while Patrick, being protected by his order, was condemned, like Simons, to imprisonment for life.

It seemed as if Warwick's existence was once more to be brought before Henry's eyes as a constantly threatening danger. This last attempt, insignificant as it was, must have made a deep impression on him, for rather more than a month after Wilford's execution, the Spaniard Puebla reports that Henry seemed in two weeks to have aged by twenty years.[1] It was then the resolve was probably taken that Warwick must be put to death on the first opportunity. This occurred shortly afterwards, and probably the farce of the new conspiracy was purposely allowed to be played a little longer.[2] A certain Cleymound, and Astwood who had been spared in January, 1495, were the chief plotters; they wanted to get possession of the Tower and set it on fire, in order, in the confusion, to escape themselves with the treasure, and to collect troops with the money. But all they really did was, that Cleymound procured a dagger for the earl.

On the 2nd of August, 1499, the great plan was agreed upon by Cleymound and Astwood with Warwick; they got into communication with Warbeck, who was lodged underneath them, for they wanted to "raise the said Peter to be king and lord, and rob the king of his crown and dignity.". Possibly the traitor was Cleymound, who accused Perkin himself of being the informer, and who, in spite of his very decided share in the affair, was pardoned. On the 16th of November Perkin was tried in Whitehall, together with his earliest confederates, Walter and Taylor, who had likewise been taken, and they were condemned " to be drawn on hurdles from the Tower to Tyburn, there to be hanged, and cut down quickly, their bowels to be taken out and burnt, their heads cut off, their bodies quartered, and the heads and quarters to be disposed of at the king's pleasure." On the 23rd of November the sentence was carried out in a milder form on Perkin and Walter. A low scaffold had been erected at Tyburn, from which Warbeck spoke once more to the numerous crowd standing round. He said he was a foreigner born, "accordyng unto his former confession, and took it upon his dethe that he was never this persone that he was named, for that is to say the second son of Kyng Edward the IVth. And that he was forced to take upon hym by the meanes of the said John a Water and other, wherefor he

Warbeck's execution.

---

[1] Berg., p. 206; on Patrick and Wilford: P. V., 770; Hall, 490; City Chron., 174*b*; Fabian's Abridgment, 685. The Chronicle gives nineteen, the Abridgment twenty years as Wilford's age.
[2] On Perkin's and Warwick's fate, see Note 14, p. 349.

asked God and the Kyng of forgiveness.   After which confession he took his dethe meekly, and was there upon the
gallows hanged and with him the said John a Water.   And
when they were dede tayken downe, and their hede striken
of and after their bodies brought to the friars Augustynes,
and there buryed, and their hedes fixed after upon London
Brigge."   Perkin Warbeck ended his adventurous career at
the age of twenty-five.

Previous to Warbeck's execution, the Earl of Warwick,
with Astwood and Cleymound, had been brought to trial.
The grand jury discharged a not very easy task   Trial and
when they extracted a great plot from the evidence execution of
laid before them.   The proceedings against the   Warwick.
other accomplices followed, but of the five commoners who
were found guilty, only two, one of them Astwood, were
executed, on the 4th of December.   The finding of the jury
against Warwick was sent to the Earl of Oxford, under
whose presidency had met the court of peers, consisting of
one duke, five earls, and sixteen barons.   On the 21st of
November, in Westminster Hall, they pronounced sentence
on the accused, who himself acknowledged his guilt, and on
the 28th he was beheaded on Tower Hill.   Henry had him
laid beside his forefathers in the neighbourhood of Windsor.[1]
It was no doubt hard for the king to resolve on carrying out
the sentence ; he preferred a conciliatory policy to a policy
of revenge, and would much rather pardon than condemn ;
but it probably seemed to him a bitter necessity for his own
preservation, and he felt obliged to disregard the murmurs
and discontent among the people.   That feeling, however,
was a right one which moved the minds of the populace—
regret that Warwick, who was so much to be pitied, should
have had to die, an innocent victim to his ancestry.

[1] At Bisham Abbey, Berks.—G.

CHAPTER IV.

RELATIONS WITH FOREIGN POWERS 1495–1503 — THE
SPANISH AND THE SCOTCH MARRIAGES.

MISFORTUNE had perpetually accompanied Perkin Warbeck
throughout his wanderings ; not one single blow he aimed at
Relations his royal rival was successful.   Directly he tried to
with Spain act alone, without the guidance of his protectors,
and France. he showed himself to be without plan, without
cleverness, and without courage.   His political importance
lay quite apart from himself, and depended on the fact that
the various Powers made use of him, or simply of his existence, for their own political ends.   In every event that concerned England from the year 1492, we find him mixed up—
in the affairs of Ireland, in the French war, in the rupture with
Maximilian and Burgundy and the commercial crisis arising
therefrom, in the complication with Scotland and in its sequel,
the Cornish insurrection.   Thus the relations of England
with all the Powers were for years influenced, and in part
controlled, by this adventurer.

If, through Perkin Warbeck, difficulties beset Henry in
his foreign relations, the political situation in Europe, on the
other hand, was for him a fortunate one, for the ambitious
grasping policy of France made the friendship of England
equally valuable to those monarchs who were trying to keep
the balance of power, and to France herself, who found
herself threatened by them.   The ruler of the island kingdom,
lying far away from the contest in Italy, had only to take
advantage of his geographical position to maintain his
importance between the two Powers, Spain and France, who
were suing for his friendship.

As the Spanish monarchs wanted to make Henry serve their own ends and draw him into the Holy League against France, they viewed with impatience all entanglements which were a hindrance to their object. For this reason their ambassador, Ayala, made every effort to reconcile England and Scotland ; for this same reason they were the only rulers who always tried to thwart Warbeck's intrigues. This, however, did not prevent them from making use of the pretender to further their own designs with regard to Henry. "If your majesties keep the so-called Duke of York in your royal hands, then you can carry out your will in all points and without hindrance in England ;" so wrote Puebla to his sovereigns, they having already sent Ayala to Scotland with his secret instructions. And though Ayala did not attain his end, either with James or Perkin, he had in fact—though decidedly against his own wish—materially helped Perkin in his last enterprise against Henry. No doubt the Spanish rulers would have liked to have Warbeck at their disposal, not only as an impostor who might be sold to Henry for valuable concessions, but also as a pretender who might be useful. It was certainly not by accident that Warbeck, who had always been called by them "he," or "he of York," or "the so-called Duke of York," should in their first letter written after his capture, appear for the first time under his own name Perkin.[1]

To the English king they had naturally always declared him to be an impostor, and even offered to give particulars as to his origin ; but as Henry still bore a grudge against many of their subjects for openly taking the side of Perkin,[2] they reserved for themselves at least the possibility of veering round, as soon as it should serve their interests to favour the pretended Yorkist prince. To this point, however, they never came, and as it is highly improbable that they believed even for a short time in the genuineness of the impostor's claim, so they alone never took his part against the Tudor.[3]

Henry's distrust was well founded, especially as he discovered that those who were urging him on against France had entered privately into communications with her, which, in the spring and summer of 1496, were continued quite

---

[1] March 7, 1498; Berg., p. 147. [2] Ibid., p. 218. [3] See Note I, p. 350.

openly through the medium of ambassadors.[1]   Moreover, the Spaniards had not been very fortunate in their assurances about Maximilian.

After the formation of the Holy League, Henry had expressed a wish to join it,[2] and this was certainly more than a mere polite form of expression, for he desired a friendly alliance with the Powers united in the League ; but to enter a warlike coalition, one member of which, Maximilian, was his bitter foe and moreover the patron of the pretender to his throne, was not to be thought of.   For the present, therefore, he prudently held back.   The danger to the Pope which had been alleged, could not be great, as he himself had not even written to England on the subject.[3]

At the same time Henry's continued friendly relations with France were a thorn in the side of the Spaniards.   A regular and polite intercourse by means of envoys was kept up between England and France, although certain complaints of piracy and injury to commerce occasionally crept in. In July, 1495, indeed, Henry declared to Ferdinand and Isabella that he was free to enter into any league, and to engage in a war ; but in the following spring he pronounced himself in favour of a matrimonial alliance, proposed by Charles, between their two Houses, and ready for a personal meeting.   He granted a reprieve of a year for the payment of sums due, and offered to mediate between France and the Powers of the Holy League.   Of course, all the time he had his own objects in view—that Charles should deliver up the Duke of Albany and take action against Scotland, who now was threatening war.   Charles seemed inclined to take advantage of this to quench the dawning influence of Spain, which threatened to become dangerous to the long-established French ascendancy in Scotland.   He proposed to James a marriage with a French princess.[4]   Why should Henry break with this friend ?   If he joined the League, it must assume a form which would preclude this necessity.   This was indeed to require much of a coalition directed against France.

[1] Berg., pp. 93, 94, 106, 118 ; Brown, No. 699 ; Letter from Charles VIII. to Isabella, April 13, 1496, in Le Roux de Lincy, Vie de la reine Anne, ii. 101, f.
[2] Berg., p. 67.   [3] See Berg., 54 ; cf. 68, 70.
[4] On the Anglo-French negotiations, see Lett. and Pap., ii. 292, ff. ; Brit. Mus. MSS. Cott., Cal., D, vi. fol. 20, f., 22, f., 26a, 28 ; French offer in Scot. : Zurita, v. fol. 135a.

The King of the Romans continued to form the chief obstacle to the designs of Spain. The Spaniards demanded the admission of Henry into the League, Maximilian opposed it; he did so in hopes of Warbeck's success, who would prove a more amenable ally against France. At all events he determined to wait the result of the contest, nor was he discouraged by Warbeck's defeat on the coast of Kent in the summer of 1495. The Pope and the Duke of Milan, as well as the Spaniards, urged Maximilian to give up his stubborn opposition; but the demands he made, whilst apparently yielding, amounted almost to a refusal. Henry was to break openly with France, and to go to war, whilst he undertook to send a force of two thousand men to Henry's assistance, and to negotiate in his behalf with Warbeck, as well as in Ireland and Scotland. Instead of the required abandonment of Warbeck, these words seemed to imply an open acknowledgment of his claims. Henry gave an evasive answer. When his envoy, Egremont, appeared at Nordlingen, Maximilian assembled all the envoys of the League who were present, under the presidency of the Italian, Ludovico Bruno, his confidential Latin secretary, who was well known to be a partisan of the pretender. He wished to insist on the conditions he had imposed, but was warned especially by the Spanish envoy not to irritate Henry by so doing, since it would undoubtedly drive him into the arms of France. Though a hostile movement on the part of England was to be desired, the chief object should be merely to prevent her alliance with France. In the end Maximilian gave in so far that Egremont was despatched with the intimation that the King of the Romans was willing to see Henry join the League. Not one word was said about the principal difficulty—Warbeck.[1]

Maximilian's attitude.

As long as Maximilian entertained hopes for his *protégé*, there was no depending upon him. In spite of papal and Venetian influence, he and Bruno expressly insisted upon his obligations towards Perkin, whilst Henry still demanded that the pretender should be given up. From the answer given to Egremont, Henry thought he had already gained something,

[1] On these relations: Brown, Nos. 652, 657, 660, 665, f., 671, f.; Zurita, v. fol. 87*b*.

and at the end of April, 1496, Sir Christopher Urswick appeared at Augsburg and presented himself to the King of the Romans. The ambassador saw little to encourage him. Maximilian, while insisting on war, had himself made no preparations for arming, and the friends of Perkin still held their heads high at court. Urswick was also informed of the prevailing dislike of England, and of the compact with the pretender in Scotland. In the face of such opposition, it was impossible for the moment to come to any agreement, and, at the end of May, 1496, Urswick was dismissed with a few friendly words, to the great vexation of the Spaniards.[1]

The difference between Maximilian's fitful, sanguine conduct, and Ferdinand's steady policy, always bent on the same goal and moving on the same lines, stood out in strong contrast in their conduct towards England. As there were rumours afloat of a marriage between Prince Arthur and the daughter of Anne de Beaujeu, it was doubly annoying to the Spaniards that England should be unnecessarily irritated by the obstinacy of Maximilian ; and thinking that the promise to fulfil the marriage treaty would prove successful, as it had once done before, not only in preventing Henry from uniting with France, but even in dragging him into the war against her, they issued full powers for concluding the negotiations on the 30th of January, 1496.[2]

That Burgundy gave up the policy into which it had been led by Maximilian's influence was certainly a notable advantage. An important commercial treaty between Henry and Duke Philip, which was concluded in London, on the 24th of February, 1496, prohibited either side from giving assistance to rebels against the other. It was specially stated that no rebel should be permitted to remain in territories under Philip's lordship belonging to the Duchess Margaret, or any other person, but that they should be immediately proceeded against.[3] This was the exact contrary to the answer given to Poynings and Warham. The Spaniards had also contributed towards bringing about this settlement. Urged by them,

---

[1] Brown, Nos. 674–677, 690, 693, 698–703, 706 ; Berg., pp. 110, 117, f.
[2] Rym., xii. 661–663 ; Berg., No. 123 ; English powers, March 5, Berg., No. 127 ; also see pp. 81, f., 84.
[3] Rvm., xii. 579–581.

the Pope had bestirred himself. He wrote to Henry, and empowered Puebla to conduct in his name the negotiations for Henry's admission into the League. They demanded the same of Maximilian, as some slight protection against his shiftiness, and, even before Urswick arrived, he had given in, and signed the power on the 18th of April, 1496. But in doing so, he had only repeated his acquiescence in the admission of Henry to the League, nor did it occur to him to give up his *protégé* on that account.[1]

It was a question whether the situation at that time would decide Henry, even without Maximilian's last concession, to join the League and thereby to secure the friendship of the other Powers, or, at least, their neutrality. It was still open to him to choose. France would have accepted his alliance as gladly as would the members of the League. For the moment, therefore, he evaded the question ; in the negotiations about the Spanish marriage also, his plenipotentiaries showed a cautious reticence. The very urgency of the Spaniards gave him a feeling of security; indeed they ordered their ambassador to conclude the marriage treaty, even if Henry did not immediately declare war against France, and conceded to the demand of Henry that if he joined the League, he should be free from any obligation to take steps against France, or contribute money for the purpose.[2] In return for this concession, Henry overlooked Maximilian's conduct, especially as he gave no more assistance worth naming to Perkin. After all, there was as little sense in the policy of the King of the Romans with regard to the pretender, as there was danger from it to Henry.

The final negotiations did not take place in England, but in Rome, whither, in April, Henry had sent his secretary, Robert Sherbourne. On the 18th of July, 1496, the agreement was concluded there in the presence of the Pope. The text of the new League was the same as the old one of the 31st of March, 1495, only that the provisions concerning help in time of war and the disposition of troops were omitted ; the members of the older League were, however, expressly bound by these earlier

Henry's reception into the Holy League.

---

[1] Berg., Nos. 120, 129, 131.
[2] These negotiations in Puebla's reports, Berg., Nos. 136, f., 143.

provisions. The announcement and conclusion of the treaty followed immediately. Henry signed it on the 23rd of September, 1496, two days after Perkin Warbeck had again been obliged to retreat over the Scottish border. The Pope sent Henry, in acknowledgment, a consecrated hat and sword, which were received with much ceremony on All Saints' Day.[1]

Though the old provisions for offence might be retained for the other members of the coalition, yet the League, in the form in which Henry was permitted to enter it, was completely stripped of its aggressive character. It was not, indeed, the admission into the alliance of this prince, with his pronounced desire for neutrality, that caused this change, but his entrance made clear the change that had already taken place. The peaceful turn in European politics, which broke up the League, originated with Ferdinand himself, the author of it.

Cordova's victories in Italy, accompanied by some successes on the Pyrenean border, had practically destroyed French ascendancy in Naples by the year 1496, and, as certain important places remained in the hands of the Spaniards, the way was prepared for their occupation of the country. The League having thus fulfilled its object with regard to Spain, there was some hope of coming to a friendly settlement by means of the negotiations actively carried on with France in 1496. Hostilities had not ceased on the border until the 27th of February, 1497, when an armistice between France and Spain was agreed upon at Lyons. The truce, which included the other members of the League, was to begin for Spain on the 5th of March, for the others on the 25th of April, and to last for the present till the 1st of November, in order that the permanent peace might in the meanwhile be settled. This armistice was extended, as the plenipotentiaries did not meet till well on in the following year at Perpignan for the final negotiations.[2]

Peaceful turn of affairs.

---

[1] Sherbourne's mission: Brown, No. 691 ; the treaty: Rym., xii. 638–642 ; Du Mont, iii. 2, pp. 364–366 ; cf. Berg., No. 146 ; Brown, No. 712. Preliminaries and execution in Italy: Brown, Nos. 713, f., 717–723 ; celebration in London : ibid., No. 725.

[2] On the negotiations and settlements between Spain and France: Berg., pp. 118, 127, f., 142 ; Zurita, v. fol. 90, 115b, 118b, f., 132b, f., 137b, f.

No one could be more pleased with this turn of affairs than Henry, for his friendship with France, as is shown most plainly by the conclusion of a new commercial treaty between them in May, 1497, was in no way shaken by his adhesion to the League. In other ways, also, pacific tendencies were making themselves felt. It was certainly no sign of dissatisfaction that Pope Alexander, even before the end of 1496, bestowed on Ferdinand and Isabella the title of the "Catholic Kings."[1] The Burgundian government now began to free itself from the influence of Maximilian, not only with regard to England, but to France, and to make overtures of friendship. The King of the Romans alone held out. But he was not to be reconciled, and when, on the 7th of April, 1498, Charles VIII., at the age of twenty-seven, died unexpectedly and without issue, Maximilian at once confronted the new ruler, Louis XII., with his claims on the Duchy of Burgundy, and began to arm for an onslaught; he could not, however, effect anything, unsupported   *Louis XII. of France.* as he was by the other members of the League. He remained completely isolated.

By divorcing his wife and marrying Charles' widow, Anne, Louis prevented the separation of Brittany from France, and he openly took up the traditional policy with regard to Italy, by assuming the title of King of France and Duke of Milan. Elsewhere his aim was peace. He at once despatched an embassage to London, where a solemn funeral service was held for his predecessor in St. Paul's.[2] On the 14th of July, 1498, the Treaty of Etaples was renewed in Paris by Henry's plenipotentiaries, and the continued payment of the sum due was guaranteed. It was only the article concerning rebels, which always played its part in all English settlements, that underwent any material alteration, and this was worded with more severity in consequence of recent experiences. Louis swore to the concluded treaty on the Holy Gospels and on a fragment of the true Cross, promising special punctuality in the payment of the money. Later, on the 1st of February, 1500, at the wish of the contracting parties,

---

[1] According to Peter Martyr, p. 89, title already conferred beginning of 1495, which Prescott also accepts, ii. 254, note; against this Zurita, v. 110*b*; cf. Gerigk., Das opus epistolarum des Petr. Mart. Königsb. Diss., 1881, p. 20, f.

[2] City Chronicle, fol. 172*a*.

Pope Alexander bound them more closely to their treaty with threats of the penalties of the Church.

Louis had not been long in making up his mind to purchase for himself the lasting friendship of England by these rather unequal concessions, even though he is said to have made great difficulties at first. He strove to abide by the treaty, which he caused to be recognised by his Estates, and the article concerning rebels came into force when in the summer of 1499, John Taylor, the partisan of Warbeck, was seized in France and handed over to Henry. Care was also taken, by means of ample pensions, to secure good friends for Louis at the English court.[1]

Maximilian had again made repeated attempts in the years 1497 and 1498 to induce the English king, for whom he otherwise displayed the most unequivocal enmity, to take the field in his interests against France, he promised to give him his support in an attack on Guienne; there was even some idea of investing him with Brittany.[2] Designs such as these were not likely to interfere with Henry's peaceful projects, but it must have been a far greater disappointment to the King of the Romans, when, in spite of all his efforts to the contrary, his own son Philip made peace with France. By the treaty of Paris of the 2nd of August, 1498, Philip, amongst other things, renounced this very Duchy of Burgundy reclaimed by Maximilian, and did homage to the French king for Flanders and Artois.[3]

On the 5th of August, only a few days later, followed Louis' agreement with the Spaniards, at Marcoussis. They were naturally mainly interested in discussing the arrangement about Naples, and here the Spanish design of a partition of that kingdom formed the basis of the understanding ; but on these ulterior plans the treaty itself was for the present silent, it only dealt with peace and friendship between the two Powers.[4] It was this contract which completely shattered

---

[1] Powers, conclusion, and ratification: Rym., xii. 681–695, 706, f., 710–712, 736–738, 762–765; cf. Berg., p. 151; Exc. Hist., 118; receipts for payments and some assignments for 1498–1500: Rym., 698–700, 712, f., 732–734, 749, f., 753, f., 769, f. ; cf. exaggerated statements in Brown, No. 799; Berg., p. 227 ; also see Berg., pp. 187, f., 192; Brown, No. 776.

[2] Ulmann, i. pp. 445, f., 479; Chmel., p. 167, f. ; Berg., p. 157.

[3] Du!Mont, iii. 2, p. 396, f. ; Molinet, v. 90–93; Berg., pp. 183, f., 192, 193; cf. Ulmann, i. 588, f.

[4] Du Mont, p. 397, ff. ; cf. Berg., pp. 149, 190, 195.

the Holy League ; Maximilian alone struggled to escape from
these trammels of a peace thus imposed on the whole of
Western Europe.

Never yet had the efforts of Henry and his Spanish friends
followed so completely on the same lines, as now in this time
of a universal agreement for the preservation of peace. The
Spaniards would indeed have preferred that Henry should
have joined in the old war league, but this merely with the
object of bringing the English king into more direct opposition to France. This time they were in the disagreeable
position of being forced to give in to English demands, for,
what now seemed to stand like some menacing spectre in the
background was the dread of any influence from England
that might injuriously affect that diplomatic war just embarked on with France, and also of the possibility of an
increase of strength to that country by her closer union
with England. Thus it came about that Henry, in the very
year that saw the attack on him by the pretender in league
with Scotland, managed, by a clever use of the European
situation, to achieve one success after another ; the defeat of
Warbeck was also a defeat for Maximilian, who was reckoning
on Warbeck's success.

Finally the Spaniards endeavoured, by the help of the promised treaty of marriage, to make Henry assume a more hostile
attitude towards France, while their own efforts for
peace made it more easy for them to drop their
original demands for war. In return, the marriage
treaty was at all events to be accompanied by a
covenant binding England more closely to Spain,
The new Anglo-Spanish treaty of marriage.
and by the long-wished-for concessions with respect to trade.
But here, too, Spain had to yield ; the treaty in London of the
1st of October, 1496, rested only on the marriage conditions
of the treaty of Medina del Campo, without taking into consideration the special wishes of the Spaniards—no alliance to
bind England, no commercial conditions, only the marriage
of Arthur and Katharine, formed the contents. The questions
as to the dowry and jointure remained as before, except that
some points hitherto uncertain were cleared up, and while
Katharine's right of succession in Spain was again secured to
her, Henry on his part confirmed by a special document the

right of succession of Arthur and his descendants in England before his brothers and sisters.

On the 1st of January, 1497, the Catholic kings executed the new treaty, and empowered their ambassador, Puebla, to arrange the formal betrothal in England by proxy; at the same time they now pressed for the conclusion, at least, of a closer alliance; they even spoke again of a war against France. At this moment Ayala was beginning his work as intermediary in Scotland, and they were still hoping to get Perkin into their hands as a useful tool against Henry. The plan failed, and since their wishes for closer alliance and facility for trade were reserved for future settlement, Henry had a pledge for the punctual fulfilment of the marriage treaty. That he intended to keep what he had got is shown by the promise to lessen the customs duties " in honour of the joyful arrival of the princess Katharine in England." He even hesitated about the execution of the marriage treaty, and did not sign it till the 18th of July, 1497, when the Cornish insurrection rendered Spanish intervention in Scotland absolutely necessary to him. A month later, in the presence of the court, at Woodstock, the solemn betrothal took place, when Puebla, as directed by his instructions, represented the princess. It is this which probably explained the second ratification of the treaty by the Spanish monarchs, on the 4th of February, 1498, at Alcala.[1] The September of 1497 saw a truce with Scotland, concluded for Henry with the help of Spain, and by October the troublesome pretender was in his power. The new political schemes and entanglements into which Maximilian had plunged, caused a temporary cessation of hostilities even with his rival; though his feelings towards Henry had by no means changed,[2] and were only waiting fresh opportunity to burst forth with renewed activity.

The English king and the Spanish monarchs were able on the whole to congratulate themselves on their success. The Spaniards, the acknowledged leaders of European politics, in whose name a new world had been disclosed in the western hemisphere, had driven Charles VIII. out of Italy, and by the truce of Lyons had gained for the present a free hand in

---

[1] On the marriage treaty, see Note 2, p. 351.
[2] Cf. also Zurita, v. 121b.

Naples; moreover, they had kept possession of Cerdagne and Roussillon, concluded an agreement for the projected double marriage with the children of Maximilian, and finally had prevented the dreaded union of England with France.

But Henry had maintained his position with peculiar cleverness in the midst of a crowd of domestic and foreign difficulties, which beset him on every side. Foreign observers agreed in saying, that England for many years had not obeyed any monarch so well as the Tudor; his throne from hence-forth stood secure. His position with regard to foreign affairs was completely changed; he who at first sued for friendship, now found his friendship sought by all, and that this fact was recognised is proved by the price which Spain paid for the renewal of the friendship with England.

The further settlement of the general question and the completion of the marriage itself were, in due course, to follow the last marriage treaty with Spain. That this treaty was so advantageous for Henry was due, not only to the European situation being favourable to him, and to his own cleverness or the lucky accident that Warbeck did not succumb to Spanish blandishments, but in great part to the inadequate and undignified diplomatic representative of Ferdinand and Isabella in England.

Among the plenipotentiaries of foreign powers accredited to Henry's court, Roderigo Gondesalvi de Puebla, doctor of civil and canon law, who permanently resided there, played a peculiar part. He was at first only temporarily in England, in 1488 and 1489, then permanently, from 1494 till his death in 1509. In the year 1496 were heard the first complaints of his indifferent despatches, his sovereigns heard nothing from him about the great Cornish insurrection, and they suspected that their ambassador represented English rather than Spanish interests. At the same time Puebla was filled with the deepest jealousy of each one of his official colleagues, who appeared in England. In this he was to a certain extent justified when his monarchs left him in ignorance of a difficult task which Ayala had fulfilled with regard to Perkin Warbeck; it was just on this very Ayala, so far superior to himself, that he poured forth the vials of his wrath, whilst

Doctor de Puebla.

he blackened his rival's character in every way with the hope of damaging his reputation with the kings. They, however, caused inquiries to be made about Puebla's own behaviour by the two ambassadors, Londoño and the sub-prior of Santa Cruz, who passed through England to Flanders in the spring of 1498.

Their suspicions that Puebla was working more for England than for Spain found special confirmation from his failure to take advantage in his sovereigns' interests of favourable moments, such as the great rebellion of 1497, and from his careless handling of the customs question, which had roused against himself the animosity of the Spanish merchants, who complained that they could get nothing out of Henry by his means unless they bribed him ; no captain, no common sailor even could get what he wanted without money. It was said he carried on the trade of an attorney, and was covetous and usurious. Now, however, he got into evil case, as his salary was not paid him in spite of all his complaints. In June, 1500, he begged for at least a third of the arrears due to him, and this third alone he reckoned at eleven hundred ducats.

This somewhat explains his scandalous mode of life. For three years he lived in the house of a mason who harboured

Puebla's conduct.

loose women, and he dined daily for twopence at the same table with this company. He could take his meals still more cheaply and comfortably at court ; and a courtier, when asked by the king what was the reason of Puebla's coming, answered with a sneer, "To eat." He was certainly not looked upon with much respect by the English, and still less by his own countrymen. One opinion of him may suffice. This describes him as a liar, flatterer, calumniator, beggar, and doubtful Christian. Henry is not likely to have had a much better opinion of him ; he knew, however, how to make clever use of him, and to attach him to himself by small favours and the prospect of greater rewards. But with good reason his masters were pointedly silent about the plan of giving him an English bishopric, or of marrying him to a rich wife in England. They treated in the same way the wish he expressed, when in financial difficulties, that they should hand over to him the civil and criminal jurisdiction over the Spaniards residing in England; although, when preferring this request, he enclosed the document granting him the appointment, prepared for signature. It may be that they wished to keep him in a state of dependence, for it was only Puebla's satisfactory relations with Henry which induced them, in spite of all the bad reports, and all their own unfavourable experiences, to leave him at his post. In any negotiations of importance they associated with him capable men like Ayala. However much Puebla's jealousy and vanity might rebel against this, all his boasting about his own superiority and experience was of no avail. They signified their dissatisfaction sometimes ironically and often plainly enough to the vain and foolish man, whom they occasionally smoothed down again by fair words. But still this most original and comical diplomatist continued to be kept at the English court.[1]

In all subsequent negotiations, Puebla did not belie his nature. The next task for diplomacy to undertake was a closer alliance with England, strongly insisted on by the Spaniards, as a supplement to the matrimonial treaty. The position of affairs, however, was quite different from what it had been in March, 1489, when Spain had compelled her ally to take part in her war with France. Desirous of peace, she had sent Londoño to England with an official communication of her pacific intentions, while Henry, now that he was sure of his affair, even began, at least in Puebla's presence, to speak of warlike plans against France. The Spanish draft of the treaty of alliance did not please him; the wording of the clauses on rebels, so important for him, offered in particular considerable difficulty, and Puebla calmly confessed that in this matter he had exceeded his powers.

On the 10th of July, 1499, a settlement was effected in London, in which the earlier treaty of Medina del Campo served again as a general basis. Certain of the single clauses on friendship, help in war, freedom of trade, and protection against rebels, were now drawn up more precisely, and the treaty was to hold good for the present rulers and their successors. England now

Treaty of alliance with Spain.

---

[1] On Puebla, see Note 3, p. 351.

stood, not only in appearance, but in fact, on a footing of equality with her ally.   Puebla tried to make the most, to his somewhat dissatisfied sovereigns, of the difficulties overcome, the excellence and great importance of this treaty, which, with evident self-satisfaction, he characterised as "a master-stroke of diplomacy."[1]

On the subject of the marriage treaty also, the fulfilment of which was to wait for some years, owing to the youth of the betrothed pair, there were now various unnecessary delays, originating more in a certain distrust justified by former experience, than perhaps in a wish on either side to postpone the agreements.   That both parties were in earnest was shown by their efforts to secure the papal dispensation, in order that a formal marriage by proxy might be concluded before the young couple had reached a marriageable age. This marriage took place immediately after the arrival of the dispensation in the summer of 1498, and in pursuance of a special power sent by Katharine to Puebla, was repeated once more in due form on the 19th of May, 1499, at Bewdley, Arthur's country seat.   After vows exchanged, he and Puebla —who represented the princess—laid their hand in each other's, whereupon both declared the marriage concluded, and that they regarded each other as man and wife.   The newly married children, who had not yet made each other's acquaintance, now exchanged their first affectionate letters, in which they spoke of love and longing, and expressed the hope that they should often hear from each other.[2]

Some difficulties were raised on the question of sending Katharine over to England, which was to be on the completion of Arthur's fourteenth year, and therefore in 1500.   The English, on their side, were for pressing on the date ; the

---

[1] See the treaty in the Spanish ratification of January 20, 1500, in Rym., xii. 741-747, and Du Mont, iii. 2, pp. 414-417 ; extract in Berg., pp. 210-212. Zurita, v. 164a, incorrectly considers it a confirmation, not a supplement, of the marriage treaty.   On the previous negotiations, see Berg., pp. 132, 149, 180, f., 187, 194, 196, 197, 203, f. ; the ratifications in Rymer, as above, and 751-753 (here wrongly referred to the marriage treaty) ; Berg., Nos. 251, f., 261 ; the last negotiations, ibid., Nos. 254, 257, 265, 268.

[2] On the dispensation, see Berg., pp. 148, 160, 168, 185; on the two ceremonies, ibid., pp. 190, 209, f. ; Rym., xii. 756-759; cf. Berg., p. 203, Arthur's letter in reply to one from Katharine, Oct. 5, 1499 : Berg., p. 212. Ratification of the marriage : Berg., Nos. 247, f., 290 ; Rym., 761 ; cf. Berg., No. 268.

princess ought, they said, as soon as possible to become accustomed to the new life and foreign tongue. The queen and the queen-mother suggested that she should at least exercise herself in French, for which she had opportunity, because English ladies did not understand Latin or even Spanish; and it was pointed out to her that to accommodate herself to the English customs and mode of life would not be easy. On the subject of a suite which was to accompany Katharine, there were differences of opinion. Henry and his queen begged that the ladies might be of good family and handsome—at least, that none of them should be strikingly plain; and they wished to reduce the number of Spanish servants, whilst Ferdinand and Isabella wished to increase it, but expected the English king to pay the salaries.

Final negotiations.

In spite of the assurances of the Spaniards that they would adhere to the appointed date, the preparations for the princess's departure were still delayed: having regard, therefore, to the approaching stormy season of the year, Henry declared himself ready to agree to a further postponement till June, 1501. Meanwhile, as Arthur had now reached an age when he could be party to a treaty, the Spaniards insisted on a repetition of the wedding ceremony, already twice performed. Apparently they were filled with anxiety lest their ally should at the last moment leave them in the lurch. After some additional delays, Henry gave in, and the ceremony was again repeated on the 22nd of November, 1500.[1] The tables were now turned. The cause of the Spaniards' anxiety was the friendly relations which were begun in the year 1500 between Henry and the Archduke Philip, and which culminated in a personal meeting between the two rulers. In June, 1500, Gomez de Fuensalida went to England, charged with a secret commission, to be concealed even from Puebla, to inquire whether there was any foundation for the report that Maximilian wished to frustrate the Spanish marriage of the Prince of Wales, and to substitute another.

[1] On these negotiations and the second marriage by proxy: Berg., pp. 156, 178, 226, 245, 246, f., 251, f., 254, f., 259; Mem., p. 405; Lett. and Pap., i. 122, f.; Berg., 239, 240-244, 248-250, 253-257.

The real object of this embassage was hidden in somewhat peculiar fashion under the pretext of a commission to assist Puebla in introducing an alteration into the marriage treaty ; and to Puebla himself this pretended commission was made specially emphatic by the censure of his bad mode of conducting business on this occasion. At the same time, after all the firm and binding covenants, the proposed change was to be a feeler to discover Henry's true state of mind ; so Fuensalida, to Puebla's annoyance, very soon brought forward the matter for discussion, but without achieving any special result. The whole commission was now withdrawn by fresh instructions from Spain, and Puebla was left to splutter forth his suspicion, jealousy, and self-conceit on the subject of this new rival. It must have been extremely annoying to him that even Henry requested King Ferdinand to leave Ayala, who had already been recalled, in England, till the arrival of Katharine, though Puebla had begged that this rival, who had become a constant nightmare to him, might be removed. Nothing, therefore, was left him but to indulge in fruitless anger and pathetic lamentations over his unappreciated talents as a diplomatist.

These customary petty jealousies on the part of the ambassador disturbed the progress of affairs as little as did the Spaniards' temporary distrust of the honourable intentions of England. This feeling had indeed been increased by Fuensalida's first reports, when he heard on his journey through France of the meeting between Henry and the archduke near Calais, and of the consequent surmises of the French. Towards the end of the journey, however, this distrust was removed. The best witness for Henry's good faith was afforded by the preparations for the wedding in England, and by the distrust again exhibited by the English in Fuensalida's own masters. The wedding ceremony had been once more repeated, according to their express wish, and they now sent to beg Henry to exercise some moderation in the festivities for which he was making ready. The king was said to have spent in France £14,000 on jewels alone for the wedding.[1]

Once more the departure was delayed, the reason given

being a rising of the Moors in Ronda. On the 21st of May, 1501, the princess left her parents in Granada, but did not arrive at Corunna till the middle of July. On the 25th of August the squadron set sail, but was driven back to Laredo by a storm; it set out again on the 27th of September. A spell of fine weather was followed by a strong south wind. The waves rose high, and, as if the storms on her passage were a foreboding of all the sorrows of heart that awaited the Spanish princess in her new home, foul weather accompanied them throughout the voyage, till they landed in Plymouth on the 2nd of October.

Forthwith the English prepared a fitting welcome. Henry greeted his future daughter in a French letter; many nobles hastened to receive and escort her. But Henry did not set out to meet her till the 4th of November, and Prince Arthur joined him on the way. When the Spanish prothonotary announced to him Ferdinand's instructions that no one was to see the princess at present, the king replied, after consulting his council, that as soon as she set foot on English soil the Spaniards were relieved of their office as her guardians, and that any further orders would be issued by the king of England. He met Katharine at Dogmersfield, and soon after him Prince Arthur greeted her. Then they separated. Katharine arrived at Lambeth on the 9th of November, where she remained till the day of her state entry into London. Henry went by another way to Richmond, then to Baynard's Castle, in London, whither his wife Elizabeth followed him.

On the 12th of November Katharine entered the capital. When she arrived at London Bridge, women in the garb of the Saints Katharine and Ursula welcomed her with a Latin distich and a longer poem in English, and at Gracechurch Street, Cornhill, Soper Lane, and Cheapside, the procession was greeted in the same way. The young Spanish princess could hardly have understood the meaning of the lengthy verses, and as little of the speech of the Recorder, delivered in the name of the citizens in Cheapside, where the Lord Mayor with the aldermen on horseback awaited the future queen. But pomp and splendour greeted her on all sides. The streets were richly decorated; costly draperies hung from all the windows, and wine flowed out of conduit pipes, to the delight of the crowd. Her procession stopped at the Bishop of London's palace, and here Henry appeared shortly after, with his wife and mother.

On Sunday, the 14th of November, 1501, the marriage ceremony took place, in presence of a crowd of spectators, Conclusion at St. Paul's, on a great platform extending from of the   the west door to the choir. The Archbishop of marriage. Canterbury celebrated mass, and then the bride, accompanied by the Spanish ambassador and young Henry of York, returned to the bishop's palace. Her jointure had been solemnly adjudged to her in the church itself, and the half of the dowry that was due had been brought thither and paid over to her.

Then followed a splendid banquet, and days of endless festivity. At Westminster there were tournaments, and in the Hall again the favourite allegorical representations. The royal party themselves led off the dance before the assembled guests, and it delighted them all to see how young Henry, throwing aside the state robe which hampered his movements, gaily went on in his doublet. Thus day after day they continued with dancing, feasting, play, and tournament, bearing with astonishing endurance for two whole weeks the monotony of this gay round of revelry. Henry himself informed Katharine's parents of all that had taken place. He vowed he would be a second father to her, a promise he was to ignore for a long time.

With noisy rejoicings and the gorgeous display of his immense wealth, the king had solemnized the union of the two princely Houses. The goal was reached for which he had striven ever since his accession. An idle rumour declared that it was not till the execution of the Earl of Warwick that Ferdinand considered the throne of the Tudor to be firmly established, and gave his consent to the marriage contract; but, in fact, that contract had been decided on before Warwick's death, and Henry had already given ample evidence of the security of his throne.[1]

If of late years English and Spanish policy had been following the same course, it was not, as before, because

---

[1] On Katharine's journey, reception, and wedding, see Note 5, p. 353.

England gave in submissively to the wishes of her stronger ally; rather it was Spain who now was the one to yield. The Spaniards rendered far more direct services to the English king than the English king did to them, and while their own marriage negotiations were still going on, Spanish policy gave its aid, as it had done before, to English policy in Scotland. Out of the truce and treaty of peace with that kingdom was to spring tnat matrimonial alliance, so full of importance for the future, which, as well as the Spanish alliance, Henry was able to regard as his peculiar work.

That Henry was genuinely in earnest in his peace policy, and pursued it for its own sake, is nowhere more clearly shown than in his dealings with Scotland. His inclination for peace impelled him to go to the **Scotland.** furthest limit at which he could allow a less powerful neighbour to meet him; for had not his proposals of a marriage for James been totally disregarded by the latter? When at last, in the year 1497, Henry was rousing himself to serious retaliation on account of Scotch hostility, the Cornish insurrection forced him back into his old pacific policy. In December, 1497, after the fresh onslaught in the autumn had been repulsed, the final treaty was concluded, to last the lifetime of the two monarchs. Henry helped to keep Scotland isolated, for by maintaining friendly relations with France he withdrew from Scotland the support which she had found hitherto in all her struggles with England. Besides this, Henry's other ally, Spain, was now working in the most decided way in accordance with the king's wishes; with Perkin's capture the ostensible reason for the continual fighting had at last been removed.

Henry showed himself, indeed, not quite satisfied with the conditions of the December truce; the guarantee against future support given to rebels seemed to him insufficient. But his attitude being on principle conciliatory, he was ready to make concessions, and James's annoyance at his demand would have been without importance, if an unfortunate occurrence on the Border had not added fuel to the flame. Some time in June, 1498, some young Scotchmen appeared in a very suspicious way before Norham, against which place James's last attack had been directed. As they would not answer any questions about their intentions, high words soon led to blows. The Scotch, who were in the minority, were driven away, leaving some of their number on the field ; the English pursued, and some pillaging took place within Scottish territory. James, who would gladly have again drawn the sword, resolved on making a complaint to Henry, who thereupon sent to him his experienced negotiator, Richard Fox, Bishop of Durham, while James begged Ayala, then in London, to act as intermediary.

Ayala, who had received 'further instructions from home through Londoño, promised to do his best, although he almost despaired of being able to persuade the hostile neighbours to agree to a lasting peace. Besides, he now met with difficulties from Henry. It appears that during the negotiations carried on at Melrose between James and Fox about the late occurrence, the scheme of a marriage which had already been mooted was seriously discussed, and that James at last gave his consent to it. As soon as Henry felt tolerably sure of carrying his point, he held back and feigned hesitation. Perhaps he was thinking less of the Scotch than of the Spaniards, who had involved themselves pretty deeply in the pretended negotiations for James's Spanish marriage. They would have been placed in the greatest embarrassment by Henry's withdrawal, for James treated the question of his Spanish marriage so much in earnest, that Ayala, in order not to vex him, advised his sovereigns really to give him the hand of their third daughter, the Infanta Maria, who, eventually, was married in Portugal.

Perhaps Henry knew of this, when by an unexpected question about the Infanta, during an interview with Londoño, he made himself certain that he would risk nothing by now bringing forward his scruples on the subject of the Scottish marriage. Margaret, who was born on the 29th of November, 1490, was really much too young, and besides, weakly for her age ; the time of waiting would therefore in any case be long. The king also spoke of the opposition of his mother and wife, on account of the bad effect it was likely to have on the health of the child. It was at that time believed that Henry would rather marry her to the Crown Prince of Denmark, who was then also a child, than to the king of Scots, who was so much

her elder.   Henry seems especially to have striven to put
pressure on the Spaniards ; he was then particularly anxious
to obtain their mediation on account of the Border difficulties,
and at the beginning of 1499, therefore, plenipotentiaries were
again actively at work settling the indemnities to be paid on
both sides.

The marriage negotiations were still dragging on.   It was
thought that Scotland's relation with France had something
to do with this ; Henry therefore considered it Negotiations
necessary to assure the Spanish monarch that the for marriage
Scotch affairs were not going so badly as they and alliance.
supposed.   We do not know the details, but anyhow Henry
was successful in his tactics.   On the 12th of July, 1499,
a treaty of peace and political alliance was once more
concluded at Stirling, between the English and Scotch
plenipotentiaries, which in every particular fulfilled Henry's
wishes, and met the objections he had made to the preceding
treaty.   The bond was drawn closer.   Henry protected himself against any help which James might perhaps give to his
former friend Perkin and his accomplices, then still living ;
for on that score he was not without misgivings.

In the never-ending series of English and Scotch treaties,
no sooner made than broken, a settlement had at last been
arrived at, which contained real guarantees of peace.   This
new covenant therefore marked one stage in advance towards
that last and strongest union after which Henry, though he
seemed to be evading it, was constantly striving.   Preliminary
discussions seem to have gone on in London with the Scotch
ambassadors.   On the 11th of September, 1499, Henry again
empowered Richard Fox to negotiate about the marriage
and dowry.   How the Spaniards managed to withdraw their
own matrimonial offer we do not know.   Some doubts still
arose, because of James's possible intentions with regard to
the hand of Maximilian's daughter Margaret, or of a French
princess ; but after some further proceedings, in October,
1501, he despatched his plenipotentiaries, who appeared in
London on the 20th of November, just at the time of the
festivities in honour of the Spanish marriage.   Their negotiations were still going on when the new year began ; the
capital did not fail to honour the foreign dignitaries with a

banquet, to which they responded by a poem in praise of
the city of London. On the 24th of January,

Conclusion of
the treaty. 1502, the treaty of marriage and alliance was
finally drawn up in three separate documents.

The marriage treaty determined that Margaret should be
handed over to her husband not later than the 1st of
September, 1503 ; the rest of the treaty mainly dealt with
the financial settlements. With suspicious caution, which led
to the most minute details, English interests were safeguarded
as much as possible in the question of jointure and dowry.
In return for the £2000 jointure, a dowry of only 30,000
English nobles or £10,000 was given. The payment was to
be made in three yearly instalments, and to cease at once
if Margaret died childless within that time. James was
expressly bound to undertake the maintenance of the young
queen's court, of which twenty-four English servants were to
form part. The treaty of alliance made at the same time
widened and strengthened that of 1499. It was to hold good
for ever ; each party was to supply aid in time of war to his
ally, if the other were attacked by "a king, prince, or any
other person ;" intercourse in commerce and on the Border
was regulated, as well as protection for the same and the
punishment of any deed of violence. The new treaty was to
guarantee peace as securely as possible, and this especially
by means of the strong bond of matrimony. It cannot
therefore but strike us as strange and regrettable that Henry
should have insisted, in such an emphatic and obtrusive
manner, on the preservation of the smallest and pettiest
money interests, when such great issues were involved.

On the 25th of January, 1502, the very day after the
signing of the three documents, the marriage was celebrated
at Richmond, when Patrick, Earl of Bothwell, acted as proxy
for his king. The court, the ambassadors of Spain, France,
Venice and the Pope, were present, together with a large
number of English notables. The Archbishop of Glasgow
performed the ceremony ; a flourish of trumpets brought the
solemn act to a conclusion. The Scotch plenipotentiaries
dined at the royal table, tourneys and more banquets followed,
whilst from St. Paul's Cross in London the completion of the
marriage was announced to the people, and in the church Te

Deum was sung. Bonfires blazed, and beside each fire a hogshead of wine was tapped for the benefit of the thirsty populace. Distribution of prizes, and again banquets and tournaments went on for the next two days, after which the Scotchmen were sent back to their homes with the customary presents.

In spite of all the obligations imposed by the treaty, many a moment of doubt and insecurity was to follow. Cause for anxiety continued to exist in consequence of the relations between the Scottish king, who was an ardent lover of women, and the beautiful Lady Margaret Drummond, till that hindrance was removed by her somewhat mysterious death, which occurred in the same year as the conclusion of the treaty. A mistake on the part of James called forth fresh correspondence. When swearing to the treaty, he—the king of a country from the earliest times on friendly terms with France—had given Henry the title claimed by him of King of France. On the 10th of December, 1502, James renewed the oath in another form ; and, on the 17th of December, he ratified the treaties, as Henry had done before him on the 31st of October. This led Henry to demand of James at the last minute the assurance that he would not renew his " old league and covenant with France." Shortly before Margaret crossed the border, James, indeed, undertook not to renew the alliance for a time, but would not pledge himself to more than this.

It was the necessary postponement of the marriage in consequence of Margaret's tender age, which contributed to lengthen out the proceedings. In the year 1503 Henry again made James specially promise that he would not demand his bride before the date fixed, also, that he would have the treaty ratified by the Scotch parliament, and Henry sent special envoys to Scotland with a view to ascertaining exactly the value of the landed estates assigned for Margaret's jointure.

The bride was given over to her husband in conformity with the conditions of the treaty. Henry himself superintended most carefully the clothing and equipment of his daughter, in which he seemed to be particularly desirous that, where possible, the red rose of the Lancastrians should

L

be introduced. He accompanied her from Richmond to Collyweston, in Northamptonshire, the favourite residence of his mother, and there, on the 8th of July, 1503, Margaret took leave of her family.

Through Newark, York, Durham, and Newcastle, the stately procession moved slowly towards Berwick.   The young queen travelled in a litter, but whenever the authorities of the counties and towns came forward to greet her, she appeared richly attired, mounted on an ambling jennet. In the towns through which she passed, especially in York and Newcastle, she was given a brilliant reception ; the bells pealed from the towers, a crowd of curious spectators thronged the gaily decorated streets, whilst the bands which accompanied her poured forth their melodies.   A retinue of richly dressed, well-mounted noblemen surrounded Margaret as, on the 1st of August, with her escort of some two thousand horse, she approached the Border.   There, at Lamberton Kirk, the Archbishop of Glasgow greeted her in the name of the king. Two days afterwards, near Dalkeith, her husband met her, approached her with his head uncovered, kissed her, and, after greeting her escort, stepped aside with her alone. After they had dined together, music struck up, and the queen danced before James with Lady Surrey. She did the same on the following day, when James surprised her playing cards with her ladies. He, in return, displayed his proficiency on the clavichord and lute, and on bidding her farewell, he sprang into the saddle without touching the stirrups, and galloped away, let follow who would. On the 7th of August they entered Edinburgh, Margaret sitting on horseback behind her husband. The marriage was celebrated by the Archbishop of Glasgow with great pomp in the chapel of Holyrood Palace.   Days of festivity followed, with church services, knightly games, and banquetings ; the ceremonies connected with his marriage had cost the king a good round sum.

Thus was concluded the union, which, according to its promoter's wish, was to bring about a long and peaceful connection between two neighbour countries, ever jealous of each other, and hitherto in a state of perpetual and useless warfare. Be the story true or not, nothing shows more

[margin note:] Margaret's journey to Scotland and marriage.

clearly the sagacity of deed and thought in the wise Tudor
than the answer which he is reported to have given to the
anxious question whether, by hereditary succession, England
might not at some future time fall to a Scotch prince ; and
if it were so, he replied, he did not see how this would do
harm to England, for England would not fall to Scotland,
but Scotland to England, since the lesser was always drawn
to the greater.   Seldom has the course of history more fully
justified word and deed of political wisdom.[1]

COMMERCE AND DISCOVERIES.

In the tangled web of English politics from the year 1490
to 1500, it is necessary to separate the individual threads
which touch and cross each other in every direction, if we
would take a general survey of the whole. During that
period, Henry, in spite of all domestic and external difficulties,
pushed the commercial interests of his country in accordance
with the principles already adopted, not only in the same
channels as heretofore, but even ventured on new and as yet
untried ground.

Perkin Warbeck's intrigues had exercised a marked
influence on the trade between England and the Low
Countries, for a serious stoppage of trade had *Commercial*
been the result of Henry's interdiction, and the *relations*
Londoners' hatred of the foreigner culminated *with the*
in the attack on the Steelyard in October, 1493. *Netherlands.*
And yet, in spite of incessant hostility on the part of the
ever-restless Maximilian, it was during the quarrel with the
Burgundian Netherlands that the first step was taken towards
an adjustment of difficulties.   Whilst Perkin was still in Scotland, and Spain was strenuously urging Henry to join the
Holy League, Burgundy concluded, in February, 1496, commercial peace with England, although the King of the Romans
still openly showed his aversion to the English king.   The
constant state of war had become extremely burdensome, and
encounters on the sea were frequent between the people of
both countries.   After a Burgundian embassage had opened,
in London, preliminary negotiations, the details of which are

---

[1] On negotiations and settlement of the treaties of marriage and alliance with
Scotland, see Note 6, p. 354.

not known to us, Philip and his council at Brussels, on the 14th of December, 1495, gave instructions to the Lord of Beures and five companions, and sent them to London, where they arrived on the 1st of February, 1496, and were quartered in Crosby Hall. On the 24th of February they concluded a treaty as a basis for future commercial relations, the general political conditions of which we have already been able to touch on.

No further burdens than those that had been customary for the last fifty years should be laid for the future on the merchants of either country; the free interchange of all kinds of goods was only so far restricted that, if occasion arose, the export of the necessaries of life might be prohibited; not only trade, but the fisheries were made free. Traders should enjoy every protection; piracy, as much as possible, be put a stop to; the people, as well as their rulers, should cease from hostilities, and mutually support each other; orderly and just dealing was promised.

If this treaty of peace contained the sum of all the general regulations by which an unrestricted and successful commercial intercourse was possible, the period immediately following it did not, unfortunately, fulfil the hopes which such agreements justified. On the whole, the preceding rupture must have been less felt by England than by her rival. Henry, indeed, showed a favourable disposition towards Burgundy. He expressed this also by his hospitable reception of the ambassadors; but in other respects, odd as it may appear, the peace was not assented to with pleasure in England. Only after much resistance did the Londoners, at Henry's demand, resolve on affixing the seal of their city to the document, and the Lord Mayor considered it necessary to issue a special manifesto in order to justify this compliance. The same command was sent to other towns, such as Canterbury and Southampton.

But after all it was from the Low Countries that fresh difficulties arose. As early as June, 1496, Henry protested emphatically against a duty imposed in Antwerp on English cloth, contrary to the treaty; the Spanish monarchs tried to smooth over these disagreements, but they lasted on into the following year. Henry passed from threats to the actual removal of the English mart from Antwerp to Calais, where a special duty was levied on Burgundian merchants. It was not till the 7th of July, 1497, that an understanding, arrived at in London, abolished the Antwerp duty. English cloth was to have free admission into all Philip's dominions except Flanders, and any fresh violation of the treaty, on the part of Burgundy, was to give Henry the right to annul all other treaties; on the other hand, the question of the corresponding English duty was to be settled at Bruges.

But the ill feeling once firmly rooted was not easily removed by new treaties, nor can we quite determine how far outside influences, perhaps again that of the King of the Romans, had to do with it. The conference at Bruges in April, 1498, was without result; the proceedings, however, were continued in London, where, at the end of July, the Bishop of Cambray appeared with three colleagues. Henry did not issue his powers till the 25th of August, and we do not hear of any treaty being concluded. We cannot attach much weight to the Spaniard Puebla's assertion that the result was a satisfactory one, for he only made use of the occasion to sing his own praises with childish vanity, and to pose as the friend in need, who had come to the assistance of the helpless parties with a solution of the difficulty. Still, he was not altogether wrong, for the ambassadors were respectfully dismissed, and the English merchants received permission to return to Antwerp, where, having been greatly missed, they were given a splendid reception, amid general rejoicing. It is evident, however, that no distinct settlement was arrived at, for it was necessary to call together a conference at Calais in March, 1499, with a view to a fresh agreement.

If the treaty of 1496 determined the general principles of commercial relations, the one concluded on the 18th of May, 1499, regulated the numerous individual difficulties. Henry, in this, as in all commercial questions, held with tenacity to the standpoint of English interests, and managed step by step to gain his end. The merchants of the Low Countries received a slight abatement of price on the English wool sold by the Staplers at Calais, and also a guarantee of honest packing. Delegates from the Staple

Agreement with the Netherlands.

merchants themselves were admitted to these negotiations, and signified their approbation.   In return for this, English cloth was relieved from the still-existing customs duties ; the whole trade was put on a freer footing, but the retail sale of English cloth was not permitted in the Low Countries themselves.   The English, too, gained an important point in the permission to export coined, or otherwise wrought, precious metal.

The settlement had been dragging on slowly enough for many years, but nevertheless Henry had managed practically to secure the advantage on his side ; the rivalry between Flanders and Brabant contributing still further to improve the favourable position of the English.   Other political questions arose incidentally in connection with this question of commerce, which largely affected the relations of England and Burgundy ; thus Henry showed himself dissatisfied with the securities to be provided for him by the February treaty of 1496, against the intrigues of the Duchess Margaret, and although the duchess herself, in the autumn of 1498, begged his forgiveness and gave reassuring promises, the king demanded new and more severe measures against her. If more friendly relations were the immediate result of the commercial agreement, the last settlement had not long been made before commerce was adversely affected by a new political dispute.[1]

Henry having, with more and more astuteness, succeeded in turning the political situation to his own advantage, had thereby made it possible for himself to enter the Holy League without endangering his friendship with France.   This friendship of France was of great value to him with regard to Scotland, as was also the increase to his revenue by the payment of the French treaty debt ; and he managed especially to make it useful for English trade.   The trade with France was by no means of the same vital importance for England as was that with the Netherlands, still it was important enough to play its part in the mutual relations of the two countries.   In spite of the Navigation Act which had sensibly affected France, the first

The trade with France.

---

[1] For the negotiations and commercial settlements with the Netherlands, see Note 7, p. 357.

treaty concluded by Henry (on January 17, 1486), immediately after his accession, had been extended, and perfectly
free intercourse established, while all the special burdens
introduced within the last twenty-two years had been
abolished ; perhaps, as a consequence of this, the Navigation
Act was not renewed in the second Parliament.

The state of war which followed naturally affected
commerce prejudicially, and even after war had ceased, new
imposts, burdensome to the English, remained, which Henry
was able to point to as justification for the Navigation Act,
which was extended and came into force in June, 1490. In
this Brittany, after its annexation, was naturally included.
The treaty which Henry, on the 2nd of July, 1486, had concluded with the Duke Francis—in its commercial conditions
only a repetition of a treaty of Edward IV. (July 2, 1468)—
had already expired, at the death of the old duke. In
December, 1494, Henry complained emphatically of piracies
committed by the inhabitants of Brittany and Normandy, of
the uselessness of all claims for damages, and of the treatment of English merchants, especially in Bordeaux. He
therefore made Charles VIII. pay him a heavy price for his
neutrality during the Neapolitan war, for we find that on the
11th of April, 1495, Charles signed at Naples a decree which
gave back to the English their ancient trade privileges. A
duty levied, in spite of this, at Bordeaux, had to be taken off
again, and the sums overcharged had to be refunded.

Henry took good care not to disturb a state of affairs so
specially favourable to his own interests ; a new settlement at
Boulogne, on the 24th of May, 1497, was made only for the
purpose of meeting the heavy damage done by the piracy
which then prevailed everywhere. It was England who
reaped all the benefit ; and bitterly did Bretons and Frenchmen complain of the restrictions they had to suffer, both on
imports and exports, of impediments to traffic, and annoyances in the way of customs duties; how for every infraction
of the law they were threatened with the seizure of their
goods, whilst the English enjoyed in France privileges
hitherto unknown. In their replies the English brought
forward fresh justifications and subterfuges for such grievances,
but of redress they said not a word.

Besides this, the English took advantage of the war between France and Spain, to try and get into their hands the trade of the two countries. It appears, indeed, that the Spanish government had to interfere in the matter in the summer of 1496, and forbid English ships bound for France to sail from Spanish ports. In France, on the contrary, things remained as before. Louis XII.'s later attempt (in the year 1504) to hinder exportation seems to have resulted in nothing. We hear once again that, in March, 1508, French emissaries were negotiating in England about commercial affairs, otherwise all the authorities are silent on the subject. Nothing further ensued to ruffle political friendly feeling, and Henry kept firm hold of the advantages he had gained.[1]

The same thing happened with the Hanse towns, except that with them commerce alone, and not mere political rela-

The situation of the Hanse merchants.

tions, came into question. The whole condition of affairs was uncomfortable, as Henry only put matters off in order, by continual annoyances and persecutions, to compel them to sacrifice their privileges, or at all events to concede more to the English. After the Antwerp diet, the strained interpretation as to the wares of the Hanse Merchants had indeed been allowed to drop ; yet the Hanse merchants at once renewed their old complaints of oppressions, and especially of the obnoxious regulation, which compelled them to have the cloth intended for export dressed in London.[2] At the same time they were ever threatened with the union between Henry and Denmark. In 1492, the Danish chancellor himself went to London, and later, in 1495 and 1496, negotiations were carried on, the details of which, however, we do not know.[3] Henry took advantage of the outburst of popular feeling at the time of the rupture with Burgundy and the consequent attack on the Steelyard, in 1493, to exact caution money to the amount of £20,000, that the Hanse merchants would not carry on any trade between England and Burgundy. They even had to submit to the intrusion of customs officers into the Steelyard and to the seizure of

[1] On the Anglo-French commercial relations, see Note 8, p. 358.
[2] See above, p. 73.
[3] See authorities, Note 13, to Chap. II.

goods.[1] The Hanse towns were already thinking, as a counter-measure, of forbidding their merchants to frequent the mart set up at Calais. Furthermore, they were dissatisfied with their merchants in London, whom they reproached with dishonesty, bad methods of conducting business, extravagance and luxury in dress, and with constantly frequenting taverns and houses of ill-fame; saying they ought the rather to make sober use of their privileges, and not do anything to prejudice the English against them.[2]

Under various pretexts the proposed diet was repeatedly postponed. The interdiction on trade with the Netherlands did not end till the commercial peace of January, 1496. The newly imposed duty on English cloth in the Netherlands pressed on the Hanse merchants also; and Cologne, especially, complained of the embargo which then lay on the importation of manufactured silk goods into England. Henry met these complaints with fresh insult. Instead of a regular diet, he proposed at the beginning of 1497 a conference between their ambassadors at Antwerp on the grievances alleged on both sides since 1491; but when in June his representatives arrived at Antwerp, they required from the Hanse commissioners formal and general authority from all the towns, which in the given time could not have been procured, and from the character of the meeting had not appeared necessary. As a substitute for this, a full power was procured in all haste from the chief town, Lubeck; but when it arrived the Englishmen had already taken their departure.[3] All this trouble had been without result, and Henry's arbitrary conduct was only more clearly shown than ever.

During the interval that elapsed before a diet was really held at Bruges, in June, 1499, Henry had made a fresh attempt to open up the Baltic trade. Dantzic having obstinately opposed all the English demands, it is probable that Henry hoped *The Riga Covenant. Diet at Bruges.*

---

[1] Hanserec., iii. Nos. 259–264, 285–288; Schanz., ii. Urk. Beil., 407, f.; cf. Hanserec., iv. No. 13, § 2; Schanz., p. 411.

[2] June, 1494: Hanserec., iii. No. 360; Weinreich's Danz. Chron., 778, for 1489; cf. Hanserec., No. 353, §§ 50–61, 73, 90, f., 101.

[3] On the negotiations in Antwerp, see especially the leading report: Hanserec., iv. No. 8 or No. 10 (Rym., xii. 651, f.), 19, 21; the Lubeck power, July 9, 1497: No. 11; cf. 12, 16; Hanseatic complaints, Nos. 13–15; Schanz., ii. Urk. Beil., pp. 409–413.

to turn the trade with the East away from Dantzic to some other centre ; in any case, to break through at one point, in the interests of Englishmen, the exclusive Hanseatic trade system.   He entered into an agreement with Riga, which was not one of the contracting parties in the Utrecht treaty, and on the 26th of November, 1498, a settlement was made at Westminster, accepting the English interpretation of the Utrecht treaty, with the highest warrantable privileges. Besides this, any existing English bonds were to be declared cancelled, and the mutual ratifications of these conditions were to be exchanged at Calais within five months.[1]

At this juncture, in April, 1499, King John of Poland wrote both to Henry and to Lubeck, with a view to mediating. He advised some concessions, if privileges were guaranteed in return.[2]   When the negotiations were opened in June at the Bruges diet, the English resorted to their old tactics. They required full powers, and refused especially to agree to any discussion on existing parliamentary statutes: his majesty the king would nobly fulfil all that was properly his duty to do.   The Hanse deputies brought forward their old accusation of the unsettled grievances of 1491, and they again cut short any attempt to tamper with their privileges. They said they did not come to that diet to give up one iota of their privileges ; they would defend themselves in that matter like men.

The Hanse deputies were beginning to think of breaking off such idle negotiations, when the Englishmen once more consulted their king, whose answer, dated the 9th of July, 1499, decided the fate of the diet.   Not a word of concession was spoken.   His own demand about Prussian trade was persisted in, and a court of arbitration, proposed by the Hansa, was refused.   As Henry was only wishing to avoid an open rupture, everything else could remain as before.   After more disputing, a general outline of the final protocol (July 20, 1493) was agreed to—that things were to remain as they were till the 1st of July, 1501.   When the almost contemptuous suggestion was made to the Hansa that

[1] Rym. xii. 700–704 ; Hanserec., iv. No. 128, f. ; cf. letter of the London Hanse to Lubeck, February 20, 1499 ; ibid., No. 131.
[2] Schanz., Urk. Beil, 414–417 ; Hanserec., iv. No. 140.

they had better trust their cause to the mercy of the king, they plainly answered that the towns well knew what they had had to endure in England, "which they would fain have written with a pen of iron on a hard flint-stone, that they might never more forget it."

They were able to retaliate by frustrating Henry's hopes in the compact with Riga. If Riga had any desire to separate from the Hanse league, it did not last long. An English bond of the year 1409, specially mentioned in the treaty with Riga, lay in the Hanseatic counting-house at Bruges, and the messenger who was to demand the payment of it there, and probably also carried the ratification of the treaty with him, was at the same time charged with special recommendations to the Lubeckers.[1] The Hanse merchants of Bruges thought it advisable not to hand over the bond, but rather to take away from the messenger his other papers. They behaved as if it had only been a question between England and Riga of the reception of the latter into the treaty of Utrecht, and Lubeck, on the strength of her right as the chief town to announce this, took the whole matter into her own hands. In July, 1500, Riga acquiesced. She acknowledged Lubeck's precedence, assented to the Utrecht treaty, and only added to it a clause, no longer of much importance, in favour of the peace concluded with England. Lubeck announced to Henry Riga's readmission into the league, and begged she might be entitled to the Hanseatic privileges; whereupon the king, without mentioning the still unaccomplished ratification, declared that the treaty with Riga should remain as before. The Hanse allowed the matter to rest for the present. Riga announced formally at a diet of Livonian towns, and also in a special document, that she had never thought of separating from the Hanse league.[2]

Thus the upshot of the business was that it ended in smoke. This renewed attempt on the part of Henry to encroach on the Hanse merchants in the field of the Baltic trade had failed, and this time finally. Now a somewhat more peaceful period was about to begin, even though both parties held to their own views. The projected new diet was finally put off to

[1] See above, p. 153.
[2] Respecting the Bruges negotiations and the result of the Riga alliance, see Note 9, p. 359.

1504; but before that time had arrived, an unexpected change had taken place in Henry's attitude. For the first time his relation to the commercial league was connected with other political questions. We shall have to consider these circumstances later.

Henry's policy with regard to the Hanse merchants was really a breach of treaty, thinly veiled by quibbles. His aim was ever the same—to oust the Hansards from their English trade as much as possible, and to break down their monopoly on the Baltic. The Hanse towns, when opposing the advance of the English into Prussia, had laid down the rule that the burghers and inhabitants of the towns ought always to have greater advantage than outsiders.[1] This dictum Henry turned against themselves. It was not possible that a condition of affairs resting on such a one-sided advantage for the Hanse league could continue ; sooner or later the growing mercantile power of England must burst the fetters of the Utrecht treaty.

We have already seen how the king followed out the same clear idea in mercantile policy in the south, as well as in the north; just at this time he held still more firmly to it with regard to Venice than to the Hanse towns. His relations with Venice were peculiar, for, though a war of tariffs was going on about the wine, in other respects perfectly friendly relations prevailed. General politics had something to do with this, for Venice was sparing no pains to induce Henry to join the Holy League, and for this purpose endeavoured to mediate with the King of the Romans. After Henry's admission into the league, Andrea Trevisano was, in November, 1496, appointed permanent ambassador in London; and in the following October, after his arrival, Henry gave him a public reception into the town, granted him audience with much ceremony, and, a few months later, conferred on him the honour of knighthood, but he flatly refused the request that he would take off the English duty on wine, and demanded that the Venetian customs dues should first be remitted.[2]

He gained the day, for in June, 1490, the Signory

Venice.

---

[1] Hanserec., No. 514, § 93.
[2] Brown, Nos. 728–730, 736, f., 740, f , 754, 764.

abolished the extra payment imposed on foreigners, while
Henry allowed his customs law to remain, and only conceded
by royal decree a reduction of one noble (6s. 8d.). Even
with this, his subjects reaped the greater benefit, and in spite
of all prayers and threats from the Venetians, Henry kept
firmly to his point.[1]

During this time, other commercial intercourse was going
on undisturbed; the Flanders galleys took their usual
voyages; only some natural excitement was created when
French seamen were bold enough to seize a captain and
several respectable Venetians in the English port of Southampton, and to extort from them a ransom. When, in 1497,
the galleys did not come as usual, Henry himself urged that
they should be sent off, and Venice at once was made to feel
the deficiency in the supply of English wool.[2] Later, on the
1st of May, 1506, Henry granted to the Venetians special
facilities over all foreigners for the purchase and export of
wool and tin.

As the Flanders galleys made successful voyages, and
often had not room in their holds for all the goods bought in
England, there was no cause for complaint about dullness of
trade. The commanders of the galleys reported on the excellent reception they continued to meet with; in 1506, the
king once invited the captain to his table. If any damage
had been sustained by a ship, artisans and necessary material
were at once placed at their disposal, and when some
Venetians were attacked and slain in England, care was
immediately taken to offer satisfaction, and to punish the
murderers.[3] In fact, having gained what he wanted for
English shipping, with respect to the duty on wine, Henry
tried to make up for the injury thus inflicted by friendly
advances in all other ways. When the League of Cambray,
shortly before his death, had agreed together to overthrow
the Republic, he would not be a party to it; in fact, he urged
very strongly that Venetian ships, trading with England,
should not be interfered with.[4]

[1] Brown, Nos. 798, 832; subsequent decree of Henry VIII.: Schanz., ii. Urk.
Beil., p. 382, f.; cf. i. 141, f.
[2] Ibid., Nos. 639, 659, 673, 736, 739; cf. No. 813, f., 839.
[3] Ibid., Nos. 782, 887, 898, 931.
[4] Ibid.. Nos. 939, f.

Between England and Spain also, there was the same double relation—political friendship existing alongside of a war of tariffs. Here too, Henry, in spite of his earlier pliancy, and of the later closer bond between them, held obstinately **Commercial** to the advantages in customs which he had wrung **disputes with** from the Spaniards through a misunderstanding **Spain.** on their part in the treaty of Medina del Campo. The Spaniards had constantly complained, during the treaty negotiations, of the unfair burdens laid upon their merchants. Henry went so far as to promise some concession, but afterwards had become more stiff again, and had included no sort of commercial settlement in the marriage treaty of 1496 ; finally, he held out the prospect of a regulation of the customs as a reward, should the Princess Katharine be really sent to England.   In return, the Spaniards revenged themselves by stopping the English carrying-trade between their country and France ; but though they demanded securities from every outgoing ship that it would not run into any French port, and even detained many, they conceded so far as to relinquish their demand for securities from the traders, and contented themselves with a general authoritative promise from the king. And yet, in September, 1496, before the conclusion of the marriage treaty, they threatened to enact as a counter-measure, that the same heavy duties should be levied on the Englishmen in Spain.[1]

In the treaty of alliance of the 10th of July, 1499, it was at last decided that, besides enjoying freedom of trade, the natives of both countries should be treated by each contracting party as his own subjects, but "with full preservation of the local rights, laws, and customs."   By this means the article in the old treaty objected to by the Spaniards was set aside.

But from this clause concerning local rights and customs, much friction arose, for Henry held to the Navigation Act, which deprived the Spaniards of the right to import into England wine and woad, and he, on his part, could complain that in Spanish ports the freighting of foreign ships was as a rule more strictly forbidden than in England by his law. Isabella, however, denied this (March, 1501), and asserted that Spanish ships only had the right to be freighted first,

[1] Berg., pp. 106, 107, 114, 119, 123.

and that in every country native shipping enjoyed the same protection.[1] In spite of the treaty, the struggle over navigation policy continued, until, in this matter also, redress was obtained by a change in the other relations of the two states.

Meanwhile the Spaniards had been for a time threatened by English competition in a direction where they believed themselves supreme ; for from England some **English voyages to the West.** apparently promising attempts had been made to take part in the discoveries and conquest of the western world.

The starting-point for all undertakings of the kind was Bristol, on the estuary of the Severn, which opening into the ocean, sent forth the dwellers on its banks not so much to the old continent as to the unknown **The men of Bristol.** regions of the West. Early attempts were made by the daring mariners of Bristol to draw aside the mystery which hung over the western ocean. The men of Bristol were in constant communication with the great seamen of other nations ; Christopher Columbus is said to have started from Bristol, in February, 1477, on his first, though somewhat apocryphal voyage to the north-west. Thomas Lloyd sailed from there in July, 1480, for the "Island of Brazil to the east of Hibernia," till tempestuous weather compelled him to return. The desire still prevailed to reach this mysterious Atlantic island of Brazil, with its seven cities on the other side of Ireland, and thence to pass on to India ; and in the year 1498, Ayala informed his sovereigns that for the last seven years, the people of Bristol had, every year, "sent out two, three, or four light ships in search of the island of Brazil." Ayala declares the moving spirit in the enterprises to be "the citizen of Genoa."

This man, John Cabot, was born in Genoa, and had, in 1476, been given rights of Venetian citizenship ; it is not known when he came to Bristol, with his three sons, **Cabot.** Ludovico, Sebastiano, and Sanctus. He was the leader in the Bristol voyages of discovery, but these first attempts did not achieve any result, until Cabot succeeded in gaining Henry's interest and support for his cause.

It is said that Christopher Columbus had also applied to

[1] Berg., p. 254.

the English king when, having been dismissed by Portugal in 1484, he had to wait long years in Spain, before he received the means for his first voyage of discovery in 1492. In the mean time he sent his brother Bartholomew to England, but he was robbed by pirates, and arriving penniless, had to earn his bread by drawing maps. With one of these he succeeded at last in gaining the attention of Henry, but it is doubtful whether Henry, in the year 1493, acceded to Bartholomew's request, as he had already heard of Christopher Columbus's first success. Be this as it may, it was in any case too late, for when Bartholomew returned home, his brother had already started on his second voyage, and remained in the service of the Spaniards.

Possibly this helped Cabot, when, towards the end of 1495, he applied to Henry, and explained his plans by means of a map of the world, which he had sketched. We know that Henry approved of Cabot's proposals, for, in January, 1496, we find Puebla writing home on the subject, and Ferdinand and Isabella forthwith made haste to prevent such competition. They offered timely words of warning, and represented the whole affair, as suggested by the malice of France, and intended to draw off Henry from other and more profitable things. Such enterprises, they urged, were very uncertain, and pointed to the losses incurred by Spain and Portugal as a warning. But Henry had already, on the 5th of March, 1496, signed the patent which empowered Cabot and his sons to sail in search of all unknown lands, with five ships, and such crews as they desired. They were to carry the king's flag, to plant it in the discovered territory, of which they were to take possession, and govern in the king's name. They were to exercise there an unrestricted monopoly of trade, and only to pay a fifth part of the profits to the Crown.. All English subjects were invited to further the undertaking.

The chief point, however, was to secure Henry's pecuniary help, whereby others should be encouraged to contribute to the enterprise. For this, unfortunately the time chosen was most inopportune, for how could Henry, overwhelmed just then by other political tasks, think of such novel, doubtful, and far-reaching undertakings! But after James IV., and Perkin

Warbeck's invasion had been repulsed, after Henry had entered the Holy League, and the new Spanish marriage bond had been concluded in the autumn of 1496, the king not only had his hands more free, but also had ample means from loans and taxes at his disposal. The patent, it is true, spoke of the enterprise being at the cost of its promoters, but Henry was fully determined to fit out a ship himself; it is possible that merchants both of London and Bristol helped also, and laded the ship with some of their goods.

Cabot's little fleet at last started, in May, 1497, at the favourable season of the year. On the 24th of June he touched the mainland of North America, probably on the coast of Labrador, and sailed along it towards the north-west. " He saw no human being, but he brought to the king certain snares which had been set to catch wild game, and a needle for making nets ; he also saw some felled trees, and therefore supposed there were inhabitants." He and his English companions spoke highly of the quantity of fish in the waters they had visited, saying that with such a supply, Iceland would no longer be necessary to England. Three months after he set sail, Cabot was again at home, and laid before Henry a chart of his discoveries ; the king seemed pleased, and ordered ten pounds to be paid " to hym that founde the new Isle."

Henry at once made plans for sending out a new fleet the next year under Cabot ; ten or more vessels were talked of, to be manned with criminals ; the founding of a colony was kept in view, men dreamt of an abundance of rich spices, and wonderful tales were told, how that the seven cities and the land of the great Khan had been discovered. Cabot was the hero of the day ; he again took up his abode at Bristol, and received a yearly income of £20. A Venetian reports that he was styled the Great Admiral, and that high honour was paid him. "These English run after him like mad people, so that he can enlist as many of them as he pleases, and a number of our own rogues besides."

Henry's new patent of the 3rd of February, 1498, did not show the same extravagant hopes as the first. Cabot was permitted to fit out six vessels of as much as two hundred

M

tons' burden, without having to pay more for them than the king himself, and to man them with any Englishmen who might volunteer their services. Here again Henry seems to have gone beyond what he promised, for he probably had the vessels equipped himself, showed himself greatly interested in the matter, and often spoke of it to the Spanish ambassador. Some time in April or May, 1498, the second squadron, counting five ships, provisioned for one year, set sail. One vessel was driven by a storm into an Irish port, the rest continued their voyage ; they were expected to be back in September.

Apparently John Cabot died during the voyage. It is altogether extraordinary that we have no reliable account of a voyage of discovery undertaken with such great hopes ; no doubt the success did not come up to the extravagant expectations that had been formed. This specially affected John's successor, his son Sebastian, as the king did not place the same confidence in him as in his father. For years the name even of the seafarer remained forgotten.

But the merchants of Bristol took upon themselves his father's work, and were never tired of seeking for the north-west passage to the coveted Indies. The king's active participation was somewhat cooled by his first disappointments, even though his interest long remained keen. On the 19th of March, 1501, he granted a new patent to make voyages of discovery under the royal flag to several citizens of Bristol, and to some Portuguese who were living there and had come from the Azores ; in this patent a definite scheme of colonization was put forward, with rights of trading and of jurisdiction for the discoverers ; of course the acquired territories were to be under English supremacy. How far the new undertaking succeeded we do not know. In January, 1502, "the men of Bristoll that founde th'Isle" again received a small reward, and in the same year, according to a report of the London Chronicle, three men were brought to England "out of an Iland founde by merchaunts of Bristoll farre beyond Ireland, the which was clothed in Beests skynnes and ate raw flessh, and were in their demeanour as Beests." No one understood their language, but the king had them provided for at Westminster, and after an interval of two years, two of them who were still living there were found—"clothed like Englishmen, and could not be discerned from Englishmen."

It appears that a squabble had broken out in the trading company to which Henry granted the last patent, for from a new one of the 9th of December, 1502, we find three members excluded; in other respects it was like the former, only that instead of the licences being for ten years, they were granted for forty, and an article added to the effect that if they should discover countries for which others had already received patents, but had not succeeded in discovering them, they could without scruple take possession of them.

We hear nothing of any success this time, but in September, 1503, a sum of £20 was again paid over to Bristol merchants, and certainly voyages to the west continued, as is proved by payments in gratitude for rare animals, some of which were brought from thence for the king. The spread of Christianity was also not forgotten, for we twice hear of clergymen going out in the ships.

The voyages of discovery under Henry VII. were attempts which had after all no lasting results. The cause of this is obvious. The discoverer sailing from Spain was led in his voyages westward to the tropical clime of Central and South America, while Cabot and **Unsuccessful attempts.** his followers, who tried for the north-west passage, arrived at the more inhospitable north, which did not possess such evident riches as metals and spices. As these were the only things sought after, it was but natural that Henry's ardour, thus disappointed, should soon cool. The history of discovery under the first Tudor remains therefore only an episode; but it shows how Henry, whose mercantile policy embraced the whole known field of commerce in Europe, also turned his eyes towards the unknown regions; and it was to his intelligent support that Cabot owed the achievement of setting foot on the American continent, even before the Spaniards. England especially ought not to forget those bold pioneers, the merchants of Bristol, who with untiring energy and daring first led the way to future greatness for their countrymen.[1]

The Spaniards at least were freed from one cause for

[1] On the history of discovery, see Note 10, p. 359.

anxiety: England still left to them the precedence in the New World, for Henry still confined himself to the one field of conflict in Europe. Here, however, he had gained for his new dynasty its position in this the most difficult and yet most successful period of his whole reign, and nothing bears witness more truly to the strength of this position as compared with that held in the preceding decade, than the last effort of the Yorkist party against the Tudor dynasty in the revolt of Edmund de la Pole, Earl of Suffolk.

CHAPTER V.

THE EARL OF SUFFOLK.

WE have not forgotten John de la Pole, Earl of Lincoln, who, as leader of the conspiracy against Henry in the year 1487, was slain at Stoke. His father, Duke John of Suffolk, husband of a sister of King Edward, survived his unfortunate son by many years. On his death, in 1491, Lincoln's brother, Edmund de la Pole, would have succeeded as heir to the family title and property, but that both were regarded as escheated to the Crown, in consequence of his brother's attainder. It was only by a special compact with the king, concluded on the 3rd of February, 1493, and confirmed by the Parliament in 1495, that Edmund received back a portion of his property; but he still had to produce a sum of £5000, to be paid in instalments, and, for this, was obliged to put in pledge portions of his reacquired possessions. As his reduced income no longer corresponded to the dignity of a duke, he had to be content with the title of the Earl of Suffolk. He appeared, however, publicly at court, took part with distinction in the tournaments which were held in honour of Prince Henry's elevation to the dignity of Duke of York, and was present at the entry and reception of the foreign ambassadors; but the sense of the injury done him by the confiscation of his inheritance was fostered by the ambition of a prince sprung from the royal House, whose elder brother had once been destined for the throne, and seems to have rankled in the mind of the hot-headed young man.

A special event led to the crisis. In the year 1498, he killed a man in a squabble, and, although he afterwards received the king's pardon, he felt his honour insulted because, although a peer, he had been indicted for this crime **Suffolk's first** before a common court of justice. He escaped **flight and** from England in the summer of 1499, and betook **return.** himself to Flanders, but stayed awhile on English territory with Sir James Tyrrel, the governor of Guines, near Calais. In August, Henry made inquiries about him from his friends ; whoever could give any information should be detained ; the ports also were watched. In September, 1499, Sir Richard Guildford and Richard Hatton went as envoys to the Archduke Philip, and were specially commissioned to induce the earl to return.

Suffolk's whereabouts had been discovered, and it appears strange that Henry should have tried in a friendly way to persuade him to return, when he might have seized him while still on English territory. Possibly it was in consequence of the last conspiracy attempted just at this time by Perkin Warbeck, in whose ruin the Earl of Warwick had been involved, that Henry treated his less dangerous kinsman of the house of York with remarkable lenity, and tried to attract him to his side by kindness. Henry was even prepared to make terms, and only threatened that he would deprive Suffolk of all foreign aid, especially from Philip. In order publicly to make known their friendly agreement, Suffolk was to return alone, without Guildford, and to bring Sir James Tyrrel with him. Probably the envoys did not even find him on English territory ; he had already escaped over the border to St. Omer, but shortly returned, and resumed his old position at court.[1]

At the same time Henry seems to have thought it ominous that Suffolk should have tried to gain over Philip of Burgundy to his side, although Philip had apparently intended to send away the earl at Henry's request. The king informed him minutely of what had taken place, for he wished to avoid any danger to the newly secured commercial treaties, and to give to their friendship the appearance of still greater firmness. The Spaniards at that time were in some anxiety about this increasingly friendly relation, for the two princes were preparing for a personal interview. On the 3rd of May, 1500,

[1] On the Earl of Suffolk and his first escape, see Note 1, p. 362.

Henry landed at Calais with his wife and a splendid retinue, and, during the month he stayed there, many more nobles arrived, amongst whom was the Earl of Suffolk.   Henry probably was desirous that he and his brothers William and Richard should show themselves just then in the royal retinue.

. For some time longer negotiations went on between Calais and St. Omer, where Philip had appeared, about the ceremonial details of the meeting, and about the political questions to be decided and which had **Henry and Philip.** to be clearly defined beforehand.   Besides the general covenant of friendship, a double marriage was projected between Henry of York and his sister Mary with Philip's daughter and his infant son Charles, then only four months old.   On the 9th of June, 1500, the king and archduke met on English ground, not in Calais itself, but near the church of St. Peter, situated not far from the town. All the festivities, reception, and banquet took place with every show of mutual respect and friendship.   Philip wanted to hold the king's stirrup for him to dismount, but this he would not allow.   No doubt the terms of former treaties, as well as the projected alliances, were discussed, but the matter did not advance beyond words and promises.   Henry stated emphatically before Puebla that the meeting was only intended to show their friendship to the world, and the anxious fears of the Spaniards, increased still more by what had transpired about the marriage negotiations, were soon dissipated.   On the same day that they had met, Henry and Philip took leave of each other.   Philip rode back to Gravelines ; the king landed at Dover again on the 16th of June.

This new friendly compact had no sooner been made than misfortune befel the king.   On the 22nd of June he buried, at Westminster, his third son, Edmund, born in March, 1499, who had died on the 12th of June, even before his father's return, at Hatfield, the property of the bishops of Ely. Somewhere about this time the sweating sickness broke out for the second time in England, beginning mildly at first, but afterwards spreading rapidly and claiming numerous victims, especially in London.   It lasted through the summer and autumn, and it was not till December that Puebla could report that it had quite died out in the kingdom. The king's country seat at Sheen was also burned down, and the palace of Richmond erected in its stead; it was, in fact, at this time that Henry developed great activity in building.[1]

This could be pointed to as an evidence of tranquillity at home, in the same way as, after the death of Warwick, Suffolk's appearance with the king at the festivities at Calais was to bear witness to the peace between Tudor and York. But the peace did not last long; Suffolk's restless spirit drove him again to venture on the enterprise he had before only begun. The events that followed his first flight seem to have suggested to him not to apply again to Philip, but to the old antagonist of the Tudor, the King of the Romans. This time he did not set to work without a definite plan, but waited till he thought himself sure of a good reception.

Sir Robert Curzon, the captain of Hammes, near Calais, had, in August, 1499, been given leave of absence at his Sir Robert Curzon at the court of Maximilian. repeated and earnest request, that he might fight against the Infidels. He entered the service of Maximilian, and so distinguished himself that he was created a baron of the Empire. Before this we find him incidentally mentioned at court festivities; at the tournament in honour of Henry of York, he fought by Suffolk's side, with whom he must have stood before that time in friendly connection, as he is said to have owed to him his elevation to the dignity of knighthood. When in a conversation with Maximilian he alluded to Suffolk, Maximilian declared himself ready to lend substantial aid to any man of King Edward's blood to get back his rights, but, in view of the political situation at the time, he recommended peaceful methods.[2]

Well might the condition of affairs dispose Maximilian to make such a reservation, for his vacillating policy had for the last few years everywhere suffered shipwreck. While he was vainly trying, after Louis XII.'s accession, to carry out his plans with regard to Burgundy, French interference increased his own difficulties; this was the case in his war

---

[1] On the meeting with Philip and events connected with it in England, see Note 2, p. 363.

[2] On Curzon, see Note 3, p. 364, and comments by Mr. Gairdner, p. 441.

with Gueldres and in the war of the Swabian League with
Switzerland, which both ended disastrously for the Empire.
In vain Maximilian tried to force his son Philip to give up the
treaty of Paris; Louis not only firmly kept his friends, Spain,
England, and Burgundy, but gained new ones as   The
well.   For, in February, 1499, he formed the league European
with Pope Alexander VI. and Venice, Maximilian's situation.
enemy; by a treaty of the 15th of March, he secured to himself, at last, the mercenaries of Switzerland, and even made
covenants with German princes.   Thus he tried to hold a
troublesome rival in check, and to make for himself allies
or secure neutrality, before he entered upon his great work
of making the title of duke, which he had already assumed,
a reality, by his conquest of Milan.   Ludovico Sforza, the
threatened duke, alone adhered to Maximilian, and the latter
seriously cherished the idea of making him a member of the
Swabian League.[1]   But with the same ease as Charles VIII.
had before conquered Naples, Louis XII. now overthrew Milan,
and on the 6th of October, 1499, made his entry into the
conquered town.   Sforza had been for a time reinstated, when
he fell, in April, 1500, into the hands of his powerful opponent,
who kept him in strict custody.   Louis had now got into his
hands this splendid prize, and for years it was carefully guarded
by France.

This victory was a severe blow for Maximilian, who before
had proposed a division of their claims in Italy, with the
Po as the line of demarcation; to this were added defeats
in his Imperial policy at home, the establishment of an
Imperial Council of Regency, which, against his wish, showed
itself prepared to make friends with Louis, and even to agree
to his investiture with the Duchy of Milan, while soon after,
the growth of the power of France, so strenuously opposed
by Maximilian, was still further increased by a second conquest of Naples.

Louis XII. had by no means given up the claims of his
predecessor, the only difference was that he went to work
more systematically; for while Charles VIII., by his expedition
against Naples, had called forth against himself the opposition
of all Europe led by Ferdinand, Louis undertook it in close

---

[1] See Ulmann, i. 773, f.

combination with Spain. The idea of a partition of Naples
had originated with Ferdinand himself, and a secret treaty at
Granada, on the 11th of November, 1500, was the first step
towards the realisation of this project. Their joint conquest
of Naples achieved, Apulia and Calabria were to fall to
Ferdinand, and at the same time his possession of Roussillon
and Cerdagne was to be confirmed afresh. In June, 1501,
the French troops had already arrived in the neighbourhood
of Rome, and Pope Alexander ratified this iniquitous compact which aimed at dividing by sheer force the possessions
of a weaker power. It was then that Ferdinand's own plans
with regard to Naples were divulged ; the power of the false
Aragonese collapsed hopelessly, and the last king, Frederick,
became the prisoner of Louis, who kept him in honourable
confinement.

While all this was going on, Maximilian was completely
thrust aside. All his hostile plans against France had failed,
and it seemed as if he were resigned to his fate, for, after
a long resistance, he gave in at last to the persuasions of his
son, who, far from himself breaking with France, pressed his
father to a reconciliation with his enemy. On the 10th of
August, 1501, a marriage was agreed upon between Louis'
daughter Claude and Charles, who had already been
promised to Mary of England ; but it was not till October,
at Trent, that friendly overtures between Maximilian and
France first vaguely began. Maximilian had certainly some
reason for holding aloof, for he was aware of the plan then
already existing of marrying Claude to Francis of Angoulême, the presumptive heir to the throne ; but in the end
he was successfully drawn into the league with France, even
to the more close-binding settlements between Louis and the
Hapsburgs at Blois and Hagenau (24th September, 1504, 5th
and 7th April, 1505).

The unfortunate experiences of the last few years, and
the uncertainty of his political situation, might well discourage Maximilian from making fresh ventures. His friendly
relations with France had just begun ; yet he had not
abandoned his older connection with Ferdinand.[1]   Meanwhile,

---

[1] On Maximilian, see Ulmann, ii. 99–118 ; cf. earlier Lanz., Introd. to Mon.
Hapsburg, ii. 1, p. 61, ff.

after the conquest of Naples, the alliance between Ferdinand and Louis was breaking up.   It was at this moment that the Earl of Suffolk appeared at the court of the King of the Romans with a request for aid against Henry of England, the friend of Ferdinand, Louis, and Philip.

Although Maximilian's consent, probably communicated to Curzon before the end of 1499, was given from the first under strict reservation, although it could not but appear doubly questionable in view of the subse- quent change in the political situation, the un- reflecting Suffolk was satisfied.   In August, or even in July, 1501, some months before the marriage of Arthur and Katharine, he made his escape for the second time from England, accompanied by his brother Richard, and hastened to the Tyrol.   Provided with letters of recommendation from Curzon, he at once announced his arrival to the King of the Romans, and after some interchange of communications they met at last at the end of September or beginning of October, at Imst, in the valley of the Inn.

This time Maximilian might have had at his disposal, not a probable impostor, but a man who could bring forward definite claims to the throne.   In the existing state of affairs, however, Suffolk had to be satisfied with an evasive answer and the promise of a safe refuge in Maximilian's dominions. After waiting for six weeks at Imst, while the king in the mean time had gone off to Botzen, Suffolk at last received from Maximilian's treasurer, Bontemps, the offer of a few thousand men.   Thus matters remained for the present ; Suffolk, at Maximilian's wish, took up his abode at Aix la Chapelle, and there he was forced to wait.

Suffolk met with nothing but ill-luck, for before he had reached Maximilian, the latter was already on good terms again with Henry.   When the Anglo-Burgundian settlement was concluded in May, 1499, Henry also endeavoured to restore more satisfactory relations with Philip's father.   But although good results were reported in England, nothing transpired for a long time, till at last, even in this quarter also, the newly confirmed friendship with Burgundy bore fruit. Not only with regard to France, but also to England, the peaceful tendency of the Burgundian policy succeeded with

Maximilian; he entrusted the management of the affair entirely to his son, who, in the summer of 1501, made known to Henry his father's desire to enter into a closer relationship with England. The phrases employed between two such old antagonists about renewing ancient friendship, strike us as rather strange, but behind there was a very plainly expressed desire on the part of Maximilian to seal this new friendship with an advance from England of fifty thousand crowns for his Turkish war ; the two kings, besides, were to wear, as a sign of their unity, their respective orders of the Garter and the Golden Fleece.

Nothing could be more opportune for Henry than this reconciliation at the time of Suffolk's second flight ; for he **Henry's measures against Suffolk.** might now hope that not only in England itself, but also with the one uncertain foreign power, successful measures might be at once taken against the rebel. In his own kingdom he acted in the same way as at the time of Warbeck's insurrection. Measures for security against possible adherents were taken, and on the 7th of November, 1501, Suffolk and Curzon, with five other confederates, were publicly denounced and condemned as traitors at St. Paul's Cross in London. Suffolk's nearest kinsmen were taken into custody ; his brother, Lord William de la Pole, his cousin by marriage, Lord William Courtenay, son of the Earl of Devonshire, Sir James Tyrrel, who had helped him in his first flight, and Sir John Wyndham. Tyrrel, Richard III.'s accessory in the murder of the sons of Edward, was, according to Suffolk's assertion, misled only by false pretences to surrender Guines. The two lords were consigned to the Tower, and later, in October, 1508, we hear that Courtenay and the Marquis of Dorset were taken over to Calais, where they were kept in confinement till Henry's death. Tyrrel and Wyndham suffered the extreme penalty —their heads fell on Tower Hill on the 6th of May, 1502 ; many of their confederates were executed after them ; accomplices were discovered and captured at various places, and upon all of them Parliament passed a Bill of Attainder in the year 1504.[1]

[1] On Suffolk's second flight, his first connection with Maximilian, and the prosecutions in England, see Note 4, p. 365.

At the same time Henry had made use of his friendly relations with Maximilian to cut off from Suffolk any possible help from abroad, and acquiescence in the desire of the King of the Romans for English golden crowns promised him success.   On the 28th of September, 1501, he gave instructions to Sir Charles Somerset and William Warham, in which he was careful to demand from Maximilian special assurances against the rebels, and their immediate extradition.   After the conclusion of the treaty, a money loan should be paid to Maximilian for war against the Turks, and in fact fully £10,000 or fifty thousand crowns were held out as a prospect to him, if he accepted the article about the rebels in the binding form desired ; in that case Henry was prepared to give the money, not as a loan, but as a present.   The project of a marriage between Henry of York and Philip's daughter Leonora was again touched upon ; for the rest the instructions of the ambassadors referred to the clauses concerning rebels and the payment of money, the two questions of most importance to the two princes.

Negotiations and treaty between Henry and Maximilian.

The negotiations were carried on at Antwerp ; and here again Burgundian officials, Cornelius de Barges and Jodokus Praat, acted as plenipotentiaries for Maximilian.   The English ambassadors are said to have been commissioned also to make use of the mediation of Ayala, then staying in the Netherlands.   But still Maximilian would not cordially adopt friendship with England ; his representatives were not sufficiently empowered, they had to ask for fresh instructions, and till these arrived the patience of the Englishmen was put to a severe test.   As these negotiations dragged slowly on, both parties reproached each other with wishing to procrastinate ; when the Burgundians refused the ratification of the treaty by the Pope, they had to submit to being told that, after the experience of former treaties, Maximilian's signature alone would not be sufficient.   With regard to the demand that the rebels should be banished from the Empire, it was maintained that Maximilian, in free towns of the Empire, like Aix la Chapelle, had not sufficient authority for this ; help should be refused to them, but in return Henry should guarantee them security for their life and property ;

at the same time the largest sum demanded, fifty thousand crowns, was insisted on.

The Englishmen, tired of waiting, were already threatening to take their departure, when the messenger at last appeared with the powers, dated the 24th of April, 1502. On the 19th of June a general commercial treaty, comprised in a small number of articles, was agreed upon, and also on the next day the payment of a sum of £10,000 for the Turkish war was promised, in return for which Maximilian undertook not to countenance rebels against Henry, but to oppose them in every way, and to prevent their being supported in the Empire. In a treaty of alliance for the lifetime of the contracting parties, he undertook furthermore to send out of his dominions all such rebels, and should they prove refractory, to punish them like criminals. The money was paid in London on the 1st of October, but the treaty was not announced publicly till the 22nd of October, and not sent to the sheriffs to publish in the counties till the 11th of November. A proclamation, identical with that of the preceding year, was issued from St. Paul's Cross against Suffolk and his confederates, and this more emphatically than before, on the strength of a bull from the Pope, which shows that Alexander VI., like his predecessor, took the side of the English king against his rebellious subjects.

Henry seems to have been in no hurry publicly to announce the treaty, for it was not specially advantageous to himself. He had been obliged to pay a very high price, and had only received, in the ambiguous form of the double agreement, a very insecure return, considering the enmity so often exhibited towards him by Maximilian. It was, however, of importance that Maximilian had expressly promised this time to deny protection to English rebels who had fled the country.[1]

Suffolk had even less reason to be pleased than Henry. Maximilian had pledged himself so deeply to the earl that he dared not entirely desert him ; hence probably the slow progress of the negotiations, and the attempt to gain more lenient terms for the fugitive. Maximilian could always regard him as a useful tool ; it was owing to him that he had secured a substantial sum of English money, and he therefore

[1] On the negotiations and settlements with Maximilian, see Note 5, p. 366.

put him off with fresh schemes and excuses. There was some talk of embassies to the King of Denmark, to gain his alliance against Henry, and a prospect was held out to Suffolk of money to enable him to travel to Denmark himself. But he received nothing ; it was even hinted to him occasionally that the protection already afforded to him ought to suffice, and that he should not make himself burdensome by further demands.

Suffolk was therefore compelled to run into debt at Aix la Chapelle for the necessaries of life. In May, 1502, he appealed for help to Maximilian, both in person and through his faithful servant, Killingworth, and the treasurer, Bontemps. Abundant promises had been made him, he urged, but he had been put off and disappointed, while his property in England had been confiscated, his friends seized and executed. He would hear nothing of an amicable arrangement with Henry, which had been proposed to him, for he and the king could not both live in England without harm coming to one or other of them. Maximilian repeatedly urged on him this peaceful settlement, and yet let fall certain remarks before Killingworth, as if there were a possibility that at no distant date his friendly relations with the English king would cease ; but he refused absolutely to recognise any obligation to give the earl assistance, alleging that he had never promised it.[1]

Suffolk at Aix la Chapelle.

Suffolk was even in fear of spies, whom Henry had sent out, possibly with a commission to arrest the fugitive. The king also applied to other Powers for their co-operation. The Spaniards informed him, in April, 1502, that they were demanding, through their ambassador, Don Juan Manuel, the surrender of the fugitive; and they drew Maximilian's attention to the fact, that Henry might perhaps be won over to their side against France. But, as before in the case of Perkin Warbeck, they desired to get the pretender into their own power, and the unsatisfactory manner in which these instructions were carried out was afterwards brought forward as the motive for Ferdinand's displeasure against Manuel. Louis of France had also been requested by Henry to give

---

[1] On Suffolk and Maximilian, see reports and letters, Lett. and Pap., i. 137–143, 147–149, 178–185, 187.

him his support, and especially to use his influence with his German friends. Henry declared himself ready to pay as a price for the rebel from ten to twelve thousand gold crowns.[1]

It was his special aim to induce Maximilian to see to the proclamation of banishment in various large towns, as required by the treaty. At first Norroy Herald was appointed to do this, as well as to bring over the insignia of the Order of the Garter, but after Henry had received Maximilian's ratification of the treaty and had paid the promised sum, he despatched Sir Thomas Brandon and Nicholas West, who were at the same time to receive the oath of the King of the Romans to the treaty.

The departure of the ambassadors was delayed, and they did not arrive in Cologne till the beginning of January, 1503 ; there Maximilian kept them waiting, and finally appointed to meet them at Antwerp, where he received them on the 1st of February. After some further proceedings, he took the oath on the 12th of February, in the church of St. Michael ; a Te Deum was sung, and in the evening bonfires were lighted in the streets and squares. Maximilian refused the investiture with the Garter as unnecessary, because he had already received the Order, and he preferred to wait till he could arrange for the performance of the ceremony by proxy in England. In the same way the ambassadors received evasive answers to their demand for a proclamation of banishment in the large towns, especially in Aix ; the King of the Romans now and then treated these questions more lightly than they liked, at all events he insisted on delay until his own ambassadors should have spoken with Henry. From the lengthy account sent home by the Englishmen of all their efforts and arguments, we gain the impression that the cunning Maximilian had led them by the nose ; he passed lightly over awkward points, and with the most amiable geniality set aside the fulfilment of the agreements he had only just sworn to ; it was, in short, very evident that, being now in possession of his £10,000, he thought no more of

---

[1] On the relations with the Spaniards: Mem. 410, Berg., Nos. 315, 346; Zurita, 241b, f., cf. Mem., 267, f., Berg., p. 364; on Louis XII. : Lett. and Pap., ii. 344, 348–350, 352, f., 361; Champollion, Lettres des rois, ii. 516, 521–523, 526, f., 536, f.

loyally executing the treaty. We only hear that he condescended to inform the town of Aix that he was bound by his treaty to give Suffolk no more assistance ; nevertheless, he sent at one time a thousand, and again, in July, 1503, two thousand gulden to help pay the earl's debts.[1]

He now despatched an embassage for the purpose of receiving Henry's oath. Conducted by the Margrave of Brandenburg, this embassage arrived in London at the end of March, 1503, and was quartered in Crosby Hall. On the 30th of March the king received it at Baynard's Castle. After a solemn mass, and while a Te Deum was being sung, Henry swore to the treaty in St. Paul's Church, on the 2nd of April. Bonfires were also lighted in London, and casks of wine were set out for those who desired to drink. The reception of Maximilian into the Order of the Garter took place in due form ; the usual contribution of £20 to the Chapel of the Order, St. George's, at Windsor, Henry paid out of his own pocket. On the 5th of March he had already, for the third time, caused the rebels to be proclaimed as traitors, and he required Maximilian to do the same. The form of the proclamation throughout the empire was determined, and Norroy Herald, who brought the insignia of the Order, which had been so earnestly pressed on the King of the Romans, was to see that this proclamation was issued.[2]

It took Henry a very long time to gain his end with Maximilian, and he could never feel safe from fresh counter-influences. Meanwhile the fugitive, scantily provided for, found an asylum, not an enviable one certainly, but which afforded him protection in **Maximilian's delay.** spite of Henry's reiterated demands. Henry behaved as if the capture of Suffolk were simply an affair in which his honour were concerned. He was never in any danger of a direct attack from Suffolk, as before from Perkin Warbeck, for no prince ever thought of arming in favour of one who from the first was only a hunted fugitive. To get hold of him was the difficulty, and Henry only partially succeeded in limiting the number of hiding-places open to the rebel. Circumstances, however, arose which caused his capture to

[1] On Brandon and West's mission, see Note 6, p. 366.   [2] See Note 7, p. 367.

appear to the king as something more than an affair of honour.

Suffolk himself, of course, spoke of his favourable prospects. He hinted at Henry's somewhat uncertain health, and therein, no doubt, hit upon a point of some importance ; for, should Henry die, the dynasty would then depend only on Prince Henry, an early death having, on the 2nd of April, 1502, brought Arthur's youthful married life to an abrupt conclusion. Hardly a year had passed after this when, in the night of the 11th of February, 1503, Queen Elizabeth died in childbed. But still severer blows had been sustained by the king in two deaths outside his family. In October, 1500, his Chancellor, Morton, had been taken from him, and Reginald Bray soon followed Elizabeth. Good and strong props to the Tudor throne were thus removed, and there was more talk on the subject than the king liked.[1] From all this it is easy to understand that Henry could not treat the affair of Suffolk lightly, however little it might threaten actual danger. He kept his eyes open. In July, 1503, eight men had again to answer a charge of high treason, and four of them were executed at Tyburn.[2] It was this year, however, which saw the fruit of long and difficult diplomacy in the Scotch matrimonial contract. Possibly it was in consequence of the somewhat uncertain situation of affairs that Henry, without any pressure of urgent necessity for money, again summoned a Parliament after an interval of six years. The session was opened on the 25th of January, 1504, by William Warham, Morton's successor in the chancellorship and archbishopric.

Many a law passed at that time bears directly on recent events. The prohibition of unauthorised assemblages was renewed ; the careless guarding of prisoners was punished, many persons suspected of treason having thereby made their escape ; and many measures for reform were resolved upon. The new Bill of Attainder affected directly the earl and his friends ; lands, offices, and dignities of those already executed, as well as of those still living, were confiscated. It is remarkable that Curzon, who elsewhere was always named

Henry's position.

---

[1] Cf. Lett. and Pap., i. 231-240; Suffolk's words, ibid., 180.
[2] Fabian's Abridgment, p. 688.

with Suffolk, should be omitted here ; Henry always reserved
to himself in all attainders the right to pardon. The Parliament, however, did not escape having to make a grant,
nor did the Convocation of York which sat in the same
year.[1]

One enactment—the result also, as far as we can see, of
Suffolk's revolt—affected to a serious extent England's commercial relations. Suffolk had found refuge in an important
imperial town. Henry therefore demanded that a proclamation should be issued against him, especially in all the larger
towns of the Empire. But as he felt very doubtful of
Maximilian in the matter, he addressed himself to the representative of the power of the towns—to the Hansa. If he
gained this, he might hope to close the gates of the leading
towns to the rebel, and to deprive him of any assistance in
money. The first really important political measure resulting
from Suffolk's intrigues was the Act of Parliament of 1504.
It protected the men of the Hansa against any adverse
ordinances then and in the future. Only one condition was
imposed, that these privileges must not clash with the freedom
and privileges of the town of London.

Such was the astonishing decree by which Henry broke
the line of policy which he had continuously pursued for
more than a decade with the men of the Hansa, *Change in*
and thereby gave up at one stroke everything he *Henry's*
had wrung from them during that period. He had *relations with*
been obliged to recognise in the struggle with the *the Hansa.*
Hanseatic league, especially after the failure of the treaty
with Riga, that his power did not yet extend far afield, and
that he must therefore grapple with his rivals in England
itself. This he had never failed to do, careless whether he
was within his own rights or not ; and now, by a short enactment, he placed himself in the most striking contradiction to
his whole previous policy.

This step is almost incomprehensible ; indeed, no other
reason can be found for it than that it had reference to
Suffolk, and there the gain that might be hoped for stood

---

[1] On the Parliament : Rot. Parl., vi. 520, f., 526, 532–542, 546, Stat., ii. 654,
f., 657–660, 669, 675–682, 685, f., Fab. Abridgment, 688, Hall, 498 ; P. V.,
775 (with wrong date, 1502); on Convocation : Wilkins, iii. 649.

in startling disproportion to the price he had to pay. It was a blunder—a blunder so much the greater that Henry never really allowed the change intended by this law to be carried out. The decree was the outcome of a momentary political situation, and Henry tried to free himself from it as soon as the occasion had passed; but by this fresh breach of faith he made his relations with the league of the towns more difficult than ever, and, moreover, there was naturally no appearance of any effect being produced in the desired direction.

His policy with regard to the Hanseatic merchants fell back, in spite of the new Act of Parliament, into its old channels. One significant clause in the Act had been that which gave preference to the privileges of the Londoners, and Henry also secured a free hand for himself, when, on announcing the decision of Parliament to the Hanse merchants, he declared that now their privileges had been sufficiently cared for, the diet might be postponed until he considered it to be necessary. He had not delivered up the sum of £20,000 already given in pledge, and when in 1504 a new quarrel arose with the Netherlands, he demanded further security against the Hanseatic carrying trade. Again there were the old complaints about overcharge in customs in England. Then, as was to be expected, in July, 1508, a year after the conclusion of the struggle with Burgundy, Henry declared the sum he held in pledge to be forfeited, in consequence of illegal export of cloth. So much for the promised protection of Hanseatic rights! This parliamentary measure had only, as a matter of fact, interrupted, and not altered, Henry's commercial policy with regard to the Hansa, and thus this curious effect of Suffolk's appearance on the scene resolved itself into a mere transient and useless politico-commercial episode.[1]

Though the existence of Suffolk as a pretender was not without importance for England, and occupied, to a great extent, Henry's thoughts, it did not, after all, present any real danger to the kingdom. As regards the conduct of

---

[1] Respecting the last change in Henry's policy with regard to the Hansa, see Note 8, p. 367.

Maximilian, Suffolk had more just cause for complaint than had Henry, notwithstanding that the latter had expended two sums of money ; for, though the exile was allowed to remain unmolested in Aix, he could, indeed, hardly find safety there from his creditors, and the uncertainty of his fate was such as to make him despair.

Apparently Maximilian did not desire that he should be driven from Aix. He preferred to reserve him to be made use of against Henry, should opportunity serve, or perhaps to hand him over for another considerable sum. Suffolk himself longed to escape from this state of uncertainty. He had thought of applying to the Count Palatine ; but Henry, hearing of it, begged the French king to interfere. Again fresh hopes were aroused in the exile by his friendly connection with Duke George of Saxony, the Lord of Friesland.

In March, 1504, we find the duke's plenipotentiary, Wilhelm Truchsess zu Waldburg, engaged in negotiations with both parties—with Suffolk and with King Henry. Duke George had received from his father the newly acquired Duchy of Friesland ; but as yet had not **Duke George of Saxony.** succeeded in establishing his full power in the country, for the town of Groningen offered him the most obstinate resistance ; and it was to overcome this that he hoped to gain Henry's help. If his ambassador at the same time was treating with the Earl of Suffolk about assistance in troops and money for an attack on England, and about a refuge in Friesland, his aim was evidently to lure the earl into his net, and to make use of him for his own ends with Henry. Suffolk was at this time with the King of the Romans, making fresh attempts to get help. His brother Richard therefore negotiated in his stead with Waldburg, and they discussed the question of armed support, and of paying the earl's heavy debts in Aix. How far they came to any binding agreement we do not know, but Waldburg's promises satisfied the earl completely, while he probably received from Maximilian nothing but his usual fair words. The hope that Suffolk's debts would be paid induced his creditors at Aix to let him depart, and only to detain Richard as a hostage. Shortly after the negotiations with Waldburg, towards the middle of April, Suffolk disappeared from Aix, evidently without Maximilian's knowledge, and against his wish.[1]

The fugitive's hopes, however, were destined to be frustrated. He had procured for himself, for his journey through Gelderland to Friesland, a safe conduct from Duke Charles of Gueldres, who equally with Duke George might entertain hopes of making use of Suffolk for his own ends. Charles disregarded the safe conduct, and caused him to be captured and kept in close confinement in Hattem, on the Isel, close to the northern border of the duchy. Thus Duke George was disappointed in his expectations.[2]

The result of all this was that Suffolk got involved in a new set of political quarrels. Charles the Bold had incorporated Gelderland into his Burgundian possessions. Charles of Egmont, the descendant of the dethroned ducal house, had, in 1492, been released from the captivity into which he had fallen in France. He was a brave and shrewd man. France willingly gave him help, and he was supported at the same time by the people of Gelderland, eager for independence, and began a struggle with the Hapsburg lords of Burgundy, which he obstinately maintained for several successive years in a perpetual and devastating warfare. The alliance of the Hapsburgs with Louis XII. changed the situation to the disadvantage of the duke, and though Maximilian, led by the Burgundian policy, allowed himself to be drawn into an alliance with France, he succeeded in return in involving Philip in the war with Gelderland up to August, 1504.

Suffolk in Gueldres.

Suffolk was then already in the hands of the duke. Henry VII. himself declared that Charles claimed an exceptionally high ransom for the earl. Later there was a rumour in Antwerp that Henry would even stir up and support Charles against Philip.[3] But of negotiations between the king and the duke nothing has transpired. More intimate relations did not exist, or Henry would not have been, in the summer of 1505, in complete ignorance of plans in Gelderland with regard to Suffolk—whether Maximilian or Philip had a hand in the game, whether Duke

---

[1] See Note 9, p. 368. [2] Lett. and Pap., i. 260–262.
[3] Brown, No. 846, f., Berg., p. 335. Ulmann, ii. 168, attaches too great weight to these rumours.

Charles was friendly to the earl, where he kept him, and whether as a prisoner or not.[1]   The fugitive was, in fact, withdrawn for a time from immediate contact with English politics, for he served the duke as a hostage against Philip, and that such a hostage should have any value for Philip showed that a change had taken place in Anglo-Burgundian relations.

In the autumn of 1504 these two countries were again engaged in an open war of tariffs.   All the treaties, even the personal meeting between the rulers, had only been **Fresh** able to secure to their states for a few short years **commercial** that amicable intercourse which was so urgently **difficulties** necessary.   Complete information as to the exact **between** cause for this condition of affairs is not to be had. **England and** Probably Burgundy, as before, opened hostilities **the Low** by imposing new customs dues, which Henry vainly sought **Countries.** to resist by a special embassage in August, 1504.   The Spaniard, Don Juan Manuel, seems to have been the moving spirit.   Accredited to Maximilian, he remained permanently in Brussels, at the Burgundian court, and exerted his influence there in defiance of his own king's wishes, and finally even against his interests.   He had already been trying to work upon Maximilian in a spirit hostile to England, and, later, he induced Philip also to carry out his wishes by decided action against Henry.   For this Suffolk could evidently serve them as an important tool, and the duke of Gueldres might very well hope, while he held such a prize, to make a good bargain with Philip.

He may therefore have himself set the rumour afloat that Henry was supporting him.   Philip showed himself to be really anxious about the matter.   He made representations to Henry, tried to calm his fears about Suffolk, and spoke of his own correct behaviour with regard to Richard de la Pole ; but it was said that he wanted all the time to make use of Richard, in default of the elder brother, against the English king.[2]

In one way, however, the capture of Suffolk was unfortunate for Duke Charles—two Powers, who were friendly towards

[1] English ambassadors' instructions, Berg., p. 352.
[2] On the beginning of the new war of tariffs, see Note 10, p. 368.

England, now turned against him. Louis of France demanded the surrender of the earl into his hands, promised his good services if his demand was complied with, and held out a prospect of an equally welcome sum of money from Henry. James of Scotland, however, who, earlier, had received a promise from Charles that he would prevent Suffolk from passing through Gelderland, and who now, instead of the fulfilment of this promise, was met with prevarications and even a request for help, wrote to the duke a highly significant letter, telling him in plain words what he thought of his conduct, and demanding the immediate dismissal of his *protégé.*

It sounded from these communications as if Suffolk had had a hospitable reception from his new protector ; but this was not the case. Suffolk tried to escape from his captivity in Hattem, and, having managed to find friends outside, he received in December, 1504, mysterious hints of secret plans progressing satisfactorily ; but no result appeared, and he achieved no more, when, in July, 1505, he tried to gain a hearing with Charles himself. Then, however, help came from without. In the middle of July, a Burgundian flying column, under the captain Von Lichtenstein, was called by the inhabitants of Hattem into the place, occupied it, cut off the greater part of the garrison, who happened to be absent, and, strengthened by reinforcements, besieged the fortress, which was only feebly defended. Philip's forces were at that time having some success. The leading town of Zutphen, situated in the heart of the country, had fallen into his hands, and shortly afterwards, after the surrender of Hattem, Suffolk became his prisoner. On the 27th of July, 1505, Charles was obliged to sue for peace, to make submission, to deliver up many fortified places, and to promise he would accompany Philip on his intended journey to Castile.[1]

From Antwerp the siege of Hattem had been watched with the greatest interest, for the sake of the prisoner who lay there, and great joy prevailed at the result, for now they hoped "to put a curb into the mouth of the king of England." The Netherlanders, indeed, had cause to rejoice over better prospects, for the war of tariffs had till now not been very

[1] Respecting Suffolk's imprisonment in Gueldres, see Note 11, p. 369.

fortunate for them. Henry had met the new imposts by a decree of the 15th of January, 1505, which opened in Calais a free market with quarterly fairs, for merchants who formerly traded with Antwerp. Tolls on exports to the Burgundian provinces were imposed, to which Philip replied by raising his own duties ; both parties prohibited entirely any imports from the opponent's country.

These dissensions with the Netherlands were probably in part the cause why Henry did not break off the negotiations with Duke George of Saxony, which were still dragging slowly on. In the hope he had founded on Suffolk, the duke was bitterly disappointed ; with the pretender no longer in his possession, he could offer but little in return for his own requests for help, for his promise to give Henry the same support, should he ever need it, could hardly have been considered an equivalent. Waldburg conducted the negotiations in England in the summer of 1504, and at Calais, with Dr. West, in March, 1505. The Englishmen, as usual, spoke of Suffolk with great contempt ; to them he was no more than a "scullion," and a "runaway youth ;" notwithstanding, therefore, repeated earnest appeals, the duke's request for help was, under various pretexts, refused. West, who made use of the opportunity to get the duke to present him with a good Frisian horse, brought to Calais the draft of a treaty, already executed by Henry, containing a covenant for mutual alliance and defence, couched in general terms, but, according to Henry's wish, formulating with special severity the article on rebels. The king having added a promise to interpret these provisions less severely, George executed the treaty in this form at Dresden on the 30th of December, 1505.

This transaction was not of much importance ; George gained from his alliance with England little or nothing, while Henry got a certain amount of security as regarded Suffolk ; he had seen, moreover, that he could gain his ends in the Netherlands without foreign aid. Envoy after envoy was despatched to England with a view to an accommodation of the dispute, but their efforts were useless ; Henry put forward demands, but offered nothing in return. He was conscious of his advantage, for

Treaty with Duke George.

the removal of the market to Calais had decidedly been productive of good results ; he could reckon on the hostile feeling
in his subjects towards Philip, and while the Burgundian
government had been already obliged to modify the prohibition of imports, we hear of no damage to English trade,
nor of losses to the king in customs.[1]

As it was entirely to his advantage that the losses should
be keenly felt by his opponent, it is very astonishing to find
that the king should have most generously supported with
his money this same opponent, at the very time when he was
making efforts to damage him commercially. We are not
acquainted with the details of the agreement, we only know

*Henry and
Philip.*
that Henry granted Philip a loan to a considerable
amount, of which the greater part was handed
over to him on the 25th of April, and the rest on
the 27th of September, 1505, "for his next voiage unto
Spayne." [2]

Philip at that time stood in a double relation to Henry, as
Lord of the Netherlands and Burgundy, and as King of
Castile. The union between the Spanish kingdoms of Castile
and Aragon had been severed on the 26th of November,
1504, by the death of Isabella ; her son John had died
before her, so had her daughter Isabella, married to the king
of Portugal, and also their young son Miguel ; the Castilian
throne, therefore, fell to Joanna and her husband, Philip.
As Joanna was already showing symptoms of that condition
of mental disease into which she was afterwards irrevocably
to fall, and therefore was incapable of governing, Isabella
had appointed Ferdinand regent. To this, however, Philip
demurred. Disaffected nobles, who objected to Ferdinand's
harsh government, entered into communication with him, and
Don Juan Manuel, in particular, gave him counsel in the
matter. After issuing a manifesto against Ferdinand's
regency, Philip made preparations to start for Spain himself,
but the Gelderland war, now more burdensome to him than

---

[1] See Note 12, p. 370.
[2] In the Privy Purse expenses, Exc. Hist., pp. 132, 133, are noted on the
25th of April £108,000, and on the 27th of September £30,000, together, therefore, the extravagant and improbable sum of £138,000. Here there must be
some error, for even if we take the same sum in gold crowns (£27,600) it would
still be extraordinarily high, but might be possible.

ever, together with the commercial dispute with England, detained him in the Netherlands, and Ferdinand meanwhile contrived to damage him by gaining over Louis of France, who, till then, had been a constant friend to Philip.

This dissension between Philip and Ferdinand was very welcome to Henry; a change was setting in in his relation with Spain, which made him view with satisfaction any difficulty for Ferdinand, such as that involved in Philip's journey to Spain. Henry hoped by his war of tariffs with the Netherlands to effect an essential improvement in England's position, and therefore continued to carry on the struggle; but because he thereby interfered with Philip's revenues, and could not help feeling that this in addition to the cost of the war in Gelderland might put a stop to Philip's journey to Spain, he gave back to the King of Castile for this journey, double and treble of what he took from him as Duke of Burgundy.

It can scarcely be doubted that in making these arrangements, Henry had had in his mind, in some form or other, the Earl of Suffolk, in whom the Netherlanders hoped they possessed the price for the removal of the interdiction on their trade. Philip, however, at once parted with his valuable hostage. By the beginning of August he had already given orders that Suffolk should be taken to Wageningen in Gelderland, and there given up. It was alleged later that this was done out of regard for the provisions of the treaty with England, and it is possible that this may have been the case, for Henry's second payment was still owing, which Philip was not to receive till September. Philip did not wish to hand over to Henry a prisoner of such importance to the Netherlands, and could find a pretext for surrendering him to Charles of Gelderland in the claims which Charles still had against the earl.

Charles had troubled himself very little about providing for Suffolk's support; after Hattem had been taken, the rescued prisoner besieged his new protector and his counsellors for money, and even for the most necessary articles of clothing. He tried to free himself by flight from his new captivity in Wageningen, but was caught near Tiel, and from that time kept in stricter confinement; only one servant had access to him, and the garrison of the town was strengthened. In spite of this he kept up communication with his friends, **Suffolk's** through whom he entreated Philip to release him **second** from "this man's hand." He said he was there **captivity in** by Philip's orders, and would always be ready **Gueldres.** to serve him. He foresaw with much anxiety the possibility of a new breach between Philip and Duke Charles, in which case he should regard himself as a lost man.

Mention had from time to time been made, though with little justice, of the expenses incurred by the duke on behalf of his prisoner, and now Suffolk, in order to escape from the power of the Duke of Gueldres, was obliged to pledge himself to pay, as compensation for his own and his servant's keep, a sum of two thousand florins ; after the payment of the first instalment of five hundred florins his full freedom was assured to him.   A Spanish merchant residing in Antwerp was prepared to guarantee the payment of the money.

Could the whole transaction have been anything else but a manœuvre to take in Henry?   What reasons could Philip have had for giving back to the unreliable Duke of Gueldres, whom he had already defeated, a hostage of such value as Suffolk, and how could a merchant have been so foolhardy as to risk good money on a man who was over head and ears in debt, unless this Spaniard had received good security, perhaps from the new Castilian king himself?   Suffolk's liberation, that is, his surrender to a new gaoler—to Philip, did not take place till Philip had received the last payment from Henry.   Thus it was Henry who found himself cheated ; with his advances in aid of Philip's journey to Spain, he had probably himself paid the so-called ransom for Suffolk, but without getting him into his hands in return.

For Philip now thought no more of surrendering Suffolk, and no compliance was made with Henry's often-repeated wish.   He tried, however, by other inducements to persuade the king to remove the customs dues.   Either he or his father offered him the hand of Margaret, who through the death of her second husband, Duke Philibert of Savoy, had again become a widow.   The projected marriage of the Princess Mary with Charles and another personal interview were again

proposed. Manuel's sister, Donna Elvira, a maid of honour
to the Princess of Wales—even the princess herself—were
drawn in as intermediaries; but Henry, who merely seized
with more eagerness upon the proposal for his own marriage,
held obstinately to his demands—that the Flemish customs
dues should first be taken off, and that Suffolk should be
surrendered.

Suffolk's situation had once more changed for the worse.
In the middle of November, 1505, we find him again kept
like a prisoner in the castle of Namur. Not only
his own hopes, but those of his creditors at Aix, Suffolk at
Namur.
had been grievously disappointed by the course
affairs had taken since his flight from their town. They had
applied in vain to Philip, and, since the taking of Hattem,
empty promises were the only consolation they could get
from Suffolk himself. His brother Richard, whom he had
left behind as a hostage, was assailed by impatient and angry
creditors in the open street. Suffolk, they cried, was a base
deceiver, and they intended to accuse him publicly of perjury.
Richard felt bitterly the humiliation and also the danger of
his position; he hardly dared to appear out of doors for fear
of being either given up to Henry or assassinated. At the
same time he incurred Suffolk's displeasure by the mode in
which he was conducting the negotiations they had opened
with Hungary about a new place of refuge. He was reproached with caring more for himself than for his brother,
and any hope of getting help from Suffolk was quite taken
away from him. In his distress he longed that God would
remove him out of this world, he had shown himself in many
things a good brother, and yet Suffolk was now treating him
so cruelly.

In his conduct towards Richard, Suffolk seems to have
been ungrateful and unjust, but his situation might indeed
excuse much. Hopes were being constantly held out to him,
while all the time nothing was done; for instance, he was
told that the ships collected together by Philip for his
Spanish expedition were destined for him. One friend, an
unpaid creditor of Perkin Warbeck's, spoke of enlisting in his
favour the King of Denmark and the Duke of Pomerania.
Meanwhile, hearing nothing definite about his fate, he lived

on such. promises and on the money of his friends, and had
very little freedom to move about. In December, 1505,
Killingworth, who had been sent to Philip's court, wrote to
him that nothing was left for him but to patiently bide his
time.

The unhappy adventurer excites our compassion, begging
for alms at every princely door, and having, for the sake of a
few miserable crumbs, to submit to the most contemptuous
treatment. Refused everywhere, deprived of all hope of
foreign aid; but yet retained as a possibly useful tool for
foreign policy, what remained to the banished man in his
despair? He took the only step left him, which
hitherto he had despised. He appealed to the
English king, that rival who stood in calm security,
watching his fruitless hostile efforts.

Overtures made by Suffolk to Henry.

But here too he was unlucky, and only made himself
ridiculous. For he, the fugitive, who was forced to beg for
bread and respectable clothing, sent off from Namur on the
24th of January, 1506, his followers Killingworth and Griffith
and empowered them in pompous phraseology, as Duke of
Suffolk, to treat with Henry's representatives, asking from
the king full forgiveness and the restoration of all his
dignities and lands, and the release of his brother William
and his friends, while in return he condescended to promise
that he would be a loyal subject to the king. But about this
time sinister rumours had reached Namur as to his future
fate, and he alone still remained hopeful. For Philip, by
then, was in Henry's kingdom, detained as an unwilling
guest, and it had already been decided that Suffolk was to
return there in somewhat less splendid style than he in his
high-flown language had seemed to imagine.[1]

Philip and his wife had been waiting at Middelburg, in
Zealand, for a favourable wind, and on the 7th of January,
1506, they were able to embark at Arnemuiden.
Among their numerous suite was the Venetian
ambassador, Quirini; but the Duke of Gueldres,
contrary to his promise, was absent. On the 10th of
January, at the full moon, the fleet of forty sail put to sea,
and amid thunder of cannon and strains of music sailed past

Philip in England.

[1] On Suffolk's history from August, 1505, to January, 1506, see Note 13, p. 371.

Calais. It was said that Philip had tried to come to a previous agreement with Henry in order to ensure a safe passage to Spain, should chance cast him ashore on the English coast. This foreboding was soon to be realised.

A strong wind having got up in the night following the second day of the voyage, the ships were driven rapidly towards the south, but after a calm, the wind shifted and increased to a frightful gale. In London even it caused considerable damage, the weathercock on St. Paul's steeple being blown down. The Burgundian fleet was scattered, and, on the 16th of January, Philip, who had given himself up for lost, was driven on shore at Melcombe Regis, opposite Weymouth ; eighteen ships put in at Falmouth, and the rest, with the exception of a few that foundered, got to land at various places.

Although his Spanish counsellors advised Philip to put to sea again as soon as possible, he preferred to announce his arrival to Henry and await an answer. He intended to visit the king and the Princess Katharine, and then, as soon as possible, to depart. But things were to turn out otherwise. He was detained hospitably on the coast, while Henry made ample preparations to receive him with splendour at Windsor. The Prince of Wales came to meet him at Winchester, and on the 31st of January, Henry, at the head of a brilliant retinue, welcomed him a couple of miles outside Windsor. The two monarchs vied with each other in civilities and outward expressions of friendliness ; and Henry did not shrink from the most lavish expenditure to do honour to his guest. But the guest was afterwards to make him rich amends for the expense incurred. Philip had announced his intention of soon joining his followers who were awaiting him at Falmouth ; they, however, waited on in vain for their lord.

Henry did not allow such a favourable opportunity to slip. We hear of private interviews between the kings, and also of others with their counsellors. On the 9th of February, Philip was solemnly installed as a Knight of the Order of the Garter, and on the same day, after hearing mass, he signed and swore to a new treaty of alliance, drawn up in two separate documents. The investiture of the Prince of Wales with the Order of the Golden Fleece concluded the ceremony. By this treaty the contracting parties bound themselves to mutual support against every aggressor, though this aggressor were an ally of one of themselves ; one provision in it was of special importance to Henry—that neither of them should suffer any rebels against the other to remain in his dominions, but must deliver them up at once on the other's demand.

Thus Suffolk's fate was sealed.   Joanna also arrived for a short visit the day following the signing of the treaty, and Philip then moved on to Richmond to see the new buildings there, and on the 15th of February, unasked, as a superficial observer supposed, he offered to surrender Suffolk to the English king, a confidential counsellor being despatched to the Netherlands to fetch the prisoner.

The surrender of Suffolk.

As we said, Philip had undertaken to deliver him up to Henry before his own departure.   It was not till the 2nd of March that he took leave of Henry, and travelled by slow stages eastwards to Falmouth.   Illness also detained him on the way, so that he did not arrive at the seaport till the 26th of March.   The provisional regency at Mecklin had made difficulties at first about relinquishing the hostage, hitherto so carefully guarded, before Philip should have at least left England in safety.   Fresh orders therefore had to be sent, and on the 16th of March, 1506, Suffolk was handed over to the English at Calais, brought on the 24th under strong convoy across the Channel, and conducted through London to the Tower.   Henry had promised his guest, not indeed by treaty, but in a solemn and binding form, to spare the life of the prisoner.

Although the hopes which Suffolk had indulged in of late were groundless enough, yet this turn of fortune was a sad one.   That he, though a man of high descent, not only failed to play a part as important as did the impostor Perkin Warbeck, but was scarcely better than a hunted wild beast, nowhere sure of his life, was chiefly due to the complete change that had taken place in the position of the Tudor king at home and abroad.   But the foolhardy, hot-headed young man, prompt to take offence, and as easily deluded by every empty promise, had without due reflection plunged into adventure, and now was to reap the fruit of his own folly. Henry indeed kept his promise, and it was left to his successor to bring the eager champion of Yorkist claims to the scaffold.

In spite of his unjust behaviour to his brother Richard, it speaks well of Suffolk's character as a man, that he had in the time of his misfortune faithful servants and friends, who to the last never forsook him. Even after his surrender, the faithful Killingworth made every effort to save his master, by reminding Maximilian of his former promises ; but finally he had to beg for assistance to pay his own debts contracted in Suffolk's service. He tried if he could at least secure safety for Richard, who was still at liberty, and asked Maximilian to appoint some place where he might live in security. No one dreamt any longer of great undertakings. After his brother's capture Richard had made his escape from Aix, and in the autumn of 1506 he appeared in Hungary, where he had established friendly relations the year before. Here Killingworth joined him, and from here he made his application to the King of the Romans. Although his surrender also was insisted on, Richard continued at liberty. He finally found a permanent refuge in France, and there rose to high honour after the rupture with England, which occurred in the reign of Henry VIII. His contemporaries knew him under the name of the " White Rose." He distinguished himself in the service of France both on land and sea, till, in 1525, he fell at Pavia, that battle so disastrous for Francis I.

Suffolk's intrigues formed the last noteworthy attempt made by the House of York against the Tudors ; and Henry, by the treaty he had extorted from Philip, had relieved himself of that difficulty. Instead of using Suffolk as a hostage, Philip had been forced himself to serve as a hostage for Suffolk's surrender, and everything he had hoped to gain by means of the rebel had been completely lost. Henry tried to turn Philip's involuntary presence in England to further purpose, on behalf of the commercial relations with the Netherlands. Of the negotiations themselves we know nothing ; Henry gave up the idea of a definite settlement before Philip's departure, and contented himself with his authorisation. Before Philip parted with the English king at Windsor, on the 1st of March, Philip alone, and then on the

14th of March, he and his wife together, issued powers for the marriage treaty already proposed between Henry and Margaret, the sister of Philip. This treaty, which we shall have to consider in another connection, was brought about

Philip's departure.

on the 20th of March. It must have cost Philip a still greater struggle before he brought himself, after long hesitation, to sign, on the 4th of April, 1506, a power for the preliminaries of a final settlement of the trade question.

Well might he long to get out of England, as he waited at Falmouth for four tedious weeks from the 26th of March. There his fleet had assembled, and some Spanish ships also had been sent by Ferdinand to make up for the losses sustained. Till their arrival at the seaport town all the expenses of Philip and his retinue had been generously provided for by Henry. Then, however, Philip was left to himself, and found the prolonged visit a severe strain on his purse. The Venetian, Quirini, complained bitterly of the poor and yet costly living in the provincial town. They must all have felt relieved when, on the 23rd of April, 1506, they quitted the shores of England.

Shortly after, on the 30th of April, the new commercial treaty was finally concluded in London. The contents of it

The new commercial treaty.

might already be surmised from Philip's power, which had merely dealt with the English complaints of violations of the former treaty and of the existing usages in trade. It was determined therefore, that for the Netherlanders the tolls agreed upon in 1496 should hold good, while the English should be exempt from certain local tolls in Zealand, Brabant, and Antwerp, and that any proposed increase of tolls should be announced a year beforehand. The wholesale sale of English woollens was not only again permitted throughout Burgundian territory, but, with the single exception of Flanders, sale by retail was also allowed, as well as the dressing and finishing of the cloth. All merchants trading in English woollens were to be subject to the same favourable customs dues as the English. In return, the Netherlanders only received, beyond the renewal of the treaty, protection against cheating in the sale of English wool at Calais, by means of a precise system of marking the

different sorts of wool, and a previous examination of the
goods. Philip's kingdom of Castile was expressly excluded
from these provisions.

Philip had been compelled to pay dearly for his previous
obstinacy; at the end of the struggle he found himself
beaten at all points. For Henry, too, the only complete
success lay in the surrender of Suffolk; the treaty of commerce was after all a prize of doubtful value. The king had
committed the serious error of making use of the enforced
situation of his rival to press unreasonable demands, which,
if literally carried out, would have perpetually menaced the
mercantile and industrial prosperity of the Netherlanders,
and even completely annihilated it by English competition.
Hence the concessions possible only on paper were impossible
of fulfilment; indeed, the extortion of such unreasonable
concessions might very well endanger privileges which had
hitherto been assured.

The Netherlanders were not able quietly to accept this
treaty made by their duke; but apart from any pressure of
public opinion, Philip from the first was disinclined to execute
the treaty concluded by his plenipotentiaries. The ratifications were to take place within three months—the English
one is dated the 15th of May, 1506—but on the 31st of July
Henry's ambassadors were still vainly waiting at Calais for
the conclusion of the marriage treaty, which had been due
already for weeks. Of the commercial treaty not a word had
yet been said.[1]

The general situation of affairs, however, seemed to promise
well for the fulfilment of Henry's hopes. The quarrels with
Ferdinand brought Philip to the verge of a civil war in
Castile. There were difficulties, even with the Castilian
nobles who had joined his party, and the Duke of Gueldres,
always ready to break treaties, seized on this opportunity for
a new insurrection, with the assistance of France. Louis XII.
at first denied that he had sent aid, but at last confessed it
plainly to Courteville, Philip's ambassador.[2] Henry according

---

[1] On Philip's voyage, his stay in England, and the settlements with Henry,
see Note 14, p. 372.

[2] Courteville's reports, etc.: Le Glay., Nég. dipl., i. 130-180, with two
supplements, also less complete and exact in van den Bergh, i. 1-64; cf. Lettres
du roy Louis XII., etc., i. 56-77.

to the treaty of alliance was under the obligation to protect the Burgundian provinces; he went so far as to promise assistance in troops to the stadtholder, William de Croy, Lord of Chièvres, on the strength of an article in the treaty, and began as usual to make a show of active preparations. But at first he confined himself to diplomatic overtures with Duke Charles, whom he reproached in no measured terms for his breach of treaty; and proceeded in the same manner with Louis of France and the Netherlands.

The government of the stadtholder had to behave in a conciliatory way; especially as the unstable commercial relations were causing such damage to the trade of the Netherlanders that they were almost disposed to regard the unfavourable treaty as the lesser evil. Chièvres counselled his master to pretend acquiescence in the proposed negotiations with France, and even to send to him in case of necessity the execution of the commercial treaty. He found some consolation, however, in the stipulation that any increase of the customs dues should still be announced a year beforehand.

In France, too, Henry was so far successful as to prevent the reinforcements of troops to Gelderland, and to cause proposals of intervention to be made to the duke, who tried to justify his behaviour to Henry. Not content with the proffered truce, he even demanded a secure settlement, and declared himself ready in return to submit to an Anglo-French court of arbitration. Though Louis's acquiescence in Henry's policy of mediation was not very sincere, outwardly this policy had been successful, and Henry at once made use of this by inviting Philip also to submit to the court of arbitration. He had, however, cause for displeasure, for he learnt that the treaty had been executed and sent to Chièvres on the 2nd of September, without his having himself managed to see anything of it.[1]

At this moment an unexpected event occurred: Philip, after a short illness, died at Burgos on the 25th of September, 1506. In his letter of condolence to Maximilian, Henry at once expressed his willingness to execute the still unconcluded treaty. Maximilian, however, in reply, only spoke of the assistance he hoped Henry would

The death of Philip.

---

[1] For these attempts at mediation, see Note 15, p. 374.

render to the children of his son, and took the opportunity of slipping in a request on his own part for a loan of 100,000 crowns.[1]

Margaret, who was placed at the head of the council of Regency for her nephew Charles, herself urged the resumption of commercial relations, but passed over in silence the last settlement in London, and indicated the treaty of 1496 as the desired basis for commercial intercourse.   Henry gave vent unreservedly to his annoyance at the downfall of his hopes, but behaved in a very conciliatory manner, and promised, out of special regard for Margaret, to permit the resumption of trade with the Netherlands.   He forwarded at the same time the draft of a commercial agreement, with a view to obtaining the necessary securities for Englishmen on the renewal of inter-course, and insisted that it should be signed and returned within fourteen days.

Commercial settlement with Margaret.

This preliminary settlement, which was sent from England in May, and was ratified by Margaret and her counsellors on the 5th of June, 1507, consisted of five articles ; it regulated commercial intercourse according to the earlier treaties, but conceded to the English, at least in the main, the reductions on customs granted by the treaty of 1506 ; in return the claims for English cloth were allowed to drop.   On the 17th of June the merchant adventurers received permission again to enter the provinces of the archduke with their wares.[2]

The two treaties agreed upon with Philip not having yet been confirmed, Henry took advantage of this to declare himself freed from the obligation of rendering assistance against Gelderland.   For the rest he insisted only on what was possible of attainment and by this means secured to the English ample advantages in customs, though compelled to relinquish his desires with regard to the English cloth industry. Thus the new agreement, considered only at first as pro-visional, remained for years under Henry VII., and his son the solid basis for commercial intercourse between the two countries.

[1] Chmel, pp. 267, 278-280; Berg., No. 499.
[2] Commercial agreement in Rym., xiii. 168-170, cf. Gachard, i. 460, f. : Henry to Marg. and Berghes : Lett. and Pap., i. 327-337 ; Decree for the Merch. Advent., Schanz., ii. Urk. Beil., p. 576, § 14.

We cannot help wondering that after Philip's death Henry should so suddenly change his policy, and show himself prepared to give way, for though the favourable circumstance of Philip's simultaneous difficulties in Castile and the Netherlands had ceased with his death, Henry still found himself at the time in so advantageous a position with regard to Burgundy, both commercially and politically, that his prospects of success appeared but slightly affected ; yet he gave up everything. Two treaties had not been confirmed by Philip. Henry now abandoned the commercial treaty, hoping by that means to secure the marriage treaty, which must necessarily afford him full compensation, by the close connection he would thereby form with the Netherlands, since his chosen bride, Margaret, was the Regent there during the minority of her nephew Charles. This matrimonial design, however, forms one of a long series of marriage projects for himself and his children, at which Henry worked indefatigably during the latter years of his reign, and which lends to that period its peculiar character.

CHAPTER VI.

MATRIMONIAL SCHEMES OF HENRY VII.'S LAST YEARS.

THE age in which Henry VII. lived was an age of marriages ;
scarcely any alliance took place between two Powers without
the plan of a matrimonial union between the royal Houses
being proposed, and seldom were more important marriages
concluded. Henry followed the custom of the times. The
safety of his own, and still more of his son's dynasty, rested
to a greater degree than he was willing to admit on his own
marriage with Elizabeth of York, and the unions proposed
and brought about by him with Spain and Scotland, were
to prove of the greatest importance for his country and his
dynasty. The matrimonial policy of his later years presents
a different picture. He proposed alliances now on this side,
now on that ; evolved the most extraordinary plans ; began
much, yet effected little. The first impulse was given to these
schemes by the fact that on Arthur's death, Henry, who was
still unmarried, succeeded as Prince of Wales, and that a year
later the hand of the king himself became free.

After the wedding, Arthur had retired into his princi-
pality of Wales, where a council composed of capable men
surrounded him. His tutor Bernard André, who,
courtier-like, was, however, inclined to exaggerate, **Death of Arthur.**
praises in the warmest manner his ability and
character ; unfortunately Arthur was delicate in health, and
on the 2nd of April, 1502, died unexpectedly at his castle
of Ludlow. For the king this was a heavy blow. When
his confessor brought him the sad news, he sent for his wife,
who tried to console the afflicted father with words of comfort,
only to break down so completely under her sorrow after she

had left him, that her attendants sent for the king, who in his turn tried to comfort his wife, as she had him. The prince's body was brought from Ludlow to Worcester and there buried with great pomp before the high altar of the cathedral.[1] What was now to be the fate of that alliance between the two dynasties, of which this marriage thus early dissolved had laid the foundation? Once more the political situation served Henry in good stead. As the treaty for the partition of Naples between France and Spain had not indicated with sufficient precision the limits of their mutual claims, strife broke out almost immediately after their common victory, and the confederates turned their weapons against each other.

This new war with France could not fail to make the attitude of England appear of the highest importance to the Spanish monarchs, especially since reports had early reached them of an enticing offer from the French of a marriage between Henry, the new Prince of Wales, and Margaret, afterwards the well-known queen of Navarre, sister to Francis of Angoulême, the presumptive heir to the throne.[2] The Spaniards must therefore lose no time if the old compact were to be preserved in the same form after Arthur's death. If the first union had been sought by the Tudor king, to gain the friendship of Spain, now it was the Spaniards, who in their desire for the friendship of England, came forward with the new scheme of marriage.

No sooner had the messenger bringing the sad news been received, than, in the beginning of May, 1502, Ferdinand,

Prince Henry and Katharine. Duke of Estrada, was despatched on a special mission to Henry. He had a power to conclude a marriage between Katharine, now a widow, and her brother-in-law Henry. Ferdinand and Isabella were anxious to renew, word for word, the old treaty of alliance, which promised protection for all territories of which the parties were at the moment in possession, in order that they might thereby include their recent Italian acquisitions, Apulia and Calabria, which were threatened by France. They even

---

[1] P. V., 772; Leland, Coll., v 373-381; cf. City Chron., fol. 201b; Hall, p. 497; Arundel, p. 41; Wrioth., p. 5.
[2] Berg., p. 272; cf. Lett. and Pap., ii. 342, f.

thought they could induce Henry to render them assistance in arms against France by holding out to him the attractive prospect of regaining Guienne and Normandy. Their instructions to their ambassador sound particularly explicit; they set to work with the greatest eagerness, before even ascertaining whether Katharine might not have hopes of a posthumous heir, who would cut off Prince Henry from the succession. It was not till a month later that the Spanish monarchs thought of obtaining definite information on the subject from Estrada.

They were unwilling, however, that their own wishes with regard to the new settlement should be brought too prominently forward, and hence Estrada was instructed to urge that Katharine should at once be sent home, that the hundred thousand crowns of the dowry should be paid back, and her widow's jointure assigned to her. The natural desire of affectionate parents to see their child again was to be the ostensible reason for their demand; but the real object was simply to drive Henry to make the first proposal of a new scheme of betrothal, to which Estrada might then assent "without betraying that he himself had any special desire in the matter."

Again Puebla was not intrusted with this business of more than usual importance, and it was left to Estrada to decide how far he should be admitted into confidence. But it so happened that the question of the new betrothal was mooted, possibly on Puebla's suggestion, between him and Henry, independently of the action of the Spanish monarchs, and they therefore learnt through Puebla that the ground in England was favourable to their plans. There was to be no further mention of any proposals to attack France, but the new betrothal treaty was to be settled as soon as possible; they contented themselves, as before, with drawing off Henry in this way from an alliance with France. It must, therefore, have been very galling to Puebla to find himself ordered to follow in everything the directions of Estrada. In the event of a refusal, the demand was to be adhered to that Katharine should be sent back to her home, and, above all, that the dowry already paid should be returned. They endeavoured to enforce, by a judicial opinion, Henry's obligation in the matter ; and they declared the king would be a monster of iniquity, should he keep the money in defiance of all laws, human and divine.[1]

Henry's friendship, or at least his neutral attitude, became more and more necessary to them, for their arms, during the year 1502, had not been successful in Italy, and in the same year their disagreement with Philip became more marked, when he appeared in Castile for the first time with his wife, in order to receive homage as heir to the throne. The journey there and back led them through France ; the Spaniards had found themselves compelled to intrust Philip, on his return home, with powers to negotiate for peace with Louis, but to England they sent strict injunctions that no engagements entered into in their name by their son-in-law should be considered binding without their express approval.[2] They refused to recognise the treaty concluded at Lyons on the 6th of April, 1503, as it went beyond the instructions given.

Henry having from the outset shown himself prepared to come to terms on the marriage treaty, the matter was quickly *The new* arranged ; a draft was ready prepared by the 24th *marriage* of September, 1502, and on the 23rd of June, 1503, *treaty.* the ratification took place at Richmond. The dowry for the first marriage was taken on for the second, and, on the part of the Spaniards, all claims on the sum already paid were given up ; the rest was to be paid on the conclusion of the marriage, in London, for the date of which the end of Henry's fifteenth year was fixed.

The papal dispensation was necessary for this union between Prince Henry and his brother's widow, and, to *The papal* obtain it, the question arose, how far the marriage *dispensation.* of Arthur and Katharine, confirmed by the Church, had been actually consummated by the married couple, who were then almost children. After Arthur's death, the customary month had been allowed to pass before the title of Prince of Wales, with the revenues, were handed over to Henry. The result of the inquiries instituted by desire of the Spaniards as to the actual consummation of the marriage

---

[1] On the first preliminaries for the new marriage treaty, see Note 1, p. 374.
[2] Isabella to Estrada, May 4, 1503, Berg., No. 363.

is to be found in Ferdinand's communication to his ambassador at Rome, wherein he stated that notwithstanding the marriage, no such consummation had taken place, but that it was well known in England that Katharine was still a maiden, as pure and untouched, as she herself asserted at a subsequent date, as "when she left her mother's womb." It was only to protect the new union against any possible objection such as Ferdinand feared might be raised through the cunning of the English, that the treaty of the 23rd of June asked for the papal dispensation, even in the event of the earlier marriage having been consummated.

Two days after the treaty had been concluded, the ceremony of betrothal took place in the house of the Bishop of Salisbury, in Fleet Street, London. This time the business was not confined to the marriage treaty. The quarrel between Spain and England over their navigation policy will be remembered, when the import of wine and woad into England was restricted, and in both countries a prohibition was laid on the freighting of foreign ships with export goods, so long as native ships lay in the harbour. That the English in this matter should be treated by the Spaniards as the Spaniards were by the English, seems to have been regarded by Henry as a violation of the stipulation in the treaty of 1499, that both nations should be placed on an equal footing, and to have been met by him with an increase in the export tolls on woollen and other goods for Spain. He had further-more cause for complaint against the Spanish seamen, who had seized a French vessel in an English port, and who, by their piracies, were constantly molesting both Englishmen and foreigners.

In order to gain over Henry to the new marriage treaty, the Spaniards promised to remove, in favour of the English, the restriction on exports, and, accordingly, a treaty of commerce and amity on these conditions, also dated the 23rd of June, 1503, accompanied the marriage treaty. But much time was to elapse before the provisions in the treaty, either concerning trade or the marriage, were carried out.[1]

On the 24th and 30th of September, 1503, Ferdinand and Isabella confirmed the treaty of marriage; on the 3rd of

---

[1] On the various treaty conditions, see Note 2, p. 374.

March, 1504, Henry did the same. The Spaniards had taken
special pains at once to obtain the papal dispensation in the
form agreed upon, but here the two Powers encountered their
first difficulties. On the 18th of August, 1503, Pope Alexander
VI. died; on the 18th of October following, his successor,
Pius III., also died, and on the 1st of November, was
succeeded in the papal chair by Giuliano da Rovere, who
assumed the name of Julius II. Henry tried to ingratiate
himself with the new Pope; he was the first among the
princes to notify his obedience. This he coupled with a
petition for the dispensation, promises of which Ferdinand had
already secured from Julius, both before and after his election.

It is not very easy to see why Pope Julius, in spite of his
friendly assurances, should have postponed the fulfilment of
his promises. The difficulties of the case, the necessity of a
closer investigation, even doubts as to his own power to grant
the dispensation, were put forward; finally, one of the
cardinals, commissioned to make the inquiries, fell ill. In
July, 1504, the Pope assured Henry that he was prepared
to grant the dispensation. Robert Sherbourne, the dean of
St. Paul's, he said, should bring it with him when he came
home; yet Sherbourne came without the bull.

It was the English king whom Julius wished to keep in
suspense; the Spaniards attained their object more quickly.
They had been far more energetic about procuring the
dispensation in Rome, and it was said that Isabella desired
to see it before her death, which was fast approaching. The
Pope was prevailed upon to issue a brief, which should
correspond exactly to the bull that was to be granted, and
which should be sent as a consolation to Isabella, in order
that she "might depart out of this life with a quiet mind;"
it was ante-dated the 26th of December, 1503.

Shortly before Isabella's death Ferdinand sent the original
of the brief itself to England, much to the annoyance of the
Pope, who declared that he had granted it to the Spaniards
only under condition of the strictest secresy. Now he was
bound also to England, and at the same time deprived against
his will of every pretext for withholding any longer the bull
itself. He therefore promised to send it off to England by
Silvester de Giglis, Bishop of Worcester, accredited to Rome

by Henry. As nothing more is mentioned of the matter, we suppose Julius must have kept his promise, and that the bishop brought the bull in the spring or summer of 1505 to England.

The bull was also ante-dated the 26th of December, 1503. It was worded more clearly and precisely than the brief, and as the latter had done, granted the dispensation to include the case of the actual consummation of Katharine's former marriage. The bull was then considered fully sufficient to enable the marriage contract to be concluded. It was not till later, when, in the matter of the divorce of King Henry VIII., the marriage itself was objected to as illegal, that defects and oversights were discovered in the papal dispensation, on the authority of which the marriage had been contracted.[1]

Henry also had honestly bestirred himself in the matter, and yet, when the execution of the treaty on both sides had long since taken place, and after the dispensation had been granted, and probably also after Katharine's marriage ceremony had been performed by proxy in London, the king suddenly drew back.[2] On the 27th of June, 1505, the day before Prince Henry entered his fifteenth year, the prince placed on record, in the presence of Bishop Fox, that he did not recognise the marriage treaty contracted when he was still under age. Although the prince main- Prince Henry's pro- tained that he was acting of his own free will, it test against is obvious that herein the boy was only following the marriage. the command of his father, and this was also the opinion of Bishop Fox himself.[3] This postponement of the marriage marks one of the most peculiar moves in the very eccentric policy of the king's later years. Once again, indeed, in September, 1505, he declared that the wedding should be solemnized in conformity with the treaty, and that Ferdinand till then ought to keep the rest of the dowry in readiness; but neither one thing nor the other was done.

Commercial relations played a most important part in this very uncomfortable state of affairs. The Spanish sovereigns

---

[1] On the brief and bull for the marriage dispensation, see Note 3, p. 376.
[2] Cf. also Lett. and Pap., i. 247, f.; Mem., p. 241; Berg., No. 545, also Berg., ii. No. 2, and the article in question: Rym., xiii. 82.
[3] Report in Herbert, Life of Henry VIII., pp. 387-389; Berg., No. 435; Fox's later examination, April, 1527; Brewer, iv. 3, p. 2588.

had promised in the treaty that the restrictions as to freightage should be taken off in favour of the English ; but it was not till after the exchange of ratifications, and after the formal betrothal on the 16th of November, 1504, that their decree was issued, by which the English in Spain were to be treated on the same footing with their own subjects.   English merchants from Seville and Cadiz first brought home the joyful news.   Henry responded on the 12th of March, 1505, with a similar proclamation.   He left the Spanish merchants free to transport their goods at will in either Spanish or English ships.   Other nations, however, were excepted.[1]

But when Englishmen appeared at Seville in the summer of 1505 with their goods, and wanted to ship wine and oil as return cargo, they were forbidden on the spot to do so, and had to make their return voyage with empty vessels and at heavy loss.   Henry made the most severe reproaches to the Spanish ambassador, who put forward various excuses, alleging that the reason lay in the difficulties of Ferdinand's position in Castile after the death of his wife, although the proclamation had been issued in her name also at Seville.   The Castilian Cortes, on the other hand, decreed that English, Flemish, or other foreign ships might not be freighted in Andalusia, so the counter-measures exacted by Ferdinand could not help much in the matter.   As was understood afterwards in England, this was really the result of the fundamental opposition on the part of an influential party to commercial intercourse with England, which took money out of the country and brought nothing in return but the English woollens, whereby the native industries were damaged.[2]   As far as we know no more changes were introduced during Henry's life ; but if the trade with Spain was not of sufficient importance to make these inconveniences especially felt, they were enough to make the relations between the two kingdoms still more unsatisfactory.

Troubles with Spain.

[1] The two decrees : Berg., No. 405, and Rym., xiii. 114, f. ; Berg., No. 424 ; cf. Lett. and Pap., i. 242 ; Berg., No. 407, and an undated communication to the Spanish ambassador in England in the Record Office.   The special permission to the Spaniards was really unnecessary, as the English Navigation Act had expressly excepted foreigners from the restriction on freightage (Stat., ii. 535) ; in practice therefore Henry exceeded the letter of the law.

[2] Berg., No. 438, f., 442 ; Mem., p. 436 ; cf. on the whole commercial relation, Schanz., i. 274-277.

For the rest, the discussion between Ferdinand and Henry turned only on the conclusion of the marriage and the payment of the dowry, and the Princess Katharine, innocent in the matter as she was, found herself in consequence of it in the most distressing position. **Katharine's position.** Henry neither gave her back her dowry, nor let her have the use of her widow's jointure, while from Spain there arrived strict orders not to part with her gold and jewels ; only for political purposes might she occasionally raise money on them.   In the summer of 1504, Henry—at least according to his own assertion—ordered £300 to be paid to her, but in the following March she appealed to Puebla for help, as she had been obliged to contract debts in order to get food.   She was, however, always filled with the greatest mistrust for Puebla, for he did nothing for her ; in fact, she regarded him as the cause of all her misfortunes. Her household must indeed have presented a sorry appearance, for none of them received their salary, or knew how they could support or dress themselves.   Fair words, to one who also was often out of health, could be of little help, and both Henry and Ferdinand behaved very shabbily to the unfortunate young princess.

Katharine was, in short, the victim of a political quarrel. She began early to taste that cup of sorrow which she was destined to drink to the very dregs in England.   Henry's behaviour towards the princess went so far that, in the year 1503, shortly after the death of his own wife, it was rumoured that he, the elderly father-in-law, had designs on her hand.[1] This was, however, an unfounded rumour, and nowhere else do we hear that Henry really made such a mistake as that.

In any case, on the death of Elizabeth, he at once entertained the question of a second marriage, and during the last years of his life he was actively occupied in various schemes to this end, although without success.   The news of his supposed designs with regard to Katharine had awakened great apprehension in Spain, and Isabella rejected in the strongest way any possibility of their accomplishment.   She therefore seized the opportunity to propose another plan to the king, which should set these first ideas entirely aside,

[1] See Note 4, p. 378.

and bind Henry still more closely to Spain. She directed his attention to her niece, the Queen of Naples.

This title was borne by two princesses, mother and daughter, both called Joanna, who lived together in Spain.

Joanna of Naples.

The elder, Ferdinand the Catholic's sister, was the widow of Ferdinand I.; her daughter was the widow of his nephew, Ferdinand II., of Naples; it was the younger Joanna who was proposed as a bride for Henry. Henry at first made no response; but in January, and again in June, 1504, Estrada was instructed to repeat the proposal, and Puebla asserted that the king often spoke of it, and himself wished for the marriage. Henry also asked for Joanna's portrait, and for a statement of her age. He really only expressed his acquiescence in the scheme by requests which had for their object to delay the matter and to keep for himself a free hand with Ferdinand; yet they show that the king, who could scarcely be still attractive to a young woman, was very fastidious on the point of feminine charms. For all the treasures of the world he would not have this promised bride, if she were ugly.[1]

Things had changed very much. Once the Tudor king had begged the favour of being admitted as a kinsman into the Spanish royal House, now he was doubtful whether he would ally himself afresh with Ferdinand, who at this time was forced to contend with Philip for the great central Spanish kingdom of Castile. Henry openly held out hopes that he would treat with both parties, as both were seeking his alliance.

In the autumn of the same year as the war of tariffs, which began in 1504 between England and the Netherlands, the proposal of a marriage between Henry and Margaret had been made by Philip, or rather by his father Maximilian. The express reason for this proposal was to thwart the Spanish schemes with regard to the widowed Queen of Naples. Thus Henry found himself in a most favourable position between these rival competitors for Castile; and in the same way he was able to take advantage of the disputes which had arisen between Ferdinand and Louis of France.

[1] On these negotiations, see Berg., pp. 303, 324, 327, 333, f. 338; Lett. and Pap., i. 241 (the abstract in Berg. is slight), 344.

As far back as July, 1502, immediately after Arthur's death, Isabella had been in some anxiety on account of the French proposals for a marriage between Prince Henry and Margaret of Angoulême. The plan did not meet with much approval in England. It appears to have been again mooted in the autumn of 1504, and Henry fell in with the idea, but in a different way. In June, 1505, French ambassadors again appeared at his court, and in August he despatched his own plenipotentiaries; he proposed to Louis XII. a personal interview, and by the remark that if he thought of marrying again he would wish most for a marriage with Margaret of Angoulême, he hinted that he might himself come forward as a candidate in the place of his son. In France the idea of his marrying a young girl of thirteen was actually accepted, whilst in England his marriage with Margaret's mother Louisa was spoken of; a close treaty of alliance was to accompany this, and extend to their successors.[1]

Marriage negotiations with France.

Henry had, however, no serious intentions in the matter, no alteration being necessary in his relations with France; and the object to be gained by playing off this alliance against Ferdinand passed away, owing to the Spaniard's reconciliation with his former rival. Ferdinand had, in fact, begun to work for a new and closer alliance with England, and Henry, though he had no thought of enmity with France, tried to bind the Spanish king under the same one-sided obligations as had been imposed in his own case some time before in the offensive clauses of the treaty of Medina del Campo. Ferdinand refused this, and a fresh proposal from England allowed to each party almost entire freedom of action; meanwhile his own reconciliation with France made any further hostile alliance against France quite superfluous.[2]

After Isabella's death renewed hostilities between France and Spain seemed imminent on the Pyrenean border and in Naples, which by that time had been quite taken out of the hands of the French; but Louis XII., having obtained the investiture of Milan, the end

Spain and France.

---

[1] On these Anglo-French relations, see Note 5, p. 378.
[2] On these negotiations and schemes, see Berg., p. 334; Lett. and Pap., i. 241; Berg., Nos. 407, 416, 419, 421, 432-434.

he had in view when he made friendly overtures to Maximilian, gave up all idea of further conquest in Italy, and accepted willingly Ferdinand's offers of alliance. The contest for Naples was concluded by the treaty of Blois (October 12, 1505), when Ferdinand received as a marriage portion with the hand of Germaine de Foix, the niece of Louis XII., a girl of eighteen, all French claims on Naples, claims which were to revert to France should there be no children of the marriage. Any further concessions to which Ferdinand had to agree were counter-balanced by the fact that Philip could no longer reckon on the support of France.[1]

Ferdinand now tried to draw the English king as well as the French to his side; but Henry guarded himself against
Henry's any binding concession, and retained the liberty
ambassadors of joining the party which should offer him the
visit Joanna. greatest advantages. Francis Marsin, Thomas Braybrooke and John Stile went to Spain as his ambassadors. In the course of their journey to Ferdinand's court they touched, on the 22nd of June, 1505, at Valencia, in the neighbourhood of which the two queens of Naples resided. They introduced themselves as the bearers of letters and commissions from the Princess of Wales; but this pretext was only to afford them opportunity for making those investigations as to the person, character, and mode of life of the younger Joanna, with which their king had charged them. They had been given a set form of questions, which they had simply to fill in with their answers under each head, to satisfy, as far as was possible, the astonishingly indiscreet curiosity of the king. The paper with these questions and answers is the drollest amongst the political documents of the time of Henry VII. with which we are acquainted. The king desired information as to her household, costume, speech, and manner. As an ample mantle concealed the figure of the queen, he had to be satisfied with the information that she was not painted, that she had a pleasant countenance, a clear complexion, brown hair, grey-brown eyes, and a slightly hooked nose, round arms, with delicate hands, a graceful neck and

---

[1] Treaty of Blois: Du Mont, iv. 1, pp. 72-74. It is an invention of Henry's panegyrist André, Ann:, 88, f., that Henry originated and kept up this friendliness between Ferdinand and Louis.

full bosom. Henry wished to be informed of the minutest
details: whether she had a tendency to a beard, whether her
breath was sweet; and the ambassadors even accomplished
the somewhat difficult task of answering this last inquiry.
One piece of information proved less satisfactory. She was
certainly entitled to an income of thirty thousand ducats, but
her property in Naples had been confiscated, and Ferdinand
paid her only a yearly pension of some fifteen to sixteen
thousand ducats. The Englishmen's efforts to obtain a
portrait of her were not successful, and they heard, moreover,
that Joanna's mother and a faction in Naples were desirous
she should marry a far younger man, the Duke of Calabria,
son of the last king of Naples, who died in France. Some
would, indeed, have preferred this young man as a husband
for Katharine, rather than an Englishman.

In Spain, and also in Antwerp, it was rumoured that the
marriage was already decided on; it was only considered
doubtful if the young princess would accept an elderly
husband. We do not know how far Joanna was asked her
opinion. In any case, notwithstanding the favourable report
of his ambassadors, Henry thought no more of a marriage
with her. Other matters had more influence with him than
a pretty face and fine figure; the inquiries of his ambassadors
at the court of the queens were of quite secondary importance to the real object of their mission. This was to inform
himself of Ferdinand's position in Castile, the state of public
feeling about the intended journey of Philip to his kingdom,
and the attitude of the nobles and of the neighbouring
kingdom of Portugal. The fact was that Henry had a large
pecuniary interest in the matter, from the advances he had
paid to Philip, whereby he had done his utmost to increase
the difficulties of Ferdinand's position. From Ferdinand
himself these objects of the ambassadors were concealed
under pretext of negotiations like those already carried on
in London, concerning the dilatory execution of the marriage
treaty of the 23rd of June, 1503, and the treaty of alliance
which was now to be renewed.

Having continued their journey, the ambassadors arrived,
on the 14th of July, 1505, in the royal camp at Segovia, and
on the 17th had their first audience. In a later interview

they were assured by Ferdinand's confidential adviser, Almazan, that his king, in accordance with Isabella's will, was determined to keep in his own hands the government of Castile,[1] whilst, on the other hand, they heard that the king's oppressive rule was not much liked there, and that men were longing for Philip's arrival in hopes of a mitigation of the taxes, but that various factions existed, that there were fears of future troubles, and that the king of Portugal was on the side of Philip.[2]

News about Ferdinand.

This was news which made the alliance with Ferdinand, hitherto so much desired by Henry, seem less worth striving for, and prevented him from regretting his own heavy contributions towards Philip's expedition to Spain. About the same time that he sent off Marsin and his colleagues, he despatched Antony Savage to Maximilian and Philip, in order to find out how matters stood with them, especially concerning Philip's plans with regard to Castile and Suffolk, and further, whether Maximilian was in earnest in his offer of the hand of Margaret. He showed himself much less curious in his inquiries about Margaret than about Queen Joanna ; it was her dowry that principally interested him. This time also he was more fortunate, for he received two portraits of Margaret. Besides political considerations, one point weighed strongly in her favour as compared with a Neapolitan princess dependent on a Spanish pension, that she as widow of the former heir to the Spanish throne and of the Duke of Savoy, possessed a double widow's jointure. Maximilian favoured the marriage, and issued his power on the 16th of November, 1505 ; but nothing had as yet resulted from it, when Philip on his voyage was driven ashore in England. This matrimonial scheme, in fact, originated entirely with Philip and his father ; yet Henry did not fail to turn to account the favourable opportunity afforded him.

Henry VII. and Margaret.

We know that Philip drew up his power on the 1st of March, 1506, and that the conclusion of the treaty took place on the 20th of March, before he had reached the coast at Falmouth. The most important points came first ;

[1] Cf. Ferdinand's similar remarks to Henry, Nov. 26, 1504. Mem., p. 415.
[2] On this mission, see Note 6, p. 378.

the dowry of 300,000 crowns — each crown reckoned at four shillings—and Philip's obligation to pay yearly 18,850 crowns for his sister's Spanish jointure, and 12,000 crowns for her allowance as duchess-dowager of Savoy. Henry was to have free control of these sums, and Philip was to be held to punctual payment, under threat of papal excommunication. Margaret's widow's jointure in England was fixed at 20,000 crowns. The same thing happened to Henry with the treaty of marriage as with the commercial treaty: he had to wait a long time for Philip's ratification; but, at last, on the 16th of July, 1506, this was procured, together with a strict promise to pay with punctuality the stipulated sums.

One important question, however, remained — whether Margaret herself was agreeable to this disposal of her hand. Just once, in November, 1505, it had been considered desirable to put the question to the lady, who was residing on her widow's estate in Savoy, and, according to the report of the Venetian, Quirini, in December, her answer was not favourable. But to overcome a weak woman's will would not, it was hoped, be difficult, seeing that her father and brother concurred in bringing their influence to bear on her. Both, in accordance with the treaty of the 20th of March, 1506, were to engage to do all in their power to gain Margaret's written agreement before the 1st of August. The time passed by, and in October Henry awoke to the distressing conviction that Philip and Maximilian's ambassadors could get no other answer from Margaret, but that, after her sad experiences, she was afraid of another marriage.

At this moment Maximilian and Philip were unwilling to put Henry out of humour; he might therefore look for a fulfilment of the commercial treaty. The King of the Romans ascribed his daughter's refusal to the machinations of the French, but promised for his part not to relax his efforts to bring about the match. In Burgundy also they imagined themselves sure of Henry, "who is still hoping for a union with Madame of Savoy, whom he desires to have more than any one in the world." [1]

Contrary to all expectation, the suitor himself threatened again to withdraw. After Philip's death, in September, 1506,

---

[1] On the marriage treaty and further negotiations, see Note 7, p. 379.

Joanna of Castile had fallen into a melancholy condition
of mental incapacity ; yet, insane as she was, a royal crown

Joanna of
Castile.

was the prize that would accompany the bestowal of
her hand. From the first it was evident that Ferdinand would do all in his power to prevent a second
rival like Philip from supplanting him in the government of
Castile. It is therefore inexplicable that Henry should have
applied to him, and still more so that in his calculations of
political advantage Henry should so far forget all human
feeling as to seek in marriage a woman who was known to
be mad ; nay, he even compelled his daughter-in-law Katharine, Joanna's sister, to make the obnoxious proposal in his
name. This much of shame was, however, left him, that he
kept his scheme as secret as possible. A few members of his
council and Puebla were alone admitted to his confidence.
Puebla seconded him loyally. He wrote that Joanna could
find no better husband, and, when united to King Henry, she
would soon recover her sound reason ; that the English, too,
did not seem to take much account of her insanity, as she had
already shown her malady would not prevent her from bearing children ! that Henry would not be likely to interfere
with Ferdinand in the administration of Castile, especially
when Joanna was living in England ; and a fixed yearly sum
would alone have to be paid to England out of the revenues.
Henry probably hoped by this means to recoup himself for
his own expenses, the large loan he had made to Philip having
been irrevocably lost at his death. Katharine was repeatedly
made to write for Henry on the subject. He endeavoured to
work upon her and her father by declaring void the marriage
compact between her and his son, because the dowry had not
been remitted, while she complained of the humiliating
contempt to which she was subjected on that account in
England.

Ferdinand was sagacious enough to put the English king
off with a semblance of agreement ; he even did not hesitate
to commission Katharine to act as his representative in these
marriage negotiations together with Puebla, whom she hated.
He made ample promises to do his utmost in the matter,
being desirous in any case to keep it in his own hands ; he
was, moreover, convinced that the poor mad woman, who in

her infatuation refused to part from the body of her dead husband, would never be induced to contract a new marriage. And if by this procrastination the union already decided on between Henry and Margaret were broken off, Ferdinand would have achieved all he could wish for. Accordingly all his answers were guarded by conditions. He protected himself behind Joanna's wishes, who, he said, if ever she married again, should receive no other husband than the king of England, so distinguished for his virtues. Meanwhile these delays placed Henry in the most uncomfortable situation with regard to his suit for the hand of Margaret, and Ferdinand, whose paternal heart was, in such matters, not easily affected, was only too well pleased that his daughter, and not he, should bear the brunt of Henry's anger. Henry now pressed on his cause with more and more vigour. Puebla was made to write that his love was marvellously great; Katharine was compelled even to inform Joanna herself of the deep impression which she had made on the king during her short visit to the English court in February, 1506, and of the sorrow he had felt at her departure. Henry outdid himself in such evidences of want of taste as this; he was incited to press his suit more strongly by a rumour that Joanna was about to marry a French noble—the Lord of Foix.

Ferdinand expressly denied any such projects; at the same time his account of Joanna was not very satisfactory. She was still causing Philip's corpse to be carried about wherever she went, and would entertain no thoughts of another marriage. He reported her condition as indescribable. She had to be treated with the greatest caution, and could not be contradicted. And so the matter rested. Very strange it was that Henry should not from the beginning have perceived the true state of affairs, and that he should engage in a fruitless negotiation, which brought him neither profit nor glory.[1]

[1] First mention of Henry's marriage project in Ferdinand's letter in reply, March, 1507: Berg., p. 405; even Bishop Fox was not initiated into this transaction: Brewer, iv. 3, p. 2589; also see Puebla's and Katharine's letter, April 15, Berg., pp. 409-413; Ferdinand's letter, May 19, p. 415. For the rest, the same correspondence principally by Ferdinand, Katharine, and Puebla, of the May of 1507, till the summer of 1508: Berg., Nos. 522-524, 526, f., 541, 543, 545, 548, 551-553, 575, 577, 586; cf. also No. 588, Col. de Doc., xxxix. 444, f., Zurita, vi. 154b, f.

The only result of this interlude was that the relations between the two kings became more strained than ever ; Henry tried by obstinately holding back in the affair of the marriage of their children to make Ferdinand more inclined to yield. Other plans for Prince Henry were spoken of, a match with Philip and Joanna's daughter Eleonora, and again with Margaret of Angoulême, but it was not till the end of 1508 that there was any mention of Henry's consent to the French proposals.[1]

Increase of ill feeling between Henry and Ferdinand.

It would seem, however, that Henry had no serious intention of carrying out these schemes, nor of really breaking off the marriage already agreed to. In these divers projects his sole object was to put pressure on Ferdinand with regard to his own marriage with Joanna, and the payment of the hundred thousand crowns still due of Katharine's dowry. But Ferdinand was content to let him wait, while Katharine alone suffered. The poor princess was spared no vexation. Her physician on one occasion announced that she had recovered her bodily health, that her only suffering was from troubles of mind, which lay outside the province of medical skill. She and her attendants positively endured privations. No promise made at the time of her marriage was kept. She was treated worse than any other woman in England ; and she scarcely ever received money from either Ferdinand or Henry to afford her even temporary assistance.[2] To Henry, Ferdinand insisted emphatically on the fact that the marriage once concluded could not be dissolved ; as for the dowry, after having twice succeeded in obtaining a postponement of the date of payment, he at last really held out hopes of paying. At the beginning of 1508, our old friend Fuensalida, now governor of Membrilla, was sent over to England ; but as soon as Henry was offered the payment in the form agreed to by treaty, he demanded the whole sum in coin, whereas, according to the treaty, a portion of it was to be covered by the valuables in Katharine's possession. Ferdinand, who had already once gone so far as to threaten war, now showed

---

[1] On Eleonora : Theimseke's account, June 14, 1508 : Lett. and Pap., i. 345, f. ; Berg., No. 584 ; on the French marriage : Berg., pp. 437, 460, 467, f. ; Lettres de Louis, i. 126–128 ; cf. Zurita, vi. 154*b*.

[2] On Katharine's situation, see Berg., Nos. 515–517, 532, 539, 541, 543, 545, f.

himself intensely irritated with this and with the treatment
of Katharine, but notwithstanding his angry remonstrances,
he gave way on all points, and sent the necessary instructions
to the Italian bankers, Grimaldo and Vivaldo. He only
impressed caution on his envoy, saying the payment was not
to be made if Henry did not permit the completion of the
marriage, " for when one has to deal with people of little faith
and honour, caution is necessary." Finally he intimated that
the English were even capable of poisoning Katharine in
order to keep her dowry.

Ferdinand had been obliged again and again to give way,
and his words convey his annoyance. On the other hand,
Henry took a certain pleasure in paying out his old ally for
humiliations of the same sort, which he had suffered at
Spanish hands during the first years of his reign. Scarcely
had he extorted all the concessions, when he suddenly
announced that, as the payment had been delayed, the treaty
was dissolved, and that the marriage should therefore not
take place. At the same time he began to intrigue against
Ferdinand with other foreign Powers. Finally he refused
any longer to admit the Spanish ambassador to audience,
and when Fuensalida rode to the palace he was denied
admittance by the guard, who seized his mule by the bridle
and compelled him to turn back.[1]

Thus the end was bitter enmity between the two monarchs.
They did not advance one step towards reconciliation, and
Katharine in a letter to her father poured forth despairing
lamentations. She declared she could no longer endure her
position, that she only received the barest necessaries of life,
doled out to her like alms, that she had to sell her household
effects, and if Ferdinand did not soon send her assistance
something might happen, which neither he nor Henry would
be able to prevent. The unhappy princess, who had experienced trouble enough for her three and twenty years,
declared in what proved to be her last words before the
death of the hard-hearted English king, that she feared she
could not survive the trials she had had to endure.[2]

[1] For Fuensalida's mission, see Ferdinand's orders, Berg., Nos. 586, 588 ; cf.
ibid., ii. No. 1, or else André, Ann., pp. 109, 110, Zurita, vi. 159*a*; Mem.,
435, Brewer, i. No. 8 ; instructions for payment : Berg., No. 590 ; Col. de
Doc., i. 358, f., xxxix. 446.
[2] To Ferdinand, Mar. 9 and 20, 1509, Berg., No. 603, f. ; cf. Zurita, vi. 155*a*.

Henry's own matrimonial project does not afford a
sufficient explanation for his constant refusal to conclude
the marriage of Katharine and young Henry, and certainly
not for his insulting withdrawal at the last, when there could
have been no more talk of his own hopes of Joanna. The
real aim of Henry's policy with regard to Ferdinand was still
to compel him to give his consent to another marriage project, for not only had Henry, in spite of his designs on
Joanna, continued to try to move the cold heart of Margaret,
but at the same time and with better result, the marriage
already proposed between the Archduke Charles and the
Princess Mary was being negotiated. It was the hope of
marrying his daughter with the heir presumptive to the
enormous dominions belonging to the Spanish and Hapsburg
Houses, and of extorting from Ferdinand his formal agreement to the match, that determined Henry's attitude with
regard to the Catholic king.[1]

As far back as the year 1499, the Duke of Milan had
talked to the king of a marriage for Mary with his eldest
son. Then during the meeting at Calais, Mary's marriage
with the Archduke Charles had been discussed, but the plan
was frustrated by the treaties of Lyons and Trent, on the
5th of August and 13th of October, 1501, which bestowed on
Charles the hand of Louis XII.'s daughter Claude. But the
French king had never been in earnest about this, and after
his investiture with Milan and his treaty with Ferdinand he
made known without reserve the other wishes he entertained.
Claude's marriage with Francis of Angoulême was announced
formally in May, 1506, in presence of the Estates assembled
at Tours.

Upon this the hopes of the English revived. Already
during Philip's involuntary sojourn in England, compacts,
either by word of mouth or by letter, had been
made about Charles and Mary, the exact purport
of which, however, we do not know. Perhaps there
was a desire to make up to Henry for his disappointment
with regard to Margaret ; at any rate Maximilian, writing on
the 14th of September, 1506, to the English king, told him
of Louis's breach of faith, and proposed, as from himself, the

Princess Mary
and Archduke
Charles.

[1] For this, cf. Zurita, vi. 155*a*, 159*a*.

marriage of Charles with Mary; Philip's consent, he said, had been secured by him. In fact, in July, the English envoy, Dr. West, had already spoken on the matter to Philip at Valladolid.

At that time three subjects stood ready for negotiation—the still undecided question of the commercial treaty, the marriage of King Henry with Margaret, and of Charles with Mary. After Philip's death the agreement about trade was the first to be concluded, and the prospects for Henry himself were the most gloomy. Notwithstanding his efforts to win the insane Joanna, he had prosecuted with energy his suit to Margaret, with a view to securing a bride in any case, and on account of these negotiations had urged as strongly upon Ferdinand the necessity of coming to an agreement about the marriage of Charles and Mary. It was his hopes with regard to Margaret which led him to concede so much in the commercial treaty of May, 1507; in the autumn, negotiations were carried on still more vigorously, and Henry tried to make a favourable impression on the archduchess by a present of six horses and several greyhounds. Margaret does not seem to have been averse to marrying again, for she must have previously expressed **Margaret's refusal.** some desire on the subject, when her father wrote to her that in no case would Henry consent to her marriage with the Prince of Wales. The son, apparently, would not have been displeasing to her, but Maximilian sought in vain to win her for the father; he was anxious that she should at least keep Henry in good humour in order to prevent him from combining with France and Spain. He promised to stipulate in the marriage contract that she should remain mistress of the Netherlands and live there four months in the year. Puebla was told by Henry that she had written very amiably, and the letter itself was read to him by the king, but all arguments of a personal and political nature, even the suggestion that she would thereby endanger the marriage of Charles and Mary, were of no avail. Margaret excused herself on the grounds of her former ill-luck in marriage, of her fear that she would not have any children, and therefore would be displeasing to Henry; she also laid stress on the unsuitable dowry agreed upon with Philip. To this answer once given, she held firm.

Though it appears from this that Henry himself was not very successful in his efforts to obtain a bride, the other matrimonial alliance between the two royal Houses was, after tedious negotiations, brought to a successful issue in the year 1507. Henry's plenipotentiary met those of Maximilian and Margaret at Calais, and on the 21st of December concluded two treaties of marriage and alliance ; the betrothal was to take place at Easter, 1508, and within a fortnight after the completion of Charles's fourteenth year the marriage was to be solemnized by proxy in England, and in like manner at the court of Charles ; in default of the final conclusion of the marriage and the payment of the first instalment of the dowry, fixed at two hundred and fifty thousand crowns, heavy money penalties were to be incurred. The treaty of alliance of the same date contained the usual obligations for mutual defence, and for protection against rebels.

Marriage treaty for Charles and Mary.

With much satisfaction Henry announced the conclusion of this treaty to the city authorities. He laid great stress on the advantages to be gained by this new alliance, especially with regard to the free and safe commercial intercourse with all those countries over which Charles would one day rule. The occasion was celebrated in the metropolis by popular rejoicings and bonfires, and the nobles of the country began to exercise themselves in knightly games, in view, it was reported, of the tournaments which would be held in honour of the betrothal.

In July, 1505, the English ambassadors had been received in Spain in a friendly and conciliatory spirit. Ferdinand appeared willing to promote, to the best of his power, a marriage between his grandson Charles and Mary. Now, the treaty having been concluded, the king seemed somewhat put out ; he regretted that Henry had not communicated with him beforehand, as he had shown himself favourable to the compact. But his attitude became more hostile when Henry urged upon him, together with the other claims on his compliance, the express obligation to ratify this marriage. Henry was able to adopt this firm attitude towards Ferdinand because of his close alliance with Maximilian and Burgundy. As Katharine, too, somewhat later suggested, Henry, after this matrimonial treaty, would no longer consider Ferdinand necessary to him.   Ferdinand expressed himself openly. From what his ambassadors told him, this marriage, instead of increasing their friendship, would, he believed, have a contrary effect.   He wondered that so sagacious a king as Henry should ask him to approve of a treaty of which not even a copy had been sent him : for even the most ordinary men are not, as a rule, supposed to sign documents without having studied them.   He promised, indeed, to show himself favourable to it, if in return the contract between Katharine and young Henry should at last be concluded ; but, in spite of these assurances, he was really resolved not to concur in an alliance thus directed against himself.[1]

That all the princes should seek the friendship of Henry arose once more from the general political situation of the last few years, for, while the attention of **The European situation.** the great Powers was turned to Italy, Henry remained in the advantageous position of a spectator not immediately concerned in the affair.

After the renewed contest for Naples between Ferdinand and Louis XII. had been decided in Ferdinand's favour, the enmity, which till then had existed between these two monarchs, yielded to a peaceful accommodation.   Almost at the same time, the friendly understanding which had been with difficulty arrived at between Maximilian and France gave place, in consequence of the rupture of the marriage treaty, to a renewal of hostility.   In the year 1506 French assistance, hitherto always granted to the Duke of Gueldres, had been withheld ; but, in the following year, Louis made use to the full of the opportunity afforded him by this pugnacious firebrand to harass the Regent's government in the Netherlands, and give them no time to breathe.

The King of the Romans saw with displeasure that Louis had, by his campaign of 1507, re-established his ascendancy in North Italy, and that Ferdinand, after remaining some time in Naples, was able to leave it a secure possession for his crown.   But Maximilian was especially angered by the stand made by the other Powers interested in Italy against the

---

[1] On this union of Charles with Mary and accompanying negotiations, see Note 8, p. 379.

scheme he had formed of an armed expedition to Rome for the purpose of getting the imperial crown, which had not yet been bestowed on him. At the same time the idea had again arisen in his mind of regaining the old imperial ascendancy over the Pope and the papal dominions.[1] These extravagant schemes were shattered at the very outset. He once more assumed at Trent, on the 4th of February, 1508, the title of Roman emperor elect ; but the campaign he opened with Venice ended in his defeat, and he was forced, on the 6th of June, to conclude a three years' truce.

He had tried to gain the friendship of England against Spain and France, the two Powers which stood in his way ; and it was in the midst of these great political schemes that the negotiations with Henry had been carried on, and the marriage treaty of December, 1507, concluded. Henry showed himself quite ready for any move against Ferdinand. Naples, as well as the whole of the Aragonese inheritance of Maximilian's grandson Charles, had, for a while at least, been imperilled by Ferdinand's second marriage. Maximilian constituted himself Philip's heir, and contested with Ferdinand the regency in Castile, in the interest of the insane Joanna and her young son Charles. Henry himself had already expressed his readiness to help in furthering any claims Maximilian might make on the regency, when the emperor made on his part the same proposal to the English king through Andrea de Burgo, who arrived in London on the 4th of July, 1508.

It is said that negotiations were entered into for a personal meeting between Henry and Margaret and her father. The young Charles was to be sent to England. Henry was, at his own expense, to secure for him the possession of Castile, to marry Joanna, and, as stepfather, to undertake the direction of affairs there, with the authorisation of the emperor, Charles's *de facto* guardian. In return, Maximilian was to receive a share of the revenues, and, what he most desired, help from Henry against France. The king, in part at least, fell in with these ideas. He characterised Ferdinand's administration of Castile as a usurpation, which was only made possible

[1] See on the subject, Ulmann, Maximilian's designs on the papacy, pp. 9–11, also by the same, Max. l. ii. 308 ; cf. ibid., also on Maximilian's whole situation at the time.

by union with France ; and, in order to sever this union, he was prepared to marry the Prince of Wales to Margaret of Angoulême ; he actually made plans for a great European coalition to the exclusion of Aragon, which he expected would soon put an end to Ferdinand's power in Castile.[1]

This friendly answer contained, however, the unpleasant truth that Henry was averse to lending Maximilian aid against France. This was vexatious, as it was France alone that enabled the Duke of Gueldres to continue his resistance so long ; but at that time Henry entertained less than ever any idea of hostilities against Louis, from whom he was just expecting another payment due to him by treaty. In response, therefore, to the pressure put on him by Margaret's envoys, he only showed himself prepared to act as a mediator. He certainly could not plunge into war for an affair that concerned him so little ; but as he openly declared that it would never do for Louis to permit the Duke of Gueldres to be annihilated, the old anxiety again arose whether he might not definitely take the side of France, while in France also they did not feel confident of his neutrality. The French, therefore were glad to possess in Richard de la Pole a good ally in the event of any possible hostilities on the part of Henry, and a plan was made, should these occur, of sending a French body of troops to Cornwall under the command of Richard.[2]

We can hardly suppose that Henry's attitude had any influence on the schemes of the various princes concerned. Maximilian was chiefly affected by the shipwreck of his plans in North Italy ; he agreed to accommo- dation on pressure from his daughter, and em- powered her, on the 23rd of July, to conclude a truce for two months with Charles of Gueldres, pending further negotiations, and to come to an understanding also on the subject with France. But it was not till the following October that the duke, deserted by France, was forced to make a truce, which was extended till the conclusion of the negotiations going

Maximilian's vacillating conduct.

---

[1] On these negotiations : Lett. and Pap., i. 360, f. ; Lettres de Louis XII., i. 124-130 ; abstract in Berg., No. 600, especially also Zurita, vi. 163*a*, 163*b* ; cf. van den Bergh, p. 119, André, Ann., 122, f.

[2] See reports from Margaret's ambassadors, June and July, 1508 : Lett. and Pap., i. 342, 344, Berg., No. 584 ; Lett. and Pap. 350-360 ; van den Bergh, i. 115, f., 123, f., 126, f. ; Lett. and Pap., 365, f. ; van den Bergh. p. 132, f.

on between the emperor and France.   These were held at
Cambray, and were to be conducted by Margaret in the
interests of Maximilian, and by the Cardinal d'Amboise as
Louis's representative.

The prospect of an understanding with France made
Maximilian alter at once his attitude towards Henry.
Already there was much that was unaccountable in the
relations with England since the conclusion of the treaties of
marriage and amity in December, 1507.   On the 22nd of
February, 1508, Maximilian executed both treaties, and the
treaty of alliance a second time on the 26th of March, in
conjunction with Charles; the required written securities of
important persons, towns, and corporations, were also in part
obtained; but Margaret's ratification, and that of her own and
her father's pecuniary obligations, which were specially to be
fulfilled, were not forthcoming; nor did her envoys appear,
who were to hand in the ratifications before Easter, 1508, and
to perform the ceremony of betrothal.   One excellent excuse
for postponement was afforded by a severe illness which
attacked Henry in February, 1508, and from which he only
slowly recovered in the course of the summer.   Henry
well knew how he could best gain over the needy emperor,
and, on the conclusion of the treaty, promised him, in return
for satisfactory securities, a loan of a hundred thousand crowns,
for which Maximilian had petitioned when their friendly overtures were beginning in December, 1506.   In return, Henry
urged the immediate despatch of the embassy for the
betrothal.

But Maximilian had not even yet renounced the hope
that the treaty of marriage, broken off by Louis, might still
be renewed; and in July, 1508, he stated quite openly in
presence of his daughter, that his main point in the conclusion of the treaty with England, had been the prospect
of receiving a large sum of money from Henry; he intended
now to take no further steps until he had ascertained that
Henry was satisfied with the securities offered for the loan.
He was quite silent about a personal interview, and Henry
asked his ambassador, later, whether anything had been said
on the subject.   In July, 1508, the king expressed more
emphatically his old desire for a marriage with Margaret, but

Maximilian now showed himself indifferent to a scheme which he had before so zealously urged.

In the month of August, Henry sent to the Netherlands a special envoy to hasten on the matter, and this envoy was none other than his chaplain, Thomas Wolsey, whom he had already, at the beginning of the year, intrusted with a mission to Scotland, and who was afterwards to become the great adviser of his son. We learn nothing as to the details of this first journey of Wolsey's to the Netherlands; probably his mission was then to set aside the obstacles which still stood in the way of the marriage of Charles and Mary. In this he succeeded, for on the 1st of October, 1508, Margaret executed the marriage treaty, and, on the 11th, followed engagements as to the fines fixed by the treaty, should the marriage not take place.

Wolsey.

Wolsey, who appeared for the second time in the Netherlands at the beginning of October, announced the arrival of a solemn English embassy, under the leadership of the Earl of Surrey, which had been prepared by Henry in July. On the 11th of October, Maximilian sent out from Schonhoven the Lord of Berghes, with several companions, empowered to exchange ratifications in England, and to conclude the betrothal there in the usual manner; another power, signed by Maximilian and Charles, but for Berghes alone, followed on the 27th. It was not till after the reception of the Englishmen at Antwerp on the 31st, that his embassy set forth and was received at Greenwich on the 7th of December by Henry, who did not conceal his displeasure at the protracted delay. The solemnisation of the marriage took place on the 17th, in presence of the king and numerous witnesses. Berghes, as proxy for Charles, held Mary's right hand in his, declared, in the French tongue, that he took her for his wedded wife, and the princess having replied in the same manner, he kissed her, and placed a gold ring on her middle finger, as a sign that the union was accomplished.

Marriage by proxy in England.

The financial settlement, described by Maximilian as the most important point, followed this ceremony. We have no exact information on this subject. The emperor left in pawn, for fifty thousand crowns, a large precious stone, called " la

Q

riche Fleur de Lys," in a costly setting ; a considerably higher sum, however, was paid him.[1]

Thus, as far as was possible at the time, the union of Charles and Mary was completed ; the only one of all the marriage projects of Henry's last years which might, in the future, promise a successful issue ; but a fate seemed to hang over the work of the king's later life, and this project also in the end fell to the ground.

Meanwhile he had not forgotten to prosecute the scheme for his own marriage, and this was Wolsey's chief task on his *Last efforts* second mission. Henry wished to leave no stone *for the hand* unturned. The prospect of a substantial reward, *of Margaret.* should the desired end be attained, was held out to the Bishop of Gurk, to whom Wolsey was specially recommended, and who already held an English benefice. But this last attempt on Henry's part proved fruitless ; his former ally, the emperor, now made difficulties, and it was in vain, too, that Henry tried to move Margaret by a letter addressed directly to herself. From this letter we learn more in detail what his views were. He wanted, as the husband of Margaret, to take into his own hands the administration of the Netherlands, and to the Bishop of Gurk was held out the promise of the entire direction of affairs under the king. It is possible that even this last effort was not made in earnest, for we are told that Henry had already declared himself prepared to renounce Margaret, if he could succeed in obtaining the hand of the insane Joanna and the regency of Castile. Whatever further advantages Henry may have expected from these two projects, whatever he may have imagined he could in the end achieve, the one plan was just as unlikely to be realised as the other.[2]

Now it was that Henry displayed his hostile feeling towards Ferdinand more plainly than ever. At the express desire of the archduchess, he had sent an emissary to the conferences, held at Cambray, by Margaret and the Cardinal d'Amboise; and here, too, more even than in the negotiations we know of with Maximilian, he endeavoured to work against the interests

---

[1] For the negotiations in the year 1508, on the marriage treaty till the conclusion of the betrothal, see Note 9, p. 380.
[2] On Wolsey's mission, Lett. and Pap., i. 426-452 ; cf. Zurita, vi. 1636.

of the Catholic king.   Not only was the union between France
and Aragon to be severed, but the usurper Ferdinand was
to be excluded from all future alliances.[1]

But no one gave heed to such propositions, the fruit of
mere personal animosity.   England took but little share in
the treaty at Cambray of the 10th of December, 1508.   Here
the affair of Gelderland was the only question settled in
accordance with earlier proposals of Henry's, the kings of
France, England, and Scotland being appointed arbitrators ;
for the rest, the contract between Charles and Claude, the
renewal of which Maximilian had so long desired, remained
unfulfilled, and Louis's investiture with Milan was again confirmed, on payment of a sum of money.   The Pope, the
kings of England and Aragon, and the princes of the Empire
were named protectors to guarantee the execution of the treaty.

Still less was there any question of the exclusion of Ferdinand from the secret treaty of alliance formed at the same
time, and known as the League of Cambray.   This league
was based on the same iniquitous political morality as the
earlier Franco-Spanish treaty for the partition of Naples.   The
Powers whose interests were in conflict in Italy made common
cause against one victim, Venice, and to each confederate
was apportioned, by way of satisfying his claims, a share of
the common spoil.   At first the compact was only made
between the emperor and France, but the Pope and Ferdinand
soon joined it, and Henry, who was also free to enter it, alone
kept aloof.   He only lived to see the first preparations for an
attack on the Republic.[2]

The admission of Ferdinand, which ran directly counter
to all Henry's stipulations, would in any case have predisposed
him against the League.   The feeling of dislike, Final rela-
nay, of hatred against the Aragonese king was tions with
almost the main factor in his policy during the Ferdinand.
last half of the year 1508.   In vain do we seek for any really
substantial ground for this behaviour ; quite at the last, however, it seemed somewhat to change for the better.   No doubt

---

[1] On Henry's participation in Cambray : Lettres de Louis, i. 122, f. ; Lett.
and Pap., i. 447 ; Le Glay, Négoc. Dipl., i. 219-221 ; Lett. and Pap., ii.
365-367 ; Eng. memorial : Lettres de Louis, pp. 124-130 ; Berg., No. 600.
[2] The treaties of Cambray in Du Mont, iv. 1, pp. 109-116 ; Le Glay Négoc.
Dipl., i. 225-243.

the settlement of December, 1507, between Charles and Mary had been, to say the least, unpleasing to Ferdinand, but the fact once accomplished, he showed himself still more prepared to give in.   In Spain there were many complaints of contemptuous treatment by England, and also of damage done to trade ; but Ferdinand promised that he and Joanna would ratify the marriage treaty as soon as Maximilian and Margaret should have done the same.   He only insisted that Katharine's marriage should first be completed ; he declared that he had bound himself to this by oath.   Henry's attitude, too, gave hopes of a change ; by a special envoy he announced his wish for the accomplishment of the marriage contract.[1] But Henry VII. never fulfilled these better intentions ; that was reserved for his son.

Henry's relations with Spain had ended in a manner which could hardly have been expected from the way they had begun.   It was in his dealings with that country that he made his first attempts in politics, and grew to be a master, and nowhere can we trace more clearly the decline of his policy during the last period of his life.   Quite apart from the fact that this policy was from the outset obviously impracticable, his unworthy conduct towards Katharine, and his wooing of the insane Joanna, are episodes which we would willingly obliterate from the history of the first Tudor king.

RELATIONS WITH ROME, SCOTLAND, AND IRELAND.

As had been the case with the Holy League, so now with the League of Cambray, a pretended danger to the Pope was made to serve as a cloak for the political selfishness of the Powers.   It was a mere pretext, but for no one more so than for the English king.   The conflicts in Italy concerned him but little, the relations between him and the states of Italy being of slight importance.   This also was shown in Henry's relations with the Roman Curia.   The prompt recognition of his sovereignty by Innocent VIII., whose bull was expressly confirmed by Alexander VI. (October 7, 1494), had been of

---

[1] On these last negotiations, see Stile's report to Henry, April 26, 1509, Mem., pp. 431-448; abstract in Brewer, i. No. 8, and an instruction of Ferdinand's of about the same date, but not sent off : Berg., ii. No. 1.

value to him; so had the intervention of the papal Curia against the rebels who had defied that recognition. Hence his relations with the Pope were marked by a courteous friendliness, which was never seriously affected by slight differences of opinion.

All three Popes, Innocent VIII., Alexander VI., and Julius II., had sent the consecrated cap and sword to Henry, and on each occasion these had been received by him with befitting solemnity. Innocent, however, showed himself somewhat disinclined to raise Morton to the dignity of cardinal, and it was left for Alexander VI. to comply with the royal wishes. Julius II. also hesitated for awhile before he acquiesced in the request for a dispensation for the marriage of Henry and Katharine. Henry in return showed himself somewhat unyielding on the question of the alum trade, which materially concerned the financial interests of the Curia. In defiance of the papal monopoly protected by the Church's ban, a Spanish ship carried alum from Piombino in Italy in the first year of Henry's reign, and had been captured by Englishmen. The Pope's representatives declared the cargo forfeited, but the English judges decided that the goods of a merchant travelling under the king's safe conduct were under English protection, and they proved by numerous precedents that the Pope could not encroach on the king's temporal prerogative. When, at a later date, a similar case arose, Henry went so far as to promise to protect the Pope's interests, but frequent complaints of a repetition of the offence during the years 1505 and 1506, when the destruction or seizure of the goods was demanded by the Pope, show that this promise was not kept by England.

With a view to giving a special dignity to his dynasty, which he regarded as the lineal descendant of the House of Lancaster, Henry ardently desired that this House *Proposed* should, by the canonization of the royal martyr *Canonization* Henry VI., add a new saint to the Church of *of Henry VI.* England. He therefore addressed a request to all three Popes, Innocent, Alexander, and Julius, but received from them all nothing beyond evasive answers, and instructions to the Archbishop of Canterbury and others to collect the necessary information on the life and acts of the proposed saint. Henry's assertion that miracles had been wrought at the tomb of the last of the House of Lancaster was not considered sufficient, and Rome was careful not to raise to this high dignity a king well known to be weak in intellect. All that Julius would grant, was permission for the solemn removal of the bones of Henry VI. from Windsor to Westminster.

It is evident that in determining the line of demarcation between the prerogatives of Church and State, Henry acted Visitation with caution, though at the same time with the of the distinct resolve in no way to relinquish his kingly monasteries. authority. He insisted from time to time that he had no intention of interfering with the rights of the Church, and in matters connected with Church reform he left to the ecclesiastical authorities a perfectly free hand. Monastic discipline had suffered somewhat during the civil wars, and there was need of drastic reform. To this end, in Henry's first parliament, the bishops were empowered to exceed their proper authority, and to impose secular punishments for immorality on clerics under their jurisdiction. At the beginning of the year 1486, the Convocation of Canterbury passed resolutions condemning the disorderly conduct of the clergy, who spent whole days in taverns, and did not even conform to the rules of dress and tonsure. In March, Pope Innocent commissioned Morton to institute a strict visitation, and to punish offenders. The archbishop forthwith opened proceedings against the Benedictine monastery of St. Albans, where the abbot had squandered the property of the monastery, had permitted laxity in discipline to increase, and had set an adulteress over a nunnery under his authority. Morton himself made a visitation throughout many dioceses, but we have a more detailed account of a visitation undertaken by Bishop Goldwell in the diocese of Norwich. He there discovered scandals of various kinds— lax monastic discipline, intercourse with the world, and participation in its pleasures, admission of women within the precincts, and gross mismanagement of the property of the monasteries. We also know that Henry himself gave permission to Lawrence Burelly, Vicar-general of the Carmelite Order, to inspect the English religious houses.

Henry maintained his influence in ecclesiastical matters

by his appointments to bishoprics. These were generally only conferred on Englishmen, except when Henry desired to reward or bribe a foreigner. In this way, in 1497, John de Giglis obtained the bishopric of Worcester, which on his death shortly after, in 1498, was given to his brother Silvester, who had acted in Rome as Henry's representative, with Cardinal Hadrian of Castello, appointed in 1504 Bishop of Bath and Wells. The election by the chapter, which took place after the royal permission had been granted, was always in accordance with the king's recommendation; and in the case of Worcester the temporalities of the see had already been handed over by the king to John de Giglis before the *congé d'élire* had been granted. The elevation of William Warham to the see of Canterbury as second successor to Morton is noteworthy. The king emphatically commended the choice of Warham to the prior and chapter of the cathedral, and on the 24th of January, 1504, followed the bestowal of the temporalities. The installation and the administration of the oath were accompanied by much ceremonial; in a detailed description of the solemnities, even the bill of fare for the various classes of guests is not forgotten.[1]

Although Henry made concessions from time to time, he was careful to maintain his kingly prerogatives. He was lord over his clergy, and drew from their ranks his most able ministers, such as Morton, Fox, and Warham. With him the interests of the State were paramount, and this is clearly seen in his dealings with the Curia on the very important question of war against the Turk.

Ever since the crusades, war against the Infidel had continued to be regarded by Christendom as the highest ideal; it was extolled, ardently desired, and promised, but, as the political interests of the European Powers pushed themselves to the front, the enterprise itself receded further and further into the background, till at last the cry became a mere pretence wherewith each might hide the real aim of his selfish policy. The Pope declared that war with the Turks was the ultimate object of the Powers combined together in the Holy League against France; but these Powers could not more strongly have belied his words than they did by their League

---

[1] On these ecclesiastical matters and the relations with the Curia, see Note 10, p. 382.

of Cambray, made some years later against Venice, one of the strongest bulwarks of Christendom towards the east—Venice, which towards the end of the century had for many years carried on an exhausting war against the Turks.

The Turkish war, further, supplied the Pope with a welcome pretext for imposing a crusade tax which should *Henry and* fill the papal coffers. Henry was the prince least *the Turkish* interested in these matters; yet, when he returned *war.* home after the victory at Stoke in 1487, John de Giglis was sent as papal nuncio to him, with a request for a crusade tax. The attempt does not seem to have been very successful, and when, two years later, Malvezzi appeared with fresh papal indulgences ready for sale, the situation was little favourable for his purpose. Henry, indeed, permitted the papal bull to be promulgated, and Morton himself communicated it to his suffragan bishops, but the task of making the collection was left to the papal emissaries alone. They imagined the bishops to be favourable, but their hearts sank when, on one occasion, having opened their collecting-box after it had been passed round at court, they found that the contributions of the royal family and the assembled dukes, earls, and high officials, only amounted to eleven pounds and as many shillings. Henry, however, at least renounced his claim to any share of the moneys collected. An equally unfavourable moment was selected for a proclamation of a sale of indulgences in the year 1497, just when Henry had succeeded in suppressing the Cornish insurrection; he therefore strongly urged upon Alexander to defer his scheme, at any rate, for the present.

On one occasion it was pointed out to the Pope as a special merit of Henry's that he, unlike other monarchs, had himself made over to the Roman chair two subsidies for the crusade. Ferdinand and Isabella warned him expressly not to trust such money to Alexander VI., as he was capable of using it for other purposes.

The increasing danger threatened by the advance of the Osmanli from Hungary on Carinthia and Carniola, more especially the serious condition of Venice in the Mediterranean, and the fall of Lepanto, followed shortly afterwards by that of Modon, awakened the anxiety of the whole western world. Ferdinand and Louis XII. sent assistance, all turned also to Henry, and urgent requests for help were sent to England during the years 1500 to 1503.

The king received these appeals with some coldness; he went so far, indeed, as to empower Gigli and Cardinal Hadrian in February, 1500, to represent him at a congress in Rome. They were to take part in the deliberations, but were not authorised to make any settlement. In the same way, he had sent to the kings of Spain and France to express his sorrow at the disastrous state of affairs, but regretted that the distance at which his kingdom lay prevented him from giving any substantial help.

Pope Alexander at once tried to utilise the situation in his own fashion. The jubilee year of 1500 had attracted crowds of pilgrims to Rome; but in order that Crusade tax the blessing of absolution might be extended to and plans for those who were unable to visit the holy places, a crusade. nuncio, Gaspar Pons, was despatched to England at the end of 1501. The proceeds of the indulgences which he had to sell were to be devoted to the Turkish war. Pons had been given the highest powers of absolution, and was provided with a scale for the sale of indulgences, graduated according to the income of each person. The tax of a tenth, which was to have been imposed on the clergy, was by the Province of Canterbury redeemed by a payment of £12,000, but York agreed to the tenth. Pons reaped a golden harvest. Henry himself contributed £4000, but did not desire to hear further about the crusade. It was a noble thing, he said, that the Pope should wish to promote peace among the princes of Christendom, for this holy purpose; he himself, God be thanked, had long been at peace with all of them; he could, however, offer no help, the claims upon France, Spain, as well as Hungary and Poland, were greater.

As had been shown by his gift of money to the Pope, Henry had not altogether held back from the common cause of Christendom, and this he further proved when at the beginning of 1502 the envoys of the most hard-pressed powers, Venice and Hungary, came over to England. It was reported that he dismissed them in the roughest way, saying, whoever had not the means to carry on war with the Turks ought to make peace; but in fact he promised assistance in money to the Hungarian ambassador, and sent one Geoffrey Blyth to King Ladislaus to treat in the matter. There was considerable delay before payment, but it was finally made, though to what amount we do not know. Henry showed himself much more active, however, when his own interests were involved, and in June, 1502, he sent off £10,000 to Maximilian for his Turkish war, in order to prevent him from supporting Suffolk any longer.

The sacrifices, however, which Henry made for the great cause of Christendom were certainly not heavy, and he steadily refused to give any assistance in men and ships; the ruler of the island kingdom of the West left the defence of the East to those who felt themselves most in danger.

Some time after, when Louis XII., stirred up by Portugal, was negotiating with him about a crusade, we hear him expressing quite different sentiments. Then Henry spoke of a crusade as if it were the ardent desire of his heart, from the fulfilment of which he had been hitherto withheld, but which he now hoped to set on foot, to the praise of God, with the aid of France and Portugal, and perhaps even to take part in it himself.

We might at first suppose this to be mere talk, but many things seem to have weighed upon the king's mind towards the end of his life, concerning which he desired to make his peace with Heaven. In the year 1506 the knights of Rhodes had appointed him their patron, and in May, 1507, he invited Pope Julius to summon the princes of Christendom to a war against the Infidel. "He had always aimed at peace, and had never striven after conquests. It was repugnant to him to shed Christian blood, but he would willingly shed the blood of unbelievers." The letter was read before the college of cardinals, and a copy sent to various courts. The Pope declared he had been so much overjoyed at it that he had read it through ten times, but added that for his part he did not need such admonitions. When, however, the time for action arrived, the Pope excused himself. He did no more than show his goodwill by an invitation to Henry to join him in mediating between Maximilian and Louis XII., and trying to turn their arms against the Turks. Yet Henry did not so easily relinquish his idea; he tried to overcome the papal scruples, and spoke to others of a crusade against Africa, and of an armed expedition he proposed to make into Hungary; he also permitted the Pope to proclaim an indulgence to raise funds for building St. Peter's Church. Shortly before his death a reminder came once more from Rome. The failing king commended the idea, but said his bodily condition made it impossible for him to comply with the summons.[1]

Thus in the question of a crusade, his policy was as uncertain as it was in other directions. Instead of quietly holding to the standpoint of English interests, he indulged in far-reaching schemes and ideas, perhaps he even went so far as to believe that he would be able to carry them out. In any case this was never to be, for at that moment the Pope had joined the League of Cambray, and was making preparations for the overthrow of Venice.

When announcing his willingness to take part in a Turkish war, Henry made an assertion in which he was fully justified, namely, that he was then at peace with the other Powers. However strained his relations with Ferdinand might be, the sagacity habitually displayed by these two monarchs would have prevented any definite rupture between them. The danger that threatened the friendship with Scotland, founded upon the matrimonial alliance, was also only transitory.

Here at first matters had gone on quietly and peacefully. The modest English dowry had been paid with punctuality, and James, going beyond the assurance which he had at first only given by word of mouth, entered on the 12th of July, 1505, into a written agreement not to renew the old alliance of Scotland with France.[2] The very plain-spoken letter he wrote to Charles of Gueldres with regard to Suffolk had been quite to Henry's mind. He now continued to behave with coldness to Duke Charles, and, following the example set by England, merely responded to appeals for help by declaring himself, in June, 1506, willing to act as a friendly intercessor.

Troubles with Scotland.

---

[1] On the Turkish war and crusade taxes see Note 11, p. 386.
[2] Ayloffe, p. 316.

He had previously entered into a correspondence with Charles's antagonist Philip during Philip's residence in England.[1]

But his conduct was now soon to undergo a change. It was certainly not with the view of promoting Henry's interests that James interfered in Irish affairs. The elder O'Donnell, who had assumed the position of a ruler in Ulster, was dependent on James, and his son even called him a subject of the Scotch king. He did not, it is true, receive any armed help in his perpetual feuds, but both father and son received from James the assurance of his confidence and good-will.[2]

The fact was that French influence was making itself felt in Scotland; and here came into play those doubts which had arisen in France as to Henry's possible attitude with regard to the war in Gelderland, which, stirred up by France, had just broken out again. In January, 1507, James had already written to Henry, this time clearly in the interest of Duke Charles, threatening that if Henry took part with Charles's enemies, his own alliance with England must be dissolved, and the sword again decide between them.[3] It was a further source of annoyance to Henry that Scotchmen, among whom were men of high rank, travelled through England in disguise and without passports, and even took with them the envoys of foreign Powers. In this manner, James Hamilton, Earl of Arran, and his brother, Sir Patrick Hamilton, of Kincavill, went over to France in the year 1507. In the following January, when they were about to return in the same way, a gentleman, named Hugh Vaughan, went on the king's bidding to meet them, and conducted them up to London. Banquets, hospitably provided for them by the city authorities, and a solemn reception by the king, could not disguise from them the fact that they were prisoners.

Arran's imprisonment.

Henry, in a letter of the 23rd of January, 1508, written with his own hand, made complaints to James, and in March sent off Thomas Wolsey to Scotland to adjust the matter. James spoke of the perpetual warfare on the Border between their respective subjects, and Wolsey was forced to confess to Henry

---

[1] Lett. and Pap., ii. 211-213, 207-210; Epist. Reg. Scot., i. 6-9, 30-34.
[2] Lett. and Pap., ii. 237-242.
[3] Jan. 8, 1507, ibid., 225-229; Epist. Reg. Scot., i. 40-44.

that, according to the information he had gathered, the offences of Englishmen were to those of Scotchmen as four to one. James was especially indignant about the treatment of Arran. He allowed that this nobleman had acted in contravention of treaties, but asserted that it had been against his will, and that Henry had therefore no right to be dissatisfied unless James, on receiving his complaint, had refused to punish the earl. He firmly rejected the offer made by Henry that he would release Arran, if he would promise on oath to return again to England, and declared that if Arran acceded to such a condition, he would hang him when he came back to Scotland. He insisted that Henry had no right to punish the offender, but should, in accordance with the treaty, leave that to his ally.

James assured the ambassador in the most solemn manner of his own loyalty to the treaty, and Wolsey, too, was of opinion that he, the queen, and the Bishop of Murray did adhere to it; but that the Scottish nation, nobles as well as commoners, were demanding a renewal of the league with France. Wolsey proposed a personal meeting between the kings, and James seemed inclined to the idea, though his councillors were against it.

Conflicting reports now reached his country of the manner in which Arran was being treated in England. It is clear that Henry surrounded him with guards and cut him off from intercourse with others. A Scotch doctor, who had secretly gained access to his countryman, was turned out with rough words and "almost with violence" by Vaughan.

Of the final settlement of this affair we have no exact information. In March, 1508, James had made a request for a safe conduct for the Bishop of Murray.[1] On the 16th of June the bishop came to London, and there remained till the 20th of July, about which time the Scotch lords were set at liberty. There exists an agreement to return to England, dated August 8th, made by Sir Patrick Hamilton in the same form which Henry had demanded from Arran, and Arran, on the 13th of August, went security for his brother.[2]

---

[1] Lett. and Pap., i. 341; Bain., iv. No. 1748.

[2] The two bonds in Ayloffe, 316, f.; only they belong to the 23rd, not to the 24th year of Henry's reign. See also on Arran's affair : André, Ann., pp. 105-107, f., 120, 123-125, especially Wolsey's report in Pinkerton, Hist. of Scotland, ii. 445–

Possibly this middle course had been adopted that both parties might to a certain extent get their own way, but Henry's aim in imposing this obligation is not quite clear; at any rate, thus the affair ended.

Henry had followed Wolsey's wise counsel, and had not insisted on a condition which James regarded as incompatible with his honour, and therefore would, in no case, have granted. It was obviously best, under the circumstances, to cement the alliance by concession, for it was only thus that Henry could succeed in obtaining fresh guarantees against a Franco-Scottish compact. The attitude of Scotland shows very plainly the importance she attached at all times to a policy of peace with France. That Henry was satisfied with the manner in which Wolsey had conducted this affair is shown by the fact that the king employed him immediately afterwards on a mission to the Netherlands. It seems that James had considerable trouble in holding to the alliance with England against the current of public opinion in his court. The picture of the chivalrous king, as it stands out before us in Wolsey's report, is drawn with something of the same sympathetic feeling that we find in the earlier description of him given by the Spanish Ayala. The friendship between England and Scotland continued so long as Henry VII. lived. It was not till the political relations had completely altered, under the reign of his son, that the old enmity between the neighbour countries again broke out.

Reconciliation between James and Henry.

Of Ireland, which had earlier been the centre of disorder, there is not much to relate during these latter years of King Henry. The country remained as before in a condition of primitive barbarism, distracted by race feuds. Although Henry had left the government almost entirely in the hands of the Lord Deputy Kildare, some few measures were taken, based on the principle laid down by Poynings' Act, that if all Ireland could not be brought under control, at any rate the

Ireland.

450 (wrongly attributed by Pinkerton to Dr. West; see, on the other hand, Gairdner, in Lett. and Pap., i., Pref. p. lxi.); on the proposal of the personal meeting, cf. the letter from James to Charles of Gueldres, undated, but probably of 1508, Lett. and Pap., ii., Pref., p. lxxii., f.

districts under English rule should be made as English as possible. Thus an Irish parliament in 1498 was made to enact that English dress and arms should be worn, and that the upper classes should ride "in a saddle, after the English fashion." The dwellers within the Pale were thereby compelled to adopt English manners, and attempts were made to separate them as much as possible from uncivilized Ireland. A subsequent parliament, in the year 1508, had to give a general order forbidding commercial intercourse with the wild Irish; with England alone was traffic in horses permitted. In spite of all the efforts at a closer union with England, good care was taken to protect the English against bad Irish money.[1]

Kildare kept himself in favour with the king. In the year 1503 he remained for three months in England, and took back with him his son, who had been held there as hostage, and who soon afterwards was raised to the dignity of Lord Treasurer. The perpetual and endless internal struggles are without general interest. The Lord Deputy himself often took up arms. In 1504 he gained a victory at Knockdoe over his son-in-law, the Lord Clanricarde. He sent, through the Archbishop of Dublin, a special report of this feud to the king, and Henry allowed him to act in the matter as he willed.[2] Not only these destructive combats, but constant sufferings from failure of crops, cattle disease, and famine checked the development of the uncultivated land, so that Henry might rest satisfied when the parliament of the English Pale voted him from time to time grants of money.[3] He took a prudent middle course with regard to Ireland, and thus at least made secure for himself the modest power which he possessed there. After describing the year 1504, the Irish chronicler Ware remarks that he is now coming to more peaceful times, which will therefore have fewer great deeds and stirring events to offer, "for peace, golden peace, gives not to the historian such material for description as does war." Thus Ireland also was in the enjoyment of peace when the days of Henry VII. were drawing to a close.

[1] The various enactments in Lett. and Pap., ii. 372, 376, f., 380; cf. Ware 68, f., 93; Gilbert, Viceroys, p. 463, ff.
[2] On Kildare, see Ware, 78, f., 83, f.; Lett. and Pap., ii. 378; cf. André, Ann., p. 115.
[3] Ware, p. 93, f.; Lett. and Pap., ii. 380, cf. 376.

With all the errors of his latter years, Henry still remained true to the leading principles of his policy.   His later schemes were not, indeed, productive of good, but they were not able to spoil what had already been accomplished.   It seems as if Henry himself had desired to sum up his work when, in making the announcement of the marriage treaty of December, 1507, he wrote thus to the city : " This our realm is now environed, and in manner, closed in every side with such mighty princes our good sons, friends, confederates, and allies, that by the help of our Lord the same is and shall be perpetually established in rest and peace and wealthy condition." [1]

Peaceful close of the reign.

It has been easy to form a mistaken idea of the foreign policy of the king, unaccompanied as it was by the noise of war and martial glory.   What it did was to serve as a wall of defence round the kingdom.   Assured peace, an honoured position among the Powers, English trade pushed to the front in the general competition, quiet and security at home under the newly consolidated power of the Crown, rendering for the first time possible a prosperous administration of internal affairs,—all this would have been impossible without the prudent, clear-sighted, judicious, and far-seeing policy of Henry VII.

[1] Halliwell, i. 194-196.

CHAPTER VII

WE have been able to see how closely Henry's state policy, properly so called, had become bound up with his commercial policy. Trade with the Netherlands still formed the central point of England's mercantile interests; next in importance to it stood that with the countries bordering on the Mediterranean and the Baltic. Among the schemes projected by Henry for the advance of England's trade, some were not crowned with success. The attack upon the men of the Hanse towns in their own field had completely failed; nor, after the first attempts, had any further expeditions to the West been undertaken; yet, with the increased stability of the Throne and State, the English merchant could venture forth with more energy and boldness.

Closely connected with his commercial policy were Henry's efforts to encourage English shipping as a means of furthering trade. The Parliament of 1490 had renewed the first Navigation Act, which had for a while been in abeyance, had forbidden the importa- English shipping. tion by foreigners of Toulouse woad-dye, as well as of French wines, and had laid certain restrictions on freightage by foreign ships to English ports. Unfortunately direct information as to the success of this law is not to be obtained; but that it was successful is seen by its gradual extension, and especially by the fact that Henry ventured to entrust the export of woollens for the Netherlands, which he was particularly anxious to promote, to English merchant vessels exclusively. This export of woollens, as also a considerable portion of the general trade between England and the Netherlands,

R

still continued to be forbidden to foreigners, even after the removal of the last interdiction on trade during the years 1504 to 1507. Henry took away the sum deposited in pledge with the men of the Hansa, on the ground that they had disregarded this interdiction, and all importation of goods from the territories of the Archduke Charles was forbidden them when a new ten years' charter was granted to the Venetians for trade with England (March 24, 1507).[1] With the increasing efficiency of English merchant vessels, the hitherto indispensable assistance of foreigners had become less necessary.

As these merchant vessels could at any time be requisitioned by the king for the service of the State, to increase their number was of the greatest importance for the protection of the country. Usually the vessels were either hired or forcibly requisitioned for the king's service from the proprietors, whether foreigners or not; but Henry thought it well, instead of depending entirely on vessels thus obtained, to secure supremacy for himself over the neighbouring seas by creating the nucleus of a royal fleet. Perhaps it is vessels of this fleet which are meant when, in the items of expenditure, "the king's ships" are mentioned, amongst which the *Sovereign* is often named, together with the *Mary of Portsmouth*, and the *Swan*. The *Great Harry* acquired a certain celebrity, and was subsequently re-christened the *Regent* by Henry's son.[2] It is true that, as far as we can learn, these beginnings were small and modest; still the honour remains to Henry of having, in this matter also, taken the first step, and shown the way to his successors.

The king's example served to foster the spirit of enterprise in his subjects, as was the case with the encouragement he gave to Cabot. Towards the end of the century an Italian observer mentions fishery and navigation as the principal occupations of the English people, and the intelligent Polydore Vergil commends Henry especially for having made England rich by the support he afforded to commerce, "in order to improve this art, which is at once useful and excellent for all mortals."[3] In the first place, this policy of

[1] Rym., xiii. 161–166.
[2] Campb., ii. 444, 475; Exc. Hist., pp. 92, 122, 130–132.
[3] Relat., p. 23; P. V., 780.

the king's affected the two great English trading companies—
the Staplers and the Merchant Adventurers.

It was the merchant adventurers who almost exclusively
reaped the benefit of a commercial policy, the object of which
was to exclude the foreigner, and to open up for
the native trade new paths and fields of commerce ; The Merchant
Adventurers.
for it was the export of woollen goods, their special
commodity, which Henry endeavoured to foster, rather than
of wool, the commodity of the staplers.   The merchant
adventurers formed a loose association extending over the
whole country, and a sign of their rising prosperity is shown
in an attempt made to form in their midst a closer, but also
more stable and self-dependent association.   This attempt
originated with the London merchants.

Once already very vigorous and successful efforts had
been made by the Londoners to obtain a monopoly, by
keeping in their own hands as much as possible the whole
trade of England which passed through London.   In Henry's
third Parliament, 1487, there came up for discussion an
ordinance of the city authorities, which forbade the citizens to
frequent other markets in England outside the metropolis.
They considered themselves possessed of sufficient power
in the metropolis of commerce to exercise this pressure ; but
at once great lamentations arose over the ruin which threatened the other markets, where the inhabitants of the neighbourhood, who would now be obliged to come to London, had
hitherto bought their goods.   The Parliament reversed this
ordinance, and prohibited it from being re-enacted on penalty
of a substantial fine.

The new measure proceeded, not from the town itself, but
from the principal merchants, under the leadership of the
Mercers' Guild.   In certain places on the Con- Merchant
tinent, especially at Antwerp, the merchant ad- Adventurers
venturers, in order to defray the expenses of and Staplers.
management, levied a toll on their merchants, amounting at
first to half a noble, afterwards to a hundred shillings
Flemish.   The Londoners, who were in the ascendant at
Antwerp, carried their point, and required that every merchant trading with the Netherlands should pay an entrance
fee of £20.   This was certainly intended to be the first step

towards getting the trade with the Netherlands into the
hands of the richer merchants, who could easily pay such
a duty. The rest of the trading class would thereby be
brought into a state of dependence on a ring of London
monopolists, and the wider association hitherto existing
would be replaced by a narrow and exclusive corporation.

The effect of this was seen at once ; the other merchant
adventurers withdrew from Antwerp, but laid a complaint
before the Parliament of 1497, pointing out the injury thus
threatened to the export trade in woollens, and the rise
which would ensue in price of imported commodities. Ready
as Henry was to further English trade at the expense of
foreigners, he entirely discountenanced such selfish action
in England itself. An Act of Parliament declared trade with
the Netherlands free, and only permitted the levy of a toll of
ten marks. Any further taxation by English subjects for
the benefit of themselves or their company was forbidden on
penalty of a fine of £20, and the payment to the injured
person of ten times the amount of the impost.[1]

This enactment for preserving freedom of competition was
not directed against the merchant adventurers in general,
but against a certain section of them, those, no doubt, the
most powerful. Some consolation, however, was afforded to
the Londoners, for after having on one occasion disregarded
their complaints directed against retail dealing by foreigners
in their town, Henry was finally induced, on the 21st of May,
1498, in return for the payment of £5000 to the royal coffers,
to confirm to the Londoners their privileges, and to restrain
foreigners from trading, except through the medium of the
citizens.[2] Hence the privileges of the Hanse merchants,
when subsequently renewed, were still restricted as far as
regarded the town of London.

Though Henry had discountenanced attempts at exclusiveness within the circle of the merchant adventurers, he
was nevertheless ready to strengthen the position they already
held as a company, and to give them a stronger central

---

[1] On the action of the Londoners, 1487, see 3 Hen. VII. c. 10, Stat. ii.
518, f. ; the history of the new movement is given by the statute 12 Hen. VII.
(1497), c. 6, Stat., ii. 638, f. ; cf. Anderson, i. 550, f. ; Schanz., i. 341, f.
[2] Schanz., i. 419, Note 3 and 420, Note 1 ; ii. Urk. Beil., p. 595.

administration. On the 4th of March, 1499, he granted permission to the company to assume a coat-of-arms of their own, and on the 9th of November, 1500, he confirmed the ancient charter of Henry IV. His decree of the 28th of September, 1505, however, went still further. The removal of the market to Calais in January, 1505, during the course of the commercial quarrel with Philip, had aroused in Henry himself a desire for a stricter organisation of English merchants, which would facilitate the carrying out of such measures. An elected governor and twenty-four assistants, likewise elected out of various guilds, were to have the direction of affairs and the right of pronouncing judgment within the company, and were to be allowed to punish resistance to their decisions. By a supplementary decree of the 24th of January, 1506, they obtained the right to call all their members together to a congress in London or any other place. Their enactments were not, of course, to encroach on the royal dignity and prerogative ; with this proviso, all merchant adventurers were to submit to them, and the king promised them his support on all occasions.[1]

The head-quarters of this authority was at first Calais, but, after the conclusion of the commercial conflict, it was removed to the Netherlands ; and thus it was not in London, but at the centre of the merchant adventurers' foreign commerce that this authoritative administration, armed with such extraordinarily strong powers, was created, facilitating any transaction between the king and the company, preventing any separate action within the body itself, and yet not possessing the right to interfere beyond its own sphere.

This was just the point against which it was necessary to guard, for once already Henry had been obliged to take the ancient Company of the Staplers under his protection against the Merchant Adventurers. While the staplers held the monopoly of the rich export trade for the Continent in raw materials, wool-fels, hides, lead, and tin, as well as wool, many of them also traded individually in other articles, more especially in cloth, outside the Staple. In November, 1504,

---

[1] Schanz., ii. Urk. Beil., pp. 549–555 ; cf. p. 576, § 12–14 ; before this, p. 575, § 8, and pp. 545–547 ; ibid., i. 342 ; Schanz. forgets the English computation when he places the grant of a coat of arms in 1498 instead of 1499.

the merchant adventurers instituted a law-suit before the Star Chamber on this subject, because these same staple merchants had, in such cases, objected to submit themselves to the authority established by the merchant adventurers. The court decided that any member of one corporation, who should take up the trade of another, must become subject to the regulations of that other. The exact scope of this decision had not been well thought out. The merchant adventurers, who at that time had been transferred to Calais, the ancient head-quarters of the staplers, at once demanded from the Staple merchants trading in cloth, a duty of ten marks, and, in default of payment, confiscated the goods. Henry immediately decided (June 25, 1505) that the sentence was to be understood thus: no pressure was to be put on merchants to enter the company, and only the usual duties might be levied on the goods, which were to be forthwith restored to the owner.[1]

Henry had no intention of sacrificing the Staple, which had for long been the foster-child of the Crown ; it was on the revenues of the Staple that the extremely expensive maintenance and protection of the English continental port of Calais depended. The Italian narrator remarks that "the Castle of Rhodes itself could not be more strongly guarded from the Turks than was Calais from the French."[2] The Parliament of 1487 resolved that the whole proceeds of the duty levied on wool and skins should be handed over to the staplers. Out of this they had to provide the yearly sum of £10,022 4s. 8d., for the garrison of Calais and of the border forts ; and in the event of their not receiving from the king a safe escort for their goods to Calais, they were to keep back, out of the customs dues in excess of this sum, the cost for protection on the sea. Besides this, they had also to contribute towards the London custom-house officials and the judges. The law remained in force sixteen years, and was renewed, with slight alterations, in 1504, for the same number of years. Both times it was expressly enacted that the Staple should not be removed from Calais.

[1] Schanz., ii. Urk. Beil., pp. 547–549 ; Gross, Gild. Merch., i. 149, is therefore wrong when he speaks of the compulsion "to join both companies."

[2] Relat., 45 and 50 ; the assertion that Berwick too was kept up by the Staple is incorrect.

Notwithstanding the increase in other kinds of exports, the duty on wool amounted to 36 per cent. of the entire revenues derived by the king from the customs; the staplers paid in customs dues nearly 33⅓ per cent., and those who were not members of the Staple even as much as 70 per cent. on the value of their goods. The average duty on wool was quite sufficient in Henry VIIth's reign to cover the required amount. Hence the export of wool continued to be most necessary to the State; nor must its political importance be underrated, since the need for wool kept both the Netherlands and Venice to a certain extent economically dependent on England—a circumstance of which Henry often enough took advantage. This was the reason why Henry also protected the Staple against the younger and more aggressive company of Merchant Adventurers. Few felt the importance of a policy of peace with the Powers of the Continent more than the Staplers, whose market lay beyond the sea; it was they who had felt most severely the stoppage of trade during the wars of 1491 and 1492, the more so as they had also suffered great losses from the ruin of their debtors, during the disturbances in the Netherlands not long before, in the year 1488.[1]

The merchants of the Staple were possessed of many privileges and enjoyed in their business relations greater independence than did others. This was especially the case with the freedom allowed them in the exchange of money; for, as a rule, the business of money-changing could only be carried on under a royal licence, and in 1508, this was farmed out for one year to a Florentine, named Corsy, for a sum of £240.[2] Henry had a special dislike to the business of money-lending; for, concerning usury he adhered to the view of the Middle Ages still supported by the Church, according to which capital in money was unproductive, and interest on loans or on money-lending in

Laws against usury.

---

[1] The law of 1487: Rot. Parl., vi. 394-397, cf. Schanz., ii. 16, f.; of 1504: 19 Hen. VII. c. 27, Stat., ii. 667-669, Rot. Parl., 523-525, cf. 19 Hen. VII. c. 22, Stat., p. 665; Henry's decree, which followed in the ensuing autumn, is in the Record Office. On the amount of duty, see examples in Schanz., ii. 6, 14, 29; ibid., p. 46, also on the effect of the war years; on the damage from the war in the Netherlands, see the evidence in a later memorial in Pauli, Drei volkswirtsch. Denkschr., p. 21.

[2] Stat., ii. 515, 669; Rym., xiii. 216.

general was illegal. Hence a statute of the year 1487, forbade the receiving of interest, "that is to say, if any one for £100, which he receives in goods or in any other way has to pay £120 or to give security for the amount." A penalty of £100 was laid on every transgression, and as these occurred mostly in towns which had privileges of jurisdiction, the duty of inquiry and passing judgment against the offenders was not left to these towns, but was undertaken by the Crown, and entrusted to the chancellor or to the justice of the peace of a neighbouring county, except that to the Church was reserved "the healing of souls, according to her laws."

This measure apparently did not meet with much success, for at the opening of the Parliament of 1495, the Chancellor Morton expressly brought forward the subject of avaricious money-making and usurers ; and a new law declared, some what less bluntly than the former one, that by usury was to be understood lending money on interest, taking advantage of the necessitous condition of another, and buying back from him more cheaply within three months goods which had been sold to him, the taking of land and other things in pledge or drawing an income from them, until the sum lent had been repaid ; the penalty was to amount to half the value of the things held in pledge.[1]

To hold to such antiquated views, and to oppose for any length of time necessary economic advance was, after all, useless trouble. The intention of the legislator, however, was a good one, for he was anxious to do away with a supposed danger to steadiness and fair dealing in commercial intercourse. Measures such as these had their origin in the same solicitude which Henry also displayed about the external instruments of commerce, and which formed a not inconsiderable portion of his commercial and economic policy. In the foreground, naturally, stood the most important medium of commerce—money, both with regard to the quantity to be drawn into the country for purposes of exchange, and to its quality. It was everywhere an evil that the small supply of the precious metal was never equal to the amount required, and England suffered from this as much as other

The currency.

---

[1] On the laws on usury, see Note 1, p. 384.

countries. It was not therefore from any theory of mercantile principles, but from the urgent claims of necessity, that every means had to be adopted to preserve and increase the invaluable store of precious metals. England's own production could scarcely count for anything, and yet Henry tried, in 1492, to meet in some measure the difficulty by reviving the neglected mining industry, and gave to the merchants of the Metal Staple of Southampton a comprehensive licence for working mines, with special rights and privileges.[1]

The importation of the precious metals was above all deemed essential, and to promote this an effort had previously been made by the decree that every merchant **Money,** must bring home in return for his exported goods **weights, and** a certain quantity of bullion; but this decree **measures.** could not be enforced, and was allowed to drop. In its place Henry VII. pursued the more judicious and ultimately successful course of increasing the exportation of English goods, and by law forbidding the export of the money thus brought into the country. Though for political purposes Henry paid out considerable sums, he compensated for this by his successful financial treaties, but accomplished most by his peaceful policy, whereby he put an end to the wars hitherto waged by the kings of England on the Continent, which had drained the largest amount of money from the country.

If the English merchant could no longer be compelled, without imposing too great a restriction on commerce, to bring back with him money in return for his exported goods, the foreign merchant might at all events be prevented from taking money away with him in exchange for his goods. In this Henry followed closely the example set by his predecessors on the throne, except that he expanded their laws and made them more severe. The original statute, which included all previous regulations, was issued in 1478 in the reign of Edward IV.; it forbade the exportation of gold and silver, without an express permission from the king; an alien was compelled to expend again on other commodities the money he had acquired by the sale of his goods, and to

[1] June 24, 1492; Lett. and Pap., ii. 373.

take a receipt for it. Edward's law had expired at the end of seven years; in 1487, the last-named article in it was renewed for an indefinite period, and extended to traders from Ireland and the Channel Islands. In the year 1490, a new law prohibited the exportation of all coins and precious metal for twenty years; no native was allowed, either by purchase or money exchange, or in any other way, to give money or any precious metal to a foreigner, who was only permitted to take ten crowns in cash out of the country. In 1504 it was forbidden to take away more than six shillings and eightpence to Ireland.

These laws were strictly enforced, and attained their object. Our Italian narrator speaks with enthusiasm of the wealth in silver plate possessed by private persons in England, and particularly by the Church; he admires the great number of goldsmith's shops. Polydore Vergil also lays great stress on "the enormous quantity of gold and silver" which was brought into England by traders during Henry's reign.[1]

The quality as well as the quantity of money was a subject of constant anxiety, and Henry resorted to severe measures for the purpose of preventing the serious increase in the amount of debased coin. The greatest difficulties arose from technical imperfection in the stamping, from the influx of foreign money of inferior value, and the fraudulent depreciation of coins by clipping. Since, owing to the deficient supply of the coin of the country, foreign money could not be excluded, its circulation was permitted within certain limits. Henry's third Parliament, however, considered it necessary to enact that the forging of foreign coin as well as of that of the country, should be punished as high treason. The bad Irish small coin caused much annoyance, and its acceptance was repeatedly prohibited. Hitherto the principle was strictly adhered to that current coin did not lose in value by wear, although owing to the bad minting this wear was very great; pieces therefore had to be accepted in payment "even when they were small and light." With regard to silver coins especially, there was general confusion and

---

[1] The various laws, 17 Ed. IV. c. 1; 3 Hen. VII. c. 9; 4 Hen. VII. c. 23; 19 Hen. VII. c. 5, § 4; Stat., ii. 452–461, 517, f., 546, 651; cf. Schanz., ii. Urk. Beil., p. 526; Relat., 28, f., 42; P. V., 780.

uncertainty ; the difficulties here were great, owing to clipping, counterfeit coin, and the importation of bad Irish pieces. Parliament therefore, in the year 1504, took seriously into consideration the whole question of the coinage.

A statute declared [1] that gold coins were only to be accepted when of full weight, but the silver coins stamped in England, the groats (four pence), half groats, and penny pieces might be passed even when imperfect, provided they bore the royal stamp ; clipped pieces were to be refused. For the future new coins were to be stamped with a circle round the edge to prevent clipping. On the strength of this law, Henry proceeded with real reforms, over which his panegyrist André goes into ecstacies, without, unfortunately, in spite of all his flow of words, vouchsafing us definite information. A royal proclamation of the 27th of April, 1505, made death the penalty for clipping coin ; the value of clipped coin was to be determined by its weight, and it could be only exchanged at the Mint in Leadenhall, London. It was about this time that a false coiner of the Tower was hanged at Tyburn as a warning and example.[2]

Concerning the gold and silver used for purposes other than coinage, the law also laid down certain fixed regulations, for whenever there was scarcity in money, many articles made in the precious metals had often enough to find their way to the Mint. In order therefore to keep some hold on workers in silver, they were made to conform to the regulations issued from the Royal Mint. Henry no doubt, in framing these enactments, as also in the matter of the exchange, tried to secure some advantages for himself ; but when, in May, 1499, Ayala reported of him that he kept all the good gold pieces for himself, and paid only with bad coin, we suspect this usually favourable witness had just been somewhat annoyed by Henry's stubbornness over the commercial negotiations. Ayala had, in fact, even spoken of a diminution in the royal revenues, and a falling off in the trade of England. Had Henry been guilty of such an

---

[1] 19 Hen. VII. (1504), c. 5, Stat., ii. 650, f. ; the earlier laws and ordinances : 4 Hen. VII. c. 18 ; ibid., 541 ; Lett. and Pap., ii. 372, 376, 377 ; cf. 17, Ed. IV. c. 1, Stat., p. 452, f.

[2] André, Ann., p. 81, f. ; the Proclamation : Lett. and Pap., ii. 379 ; also Fabian's Abridgment, p. 688, f. ; City Chron., fol. 206*b*.

attempt, it would soon have been put a stop to by his own law, which required full weight for every coin in circulation. It is possible, however, that Henry's activity in accumulating treasure had had a perceptible effect on the otherwise slender store of money in the country.

More serious than the question of the coinage was the uncertainty in weights and measures, for when Henry came to the throne, their condition was chaotic. A law passed by his fourth Parliament of 1491, repeated the ordinance often issued since the Great Charter, that one standard of measure and weight should be adhered to. The confusion was attributed to the standard measures not being sufficiently known, and the Commons begged the king to have these made in metal at his own cost, and sent to the larger towns in order that the measures in use there might be altered in conformity with them. But for some reason or other the Government retained these standard measures until the Parliament of 1495 gave orders that they should be distributed by the members of the lower House throughout their own electoral districts. It happened, by some mistake, that for bushels and gallons, incorrect standard measures had been made ; but in 1497 these were called in by order of the Commons, and replaced by correct ones. Thus the difficulty had been firmly grappled with, and confusion and uncertainty removed by definite legislation. But the chief gain lay in the better means of enforcing the laws, now that a strong authority existed at the head of a better organised administration.[1]

When speaking of the media of commerce, we must not forget the roads by which commerce travelled, and these
Roads and other ways of communication. certainly at the beginning of the reign were very insufficient. Henry's attention was devoted almost entirely to the great continental trade, and for it the sea, that general road for intercourse, lay ready. England herself, moreover, possessed her great estuaries, navigable for all large vessels for some distance up into the country. The seafaring merchant was exposed, however, not only to the dangers of the sea, but also to the piracy which was carried on on all sides, often in quite a recognised way.

[1] See Note 2, p. 385.

In all complaints and grievances, injury inflicted by piracy always stood foremost. Henry did his best to ensure safety in the Channel, and compelled the merchants of the Staple to contribute to this purpose. No doubt the frequent calling out of the little royal navy had the same object in view. We hear occasionally of men being enlisted to ensure safety on the sea.[1]

In his commercial treaties, Henry made agreements for mutual obligations of protection and compensation, especially with France and Spain. Of course he had only his own subjects' safety in view, for they themselves carried on the existing practice of piracy just as much as the others; and possibly Henry often permitted, and even encouraged it in the pursuit of political or politico-commercial interests, as he did for a while against the Netherlands, the Hanse merchants, and Denmark, when at variance with them.

That the care taken to foster trade within the country was small, as compared with that bestowed on the foreign trade, is evidenced by the condition of the roads. The maintenance of high-roads and bridges devolved upon the parishes or else on the whole county. When the drying up of the arm of the sea between the mainland and the Isle of Thanet had advanced so far that in the marsh thus formed the ferry-boat had scarcely sufficient water to float it, the king allowed the neighbouring inhabitants to build a bridge, but at their own cost. The authorities of the towns had also to be looked after, to see that they kept in good condition the principal streets used for the traffic which passed through them. Winchester and Bristol received a reminder on the subject from Parliament, and four years later the latter complied with the order.[2]

Little care was taken about other roads, most of them were very unsafe, and assaults, robberies, and murders were of daily occurrence. This seems to have been the case especially in the south-west; for in January, 1506, Quirini the Venetian, cast on shore at Falmouth, preferred to wait there several months for Philip, rather than to trust himself alone on the dangerous road to London. It was often necessary,

---

[1] Receipt of Mar. 19, 1487, in the Record Office.
[2] Rot. Parl., vi. 331, 333, f., 390, f.; cf. Ricart, p. 47, f.

when the king was on his journeys, to make roads for him, and he even caused works of the kind that were urgently needed to be undertaken at his own expense, but this was generally not very serious. He also left in his last will a sum of £2000 for the construction of good roads and bridges between Windsor, Richmond, Southwark, and Canterbury; they were to be sufficiently wide for two waggons to drive abreast.[1]

The harbours and estuaries were used only for the foreign trade. When the merchants of Southampton complained of the stopping up of the harbour by bars and other arrangements for the fisheries, the right was conceded to each person to remove such hindrances (1495), and to replace them was forbidden under threat of punishment. A law also enacted that the navigation of the Severn should be kept free.[2]

The king seemed himself to put obstacles in the way of the trade of the country, when he allowed such an extra- **The woollen cloth industry.** ordinarily high customs duty to be imposed on an export commodity like wool. Financial considerations, especially the importance of protecting Calais, could certainly not have been the sole motive for this, for it is striking to note, that while 33⅓ and even 70 per cent. on the value of the goods were exacted as the duty on wool, a duty of only 7 to 9 per cent. for foreigners, of 1 to 9 per cent. for natives, and even for the Hanse merchants only 1 to 7 per cent. was levied on exported woollen cloth.[3] The Italian narrator explains shortly, and to the point, the reason of this high duty on wool. "Such a high duty was imposed in order that wool might not be exported in an undressed state, but that cloth might be manufactured in the kingdom."[4] A good part of Henry's commercial policy, and still more of his customs policy, was in the interests of English manufacturers. We have already often noticed this, and especially the way in which Henry fostered the cloth industry, and gave it his support in its competition with foreign countries.

---

[1] Will of Henry, p. 21 ; before this, see Brown, No. 867 ; Exc. Hist., pp. 94, 114, 130.
[2] 11 Hen. VII., c. 5 (1495); 19 Hen. VII. c. 18 (1504) ; Stat., ii. 572, 662. f.
[3] Numbers according to the table in Schanz., ii. 6.
[4] Relat., p. 50; the English translation of this passage is inaccurate.

The protective measures Henry adopted for this purpose were not the result of new ideas. We find them mostly to be the further development of earlier measures, which, at first mere experiments, had often been re-modelled, and were now energetically and successfully carried out. But Henry's commercial policy, devoted also to the interests of English industry, and destined to open up new fields of traffic for English woollen cloth, was altogether his own. We must remember the bitter struggle carried on on this account with the Netherlands and with the Hanse towns, especially with Dantzic.

It was Henry's custom to make a move in several quarters at the same moment. While trying to extend the area of trade, and to lighten the conditions of the market, he endeavoured also to facilitate and increase production.

Woollen cloth was always the special object of his care. By extreme taxation he checked the exportation of the raw material, wool; and furthermore kept in force a statute of Edward IV.'s of the year 1467, which restrained foreigners and naturalised aliens from exporting unwoven worsted, and also cloths which had not been previously fulled in England. This law he extended in 1487, enacting that the carding and shearing of cloth must also take place in England. As he himself subsequently declared, though he included Englishmen under this restriction, he was ready to grant exceptions. The stipulation that the cloth must be sheared formed one of the special grievances of the Hanse merchants, who alleged that the cloths were spoiled by the English shearmen, and the price unduly raised; also that cloths were sheared which were not fit to stand it.

English spinners and weavers gained an important advantage from the statute of 1489, as it reserved for them for a period of ten years, from the 1st of March, 1490, the right to purchase unshorn wool, or the right to purchase beforehand until the 15th of August wool growing for the following year, and at the same time prohibited the foreign merchant from purchasing shorn wool from the time of shearing till the following 2nd of February, so that there should only remain for him what the English merchants had discarded. This was simply an extension, with trifling alterations, of a

law of Edward IV., although the fact is nowhere stated in
the statute. To the Venetians alone was permission given,
by the decree of the 1st of May, 1506, to purchase wool at
any time after the 15th of August.

Attempts were made by special legislation to meet the
case of local cloth industries. The centre of the English
cloth industry was the county of Norfolk, and in order to
check the decay of the worsted industry in the chief town of
Norwich, an exception was made in its favour to the stringent
law of Henry VI. concerning apprentices, which had only
allowed the children of rather well-to-do parents with a
yearly rental of one pound to enter the trade. Parliament
removed this restriction in 1495, so far as Norwich was
concerned, and in 1497 for the whole county. However, a
heavy visitation befell Norwich about ten years later, when
in May and June, 1508, two conflagrations reduced almost
the entire town to ashes.

Silk weaving was a kindred industry possessing at that
time some importance, and was apparently sufficient to meet
the requirements of native consumers. As far
Silk weaving. back as 1455, in Henry VI.'s time, silk weavers
both male and female, had made bitter complaints of the
excessive competition in the trade, especially from the
Italians, and for a while the import of silk was entirely forbidden. After a long interruption of this prohibition, a statute
of Edward IV. again forbade the importation of silk goods for
four years; Richard III. extended it to ten, and Henry, in
his first Parliament, to twenty years. It was expressly stated
by the Parliament of 1504 that this enactment only concerned
certain definite fabrics already specified in the earlier statutes,
and that all other silk, manufactured or raw, should be free.
The statute was to hold good for an indefinite period. This
restriction aroused bitter feeling among the merchants of the
Hansa, especially at Cologne, which was the most affected,
but all complaints were in vain.

Meanwhile Henry was careful not to give in to the wishes
of his own subjects for heavier restrictions on the foreigner
and on foreign products. The extravagant regulations of
Edward IV. and Richard III., which checked the importation
of articles in which the English manufacture was still far

inferior to the foreign, were not adhered to by him, for in this matter he protected the consumer, and allowed native industry to be stimulated by foreign competition.[1]

Henry was guided especially by a desire to protect the consumer whenever the commercial and industrial classes displayed an inordinate greed for gain, such as in the attempt at monopoly made by the Londoners, **Trade guilds.** and by the branch of the merchant adventurers in the metropolis. In the same way he set himself against every effort for independence on the part of the guilds. The position acquired by the guilds in England was by no means the same as that they held in Germany ; a statute of Henry VI. (1437) interfered materially with their rights of self-government, and required them to submit their charters and every by-law to be issued by them in the future to the approval of the authorities of their town and county. This law had expired, and the selfishness of the guilds made its loss occasionally felt. Thus in the year 1501, in consequence, it was said, of fraudulent dealings on the part of the bakers, a great scarcity of bread arose, although there was a sufficient supply of wheat, and the price of corn did not stand specially high. What the bakers exactly did we do not know, but their action possibly recalled to men's minds the forgotten law, which was accordingly renewed in the Parliament of 1504, with a reference to many guild by-laws issued in the interval, and with this noteworthy alteration :(that the control of the guilds and other companies should no longer be entrusted to the authorities of the town, but to the Chancellor, the Treasurer,)and chief justices, or to the judges of assize when on circuit. (By this means all companies were placed under State inspection, and the by-laws they issued had to receive the sanction of the Government.) This was the first step towards depriving them of all independence, and making them mere instruments of the king.[2]

---

[1] On industrial policy, see Note 3, p. 385.

[2] Guild statutes, 15 Hen. VI. c. 6, and 19 Hen. VII. c. 7: Stat., ii. 298, f., 652, f. ; cf. City Chron., fol. 182a. The more general scope of the laws to which Ochenkowski, p. 142, makes objection is of importance, because the limits of the king's interference were by them to be extended as far as he desired. The very essential difference between the two laws has been overlooked till now, even by Cunningham, pp. 454-456

The inspection of industries by the State was not, however, first introduced on this occasion, for Government had **State control.** for a long time exercised a control over wares and the prices of wares. With regard to the cloth industry, in particular, Henry had merely to adhere to the statutes of his predecessors, especially those of Edward IV. and Richard III., which had determined the size, weight, and quality of the cloth, and had regulated the work of inspection. Henry only removed, at least for a time, the penalties attached to Richard's ordinances, which had been found to interfere too much with the industry. When the entry of apprentices was made easier into the trade of the worsted shearmen of Norwich, the same law provided that no one might become a worsted shearman who had not served a seven years' apprenticeship. The control, at first confided to the masters, was afterwards taken away from them, in 1504.[1]

The mode of manufacture was also considered by the law, as, for instance, when the simpler and much-used method of singeing off was forbidden for fustians; and as early as Henry's first Parliament, regulations were made about the work of the tanners, and the division of labour between them and the leather-dressers. Even the stuffing of beds attracted the attention of king and Parliament. On the complaint of two London parishes in the neighbourhood of St. Paul's, of the poisoning of air and water by the butchers close by, butchers in every town, with the exception of Berwick and Carlisle, were forbidden to exercise their trade within the walls.[2] The cloth-workers and tailors were accused of claiming too large profits in the retail trade ; and for the hat and cap manufacturers the law set a limit on prices, which was certainly far below their demands. On the other hand, protection was afforded to stationary handicrafts against the hawker's trade.[3]

In many of these industrial Acts of Henry VII.'s, the express aim was to discourage sloth and idleness, and this was insisted on when the licence for mining was granted on

---

[1] The laws, 12 Hen. VII. c. 4 ; 11 Hen. VII. c. 11 ; 19 Hen. VII. c. 17 : Stat., ii. 637, 577, f., 662.

[2] 1 Hen. VII. c. 5 ; 4 Hen. VII. c. 3 and 22 ; 11 Hen. VII. c. 27 ; 19 Hen. VII. c. 19 : Stat., ii. 502, f., 527, f., 545, 591, 663, f.

[3] 4 Hen. VII. c. 8 and 9 ; 19 Hen. VII. c. 6 ; ibid., p. 533, f., 651, f.

the 25th of June, 1492, and yet still more strongly in his agrarian legislation.

In the reign of Henry VII. that great agrarian revolution first made itself really felt, which in the following century was to culminate in a most serious crisis, notwith- **Beginnings of** standing all the efforts of legislators to avert it. **the agrarian** Of all the productions of English husbandry, **revolution.** wool was the most important. The favourable conditions of the English climate for grazing and the breeding of live-stock, gave it an important advantage over all other countries. We have seen already how English wool commanded the market. From the "Italian Relation" we learn that agriculture was only carried on for home consumption ; "because were they to plough and sow all the land that was capable of cultivation, they might sell a quantity of grain to the surrounding countries ; " but the deficiency was made up for by the great abundance of cattle, "especially they have an extraordinary number of sheep, which yield them a quantity of the best wool."[1]

Besides the constant need for wool on the Continent, it was also now in demand for the cloth industry at home, which was fostered in every way by the State. The rapid rise of England as an industrial and commercial State, based chiefly on the production and export of wool and cloth, necessarily affected English agriculture. In a country with an open line of coast, accessible on almost every side, with rivers navigable far inland, and few natural hindrances to intercourse in the interior, the same change affected larger districts with greater ease than was the case elsewhere.

Little wonder that all husbandry tended in that direction which promised the highest profits, especially as another circumstance contributed to the same change. In England the dues on the land were already converted into money charges, and the landlord naturally preferred to collect his rent from a few larger farmers than from many small ones. Much land was now enclosed, by throwing together small pieces of ground into larger farms, and this, coupled with the change to a style of agriculture more suited to the special circumstances of England, could only have been

[1] Relat., p. 10,

regarded as a blessing, where the land was divided into a number of small holdings, if the small copyholder had not been thereby pushed out. Unfortunately, in consequence of the attractive profits to be obtained from breeding live-stock, the land hitherto arable was at the same time converted into pasture. 'Land was thus withdrawn from both plough and ploughman, the small owner was not only thrust out of his former holding, but work and livelihood were taken away from the agricultural labourer in general, since the keeping of stock only necessitated a small amount of man's labour.

In the first years of Henry's reign, the evil consequences of this change had already made themselves felt. From the Isle of Wight came complaints that houses and villages were razed to the ground, fields hedged round and converted into pasture, and that farms which formerly were divided among several, now came into the hands of one man ; that the island, so important for the protection of England, was becoming depopulated, and inhabited only by cattle. From all parts of the kingdom came reports of the great evils produced by the demolition of dwellings and the conversion of ploughland into pasture, "whereby idleness, the cause and root of all evil, begins daily to grow." In some places, where formerly two hundred men found occupation, now there were only two or three herdsmen.

Henry's third Parliament, during the session of January and February, 1490, enacted that no one in the Isle of Wight should occupy a farm at a rental of more than ten marks, that contracts not in accordance with this should be annulled, and that throughout the king- dom the owners of houses, which in the course of the last three years had been let with twenty or more acres, should be compelled to keep up those houses.

Legislative interference.

Henry, in the interest of agriculture, made strenuous efforts to restrain the keeping of live-stock ; the heavy duties on wool were designed for the same object, as were the restrictions on the purchase of wool. His aim was to lower the price and to make its pro- duction less remunerative ; only where the English cloth industry was concerned was freedom permitted and develop- ment encouraged. But this, as well as subsequent still more

The export of cattle and corn.

stringent enactments, serve only to show how futile is the attempt to stem the tide of a great economic movement, progressing by natural laws, by combating its consequences without inquiring into its deeper causes. It was necessary that England should pass through this crisis, with its mighty social convulsions.

The amount of production was gradually becoming insufficient to meet the increasing demand for wool ; keeping stock was, besides, not only cheaper than growing corn, but also more lucrative, on account of the lowness of the normal price of corn. This low standard of prices, partly accounted for by improved methods of farming, shows that, in spite of the enclosures and the newly converted pasture land, England still produced a sufficient quantity of bread-stuffs for her own consumption. Legislation did not concern itself about these economic causes, for the new movement was not inspired by a desire to provide sustenance for the people, but was actuated, as it expressly stated, by social and political considerations. These, too, were the motive of Henry's attempt to facilitate the entry of the superfluous agricultural population of Norfolk into the wool industry.

As an export, corn was not an article of great importance ; as yet, under normal conditions, the countries of Europe had not needed any importation of grain. Export from England was legally free ; only once did a royal edict forbid it, when, in 1491, war was imminent, and, owing to a bad harvest, the price of corn rose high. Strange though the policy appears on the part of a government which aimed at the encouragement of agriculture, the export of corn seems sometimes to have been subject to restrictions, otherwise it would not have been necessary for the Pope, in 1504, when there was a dearth in the States of the Church, to beg for a special permission that corn might be exported from England, which was granted readily enough. The request was repeated in the following year. The export of horses was strictly limited, that of mares entirely forbidden, as also, we are told, the export of cattle.

The object was to retain in the country its own material for breeding stock, a matter of special importance with regard to English sheep. A statute of 1423 had interdicted their export without special license from the king; but Edward IV. abused this right to grant permission, when he allowed his sister, the Duchess Margaret of Burgundy, to export annually, without paying any duty, not only one thousand oxen, but also two thousand rams. He was subsequently accused of having allowed the breed of Spanish sheep to be improved by English sheep, so that their wool was able to compete with the English wool. Henry was hardly likely to follow Edward's example in this, and the license to Margaret was in his reign withdrawn. But one case has come under our notice, which occurred during the first years of his reign, when he allowed a certain William Tyll to export to Picardy, in English ships, a hundred oxen and six hundred sheep. At other times also sheep were, as a matter of fact, exported.[1]

True, the policy was often vacillating and contradictory, the means employed frequently in opposition to the end in view; but, in all these measures, certain leading ideas were always prominent. In all the legislation, especially in that relating to agriculture, social and political considerations were always recurring with peculiar significance; besides the maintenance of a rural middle class, there was the desire to keep the king's subjects from idleness, and to take care that "the poor common people might get work and occupation," and that not so much for the support of life, as on account of the demoralizing influence which idleness, the mother of all vices, has on men.

Mendicity, vagabondage, and crime abounded in England. In spite of all the severe penalties, there was no country in the world, according to the "Italian Relation," "in which there are so many thieves and robbers as in England, so that few can venture out in the country except in the middle of the day, and still fewer at night in the towns, especially in London. People here are taken up every day by dozens, like birds in a covey, yet, for all this, they never cease to rob and murder in the streets." The struggle against vagabondage was an attempt to close up one of the sources of crime. The laws against vagrants were of old date, but the severe punishments which were imposed by a statute of Richard III., in 1483, in re-enactment

Laws against vagabondage.

---

[1] On the agrarian policy, see Note 4, p. 385.

of an ordinance of Edward III., were done away with by
Henry in 1495.) The vagrant who had been taken up was to
be set in the stocks for three days, and fed on bread and
water, and then to be released; if he returned, he would be
punished by six days of the stocks. Every beggar incapable
of work was compelled to return to the hundred " where he
has last resided, or where he is best known or was born," and
there to remain without begging out of the said hundred ;
scholars, soldiers, and sailors were required to show a certifi-
cate from their University, their superior officers, or other
authorities. (These regulations were improved upon by the
statute of 1504, which adjudged to the vagabond who had
been taken up, only a day and a night in the stocks, and also
carried out more definitely the idea of a house for relief.) The
vagrant was made to return to his native place, or to the
place in which he had lived for three years ; the relief, however, merely consisted in the permission to beg. The over-
seers were threatened with punishment for any carelessness,
and the crown officials and the judges were given the supreme
control.[1]

This greater leniency towards vagrants, who were not
criminals, was in accordance with Henry's endeavour to
meet the evil not only by prohibition and punishment, but by
definite measures of reform. Various statutes already mentioned were framed with the object of providing opportunities
for work—such as the Navigation Act, for sailors ; the
measures for the protection of industry, for artisans ; the laws
against enclosures, for agricultural labourers. At the same
time an attempt, though in strictly dictatorial fashion, was
made to promote the interests of the workman himself, by
regulations with regard to labour, hours, and wages.

On the whole, the condition of a workman in the fifteenth
century was not an unfavourable one when we remember the
low price of the necessaries of life, especially of
corn. Wages remained almost stationary for more
than a century, at a fair "living" rate, which
was nowhere exceeded except in London.[2] Attempts to

Condition of
the workman.

---

[1] Laws on vagabonds, 7 Rich. II. c. 5; 11 Hen. VII. c. 2; 19 Hen. VII.
c. 12 : Stat., ii. 32, f., 569, 656, f. ; cf. on this legislation Stephen, Crim. Law,
iii. 266, ff. ; also Relation, pp. 34 and 36.
[2] Rogers, iv. 219, 490, f., 514-520.

restrict by law any rise in wages were not a novelty. Similar attempts had been made, about the middle of the fourteenth century, under Edward III., and had been frequently repeated, though without success. A statute of Henry VI., which only aimed at adjusting wages to the standard which prevailed outside London, exercised no visible influence. This also regulated the relations between master and servant; no servant was allowed to leave one situation without having first secured another. As a supplement to this statute, the Parliament of 1495 undertook a fresh measure. The normal rate of wages was somewhat raised; though the summer wages, fixed at 6*d.* daily for carpenters, masons, and brickmakers, tallied with the average of the preceding three years. A male domestic servant was to receive annually, in addition to money for clothes, 19*s.* 8*d.*; a female servant, 14*s.*; a child under fourteen, 12*s.* 8*d.*; 2*d.* were deducted from a labourer's daily wages for his board.

These were the highest wages generally allowed. In places where the usual wages were lower they had to remain so. Every workman who was not distinctly otherwise occupied, was compelled to work for the legal wage, and half-days were to be paid only as half, holidays not at all. Whoever left unfinished any work he had engaged to do, was with exceptional severity punished by one month's imprisonment and a fine of one pound.

The law is especially interesting in its endeavour to regulate work, and to punish those workmen who did not earn their wages, who came too late and left too early, sat too long over meals, and spent too much time in sleep. From the middle of March to the middle of November each workman had to be at work at five o'clock in the morning, half an hour was allowed for breakfast, an hour and a half for the midday meal, while work did not cease till between seven and eight o'clock in the evening; in winter it lasted from daybreak till dusk. A penalty was incurred not only by the workman **Social** who demanded higher wages, but by the master **principles.** who paid them. There was not much object in regulating the rate of wages, when, without such regulations, they had for a long time remained so extraordinarily steady, and Henry seems soon to have come to

this opinion. As early as the Parliament of 1497 the clauses
on wages in the earlier statute were repealed, although
enactments about compulsory labour and hours of labour
remained in force.

Thus the workmen, and especially the domestic servants,
were kept in strict dependence and discipline. This was the
case also with the apprentices during their seven years'
apprenticeship. Moreover, the law deprived them of most
amusements. Games, such as cards, dice, and ball, were only
allowed them at Christmas under the supervision of the
master and in his own house; offenders were to be set in
the stocks for a day. The apprentices, servants, and day-
labourers had by no means an enviable lot; they were kept
for the most part very closely to work by their employers.
One result of this severity and of the specially long period of
dependence for the apprentice, always struggling after liberty
in his work, was that he burst through this constraint as soon
an opportunity offered. The storming of the Steelyard in
1493 is an instance of this, when the apprentices opened the
attack, although we do not know how far their masters may
have secretly aided and abetted in the riot against the hated
foreigner.[1]

Existing relations were strained rather than improved by
this legislative interference, which bore the stamp of Henry's
policy with regard to workmen, and was carried out con-
sistently in all his enactments. The aim of the legislator was
to give as far as possible full opportunity for work, and then
to threaten idleness with punishment, while those incapable or
unwilling to work were to be despatched to the place where
they were known and could be watched. Diligence and
industry were to be awakened by increasing the supply of
work and compelling all to labour. This was not, however,
to show a care for the workmen in the modern sense. The
lower classes were to be kept steady and obedient in their
proper place in the State, and compelled to work for the
benefit of industry and agriculture, for which their services

[1] The various laws, 23 Hen. VI. c. 12, Stat., ii. 337-339 (cf. Schanz, i. 662;
Rogers, iv. 516); 11 Hen. VII. c. 22; ibid., 585-587 (cf. Schanz, 663, f.;
Rogers, 518, f.); 12 Hen. VII. c. 3; ibid., 637; 11 Hen. VII. c. 2; ibid., 569;
cf. 19 Hen. VII. c. 12; ibid., 657; Relation, p. 24, f. Cunningham, p. 483,
says the statute of labourers of 1495 is "evidently conceived in a spirit hostile to
the worker," an opinion as correct in a modern as incorrect in an historical sense.

should be obtainable at as cheap a rate as possible. Henry's social policy was in its nature distinctly educational. Besides aiming at the promotion of industry and public order, he was careful to consider what was then regarded as the moral welfare of the lower classes, and to these ends severe restrictions on their exterior well-being were held to be necessary.

All the care bestowed by the State upon trade, industry, and agriculture, upon the medium of exchange and the regulation of industry, as well as upon the condition of the worker, started from one point of view, and, except for occasional deviations, worked for one end. It is true that this solicitude bears often a twofold aspect; it opens new paths, and at the same time clings to traditional prejudice; as a whole, it constantly endeavoured to hold to existing usage, and to construct by enlarging upon it. Into all branches of labour this activity on the part of the State thrust itself, now promoting, now restraining. The Government created for itself in those matters where hitherto it had possessed no power—as in the case of the guilds and the legislation on usury—a possibility of immediate legal interference: and this idea may have had some influence in the organisation of the merchant adventurers into a closer corporation. Everywhere, along with this increasing activity of the Crown in all branches of economic life, their dependence upon the Crown was made the more complete.

MONARCHICAL REFORMS IN JUDICIAL PROCEDURE.

The legislation of Henry VII., with regard to the administration of justice, was one special outcome of his monarchical policy. We must here refer to what has been already said. Even throughout the period of the civil wars the laws and regulations of England had, it is true, been preserved, though the strength to enforce them had been wanting. They had been compelled to give way before the violence of a powerful nobility. War and internal disorder had, in fact, constantly favoured the supremacy of the nobles; individual lords kept in their pay bands of armed retainers, wearing their own particular badge, with whose assistance they formed a most serious obstacle to all orderly exercise of the law. In league with the sheriff, they had, by

Judicial reforms.

an arbitrary packing of the juries, by the corruption, and still more by the intimidation of the jurymen, overawed the county courts.

This disorder had now in a great measure ended in its own destruction, for in the sanguinary battles of the Wars of the Roses, the English nobility had been well-nigh exterminated. It was very important now to gain security against a renewal of this state of things. As the laws of the realm, and especially the courts entrusted with their preservation, had shown themselves powerless, some reliable substitute must be found to supply this deficiency in the law, and these shortcomings in the exercise of justice. An Act passed by Henry's second Parliament in 1487, The Star Chamber. which is generally considered to be the origin of the Court of the Star Chamber, supplied this want, and became the groundwork of all further reforms in justice.

Neither this court, nor its name, were new. For a long time the Privy Council " in the Star Chamber " had exercised an extraordinary jurisdiction, in addition to that possessed by the Chancellor. Their duty was to intervene where the common law had failed. The Commons, however, repeatedly raised objections to this judicial court, depending as it did upon the king alone. They did not deny the general necessity of an extraordinary jurisdiction, but merely demanded the co-operation of Parliament, and especially the abolition of the abuse of bringing up before the Council cases which fell under the common law. In the year 1483 a statute was passed requiring that persons who, " on account of serious disturbances, extortions, oppressions, and great crimes against the peace and the laws," were summoned by the king to answer for the same before the Council or the Chancellor, should be compelled to appear, under heavy penalties ; but this law was only in force seven years, and " no case amenable to the laws of the land " was allowed to be dealt with in this manner.

This royal jurisdiction, which had hitherto only rested on custom, and had only once been confirmed, in an indefinite way and for a limited period, by the Act of 1453, was now, by Henry's statute of 1487, placed upon a firm legal basis, and given a definite shape, within definite limits. The new statute entrusted to a special committee alone, and not to the whole Council in the Star Chamber, the hearing of judicial causes. The Chancellor, Treasurer, and Keeper of the Privy Seal, or two of them at least, were to act as judges in this new tribunal, and were to add as their colleagues a bishop and one temporal peer from the Privy Council and the Chief Justices of the Courts of King's Bench and Common Pleas, or two other judges as substitutes. They had the right to summon, examine, and punish in the same way as if the accused " had been convicted by the ordinary legal procedure." Just those abuses which had been felt in the past came within the cognizance of the court; that is, the maintenance of retainers in livery, the neglect of duty on the part of the sheriffs, as in the empanelling of the jury, the bribing of jurymen, rioting, and illegal assemblies. Speaking generally, they were the same crimes against which Henry had endeavoured to guard by the oath he had compelled his Commons and barons to take in his first Parliament.

The new statute itself did not, it is true, make use of the name of Star Chamber, yet it laid the foundations of the legal existence of the later court of justice permanently called by that name. As it addressed itself to the evils that were most severely felt, Henry could be certain that the Commons would cheerfully acquiesce in it. (The real importance of the Star Chamber statute is not, after all, of a judicial, but of a political nature, for beyond its immediate object—the subjection of the aristocracy—it became the legal foundation-stone of the structure of monarchical supremacy in the State.)

The Star Chamber Act had dealt with the untrustworthy sheriffs, and the subsequent Parliaments went still further in this energetic control of the officers of justice. For all royal suits the judges were to examine the lists of jurymen drawn up by the sheriff, and to demand any alterations that might be necessary. Sheriffs and their subordinate officers, who made use of their authority in an unlawful way, for the purpose of enriching themselves, were threatened with penalties ranging from £20 to £40. In the same way penalties were attached to carelessness in the execution of the law of vagrants by the sheriff, or in the superintendence of prisons, which was entrusted to him, and

for breach of duty in the punishment of those concerned in
riots and conspiracies.   In this last enactment the justices
of the peace were also included, against whom a stringent
statute had been passed, in case they should fail to carry out
the laws, and thereby do harm to the subjects of the king ;
" for nothing is more agreeable to the king than to know that
his subjects live at peace under his laws, and increase in
riches and well-being."   Whoever had a complaint to make
against a justice of the peace was to address himself for satisfaction to the justice himself ; and, failing him, to the judges
of assize on circuit, or to the king and Chancellor ; the offending justice of the peace was to be dismissed from his office.
The law was to be announced publicly in the usual manner.

By these severe threats of punishment—which, however,
were not new—a more strict administration of justice was
insisted upon, and the official was thereby made to feel more
strongly his dependence upon the Crown.   Improved discipline
was thus secured, and at the same time the officers of justice
were brought more strictly under the control of the royal
power.   Not only was the administration of justice to be
more dependent on the Government, especially on the court
of the Star Chamber, as the representative of the king, but
the decisions of the courts themselves seemed likely to be
brought under the same control.

The Parliament of 1495 created a permanent final Court of
Appeal, from which each man, who believed himself injured in
his rights by the packing of the jury or by their
verdict, could get justice.)   The mode varied in   Court of
                                                       Appeal.
civil and criminal cases.   Hitherto, in a civil case,
any appeal against the verdict of a petty jury had been
extremely lengthy and expensive ; for the future, in suits
involving £40 and upwards, every one was free to appeal
from the petty jury to another jury specially summoned for
the purpose, which had the right to reconsider the decision
of the petty jury.   If the special jury reversed the verdict of
the petty jury, each member of the latter was fined £20, and
could never again be sworn before a court.   The law was
renewed by the subsequent parliaments, so that it still stood
in force at the time of Henry's death.

In criminal cases the law, with regard to the jury, was

different. If, in a cause instituted in the interests, or in the name of the king, or by private individuals, a party felt himself aggrieved by the judgment pronounced, he should, within a period of six days, address himself with his complaint to the presiding judge, who had to forward the complaint to the Chancellor; the Chancellor summoned the accused before him, before the Treasurer, the Chief Justice, and the Clerk of the Rolls for examination and punishment. As a previous statute had already provided against a culpable delay in the execution of a sentence caused by the demand for a fresh trial, so here the complainant, if non-suited, was punished.

All these laws were only to hold good for a limited period ; the last was not even renewed in 1504. This statute had, in fact, been a further step onwards in the same direction as the law of the Star Chamber, which had already dealt with the bribing of jurymen ; for, as in the case of the control over sheriffs and justices of the peace, an appeal against the verdict of the jury was referred to the Court of the Star Chamber. (A vicious circle was thus formed ; in causes affecting the Crown, appeal was to be made to a court entirely dependent upon the Crown ; that is, to the Crown itself. Every question concerning any interest of the king was, so long as this law was in force, from the first referred to the Star Chamber for its final decision.) In practice this was carried still further, for quarrels, as, for instance, those between the merchant adventurers and the staplers, as also civil causes, were brought before this court. Finally, it was to the Star Chamber, including in itself also the jurisdiction of the Chancellor, that the execution of the laws against usury and the control of the guilds were committed.

The tendency of this judicial legislation was to increase the prerogative of the Crown, but this was a blessing for the Tendency of country ; after all the disorder in the kingdom, the judicial a firm power again existed which could enforce legislation. the exercise of law and justice. Here, as with Henry's legislation in general, the question how far he adopted or altered existing laws is not essential, but it is important to note that they were remodelled on a uniform principle, and executed with energy.[1]

[1] On Henry's judicial legislation, see Note 5, p. 387.

Henry strove earnestly to do away with the evil of insecurity in matters of law, and one of his most important and fair measures for this object was the first statute of that Parliament which met in October, 1495, after Perkin Warbeck's attempted landing. Not only were Henry's adherents, but far more the former adherents of the House of York, to be secured against prosecution, if they remained loyal to the new government. And it may be regarded as an assurance of his own conciliatory intentions that Henry, about this same time, caused the tomb of his fallen rival, Richard, at Leicester, to be erected, if not in a splendid, at least in a suitable style.[1]

⌈Henceforth the aristocracy, kept in check by the law of the Star Chamber, could not easily disturb the peace and order established by the king⌉ but there still remained the Church, the one power in the State which was able to interpose serious obstacles to the execution of his laws. We have already seen that Henry's relations with the Pope were satisfactory; at the same time the old English desire for independence of Rome had been kept alive, and was displayed from time to time in the judgments which the judges delivered upon the complaints made by the Pope on the subject of the trade in alum. Otherwise Henry respected the rights of the clergy; his first Parliament even strengthened the judicial power of the bishops over immoral clerks. Only on two points was any objection raised—the so-called benefit of clergy, and the right of asylum.

Benefit of clergy consisted in the privilege of being handed over by the secular judge to the bishop, except in cases of treason. As in the Middle Ages a knowledge of reading was for the most part limited to the clergy, the ability to read was accepted as a proof that a man was a cleric, and this still continued even when education was much more widely diffused. Whoever could read asserted his claim to benefit of clergy. It followed, therefore, that a serious obstacle was put in the way of the execution of justice, and an Act of 1490 drew attention to the fact that people who could

Clerical privileges.

Benefit of clergy.

---

[1] The law, 11 Hen. VII. c. 1, Stat., ii. 568; cf. Blackstone, iv. 88, f.; Stephen, New Comment., iv. 153-155; against this, Hallam, i. 9, f. £10 1s. "for King Richard's tomb," are entered on Sept. 11, 1495: Exc. Hist., p. 105, the inscription on tomb in Buck, Rich. III., p. 149.

read were encouraged to commit murder, robbery, and theft, because on every repetition of the offence they were again admitted to the benefit of clergy.   The law accordingly provided that every man who did not directly belong to the clerical order could only profit by clerical privileges once ; but if he were indicted for murder, he was to be branded with a letter M on the ball of his left thumb, for other crimes he was to be marked with a T (thief).   If, on a repetition of the offence, a man branded in this manner could bring forward no testimony from his superior that he belonged to the clerical order, he was to lose the privilege.

In the same way the Parliament of 1491 disputed this benefit of clergy for deserters during the preparations for war against France, on the grounds that their offence was directed against the welfare of king and realm ; and a law of 1497 enacted the same in the case of any one who had murdered his lord or master.

And yet, in spite of restrictions such as these, a state of affairs was suffered to continue, in which an assurance of almost complete immunity for the first offence positively encouraged a special class of men to crime.   If, notwithstanding the more strict administration of justice, robbery and murder were still rife in England, the fault must in great part be ascribed to this antiquated privilege.   That some consciousness of this existed in men's minds may be seen in the first restrictions ; and it is said that the very first of these laws was suggested by Henry himself, and that he had been moved thereto by what he had seen in France.[1]

The right of asylum in ecclesiastical houses was just as serious an abuse.   Every church afforded to the fugitive its protection for forty days, specially favoured places did so for his whole life.   The ordinances which Henry succeeded in obtaining from Popes Innocent VIII., Alexander VI., and Julius II. concerned solely the abuse of the right of sanctuary by criminals, who made the sanctuary serve as a place of refuge whence they might start again upon a fresh career of crime.   Thus Innocent VIII.'s

Right of asylum.

[1] On benefit of clergy, see 4 Hen. VII. c. 13 (by Stephen, Crim. Law, twice wrongly dated, 1487, pp. 462 and 463) ; 7 Hen. VII. c. 1 ; 12 Hen. VII. c. 7 : Stat., ii. 538, 549, 639 ; also P. V., 770, f. ; Relation, p. 35, f. ; on the whole question : Reeves, edit. Finlason, iii. 164–167 ; Stephen, as above, i. 459–464.

bull of the 6th of August, 1487, confirmed by Alexander VI. on the 3rd of August, 1493, provided that, should a robber or murderer seek refuge in the sanctuary a second time in consequence of a fresh crime, he could be taken out by the officers of the king; a man suspected of high treason should be watched from the very first, in order to guard against further crimes. This enactment was, by the bull of Julius II., dated the 20th of May, 1504, extended to all criminals, who, moreover, when they quitted the place cf refuge, were neither to be readmitted to that or to any other sanctuary. The right of asylum had also been abused by fraudulent debtors, who made a show of handing over their property to a third party, and lived in a sanctuary on their income, leaving their creditors unsatisfied; an Act of Parliament of 1487 declared therefore that such assignments of property were illegal.

The strongest opposition to ecclesiastical privileges proceeded from the judges. Though in a few cases, as in the laws against usury, ecclesiastical jurisdiction received especial respect in the legislation, the privileges of the Church were in the main disliked, nay, hated. The judges especially alluded to them in their decisions with disrespect and open contempt, and ruled, where possible, against the principle of such privileges. They did their best to set aside ecclesiastical jurisdiction even in those questions that belonged to it of right, and whenever they could overrule an appeal to the right of asylum, they indulged in specially cruel punishments. We know, for example, the sentence on Humphrey Stafford in the year 1487, when the judges rejected the plea of right of asylum, as powerless to protect the traitor.[1]

On the question of the claims of the ecclesiastical jurisdiction, the judges stood forward as champions of the royal authority, and in this particular supported Henry's endeavours to strengthen the prerogative of the Crown. As the English judicature had failed directly the strong support of a monarch had been withdrawn, it was undoubtedly a blessing for the

---

[1] On right of asylum, see Relat., p. 34, f.; Reeves, edit. Finlason, iii. 190, f.; 3 Hen. VII. c. 5: Stat., ii. 513; cf. Year Book, 3 Hen. VII. fol. 12a; also More's Utopia, p. 83; the papal bulls in Rym., xii. 541, and xiii. 104, f. On the conduct of the judges, Finlason gives many characteristic examples from the Year Book and Keilwey. Reports in Reeves, edit. Finlason, iii. 131–133, 167–169, 190, f., in the notes.

T

country, that an impartial royal power should again take law and justice under its protection, and be able to execute them with its own strong hand.   But as soon as this impartiality no longer existed, and the power of the Crown was misused to serve the personal interests of the king alone, then the most serious and most profound apprehensions could not fail to be awakened.   Unfortunately this was the case during the reign of Henry VII.

In the Parliament of 1495—a fruitful one in legislation— a noteworthy statute was passed.   It stated that many excellent laws had been made, but were not kept, and the prosecution of offenders was hindered by the corruption of the jurors at the sessions. Wherefore the judges of assize and the justices of the peace were empowered on the information of any private individual to decide upon the initiation of judicial proceedings ; and the judge who authorised these then referred the matter to his own court, and again awarded punishment according to the measure of the violation of the law.   It was only required that the informer should be resident in the county, and should, if his information was proved to be wrong, pay the costs of the defendant.   Treason, murder, and the more serious crimes in general, involving loss of life and limb, were excluded from this Act, as also cases involving forfeiture of property to the informer.[1]

The statute of 1495.

It was a revolutionary law, directly in opposition to the fundamental principles of English jurisprudence ; the legal officer, dependent on the king, took the place of the grand jury—he was public prosecutor and judge in one person. Here again Henry introduced into England a custom with which he had become acquainted in France ; for the technical expression " information " used in France for the same procedure was adopted.[2]   If the system thus begun had been continued in England, a purely bureaucratic criminal prosecution by officials would have been established here, as it has been in France.   It was the first step towards doing away with the jury.

This law was at once put to the worst possible use, for the

---

[1] 11 Hen. VII. c. 3: Stat., ii. 570 ; Relat., p. 34, shows that the required punishment of unjust accusations was not carried out very strictly.

[2] Cf. Schmidt, Staatsanwalt und Privatkläger, pp. 100, f., 106.

king's advantage. Polydore Vergil, who reports things on his own personal observation, describes the method pursued as follows. Having found himself unable to take money from his richer subjects illegally, it occurred to Henry that almost every one of them might be convicted of offending against existing laws. He began therefore to impose on such offenders light money penalties. For this he appointed two Exchequer Judges, the lawyers, Richard Empson, whom he subsequently knighted, and Edmund Dudley. Empson and
Dudley. These now gathered round them a crowd of informers, eager to compete for the king's favour, "and in their greed for money, paid too little heed to their duty, to their own danger, or to humanity, although they were often admonished by persons of importance that they should act with more moderation." Polydore Vergil also characterises, as strange in the telling and lamentable in reality, a procedure which was called by the name of justice, but was rather a criminal abuse made possible by the corruption of the courts. A completely unsus- Legal abuses
and exactions. pecting person was accused before the judge, and if he did not respond to the summons—of which very often, as he lived at a distance, he had no knowledge—he was condemned, his goods were confiscated, and he himself put in prison ; his property, however, was not forfeited to the informer, but to the king. "Men thus condemned were marked for the future as outlaws, that is, deprived of every civil right which the law gives to man." The result of this procedure is obvious enough ; large sums were extorted for the benefit of the royal treasury, and all sorts of possible or impossible claims for the royal prerogative could by the help of easily procurable accusations be brought forward and established. The character of this law is best described in a statute of Henry VIII.'s first Parliament, by which it was repealed, on the grounds that, as was well known, many dishonest, cunningly devised, and false accusations had, on the authority of this Act, been made against various subjects of the king to their great damage and wrongful vexation.[1]

[1] 1 Hen. VIII. c. 6: Stat., iii. 4 ; P. V.'s account, 775 and 778 ; after him, partly incorrect, Hall, pp. 499 and 502, f. ; Dudley was not a knight, as Pauli states, p. 628, but only an esquire.

We are acquainted with some cases, which aroused especial attention.   One of these was the action taken against the London alderman, William Capell, of the Cloth-
Capell.   workers' Guild, who from 1489 to 1490 had been one of the sheriffs of the city, and was subsequently knighted. Five years later he was charged with having sold goods to foreigners without requiring in return immediate payment in money or in other goods, and "thereupon condemned by the king to pay £2744, which fine was subsequently reduced by the royal mercy to £1615 6s. 3d., of which £732 were to be paid at once, and the rest within three years."   Even then Capell was by no means free, his riches had attracted too much the attention of the exchequer officials ; but no legal pretext to touch him could be found until he became Lord Mayor of London (1503–1504).   It was a disastrous year for the town, as many destructive fires had taken place ; we do not know, however, for what failure in the execution of his official duty it was that Capell, towards the end of 1507 or the beginning of 1508, was arrested at the suggestion of Empson and Dudley, and delivered over into the charge of the sheriffs.   Shortly before this, these two had caused Thomas Kneysworth, of the Fishmongers' Guild,
Kneysworth.   the Lord Mayor for 1505–1506, to be put in prison with his two sheriffs, Shore and Grove, until they purchased their freedom for £1400.   It is possible that André is referring to Kneysworth when he relates that in July, 1508, a former Lord Mayor with his two sons died, according to some from grief of heart at the loss of their wealth, according to others, from a disease then prevalent.   Capell this time remained obdurate, in spite of the attempts made to coerce him, by taking him from the charge of the sheriffs and shutting him up in strict confinement in the Tower, where he remained until the death of the king restored him to liberty. Henry's death appears also to have been the salvation of Sir Lawrence Aylmer, the Lord Mayor who was taken into custody with his sheriffs at the end of his year of office, in 1508.[1]   We can form an approximate idea of the number of

---

[1] City Chron., fol. 143*b*, 154*a* ; Fab. Abridgment, pp. 685, 686, 689, 690 ; Arnold, pp. 38, 42, 43 ; Grey Friars' Chron., p. 29 ; André, Ann., pp. 108, 126 ; cf. Year Book, 10 Hen. VII., fol. 7.

notes of hand thus extorted, from the fact that quite half a
hundred of them, all dating from the last two or three years
of Henry VII., were declared null and void in the first two
years of his son's reign.   The sums in question were from
£50 to £100 ; the Earl of Northumberland, however, was
fined £10,000, of which Henry VIII. remitted £5000 ; it is
not known if he was compelled to pay the other half of this
enormous sum.   Two townsmen had made themselves
answerable for 9000 marks, of which 2450 had already been
paid, and Corsy, the farmer of the money exchange, had
to disburse considerable sums.   In many of the orders by
which such bonds were cancelled, these significant words
are found—that obligations had been incurred on the unreasonable instigation of certain counsellors of the king,
"against law, right, and conscience, to the evident over-
burdening and danger of our late father's soul." [1]

Henry VII. himself had felt some qualms of conscience.
On the 19th of August, 1504, a royal decree was addressed to
the sheriffs, to the effect that the king, having always striven
to deal justly towards his subjects, and never to lay claim
unfairly to any one's property and goods, announced, for the
unburdening of his conscience, that any man who felt himself
aggrieved might, within two years, present his complaint in
writing, whereupon he should receive all reasonable satisfaction.   We do not hear of any fulfilment of this promise—in
fact, the evil rather grew worse during the last two years ; and
the chronicler Hall remarks that the execution of this design
having been prevented by Henry's death, which, however, did
not occur till five years later, it was repeated in the king's
will ; "but in the meane season many men's coffers were
emptied." [2]

Empson and Dudley by no means always acted in the
interests of the king.   They were far more often concerned
with their own private advantage, making for that
purpose a most unscrupulous use of the king's   Sir Robert
name and influence.   They certainly did not   Plumpton.
always adhere to the principles of the law of 1495, but managed

---

[1] Brewer, i. Nos. 63, 313, 317, 464, 575, 578, 697 ; especially Nos. 945, 961,
1026, 2036 ; also 1386, 3079, 4116.
[2] Rym., xiii. 107 ; P. V., 775, f. ; Hall, 499.

in every way to make the courts serve to their own profit. An example of this, and of the tenacity and energy with which they dogged their victims, is afforded by Empson's legal proceedings against Sir Robert Plumpton, as far as can be gathered from the somewhat complicated story preserved in the family correspondence of the Plumptons and in other papers. It is not possible to follow it in detail.

In February, 1497, the first signs were visible that Empson —of course as the legal representative of others who had claims on Sir Robert—had some design in view. On the 2nd of May, 1499, the knight was dispossessed of various portions of the Plumpton family estate, by order of the king's council; in November, 1500, he was threatened with a lawsuit at the next assizes, and was advised to gain over the sheriffs and other friends in the various counties in which his estates lay; these included besides Yorkshire, Nottingham, Derby, and Stafford. Some sympathy was felt in the fate of the persecuted man. "May God give you the power to resist and withstand the utter and malicious enmity and false craft of Master Empson and such others your adversaries, which as all the great parte of England knoweth, hath done to you and yours the most injury and wrong, that ever was done or wrought to any man of worship in this land of peace." [1]

Empson's legal machine, however, worked too well, and in 1501, Sir Robert was deprived of his domains in three of the four counties, York being excepted, and, in 1502, of Plumpton also; Empson received as his reward the estate of Kinalton, and married his daughter to the son and heir of his successful client.[2]

But the knight was not disposed to give in quietly. At the first the complainants stood somewhat in fear of his and his servants' vengeance; having lodged an appeal, he tried to assert his rights by force, and evicted the farmers who refused any longer to pay him their rents. At the same time Plumpton tried, as a last resource, to appeal to the king's mercy, and begged that Henry, his Council, or two judges, might pronounce the decision; although he had

---

[1] Plumpt. Corr., p. 162 ; before this, see ibid., pp. 121, f., 147, 151, 153, f.; cf. 161, and Acts of the Court of Requests, p. 22.

[2] Plumpt. Corr., p. cvi.–cx., 165, f. ; cf. a receipt to Empson, Mar. 22, 16 Hen. VII. (1501), in the Record Office.

already been warned that he would "get little favour." He was so far successful that Henry appointed him a Knight of the Body, and thereby protected him from personal imprisonment, and, further, insured to him the usufruct of his manors of Plumpton and Idle. The lawsuit continued. The family were completely ruined through all the expense and pressure they had had to bear, and in Henry VIII.'s reign, the unfortunate Sir Robert, now no longer protected by his position at court, was consigned to a debtor's prison, where for a long time he ate his scanty fare in a dungeon. Not till his hard-hearted opponent Empson had met his death on the scaffold, was an agreement entered into between the two parties.[1]

In the whole case there had been no question of the interests of the Crown; the advantage accruing to it consisted solely in the dues to be paid. Probably this may have been the reason why the Under-Treasurer, Sir Robert Lytton, deaf to all entreaties for delay, exacted from Plumpton the payment of his debts.[2] This was one case among many, possibly a bad one; but it is obvious that a misuse of the power of the law, as exercised against the London citizens and Plumpton, could not fail to have aroused much bitter feeling. Though the heaviest guilt lies on the two assistants, much still attaches to the king himself. Nothing could be more serviceable to the country after the Wars of the Roses than a severe and rigorous administration of justice; on the other hand, nothing could more undermine all respect for the law than the financial abuses which Henry allowed to be carried on by Empson and Dudley, under the legal authority of the king. In Henry's administration of justice there may be traced an irreconcilable contradiction, for ideas which were good and sound in their conception degenerate in his latter years into mere caricature. This is identically the same change which we have observed in his general policy; and it is just this discrepancy in his conduct at the close of his reign, which has contributed so much to the harsh judgment passed on his whole mode of government.[3] The

[1] Plumpt. Corr., pp. 122, f., 165, 167, ff., 183, 186, f., 196, cx., cxi.-cxiii., cxvii. f.   [2] Ibid., p. 165, f.
[3] Cf. especially Blackstone, iv. 554, who says extortion was the only object of Henry's legislation; repeated word for word by Stephen, New Comment., iv. p. 480.

only result of these abuses of the law was, that his successor found himself obliged to sacrifice to the popular clamour a statute so important to the power of the king as that which, in the interests of judicial reform, made the judge, who was dependent on the Crown, take the place of the jury. Empson and Dudley fell victims to the same popular hatred, and lost their heads on the scaffold. The wrongs of men who, like Sir R. Plumpton, Capell, and Kneysworth, had been by them almost done to death, were thus avenged.

ADMINISTRATION OF FINANCE.

The fiscal oppressions associated with the names of Empson and Dudley are the darkest spot, not only in the judicial administration, but also in the financial policy of Henry VII., and the judgments of posterity on him have thereby been prejudicially influenced.

Henry's financial policy.

Still, if we compare what we know of Henry's commercial and industrial policy with the reckless ideas on finance, which in these questions guided the monarchs of the Middle Ages, the contrast between them is evident. Where the public interest and his own financial interest were alike concerned, the former was regarded by Henry as the most important, and determined in the main his course of action.

No doubt Henry was consulting his own interests in departing from the policy of Richard III. towards foreigners, and forcing them, with the exception of the Hanse merchants, to pay far heavier customs. And yet, if the question of the customs duties had been paramount with him, he would not have tried at the same time to supplant the foreigners by his own English trade, the efficiency of which was constantly on the increase. The high duty on wines imposed on the Venetians served solely for Henry's navigation policy, and was at once reduced when that end had been accomplished. The raising of the customs duties, so often objected to by the Spaniards in the interest of their merchants, was certainly beneficial to the royal treasury, but it also served Henry materially as an expedient for furthering the other political demands he was making from Spain ; and these having been secured, the duties were reduced.

It is only in the support of the Staple and of the high

duty on wool that any advantage to the Crown seems to stand out prominently. This most secure source of customs revenue was, however, exclusively devoted to the object of preserving Calais—an important one to the State—and the heavy charges laid on wool had for their principal object, even in the eyes of contemporaries, to further the cloth industry. Had Henry herein allowed himself to be swayed by purely fiscal considerations, he would hardly have issued enactments which were intended to restrict the purchase of wool by foreigners, and especially to limit the production of it.

Henry had promoted commerce, even from his own funds. For instance, he contributed to Cabot's expeditions to the West, and gave help to merchants on other occasions by advances out of his own private purse.[1] No doubt his far-seeing commercial and industrial policy operated so far to his own advantage, that, with the growth of trade, the whole receipts from customs increased. For the rest, we cannot insist too strongly on the point that Henry's economic policy was determined by other political interests—as, for instance, with regard to the Netherlands—rather than by any temporary and shifty financial interest of the Crown.

We must the more acknowledge this, since the creation of an independent, secure, and well-regulated system of finance was one of the most important and difficult tasks of Henry's reign, for the fulfilment of which any *Henry's* useful expedient would be welcome. He had to *revenues.* make good the deficit of the preceding decade. He found ruin in the exchequer as well as everywhere else. The revenues of the Crown had to be regulated, the sources from which they were derived made as productive as possible, new ones opened, and those which had been diverted from the Crown in the civil war, recovered. These were tasks which, added to the claims put forward on all sides upon the king, were as easy to undertake as they were difficult to perform.

Of the ordinary revenues of the king, the most important, the amount of which could also be most exactly estimated, were those derived from the landed property of

---

[1] P. V., 780: "mercatoribus . . . quos ille sæpenumero pecunia mutua data gratuito iuvabat."

the Crown.   Next to these, stood the varying but yet usually lucrative customs duties, then the taxes less certain in amount—such as the still-surviving feudal dues —the judicial fines, the profits from the Mint, and the business of exchange. Among the extraordinary revenues, the grants made from time to time by Parliament stood first, and to these were added the benevolence levied once by the king, confiscations of the property of outlaws, and the payments agreed upon by international treaties.   The revenues from confiscated property, besides those payments made at intervals to Henry by France after the treaty of Etaples, must also be added to his regular income.

Crown lands.

To render this secure, and to increase it, was an important object with the king. The revenues from his landed property formed the bulk of his capital.   The possessions of the Houses of York and Lancaster, the property which, after the ruin of so many families, had fallen in or had been confiscated, were all collected together in the hands of Henry VII.   Much had been squandered away in the time of Henry VI.   Henry VII.'s first Parliament required the restitution of all the Crown lands which had been given away since the 2nd of October, 1455.   The Parliament of 1495 went still further ; the fiscal agents even went back to the times of Richard II. and Edward III., to recover such alienated property.   In spite of all limitations, these laws resulted in great harshness and frequent perversion of justice.   An attempt was made in 1495 to increase the revenues of those portions of the property of the Prince of Wales which were farmed out ; contracts which had till then held good were simply repudiated.   It was a harsh and severe system of retrenchment, after the disorderly extravagance of the preceding period.   The total income from the private property of the Crown, to which belonged that of the Prince of Wales and of the duchies of York and Lancaster, amounted—according to the reckoning of the Italian narrator—to 547,000 crowns, or £109,400. Proscriptions had contributed much to increase this source of Henry's income ; he seems also occasionally to have added to his landed property by purchase.[1]

---

[1] On the parliamentary measures: Rot. Parl., vi. 336–384, 459–462, 465–469, Stat., ii. 592, f., 594, 597–601 ; cf. Campbell, i. 250, 381, f., 385, f., 409, 461, f.,

Next came the much smaller revenues from tonnage and poundage, and from the customs. Formerly these had only been granted to the kings for stated periods and definite objects. Henry V., after his victory at Customs and other duties. Agincourt in 1415, was granted them for the remainder of his reign ; Henry VI., not till 1453 ; Edward IV., in 1465 ; and Richard III., in 1484. We know that the first response made by the Commons in Henry VII.'s first Parliament, to their speaker's address, was to confer their grant on the king for his lifetime. By this means the customs were converted for the lifetime of the reigning king into an assured revenue for the Crown ; and the result of Henry's commercial policy—if we take the yearly average of three periods of eight years each since his accession—was that these customs rose from £32,600 to £37,700, and finally to £42,000, that is, by quite twenty-eight per cent.[1]

A far more assured source of revenue—though from its nature variable—was afforded by the old feudal dues, especially from the king's right of wardship over the children Feudal dues. still under age of deceased vassals, from the administration and usufruct of their estate, and from the "relief" upon the acquisition of the fief, and the dues on the marriage of the heiress. Henry insisted very strongly that the freeholder with a land-rental of £40 should receive knighthood and pay fees for the same. The frequent repetition of this order issued to the sheriffs shows that it was evaded whenever possible, and that it must have been a question of considerable importance to the royal revenue. It was part of Empson's duties to hunt out defaulters in this particular, and bring them up for punishment.[2] Twice over the law enjoined not only the duty of money payments, but also that of serving in the army, on all holders of offices and estates conferred by the Crown.[3]

496, f., 545, f., ; ii. 67, 251, ff., 255, f., 261, 418 ; also see Relat., pp. 47-49 ; Exc. Hist., p. 120.

[1] The average is calculated from Schanz's tables, ii. 46, and given in round numbers. The estimate of £40,000 given in the Ital. Relat., p. 50, comes wonderfully near the right proportion. Grant by Henry's first Parlliament : Rot. Parl., vi. 268-270. Gairdner's remark is not quite exact, Hen. VII., p. 38, "the grant of tunnage and poundage, usually passed at the commencement of a reign," for at the most it could only apply, before Henry, to Richard III.

[2] Campb., ii. 76 ; Rym., xii. 770 ; Lett. and Pap., ii. 378, 379 ; Plumpt. Corres., p. 151.

[3] 11 Hen. VII. c. 18, and 19 Hen. VII. c. 1 : Stat., ii. 582, 648, f. ; Rot. Parl., vi. 525, f.

Included in the king's income were also the revenues from the Annates on appointments to bishoprics, although

Annates. Henry often resigned these in the newly appointed bishop's favour; the revenues from coinage and the farming-out of the exchange business, and occasional payments on the bestowal of offices, even when at the same time Henry granted compensation for official expenses.[1] Finally, we must not forget the imposition and extortion of judicial fines, which led at last to such crying abuse.

Henry endeavoured to augment these ordinary revenues as much as possible, that he might thereby provide for all State

Parlia- mentary grants. expenses, and be relieved from the necessity of drawing upon parliamentary grants—the principal source of his extraordinary revenues. We have already noticed these various grants and the object of them. In 1489, on the occasion of a vote of £75,000 for the war, the usual form of levy was departed from; out of each man's yearly income a tenth part was to be paid, and on personal property of ten marks and upwards, 1s. 8d. on every ten marks capital. The assessment and collection proved so faulty that only £27,000 came in, and perhaps this was the reason why the old form of a fifteenth and tenth was reverted to. A "fifteenth and tenth" was originally a levy to these amounts on personal estates; since the time of Edward III. it was understood to mean a sum of £37,000 to £38,000, fixed portions of which were to be contributed by each separate parish in the counties and towns. By this means a definite standard of taxation was obtained, and, when required, many fifteenths and tenths were granted.[2] In the last Parliament of 1504, when no special reason for making a demand on Parliament existed, Henry bethought him of claiming the old English feudal aid due on the knighting of his eldest son, and the dowry of his eldest daughter, although Arthur's knighting had already taken place on the 30th of November, 1488, and the prince himself had been dead nearly two years. It is said that to this demand a serious opposition was raised, under the

---

[1] An entry of the revenues from vacancies at Canterbury, Chichester, and London, Oct. 19, 20 Hen. VII., in the Record Office. Payment for a shrievalty in Brewer, i. No. 996; cf. the order, Dec. 21, 1508, in the Record Office.

[2] In the Relation, p. 52, the amount is given exactly at £37,930, but the author is incorrect when he calls this sum only a "fifteenth."

leadership of young Thomas More, which resulted in a considerable reduction of the original amount, and that Henry revenged himself for this in a somewhat undignified manner on More's father, by condemning him, on some pretext or other, to a fine of £100, and keeping him in the Tower until he paid.[1]   In the end, however, a show of polite accommodation was arrived at; the Commons offered £40,000, and the king took only £30,000.   During the twenty-four years his reign lasted, Henry did not demand more than five parliamentary grants, of which the second was merely to supply what was needed to bring up the first to the required estimate, and of these grants only two were made from 1492 to 1509, a period of nearly eighteen years.

The disorders, which on two occasions were associated with the levying of these direct taxes, show how unpopular they were, and this led Henry, in the autumn of 1491, before the French war, to resort to a bene- **Benevolence.** volence, an imposition pressing solely on his wealthier subjects.   Various obligations then incurred not having been fulfilled, the Parliament of 1495 granted him the power of collecting the arrears of these so-called voluntary presents to the Crown, in the same way as with assessed taxes, under severe punishment for the refractory.[2]   It looks very much like extortion, that Henry, after having granted privileges to London, on the 21st of May, 1498, which then brought him in £5000, should, scarce seven years later, demand the payment of five thousand marks for a fresh confirmation of these privileges.   To his extraordinary revenues must be added the profits which he made from mercantile ventures, undertaken on his own account, in wool, tin, and wine.[3]

Temporary money difficulties Henry met by loans.   In the very first year of his reign he asked for £4000 from the city, but had to be content with half that sum; in the following year he borrowed smaller sums from **Loans.** private persons, and did the same on the occasion of the

---

[1] Roper, Life of More, p. 7, f.; cf. Seebohm, as above, p. 144, f.   On Henry's parliaments and their grants, cf. Stubbs, Seventeen Lect., pp. 357–360.

[2] 11 Hen. VII. c. 10, Stat., ii. 576, f.

[3] Notes of expenditure show this, as on May 16 and June 16. 1494, July 15, 1496, May 24, 1497, Oct. 23, 1500: Exc. Hist., pp. 98, 108, 111, 124.   Pauli, p. 340, remarks the same, but founds it on the passage in P. V., 78, and Hall, p. 505, which he misunderstands; see above, p. 281, Note 1.

preparations for Elizabeth's coronation. In this case the king showed that he was to be trusted, and two loans obtained from the city, in the third year of his reign (1487–88), together amounting to £6000, were also punctually repaid in the following year.[1] When in November, 1496, he wished for a loan in advance of £10,000 for the Scottish war, in anticipation of the grant to be made by Parliament, the city only gave him £4000; but loans for £40, £20, or even £10 were at the same time raised in different parts of the country, from a great number of wealthy persons, to whom the king addressed himself in a special letter, signed by his own hand, promising to each punctual repayment before the following 30th of November. His commissioners did not receive everywhere the sum demanded, sometimes not more than the half, but yet the considerable sum of £58,000 was collected, and, as far as we can see, duly repaid. Henry justified the credit which he enjoyed. Among his items of expenditure, payments of debts of this kind are often noted, but the creditor is never named, and only sometimes the purpose of the payment. The queen also was often obliged to borrow money; she applied to strangers as well as to her husband, who, even from her, required punctual repayment.[2]

Only in sudden emergencies did Henry resort to larger loans of this kind, or to grants from Parliament or to benevo-

Regulation and control of expenditure. lences. That he was enabled to free himself more and more from all these external aids, especially from the necessity of calling parliaments, he owed in the first place to his firm policy of peace; next, to the increase of his ordinary revenues; lastly, to the severely economical administration of his finances. The arrangement he adopted was as follows: for important expenditure recurring regularly, certain fixed and permanent revenues were assigned, as we have seen, in the appropriation

[1] On these first loans, see City Chron., fol. 141*b*, 142*b*; Fabian's Abridgment, p. 683; Receipts of Feb. 23, Dec. 1, 1487, in the Record Office.

[2] On the great loan, see City Chron., fol. 161*b*, 162*b*, 172*b*; 3 Rep. of the Hist. MS. Comm., App., p. 420. A considerable number of Privy Seals, partly in bad preservation, all of Dec. 1 (1496), are among the unpublished manuscripts of the Record Office. The Commissioners noted each time the sum received underneath. The Abbot of Battle asks to be specially excused for having contributed only £20 instead of £40; Letter of July 29 (1497), ibid.; also see Exc. Hist., pp. 92, 93, 95, 97, 103, 110, 111, 116, 118, 127, 132; cf. Nichols, p. ciii.

of the Staple customs to the maintenance of Calais.   In the same way, for the protection of the north against Scotland, certain revenues were apportioned by law to Berwick and Carlisle ; the safety of the northern bishopric of Durham was to be provided for out of the revenues of the bishopric, on which account Henry left the see vacant for a long time, and, when the appointment was made, diverted, with the approval of the Pope, a portion of the income of the see towards its defence.[1]

The oppressions connected with the maintenance of the royal court when in progress were a grievance of long standing. After Edward III.'s time judicial measures promised a remedy, but these were never carried out, and the complaints continued.   The court officials took from the surrounding inhabitants more than was necessary ; they used compulsion and extortion, and forgot to pay.   In Henry's first Parliament, the Commons protested against the " constant appropriation of property and cattle for the expenses of the royal household, for which the owners do not receive satisfactory and proper payment."   Henry, who was endeavouring to secure popularity for his new dynasty, adopted a more effectual measure for redress, by getting Parliament to grant £14,000 a year for the expenses of the royal household, and assign for the purpose definite sources of revenue, such as land dues and customs.   By this means the king guaranteed as it were the possibility of payment, which up to that time had depended on bare promises, and likewise managed to separate the expenses of the royal household from those of the State. In 1495 the Act underwent modification in certain particulars. It was on the same principle that £2105 19s. were appropriated for the king's wardrobe.[2]

Expenditure was thus from the first regulated in detail, but Henry nevertheless kept a strict eye over all the accounts, both of State and court.   Among the printed and unprinted records bearing on the history of Henry VII., a remarkable number of statements of accounts are to be met with, often

---

[1] Berwick and Carlisle : Rot. Parl., p. 394 (1487), and 11 Hen. VII. c. 16, Stat., p. 626, f. ; Rot. Parl., 496, f. Durham.   Letter of Julius II., April 17, 1508 ; Reg. Brev., Julius II., tom. vii. 164.

[2] Rot. Parl., pp. 299–304 ; 11 Hen. VII. c. 62, Stat., pp. 627–630 ; Rot. Parl., pp. 497–502.

drawn up in a very neat and ingenious fashion. The king demanded an exact account for everything, and we can well understand that officials, to whom this strictness was irksome, should find fault with him for his avarice. That these accounts are not exactly on the pattern of modern book-keeping does not in the least diminish their importance.

Among the most interesting of these are the accounts of the *Privy Purse* expenses for the years 1491 to 1505, which have **Privy Purse.** been preserved and published, though in a somewhat inadequate form.[1] These fragments, however, are quite sufficient to enable us to gain an insight into the variety of matters which occupied the king's mind, and especially to note and admire his careful and orderly method. Ayala relates, though with a certain amount of exaggeration, that Henry employed all the time he did not spend in public or in his Council, in writing down his accounts with his own hand.[2] This was not approved of by the Spaniard, who thought Henry was too fond of money. But this reproach of avarice against the king rests, for the most part, on a confusion between careful orderliness and avaricious niggardliness. There is no doubt that Henry often showed signs of parsimony, even on occasions when it was out of place, as in the marriage treaty with Scotland, but the failing was not one which belonged to his real nature. It was simply the result of that carefulness he was obliged to exercise, in order to establish a sound system of finance, after the extravagant prodigality of former times.

At the right moment Henry was quite ready to deal out money with unstinting hands. We need only recall the magnificence of his court festivities, the lavish splendour with which he received King Philip in 1506, the profusion of precious household possessions which he displayed on such occasions. Henry himself also had many expensive tastes. In the privy purse accounts the sum of £110,000 is set down for jewels alone; and for political purposes he expended

---

[1] Exc. Hist., pp. 87–133. Their incompleteness is shown on a comparison of the amount of the sums noted with the total amount given in the account itself; for Oct. 1, 1502, to Oct. 7, 1503, the latter is given at £90,327 8*s.* 9*d.* (p. 131), while an addition of the separate sums comes only to £62,115 19*s.* 4*d.*

[2] July 25, 1498 ; Berg., p. 178.

without hesitation very considerable amounts, as, for instance, on Maximilian in 1503, and in 1505 on Philip. We cannot but respect that strict orderliness which noted with equal care sums of thousands of pounds and the three or four shillings which the king had disbursed in alms or on a small present or salary.

The energy with which Henry imposed this exactness on himself and on his officials met with its reward. It is an evidence of the financial independence which he gained for himself at the cost of such laborious and continued effort, that he could carry on the whole current administration, and provide for court expenses out of his regular income, while at the same time he commanded without difficulty considerable sums for special purposes, and yet made his income largely exceed his expenditure. Of no single prince of his time could the same be said.

Nevertheless it is certain that England was not then rich either in population or resources. It stood below France, for example, in both respects. The levy of a tax, *Henry's strong financial position.* which after all only produced £27,000, pressed so heavily that it caused that outbreak in the north, in which the Earl of Northumberland lost his life, and the levy of two fifteenths and tenths in the year 1497, was sufficient to stir up the Cornish insurrection. On the other hand, we find that Henry alone was able to disburse large sums in quick succession, £4000 on the 16th of September, 1502, £10,000 on the 1st of October, and £30,000 on the 16th of December. His privy purse was not generally burdened with the costs of government, but yet from it were made payments to foreign Powers and for entertainment of foreign guests, and from it alone, in the financial years 1495–1496, upwards of £25,000 was paid out; in 1497–1498 over £72,000; in 1499–1500 over £46,000; in the following year about £48,000; and in 1502–1503 as much as £90,327.

Sums such as these are the best evidence of the success of Henry's financial system, supported as it was by his whole policy. Our otherwise excellent Italian observer had allowed himself to be deceived by his informants, when he estimated Henry's entire expenditure for himself and his court at

£20,000.[1] In this matter the king had taken care not to show his hand.

As to the amount of Henry's accumulated treasure, we have no reliable information. This did not consist of coined money alone. The treasure in jewels which he amassed, and his enormous wealth in gold and silver plate, were not only intended for pomp and display, but formed at the same time a secure fund of capital, a part of the royal treasure which could at any moment be realised. These treasures served especially to spread throughout the world rumours of King Henry's riches, which no doubt were of great use to him. Much exaggeration was also afloat on the subject; Ayala asserts that any gold pieces which found their way into the king's coffers never came out again, and the ambassador of the Duke of Milan estimated Henry's treasure, even in 1497, at £1,350,000, and what he put by yearly at £112,500. Peter Martyr also calls him the richest of all kings in money. He is spoken of in the same way at Venice, and Duke George of Saxony received from Brussels, at the beginning of 1509, the information that Henry "is described as the wisest and richest lord that is now known in the world."[2]

No one recognised more clearly than King Henry that in the political life of nations money is all powerful. From the outset therefore he bent his mind on creating, by means of his finances, a broad, independent, and solid foundation for his royal authority. Here too he worked so that everything should contribute to one end, and in the whole conduct of his policy he took special care not to endanger this financial security, which he had with such trouble created. By this means he became more independent, especially of grants

[1] Relat., p. 47; Ayala's estimate is almost exactly the same, Report on Mar. 26, 1499, Berg., 206, and as the Italian writer relies elsewhere on Ayala, here also he probably got his information from Ayala, or from the same source.

[2] Ayala's report, Berg., p. 206; the Milanese report, Sept. 8, 1497; Brown, No. 751, cf. No. 795, 942; Peter Martyr, Op. epist., p. 218; Heinr., von Schleinitz to Duke George, Brussels, Feb. 17, 1509, Dresd. Archiv.; cf. Faliero's Relat. of 1531: Albéri. Rélat. Venet., i. 3, p. 8. In all historical accounts it is estimated that Henry's treasure amounted at his death to £1,800,000. The only source is Bacon, p. 210, who, moreover, adds "as by tradition is reported;" Bacon also asserts that Henry had the money in his own keeping in secret places at Richmond. Henry would certainly have been prudent enough to use for this purpose the more secure Tower, where also the Mint was situated. Bacon's statements are quite unfounded.

from Parliament, than any English king before him. His financial policy was thoroughly monarchical. Upon it rested to a great extent the independence and power of the newly established Tudor sovereignty.

THE ESTABLISHMENT OF AN ENLIGHTENED ABSOLUTISM.

The life's work of the first Tudor king was constantly, and to the very last, directed towards one great object—the restoration of the monarchy by the establishment of royal absolutism in the English Constitution. If therefore, in conclusion, we wish to treat of this king's monarchical policy as a whole, we must glance back again for a moment over the history we have been relating. *Henry's monarchical policy.*

By the help of a strong monarchy alone could the England of the Wars of the Roses be saved from falling into utter ruin. Edward IV. and Richard III. had alike failed to create such a monarchy, and it was left for that man to accomplish, who overthrew the revolutionary throne of the House of York. Thus England became the prize of that Tudor dynasty which had brought her deliverance. Henry was able to make the most of his first success, and to use it to secure for the Crown a position of authority such as had long been unknown, because he always understood how to link closely together the interests of king and State, never promoting the one to the detriment of the other. In this consisted the significant character of Henry's personal rule. It was the same with his great contemporary, Ferdinand the Catholic; with both of them dynastic interests no longer existed apart from the interests of the State. For this reason no king ever accomplished more for himself and his own position in the State than this Tudor monarch.

He renounced all thoughts of a return to that mediæval policy of conquest, of which kings before and even after him dreamed, as the highest aim of their ambition; he never sought to extend his royal authority beyond the borders of England and Ireland. He realised that the strength of the island kingdom, girdled about by the sea, lay in the isolation of its natural position, that any possessions on the Continent which would bring it into immediate contact with the Powers there in conflict, instead of adding to its strength, as they might

appear to do, would in reality diminish it.   Fleets no longer
sailed with armed hosts against France ; under Henry's rule,
the ships of England bore the English merchant and English
products to foreign lands ; it was they who carried out his
new policy of conquest   The one outpost beyond the sea was
Calais, maintained at great expense, since it was necessary to
the trade with the Continent, and for holding supremacy in
the Channel.   To this insular policy of Henry's, which cannot
be too much commended, belongs also his constant endeavour
to bring about a lasting peace with Scotland, and the remark
with which he is credited on the possible future union of
Scotland with England, as the result of the Anglo-Scottish
marriage alliance he had brought about, already contains the
idea of that union of Great Britain, which was one day to
spring from that marriage.

No doubt, at first, the exigencies of the time in England
were his best allies, as they afforded him the opportunity to
exercise his power in re-establishing peace and order in the
kingdom, in protecting it permanently from all who might
create disturbance, and finally, after many unsuccessful
beginnings, in gaining for his kingdom an independent and
honoured position in the eyes of foreign Powers.   But besides
these political duties, belonging properly to the functions of
the Crown, the king had interfered in the wider field of
commerce and industry, where the English spirit of enterprise
was more than usually astir.   Here from the first he had
taken the guidance into his own hand, and had promoted or
restrained according to his own views.   He aimed at being
the leader of the State in all foreign relations, as well as the
master and guide of all the forces at home.   Thus from the
Crown came that new life which now throbbed throughout
England after many years of disorder.   Whatever of their
prerogative the kings in earlier times had been compelled
to relinquish in consequence of their own weakness, or for the
sake of obtaining help from their subjects to carry out their
policy of war, Henry won back to the full for the monarchy,
in the work he did for the State.

Not only in àll his actions was he indirectly working
for himself and his royal authority ; but he allowed no
opportunity to slip of directly furthering the power of his

dynasty. We see this clearly in his policy with regard to those marriage alliances which he so assiduously endeavoured to promote. By their means the royal upstart of *Protection of* still apparently doubtful origin would be entitled to *the kingly* take his place on an equality with the other royal *power.* families, and what his dynasty gained in Europe thereby and by the further success of his political schemes, it gained at the same time, and to a far greater degree, in England itself.

When Henry began his reign, he was obliged to revert to very primitive safeguards for his throne. He surrounded himself at once with a bodyguard, which he subsequently retained, but which never exceeded the number of two hundred men. Our Italian authority states that never before Henry's time had the Tower been so well guarded, that it was plentifully provided with material of war, especially with bows and crossbows. Against those chance dangers which in former times menaced the English kings, Henry was resolved "to protect himself by strongholds," which should also serve for protection within the country, and among these he reckoned the border towns of Calais and Berwick. From other sources we learn that Portsmouth likewise received a garrison, and Henry's endeavour to keep his forts as inaccessible as possible is shown by his order to the governor of Scarborough, to allow no foreigner residing in the town to have access to the castle. We also hear occasionally of the presence of German mercenaries in the kingdom.[1]

Henry was the first to protect his royal power by mercenaries and strong places. Means for the purpose he obtained by clever administration of his finances, and this he subsequently contrived to develop still further into one of the securest supports of his kingly independence. His legislation furnished another pillar of the royal authority; more especially that which dealt with judicial procedure, and the statutes which brought the guilds and other companies directly under the power of the Crown, or withdrew the administration

---

[1] André, Ann. (1508), p. 127. On the body-guard see P. V., 720; Relat., p. 47; Milanese report, Sept. 8, 1497; Brown, No. 751. On the fortresses, see Relat., p. 45, f.; Leland, Itin., iii. 114; cf. the Milanese report differing slightly from the Relat., Brown, as above; Henry to the Governor of Scarborough, Westminster, Mar. 8 (without year), in the Record Office.

of certain laws, as of those concerning usurers, from municipal jurisdiction.

This policy, contrary as it was to every custom of the country, shows very plainly the influence which Henry's residence in France before his accession had exercised upon him. It must have been there that he formed those theories of personal government, which he tried to introduce into the English Constitution; from thence he borrowed the idea of strengthening the defences of the country; thence those judicial reforms, which aimed at the abolition of juries. Indeed, his desire to transplant French institutions into English soil went still further, as we are told by Ayala, "He would like to govern England in the French fashion, but he cannot do it."[1]

All, however, that Henry had accomplished would have remained still of doubtful advantage, if he had been unable to protect his newly established monarchy against the two greatest rivals which confronted it in England. The most difficult part of his policy was to assert his royal authority against the two Estates assembled in Parliament—the Lords of the Upper House, and the Commons in the Lower.

It was reserved for Henry VII. to put an end for ever to the fierce struggle between the Crown and the aristocracy. The Crown We know that the Wars of the Roses, the last and the furious outburst of this long struggle, had struck Aristocracy. down deep to the very roots of both parties. And while Henry had only to grapple with a few isolated members of the rival royal House, it was but the remnants of the old nobility that were left to oppose him. To keep them in subjection, and especially to prevent them from ever rising to fresh power was not only imperative in the interests of the Crown, but also necessary for the peace and prosperous development of the country.

In the very first years of his reign, Henry began to take vigorous measures. It is noteworthy that of the three friends on whom he conferred peerages after his victory, only one was not already a peer, and he was always careful not to augment to a dangerous degree the ranks of the nobility.[2]

[1] July 25, 1498, Berg., p. 178.
[2] The lists of his creations in 47th Rep. of the Dep. Keeper, App., p. 79, ff. ; cf. Stubbs. Sevent. Lectures, p. 355, f.

In his first Parliament he exacted from the assembled lords, spiritual and temporal, a special oath that they would loyally keep the peace, while his second Parliament, by its law of the Star Chamber, put into his hand a most powerful weapon against the nobles and their excesses. By this law the aristocracy were delivered over, not to the courts of the realm, but entirely to the Crown, and the Crown then had to show that it possessed the power to execute the law effectively.

The men who stood foremost by the king's side to help and advise him in this as in other matters, were not chosen from the ranks of the great nobles of the realm. We meet in the highest offices with the names of the churchmen, John Morton, Richard Fox, William Warham, and the laymen Sir Reginald Bray, Sir Giles Daubeney, who was not created a lord till later, Richard Edgecombe, Edward Poynings, and Sir Thomas Lovell, with whom eventually were associated such men as Empson and Dudley. Except the king's own relatives, the only members of the aristocracy who can be named as occupying positions of influence are the Earl of Oxford and the Earl of Surrey, Lord Treasurer, and even they stood in importance far below men such as Morton, Fox, Warham, and Bray. The hereditary nobility had to make way before the talent of the statesman. In this Henry set the example to his successors, for the leading statesmen of the Tudors were men of low origin.

The part which the high aristocracy had played in politics was over. The estates of the old families had passed into other hands; most of them, by attainders and confiscations, had fallen to the Crown.[1] In the Upper House the aristocracy found themselves confronted by the spiritual peers, who outweighed them in number, and amongst these the leading men were Henry's firmest and most faithful supporters, whom he had thrust into high places in the Church. We scarcely hear anything more of the Upper House.

[1] That Henry, with the Stat. de finibus, 4 Hen. VII. c. 24, Stat., ii. 547, f., had especially aimed at undermining the power of the nobility as great land-owners by facilitating the alienation of entailed lands, is an assertion not in accordance with the intention of this law, which besides is only the repetition of an earlier statute. This assertion is expressly made by Hume, and again by Stephen, following Blackstone, New Comm., i. 255 ; see Reeves, ed. Finlason, iii. 136–141, cf. 129, f. ; after Reeves, Hallam, i. 11–13.

The supreme court of justice, formed of the peers of the realm, sank into an unimportant tool in the hands of the Crown.

The members of the nobility henceforward became the mere ornaments of the court; they surrounded the king on festive occasions, and solemn embassies, which did not involve any diplomatic difficulty, were confided to them. As was natural, the principal part still was theirs whenever there was a call to arms, but Henry was careful that this should take place as seldom as possible; and as to the conduct of a campaign, such as that in France in 1492, no one could have been less enlightened than the noble lords, who then took the field. Court festivities and tournaments were henceforward their principal field of action, service at court the only mode in which they could fulfil their feudal duties. For to appear at court was their duty. André, the court historiographer, considered it especially necessary to note and justify the long absence of a few lords from the court.[1] And yet this nobility, which had sunk to a position of such political insignificance, still retained its prominent social position, and it was only by promotion to the highest ecclesiastical dignities that statesmen such as Morton, Warham, and Fox could be placed on a level of equal or superior rank. Thus the old and powerful aristocracy of England was already in Henry's reign turning into a nobility of court and office, required for the sole purpose of enhancing the splendour of the Crown, but unable any longer to threaten its position.

In Henry's attitude towards the aristocracy he could be certain of the approval and support of all those who had suffered under the oppressions of powerful nobles. Polydore Vergil[2] declares that Henry "was the firmest protector of justice, whereby his people were much beholden to him, as they could now live their lives free from the vexations of the mighty."[2] Thus at the very outset he pressed on the legislation which should give greater authority to the king, because it insured for the weak the powerful protection of the law against the violence of the strong. The Commons took sides with the king; they were protecting themselves when they increased the prerogative of the Crown.

We may remember that any advance in power gained by

---

[1] André, Ann., p. 125.   [2] Pol. Verg., p. 779.

the Lower House had taken place under the rule of strong
monarchs who were able to repress the nobles;   The Crown
the same might be expected under the rule of   and the
Henry VII. His reign seems most to resemble   Lower House.
that of the first Lancastrian, Henry IV., who, having won the
throne by the sword, likewise grounded his claim on the
sanction of Parliament, and thenceforth found in the Commons
support against foes within and without. But, unlike his predecessors, unlike Edward I. and III., Henry IV. and V., the
Tudor king knew how to compel the Lower House to keep idly
in its scabbard that weapon which it had so often made use of
to resist any extension of the royal prerogative—its claim to
grant or withhold money. It was to the constant need for
money of those earlier kings that the Commons owed all the
steps they had gained ; but the Crown's financial need ceased
with Henry VII. He was independent of his Lower House,
because his financial policy made it possible for him to avoid
any dangerous conflict with it ; and accordingly he was able,
with one exception, to abstain from summoning Parliament
during the last twelve years of his reign.

We see, therefore, that Henry did not afford the classes
represented in the Lower House an opportunity of expressing
their opinion on political matters much more often than the
peers of the Upper House. Yet his whole solicitude was
directed to the interests of the industrial middle classes, and
to the smaller landowners, who were for the most part represented in the Lower House. He knew that by raising and
strengthening them, he would lay the best foundation for his
dynasty. For them, therefore, was the protection of justice
undertaken by the king, for them his many measures to
promote commerce and industry, for them the agrarian legislation in the interests of the peasants and tenant farmers,
for them, in fact, his whole endeavour to guard the kingdom
and, in his own words, to advance it in "rest, peace, and
wealthy condition."

One peculiar economic principle of Henry's should here
be noted. Polydore Vergil remarks that he did   Henry's
his best to keep down his burghers, especially the economic
richer among them, because he well knew that,   principles.
as they grow richer, men become overbearing, and allow

their actions to be controlled by money interests alone. To the Spaniard Ayala Henry had, in fact, said almost in the words of the chronicler, that he tried to keep his subjects down because riches would make them insolent.[1] In this, however, Henry did not show an inconsistency with his general views; he certainly wished to see England rich and flourishing — that was the very aim of his state and economic policy—but this wealth was to be diffused as widely as possible, and not to be amassed in the hands of individuals. While shattering the hereditary power of the great nobles, Henry sought to check the rise of others, whose new power was founded on their wealth, and who seemed to him just as dangerous. Men who were influential either from their birth or their riches were, in his opinion, likely to be tempted to stir up or to support a fresh contest for power, and cause fresh confusion and disorder in the kingdom. It was from this point of view that he restrained the efforts after monopoly made by the London merchant adventurers, and resisted the increase and consolidation of large landed properties. Viewed from the standpoint of a struggle with capital, his fiscal abuse of justice, if not excused, is somewhat freed from the reproach of personal avarice, and appears in a more generous light. Polydore Vergil, in fact, connects those cruel exactions, which resulted in the ruin of many individuals, with the principle mentioned above. Henry acted thus, he says, in order to stifle the restless spirit of party in the country, not from greed for money, although the sufferers complained that they were not so much the victims of severity as of covetousness. Henry even gave a helping hand to those who had been severely bled by his judges, as if, having been once plucked, their feathers could be made to grow again. "Certain it is that the prince, so moderate himself, did not rob his subjects above measure, he who left his kingdom in every respect in the greatest prosperity."[2]

The policy of Henry is clear enough; he wished for a comfortable, well-to-do commonalty, a numerous and wealthy middle-class, as much as possible on an equality, by whom the dependent labourer, kept by law at work and under

----

[1] Report of July 25, 1498, Berg., p. 177; P. V., 775.
[2] P. V., 775 and 780.

discipline should be employed. Interfering in all the details of life, controlling and regulating according to his own supreme will, the king should stand over all, without too many intermediate links formed either by a powerful aristocracy or by individual citizens, influential by their wealth.

Thus Henry's endeavour to establish the sole sovereignty of the Crown, unmolested by any other power in the State, stands out very obviously. Whoever raised himself above what was, in Henry's opinion, his proper sphere, was at once energetically suppressed, even though he might have hitherto enjoyed the royal favour. Hence, as we have seen, the king extended his influence to the utmost in his legislation. And that he made real use of this newly acquired prerogative, as, for instance, in dealing with the trade guilds, is shown by the occasional experience of the Londoners.

On the 6th of January, 1503, Henry bestowed on the London Tailors' Guild, together with a new charter, the name of the Merchant Taylors, and aroused thereby great discontent among the other companies. This feeling was displayed at the election of sheriffs in the year 1505, when Fitzwilliam, the candidate of the Taylors' Guild, was unsuccessful. In the next election of 1506, Henry in consequence interfered. When on the 30th of September the customary presentation of the sheriffs took place before the lords in the Star Chamber, one Thomas Johnson, who had been legally elected, was not admitted to take the oath ; and on the 10th of October came an order from the king to the Lord Mayor to set about a fresh election, and Edmund Dudley appeared in Guildhall with the express command that Fitzwilliam should be elected sheriff, "which took place at last after great difficulty." [1]

The Parliament of 1495, took from the inhabitants of the lordships of North and South Tynedale on the Scotch Border, those privileges under cover of which they had, in company with the Scots, done many deeds of violence. Henry, in like manner, interfered in the municipal government of

---

[1] Stow, pp. 876, 877, 879 ; Fabian's Abridgment, p. 688 ; Arnold, p. 42 ; cf. Grey Friars' Chron., p. 29. The Charter is printed ; I found it in a volume of miscellanies, London Companies, Brit. Mus., $\frac{10,349 \text{ d } 10}{}$

Leicester, where there had often been disturbances on public
occasions, as on the election of mayors or members of Parliament.[1] Thus rights and privileges were set aside, even with
the assistance of Parliament, if they were contrary to the
welfare of the State; and of this the king was sole judge.

Henry did not directly attack the constitutional position
of Parliament; even under his rule the judges stated expressly
that a statute, to be legally binding, must have passed through
"the full assembly of commons, lords, and king."[2] He did
not suppress the expression of adverse opinions in the
Commons, although he is said to have taken revenge afterwards for any opposition that was distasteful to him. But
the petitions from the Commons which he granted, coincided
so strikingly with his own ideas and wishes, that we can
hardly be mistaken if we seek the real originator of the
petition in the person to whom it was addressed.

He did not injure the form of the Constitution, for after
all, he found it pliant enough even when he carried measures
which violated its spirit; and in this was most
clearly illustrated the real strength of his kingly
authority. Only men who were agreeable to him
were chosen as speakers of the Lower House, Richard Empson,
in 1491, and in 1504, even Dudley, when public hatred was
already strong against both him and Empson. The name
of the "obedient Parliament" can best be applied to the
Parliament of 1495; it carried back further than any other
the restitutions of Crown lands which it granted to the king,
it raised the benevolence imposed by the king to the same
level as a tax voted by Parliament, and it was in this
Parliament that Henry passed his judiciary laws, in particular
the statute, afterwards so notorious, for the partial abolition
of the indictment by jury. One step to be noted was gained
by him when the Parliament of 1504, under the pretext of
the limited time at its disposal, granted him the right to
reverse on his own authority all the attainders which had
taken place in Parliament during Richard III.'s time and his
own; in this instance the Parliament abandoned for the life-

_Henry's
success._

---

[1] 11 Hen. VII. c. 9, Stat., ii. 575, f.; and Rot. Parl., vi. 432, f.; Campb.,
ii. 456, f.
[2] Year Book, 7 Hen. VII., fol. 14a, f.

time of the king that fundamental law by virtue of which
statutes passed by king and Parliament could only be repealed
or modified by the same authority.[1]

Thus Parliament supported the absolutist policy of the
king, who, although without outward powers of compulsion,
had succeeded in raising the Crown to its new and command-
ing position. Our Italian observer, comparing the English
of the time with the Scotch, declares that only a few of them
were loyally devoted to their king, "generally they hate the
living king and praise the dead one." Yet this same writer
testifies emphatically to Henry's success. "From the time
of William the Conqueror to the present, no king has reigned
more peaceably that he has; his great prudence causing him
to be universally feared." From other sources also we hear
that Henry held the people in subjection, as had never before
been the case; "his crown is unassailed and his rule strong
in every respect." A Milanese writer, who confirms the
opinion that the kingdom for many years had not been so
obedient to any sovereign as it was to Henry, expresses his
astonishment that the king, in spite of the small number of
his body-guard, was able to reside in open and unprotected
places in the forest districts.[2]

The above are the opinions of contemporaries before the
opening of the new century. The monarchy, having fallen
into decay with the weakness of those who held it, now rose
up again with renewed strength, when a real master stood at
the head of the State. It would be an idle question to
discuss, when determining the causes of the royal success,
whether the creative ideas originated with the king himself
or with his counsellors; the will to carry into effect
remained always with the wearer of the crown. But the
question is by no means unimportant when we are passing
judgment on the persons concerned in this success, though
the answer, which in the case of Henry's successor is perfectly
clear, with him is doubtful and obscure.

In the year 1498, Ayala asserts that Henry had been
governed by the members of his council, but that he had

[1] 19 Hen. VII. c. 28, Stat., ii. 669; Rot. Parl., vi. 526.
[2] The various opinions: Relat., pp. 32, 46; Londoño and the sub-prior's
reports, July 18; Ayala's, July 25, 1498, Berg. pp. 163, 178; de Soncinos, Sept.
8, 1497, Brown, No. 751; cf. 750.

already shaken off some of them, and had to a great extent freed himself from this control. Nine years later, according to Puebla, Henry no longer had any confidential advisers ; and Polydore Vergil, who was only acquainted with these later years, characterises his mode of government shortly and to the point. "No man enjoyed so much consideration with the king that he could venture to do anything of his own will." Henry desired that "he might not wrongly be called a ruler, but be one who would rule and not be ruled."[1]

So far as a general survey of Henry's reign allows us to form an opinion, it seems clear that the more he became himself initiated into his kingly office, the more he grew independent of his councillors. One cause of this, however, was that the men whom he chiefly trusted, had preceded him to the grave.

On the 12th of October, 1500, died John Morton, the Cardinal Archbishop of Canterbury, who, in Puebla's opinion "left no statesman behind him, to be compared with him," and whom the London Chronicle extols as "a man worthi of memory for his many greate deeds, and specially for his greate wisdom, which contynued to the tyme of his descease, passyng the yeres of eighty and odd ; in his tyme was no man lyke to be compared with hym in all thynges. Albeit that he lived not withoute the greate disdain and greate haterede of the comons of this land."[2] Above all, More, who when a boy lived in the house of the cardinal, bears in his Utopia, splendid testimony to Morton's worth : he was a man "not more honourable for his authoritie, then for his prudence and vertue. He was of a meane stature, and though stricken in age, yet bare he his bodye upright. In his face did shine such an amiable reverence, as was pleasaunte to behold, gentill in communication, yet earnest, and sage. He had great delite manye times with roughe speache to his sewters, to prove, but withoute harme, what prompte witte and what bolde spirite were in every man. In the which, as in a vertue much agreinge with his nature, so

Archbishop Morton.

---

[1] P. V., 779 ; Ayala's report, July 25, 1498 : Berg., p. 178 ; Puebla's, Oct. 5, 1507 : ibid., p. 439.

[2] Puebla, Dec. 27, 1500 ; Berg., p. 251 ; City Chron., fol. 181*b*. Morton's biography in Hook, Lives of the Archbishops, vol. v., is superficial ; what is there especially ascribed to Morton is based on mere supposition.

that therewith were not joyned impudency, he toke greate delectatyon. . . . In his speche he was fyne, eloquent, and pytthye. In the lawe he had profounde knowledge, in witte he was incomparable, and in memory wonderful excellente. These qualityes, which in hym were by nature singular, he by learninge and use had made perfecte. The kynge put muche truste in his counsel, the weak publyque also in a maner leaned unto hym. For even in the chiefe of his youth he was taken from schole into the courte, and there passed all his tyme in much trouble and busines, beyng continually tumbled and tossed in the waves of dyvers misfortunes and adversities. And so by many and greate dangers he lerned the experience of the worlde, whiche so beinge learned can not easely be forgotten."[1]

Such was the man whom we first learnt to know as the most faithful of Henry's adherents in the early days of his exile, and who, soon after his accession, held, as primate and chancellor, the highest ecclesiastical and the highest secular dignity in England, and died a cardinal of the Church of Rome.

Morton's death took place on the threshold of the new century ; three years afterwards, on the 5th of August, 1503, died Sir Reginald Bray, whom Morton himself had brought into the service of Henry before his accession. It certainly is more than a mere coincidence that from this period is to be dated that decline in so many directions, which we have noticed in Henry's policy. We meet now with no new idea, for we cannot know how long beforehand the few laws passed by the Parliament of 1504 had been in preparation, during the intermission of Parliament. The Spanish and the Scotch marriage treaties were still being concluded, the subsequent marriage treaty between Charles and Mary remained therefore the one success amid a mass of hopeless and unfruitful projects ; on the other hand, it was then that Henry's almost incomprehensible action with regard to Ferdinand and Katharine began ; then that the unfortunate commercial treaty of 1506 took place with Philip. Then, too, occurred that sudden and temporary episode in the relations of England and the Hansa, when Henry for a while gave way.

---

[1] More, *Utopia*, p. 27, translated by Ralphe Robinson, 1556 (Pitt Press Series) ; cf. p. 90, orig. edit.

To this period, finally, belong the abuse and discredit of the administration of justice, when Henry allowed Empson and Dudley to rule.

All this happened after the death of Morton. The old tact and the old firmness seemed to have vanished; the evil for the most part consisted in the degeneracy of ideas that in themselves were good. Whoever may have originated these ideas, Henry had made them completely his own, although he was now mistaken in his mode of carrying them out; it is possible that this deterioration in his latter years was connected, not only with a decay of his physical, but of his mental powers.

Nothing, however, can diminish the fame of King Henry as the restorer of the English monarchy. Since William the Conqueror no power so absolute had existed in England as that which Henry bequeathed, on firmly fixed foundations, to his successors. It was not a new edifice, like that feudal sovereignty which the powerful Norman had erected in the place of the shattered Anglo-Saxon kingdom, but an arbitrary yet constitutional monarchy, constructed with consummate art, within and upon the already existing Constitution. A new epoch had begun in England—THE PERIOD OF AN ENLIGHTENED ABSOLUTISM UNDER THE TUDORS.

HENRY'S PERSONAL CHARACTER AND DEATH.

When a monarch of such individuality and force of character as the first Tudor forms the central figure of a State which is advancing by strides to a new and important position, the historian cannot fail to take an interest in that monarch's personality. The pictures of him by Mabuse and the bronze figure by Torrigiano on his tomb, depict for us Henry's form and features.[1] Neither in figure nor countenance was he handsome; his thin form was somewhat above middle height, his face was furrowed, his eyes serious, but with a soft expression. His features bear far more strongly the impress of a certain mildness of character, than of that tenacious and energetic determination which he displayed throughout life. His hair was thin, and his mouth disfigured by loss of teeth; but

Henry's outward appearance and demeanour.

---

[1] The bust in the Kensington Museum is identical with this.

when he spoke, his grave countenance, it is said, would light
up.   The cares and anxieties of his reign showed themselves
in his outward appearance ; he was old for his years, but yet
"young for the sorrowful life he has led."   As we gaze upon
him in the picture at Hampton Court Palace, in long robe,
raised on a step behind his son, who, in short doublet, stands
with outstretched legs before him, there seems something
priest-like about the appearance of the king.[1]

Yet, though cautious and deliberate in life as in his policy,
he was not always reserved.   He was of a ready wit, and
loved to make a joking *repartee*, and was quick at times in
showing pleasure or annoyance.   There was no doubt of the
impression he made on men, for the fame of his prudence and
sagacity was far more than a mere courtly compliment.
Good evidence of this is supplied by the Spaniard, Ayala,
who, conscious that the king, for all his amiable manner,
had cleverly over-reached him on commercial questions, burst
out with the half-angry words, " He is so clever in everything,
and in this matter displays it so much, that it is a miracle."

There was much judicious calculation in the manner in
which Henry showed himself to people.   He was careful to
guard his dignity, and in no way to lower it, " for he knew
that his life was observed by many, and that therefore the
sovereign must excel all others as much in wisdom as in
power."   Henry was desirous to be thought a wise and great
man ; he anxiously avoided yielding to any weakness, and
made use of every opportunity to show himself to the best
advantage.   He wished not only to make an impression, but
also that men should speak of it ; still it is possible that, in
spite of the high opinion generally formed of him, his success
in this respect fell below his somewhat lofty expectations.
Such a desire was quite in accordance with his general
monarchical policy, where it was important that the personality of the monarch should stand high in the respect and
consideration of men.

In the whole outward life of his court, as well as in his
personal demeanour, Henry kept this end in view, displaying
on State occasions his wonderful riches and magnificence.

---

[1] Possibly Bacon had this picture in his mind when he said, p. 220, " His
countenance was reverend, and a little like a churchman."

Great sums were expended on costly materials, furniture, and jewels, and he himself took pleasure in the arrangement of festivities. He instituted for these a special and solemn ceremonial, and when we read how the Church festivals, St. George's Day, Arthur's christening, his promotion to be Prince of Wales, his knighting, his wedding, and finally his obsequies were solemnised, we cannot doubt that Henry thought seriously of the dignity and solemnity of his position as king. Added to this, he kept a liberal table, and was hospitable host.[1]

In Henry's opinion, all this belonged to his calling and to his duty as king ; his own inclinations were more simple, and he was personally very frugal.[2] Still he showed himself not averse to the more serious or to the lighter joys of life. For this side of his character we have but one source of information—the king's account-book. Its dry entries, however, give us many glimpses into his private life and that of his family, and present us even with a vivid picture.

We meet there often with the names of the king's relatives, who in State affairs played a not very prominent, and at the most a passive, part. It was, indeed, asserted that the influence of Henry's mother, Margaret, upon her son had been important, but this can scarcely have extended to political matters, for although she outlived the king, she had been unable to prevent the absurd and unworthy matrimonial projects of his latter years. Within the court itself it was otherwise ; there the aged countess had an influential voice in the organisation of ceremonial, and took the lead over the king's wife, Queen Elizabeth. Yet it was to the queen, who was usually kept in the background, that the sympathies of England were directed ; her favour with the people was to be attributed in great measure to her lack of influence with the king, who, on the whole, was not beloved.[3] Their domestic life seems to have been irreproachable, and,

Court and family.

---

[1] For the accounts as to Henry's appearance and demeanour, see the personal description by an eye-witness in P. V., 779 ; also the reports of Ayala, July 25, 1498, Mar. 26, 1499, Berg., pp. 178–207 ; Puebla's, July 15, 1498, ibid., p. 154 ; André, Vita, p. 25 ; Herald's reports in Leland, iv. 204, ff.

[2] Relat., p. 46.

[3] See the Spanish reports in Berg., pp. 163, 164, 178 ; cf. Cooper, Mem. of Marg., p. 34, f., 53, f. For the following instances taken from the Privy Purse Expenses in Exc. Hist., I do not think it necessary to give separate references.

on the occasion of Arthur's death, husband and wife displayed
a certain warmth of affection.

Henry found his greatest delight in the freedom of a
country life. He was passionately fond of the chase;
ambassadors had frequently to follow his travelling
camp from place to place, and he would some- **Henry's
recreations.**
times send word to them that, if their business was
not very urgent, they might wait, as he did not wish to be
disturbed. In his last years he was more addicted to sport
than ever; in September, 1507, he was in the country hunting,
and "going from forest to forest, from one mountain to
another; he did not remain a single day quiet in the same
place."[1] He also encouraged knightly exercises among his
subjects, anxious at the same time that they should keep
up their skill in the use of arms. As there were fears of
a decline in the art of shooting with the long bow—that
national weapon with which the English excelled—he called
in the aid of legislation to keep down the price of bows,
and to restrain the use of the cross-bow, which was coming
into vogue.[2]

The capital Henry visited with reluctance, and only for
a short time together, he preferred rather the neighbourhood,
and his favourite seat was the charming palace at Sheen, the
later Richmond, where, from a slight eminence, a wide view
is obtained over a beautiful landscape of wood and meadow,
amidst which the Thames winds its way.

Sometimes Henry gave himself up entirely to those
pleasures that were congenial to him. We learn what were
the usual occupations of both king and court, besides work
and the chase, from his accurately kept account-book. From
that, too, we get to know many of the persons belonging to
the king's household; his physicians, Dr. Holand, Master
Ralf Sintclair, and Vincent Wolff, who, judging by the
amount of his salary, must have been specially skilful; and
the queen's physicians, Master Lewes and Robert Taillour.
To a good preacher the king would occasionally give a
pound: his preference for France is sometimes shown in these

---

[1] Berg., pp. 197, 428, 439; cf. Leland Coll., 243, 248; André, Ann. for 1508.
[2] 3 Hen. VII. c. 13, 19 Hen. VII. c. 2 and 4: Stat.. ii. 521, 649, f.; cf.
Relat., p. 31; Berg., p. 438.

presents, for if the preacher had the good fortune to be a native of that country, he would receive two pounds. Music was a favourite recreation with Henry and his family; he often bought instruments, organs, and also lutes, especially for the Princesses Margaret and Mary. He bestowed regular though limited salaries on minstrels and organists, as well as on the "king's pipers." For a change, the wandering musicians of the queen or the princesses, would perform before the king; and again his purse was opened freely, when on one occasion, the minstrels of the Queen of France appeared before him. He also gladly rewarded solo performers on the organ, harp, violin, or horn, as well as the trumpeters who greeted him upon the Thames, and the children who pleased him with their singing in the church or in the garden. Composers and painters, and among poets the "Walshe rymers" in particular, received substantial recognition of their works; one Spanish musician received at one time ten pounds, and an Italian poet even twenty pounds. For his library, Henry caused some books to be procured from abroad, others to be copied; the court bookseller, Quintin, was charged with the copying of the books, and their proper get-up and binding. He encouraged the new art of printing, and gave the printer Pynson an advance of ten pounds to print a mass book. Considerable sums were often paid for books; occasionally two pounds for a single book, for several together from ten to twenty pounds, and in one entry to a Frenchman, as much as twenty-five pounds. As to numbers of volumes and titles, the account-book is, unfortunately, silent; once only does it add the detail, that one Anthony Verard received six pounds for two books entitled the "Gardyn of Helth."

Lighter recreations were not neglected. Henry was fond of games of dice, and, above all, cards—which were strictly forbidden by law to the poor apprentice boys: he often lost quite substantial sums; how much he won he does not inform us. Jesters, jugglers, and clowns seem to have afforded him special amusement; when he went to any house as a guest, his host would be careful to provide for him this sort of entertainment; and if a pretty young girl danced before the king, he was ready to reward her liberally; jugglers of various kinds, skilful swimmers, conjurors, rope-dancers, and fire-eaters had to be content with less.   Henry seems to have kept a whole troop of jesters at his court ; we read of " the foolyshe duc of Lancastre," of Dego, the Spanish jester, as well as of Thomas Blackall, and Scot and Dick 'the master fools.'" These jesters received from the king their appropriate costume ; to the Spanish fool, Dego, he also presented a horse, with a saddle and bridle.   Besides jugglers and jesters, men with physical peculiarities seem to have found favour with him ; the "grete Walshe child," " Alen the litell Scottisman," "the grete woman of Flaunders ; " possibly the " Greek with a beard " might be reckoned among these.   For rare animals, such as lions, leopards, wild cats, and foreign birds, he was willing to pay, as well as for human monstrosities ; for a common nightingale he once paid a whole pound.

Thus, with the help of the royal account-book, we can take a glance into the life of the narrow court circle, and into the favourite relaxations of the monarch.   On the same pages on which are recorded large sums for political, military, and similar objects, we find, accurately entered, a bow for Prince Arthur, new hose for Prince Henry, and the wages of the royal barber.   The king's own purchases are also found, such as a weather-glass, an ornamental sword, a dagger, an artistic glass, or a silver fork.   He supported an alchymist, who practised his art within the Tower, rewarded the monk who manufactured gunpowder, and the constructor of the first paper-mill in England.   But he would pay just as much to a woman who brought him cherries and strawberries in April, to a girl who offered him flowers, or to another who supplied him with refreshment on a journey.   Many a small but interesting trait of character is here to be traced, showing, as also do his alms to the poor and injured, that the king was not wanting in kindly feeling, and through all there is that touch of humour, which we see him display in his intercourse with men.

And yet his almsgiving, especially for religious purposes, was rather the expression of his devotion to the Church, and of that piety which, in his latter years, Henry liked to exercise, in accordance with the precepts of the Church.   Amongst the persons who had

Devotion to the Church.

received presents, we find on one occasion, a heretic at
Canterbury ; this gift is said to have been a sign of Henry's
satisfaction at having himself induced him to retract.   It
would seem, however, that the wretched man was burnt after
all.   Unfortunately in this matter Henry inherited the views
of the Lancastrian kings ; and many times during his reign
heretics perished at the stake at Smithfield.   Exposure on the
pillory and other milder punishments for heresy were also
frequent.   Heroic endurance was often displayed by these
martyrs.   On the 24th of April, 1494, a woman of upwards of
eighty was burnt ; her heresies comprised nine articles ;   " and
never wold she turne from the said heresys for noon Exhor-
tacion, but in the said false and heronyous opynyons dyed."
Henry promised the Spanish ambassador that he would per-
secute with severity the Spanish Jews, who had fled to England.

A unique present was made to the king by the French
statesman, Cardinal d'Amboise, who sent over a precious
relic, the thigh-bone of St. George, enclosed in silver.   On St.
George's Day, the 23rd of April, 1505, Henry went in solemn
procession to St. Paul's, where the holy relic was displayed
before a devout multitude.   The Convocation of Canterbury,
when sitting in August, 1504, bestowed upon the king a spiritual
favour—he was to participate in all the Church's acts and
good deeds in England during his lifetime, as well as after
his death, and at the Mass in every large church, the celebrat-
ing priest was to pray for the king's salvation.[1]

The devotion of the king and his family to the Church
was shown in religious foundations of various kinds.   The
Franciscans he especially favoured.   For the Observants,
a branch of this order of friars, he founded three houses, at
Canterbury, Newcastle, and Southampton ; for another, that
of the Conventuals, three, at   Richmond, Greenwich, and
Newark.   These he evidently continued to bear in mind, for
on one occasion he made a valuable present of books to the
friars at Greenwich for their library.[2]   We hear of chapels

---

[1] Wilkins, Concilia, iii. 649; on the relic: André, Ann., p. 82; Fabian,
Abridgment, p. 688 ; on the religious persecutions: City Chron., fol. 172a (cf.
Exc. Hist., p. 117) ; also fol. 148b, f., 157, f., 160b, 175b, 178b, 181b; Fabian,
Abridgment, pp. 685–687, 689 ; Arnold, p. 40 ; Grey Friars' Chron., p. 26 ;
Berg., p. 164 ; André, Ann., 109.

[2] Grey Friars' Chron., p. 26 ; P. V., 780 (with a mistake in the order of the
foundations) ; Exc. Hist., p. 133.

founded by Henry's wife and mother. He himself built the
Savoy Hospital, near Charing Cross, in London, destined to
afford shelter for one hundred poor persons ; and in the last
year of his life he determined to erect at Bath a large
hospital, on the model of the one in Paris. For these and
similar foundations he appropriated the revenues of ecclesiastical institutions which were falling into decay, and thereby
diverted them to better uses. To John Alcock, Bishop of
Ely, he gladly gave permission to abolish an ancient nunnery,
and to found in its stead a college at Cambridge. His
mother in like manner founded Christ's and St. John's Col-
leges in the same University, and the Bishops of Lincoln and
Winchester one each at Oxford.[1]

Henry's activity both in sacred and secular building bears
testimony to his feeling and love for architecture. On the evening of the 21st of December, 1497, a fire broke out   **Henry's**
in the palace which he had built for himself at Sheen, **activity in**
and in less than three hours the greater portion of   **building.**
the building, and the whole of its valuable contents, were
destroyed. A splendid new building was at once begun, and
was almost completed by the year 1501 ; but in consequence
of the disaster the old name seems to have become distasteful
to Henry, who therefore called the place Richmond, after his
former title as earl. He also rebuilt Baynard's Castle, in
London, and took in hand alterations at the palace at
Greenwich, which he often visited.[2]

But the most splendid monument of the architecture of
the Tudor king is the chapel in Westminster Abbey that
is called by his name. At first Henry's design was to found
a chapel at Windsor, to be dedicated to the Holy Virgin, in
which he intended one day to be interred, and to which
should be attached a hospital for the support of the needy.
To this plan Pope Alexander VI. gave his consent on the
4th of October, 1494, and allowed at the same time that the
revenues of two decayed priories in the dioceses of Winchester

---

[1] For these foundations, see Rym., xii. 284, f., 653, f. ; Brown, No. 581 ;
André, Ann., p. 123 ; Stow, p. 891 ; P. V., 781 ; Reg. Brev. Julii, P. II.
tom. ii. 685 ; Cooper, Mem. of Marg., p. 33, f., 58, 135, f., esp. chaps. 9 and 10 ;
Leland, Itin., i. 24, and iv. 117.
[2] City Chron., fol. 171*b*, 182*a*, f. ; Fabian, Abridgment, pp. 686, 687 ;
Arnold, p. 40 ; Grey Friars' Chron, p. 26, f. ; Wrioth., p. 4 ; P. V., 771 ; Hall,
p. 491.

and Lincoln should be devoted for the purpose. In the matter of granting indulgences, this new chapel was to have the same privileges as the "De Scala Coeli" at Rome. The works for the king's tomb had already been begun at Windsor, when he changed his plan and removed his new foundation to Westminster. New bulls were obtained from Alexander. VI. and Julius II., and the arrangements for the chapel and hospital were drawn up in detail; other benefices were appropriated to endow it, and the new foundation was to be placed under the immediate protection of the papal chair. In January, 1503, the demolition of the surrounding buildings having been completed, the foundation-stone was laid.[1]

Then began to rise, at the east end of Westminster Abbey, the chapel of Henry VII., which was completed by the son of **Henry VII.'s** the founder, and remains to this day one of the **chapel at** most beautiful ecclesiastical buildings in London. **Westminster.** The chapel is built in the Tudor style, with its characteristic low-pitched arch, and seems in the luxuriant richness of its ornament to defy all the stricter rules of con- structive form. The principal lines of the building, which in the Gothic style stand out clearly, are here obscured by this overhanging fretwork of stone, and the architectural form is made use of for the indulgence of the most exuberant play of fancy. Yet the architect has not carried this free- dom too far. He has kept within the limits of good taste, and all is blended into a most artistic, beautiful, and har- monious whole. At the east end of the chapel stands the sarcophagus of the royal pair, brought from Windsor and completed later, on which lie the bronze figures of both the king and queen, the whole being surrounded by an iron screen.

This chapel is a splendid monument raised for himself by the founder of a dynasty, after he had successfully passed through all dangers and all struggles and established the

---

[1] The various bulls : Rym., xii. 562–566, 591, f., 644, 672, 738–740, xiii. 60– 62, 97–103 ; cf. Wilkins, Concilia, iii. 644, 645, 648, f.   On the preparations for the building, see Exc. Hist., pp. 124, 125, 127, 129, 131, 132 ; City Chron., fol., 204*b* ; Fab., Abridgment, p. 688 ; Stow, p. 875.   That for the purchase of the soil and ground £3c,000 were given (entry of Dec. 16, 1502) is of course a clerical or printer's error ; but from Oct., 1502, to June, 1505, as far as we learn, £9600 were paid for the building to the Abbot of Westminster ; to this in the will was added £5000.

security of his throne. It stands before the world as an enduring symbol in stone of the solidity and power which distinguished the new sovereignty of the Tudors.

This taste for architecture the king shared in common with his most eminent ministers, Morton and Bray. Morton was a true Maecenas. A whole series of edifices were, after his death, attributed to him, among which the most important are the archiepiscopal palaces of Canterbury and Lambeth. He also entertained the idea of converting into a harbour that arm of the sea which was gradually closing up between the island of Thanet and the mainland. Reginald Bray, who moreover had had a share in the education of Prince Arthur, was not only a patron of architecture, but himself an architect. He laid the foundation stone of the chapel at Westminster, and to him is attributed the design of that chapel, and also the rebuilding of St. George's Chapel at Windsor; the resemblance between these two edifices is no doubt striking. Bray died on the 5th of August, 1503, a few months after the laying of the foundation stone at Westminster. He had gained wealth in his official position, and had bestowed bountiful gifts on the chapel at Windsor.[1]

There were others also who vied with Henry and his ministers in this work. The London Chronicle gives us a glimpse of the munificent public spirit of wealthy citizens, who erected churches and public buildings in London and other towns. The aldermen, John Tate, Hugh Clopton, Ralph Austry, Kneysworth, and others, hereby distinguished themselves.[2]

Henry VII. had while on the throne led a life of incessant and fruitful work, and thus he soon became old beyond his years. Towards the close of the century, when he had victoriously passed through all the dangers, domestic and foreign, which had beset him on all sides, he began to get more anxious, he attached importance to gloomy prophecies, or feared some new misfortune, should

Henry's last years.

---

[1] On Morton, cf. Leland, Itin., vii. 137, 139, f. ; on Bray, ibid., i. 117 ; ii. 10 ; iv. 10, f. ; viii. 113*a*; 8th Rep. of the Dep. Keeper, p. 331 ; and the *résumé* in the Article in the Dictionary of National Biography, v. 237, f., by Thompson Cooper.

[2] City Chron., fol. 175*a*, f., 183*a* ; Fabian, Abridgment, p. 686, f. ; Stow, pp. 862, 865, f., 878, 890.

they become known among the people. His more strict observance of religious duties seems to have begun about this
time. At last his health began visibly to decline. Early in
life he had begged for dispensation from fasting, on account
of weak health; it was not until later that he became more
strict in this as in all other ordinances of the Church.[1]
On the occasion of Suffolk's rising, a rumour was circulated
that the king was in declining health and had not much
longer to live, but it is not till the first months of the year
1507 that we hear of a severe illness. Then, however, he was
in great danger. In the summer he regained his strength by
taking frequent bodily exercise; but in the following February,
attacks of gout kept him to his room at Greenwich, and it
was not till the end of March that he slowly recovered. In
June, Henry was still very weak. All idea of his getting well
again was then abandoned—in fact, he never really recovered;
and after a fresh attack, in March, 1509, all hope disappeared.

The king indeed continued to speak of his recovery, and
occupied himself with the affairs of State, but at the same
time he made preparations for his end. His last will, no
doubt made long beforehand, bears the date of the 30th of
March, 1509.[2] He desired to rest by the side of his wife,
before the high altar in his chapel at Westminster. To complete the building, he left £5000 to the abbot, and ordered
masses for his soul, the distribution of alms, and the satisfaction of the just claims of all those who might have any
grievance against him. He remembered his counsellors and
servants, the completion of his religious foundations, also the
conclusion of the most important political treaty of his last
years—the marriage of the Princess Mary with the Archduke
Charles. His mother's name headed the list of those trusted
friends who were commissioned to carry out his last will and
testament.

To appease Heaven, a last general pardon was
*Henry's death
and burial.* granted, and pilgrimages were undertaken for the
king's recovery, but the end could not be averted.

---

[1] Brown, No. 520; 1 Rep. of the Dep. Keeper, p. 77; Berg., p. 471.

[2] On Henry's illnesses, see the authorities in Lett. and Pap., i. 233 (cf. 239,
319); Berg., pp. 408, 439; André, Ann., pp. 108, 113; Brown, No. 906 (cf.
Berg. p. 457, 460); Lett. and Pap., i. 362; Brown, No. 939, p. 945, cf. 941.

[3] Published by Astle, London, 1775.

On the 21st of April, 1509, in his fifty-third year, Henry VII. died at his beloved Richmond.[1]

On the 8th of May, a Tuesday, his body was brought by land along the south bank of the Thames to London. In the gloom of the evening, lighted up by countless torches, the long procession passed in mournful state over London Bridge. In front rode the sword-bearer and the vice-chamberlain of the town, and among the great crowd that followed them were the trumpeters and minstrels of the king, the foreign merchants, and officials of the court. The sheriffs and aldermen each carried two white roses in their hands, on horseback came two heralds-at-arms, a knight on a horse with black trappings with the king's standard, dignitaries of the Church, and the chief justices of the royal courts of law. The friars walked along chanting, with the canons of London, and the choir of the king's chapel. The lords followed them on horseback, the temporal lords on the left, the spiritual lords on the right. Sir David Owen carried a steel helmet with a gold crown upon it; Sir Edward Howard wore the king's armour, with an open vizor, in his hand the battle-axe, the head bent downward resting on his stirrup; one knight displayed on rich armour the arms of England. Alone, in front of the car, with his mace in his hand, rode the Lord Mayor of London.

Seven large horses, with trappings of black velvet, drew the car, on which lay an effigy of the deceased king, clothed in his rich robe of state, with the crown on his head, the sceptre and golden ball in either hand. Over it rose a canopy of cloth of gold. At the side of each horse marched a knight, and four lords at the side of the car, each one with a banner in his hand. Then followed the knights of the garter, according to their rank, one lord, five earls, and three barons, led by the Duke of Buckingham; esquires bore the swords and caps sent by the successive popes; Sir Thomas Brandon, the Master of the Horse, led a horse, with velvet trappings

---

[1] P. V., 779; Fabian, Abridgment, p. 690; Brown, No. 943, 945; cf. 944; Hall, p. 504, and the Grey Friars' Chron., p. 29, give the 22nd, an information from Rome, the 20th, Brown, No. 942. The 21st is certain as the date; cf. also Leland, Coll. iv. 303. Zurita, vi. 193*a*, adds that the death was kept secret till the leading men of the kingdom should have assembled. The following description of the funeral ceremonies is taken from the Herald's report in Leland, as above, pp. 303-309; some extracts from the Grey Friars' Chron., p. 29.

on which were the arms of England; Lord Darcy rode at
the head of the body-guard; gentlemen, members of the trade
guilds, and others in great numbers, formed the remainder of
the procession.

At the west doors of St. Paul's Church, where the Bishop
of London was waiting in full canonicals, the procession
paused.

Amidst clouds of incense, twelve men of the guard lifted
the heavy coffin with the effigy lying on it, from the car, the
Duke of Buckingham and five earls walked at the side and
laid their hand on the coffin, four barons held a rich canopy
over it, till it was set down before the high altar. After a
solemn dirge by the Bishop of London, the procession left the
church, and knights and heralds kept guard over the corpse.
On the following day three masses were sung, and the Bishop
of Rochester preached. About one o'clock, after the midday
meal, the coffin was borne out of the church, and the procession went in the same order as on the previous day,
through Fleet Street to Charing Cross, where the Abbot of
Westminster, with three abbots and the monks of the abbey
stood, and incensed the corpse. In the same way it was
received at the west door of the abbey by the Archbishops
of Canterbury and York, whilst the Abbey Church was lighted
up with a costly and curious light. Here also knights kept
guard by the coffin throughout the night.

On Thursday, the 10th of May, took place the interment.
After three masses had been celebrated, and a solemn requiem
by the Archbishop of Canterbury, the offerings were made
with befitting solemnity; four heralds received the king's
coat of mail, shield, sword, and the crowned helmet; then
Sir Edward Howard rode in full armour, but without a
helmet, into the church, sprang from his saddle, and,
led by the earls of Kent and Essex, stepped up to the
archbishop before the altar; two monks then led him into
the sacristy, where he took off his armour. He appeared
again in a black garment, and presented his offering, whereupon all, according to their rank, followed him with their
gifts. Meanwhile the Duke of Buckingham and the knights
accompanying him, carried in palls with slow and solemn
step, and spread them over the catafalque. The Bishop of

London preached the sermon ; then they raised the image of the king from the bier, and the choir chanted the psalm, " Circumdederunt me gemitus mortis." Again the corpse was incensed, and the insignia were taken from the coffin, upon which lay, on black velvet, a large cross in white satin.

Thus they bore King Henry to the vault. The prelates pronounced the absolution, the Archbishop of Canterbury threw earth upon the coffin, the Lord Treasurer and the Lord Steward broke their staves and threw them into the vault, and the other state officials did the same. The vault was then closed, and a pall of cloth of gold was spread over it. But the heralds took their tabards from their shoulders, and hung them on the railing round the catafalque, and cried out in French the lamentation, " The noble King Henry VII. is dead ! " Then they put their tabards on again, and with loud voices uttered the joyful cry, " Long live the noble King Henry VIII ! "

A new reign had begun.

APPENDIX I.

———◦◦———

NOTES.

INTRODUCTION AND CHAPTER 1.

1 (*to page* 10).—On the question of the murder of Edward's sons, I content myself with referring to Mr. Gairdner's exhaustive discussion, Rich. III., pp. 152–164, and to Pauli, Geschichte von England, v. 483–487. The recent attempt to rehabilitate Richard, made by A. D. Legge, The Unpopular King, ii. 42, ff., is quite superficial, and the author's account of the history of Henry of Richmond at that period is full of mistakes. The essay in the Eng. Hist. Rev., vi. (1891), pp. 250–253, by Markham, who endeavours not only to clear Richard completely, but even to stamp Henry VII. as the murderer, is quite unsuccessful. His allegations have been satisfactorily refuted, and, moreover the extreme partiality shown in his researches has been pointed out by Gairdner, ibid., pp. 444–464. I found no occasion in the further course of the history to return to Markham's essay. Markham's reply (as above, pp. 806–813), and Gairdner's rejoinder (ibid., 813–815), prove still more strongly that the former's hypotheses are quite untenable.

2 (*to page* 13).—On the place and day of Henry's birth, see André, Vita, Hen. VII., in Memorials, p. 12 ; cf. the Pref. xxiv., and Cooper, Memoir of Margaret, p. 10. The date is questionable. André gives as the day of birth " dies Sanctæ Agnetis secundæ," *i.e.* Jan. 28 ; but previously the date "Februarii kalend. decimo septimo," *i.e.* Jan. 16. A mistake in the date of the saint's day seems less probable than in the foreign Roman calendar; the difficulty cannot be solved otherwise; cf. Gairdner, Hen. VII., p. 3. A local tradition quotes another place of birth : Leland, Itinerary, v. 6.— That Henry was a posthumous child is noticed in a speech delivered before Henry VII. when he visited the University of Cambridge : " Mater deinde viro orbata te peperit orphanum," in Lett. and Pap., i. 422 ; the speech had already been printed in full in Leland,

Itinerary, ii. 156–164 ; cf. on the subject, Cooper, as above, p. 10, ff. ;
Gairdner, in Memorials, Pref. xxiv., note; and Hen. VII., p. 3, f.—
André says he heard the commendation of Henry from Andreas
Scotus himself: Vita, as above, p. 13; Leland mentions the Dean of
Warwick (Itinerary, viii. p. 29) when noting those interred in the
church at Warwick. In the Privy Purse Expenses are entered on
July 9, 1495, £2 for the king's schoolmaster : Excerpta Historica, p. 103.—On the meeting with Henry VI., see Pol. Vergil, p.
662, f.; André Vita, p. 14.—On Henry's flight to Brittany, and the
efforts made by Edward IV. and Louis XI. for his surrender: Pol.
Verg., 674 and 676; André, Vita, 17 and 23. Letter of Sir John
Paston, Sept. 28, 1471 (the rumour alluded to in it of Pembroke's
surrender was not realised); Paston Letters, iii. 17; Morice, Memoires, iii. 266–270 ; Lett. and Pap., i. 39–41 ; cf. Dupuy, Hist. de
la réun. de la Bret., i. 41.

3 (*to page* 14).—On Buckingham's connection with Morton, Pol.
Verg. gives only a few short notices, p. 697, but these go to the root
of the matter ; Hall's Chron., pp. 382–390, gives the words on both
sides in the fullest detail. In the first part (to p. 384, line 5), Hall
agrees word for word with More, Hist. of Kyng Rycharde III., pp.
88–91, which last breaks off abruptly at the words, "as our Lorde
hath planted in the parsone of youre grace." It is quite inadmis-
sible that Hall—who, however, elsewhere indulges in amplification of
details—should have invented this long continuation, which joins on
so well with the first part. We know that More's account is derived
from none other than Morton himself, in whose house More lived
in his early youth, and who, if we follow a tradition originating with
More himself, had a great regard for him (see More's Life, by his
son-in-law, Roper, p. 3, f.). George Buck—otherwise not much to be
relied on ("The History of Rich. III., 1646—an attempt at justification ")—makes a statement, which is quite possible, that Morton had
"written a Booke in latine (this Booke was lately in the hands of
Mr. Roper of Eltham, as Sir Edward Hoby, who saw it, told me
against King Richard, which came afterwards to the hands of Mr.
Moore (sometimes his servant)." According to this, More's account
rested on a written testimony handed down from Morton himself.
But we must reject the first idea which occurs, that Hall in his continuation made use of the same source, for Hall, in his list of
authorities, mentions, not Morton, but More ; so we are led to the
assumption that More's work went further in manuscript than we
have it in print, and that Hall made use of it in this form, as did
also Pol. Verg., but much shortened. For a further account of the

intrigue, which is, indeed, to be traced back to the same source, see P. V., 697–699 ; Hall, pp. 390-392. The two differ only in this, that, according to P. V., p. 697, f., Margaret entered independently into communication with Elizabeth, and, according to Hall, p. 390, not till she had heard of a similar plan of Buckingham's. As Margaret was the originator of the whole plan, I have not hesitated to follow Pol. Verg. ; a more certain conclusion cannot, of course, be arrived at. Cf. also André, Vita, p. 24, who, however, puts Henry's first and second enterprises together, and makes also other incorrect assertions. The respective claims to the throne of Henry and of his mother Margaret are touched upon first by Hume, iii. 300, then more clearly stated by Pauli, v. 521 ; cf. also Halsted, Life of Marg., 163, f.

Gairdner mentions, in Lett. and Pap., ii. Pref. xxx., f., that Henry probably did not know of the Act of Legitimation for his House ; cf. earlier, Nicolas, Mem. of Eliz. of York, in Privy Purse Exp. of Eliz., p. lx. Buckingham's cousin, condemned in 1521, certainly knew of it. Confession and deposition of the Duke's Chancellor in Brewer, Lett. and Pap. of Henry VIII., iii. 1, p. 494 ; Baga de Secretis, 231 ; cf. Gairdner, as above, xxx., note 3.—For the negotiations between Richard III. and Duke Francis, see the English instructions, July 13, 1483, Rymer, xii. 194 ; Morice, iii. 430, f.— The duke's instructions, Aug. 26, Lett. and Pap., i. 39–41 ; also see P. V., 699. André mentions the marriage project, Vita, p. 37 ; only he erroneously places it before Henry's second expedition from France. It was therefore not mere bombast when Henry affirmed, in his subsequent petition for the papal dispensation for his marriage with Elizabeth of York, that he was in a position to be able to conclude instead an advantageous foreign marriage.—Richard's proclamation of Oct. 23, 1483 : Ellis, Origin. Lett., ii. 1, p. 160 ; Rym., xii. 204, f.—P. V., whose account, p. 701, f., I have followed on the whole, gives, as the place where Henry touched the coast, Poole harbour, the Parliam. Bill of Attainder, Rotuli Parliam., vi. 245, and Contin. Croyland, 570, say, on the other hand, Plymouth.

4 (*to page* 19).—Gairdner, Rich. III., pp. 274–280, gives another account of the action of Rice ap Thomas, grounded on a family tradition which was written down quite a century later, under James I. (in Cambrian Register, pp. 81–112). This account tries very circumstantially to represent the Welshman as loyal throughout in his conduct towards the king ; but an original document cited —a letter to Richard III. (p. 86, f.)—actually shows that he made

Y

the same and equally unreliable promises of loyalty to the other side; besides, the letter is placed too early, before Buckingham's insurrection, although it bears the date 1484. The events not exactly concerning the hero himself are related from Hall, and include also the points in which he differs from Pol. Verg. Pol. Verg.'s simpler account is to be preferred to this family story, with its decided bias.

5 (*to page* 21).—Hutton, Battle of Bosworth, gives a very careful and also very full account, with good knowledge of the locality, but makes use of very unreliable material and traditions, and adds much gratuitous matter. Equally exact in the description of the neighbourhood, but just as unreliable in its statements, is Burgess's The Last Battle of the Roses. At the beginning is printed a highly-coloured and poetical account of the battle by Saville, and one in verse by Drayton, both without historical value. The latest description is given by Gairdner, Rich. III, p. 292, ff., based, in a great measure, on Hutton, whom he at the same time improves upon. Of the original authorities, Pol. Verg. has the simplest and most reliable account, 713–715; cf. City Chron., fol. 141; Fabian's Abridgment, 673.

6 (*to page* 23).—The date, according to the manuscript City Chron., fol. 141, which agrees with André (Vita, Mem., 34), who calls the day a Saturday. Fabian's Abridgment, p. 673, gives by a mistaken reading which is easily accounted for, the 28th. Gairdner's Hen. VII., p. 32, f., and the article, Hen. VII. in Nat. Biogr., xxvi. p. 71, give Sept. 3, from the short and unarranged notices, which are to be found in a manuscript in the British Museum, Harl., 541, fol. 217*b*–219*b*, but are not very reliable (see on the subject, Appendix II.). Furthermore, the notice only says that Henry came to the town on Sept. 3. This had to do with a second visit; otherwise the slowness of the journey from Bosworth to London cannot be explained. In any case, the accounts that are based on Fabian's London Chronicle should be preferred to the short and almost chance information of some unknown person (see on the subject, Appendix II.). That another visit did take place on Sept. 3, appears from the decision of the London Common Council of Aug. 31 on the reception of the king by the Lord Mayor, aldermen and guilds (Campb., Materials, i. 4–6), which generally took place on the occasion of the king's visits to the city.—The peculiar statement in Bacon's Hist. Hen. VII. (edit. by Lumby, p. 11), founded upon a misapprehension of André's words, that Henry made his entry in a closed carriage, has hitherto been generally accepted, and is always specially noted (latest by Pauli, p.

522). This mistake has been discovered and corrected by Gairdner (Mem., Pref. xxv., f.; Hen. VII., p. 33).

7 (*to page* 24).—A detailed description of the sweating sickness is given by P, V., 720, f.; after him Hall, 425, f.; shorter notices in the manuscript City Chronicle, fol. 141*a*; Fabian's Abridgment, 673; Stow, p. 860; Arnold's Chronicle, p. 38; Grey Friars' Chron., p. 24; Wriothesley's Chronicle, p. 1.; Ricart's Calendar, p. 46, f. On the nature of the disease see the earlier researches of Hecker, Volkskrankheiten des Mittelalters, and the shorter accounts in Hirsch, Handbuch der Hist. Geogr. Pathol., i. Abt. (2nd edit.), also my remarks in the Hist. Taschenbuch, vi. 8, p. 319. In the year 1551, the disease appeared for the last time and then disappeared for ever. Stow, p. 860, and Bacon, p. 12, give the 21st, the City Chronicle the 27th of September as the day when it began. As here Bacon probably used Fabian's Chronicle independently of the other known sources (see Appendix II.), the account of two witnesses stands in opposition to the City Chronicle; probably the latter contains a clerical error. When in Fabian's Abridgment, p. 673, the 11th of October is given as the date of the outbreak, it is probably a confusion with the day of its disappearance. As all these accounts are to be traced back to Fabian's London Chronicle, they only hold good for London; in the country the disease probably broke out earlier; Pol. Verg at least says, "sub primum in insulam descensum." In any case it had by no means died out over the greater part of England by the middle of October, for the abbot of the monastery of Croyland died of it on Nov. 14, 1485; Cont. Croyl., p. 570.

8 (*to page* 28).—On the first Parliament, its transactions and measures, see Rotuli Parliamentorum, vi. 267–384, especially 269, 270, 278, 287, f. Statutes of the Realm, ii. 499–508; Campb., i. 110 to 149, 209, f., especially 115, 119, f., 209, f. Contemporary reports of Gigli to Pope Innocent VIII., Dec. 6, 1485, Brown, Cal. of State Papers, Venet, i. No. 506; Campb., i. 198, f. Betanson to Plumpton, Dec. 13, and Feb. 15, Plumpton Corresp., p. 48, f.; P. V., 718, makes a short allusion to the Parliament, but in the wrong place; the sequence of facts is here especially confused by him; the events mentioned after the summoning of Parliament belong to the time before it, and indeed to before the coronation. It is a mistake of Hall's, p. 429, to take "domesticum senatum" in P. V., p. 720, as meaning the Parliament; whereas it is obvious, from P. V.'s own remark, that the Privy Council, called on p. 719 "consilium domi," is meant. See also André, Vita, 37. The Parliament sat in two sessions, extending, with a pause between them, from

Dec. 10, 1485, to Jan. 23, 1486 (see Rot. Parl., 278). No notice of
the resumption and final conclusion of the discussions is given; as
however, according to the dates of his writs, Henry remained in
London till the middle of March (see the decrees in Campb., i. to
p. 387, the last dated Mar. 13), probably the close of the session
took place at that time, for, except for this, Henry would certainly
not have put off his journey to the north, which was urgent; cf.
Plumpton Corresp., p. 50. The Parliament Rolls give no particulars as to the distribution of the various measures between the
two sessions. The actual measures themselves of this Parliament
will be treated more fully in the last chapter.

9 (*to page* 30).—The date of Henry's marriage in Hall, 424, f.,
and Brit. Mus., Harl. MSS., 541, fol. 218*a*; also André, Vita, Mem.,
38, f.; Fabian's Abridgment, 683; Ricart's Calendar, 47; papal
bull of Mar. 2, 1486, and recognition of the legate's dispensation,
July 23, Rym., xii. 294, f. 313, f.; Du Mont., Corps Diplom., iii.
2, p. 151, 154, f.; Campb., i. 337. The assertion that Henry was
not pleased at the general rejoicing (cf. Pauli, 528, f.), and especially
that he allowed his dislike to the House of York to affect his married
life, is a gratuitous supposition of Bacon's (p. 19) which has, unfortunately, passed into history.—Bull of March 27, in Rym., xii. 297–
299; Campb., i. 392–398. The altered English text, in which the
bull was published in England, in Camd. Misc., i.; cf. the outline
of a speech of the English ambassador to the Pope, in Lett. and
Pap., i. 421.

10 (*to page* 31).—André gives the date of Arthur's birth: Vita,
Mem., p. 41; the notices in the manuscript in Brit. Mus., Harl.,
541; fol. 218*b* give the Tuesday before Michaelmas; that would be
Sept. 26, when Arthur had already been baptized. Arnold, p. 28,
and after him the Grey Friars' Chron., p. 24, place the event in the
third instead of the second year of Henry's reign; Wriothesley, p. i.,
corrects this, but names the place wrongly Windsor, also P. V.,
722; Hall, 428; Fabian's Abridgment, 683. On the christening, see
the account in Leland, Collect., iv. 204–207; Stow's memoranda, p.
104, f.; cf. Cooper, Mem. of Margaret, 34, f.

11 (*to page* 34).—Lett. and Pap., i. 91–93, is an undated instruc-
tion printed from a manuscript in the Brit. Mus., Cotton MS., Titus
B., xi. fol. 13, for John Estrete's negotiations with Kildare. The editor,
Gairdner (cf. his Pref. xxxi., and Hen. VII., p. 49, f.), as Ware,
Rer. Hibern. Ann., p. 5, f., did before him, places it at the beginning
of Henry's reign, 1486. On the other hand, the catalogue of Cotton
Manuscripts, followed by Bagwell, Ireland under the Tudors, i. p. 103,

note 2, places it still earlier, in the time of Richard III. The arguments Bagwell brings forward, however, will not bear examination ; it
is quite explicable that a reference should have been made to Edward
IV., especially in dealing with the Irish ; moreover, Henry, later on,
at the conclusion of the peace of Etaples with France, pointed out
that his policy was an exact continuation of that of Edward IV.
Estrete, who certainly was in Ireland even in Richard III.'s time
(20th Report of the Dep. Keep. of Pub. Rec. in Ireland, App. 7, p.
99), remained there under Henry VII. (ibid., 99, f. ; Campb., i. 365,
ii. 155, 348).—But the tenor of this instruction bears unmistakable
reference to three letters from the Earl of Kildare and his friends to
Henry VII. (Lett. and Pap., i. 377-382), dated, without giving the
year, the 4th and 5th of June, and 10th of July. In them reference
is made to a royal letter of the 28th of July in the preceding year,
with which we are unacquainted, but in their contents the letters
give the answer to the orders issued by the king in the undated
instruction, that Kildare must appear before him not later than on
or before the following 1st of August. Further reference is made in the
instruction to letters of safe-conduct sent at the same time to the
earl ; we have, however, a pardon for Kildare, dated July 29, 1490
(Lett. and Pap., ii. 371), for all offences against the law, if he
appeared in England within ten months. A better chain of evidence
can hardly be wished for ; according to this the undated instruction
falls in the last days of July, 1490 ; it is quite usual that an instruction and some sort of document to accompany it (here the royal
letter of the 28th and the pardon of July 29,) should differ in
date by several days. Add to this that according to the Irishmen's
letters, that royal document of July 28 was written at Westminster, but
then, according to other decrees (see Campb.), Henry was not at Westminster at the end of July in the years 1486-1489; but in 1490 it can
be proved, at least, that he was still there on July 11 (Bergenroth,
Cal. of State Pap., i. p. 47). The three Irish letters therefore are in
any case, to be placed in the year 1491, as Gairdner assumes (as
above, ii. Pref. xxxvi.), correcting his earlier view (i. 377). Ware, as
above, had also assumed 1486 as the date. In this most satisfactory accordance, fixing the date almost to a certainty, there exists
no doubt, one difficulty, that in the pardon of July 29, 1490, the
term for Kildare's appearance is fixed at ten months, but in the
instruction by the mention of the 1st of August, at a whole year.
Possibly Henry may have wished to leave greater freedom of action
to the ambassador, or it may be there is some inaccuracy in the
writing ; in any case the discrepancy is not sufficient to upset the

evidence already collected, which is of importance, because according to it, Henry did not interfere in Ireland soon after his accession, but only considerably later, and the first occasion for such interference was supplied by Ireland itself, through its participation in the Simnel insurrection.

12 (*to page* 37).—The description here given of the insurrection which bears the name of Lambert Simnel differs in essential points from earlier ones. Unfortunately, Gilbert, Hist. of the Viceroys, 425, f., in his circumstantial account of the origin of the movement, supplies none of the grounds for his statements. Besides, his description (p. 427 ff., cf. p. 605 note) with its curiously Irish bias, arouses in the reader's mind the suspicion that the author wishes the genuineness of Simnel's claim to appear not impossible. The traditional narrative makes the priest Simon the centre of the plot at its origin ; Ware, Ann., p. 6, f. 9, makes his intrigues and those of Lincoln, Lovell and Margaret begin at first separately and independently, and then join together later on. That which seems more probable from internal evidence—viz. the oneness of this movement which, originating in the Yorkist party, displayed itself at first in various places, then united into simultaneous action, is supported by the various Acts of Attainder passed in the Parliament, which mention Lincoln, make the rising appear throughout as his work, and name him especially as the man who caused Simnel to be crowned in Dublin; " caused oone Lambert Symnell . . . to be proclamed . . . as Kynge of this Realme," Rot. Parl., vi. 397, cf. 436, f. 545. From this it is clear that these intrigues were already at work on Jan. 1, 1487. On Lovell's flight from England, see Paston Lett., iii. 329, Jan. 24, 1487 ; also P. V., 726, makes Lovell escape before Lincoln. —That Simnel was the son of an organ-builder is stated in the report of Convocation in Wilkins, Concilia, iii. 618, and in the account in the Carew Pap., p. 472 ; in Rot. Parl., vi. 397, is said of him, " Sonne to Thomas Symnel, late of Oxford Joynoure," in André, Vita, 49 ; "filium pistoris sive sutoris;" cf. Ware, p. 6. On the support which Simnel found in Ireland, is to be noted the letter of the Archbishop of Armagh, which, no doubt, is not objective, Lett. and Pap., i. 383, f. ; also the Book of Howth, in Carew Pap., p. 388; and Misc., p. 472, f. ; cf. Ware, p. 6 ; on the attitude of Waterford, see Carew Pap., 473. It is also remarkable that Simnel is regarded by Molinet, his French contemporary, Chroniques, iii. 152–156, as the genuine Warwick. We probably possess in Molinet's whole poetical and imaginative account a picture of how the event was described in the rumours circulating from mouth to mouth at the time.

The date of the sitting of the Council at Sheen in Leland, Coll., iv. 208; the sentence on the Queen Dowager in Campb., ii. 148, f.; 319; cf. 225, 273, 296, 322, 392, 555, 560. The suggestion of a voluntary resolve on the part of the queen, in Pauli, 536; against the above expressed assumption that this sentence was passed upon Elizabeth on account of her connection with the Yorkist rising: Nicolas, Privy Purse Exp., lxxvii. ff.; Halsted, Marg. Beauf., 172; Lingard, v. 389 f., Pauli, as above. Against this, see Bacon, p. 24, and the old account is very precise; S. W., The Hist. of the Two Impostors. It should be mentioned that Legge, ii. 51, discovers in Henry's behaviour to the queen dowager a proof that he believed another son of Edward's to be still in existence.

On the landing of Lincoln and the mercenaries in Ireland, see a letter of Henry's to Ormond, May 13, Ellis i., i. p. 18, f.; Halliwell, i. 171; Ellis incorrectly connects this letter, which has no date of the year, with Perkin Warbeck; cf. also Nicolas, as above, lxx. Henry's journey in P. V., 726, f., supported by the despatches in Campb., ii. 134–140; P. V. is only incorrect in making Henry celebrate Christmas instead of Easter at Norwich; also it is impossible that Henry should, according to Campbell, 140, be at Greenwich on April 24, when he was staying at Coventry from the 26th on; cf. Campb., as above, to p. 160; Leland, Coll., iv. 209.—Communications from Lord Howth to the king: Book of Howth, Carew Pap., p. 188, f.; cf. Ware, p. 7. Landing of the rebels in England: Rot. Parl., vi. 397; royal command to the army: Leland, Coll., iv. 210–212; Battle of Stoke: Rot. Parl., 397; Book of Howth, Car. Pap., p. 189; the notices, Harl. MS., 541, fol. 218*b*, give the day July 16; Ware, p. 12, June 20.

Lord Lovell is mentioned by P. V., 729, Hall, 439, among the slain; the decidedly more reliable account in the Herald's report in Leland, Coll., iv. 212–215, cf. Ware, p. 12. Lovell's attainder was first passed retrospectively in Henry's fifth Parliament, 1495, and this remarkable reason adduced "in the which Acte of Atteyndre the seid Francis Lovell was ignorauntly lefte out and omitted." Statutes, ii. 630, f.; Rot. Parl., vi. 502, f.; cf. Pauli, p. 542, note 1. Other punishments: P. V., 730; cf. Plumpton Corr., 54, f.; Commission to Waterford, Oct. 24, 1487: Carew Pap., p. 467; Ware, p. 14; also copied in Ryland, Hist. of Waterford, 26–28; and under date Oct. 20, in Smith, Antient and Present State of Waterford, p. 133, f.

The papal bulls and correspondence about them: July 5, Aug. 6, 1487, Jan. 5, 1488: Lett. and Pap., i. 94–96; Brown, No. 519; Wilkins' Concilia, iii. 621–623; Rym., xii. 324, f., 332–334; Ware,

p. 16; reconfirmation of the bull of Aug. 6, by Alexander VI. on July 5, 1493; Rym., 541, f.; another bull on May 16, 1488; Rym., 341–343. Extension of the power of absolution, July 15, 1495; Rym., 573, f.; cf. the apologetic letter of the Archbishop of Armagh, Lett. and Pap., 383, f.—See the whole account of Simnel's insurrection in P. V., 723–729; Hall, 428–435; Leland, Coll., iv. 209–215; Ware, p. 6, f., 9–13; André, Vita, 49–52; the latter is inexact, according to him Simnel appeared as the second son of Edward; of foreign contemporary accounts, see besides Molinet, as above, Weinreich's Danziger Chronik in Script., Rer. Pruss., iv. 763, 764.

To Chapter II.

1 (*to page* 41).—Details on the war between France and Brittany, see in Dupuy, Hist. de la réunion de la Bretagne (1880); Pelicier. Gouvernement de la Dame de Beaujeu (1882); De Maulde-la-Clavière, Hist. de Louis XII., vol. ii. (1890). England's part in this conflict is described in all these works in a very inadequate way, by no means commensurate with its importance in regard to the later relations between England and France.

2 (*to page* 46).—First offers to Brittany: Puebla's report, Oct. 11, 1488, Berg., i. No. 25. Powers of Dec. 11 to the various ambassadors: Campb., ii. 376–378; Rym., xii. 347–355; Berg., i. No. 28; Gigli's report on Henry's words, Jan. 28, 1489: Brown, i. No. 550; the orders for mustering troops of Dec. 23: Rym., xii. 355–357; Campb., ii. 384–387; in January: 37th Rep. of the Dep. Keeper, App. ii., p. 117; order to levy troops of Feb. 12, 1489: Rym. xii. 358; arrangements about war material: Campb., ii. 395. Directions, dated Jan. 26 and Feb. 25 to the master of the ordnance and the captain, Sir John Cheney, about payments, in the Record Office. Opening of Parliament, Rot. Parl., vi. 409, where, by mistake, the years 1488–1489 are given for the three sessions of Parliament instead of 1489–1490; vote of the clergy: Wilkins, iii. 626, 630; Campb., ii. 424, f., 452; see especially Gigli's report, Brown, No. 550; vote of the laymen: Rot. Parl., 420–424; City Chronicle, fol. 143*a*; Fabian's Abridgment, 683; cf. also the law, Stat., ii. 528–530. Pauli, v. 550, is wrong when he thinks that only £75,000 altogether were voted for the king in answer to his demand for £100,000, whereas it was only a question of the distribution of the levy.

3 (*to page* 48).—Northumberland's appointment: Rotuli Scot., ii. 470, f., 484, f.; Campb., i. 199, 242, ii. 240; also on the revolt, P. V., 735; Hall, 442, f., after Fabian, with additions; Campb., ii. 443, 444, f., 447, f.; Plumpton Corres., 61; Paston Lett., iii. 359–361; Brown, i. No. 553; Leland, Coll., iv. 246; account in *Gentleman's Magazine*, new series, xxxvi. (1851), pp. 463–468. Hall, and the City Chronicle, fol. 143, call the leader, John "of" or "a" Chambre; Fabian's Abridgment, p. 683, probably misled by a name following soon after, says Chamberlayne. André, Vita, p. 47–49, places the rising before Simnel's; he also sang of the death of Northumberland in a long ode. The news of it had travelled far, as is shown by Weinreich's Dantzic Chronicle, which is pretty correct as to date, Rer. Pruss. Scrip., iv. 774.

4 (*to page* 48).—Pauli, v. 549, had already rightly perceived that Henry was only drawn into the war against his own will. When Pauli wrote, the treasures in the archives of Simancas had not yet been disclosed, by means of which we can see what were the motives that actuated Henry at that time. Being in difficulties to find reasonable general grounds for this policy of war, Pauli thought he would seek them in a demand on the part of the nation, especially as Bacon, whom he frequently follows, had already hinted it (p. 52; cf. 59, f.). In the same way, Dupuy's statements rest solely on Bacon, and are, moreover, greatly exaggerated (ii. 163).—When Henry, in the treaty with Brittany, speaks of his aims at conquests on his own account in France, and even of his claims on the crown, this must not be taken as the motive for his action; utterances such as these were with him at that time, as well as later, mere empty phrases.

5 (*to page* 50).—The English powers to Spain of March 10, 1488: Rym., xii. 336, f.; Berg., No. 13; Campb., ii. 273. Spanish reply: Berg., i. Nos. 14–16. Agreement in London, July 7, 1488: Berg., i. No. 20; also Puebla's report, July 15, ibid., No. 21. As there is no mention in the first powers to the English ambassador of a marriage treaty, and as it is mentioned for the first time in the Spanish power of April 30, 1488, it would appear as if the first overtures were made by Spain. But a passage in Puebla's report (p. 6) specially confirms what would besides appear as the most natural thing, and states that the Spanish plenipotentiaries demanded of the English that they ought first to name the amount of the dowry, "as they had first proposed the marriage."— Here I take the opportunity to mention Hepworth Dixon's History of Two Queens, about the three first volumes of which I can only

repeat the opinion I have expressed elsewhere (Hist., Taschenbuch,
vi. 8, p. 286, note) on the second half. It is a very disappointing
book—too much of a romance to be worth anything as a work of
history, and yet too historical for a novel; in any case, it presents
such a reckless mixture of truth and fiction, that we must from the
outset give up all idea of getting any details from it.

6 (*to page* 54).—Powers for Savage and Nanfan of December
11, 1488, Rym., xii. 353-355; Campb., ii, 376; Berg., i. No. 28.
Herald's report: Mem., p. 157-199, short extract in Berg., i. No. 33;
the arrival of the ambassadors is also mentioned in Zurita, v., fol.
358*b*. Text of the treaty of March 27, 1489, in Du Mont, iii. 2, pp.
219-224, and, in the later execution by Henry on Sept. 20, 1490, in
Rym., xii. 420-428, Abstract in Berg., No. 34. The treaty contains a
clause which still left it free to either party to join or not in the war,
if, on the day the treaty was concluded, the 27th March, hostilities
between England and France should not yet have begun. Apparently
the Spaniards assumed that they had begun already, whereas they
did not begin until April. To this clause Mr. Gairdner (Henry VII.,
p. 92) attaches, in my opinion, too much *practical* importance. As a
whole, this article was a highly sophistical composition, and had for
its real object to postpone as long as the truce lasted, that is, till the
year 1490, the Spaniards' participation in the war already opened by
Henry in April. However, I must acknowledge that Mr. Gairdner
is justified in finding fault with me (Hist. Rev. viii. 353) for having
hitherto ignored the clause, and I alter, accordingly, the view I previously held.—With regard to the setting Guienne and Normandy
against Roussillon and Cerdagne, be it observed that the striking
contrast quite escapes Pélicier, who speaks of "les mêmes conditions" (p. 153, f.); on the other hand, see Mr. Gairdner's apposite
remark, p. 92.

7 (*to page* 59).—Maximilian's power, Ulm, May 22, 1490, in
Rym., xii. 393, f., the treaties of Sept. 11 and 13, ibid., pp. 397-407,
403-405; Du Mont, iii. 2, pp. 254-258; and Godefroy, Hist. de
Charles VIII., pp. 605 to 609; Henry's ratification: Rym., pp. 405-
410; cf. 45th Report of the Dep. Keeper, App. i., p. 338, f. Sending
the Order of the Garter, Rym., p. 403. Proclamations: ibid., 410, f.
—The negotiations with Spain: Berg., pp. 27, 29; ratificaion of
the treaty of Medina del Campo, Sept. 23, 1490: Rym., 417-429;
Berg., Nos. 53, 55; Berg. gives the date Sept. 20. Power for the
envoys bringing it over, dated Sept. 23, 1490: Rym., 429; Berg.,
No. 56. The two proposed alterations: Rym., 411, 412; Berg., No.
54, and Rym., 413-417; Du Mont, 260-262; Berg., No. 62.

Pauli, v. 554, misunderstands the proposals; he thinks that they express the concurrence of the Spanish sovereigns in Henry's treaty with Maximilian, which is certainly not the case. Possibly the tenor of the proclamation of the two treaties, printed just before in Rymer, led him into this error.—In Gairdner, Henry VII., p. 94, f., it is not put clearly enough that Henry was only making *proposals* for a treaty, though he was careful beforehand to communicate them to his ambassador in the form of a treaty fully executed on one side. Also, Mr. Gairdner only refers to the one proposal (Rym., 413-417, Berg., No. 62), and goes too far when he assumes that the two contracting parties had by it been already placed on a perfectly equal footing as regarded discontinuing the war against France; whereas, on the contrary, in the preamble the undue advantage conceded to Spain is adhered to, in accordance with the treaty of Medina del Campo, and it is only further on that this is not again sufficiently clearly expressed (Rym., p. 415). By this, Mr. Gairdner is led to the mistaken conclusion that neither might retire from the war, unless *not only* Roussillon and Cerdagne, *but also* Guienne and Normandy were surrendered.

In the very favourable notice of this first volume which my friend Mr. Gairdner has done me the honour to contribute to the Hist. Rev., viii. 351-355, exception is taken to three passages in my book. I am glad to be able to acknowledge the justice of his criticisms on two of these passages, but on this point I must hold to my original opinion. The two proposed treaties agree word for word in the preamble, which repeats the earlier agreement about Roussillon and Cerdagne, and Guienne and Normandy; and they also agree in the concluding articles on the marriage and dowry. The one proposed treaty, printed first in Rymer (p. 411, f.), stipulates besides—in the place of the old agreement repeated in the preamble—that both Powers should be placed upon the same footing, that neither, without the other, should be able to withdraw from the war or make agreements with France. The other proposed treaty (Rym., 413-417), merely adds to the preamble that undefined points in the manner, time, and place of conducting the war existed, and also that concerted action with regard to Maximilian was to be desired. In the more detailed separate provisions which then follow, the contents of the preamble are twice repeated in the form "quod neuter a bello inter duos annos . . . ingressum . . . sequentes" (this fixing of the time is new) ". . . desistet, nisi quod interim *tam* pro parte Regis Anglorum Ducatus Normanniæ et Aquitaniæ, *quam* et pro parte Regis Castellæ, etc. comitatus Rocilionis et Saritaniæ a . . . communi hoste recuperentur . . . in quo vero casu *utrique* ipsorum Regum . . . a bello desistere liceat." The actual words certainly lead at first to the view supported by Mr. Gairdner, but looking at the connection of the whole, especially when viewed with reference to the other proposed treaty, which would otherwise be quite superfluous, it follows, in my opinion, that the conception is the same as in the treaty of Medina del Campo, and that in any case the Spaniards would only thus have interpreted this provision. In this proposal Henry still retains the provision that was unfavourable to himself, whilst the other alone has for its aim (otherwise they are entirely in agreement) to demand, beyond this proposal, that the undue advantage to one party should be done away with. They were then, in fact, two alternative proposals, which were certainly neither of them accepted by Ferdinand.

8 (*to page* 60).—From the way in which the Spanish ambassador in Brittany writes to Henry about the marriage, Henry cannot have known anything about it beforehand (Berg., No. 57). The assertion repeated, but with grave doubts, by Ulmann (i. 121), that Henry had urged Maximilian to it, is based only on a statement of the unreliable Bacon, p. 77, cf. 74.—Maximilian's order to his plenipotentiaries is from Innspruck, March 20, 1490, and incorrectly assigned by Du Mont (iii. 2, p. 219), to 1489; cf. Ulmann, i. 84, note, also 120, f. Mr. Gairdner (Henry VII., p. 82) forgets that Maximilian was at that time not in the Netherlands, but at Innspruck.—In a power to an English ambassador of March 29, 1491 (Rym., xii. 438, f.), Anne was given the new title, though not in a similar power of Feb. 26 (ibid., 436–438); also see Ulmann, as above.

9 (*to page* 61).—On the withdrawal of the Spanish troops and the truce: Berg., Nos. 57–59; Zurita, v. fol. 5*b*. Mr. Gairdner (Henry VII., p. 96) thinks that the Spanish ambassadors in this matter had disobeyed their instructions, and had even asked Henry to excuse them to their own sovereigns for withdrawing the Spanish forces. Henry's intercession was only requested because the Spanish troops had not been combined with those of England immediately after their arrival in Brittany: Lett. and Pap., i. 97; Berg., No. 49.

10 (*to page* 65).—Henry's negotiations with the Pope and Milan: Brown, Nos. 613, 617. On the compacts in Brittany, see the accounts in De Maulde, Louis XII., ii. 258–260; the Parliament: Stat., ii. 549–551; cf. 556–558; Rot. Parl., 444–446; the Convocations: Wilkins, iii. 634, 635; orders for procuring material and levying troops: Rym., xii. 463, f., 477–480, cf. Past. Lett., iii. 375, f., Plumpt. Corr., 102, f., Leland, Itinerary, iii. 114; summons to the counties, Aug. 2, 1492: Rym., 482, f., 1; cf. Lett. and Pap., ii. 373,

and in the State Papers an order to Lord Darcy, Aug. 2 the year not given, to be assigned to 1492.

11 (*to page* 66).—Negotiations were going on since the beginning of the year 1492; safe conduct for the French ambassadors, Feb. 5, in Rym. xii. 470. Then the Marshal des Querdes and the English governor of Calais, Giles Lord Daubeney, were commissioned to escort them. That they negotiated at first alone is evident from the preamble of the later French instructions of July 26 for the marshal and his colleagues, which we find inserted into the final treaty of peace, Rym., 498. On June 12, Henry empowered, besides Daubeney, Stillington, Bishop of Bath and Wells, and four other colleagues, ibid., 481, f. Charles also associated several colleagues with the marshal on July 26. It is evident that these persons must be regarded as forming a peace congress, which sat on continuously, for their names appear also as signatories in the treaty of peace. The sitting ended at Etaples, where the final settlement of the treaty took place; P. V., 742, f., says it began in Calais.—On the appropriation of the galleys: Brown, Nos. 621–625; Arthur's power, Rym., 487–489. For the departure, P. V. gives by mistake the date, viii. Iduum Sept. (Sept. 6); City Chron., fol. 145*b*, and Hall, 457, have Oct. 6, which Pauli (v. 560) corrects into Oct. 2, from the list of expenses in Excerpta Historica, pp. 91 and 92; the last date is also in the Chronicle of Calais, p. 2. The account of these events in Molinet, iv. 323, ff., is inexact.

12 (*to page* 67).—The opinion of the generals: Rym., xii. 490–494; the various settlements and ratifications of the treaty of peace: 497–504, 505–511, 513, f. Du Mont, iii. 2, pp. 291–297, differs somewhat in unessential points from Rym., and adds the ratifications; cf Godefroy, Hist. de Charles VIII. p. 629, ff.; Charles's oath on the treaty: Champollion Figeac, Lettres des Rois, ii. 502, f.; French ratifications of April and May, 1496, in 45th Rep. of the Dep. Keeper, App. i., pp, 341–343; the confirmation by the English Parliament, 1495: Rot. Parl., vi. 507, f., Stat., ii. 635; cf. Rym., xii. 710–712. Proclamation in Boulogne: Lett. and Pap., ii. 290, f.; Exc. Hist., 92. Announcement and festivities in London: City Chron., fol. 145*b*, f.; Hall, 459; Fabian's Abridgment, 684; Henry's reception: City Chron., 146*a*; on the peace, cf. P. V., 743, f.

13 (*to page* 76).—Acceptance of and preparations for the diet by the towns: Hanserecesse, ii, Nos. 345, 358, 360 (cf. Nos. 355, §§ 7–12, 22), 374, f. 377, 380–388, 399, § 10 (cf. No. 406, f.) and § 11; behaviour of the Englishmen: powers, April 21, 1491, Rym., xii. 441, f.; Hanserec., No. 499, 515, § 33; Recess, No. 496, §§ 35–37,

64–67, 102, f., 106, f.. 135–138; Dantzic report, No. 514, § 12, 37, f., 41, f., 55–58, also No. 519, f.; discussions, complaints, and final settlement, Recess, No. 496, § 159, 175, 207, 215–217, 233, 238–245, 267–270, 285, 298; Dantzic report, No. 514, § 83, 87, f., 93–97, 100, 103, also Nos. 454, 497, f., 504–511; adjournment: No. 546; cf. Weinreich's Danziger Chronik, in Script. Rer. Pruss., iv. 790.

Schäfer goes into the question in Jahrbuch für National-ökonomie, N. F., vii. 104, ff., and takes exception to the account in Schanz, i. 187–189. In spite of the correctness of his various criticisms, I cannot quite concur in Schäfer's view. In his judgment of Henry's attitude, Schäfer does not sufficiently take into account the extremely difficult position of the king, both at home and abroad, in the years 1487 to 1492, which compelled him to act with caution. He carried on his struggle against the privileges of the Hansa solely by allowing and encouraging unlawful burdens to be imposed on them in England itself. The principal object which he obviously had in view in his negotiations with the Hansa was the opening up of the Baltic trade for the English. Hence his compact with Denmark should not be disconnected from his policy with regard to the Hansa. Besides being a commercial agreement with Denmark itself, the treaty contained a menace for the Hansa, resembling in its object the treaty with Florence, in opposition to Venice, concluded almost at the same time, on April 15, 1490.

As regards the Anglo-Danish negotiations, continued almost immediately after the conclusion of the treaty, Schäfer (as above, p. 111, f.) must be regarded as correct rather than Schanz., i. 188, when he says that the statements about English envoys coming to Denmark in 1491 in Weinreich's Chronik (Script. Rer. Pruss., iv. 786) are chronologically inexact, and have to do with Hutton and his companions. According to Weinreich, the Englishmen on their return were accompanied by a Danish secretary; in the Deventer report (Hanserec., ii. No. 515, § 33) on the diet at Antwerp, it is mentioned that, in May, 1491, English envoys were again in Denmark. No doubt, as Schäfer rightly observes, this is only mentioned as " vaga relacio." Nevertheless the information is not to be rejected. Some message in reply must have been sent from England to Denmark, for, in the summer of 1492, the Danish chancellor appeared in England with several companions, and set off back again at the beginning of September (letter of the London Hanse merchants, Hanserec., iii. No. 83, f.; Script. Rer. Pruss., iv. 786, note 5). It must have been a question of matters of importance for the Danish king, for not long afterwards an embassage, again headed by the chancellor, came to Henry. On Mar. 1, 1493, there is an order from Henry for money to be given to them ("and whereas th' Ambassatours of our Cousin the King of Denmark have taken their Leve of us; and entend hastily to depart into their Cuntry....," Rym., xii. 516; cf. before, Hanserec., No. 84, "aldus de kanseler wert wedder hiir komen"). For the subsequent relations, see the entries in Exc. Hist., 102 and 109; Berg., pp. 139, 252. Perkin Warbeck boasted of being in alliance with Denmark: ibid., p. 50. According to a communication from the London Hanse merchants, there was a question in the summer of 1492 of a Danish demand for concerted action against the towns. After the treaty of January, 1490, which completely fulfilled all possible English demands, these negotiations, resumed immediately after, could have been for no other object than to make additional supplementary provisions in Danish interests. Sending the Danish secretary to accompany Hutton on his return could hardly have been for any other object than to make use of the friendship of England for Denmark against the Hansa (see on this Schäfer, as above, p. 110). Open hostility against the Hansa never formed part of Henry's plan, and yet it is very possible the effect of such rumours upon the Hansa might not have been unwelcome to him. How, notwithstanding the first modest success, Henry's policy on the Baltic was in the end not productive of much result as a whole, is another question.

To Chapter III.

1 (*to page* 86).—This story of Perkin Warbeck's previous history rests upon the confession he made publicly in June, 1498 (given to the same effect both in the City Chron., fol. 168*b*–170*b*, and in Hall, p. 488, f.), which Henry had caused to be printed and circulated as widely as possible (André, Vita, 73). Against this, P. V., 746, makes the setting up of this new pretender appear as the work of Margaret of Burgundy. Hall, 462, has also adopted this story without criticism, and embellished it. We find it then in Bacon, 107, f., with further fanciful additions. These two accounts agree so far in stating that Perkin had been in Ireland and France, and from there had gone to Margaret, Pol. Verg. says for the second time. Pauli, v. 565, tries to make them coincide by supposing that in the confession Margaret's name was not mentioned, because Henry wished to spare her. Besides its obvious improbability, the idea of any

such consideration for Margaret is contradicted by the fact that Henry made Perkin repeat, in presence of the Spanish ambassador, Puebla, the assertion that Margaret knew as well as he that he was not King Edward's son (Puebla's report, Aug. 25, 1498; Berg., p. 185, f.). Mr. Gairdner was the first to do the right thing, and give the account from the confession without additions (Perkin Warbeck, p. 337, ff.; cf. 386, f., 389, and earlier, Mem., Pref., p. xxx., ff.). The fact that the confession was so welcome to the king, that he had it printed to circulate it as widely as possible, does not afford sufficient grounds for regarding it as a forgery. It also agrees, as to Perkin's later public career, with Pol. Verg., and particularly with a letter of Perkin's own from Flanders to Queen Isabella, dated Aug. 25, 1493 (first printed by Madden in Archæologia, xxvii., 1838, p. 199, f.; cf. before, 156–158, abridged in Berg., No. 85), which also places the beginning of his career as a pretender in Ireland. But as Perkin did not play any great political part, and was not generally known till he went to Margaret from France, it is easy to see how tradition came to regard her as the author of the plot. It was the view of contemporaries, for we see it also in André, p. 65, and it was handed down thus to Pol. Verg., who on his own statement described these events in 1512, therefore twenty years afterwards.

André's story (Vita, p. 65, f., 72) is very doubtful (cf. Gairdner, as above, 343), that Perkin had been brought up in England by a converted Jew, who had had King Edward IV. for his godfather. In that case it would not have been necessary for Perkin to learn English first in Ireland (Confession, Hall, p. 489). But André particularly notes this as Perkin's own declaration, which would quite contradict his confession; the blind biographer has here allowed himself to be rather imposed upon. Bacon, 105, f., gives a romantic version of the affair. On the other side, see Madden, as above, 163; Spedding, in his edition of Bacon, p. 133, note 4; Gairdner, in Mem., Pref., p. xxxiv.—The extracts from the city registers of Tournay, printed by Gairdner (Perk. Warb., 389, f.), confirm most of the statements as to family in the confession, except that, according to the latter, Perkin's father was "comptroller" at Tournay, according to the extract from the register, "pireman;" and Henry calls him "batellier" in an instruction destined for France, Aug. 10, 1494 (Lett. and Pap., ii. 294). The registers are of the years 1474 and 1475. It will agree therefore with both accounts that John Warbeck should later have become what, according to the town-book, his father-in-law had been in 1459: "Pierar Faron, piereman et cureur de toilles." A statement in a letter of the Spanish sovereigns, April 14, 1496, Berg., p. 92, that he had been a barber, is, of course, to be rejected.

The question of his name is more difficult : the registers write it Werbeque, Perkin, in a letter to his mother (in Gairdner, Perk. Warb., 385), Pierrequin Werbecque ; but in the confession he calls himself Osbeck, and Henry uses the same name in a letter to the town of Waterford (Halliwell, i. 177) and so does Zurita ; the last two, in this particular, follow the confession.   There can be no doubt as to the correctness of the first-named form, according to the two witnesses cited ; where the other comes from I am at a loss to determine.   It is not impossible that, after his long wandering, Perkin should have altered his name, or have caused it to be altered.   Bacon's conclusion on this subject, p. 106, is again to be rejected.

We can conjecture the year of Perkin's birth from a statement in a letter to Isabella, where, in his character of Richard of York, he alleges his age, in the year 1483, to have been nearly nine years, whereas at that time Richard must have been nearly eleven (cf. Madden, as above, 161, f.).   The obvious supposition that this inaccurate statement represented Perkin's own age, is exactly confirmed by a Venetian report of Dec. 31, 1497 (Brown, No. 760), which makes him twenty-three at that time.—It should be noted that Legge, Rich. III., ii. 42, seems to wish to imply the possibility of the pretender's claim being genuine ; Halsted, Marg. Beauf., 257, f., even makes feeble attempts to prove this ; cf. besides, Bergenroth in his Preface, p. lxxxiii.

The first indication of the new conspiracy is given us by John Taylor's letter of Sept. 15, 1491, contained in the parliamentary report on Hayes, Rot. Parl., 454, f. ; only it is not quite clear from the report how the Government came to a knowledge of the contents of the letter, since it is expressly stated that Hayes burnt it on receiving it.   Lingard, v. 436, and Pauli, p. 595, knew the letter, and assumed from it the existence of a special and independent plot for Warwick.   It is remarkable that, though there is mention of assistance for Warwick, the idea of freeing the earl, which had been the first object with the Abbot of Abingdon and his companions, is not even hinted at.   It is possible even that the writer of the letter may at that time have been thinking not so much of the imprisoned earl as of a substitute for him like Lambert Simnel.   Shortly afterwards Perkin himself was chosen, in the first instance, to personate Warwick.   Subsequently, in his confession, Perkin named Taylor as one of the authors and ringleaders of his

z

insurrection, as does the Milanese ambassador (report of July 13, 1499, Brown, No. 799). Taylor was tried and condemned in company with Perkin (City Chron., 176a). With the very arbitrary mode of spelling names common at the time, we find the name written, Tailor, Tailour, Taylour, Taillour, Tayllour, Tyler, and Tiler ; there is no reason on that account to question their identity. The only possibility would be to suppose a father and son, for the John Taylor of the letter calls himself "the elder ; " but this would not alter the most important question as to whether it was all one plot. Add to this, that Perkin Warbeck actually first went from Ireland to France, whither the Government, through Taylor, invited Warwick and his adherents; the notification in the letter, "there shall be helpe in thre parties out of the Royalme,"—if by the last word only England is meant—fits in for Perkin, who at once found assistance in Ireland and France, and soon entered into communications with Scotland (see Lett. and Pap., ii. 526, f.).

However, it is improbable that in this letter Taylor could have already had Perkin himself in view. According to the confession, much time cannot have elapsed between the proposal that Perkin should personate Warwick, and his denial that he had done so, which he made upon oath before the Mayor of Cork, "called Jhon le Wellen." For, according to the list of mayors in Smith, Ant. and Pres. State of Corke, i. 429, " John Lavallen " was mayor for 1492 ; his year of office had begun (idem., 421) the Monday after Michaelmas, *i.e.* Oct. 3, 1491 (the election had taken place on Aug. 29, the Monday after St. Bartholomew's Day), and therefore Taylor, writing on Sept. 15, can hardly have been speaking of Perkin himself. But Perkin's arrival in Ireland must certainly be assigned to the year 1491, for by the time he had gained over the leading Irish nobles, such as the Earl of Desmond, at the beginning of March, 1492, his alliance with James of Scotland had already taken place (Lett. and Pap., ii. 526).

There are gaps unfortunately in the story ; after piecing together as well as may be the various scattered items of information, we gather that a Yorkist plot in Warwick's name was in existence, but that the leaders, at what moment we do not know, imagined a repetition of the former attempt with Simnel—that is, to set up a pretender for Warwick—that they had conceived the plan, and had already gained support, as, for instance, in France, when chance threw Perkin in their way as a suitable person. As to what had already taken place beyond this we remain quite in the dark. The plan and whole manner of the undertaking were then altered, the participators remained as before, the plot was still directed against the Tudor king, but Perkin from this time came conspicuously to the front. On the personal history of John Taylor, see also Campb., ii. 454, cf. i. 201, f.; Rot. Parl., 504. On Hayes: Campb., i. 20, 189, 198, 211, 237, 400, 445, 459; ii. 89, 93, f.; cf. i. 296, 309. On John Walter: Madden, p. 189, note, as above, and Zurita's remarks, v. fol. 170*a*. Smith, as above, ii. 30, mentions that 1491 was a year of famine for Ireland.

2 (*to page* 89).—On Perkin's first political intrigues and the result of them in Ireland, France, and the Netherlands, the following should be noticed. Ware, p. 68, says that Perkin's letters to Kildare and Desmond were still extant in his day. Kildare's later assertion that he had not supported the " French lad " (Lett. and Pap., ii. 55), had a special object, and cannot be considered of much account. Perkin's confession tells about the invitation to France, Hall, 489; cf. P. V., 747 (Hall, 463). Taylor's previous letter shows that the connection with France had already assumed a greater political importance than is assigned to it by Gairdner, Perk. Warb., 344; cf. also Ware, p. 39.—For Perkin's evidence about Margaret, see in Puebla's report, Berg., p. 185 (cf. preceding note); according to Zurita, v. fol. 170*a*, Margaret and Maximilian believed in Perkin, a view also adopted by Ulmann, Maxim., i. 261; cf. idem. 262 on Maximilian's attitude, also Zurita, v. fol. 59*b*. Powers for Poynings and Warham, July 13, 1493, Rym., xii. 544, f.; Lett. and Pap., ii. 374; cf. the warrant for the money, in Ellis, ii. 1, p. 167, f.; Henry's order to be in readiness and his communications about Perkin: letter to Talbot, July 20, 1493, in Ellis, i. 1, pp. 19–21; Halliwell, i. 172, f.; Gairdner, Perk. Warb., 345–347. At that time or later Henry seems to have made some inquiries from Pregent Meno, who on April 12, 1495, received £300, and, later, the privileges of an English denizen, and other marks of favour (Lett. and Pap., ii. 375, f.). On the dismissal of the English ambassadors in Flanders, we only have the statement in P. V., 750; the commercial enactments on both sides: Lett. and Pap., ii. 374; Schanz, ii. Urk. Beil., 191, f., and 193, f.; cf. i. 17, Note 5; City Chron., fol. 149*a*; Hall, 467.

Attack on the Steelyard: Hanseatic letter of complaints, June, 1497, Hanserecesse, iv. p. 20; Schanz, ii. Urk. Beil., p. 410; City Chron., 146*b*, 147*a*; Hall, 468; Fabian's Abridgment, 684; Grey Friars' Chron., p. 25; cf. letter of the London Hansa to Lubeck, Oct. 23, 1493; Hanserecesse, iii. No. 259; also ibid., Nos. 274, 291; iv. No. 8, § 9. The date appears in the above-mentioned

letter of complaint, in drawing up which envoys from the London
Hansa took part ; the City Chronicle and Hall differ about it, but
the mistake is obvious; both—therefore also Fabian's Chronicle,
which forms the basis for both—give "Tewesday before Seint
Edwardes day," that is, Oct. 8 ; whilst Oct. 15, given in the Hansa
report, was the Tuesday *after* St. Edward's day.   Pauli, p. 570, gives
Oct. 12—that is, just the day before St. Edward's day, and he
quotes the City Chronicle, and therefore has overlooked the
"Tuesday."

3 (*to page* 96).—On Perkin's first communications with friends in
England, see the Bill of Attainder, Rot. Parl., vi. 504, Stat., ii. 632.
When, after the storming of the London Steelyard, the trade of the
Hansa between England and Burgundy was greatly restricted, they
were compelled to give security to a considerable amount that they
would not enter into any sort of relation with the rebels against
Henry residing in Philip's provinces : Oct. 21, 1493, Schanz, ii., Urk.
Beil., p. 408.—Description of Prince Henry's elevation to be Duke
of York, and the accompanying festivities : Lett. and Pap., i. 388–
404.   On the condemnations and executions in England the most
detailed account is in the City Chronicle, fol. 152*a*, 153*b*; shorter
in Fabian's Abridgment, 685 ; cf. P. V., 750, f. ; Hall, 467, 468, f. ;
Arnold, p. 39, and following him the Grey Friars' Chronicle, p. 25,
are not exact in the chronological order of events.   A contradiction
exists only between the subsequent act of restitution for Worseley,
the Dean of St. Paul's (Stat., 619, Rot. Parl., 489) which places the
proceedings against him Nov. 14, 1494, and the City Chronicle,
which gives as the date Jan. 24, 1495.   As both these statements
are above suspicion, we are forced to conclude there were previous
proceedings against him, possibly suppressed, but afterwards on
Clifford's information resumed, though it is remarkable that the Act
does not mention the second proceedings.—On Lord Fitzwater :
City Chronicle, 156*b*, f., 161*b*; P. V., 751 ; Lady Fitzwater received
in March, 1497, a gratification of £33 6*s*. 6*d*. : Exc. Hist., 111.

Concerning other accomplices who at first remained concealed,
extraordinary revelations are made in the statement (Mar. 14, 1496)
of a certain Bernard de Vignolles, at Rouen, which has been printed
three times : in Champollion, Lettres des rois, ii. 505–511 ; Archæol.,
xxvii. pp. 205–209; Lett. and Pap., ii. 318–323; see especially
Lett. and Pap., 318, 321, 322, f.; and cf. Madden's remarks,
Archæol., 171–178.   The reliability of this statement cannot be
proved, and against it might be argued that not only the Bishop of
Winchester, who is mentioned, remained in office, but also that John

Kendall, who was the most implicated, got off free (on him, cf. Rym., xii. 481, 579; cf. Rot. Parl., 507).

The time of Clifford's arrival in England is shown from the statement in the City Chronicle, fol. 152a, which agrees very well with the date of the pardon for him, Dec. 22, 1494, (Lett. and Pap., ii. 374); see also P. V., 751, who is only inexact in the chronology. That Clifford must have rendered the king very important services, is shown by the exceptionally high reward of £500, which was paid to him as early as Jan. 20, 1495: Exc. Hist., 100. It is mentioned also in Perkin Warbeck's later proclamation that Clifford was gained over by Henry: Bacon, Works, edited by Spedding, vi. 252. Cf. also the embellished account in Molinet, v. 47–49.

On Stanley: P. V., 751; Hall, 469, f., with additions from Fabian's Chron.; City Chron., 152a, 153b; Fabian's Abridgment, 685. André's exaggerated statements, which are also chronologically incorrect, Vita, 69, f., are of little use. Cf. also the entry, Exc. Hist., 101. We learn nothing about the grounds for the sentence against Stanley except from the notice in the City Chronicle: "was . . . found gilty of treason by a quest of diuers knyghtes and worshipfull gentilmen." A later communication to Wolsey on the occasion of the trial of the Duke of Buckingham in the year 1521, relates that Henry for a long time had entertained suspicions of Stanley: Brewer, Lett. and Pap., iii. 1, p. 490. On Stanley's possessions: City Chronicle, as above, Henry's Patents, Feb. 8 and 25, 1495; Lett. and Pap., ii. 374, f.; disbursements for the funeral and to Stanley's servants: Exc. Hist., 101, 102.

4 (*to page* 96).—On the landing in Kent and the executions I follow the circumstantial account in the City Chron., fol. 154a–156b, to which I also give the preference wherever it differs from Puebla's report, Berg., p. 58, f. Also P. V., 754, f.; Hall, 472; Fabian's Abridgment, 685; Arnold, p. 39; Grey Friars' Chron., p. 25; Wriothesley, p. 3; Ware, p. 52; Rot. Parl., vi. 504; Brown, No. 651; Past. Lett., iii. 386, 387, f. André's description, Vita, 66, f., is again not of much use; cf. also Molinet, v. 50–52. For the arming of Henry's own ships, see the entry of payment, Exc. Hist., 101.

5 (*to page* 98).—The Irish events cannot be placed in right order, owing to gaps in the story handed down to us. The account in the Book of Howth, Car. Pap., 188–190, whenever it comes in contact with other accounts, is shown to be reliable and of use, and yet, according to it, it would appear as if Simnel's overthrow, the visit of the Irish in England, and the appointment of the Earl of Surrey, which did not take place till 1520, under Henry VIII., had followed

each other in quick succession. The scene with Lambert Simnel, pleasantly described in the Book of Howth, may lead us to the conclusion that the visit took place shortly after his insurrection ; Ware, 26; Bagwell, Hist. of Ireland, i. 108; and Gairdner, Henry VII., p. 122, have placed it then.   But according to the orders sent to Edgecombe, and the subsequent correspondence with which we are acquainted (see Note 11 to Chap. I,) it must be considered as impossible that Kildare was in England, in obedience to Henry's command, during the years 1487 to 1491.   As the visit came to a successful conclusion : " After, the Lords being there a time longer than their purses could well bear, they were licensed to go to their country," and a rich present to Lord Howth is even mentioned, we may connect it with the pardon of Kildare on June 22, 1493, (Lett. and Pap., ii. 374), and place it therefore in May or June, 1493, which links the events well together.   The visit mentioned by Ware, p. 43, f., took place then in the following November, without leading to the object which Kildare was then trying to attain.   On Gormanston's appointment, see Ware, p. 42.—At the point of time to which we have assigned the first visit, Gairdner, as above, 125, has introduced a conversation of Kildare's with Henry, which is related in the Book of Howth, p. 179; but as this resulted in the appoint- ment of the earl to his post as Lord Deputy " during his life," it cannot have taken place till 1496, when the appointment was made ; see Ware, 56.

6 (to page 100).—Appointment of Prince Henry and Poynings of Sept. 11 and 13, 1494: Rym., xii. 558–562; according to Lett. and Pap., ii. 374, for both on Sept. 12 ; of Dean and Conway : Lett. and Pap., idem; cf. Ware, 41 ; idem., 43, Bedford's dismissal; on Poynings' commissions, cf. Lett. and Pap., ii. 295.—Landing and war in Ulster : Ware, 44–47 ; Act of Attainder against Kildare, Car. Pap., 483, f.   Ware tries to clear the earl from the charge of high treason made against him in the Act, but its official statements are of more weight than O'Hanlon's oath in support of Kildare's innocence; Henry's subsequent proceedings point also to his guilt. The name Fitzthomas is given in the Act in mistake for Fitzgerald.

Opening of the Parliament of Drogheda : Ware, 47 ; Measures : the Stat. of Ireland, 10 Henry VII., p. 41–57 ; cf. Irish Stat., rev. ed., p. 3 ; Car. Pap., 456, 483, f. ; Stephen, New Comm., i. 95, f. ; Gilbert, Viceroys, 451, ff. ; Thom. Leland, Hist. of Ireland, ii. 102, ff. Under the name of " Poynings' Act " was especially understood the statute passed first of all, which made the summoning of the Irish Parliament, and its legislative measures dependent upon the previous permission of the king.—Kildare's arrest : Ware, 49 ; Book of Howth, 179 ; Henry's report to France on Irish affairs, Dec. 30, 1494 : Brit. Mus. MS., Cotton, Cal., D, vi. fol. 20*b*. Offer of pardon to Desmond, Dec. 12, 1494 : Rym., xii. 567, f. ; Lett. and Pap., ii. 374 ; Smith, State of Cork, ii. 32.

The report on the siege of Waterford, Car. Pap., p. 472, is so far inexact, that it is silent about Perkin's long residence in Scotland, which followed shortly after, and places his third visit to Ireland immediately after the siege, though it did not occur till 1497 ; it also mentions, somewhat unaccountably, the Earl of Lincoln as one of Perkin's accomplices, which can only have arisen from a confusion of Perkin with Simnel. It is to this report that the incorrect statement in Smith, Waterford, 134, f., is to be referred ; he makes all the events happen in 1497. The statements in the Lord Treasurer Hattcliffe's accounts are to be connected with this report : Lett. and Pap., ii. 298–300. Cf. Brown, No. 655 ; Ware, 52 ; P. V., 755 ; and after him, Hall, p. 472, make Perkin return to Flanders again after his defeat in Kent, and not till after that go through Ireland to Scotland. Cf. Madden in Archæol., xxvii. p. 170. Poynings' reinforcements in troops and money : Exc. Hist., 100, 103, f. ; Lett. and Pap., ii. 375. Dublin's share : Gilbert, Cal. of Records of Dublin, i. p. 381.

Inquiry into the Irish in England : City Chron., 156*b* ; Hattcliffe's instruction and accounts, Lett. and Pap., ii. 64–67, 297–318 ; cf. Pref., xlv. ; other orders, ibid., 67–69 ; cf. Pref., xlvi. In the Privy Purse Expenses, Exc. Hist., 105–108, 110, a sum of rather more than £11,613 is entered for Ireland under date Nov. 2, and Dec. 1, 1495, Feb. 21, May 26, Oct. 8, 1496.—Poynings' recall : Ware, 53, f. Henry's conversation with Kildare : Book of Howth, 179, f. ; following it, shortened, Ware, 56. Kildare's reinstatement : Rot. Parl., vi. 481, f. ; Stat., ii. 612, f. Fresh appointment Aug. 6, 1496 : Ware, 56 ; cf. Exc. Hist., 109.

7 (*to page* 101).—On the events and negotiations between England and Scotland till the conclusion of the peace of July 3, 1486 : Campb., i. 31, 44, 63, 579, f., 268, 480 ; Rym., xii. 285–293, 316, f. ; Du Mont, iii. 2, p. 156–158 ; Rot. Scot., ii. 471, 473–477 ; Bain, iv. No. 1521 ; Ayloffe, Cal. of Charters, p. 313 ; Past. Lett., iii. 324. It has not hitherto been noticed that the peace probably expired after lasting a year, and had possibly been already replaced by a new settlement, but only for a year, which was then followed by the treaty of November 28, 1487, at Edinburgh (Rym., 328–331 ; Rot. Scot., ii. 480–482 ; cf. Rym., 325–328 ; Bain, iv. No.

1530). Of the intervening treaty we know directly nothing at all, we only have the treaties of July 3, 1486, and Nov. 28, 1487. In the latter reference is made to an earlier treaty, which Bain, p. 313, considers to be the treaty of July 3, 1486. As, however, the plenipotentiaries here named are not the same as those who had actually concluded the July treaty of 1486, as, moreover, in the November treaty of 1487, July 3, 1488, is named as the date of the termination of the treaty in question—and yet the July treaty of 1486 was, according to whether the clause about Berwick was fulfilled or not, to last either three years, till 1489, or one year, till 1487—it is not possible that the earlier treaty mentioned in the November treaty of 1487, can be the one of July, 1486. As, from the wording of the November treaty, no agreement about Berwick had resulted, the July treaty of 1486 must, in accordance with the stipulation, expire on July 3, 1487. At that time, perhaps even earlier, a new arrangement for a truce may have taken place, under the same conditions, but only for a year; however, already in the autumn new, and at the same time more complete, settlements had been resolved upon.

8 (*to page* 103).—On James IV. and Margaret of Burgundy, see Tytler, Hist. of Scotland, iv. 319, f., especially the note. Letter of the Master of Huntley to Henry, Jan. 8, 1489 ; Brit. Mus., Cotton, Cal, B, iii. fol. 20.—Compact with Bothwell, April 17, 1491, Rym., xii. 440, f. ; Bain, iv. No. 1571, and Ayloffe, p. 313; the latter differs in the amount of the sum paid to Bothwell, £116 instead of £266. On Bothwell, his attainder, and a yearly income paid to him from England, cf. Acts of Parl., ii. 201–203; Bain, Nos. 1534, 1570, 1576, 1581, 1584, 1602, 1606, 1611, 1620, 1624.—Resumption of the plan of an alliance with France, April, 1491 : Acts of Parl., ii. 224, 228 ; Scotch and English embassage of peace : ibid., 228 ; Rot. Scot., ii. 497 ; further relations of Scotland with France : Brown, p. 208 ; Acts of Parl, ii. 230; and with Perkin, March, 1492, Lett. and Pap., ii. 327.

Henry's compact with Angus, Nov. 16, 1491; Lett. and Pap., i. 385–387; Bain, App. i. No. 32; Ayloffe, p. 313. Fraser, The Douglas Book, ii. 91, note, doubts the correctness of the date written into the document in a modern hand, the passage in which it ought to stand being illegible in the text. But the copyist as well as Ayloffe must have had the original document in his hand before it was damaged ; if Angus really did not come to England in November, 1491, as Fraser asserts, the treaty was concluded by proxy, possibly his son. On the measures against Angus in Scotland : Fraser, iii. 134. f., as above; cf. ii. 92, f. ; Tytler, iv. 308.

The instructions, terms, ratifications, etc., for the treaty of Dec. 21, 1491 : Rym., xii. 465–470; Rot. Scot., ii. 503–505 ; Du Mont, iii. 2, p. 276–278; cf. Rym., p. 473–475; for that of Nov. 3, 1492 : Rym., p. 483, f. 494–497; Rot. Scot., 507 ; cf. Ayloffe, p. 313, with the year of Henry's reign given wrong; for that of June 25, 1493: Rym., p. 525, f. 534–540; Rot. Scot., ii. 508–512 ; cf. Rym., p. 542, 545, f. 547, f.; Rot. Scot., 512 ; Ayloffe, 314 ; Bain, Nos. 1590–1592, 1596, f.

9 (*to page* 105).—Concerning James's support of Perkin, see Gairdner, Perk. Warb., 364, f. ; on the reception in Stirling, see the Treasurer's accounts, Nov., 1495, Lett. and Pap., ii. 327–329 ; the day of his arrival is not certain; on p. 327 the 27th, and on page 329 the 20th, is given.   The speech which P. V., 755, f., makes Perkin deliver before James IV. is entire invention; but in its purport follows faithfully the rumours on his origin and career ; Hall, 473, f., repeats it with slight alterations.   On Perkin's request to Desmond, see Ware, p. 53; on the preparations for war in Scotland, see the Treasurer's accounts, Lett. and Pap., ii. 329 ; on the current rumours, Brown, No. 677.—On Perkin's marriage, the time of which cannot quite be determined : P. V., 756 ; André, Vita, 70 ; Brown, No. 727 ; Perkin's letter in Berg., No. 119 ; the writer is not named, but the editor makes it quite probable that the letter really is Perkin's.

10 (*to page* 112).—Pol. Verg., p. 758–762, is the chief authority for the history of the Cornwall insurrection up to the arrival of the insurgents before London; from that time on, the far more detailed City Chron., 162*b*–165*b*.   Here also Hall differs from P. V. (476–480) in order to follow the common original source of the city annals ; he adds especially from them some good additional details on the order of the battle, to the somewhat scanty and obscure account of it in the City Chronicle; some additional facts are also supplied by Bacon, 152, ff.

As to the date of the battle the accounts vary : the City Chronicle names Saturday the 17th, Hall, Saturday only ; the later Act of Attainder of 1504, Rot. Parl., 544, gives the 22nd.   Strangely enough, Stow, who generally refers back to Fabian, also gives this incorrect date, p. 870.   The 22nd was a Thursday, and therefore Bacon's attempt (p. 154) to make Hall and Stow agree by giving Saturday, June 22, is a double error.   On account of the notice in Exc. Hist., 112, that on June 19, Henry was on Blackheath, Pauli thinks it necessary to make the battle take place on the 18th, v. 587.   Cf. also the shorter accounts, Fabian's Abridgment, p. 686;

Arnold, p. 39; Grey Friars' Chronicle, p. 25; Wrioth., p. 3; Ricart, 48, f.; Rot. Parl., 544, f.; Brown, Nos. 743, 746, 750, f., 754; Zurita, v. 127*b*.

On Henry's preparations for war with Scotland before the insurrection: Lett. and Pap., ii. 376; Rym., xii. 647; Exc. Hist., 110, 111.—For the statements about Audley, whose father had died on Sept. 25, 1490, see in the 37th Rep. of the Dep. Keeper, App. ii. p. 723; his father had been royal commissary for the tax levied in Surrey, in 1487: receipt of July 25, 1487, in the Record Office. —Hall p. 477, f., introduces into his report, taken from Pol. Verg., an account of the march of the insurgents to Taunton, and the murder of a tax commissary; this event, which is taken quite correctly from Fabian, is only incorrect as to time, it occurred in the following autumn, during Perkin's march from Cornwall, see City Chron., 167*a*, f.

11 (*to page* 115).—Concerning the Spanish negotiations in Scotland the offer of marriage, the proposal for the Anglo-Scotch marriage, Ayala's mission: Berg., p. 97, 105, 115, f., 124, 135; Zurita, v. fol. 103*b*, f., 110*a*. (Zurita speaks by mistake of a "sister" instead of a daughter of Henry's.) Recommendation of peace to Henry, Mar. 28, 1497, Berg., p. 140; cf. Zurita, 134*a*, f.; Henry's mistrust of Spain: Berg., p. 61, 85; Puebla and the Spanish scheme with Perkin: Berg., p. 91, f. 112. Perkin's letter of Oct. 18, 1496, to Bernard de la Forse, in Spain, Archæol., xxvii. p. 182, f.; Berg., No. 165.

On Ayala's negotiations with James and Perkin: Zurita, v. fol. 133*b*, f., to whom we are also indebted for interesting particulars on the Spanish intrigues. His narrative, which is probably based on Ayala's own reports otherwise not accessible to us, is to be corrected in some passages by the other communications handed down to us, and also suffers here as elsewhere from some obscurities.

Raising money and arming for war in Scotland: Lett. and Pap., ii. 331, f.; Tytler, iv. 329, note; the merchant vessel belonged to a Breton named Guido Foulcart; see about him the subsequent letter from James to Anne of France and Brittany: Lett. and Pap., ii. 185, f., with the statement that this Foulcart, probably a Breton, had accompanied Perkin by ship to England, where he had been taken prisoner and robbed of his property. Gairdner, Perk. Warb., 379–381, supposes from this that Perkin had, between Sept., 1496, and July, 1497, undertaken another disastrous expedition (cf. the notice in the letters of the Spanish kings, Mar. 28, 1497, Berg., p. 140); but the event must certainly be taken in connection with the expedition of July, 1497, especially as Henry himself mentions a " Breton prinse " (pinnace) as a ship which accompanied Perkin (Ellis, i. 1, p. 32). Probably the confiscation of the ship was a reprisal for the injury which had been done shortly before to Robert Barton in Brittany, see Lett. and Pap., ii. 202, f. 258–260.

For the description of the Scotch attack, see in P. V., 762, f. ; after him Hall, 480, f. ; who, however, 481, f., adds details to P. V.'s short account of Surrey's proceedings, probably from Fabian's London Chronicle (cf. the original short entries in Fabian's Abridgment, 686) ; P. V.'s reliability, as well as Hall's, is shown by his agreement with what is stated in Treasurer's accounts : Lett. and Pap., ii. 332–334 ; the reports in Brown, Nos. 750, 754, are inexact.—Spanish mediation for peace : Berg., p. 135, 147, 160 ; English powers, Sept. 5, 1497 : Rot. Scot., ii. 524 ; Bain, iv. No. 1636 ; truce of Ayton, Sept. 30 : Rym., xii. 673–678 ; Rot. Scot., 521–529 ; cf. Bain, Nos. 1640, 1644 ; permanent peace in London, Dec. 5 : Rym., 678 to 680 ; Rot. Scot., 529, f.; cf. Berg., No. 186 ; Brown, No. 763 ; also Zurita, v. 135*a*; proclam. in London, Dec. 6 : City Chron., 171*b*, Fabian's Abridgment, 686.

The view which is grounded on P. V., 757 and 764, f., and is shared also by Pauli, 588, that James and Perkin's friendship had come to an end in the summer of 1497, and that Perkin had only been given a good escort on his leaving Scotland, is in contradiction to the facts described, which point to the plan of a concerted attack. Tytler, iv. 330, and Gairdner, Lett. and Pap., ii. Pref. lvii., Perk. Warb., 380, f., have already expressed doubts about the earlier view ; however, Gairdner is still of opinion that it was no more than a kind of escort of honour. The flotilla was small, means being restricted ; besides, James was putting all his strength into his own onset. It can scarcely be supposed that Perkin would have been dismissed just before James's own attack, and without any reference to it ; and that James himself encouraged Perkin's attempt on England is stated in the letter already mentioned about Foulcart, Lett. and Pap., ii. 185 : "ducem Eboracensem in Angliam transmittere per nos fuerit compulsus." Perkin himself, according to that, acted contrary to the Scotch as well as to the Spanish plan.

12 (*to page* 116).—That Perkin was summoned to Ireland by Sir James Ormond is asserted by Piers Butler (to the Earl of Ormond, Lett. and Pap., ii. Pref. xlii.), a bitter enemy of Ormond's, no doubt, but as he made the statement after Ormond's death, and referred to witnesses in support of it, we may with safety follow him. The reconciliation with Desmond was announced to Scotland by Henry

himself: Ware, p. 59; Ellis, i. 1, p. 24. On the Spaniard Guevara, see Zurita, v. 134*a*, whose narrative is somewhat obscure, but fits in well with other events which were unknown to Zurita. On Perkin's negotiations with the inhabitants of Cornwall, see the Act of Attainder of 1504, Rot. Parl., vi. 545, according to which it was really from these men that the suggestion of a landing in Cornwall first proceeded; the object of the Act may have influenced this assertion; cf. P. V., 765, Hall, 483.

On the subsequent events, down to the landing in Cornwall: Ware, p. 60, f.; Henry to the town of Waterford, Aug. 6, 1497: Halliwell, i. 174, f.; Goldsmid, Coll. of Doc., i, 12, f.; Ryland, Hist. of Waterford, 32, f.; Smith, Waterford, 135, f.; Car. Pap., 468; to Gilbert Talbot, Ellis, i. 1, p. 32, f.; Halliwell, i. 179, f.; Puebla's report, Aug. 25, 1498: Berg., p. 186; Rot. Parl., vi. 545; petition from Waterford in 1499: Ryland, 37, f.; Zurita, v. fol. 134*a*. How Perkin persuaded the captain to sail for Cornwall is not quite clear, for that his doing so was against Ayala's intentions is beyond all doubt. We may suppose that these sailors were the persons who were engaged by Ayala to convey Perkin, otherwise the firmness with which they rejected the offer of two thousand nobles for Perkin is inexplicable.—Ware's suggestion, made, however, with reservation, that Desmond had again sided with Perkin, is contradicted by Henry's own statement (Ellis, p. 32; Halliwell, p. 179).—The report in the Book of Howth, Car., Pap., 472, which makes the landing in Cork, July 1497, coincide with the siege of Waterford in 1495 (see above, Note 6), does not agree satisfactorily in its account of Perkin's escape to Cornwall with Henry's statement (Ellis, 32) that Perkin had landed with three ships (this number is also given by Zurita, 134*a*, City Chronicle, 166*a*; by a mistaken reading, Hall has four), and the remark in the report that Perkin had been brought to Henry at Exeter is also incorrect.

13 (*to page* 118).—On Perkin's career, from his landing to his imprisonment, see in particular the reports in Henry's own letters: Car. Pap., 468, f.; Halliwell, i. 175–178; Smith, Waterford, 136–138; Goldsmid, i. 13–17; Ryland, Hist. of Waterford, 33–37; Ellis, i. 1, pp. 33, 34, f., 37, cf. 36, f., 38. The narrative in the City Chronicle agrees very well with this, 166*a*–168*a*, and is grounded on the king's reports to the authorities of the town, probably the same as those already quoted to Waterford. The account in P. V., 765–767 is good (after him, with additions, Hall, 483–486), also Zurita, vi., fol. 134*a*, 134*b*, f.; Molinet, v. 78–80; also see Brown, Nos. 755–757, 759; cf. André, Vita, 70–75, and separate notices, Exc. Hist., 113, f.

—Gairdner, Perk. Warb., 384, probably following here the report, Car. Pap., 472, is mistaken when he makes Perkin not brought before Henry till he was in Exeter, for he came there later in the king's company: Exc. Hist., 114.

Instructions for the commissaries sent into the shires, Sept. 13, 1498: Rymer, xii. 696–698; their accounts: Lett. and Pap., ii. 335–337; cf. P. V., 768; Rep. of the Comm. of Hist., MSS., ii. 20; instructions of March 11, and Aug. 6, 1500: Bain., iv. No. 1663; Rym., xii. 766, f.; the account is in Lett. and Pap., ii. 337, added to the one also named of 1498, the names of the commissaries, however, make it belong to 1500.—Grant for Waterford: Smith, Waterford, 138, f.; Ryland, 37, f.—Perkin's letter to his mother, Oct. 13, 1497, in Gairdner, Perk. Warb., 384–386, cf. 387.—The return journey: Exc. Hist., 115; the extract in City Chronicle, 168b, does not correspond with the itinerary given in Exc. Hist., is, besides, obscure, and appears in this passage to have been badly copied from the original. Perkin's summons before the king: City Chron., 171a, Fabian's Abridgment, 686; the treatment he received later, P. V., 767; Hall, 486; Brown, Nos. 760–763; cf. City Chron., 172a; entries in Exc. Hist., pp. 115–117, for Dec. 18, 1497, Feb. 17, Mar. 10, April 18, May 23, 1498.

On the treatment of his wife: Lett. and Pap., ii. 73, f.; Exc. Hist., 115; City Chron., 168a; P. V., 767; Hall, 485; Berg., No. 184. The notices on her later years have been collected by Tytler, iv. 363, f.—In a Venetian report, Brown, No. 755, and also by André, Vita, p. 70, children of the marriage are mentioned; we do not hear anything of them elsewhere, and it is possible there is some error in both accounts; there could not have been many children, for Perkin did not marry till quite the end of 1495, and by September, 1497, the married couple were already separated.

14 (*to page* 120).—On Perkin's flight and punishment in June, 1498: Puebla's reports of July 17 and Aug. 25: Berg., 156, 185, f.; cf. 152; City Chron., 172a, f.; Fabian's Abridgment, 686, and, following Fabian, Hall, 488, f., expanding his former authority, P. V., 769, f. In a Venetian report, Brown, No. 768, it is assumed that Henry himself artfully caused Perkin to be urged to attempt his escape, in order to afford a pretext for keeping a stricter guard upon him. Henry's order for the prosecution to the Earl of Oxford, June 10, 1498: 10th Rep. of the Dep. Keeper, Part iv. p. 2; cf. the notes, Exc. Hist., 118.

Perkin's ultimate fate is related most in detail by the City Chron., 176a–177a; Hall, 491, again enlarges considerably on P. V., 771.

See also the indictment of the jury: Baga de Secretis, 216, f. ; the
Act of Attainder of 1504 ; Rot. Parl., vi. 545 ; also Fabian's Abridg-
ment, 687 ; Arnold, p. 40 ; Grey Friars' Chron., p. 26 ; Wrioth., p. 4 ;
Zurita, v. fol. 170*a* ; Berg., p. 213 ; Lett. and Pap., i. 114 ; Plumpt.
Corres., 141, f. The only difference between the City Chron. and
Hall, where the latter is following Fabian, is that the former (fol.
176*b*) calls the eight confederates "prisoners of the Tour," while
Hall designates the four mentioned by him as "hys (Perkin's)
kepers." Probably this is an independent, and at the same
time incorrect addition of Hall's, for among the four was
Astwood, who had been at first condemned in 1495 as a follower
of Perkin, and afterwards pardoned, and a certain "long Roger,"
possibly also a former follower of Perkin, who had been arrested
long before (see the reward entered under date Oct. 23, 1494,
in Exc. Hist. 99, to five men for "riding to feche Long Roger").
Certainly these people cannot be put down as Perkin's "keepers."
John Walter had been expressly excluded from the general pardon
for the Irish of Aug. 26, 1496 (Rym., xii. 634, f.) ; concerning his
capture, see Smith, State of Cork, ii. 31, f. ; on John Taylor's which
followed in France : Report of the Milanese ambassador, July 13,
1499, Brown, No. 799.

On *Warwick's* condemnation and execution : City Chron., 176*b*,
177*a*, f. ; Hall, 491 ; Baga de Secretis, 217, f. ; Plumpt. Corres., 142,
f. ; cf. P. V., 771. Short notice in Puebla's letter: Lett. and Pap., i.
114 ; Berg., p. 213, with reference made to earlier and more detailed
accounts ; these are now wanting, but have been made use of by
Zurita, v. 170*a*, according to whom Puebla was present at the judicial
proceedings against Warwick ; Zurita also mentions the discontent
among the people at Warwick's execution. The City Chronicle has
two mistakes, probably mistakes of the copyists, fol. 176*b*, that Warwick's trial took place on "Tuesday" instead of "Thursday," and
fol. 177*a*, the execution on Thursday, Nov. 29 (instead of Thursday
the 28th). Hall gives the correct dates, supported also by the letter
in the Plumpt. Corres., as they probably were given in the common
authority, Fabian. Henry paid £12 6s. 8d. for Warwick's burial:
Exc. Hist. 123.

To Chapter IV.

1 (*to page* 123).—The question as to whether the various princes
with whom Perkin came in contact believed in him, and for what
length of time they did so, can only be answered with more or less

probability. Bergenroth, in his preface (p. lxxix.), allows that Ferdinand, as a matter of fact, preferred the Tudor to the pretender; but thinks also (ibid., p. lxxxiv.) that all the princes of Perkin's time looked upon him as the genuine Yorkist prince. He infers this with regard to all except the Spaniards from a remark made in the presence of the Spanish ambassador by Henry, who intended, as he expressly left out Ferdinand and Isabella, to pay them thereby a politic compliment. A polite speech such as this proves nothing. In support of the view that the Spaniards also believed in Perkin, Bergenroth adduces the very specious argument that in a key to the cipher used by Puebla, under the same heading as "the Pope, the Emperor, kings, and other persons of the blood royal," Perkin's cipher is found as that of the Duke of York. But as Perkin is always mentioned in the letters under this name, it is probable that the name is included under this heading because it was a royal one, not because the person who assumed it was presumed to be of royal blood. As, however, it is quite conceivable that for a time, especially on the first announcement of the rising, the idea that Perkin's was a genuine claim had taken some hold on men's minds, the passage may possibly be understood in the way Bergenroth takes it. But the whole conduct of the (Spanish) sovereigns, to whom ways enough of getting information lay open, shows that they by no means continued to hold this view (cf. their own words, Berg., p. 92 ; cf. Zurita, v. 59*b*).

2 (*to page* 132).—Last negotiations before the settlement: Berg., pp. 122 to 127. Text of the treaty in the subsequent ratification by Henry: Rym., xii. 663–665. Abstract in Berg., p. 129, f. ; cf. Zurita, v. 100*a*, who dates the English power the 2nd instead of the 22nd of Sept.—The special assurance given by Henry of Arthur's right of succession, in an undated letter to Ferdinand and Isabella, is placed by Bergenroth, No. 169, on Jan. 1, 1497, the day of the Spanish ratification. It has nothing to do with that, and should be placed close to the date of the treaty.—The Spanish ratification and power for the betrothal for Puebla : ibid., No. 167, f. ; the further demands : ibid., Nos. 170, 175. Henry's qualified promise, on the subject of the customs: ibid., No. 182. Betrothal at Woodstock, Zurita, v. fol. 127*a*, f. ; cf. Berg., p. 132. New Spanish ratification, Feb. 4, 1498 : Berg., No. 189 ; Zurita, 139*a*.

3 (*to page* 135).—The first complaints about Puebla : Berg., pp. 109, 117, 120, 135, 147. Puebla against Ayala : ibid., 152, 155, 158, 161, 164, f., 191, 197 ; cf. later, 248, 250–252, and the same earlier, in the year 1488: p. 16. Powers for Londoño and the Sub-prior, p. 148. Reports on Puebla, ibid., pp. 161–167 ; his financial

embarrassments : pp. 112, 166, 191, 232. A salary of a 100,000
maravedi (about 1200 marks) had been promised him : ibid.,
p. 192. Henry's offers: pp. 146, 162, 163, 165, f., 167, 228,
232. Puebla mentions his request for the jurisdiction over the
Spaniards in England on June 16, 1500, ibid., p. 228, but refers to
a petition made before; possibly the reference is to an undated
letter quoted not long before by Bergenroth, No. 273. The letters
granting this petition, ibid., Nos. 274–276, are rough drafts; and
Nos. 274 and 275, the editor remarks, were written by Puebla's
secretary; No. 274 was even enclosed with No. 273. These were
therefore compositions of Puebla's own, which, however, his sovereigns
took care not to make use of. Schanz., i. 274, f., is accordingly in
error when he considers the appointment as having really taken place.
On the treatment of Puebla by Ferdinand and Isabella, see Berg.,
pp. 135, 277, 281, 294; his praise of himself, pp. 189, 195, f., 198,
250. His severe illness, in the year 1508, is mentioned by André,
Ann., pp. 104, 105, 110, 111. On the whole subject, cf. Bergenroth's
Preface, p. xix., ff.

4 (*to page* 138).—The special instruction for Fuensalida in Bergenroth, p. 234, f. (but to be placed somewhat earlier, between Nos. 265
and 266). The pretended orders to Puebla, June 6, 1500: ibid.,
pp. 220–222, cf. p. 243, f., reports on the embassage : pp. 235–238,
252. On Puebla's conduct: ibid., pp. 236, f., 248, 250–252, 254;
also Lett. and Pap., i. p. 124, f.

First we cannot help being struck by the letter to Puebla of
June 6, not only on account of the alteration demanded in the treaty
after all the binding agreements that had already been concluded, but
also because, according to it, we are to credit the Spanish Government with an astonishingly careless mode of conducting business.
In this letter the king and queen asserted they had blindly trusted to
Puebla's assurance that the marriage compact was more favourable to
them than the article concerning the marriage in the treaty of Medina
del Campo, and therefore had signed it without inquiring into it; and
that the Secretary of State had not been able to judge of the new
article, as he had never seen the old one ! It was not, they said, till
they were beginning to execute the new stipulations that they had sent
for a copy of the old ones, and then discovered, on comparing them,
how much less favourable to themselves the new ones were. This
had therefore not occurred to them till June, 1499, while the treaty
they found fault with had been already concluded on Oct. 1,
1496. They thought they might impute a good deal to Puebla, and
managed cleverly to hide it from the conceited man by making a

show of great confidence in him and by the reproaches they now cast upon him. It is possible that their order of May 25, 1500, to the secretary, Ferdinand Alvarez (Berg., p. 219), directing all the papers concerning the treaty of Medina del Campo to be sent to the court, was only written on Puebla's account. Unfortunately, the corresponding instruction to Fuensalida, on the attitude he was to assume with regard to these orders, is not extant; we only learn from himself how it was carried out. But that the order to Puebla was a mere blind is quite obvious from the other circumstances, and chiefly from the fact that the order was rescinded before it had been possible for any special negotiations on the subject to take place.

Concerning the mistrust displayed by the English with regard to the Spaniards, cf. Berg., p. 237; on the preparations for the wedding: ibid., pp. 214, 217, f., 226, 231, 253, 254, f.; Past. Lett., iii. 394. Henry's purchase of jewels: Exc. Hist., 125; scheme for the reception festivities: Hardwicke Papers, i. 1–20; Lett. and Pap., i. 404–417; ii. 103–105; grant from the city to pay the costs: City Chron., fol. 178*b*.

5 (*to page* 140).—On Katharine's journey from Granada to Coruña: Berg., pp. 252, 256, f., 258, 259. The date of her departure, May 21, is given by Ferdinand himself, p. 258; the statement of Peter Martyr (p. 127): "V. nonas Maii," is therefore to be rejected; cf. Zurita, v. 212*a*, and Galindez Carvajal, Anales breves in Col. de Doc. ined., xviii. p. 300.—Embarkation and landing: Berg., 261, f.; Zurita, 220*b*; Carvajal, 301, as above (the latter gives Aug. 26 as the date of the embarkation at Coruña). The City Chronicle, 183*a*, states that the news of the landing came to London on Oct. 4; from the context in the City Chron., we must conclude that the original source, Fabian's Chronicle, must here have been obscure, as the other documents derived from it—Fabian's Abridgment, 689, and Stow, 874—incorrectly give Oct. 4 as the day of the landing. Arnold, p. 40, and, following him, the Chronicle of the Grey Friars, p. 57, give, in fact, Oct. 8.—Henry's letter of welcome: Lett. and Pap., i. 126–128. On his journey before the meeting, see the Herald's report in Leland Coll., v. 352–356; cf. City Chron., 183*b*–184*a*.

The detailed description of Katharine's entry into London and the festivities in the town are given by the City Chronicle, 184*a*–196*b*. Hall, 493, f., endeavours, from the same account, to give a complete picture of the whole affair. He adds some things about the marriage which are wanting in the Chronicle; among these, however, it must be noted that the minute description of how the wedded couple were conducted to bed ("and there dyd that acte, which to the performaunce and full consummacion of matrimony was moost requysite and expedient"), as well as the story connected with this about Arthur's words after the wedding night, were written by Hall, after Henry VIII.'s divorce, when the chief point in question was whether Arthur and Katharine's marriage had been consummated or not. Arthur's words also played a part in the judicial inquiry of 1529. The Chronicle of the Grey Friars of London, p. 27, here independently enlarges upon Arnold, p. 40. The extract from a "printed book," likewise included in the proceedings at the trial in 1529, Brewer, Lett. and Pap. of Henry VIII., iv. 3, p. 2587, f., is a piece from Arnold's Chronicle; cf. Exc. Hist., 126, for Nov. 12, 1501.—The settlement of the jointure: Berg., No. 308, f.; Rym., xii. 780–783. The receipt for the payment of the dowry was dated Nov. 17, 1501, see Col. de Doc., i. p. 356; cf. Exc. Hist., 126, to Nov. 18: "For carage of the payment of Spain from Poules to the water, 1s."—On the subsequent festivities: Herald's reports in Leland, Coll., v. 356–373; City Chron., 196*b*–199*b*. Notice in Hall, 494. Henry's letter to the Spanish kings, Nov. 28, 1501, Berg., No. 311.

The first notice of the rumour that Ferdinand had deferred the conclusion of the marriage and the sending of Katharine for as long as Warwick lived, because, till his death, England would never be safe from civil war, is brought forward by Hall, p. 491. That this assertion could not be maintained can at once be shown by the account of the events from original sources, and it is just as easy to explain, from the coincidence in time, how such a rumour arose among the people. Bacon (p. 179) enlarges on the short account in Hall; he knows of letters that Ferdinand is supposed to have written about the matter; he represents the whole affair as a move planned by Henry in order to shift the blame of Warwick's death on to Ferdinand's shoulders. Gairdner, Henry VII., p. 174, combats Bacon's view, without, however, remembering the earlier statement in Hall; Gairdner also (Lett. and Pap., i. 113, f.; Berg., p. 213) attaches too great weight, as influencing Ferdinand's judgment of the matter, to a remark of Puebla's on the importance of Warwick's death. Pauli, p. 605, misunderstands Bacon when he says that Ferdinand took offence at Warwick's execution. Possibly Bacon and Hall's accounts are based upon Fabian.

6 (*to page* 147).—Henry's proposals of alterations with regard to the peace with Scotland of Dec. 5, 1497, in the herald's instruction, Brit. Mus. MS., Cott., Vesp., Cxvi. fol. 118, f., the actual contents of which are given Lett. and Pap., i. 424. James's words on the subject

to Ayala, Aug. 28, 1498 ; Brown, No. 769 ; the report on the Border incident near Norham in P. V., 768, following him, Hall, 487, is completed and also confirmed by the allusions in the Spanish reports, Berg., pp. 168, 190, f., and in the letter mentioned above from James to Ayala, with the help of which also the date, given too late by Gairdner, Henry VII., p. 167, can be approximately determined.

For the negotiations between James IV. and Bishop Fox at Melrose I also follow P. V., 769, only it is obvious that the attempt to ascribe the whole initiative in the affair of the marriage to James has a distinct purpose, and is made, moreover, in the supposed interest of Henry ; whereas the story, which can be supported on documentary evidence, certainly shows the circumstances to have been exactly the reverse. Pauli, p. 600, and also again Gairdner, p. 168, f., have let themselves be too much influenced by Polydore Vergil.

Ayala on the scheme of the Spanish and Scotch marriage : Berg., pp. 175, 176, 178, f. ; Henry's utterances and hesitation : ibid., 160, f., 175, f. On Henry's supposed idea of a Danish marriage, see the report of the Milanese ambassador, Nov. 17, 1498, Brown, No. 776 ; on the negotiations of the Border plenipotentiaries at the beginning of 1499 : Fraser, Douglas Book, iii., Charters, pp. 173–175 ; the supposition that Scotland had demanded that France should be included in Ayala's report, Mar. 26, 1499, Berg., p. 206 ; cf., on the other hand, Puebla, Aug. 25, 1478, ibid., 191, Henry's letter to Ferdinand and Isabella, June 15, 1499, ibid., p. 210 ; Lett. and Pap., i. 110, f. ; Treaty of July 12, 1499, with the powers, Rym., xii. 722–728 ; Rot. Scot., ii. 537, 539–542 ; Bain, iv. 332, f. ; see also Rym., 721, f., 726 ; Lett. and Pap., ii. 84 ; Henry's suspicion on Perkin's account : Lett. and Pap., i. 424 ; cf. the article in the treaty, Rym., 675.

The possibility of preliminary negotiations for the marriage in London by Scotch ambassadors is afforded by the fact of their presence in London : Exc. Hist., p. 122 ; Henry's power for Fox, Sept. 11, 1499, in Rym., 729, f. ; Bain, No. 1658 ; see besides, Puebla's reports : Lett. and Pap., i. 114 ; Berg., 213, 218, f., 225, 228 ; fresh appointment of Border commissioners : Rot. Scot., ii. 543–546 ; Bain, iv. No. 1664 ; cf. Exc. Hist., 124. The treaties of Jan. 24, 1502, in Rym., xii. 787–803 ; Du Mont, iv. 1, pp. 23–27 ; Rot. Scot., ii. 548–561 ; cf. Ayloffe, p. 314 ; Bain, Nos. 1680–1682 ; instructions : Rym., 776–779, 780, 791, f., 798, f. ; Bain, No. 1675, f., 1678 ; Henry's safe conduct, given prematurely : Rym., 772 ; Rot. Scot, 546 ; Bain, No. 1670. On the arrival and residence of the Scots in London, cf. City Chron., 198*b*, 199*b*–201*a* ; Hall, 494. Pauli's statements, p. 601, on the marriage treaty are inexact, and with regard to the stipulations in the treaty of alliance mentioned on p. 302, he overlooked that they were already included in the treaty of 1499.

On the marriage ceremony of Jan. 25, 1502, see the report of Somerset Herald : Leland Coll., iv. 258–264. The report has the date of the year 1502, which, according to the English computation, meant January, 1503, and, in the same year, Feb. 24, 1503, is placed in Rym., xiii. 54, f., the letter of thanks from the Archbishop of Glasgow and the Earl of Bothwell for their reception in England. Both dates are wrong, for it certainly cannot be supposed that the very same ambassadors, just a year after, were once again in England, and we also cannot find the smallest notice that this was so. In the letter of Feb. 24 mention is made of King James's oath to the treaty, which was taken Feb. 22, 1502 (Rym. xii. 804), signed by his own hand and enclosed in the letter, and would hardly have been detained in Scotland for again exactly a year. To this agree too the statements of the City Chron., 198*b*, 201*a*, and of Hall, 494, for 1501–1502; cf. Arnold, p. 41; Grey Friars' Chron., p. 27. In Henry's accounts the costs of the Spanish embassy are entered under date Jan. 31, and with further additions on Mar. 31, 1502, in the sum of £428 13s. 2d. : Exc. Hist., 127. Pauli, p. 601, places the conclusion of the marriage correctly, 1502, Gairdner, Henry VII., p. 182—led astray no doubt by the erroneous dates given—in the year 1503, shortly before the death of Queen Elizabeth.

On James's relations with Lady Drummond, see Tytler, v. pp. 10, 12, f.—The ratifications and twice-repeated oath of James, see Rym., xii. 804; xiii. 30–32, 43–51; Ayloffe, 314, f.; Rot. Scot., 546–561; Bain, Nos. 1690, 1693–1695; cf. Lett. and Pap., ii. 378. Pauli, p. 602, again makes a mistake when he assigns James's incautious oath to Dec. 10, for it was on that day that the second oath was taken.—James's promise not to renew the league with France, in a letter to Henry, July 12 : Rym., xiii. 12; Bain, iv. App. i. p. 441, f., placed incorrectly by Rym. in 1502, by Bain correctly in 1503. James refers to a letter of Henry's from Richmond on June 27, and Henry was there on June 27, 1503; he was just then setting out from Richmond : Leland, Coll., iv. 265, whereas, in the year 1502, on the 22nd and 28th, probably therefore also on the 27th of June, he was at Westminster : Rym., xiii. 11; Berg., No. 326.

James's last assurances with regard to the marriage : Rym., xiii. 54, 62–76; Bain, Nos. 1706–1714, 1718; cf. Rym., 92, f.; Bain, No. 1735, f.; Ayloffe, 316. Henry's power on the subject of the jointure, May 4, 1503 : Rym., 56–60; Rot. Scot., ii. 561–563; on

Margaret's outfit: Bain, Nos. 1677, 1689, 1698–1700, 1704, f., 1715–
1717, 1720–1727, App. i. No. 38; detailed description of the
journey and the wedding, in the herald's report in Leland, Coll., iv.
265–300; on Colliweston, cf. Cooper, Mem. of Margaret, 43.
James's expenses for the wedding amounted to something above
£7000 Scots (three pounds Scots were equal to one English): Rot.
Scacc., xii. 181, 182; cf. ibid., Pref., 54; on the payment of the
dowry, see Exc. Hist., 130, 133; Rym., xiii. 118, f., Rot. Scot., ii.
565; Bain, 1740; Ayloffe, 316.—Henry's noteworthy saying is
reported by P. V., 769.

7 (*to page* 150).—The Anglo-Burgundian treaty of Feb. 24, 1496,
with the powers, in Rym., xii. 576, f., 578–591; Du Mont, iii. 2,
pp. 336 to 343, where, pp. 318–324, the same treaty, with Henry's
ratification of Mar. 26, 1496, is wrongly placed in the previous year
1495. The conditions of it are given in Schanz, i. 18, ff.; Anderson, Origin of Comm., i. 545–547; cf. Rym., 601, f.; 45th Rep. of
the Dep. Keeper, App. i. p. 341; Berg., pp. 88, 95; Brown, No.
690. On the reception of the ambassadors in London, see City
Chron., 157*b*.

The name of the " Magnus Intercursus," given to the treaty,
appears neither in contemporary documents nor in the new settlements, which followed shortly after, where the treaty is designated
in the usual manner, by the date alone. Bacon, p. 146, says: "This
is that treaty which the Flemings call at this day intercursus
magnus;" and Rogers says, Six Centuries, etc., p. 320: "I suppose
this is Bacon's own name for the treaty of commerce of 1496." In
any case an authority such as that of Bacon will not be sufficient to
make us accept the name he gave, as has hitherto been generally
done. No sort of confirmation of it in any other place has come
under my notice.

Concerning molestation at sea again in the year 1495, see Lett.
and Pap., ii. 58–60; on Henry's frame of mind after the treaty:
Brown, No. 684; Berg., p. 103; his expenditure for the ambassadors:
Exc. Hist., 107; on the demand for the consent of London to it,
see in detail the City Chron., 158*b*–159*b*, with the text of the decree
by the Lord Mayor, of May 1, 1496. In the decree, fol. 159*a*, Feb.
24th is put quite correctly as the date of the treaty; but before
that, fol. 158*b*, April 3rd; this is probably a mistake of the copyist.
In the original, the proclamation, or some other enactment to do
with it, was perhaps given under date of April 3 (Henry's ratification
was of the 26th March). On the order to the other towns, see
9th Report, Part i. p. 146, and 11th Report, Part iii. p. 13.

Henry's complaints on the subject of the new toll, June 21, 1496 : Lett. and Pap., ii. 69–72; cf. Puebla, of July 11, Berg., p. 112; Spanish mediation: Berg., p. 133. Henry's further threats : ibid., 143. The new removal of the market is mentioned in a later letter of Henry's of May, 1507 : Lett. and Pap., i. 329; this removal should be placed between the treaty of Feb. 24, 1496, and the levy of July, 1497, not, as Schanz, i. 22, f., puts it, before the negotiations at Calais in the spring of 1499.

Settlement of July 7, 1497 : Rym., xii. 648, 654–657.—On the negotiations of the Bishop of Cambray in England, see the reports of Puebla of Aug. 25, Sept. 7 and 25, 1498 : Berg., pp. 189, 196, 197, f. English instruction, Aug. 25 : Rym., xii. 695, f. Payment to the ambassadors, Aug. 1 : Exc. Hist., 119. This negotiation in London has been overlooked by Schanz, i. 22 ; he makes the conferences at Calais follow immediately after those at Bruges. Hall, 483, and Stow, 872, both following Fabian, mention the reception of the Englishmen on their return to Antwerp.

On the particulars of the conference at Calais, see Schanz, i. 22–25, and the correspondence published by him, ii. 195–203; cf. Berg., p. 209 ; Treaty of May 18, 1499 : Rym., xii. 713–720; Du Mont, iii. 2, f., 409–412 ; part taken by the staplers : Schanz, ii. Urk. Beil., pp. 195, 198, 200, f. ; Henry and Margaret of York, in the year 1498 : Puebla's reports, Sept. 7 and 25, Berg., pp. 196 and 198.

8 (*to page* 152).—The Anglo-French treaty of Jan. 17, 1486, in Rym., xii. 281, f.; the commercial arrangements with Brittany, July 2, 1486 : ibid., 305–310 ; the treaty of Edward IV., ibid., xi. 618–624; cf. Schanz, i. 293, f. ; Henry's grievances in the Herald's instruction, Dec. 30, 1494 : Brit. Mus. MS., Cotton, Cal., D, vi. fol. 20, f. ; Charles VIII.'s decree, Nov. 16, 1495, which contains the edict of April 11, in Michel, Hist. du Comm. à Bordeaux, i. 376, note 1 ; cf. Schanz, i. 302. Treaty of May 24, 1497, with the fresh ratifications on the change of government in France on July 14, and Aug. 24, 1498, in Rym., xii. 690–693; Du Mont, iii. 2, p. 401, f. ; cf. Godefroy, Hist. de Charles VIII., pp. 738–743. Schanz, i. 306, f., does not notice in his statement of contents that the text in Du Mont, iii. 2, pp. 376–378, used by him is in the somewhat strange form of a ratification by Henry on Jan. 15, 1498, with a free summary of the terms of the treaty, shortened in some parts, and in others enlarged with explanations.

Complaints of the Bretons with the English answers, of the year 1507, in Schanz, ii. Urk. Beil., pp. 528–536, only an introductory fragment, moreover incorrectly dated 1497, in Lett. and Pap., ii.

72, f.; complaints of the French, the text in Schanz, 525–528, summary in Brewer, Lett. and Pap. of Henry VIII., ii. 2, No. 3521; Michel, i. 377–380, 383, f. In opposition to Brewer's date, July, 1517, Schanz, i. 302, note 7, holds to the time accepted by Michel, that is, the end of the fifteenth century. To decide this for certain is difficult, and not of great consequence for us, as the fragments quoted, similar in their purport to the Breton complaints, show a condition of feeling such as had existed among the French merchants since about 1495, and may in any case, without hesitation, be applied to the later period of Henry VII. On the English carrying trade between Spain and France, see Ferdinand and Isabella to Puebla and Henry, June 21 and 26, 1496: Berg., pp. 106, 107; cf. 119; later negotiations: André, Ann., 1508, Mem. 110.

9 (*to page* 155).—For the events in Bruges, see especially the Recesse: Hanserecesse, iv. No. 150, f.; the Dantzic report, ibid., No. 174, and the English, No. 180; Schanz, ii. Urk. Beil., 420–428; English power: Hanserec., No. 145; the Hansa grievance articles, No. 162 (cf. ii. No. 506), the English, No. 165; letter of the Hanse messengers to Henry, June 25, No. 175; Henry's answer, July 9, No. 181; Schanz, ii. pp. 428–430. A comparison of the reports is necessary, because each individual reporter only brings out those points which seem to him the most important, and all prefer to relate that wherein they imagine they have specially distinguished themselves. The Recesse and reports are not quite clear as to whether the English plenipotentiaries went themselves to England at the end of June to deliver their report or not; that they sent a messenger is expressly stated by Alb. Kranz, who was himself present, in Wandalia, lib. xiv. c. 24. On the Riga incident: Hanserec., No. 150, §§ 43, 78; No. 151, § 17, f.; Nos. 278, f., 295, § 18, f.; No. 312, § 3, f.; No. 314, f. The account in Schanz, i. 238, ff., requires many alterations in consequence of the materials recently disclosed; see Schäfer in opposition to him: Jahrbuch für Nationalökonomie, N. F., vii. 116, ff., from whose views, however, I differ in many points, especially in regard to Henry's aims (p. 118).

10 (*to page* 163).—Concerning the first voyages of discovery from Bristol, see Peschel, Zeitalter der Entdeckungen, p. 101; Ruge, ibid., p. 220, and Ruge's " Christopher Columbus," p. 36, f.; Harrisse, Cabot, p. 44, note 3; Ayala's report, July 25, 1498, Berg., p. 177; the passage on the subject is given in full in Harrisse, p. 329.

The account of Christopher Columbus's relations with Henry

rests chiefly on the history of the admiral, supposed to have been written by Columbus's son Ferdinand (extracts on the subject in Hackluyt, Voyages, Navigations, etc., iii. p. 2, f.; on this work, cf. Ruge, Christopher Columbus, p. 21, ff.); whence Peschel, p. 113, Ruge, 280, Schanz, i. 314 f., all take their information. Winsor, Hist. of America, ii. 3, contributes nothing new to the settlement of the question. The statement in the biography that Bartolommeo returned, "con los capitulos concedidos," is contradicted by the manuscript, Historia general de las Indias, by Las Casas; "no pudiendo concluir sus tratos con el rey de Inglaterra" (see on the subject Navarete in Col. de Doc., ined. xvi. 551–554); I found no allusion in any English sources. Otherwise Las Casas and the biography agree; to decide about this one divergence is hardly possible. Las Casas certainly deserves the greater confidence, only Henry, who probably already knew of Christopher Columbus' first vòyage and its results (in January, 1493, a Spaniard who brought him spices was given £2), would, if he had dismissed Bartolommeo, have been acting in a very different spirit to that shown in his treatment of Cabot later. In any case his consent remains doubtful, and we should certainly not speak beforehand with Peschel, No. 260 (whom Schanz follows), of a consent to all demands.

On Cabot's previous history ("Cabotto" was his real name): Brown, No. 453; cf. 443; Harrisse, 309–312; see also, with regard to his origin, the very full and convincing accounts in Harrisse, 1–41; Bourne, English Seamen, i. 28, 30, has some erroneous statements. See Ferdinand and Isabella's letter to Puebla, March 28, 1496, with a reference to a report of Puebla's which is unknown to us, in Berg., No. 128; this passage is given again in full in Harrisse, p. 315.— Patent for Cabot, Mar. 5, 1496: Rym., xii. 595, f.; Harrisse, 312–315; also Hackluyt, iii. 4, f.—On the first voyage 1497: letters of De Soncinos, Pasqualigos, and Ayala; Brown, Nos. 750, 752; Harrisse, 322, 324–326; Berg., p. 177; City Chronicle, 173a; cf. Exc. Hist., 113. Soncinos' subsequent letter of Dec. 18, 1497, is especially to be noticed, in Winsor, iii. 54, f., who, besides, mentions only one ship with which Cabot set sail. The bestowal on him of a yearly income from the Bristol customs revenues is dated Dec. 13, 1497; Winsor, p. 6 (the author of the section on the Cabots in the History of America edited by Winsor is Charles Deane. He did not make use of Harrisse's works). The account in Schanz, i. 316, is in some points to be corrected; from the statement in the City Chronicle, it is quite clear that Henry contributed to the enterprise, and thus perhaps roused the sympathy of the London merchants. The following words occur in Soncinos' reports: Harrisse, p. 323; Brown, No. 750: "S. Maestà mandò un Veneziano," although to that alone not much weight can be attached.

The question as to whether Cabot's first voyage of discovery took place in 1494 or 1497 has been sufficiently discussed with the fullest examination of the original sources, and 1497 decided on by Harrisse, pp. 52–60, and, following him, by Ruge, p. 501, f., note. On the voyage, see besides the full discussion in Harrisse, pp. 61–95; (summing up of the whole, p. 95, f.; cf. Ruge, p. 502), and 97–100, with which the equally detailed first chapters of Biddle's memoir of Cabot should be compared. The final result is that no satisfactory assurance as to the direction of Cabot's first voyage is as yet to be obtained. (By mistake the battle of Blackheath, in June, 1497, is regarded by Harrisse, p. 110, note, as forming part of the Scotch war which followed later.)

The second patent of Feb. 3, 1498, is printed for the first time by Biddle, 76, f., repeated by Harrisse, 327, f.; cf. Hackluyt, iii. 5; Bourne, English Seamen, i. 36. The part Henry took in the expedition is not only spoken of as prominent, but it is even stated that sending out the vessels was his work, by Ayala ("el rey . . . ha fecho armada" . . . "El rey determino de enbiar . . .") and Puebla ("El Rey . . . embio cinco naos"), Harrisse, pp. 328, 329; Berg., p. 177; in the Privy Purse Expenses, Exc. Hist., 116, f. (cf. Biddle, p. 86), in March and April, 1498, the payment of £70 is entered for Lancelot Thirkill and Thomas Bradley together, and £2 for John Carter. In Harrisse, 102, note 2, the latter sum is noted in shillings, so that Ruge, p. 502, by mistake reckons Henry's whole contribution at £110 by adding together the sums £70 and £40. We need not, however, consider these two entries as representing the whole contribution, they were only two separate payments to companions of Cabot. Harrisse, p. 102, says, "Aussi ne croyons-nous pas, malgré l'expression employée par Puebla et Ayala, que les cinq navires furent expédiés aux frais de Henry VII., dont l'avarice était notoire," and therefore, because of the old tradition of Henry's avarice, Harrisse entirely sets aside, without any further reason, this evidence from two original authorities, which to us seems decisive. Rogers, Hist. of Agriculture, etc., iv. Pref., pp. ix., xii.; and Cunningham, Growth of English Industry, p. 419, cf. 444, also represent entirely this one view with regard to the king, which really has nothing in its favour except its antiquity. Our best authorities, on the contrary, compel us to believe that the voyage of 1497 was supported by the king, and that the one in 1498 was altogether an undertaking of the king's own. According to these reports the squadron consisted of five, instead of two ships, as stated by Peschel, p. 276, and Schanz, p. 317 ; and there is no mention of John Cabot's having died before this first voyage, as Peschel, 276, and Hellwald, Sebastian Cabot, p. 16, suppose, both from a mere supposition of Biddle's, p. 81 ; cf. Winsor, iii. 59. It is possible that something in a very inexact story of Sebastian Cabot's about the first journey, full of evident mistakes, has reference to the otherwise unknown details of this second journey ; report of Butrigarius in Hackluyt, iii. 6, f.

Text of the patent of March 19, 1501, in Biddle, pp. 312–320 ; short statement of contents in Lett. and Pap., ii. 378 ; cf. Bourne, i. 309. Schanz, i. 317, only knew the purport of the patent, and does not give a full discussion of the contents till p. 318, in connection with the patent of Dec. 9, 1502, Rym., xiii. 37–42, which in the main is a mere repetition of the first. These later attempts of the men of Bristol are therefore not to be regarded as so insignificant as they appear to be in Deane's opinion (Winsor, iii. 58).

On the natives brought to England, see City Chronicle, 204*a*, enlarged upon by Stow, 875, also see the notes of expenditure in Exc. Hist. 126, 129, 131, 133 ; cf. Peschel, p. 278, note 2.—Considering the successful part played by the men of Bristol in these voyages to the West, it is a matter for surprise that the Bristol local chronicle—Ricart's Calendar—does not contain a word of allusion to these exploits.

To Chapter V.

1 (*to page* 166).—On Edmund de la Pole's partial restitution : Rot. Parl., vi. 474–477 ; on the part he took in the tournaments in honour of Henry of York : Lett. and Pap., i. 392, 394–398, 400, 402 ; shorter account : City Chron., fol. 150*a*, f. ; also see Brown, Nos. 754–794 ; later, Berg., No. 278. The date of his first flight is to be inferred from the Bill of Attainder, Stat., ii. 685, Rot. Parl., 546, which gives July 1, 1499, as the day for the forfeiture of his property ; cf. Gairdner in Lett. and Pap., i. Pref., p. xl. ; Henry's orders : Lett. and Pap., ii. 377 ; Past. Lett., iii. 393 ; the undated instruction for Guildford and Hatton : Lett. and Pap., i. 129–134 ; the approximate date of their mission is given by the payments to both, entered on Sept. 20, 1499 : Exc. Hist., 123 ; according to the instruction, Henry supposed Suffolk's abode at that time to be Calais, but Molinet, v.

118–120, is able on examination to demonstrate that he was staying at St. Omer. According to Molinet, the ambassadors came to Philip, and he tried to put pressure on Suffolk with a view to persuade him to return. P. V. also, 773, speaks of a flight to Flanders, and, in fact, to Margaret's court; this last is clearly a mistake. Otherwise for Suffolk's history, especially for the first part of his career, Polydore Vergil's account is indispensable, 773, f.; Hall follows him, 495, f., with a few additions. P. V. should, however, be set right in some particulars, as has already been done by Gairdner, Lett. and Pap., i. Pref. xxxix., f., for the confusion in the dates of Suffolk's crime and first flight. P. V. appears only to have known the date of his second flight in July or August, 1501; according to him the homicide, indictment, first flight, return, and second flight, must all have taken place in the space of a few months.

2 (*to page* 168).—Puebla, who was himself present, gives us information about the interview between Henry and Philip, but he knew nothing of the negotiations, June 16, 1500, Berg., p. 226, f.; Chronicle of Calais, p. 4; cf. 49–51; Arnold, p. 40; Grey Friars' Chronicle, p. 26; Zurita, v. 187*a*; Molinet, v. 130–132; the names of Henry's retinue in Lett. and Pap., ii. 87–92, cf. Chron. of Calais, 3, f. Concerning the previous negotiations, information is given by a letter of Henry's of June 2, to the city authorities; the text of this is given in the City Chron., fol. 178*b*–181*a*; from this Hall, p. 491, f., took his account, which enlarges upon the meagre one in Polydore Vergil, 771; Bacon did the same, 180, f. The latter makes these negotiations take place at the meeting itself, of which the original authorities say nothing; but no doubt it may be supposed that the same questions were touched upon there. Henry's remark in Puebla's presence: Berg., p. 234; on the anxieties of the Spaniards, ibid., 234–236; Zurita, v. 187*a*. The cost of his nine weeks' absence amounted for Henry to £1589 12*s*. 10*d*.: Exc. Hist., 124.

Hall and later writers, following the lead of P. V., think that Henry wished to make an inspection of Calais and its garrison; this idea probably arose from his long stay there before the meeting with Philip. But P. V. especially declares that the visit took place in order to escape from the sweating sickness, which was then prevalent in England; with him the meeting is regarded as an affair of secondary importance. Hall reduces this assertion to a mere supposition, and in this Bacon follows him, p. 180, and so does Gairdner, Henry VII., p. 175; whilst Pauli, v. 614, follows P. V. closely. But the view which connects these events must be rejected as untenable. Puebla states in a letter written from London, after the return there,

June 29, 1500 (Berg., p. 238), and also in a postscript added afterwards, that many people were dying in London of an epidemic which
had just begun to rage there ; that the disease was not yet serious,
but that an increase in the mortality was expected.   He could not
have written in this way, if Henry had fled to escape the disease nearly
two months earlier.   As a matter of fact, Henry's return coincided
with the commencement of the disease.   The notice of it in the City
Chron., fol. 181*b*, occurs among the events between the end of July
and beginning of October.   The journey to Calais had simply the one
political object, and it was only the preliminary negotiations mentioned
in Henry's own letter which delayed the meeting; P. V.'s statement
is nothing but a later erroneous supposition.   See also on the sickness, P. V., 771; Hall, p. 491; Wrioth., p. 4; Plumpt. Corres., pp. 138–
140.   The two letters in Plumpt. Corres. are inserted by the editor
in the year 1499, instead of 1500.   P. V.'s statement, which Hall
accepts (cf. also Pauli, as above), that in London alone 30,000
victims perished, is an obvious exaggeration.

Death and burial of Prince Edmund: City Chron., 181*a*, cf. Arnold,
p. 40; Wrioth., p. 4; Grey Friars' Chron., p. 26 (put under the
wrong month, "in December") ; also Puebla's account, June 16, 1500,
Berg., p. 225.   The entry of the costs of the funeral under "May,"
Exc. Hist., 124, cannot be reconciled with any of these statements.
The obvious error existing here can be explained as follows : the two
larger sums here placed together, for the funeral and Henry's
journey, were entered in a later addition, and hence the mistake arose.
The last entry before them is of April 15, the next following, of July.

3 (*to page* 168).—Curzon's leave of absence, Aug. 29, 1499 : Rym.,
xii. 729.   He is called Lord C., on account of the title given him by
Maximilian, for he was probably never an English peer; see on the
subject Gairdner, Lett. and Pap., i. Pref. p. xl., f., note 2, and
Henry VII., 186.   Mr. Gairdner also rightly objects to a presumption
of P. V.'s, 773, further enlarged upon by Hall, 495, and Bacon, 193,
f., and also repeated by Pauli, p. 615, that Curzon had acted from
the first as a spy for Henry, in the same way as Clifford had
previously done.   That on his return Curzon was again received
into favour agrees with Henry's usual course of action, and by no
means compels us to regard Curzon's case as analogous with that
of Clifford, especially as the date of his leave of absence, Aug.,
1499, two years before Suffolk's second flight, makes this idea
impossible.

This point Gairdner also brings forward with regard to the
opinion hitherto held that Curzon had followed the earl to Flanders ;

he overlooks, however, that this opinion rests only on a misunderstanding of P. V.'s, and also of Hall's. If we look closely into P. V.'s narrative, it is perfectly clear; but Hall thought himself called upon to enlarge passages that in his opinion needed explanation, by certain explanatory additions, which, however, as Hall misunderstood the originals, only twist and obscure the sense. To this inaccuracy of Hall's alone, who was again himself misunderstood, we may trace the incorrect view hitherto accepted, that Curzon followed the earl on his second flight. This mistake might have been entirely avoided, if historians, from Bacon down to the present day, had not made use of the second-hand authority, Hall—who is not clear here—instead of the original authority, Polydore Vergil, who on this point is particularly correct.

For the same reason the following noteworthy remark in P. V., 773, has hitherto been overlooked: "Cursonus . . . qui per eum in equitum ordinem venerat," in which "per eum" refers to Suffolk, mentioned shortly before, whereas Hall, p. 495, carelessly renders it by "the king."

On Curzon's interview with Maximilian there are two conflicting reports, Lett. and Pap., i. 134–149, and 150, f. The first comprises the events from 1501 to 1503, and contains many original letters. The author is evidently Suffolk's servant Killingworth. It is true that he mostly speaks of himself in the third person as "the steward," but on p. 146 he falls once into the first person. The report is strongly biased in Suffolk's favour, and the obligations into which the emperor is here reported to have entered, sound much more binding than in the other account of the audience granted to Suffolk. This latter is very deficient in places (p. 150, f.), and the name of the author is not given. It begins, "Le Roy des Romains nostre seigneur." According to it Maximilian made his statements in the presence of the Spanish ambassador. Admonitions about keeping the peace, which are not mentioned in Killingworth's account, are specially included, and nothing is said about troops and money. This account, being entirely on the side of the emperor, must also be used with caution. See besides on Curzon, Lett. and Pap., i. 394–398, 403; ii. 291; Exc. Hist., 101.

4 (*to page* 172).—As to the date of Suffolk's second escape the City Chronicle, 183*a*, and Fabian's Abridgment, 687, give August, 1501, according to the Act of Attainder, Stat., ii. 686, and Rot. Parl., vi. 546, it might have been the 20th of July. According to Stow, p. 874, Suffolk made his escape from Harwich; Zurita, v. 221*a*, places his flight too late—"al mismo tiempo que la princesa

(Katharine) arribo a Inglaterra." On Suffolk's meeting with Maximilian, see Lett. and Pap., i. 134-137, 143-145, 179.

On Henry's first relations with Maximilian : Milanese ambassador's reports, March and June, 1499, Brown, Nos. 788, f., 791, 799; preamble of the instruction for the English ambassadors, September, 1501, Lett. and Pap., i. 152, f.—Measures in England : Lett. and Pap., ii. 378; cf. City Chron., 183*a*. Proclamation at Paul's Cross : Hall, p. 496. Suffolk on Tyrell's imprisonment : May 12, 1502, Lett. and Pap., i. 181; also on the arrests and executions : Rot. Parl., vi. 545; City Chron., fol. 201*a*-203*a*; Fabian's Abridgment, p. 687; Hall, p. 496; P. V., p. 773, f.; cf. Grey Friars' Chron., p. 28; Chron. of Cal., p. 6. An inventory made room by room in the castle of Guines, with scattered notes in Henry's own hand, is among the State Papers.

5 (*to page* 174).—Instruction for Somerset and Warham : Lett. and Pap., i. 152-167. Sum of money paid to them, September 30, 1501 : Exc. Hist., 125. Zurita, v. fol. 221*a*, says that they were directed to address themselves to Ayala, then residing in Flanders (see Berg., p. 236). The reports of the ambassadors : Lett. and Pap., i. 168-177; ii. 106-112. The powers, resolutions, receipts, and ratifications : Rym., xiii. 3, f., 6-10, 12-27; cf. Du Mont, iv. 1, pp. 30, f., 34-37. Expenditure : Exc. Hist., 129. Proclamation in London : City Chron., fol. 203*b*; cf. Fabian's Abridgment, p. 688. Both speak at the same time of the announcement of a treaty of peace and amity with "the Archduke of Burgundy." Schanz, i. 28, likewise regards this commercial treaty as a renewal of the treaty of 1496 with Philip. This is a mistake of Fabian's as well as of Schanz, arising probably from the circumstance that the plenipotentiaries were officials of Philip's; but, at that time, they were acting for the emperor—indeed, the attempt they made to act also as Philip's servants was decidedly objected to by their English colleagues, Lett. and Pap., ii. 106, f. The proclamation of banishment of October 23, 1502 : City Chron., 204*a*; Fabian's Abridgment, p. 688. The orders to the sheriffs, November 11 : Brit. Mus. MSS., Sloane, 747, fol. 62*b*, f.

6 (*to page* 177).—In Lett. and Pap., i. 220-225, there is printed an undated order to Wiltshire (cf. 225-229), which Gairdner puts into the year 1503, corresponding to Wiltshire's appointment as controller of Calais, and connects, both in time and purport, with an instruction for Norroy Herald (ibid., 417-419), who was to bring over the insignia of the Garter to Maximilian, after his reception into the Order had taken place by proxy in London, April, 1503.

The order to Wiltshire, however, was written before the payment of the money to Maximilian, which followed on October 1, 1502 (Lett. and Pap., i. 222; Exc. Hist., 129), and should therefore not be connected with the later herald's instruction.   The herald, in 1503, was to see to the carrying out of the proclamations in the form in which they had been agreed upon by Henry with the ambassadors of the King of the Romans (p. 418).   The order to Wiltshire mentions an earlier form, which had been determined upon first " par le conseil du roy " on the one side alone (p. 223), and this agrees exactly with the report of Brandon and West, who demanded that the proclamation should be made " in the forme made by your grace " (ibid., p. 215).   The intended despatch of a herald, which is spoken of in the order to Wiltshire, therefore before October 1, 1502, is not the mission of Norroy Herald in 1503.   Probably on the first occasion the herald after all was not sent, for the herald's commission with regard to the proclamations against Suffolk, mentioned by Wiltshire, was undertaken exactly by Brandon and West in conjunction with their other commission about Maximilian's oath and investiture with the Order.   As a matter of fact, they only succeeded in getting Maximilian to take the oath.   On the despatch of Brandon and West, see Rym., xiii. 35, f.; Exc. Hist., 129; Brown, No. 830. Their long and often imperfect report: Lett. and Pap., i. 189–219. —Money sent by Maximilian to Suffolk, ibid., 186–188, 229, f.

7 (*to page* 177).—Of Maximilian's embassage to Henry we have accounts in the City Chron., fol. 205*b* to 206*a*, and Hall, p. 498, all following, but enlarging upon, Fabian.   Hall's statement that with the condolences for the death of Queen Elizabeth, which had happened shortly before, the ambassadors brought an offer of another marriage for Henry with the widowed Archduchess Margaret is an error; her second husband, the Duke of Savoy, did not, in fact, die till a year later.   See also the notices in Arnold, p. 42; Wriothesley, p. 5; Grey Friars' Chronicle, p. 28 (the arrangement is incorrect); Exc. Hist., 130.—The third proclamation against Suffolk and his companions took place on the " first Sunday in Lent ": City Chron., fol. 205*b*; Fabian's Abridgment, p. 688.   The Grey Friars' Chron., p. 27, is here confused in its statements.   Instruction for Norroy Herald, Lett. and Pap., i. 417–419; cf. former note.

8 (*to page* 180).—The fresh confirmation of privileges to the Hansa: Stat., ii. 665.   Henry's communication, May 24, 1504, Schanz, i. 198, note 1.—Schanz, p. 199, thinks the king wished, through the Hansa merchants, to put a pressure upon the Netherlands, where Suffolk was at that time residing.   That is not

possible, for till Easter, 1504, Suffolk was staying at Aix-la-Chapelle;
he then fell into the hands of the Duke of Gueldres, at that time at
war with the Burgundian government. Further, the date of our first
news of a fresh dispute between Henry and the Netherlands is not
before August, 1504 (Rym., xiii. 105, f.); and besides this, the Hansa
themselves were in constant friction with the Burgundian government, so that their alliance was to be obtained at small cost.—On
the renewed complaints of the Hansa, see the quotations in Schanz,
i. 200, note 1-4. Date when sum in pledge fell due, July 8, 1508,
Brit. Mus., Cott. MSS., Claud. E, vii. fol. 103.

9 (*to page* 182).—For my knowledge of the relations of Duke
George of Saxony with Suffolk and Henry, I am indebted to my friend,
Dr. F. Gess, Professor at Dresden, who very kindly placed at my
disposal his transcripts and extracts from the Dresden State Archives.
Two letters of Waldburg's to Duke George of March 17 and 24,
1504, deserve consideration. Concerning the result of the negotiations, Waldburg said to Sigmund Pflugk that he hoped his duke
"und die weiss ross Sich mit ain andern verainigen werdent," and
Suffolk himself, in a letter to Richard, makes use of the expression,
"pro quibusdam promissis inter nos factis," Lett. and Pap., i. 262.
In the same and in the preceding letter to the town authorities of
Aix, Suffolk says, it was in the hope of satisfying his creditors that
he was specially anxious to go to Duke George.

The usual dilatory conduct of Maximilian, who was always
hoping to make further use of Suffolk, is sufficient to contradict the
supposition suggested by Ulmann, ii. 85, that Maximilian had sent
Suffolk out of Aix. Add to this especially, that Suffolk in a later
message to the King of the Romans tried to justify his conduct,
which would have been quite superfluous if he had been merely
following the king's orders. Killingworth was to say to Maximilian,
as Suffolk wrote to him in his shocking English : "The favt vas nat
yn, my lord, for my lord provffered ef yovr gras weld enterten my
lord for to monnet with xii. hores, my lord vas vel contend to beed
yovr plsser, and vane my lord vas gone J bod be hend xx days to
cheke (= know) your plesser," Lett. and Pap., 254. This agrees therefore excellently with Waldburg's communication of March 17, that
"hertzog edmundt bey ror kr Mt In handlung vmb hilff Sich bear-
beytt," and again helps to fix the date of the flight so as almost to
coincide with the statement in James of Scotland's letter to Duke
Charles, Lett. and Pap., ii. 193, that Suffolk, about Easter, 1504, begged
for permission to enter Gueldres. In 1504 Easter fell on April 7.

10 (*to page* 183).—Schanz, i. 28, adopts the view that Henry

began the new commercial struggle with the Netherlands, following thereby a later statement of the Venetian Quirini of Nov. 29, 1505, Brown, No. 860. The first we hear of the dispute is a power from Henry under date Aug. 4, 1504, for several ambassadors (Rym., xiii. 105, f.), to demand a reform in the treatment of the English merchants, who in spite of treaties were suffering from the increase in the customs duties and other burdens. That this was not attended with success is shown by the next measure we know of— the removal of the English market from Antwerp to Calais, Jan. 15, 1505: Lett. and Pap., ii. 379; in the catalogue of documents of the merchant adventurers, Schanz, ii., Urk. Beil., p. 576, § 11, dated Jan. 31. From Quirini we have two accounts, July 1 and Nov. 29, 1505, Brown, Nos. 846 and 860. In neither account is he quite clear; in the second, which besides shows very erroneous ideas about Calais, he speaks of English export duties in Calais, and of counter duties imposed by Philip on English imports into Flanders, while in the first account he speaks of a general prohibition of imports into Flanders, in return for the prohibition of Flemish imports into England. From this we might suppose that Henry had first raised the export duties in Calais, whereas his instructions to his ambassadors speak, not of an adjustment of complaints on both sides, but only of complaints against the Netherlanders. This by itself would not be a very important proof, if the Burgundian author of a narrative of travels printed in Gachard's Coll. des Voyages, i. p. 460, had not himself shown the Netherlanders to be the originators of the struggle, and Quirini's statements generally in this passage are too inexact to be of any great weight. The duties in Calais were probably first raised when, by transferring the market, the whole trade was turned towards Calais, and Philip probably raised his duties to correspond, and afterwards forbade all imports. Schanz gave Suffolk's presence in the Netherlands as the special motive for Henry's action, but up to July, 1505, Philip and Suffolk had no direct relations with each other. Philip, indeed, complained to Henry of the supposed support of Gueldres by England, Oct. 29, 1504, Berg., No. 402 (cf. with the letter, ibid., p. 347; Zurita, v. 349*a*); therefore if Suffolk had anything to do with the matter, it can only be conjectured that Philip began the war of tariffs in consequence of this supposed assistance given to Gueldres. Häbler in: Der Streit Ferdinands und Philipps, overlooks almost entirely these commercial relations, of such primary importance for Henry's and Philip's relations with each other.—On Manuel, see Berg., pp. 266, 286, 369.

2 B

11 (*to page* 184).—Concerning Louis's conduct we have a Freneh account, destined indeed for Henry, but with internal evidence of trustworthiness : Lett. and Pap., ii. 140–142 ; cf. Quirini's statements, Brown, No. 853, and Lettres de Louis XII., i. 82 ; van den Bergh., i. 45.—James of Scotland's letter, undated, Lett. and Pap., ii. 192–197 ; imperfect in Epist. Reg. Scot., i. 11–16 ; cf. Lett. and Pap., i. Pref., p. xlvii.-l. ; the letter was not written before the latter half of June, 1505, as it contains a reference to a message of Charles's of June 14, Lett. and Pap., 192.

The intimations of Suffolk's plans : Lett. and Pap., i. 419, f. ; his request for intercession with Charles in a letter to an unknown person : Ellis, iii. 1, pp. 127–129 ; the editor supposes this person to have been some one at Philip's court, whereas all the allusions point undoubtedly to one of Charles of Gueldres' counsellors. Suffolk speaks with some exaggeration of a year and a half's imprisonment, and mentions letters of Philip's "sent John dae last passed ; " as the letter, besides, was written before Suffolk's first release and before the compact between Charles and Philip, it may be placed somewhat exactly at the end of June or beginning of July, 1505. The order of the Suffolk letters in Ellis is very unsatisfactory.—On the fall of Hattem and the end of the war, see the Venetian reports : Brown, Nos. 849, 851 ; and Suffolk's letter : Lett. and Pap., i. 262.

12 (*to page* 186).—On the course of the commercial war, see the references in Note 10 ; on Henry's relations with Duke George, the following are to be consulted : Henry's letters to George, July 17, 1504, and Feb. 20, 1505, to Waldburg, April 30, 1505, George to Henry, Sept. 25, 1504, orders to Waldburg of Dec. 30, 1504, and Waldburg's letters of Aug. 19, Nov. 29, 1504, April 3, 1505, in the Dresden State Archives (see before, Note 9). George's power of Dec. 26, 1504, in Rym., xiii. 120 (there incorrectly placed in 1505), and Henry's of Feb. 22, 1505, ibid., p. 114 ; the treaty in George's ratification of Dec. 30, 1505, ibid., pp. 120–123 ; Du Mont, iv. 1, pp. 74–76. As is evident from a safe-conduct of Dec. 2, 1495, Rym., xii. 575, an ambassador from the Saxon duke was already then expected in London, for what purpose, is not known. Perkin, concerning his relations with Saxony, in the letter to Isabella, Archæol., xxvii. 119 ; Berg., No. 85.

On the embassages to England : quotations in Schanz, i. 29, note 3. On the public feeling in England, Puebla reports, but always on the side of Henry, Aug. 11, 1505, Berg., 368, f. ; also cf. Brown, No. 846 ; Lett. and Pap., ii. 379. André bestows the most extravagant praises on the removal of the market, Ann., p. 83, f.

Schanz, i. 28, note 4, attaches too much weight to such compliments on the part of the court historiographer; besides, the passage in question is not from the Vita, as he supposes, but from the Annales. The English chroniclers are silent on this commercial measure; in any case, it must have been but little felt in England. The duty on wool of the staplers begins to show, indeed, a decrease in the autumn of 1503; in 1505 to 1506 it drops even to the low level of the war years 1491-1492, but the general customs receipts experienced no remarkable fluctuations as compared with other times: see the tables in Schanz, ii. 46. On the effect of the stoppage of trade in the Netherlands, Quirini gives us information: Brown, Nos. 846, 849, 860.

13 (*to page* 190).—Suffolk's complaints and petitions for release: Lett. and Pap., i. 254-257, 264. From internal evidence the letters, No. xxxi., f., were written after his release, and therefore to be placed after the letter of July 28, 1505, No. xxxv.—His surrender again to Gueldres: ibid., 266; Brown, No. 853; attempts at escape: Suffolk's letters to Killingworth and others, Lett. and Pap., i. 253, f.; Ellis, iii. 1, pp. 130-134. These are three undated letters, which from their contents and occasional references belong to nearly the same time; the allusions to various events, such as the promise of a treaty from Charles to Philip, Suffolk's residence in Wageningen, the statement that he was in Gueldres by Philip's orders, show them to be of the period of his second captivity, the autumn of 1505. It is therefore not possible to place their date, as has hitherto been done, before the conclusion of the peace on July 27, 1505.—For the assertion that Charles spent money on Suffolk: Lett. and Pap., ii. 142.

The compact between the duke and Suffolk is printed in Lett. and Pap., i. 269, f., from a corrected rough draft, which is dated Sept. 24, 1505; but the date of this draft is not necessarily the date of the final treaty. Concerning the further negotiations between Henry and Philip, see the Venetian and Spanish reports: Brown, Nos. 855, 858, 860, f.; Berg., Nos. 429, 439-441, 444; Zurita, vi. 42a, f.—Suffolk wrote from Namur on Nov. 17, 1505, Lett. and Pap., i. 272; cf. Brown, No. 860; his previous promises to Aix: Lett. and Pap., i. 261, 262; Richard's letter to Suffolk, Nov. 24, 1505; ibid., 273-275; cf. 276, f.; Ellis, iii. 1, p. 138, f. One letter from Suffolk to Killingworth has been placed by Ellis (iii. 1, pp. 125-127) among the first letters of the Suffolk correspondence, whilst it belongs to the last, about December, 1505. Suffolk speaks in it of news about "Derreke," which "Hestu" had communicated to him; but on Nov. 24, 1505, Richard sent him by "Ewstas" (Eustace, written thus in Suffolk's peculiar spelling), a letter in which he informed him he had news from " Derik " ; Richard to Suffolk, " Aken," Jan. 4, 1506 ; Ellis, p. 129, f. Ellis supposes "Aken" to be Aken on the Elbe, not far from Dessau (!), whereas Aix, of course, is meant. Zurita's statement, v. 349*b*, that Suffolk had paid Richard's debts in Aix in order to make it possible for him to undertake an expedition against England, is in contradiction to all other accounts.—On the promises to Suffolk and his real condition, see Lett. and Pap., i. 263–265, 276, f. ; Ellis, 138, f. ; Lett. and Pap., ii. 381, f.—Suffolk's commission and instructions to treat with Henry, Jan. 24 and 28, 1506, Lett. and Pap., i. 278–285 ; cf. his letter of Jan. 28 in Ellis, iii. 1, p. 140, f.

14 (*to page* 195).—On Philip's journey, see the reports of Philip himself, Jan. 27, 1506 : Gachard, Coll. des Voyages, i. 498, f. ; those of a travelling companion, ibid., 501–503; and of the Venetian Quirini: Brown, Nos. 862–865 ; further, on the journey and the residence in England, the full account of a fellow-traveller : Mem., pp. 282–303 (on the author, pp. 283, 300, 302); Abstract in Berg., No. 451, and the account in Gachard's Deuxième Voyage, as above, pp. 408–410, 415–431 ; Zurita, vi., fol. 436, gives Jan. 8 as the day of the departure, the 15th as that of the landing ; cf. also Philip's letters to Ferdinand, Jan. 20 and Feb. 22 ; Col. de Doc., viii. 371, 376, Lett. and Pap., ii. 363, f., 365.

Concerning the anxiety beforehand about a landing in England, see Quirini in Brown, No. 860; on the landing and first reception : Philip's letters, Gachard, i. 499, 504 ; Col. de Doc., viii. 370 (Lett. and Pap., ii. 364); also Zurita, vi. 43*b*; Gachard, p. 418; Mem., p. 283 ; P. V., 776 ; Paston Lett., iii. 403–406 (dated "from Wyndsouer this Saterday," assigned by the editor Gairdner to Jan. 17, whereas the interview of the 31st is meant).—The treaty of amity of Feb. 9, 1506 : Rym., xiii. 123–127 ; Du Mont, iv. 1, p. 76, f. ; Abstract in Berg., No. 452, f. ; cf. Molinet, v. 276–278 ; Zurita, vi. 44*a*.—The parting from Henry : Mem., p. 303 ; Berg., p. 379 ; the account of Philip's illness on the way is given both by Quirini, Brown, No. 869, and by the informant in Gachard, p. 429, in the same form, so that there is no doubt it is correct. Häbler's assertion (p. 88), that the illness was only a pretext, is therefore without any foundation.

Concerning the offer to deliver up Suffolk, see the accounts, Mem., p. 302 ; Gachard, 1, 431 ; Quirini, Mar. 17 ; Brown, No. 869, cf. 867 ; also the correct statements in Die alder excellenste cronyke von Brabant, etc., cap. 49 ; Peter Martyr, p. 170, ep. 300.—

Of Henry's promise to spare Suffolk, nothing transpires in the treaty settlements; it is vouched for, however, by a communication from the Lord of Croy to Maximilian, Mar. 23, 1506: Chmel, p. 229; Abstract in Berg., No. 456; and Quirini's, Mar. 27; Brown, No. 870. According to Croy's words—"a aussi promis et donné son scelle de bien traictier . . ."—Henry must even have entered into a written obligation. When, on the other hand, Quirini (cf. also Nos. 872, 874) speaks of a restitution of the property of the proscribed man, he must be under a mistake; Croy would not have been silent on the subject; besides, such a concession on the part of Henry is in itself improbable, and certainly was not carried out. The Pope supposed Henry would not keep his promise, Naturelli to Philip, April 18; Le Glay, Négoc. Dipl., i. 114.—On the surrender of Suffolk: Chron. of Calais, p. 5, f.; Fabian, Abridgment, 689; cf. Quirini, Brown, Nos. 869, 872, 874; and Grey Friars' Chron., p. 29.— Gairdner, Henry VII., p. 194, contradicts the statement that Philip had been detained in England until after the surrender had taken place, because the kings had already taken leave of each other on March 2. But Philip remained till April 26 in England, and therefore in Henry's power, and long before his arrival at Falmouth, Suffolk had been handed over to the English at Calais, on March 16. Quirini asserts (Brown, No. 869) that Philip had really entered into an agreement not to set out before; cf. the same form of expression in the Chron. of Cal., p. 5.

Arrival at Falmouth and departure: Quirini, Brown, Nos. 869, f., 878; Gachard, 430, 433, f., 450, f.; Philip's letter, Col. de Doc., viii. 375, f.; Lett. and Pap., ii. 365; Croy's letter: Lettres de Louis XII., etc., i. 70, Van den Bergh, Corr. de Marg., i. 55; Peter Martyr, p. 169, ep. 298; Zurita, vi. 44b.—On Killingworth and Richard de la Pole, see Lett. and Pap., i. 303, 306–322; Brown, No. 889.—The commercial treaty of April 30, 1506, with the instructions in Rym., xiii. 132–142; Du Mont, iv. 1, pp. 83–88; cf. the account in Schanz, i. 30–34, who also contradicts Bacon's incorrect statements concerning the origin of the name "Intercursus Malus;" it is just the same as with the name "Intercursus Magnus" (see Note 7 to Chap. IV.), it rests solely on Bacon's statement (pp. 146, 205).

Bergenroth's views (Introd., pp. cix.–cxi.) on the settlements between Henry and Philip are quite extraordinary, and still more so the reasons he gives for them. According to Bergenroth, the whole gain was on Philip's side, for, as compared with the promise to protect Philip's possessions and claims on possessions, the

surrender of Suffolk was of much less weight, especially as Philip
and Maximilian had already offered to surrender him before the
conclusion of the treaty (?). So was also the marriage treaty, because
others would have to give their consent to that, and the commercial treaty, because a treaty of that kind was of small value,
and could easily be annulled by Philip. As if Henry, with regard
to the treaty of alliance, would not have had just the same freedom,
and would not, in fact, have exercised it.—With such a method as
this, everything may be asserted and everything proved.—For the
subsequent negotiations about the treaty, cf. Henry's and Philip's
letters: Chmel, 247, f., 255; Berg., Nos. 483, 491; Lett. and Pap., ii.
158, ff.; Gachard, 553.

15 (*to page* 196).—Henry's promise of help for the Netherlands:
Chmel, p. 240; cf. Lettres de Louis XII., etc., i. 60, f., 82; Van
den Bergh, i. 38, 45. On the English war preparations: account in
Gachard, i. 466; with incorrect statements as to the object, cf. before
pp. 464, f., 477. Henry and Gueldres: Lett. and Pap., ii. 164–167;
instructions to France, Aug. 12, 1506: Lett. de Louis, 78–87; Van
den Bergh, pp. 41–50. On the attitude of France, see the letters of
Louis XII.: Lett. and Pap., i. 289–293; of Courteville, Le Glay,
183–189; Van den Bergh, pp. 68–73, 79; of Marsin: Lett. de Louis,
87–91; Van den Bergh, 73–78; of Chièvres: Chmel, p. 252.—
Attitude of the Burgundian government: Chièvres to Philip, Aug.
16, 1506; Lett. de Louis, 74, f., 76; Van den Bergh, 58, 59. Henry
to Philip and Maximilian, Sept. 16 and Oct. 1, Lett. and Pap., i.
294–300; Chmel, p. 256; Berg., No. 491. On Henry's position,
cf. Courteville's opinion: Le Glay, i. 182; Van den Bergh, p. 65.

To Chapter VI.

1 (*to page* 202).—First orders for Estrada and Puebla, May 10,
1502: Berg., p. 267; power in subsequent treaty instrument:
Rym., xiii. 80, f.; later orders: Berg., pp. 271, 273, f., 275, 278–
290, 292, 293, 296, f., 300–302, 304 f.; cf. Zurita, v. 236*b*, 306*a*.—No
word was said to Puebla of the affair of the marriage, his co-operation
then desired, but left to Estrada: Berg., p. 284; cf. 281. As, however, the first announcement of Henry's readiness for the new
marriage treaty was made through Puebla (ibid., 289, 290, 292), it
is probable that conversations between him and Henry had taken
place independently of the wishes of Puebla's sovereigns. Very
much later, in April, 1527, Bishop Fox stated in court that he had
discussed the marriage with Puebla on many occasions, but was not

sure whether it was Puebla or Henry who proposed the marriage ; he thought, however, that it was done through Puebla : Brewer, Lett. and Pap. of Henry VIII., iv. p. 2588.

2 (*to page* 203).—On the preliminary draft of the marriage treaty of Sept. 23, 1502, Berg., No. 351, gives only a short notice. The document in question is to be found in the British Museum MSS., Cott., Vesp., c. xii. fol. 261–270, and breaks off in the middle of a sentence. The treaty itself, see in Rym., xiii. 76–86 ; Du Mont, iv. 1, pp. 38–44 ; Abstract in Berg., No. 364. The abstract of the treaty in Berg., p. 307, gives as the date for the conclusion of the marriage, Henry's coming of age, that is, the completion of his fourteenth year, which would appear to be most probable, and had also been fixed in the case of Arthur ; also, Prince Henry put off the protestation he made later against the marriage to the day before the completion of his fourteenth year, Berg., No. 435. However, not only does the text of the treaty in Rym., p. 83, and Du Mont, p. 42, say the *completed fifteenth year*, but so does a later letter of Ferdinand's of April, 1509, Berg., ii. p. 1. We are therefore compelled to follow these statements. For the ratifications, see Berg., Nos. 372, f., 375, f., 378–380 ; Rym., xiii. 76, ff., and Berg., No. 393 ; the notice in Col. de Doc., i. 357, gives a wrong date for the year.—On Henry's promotion to be Prince of Wales, cf. Hall, 497. On the question of the consummation of the marriage : Ferdinand to De Rojas in Rome, Aug. 23, 1503, Pocock, Records, ii. 426, f. ; Berg., No. 370 ; Zurita, v. 236*b* ; Peter Martyr, p. 414 ; cf. my remarks in : Der Sturz des Kardinals Wolsey im Scheidungshandel Heinrichs VIII. von England, Histor. Taschenbuch, vi. 9, pp. 46, 68.—The information in Stow, p. 876, which apparently comes from Fabian's London Chronicle, that on June 25, in the house of the Bishop of Salisbury, in London ". . . was Prince Henry . . . assured in matrimonie to the Lady Katherine," can only refer to a ceremony of betrothal, for neither time nor place correspond with the treaty itself. Ferdinand certainly did not write till Sept. 24, 1504 (Berg., No. 375), to tell Henry that his ambassadors had informed him of the betrothal. Possibly this betrothal took place twice, as was often the custom. The exaggerated expression which King Henry is said to have used before the French ambassadors, that the prince and Katharine were already "married," also refers to the betrothal : Puebla's report, Oct. 23, 1504, Berg., p. 333. As the papal bull of dispensation was not issued till 1505, it could only, before that date, have been a question of the "sponsalia per verba de futuro," that is, of a *betrothal*, whereas the commercial proclamations of the Spaniards and

Henry, of Nov. 16, 1504, and March 12, 1505 (Berg., p. 337, and Rym., xiii. 114, f.), are equally exaggerated and incorrect in speaking of the conclusion of the marriage "per verba de præsenti."—On the commercial relations, see Berg., pp. 299, 308 (on this, cf. Schanz, i. 275), 317. Short statement of the tenor of the second treaty of June 23, 1503, in 45th Report of the Dep. Keeper, App. i., p. 346 ; also see Berg., Nos. 365, 370.

3 (*to page* 205).—The efforts of the Spaniards to procure dispensation : Pocock, ii. 426 ; Berg., pp. 309, 314, 326 ; Lett. and Pap., ii. 114, f. On Henry's embassage of obedience to Julius, see Reg. Brev. Jul., P. II. tom. 1, p. 256.   Julius's delay : Lett. and Pap., ii. 113–116 ; Pocock, i. 2 ; his promise to send the dispensation by Sherbourne : Pocock, i. 5 ; Herbert, Life of Henry VIII., p. 383, f. ; Berg., p. 328 ; cf. Estrada's report, Aug. 10, 1504, ibid., p. 330 ; the expression in the abstract : "the dispensation arrived," is a mistake, for the promise of the dispensation already arrived in England, cf. Estrada, Oct. 23, ibid., p. 336 ; see besides : Henry to Julius, Nov. 28, 1504, Pocock, ii. 429 (the abstract in Berg., p. 341, is not quite correct) ; Puebla, Dec. 5 ; Berg., p. 347.

The *brief* which preceded the actual bull of dispensation sent from Rome to Spain, and from there to England, has a story of its own. It receives its special importance, which justifies a closer examination, from the part it played later in the great divorce trial of Henry VIII.   Herbert, 373, f., gives the text of the brief from a copy drawn up in Spain and attested by notary in Dec. 1528. The brief is worded more shortly than the bull, ibid., 370, f. ; Rym., xiii. 89, f. ; some oversights also occur in it. As the brief was not even entered on the register, the publishing of it was perhaps somewhat hastened, on pressure from the Spaniards. Being short, it is more general in its tenor than the bull ; and a noteworthy variation occurs in the insertion of the word "forsan" into the bull touching the consummation of Arthur's marriage. Katharine considered it necessary to guard herself against the possibility of the actual consummation being regarded as completed, from the definite wording of the brief : Nov. 7, 1528, Pocock, ii. 431, f. ; Brewer, iv. 3 App. No. 211. The Bishop of Worcester mentions on March 17, 1505, Lett. and Pap., i. 243, a "copy of the bull" (copiæ bullarum), which had been sent to Spain. Friedmann, Anne Boleyn, ii. 329, considers it "very probable" that this "copy" was the brief, for the reason that it was nowhere stated that this duplicate was an exact copy of the projected bull. From this passage alone we might rather infer the contrary, but it happens that the proof which

Friedmann omitted to bring forward, can really be supplied, and furthermore converts the supposition into a certainty. The expression, "copiæ bullarum" is inexact. Julius II. himself says (to Henry, Feb. 22, 1505, Pocock, i. 7; Herb. 385, f.): "literas dispensationis . . . ex Hispania ad te missas," and Ferdinand (to Henry, Nov. 24, 1504, Lett. and Pap., i. 242) even says : " Caeterum eidem Doctori De la Puebla . . . bullam mittimus." Ferdinand sent to Henry, not a transcript, but the original of the document that came from Rome, which he again vaguely terms a "bull," whereas it was only to give the tenor of the promised bull. But the original of the brief was found later among Puebla's papers, and handed over by his sons, in 1528, to Charles V. at Burgos : Gayangos, Cal. of State Papers, iv. 1, No. 571. From this it may be regarded as certain that this document, sent to Puebla in 1504, was the original of the brief, for otherwise it would be altogether a mystery how it came to be among the papers of the ambassador. As the bull itself followed shortly after it, the brief was no longer of any value; no copy of it was made, and it was completely forgotten, until in 1528 it came to light among the papers left by the ambassador. On the Spanish side it was even wrongly asserted from the first, that this document was of a later date than the bull : Gayangos, iii. 2, p. 806. The imperial government kept the original in its hands ; the English ambassadors in Spain were allowed to examine it ; but Henry VIII. had to content himself with an authenticated copy (Herbert, as above). For the English statesmen, who, in 1528, were endeavouring in the trial for divorce to insist on the insufficient legality of the bull of dispensation, the newly discovered brief was very unwelcome, less on account of the not very important differences to be found between it and the bull, than because the brief contained a new and very direct expression of opinion from the Pope on the matter. Hence the brief was at once treated as a forgery on the English side, and this opinion has been accepted by party historians, such as Burnet and Froude, while the same view has been once more maintained in an article, anonymous, but known to be written by Lord Acton, in the *Quarterly Review* (1877), vol. 143, p. 38, f. On the other hand, Friedmann, as above, ii. 328, ff. contended for its genuineness, and I have added to his remarks in the Hist. Taschenbuch, vi. 9, p. 48, note. Each additional contribution to the history of the brief makes its genuineness seem unassailable. The principal point brought forward against its genuineness is the date : " die xxvi. Decembris millesimo quingentesimo tertio." As the Curia officially announced on May 31, 1529 (Rym., xiv. 294 ; Brewer, iv. 3, No. 5615), that it reckoned, in dating briefs, Dec. 25

as the beginning of the year, here Dec. 26, 1502, would be meant, if the year of the pontificate, also given, did not place the intended date, Dec. 26th, 1503, beyond all question. The error may thus be explained : as the brief was antedated just a year, such an error was more probably the work of a hasty scribe rather than of an intentional forger. On brief and bull, see also under the years 1528 and 1529 : Brewer, iv. 2, Nos. 3873, 4980 ; iv. 3, Nos. 5211, 5376, 5470, f., 5791.

4 (*to page* 207).—On Katharine's position in England till the beginning of 1507, see Berg., pp. 268–271, 277, 298, 321, 327, 328–330, 334, f., 350, 354, 376, f., 386, 397, f. 400, 401, 406.— Gairdner, Hen. VII., p. 190, speaks of Henry's "monstrous proposal" to marry Katharine himself; cf. Bergenroth, Pref., p. xcv. He is here assuming too much. We are only referred for this to the statement made by Isabella in a letter to Estrada, April 11, 1503, Berg., p. 295 : "The Doctor (Puebla) has also written to us with regard to the marriage of the king with the Princess of Wales, our daughter, saying that it is much talked of in England." Therefore the ambassador had only a rumour to go upon, for which any other confirmation is wanting.

5 (*to page* 209).—On the first offers of marriage from France : Baker's report, June, 1502, in Champollion, Lettres des rois, ii. 515, 519, f., Lett. and Pap., ii. 342, f., 347 ; Isabella to Estrada, July 12, 1502, Berg., p. 272 ; Puebla's report, Oct. 23, 1504, Berg. pp. 331–333; Zurita, v. 345*a* ; cf. Cardinal Hadrian to Henry, Oct. 23, 1505, Lett. and Pap., i. 247 ; on the subsequent negotiations see the answers given to the English ambassador : Lett. and Pap., ii. 125–146 ; also the entries on June 21 and Aug. 1, 1505, Exc. Hist., 133. Margaret of Angoulême was born April 11, 1492 : see Journal de Louise de Savoye, Petitot Coll. des Mém., xvi. 390 ; the Portuguese ambassador in England sends word of the plan of the marriage with Louise, Oct. 10, 1505, Lett. and Pap., ii. 146, f. ; the Venetian ambassador, Oct. 27 : Brown, No. 858; and the Flemish ambassador, July 20, 1508 : Van den Bergh, 3, 132, f.

6 (*to page* 212).—Instruction and report of the ambassadors sent on the mission to the queens of Naples : Mem., pp. 223–239, Abstract in Berg., pp. 359–361 ; and to Ferdinand : Mem., pp. 240–281 ; Berg., pp. 362–366. This curious document soon aroused interest; the earliest publication of it with which I am acquainted appeared in London, 1761 : "Instructions given by King Henry the Seventh to his Embassadors, when he intended to marry the young Queen of Naples : together with the Answer of the Embassadors," after a

fragment had already appeared in the *St. James's Chronicle* of Aug. 6, 1761. The *Gentleman's Magazine* printed a more complete copy, vol. lvii., part ii. (1787), p. 19; the absurd statements contained in it, that the suit was made in Arthur's behalf, and that Henry VIII. afterwards married Joanna, are corrected, ibid., pp. 208 and 213.—See also Quirini, Antwerp, July 5, 1505; Brown, No. 847 (cf. 858), and Puebla, Aug. 11, Berg., p. 368. The leader of the embassage, Francis Marsin, received the honour of knighthood from Ferdinand, and died Dec. 5, 1507 : André, Ann., p. 101.

7 (*to page* 213).—Orders for Savage : Berg., No. 449; treaty of March 20, 1506: ibid., No. 455; Zurita, vi., 44*b*. Häbler, p. 87, f., and note 2, speaks, instead of powers for the marriage treaty, of ratifications, and on the strength of these powers calls the conclusion of the treaty, "the exchange of the ratifications;" and as this took place on March 20, gives it as "the official date." But, as is well known, treaties were given their date and names, not from the time and place of the exchange of the ratifications, but of the conclusion by the plenipotentiaries. The remarks Häbler subjoins on the commercial treaty are inexact and not to the point. Cf. on the further carrying out of the treaty, Berg., No. 483; Rym., xiii. 127–132; Berg., Nos. 463–466; Rym., 146–155; Berg., No. 467, f. Maximilian to Henry, July 20; Chmel, 236, f.; Lett. and Pap., ii. 153–155; a very inexact abstract in Berg., No. 475; Henry to Maximilian, Aug. 12 or 19; Chmel, 247, f.; Lett. and Pap., ii. 159, f.; Berg., No. 483; cf. Chmel, 255; Berg., No. 491. Philips' ratifications: Berg., No. 474; cf. Quirini's reports; Brown, Nos. 883, 885, f.—On the negotiations with Margaret : Quirini, Nov. 29 and Dec. 20, 1505; Brown, No. 860, f.; Henry to Maximilian, Oct. 1, 1506; Chmel, 254; cf. report to Maximilian, July 30 and Aug. 8; ibid., 238, 242–244, Berg., No. 476, 480; Oct. 31, Chmel, 277; Berg., No. 496; Maximilian to Henry, Sept. 24, Lett. and Pap., i. 305, f., the abstract in Berg., No. 490 is not satisfactory.

8 (*to page* 221).—On the Milanese offers for the hand of Mary, see the Venetian account, April 1, 1499; Brown, No. 790. Information as to the settlement about Charles and Mary's m....iage in England at the beginning of 1506, is supplied us by Henry's later remarks in presence of Puebla, report of Oct. 5, 1507, Berg., p. 437 ; Ferdinand's words, Aug. 7, 1508: ibid., p. 463, f., and conversation of Maximilian's ambassadors with Margaret, Aug. 8, 1506: Chmel, p. 244; cf. Quirini, Mar. 30, 1506; Brown, No. 872; Zurita, vi. fol. 44*a*.—Maximilian's letter to Henry, Sept. 14, 1506: Lett. and Pap., i. 301–303, abstract in Berg., No. 488. On West's negotiations in

Valladolid, Quirini makes some communications, which are rather
beside the mark : reports of June 25 and July 23, 1506; Brown,
Nos. 883–886.—On Henry's present to Margaret : Berg., No. 543;
concerning his efforts to obtain her hand, see Maximilian's letters to
Margaret, Sept. 16, 1507, Le Glay, Corr. de Max., i, 10–12;
abstract in Berg., No. 547; Puebla, Oct. 5, 1507, Berg., p. 437;
answer to the English ambassadors on the part of Maximilian : Lett.
and Pap., i. 323–327; Berg., No. 560 (placed by Berg. correctly
after the treaty of Dec. 21, 1507).—On negotiations for Mary's
marriage with Charles in the year 1507, see the notices in Berg.,
pp. 430–435, 437, 442; Le Glay, Corr. i. 20, f.; the marriage treaty
of Dec. 21, 1507, with the powers in Maximilian's ratification of
Feb. 22, 1508, in Rym., xiii. 171–188; Du Mont, iv. 1, pp.
93–102; abstract in Berg., No. 558, f.; cf. the statements in
Zurita, vi. 153*b*, f.   Chronicle of Calais, p. 6; André, Ann., pp. 100,
102, f.; the treaty of amity is printed twice in the various settlements, in Rym., xiii. 189–212; in Du Mont, iv. pp. 103–109;
abstract in Berg., No. 557; Henry's letters to the Lord Mayor and
aldermen : Halliwell, i. 194–196; see also André, Ann., pp.103–106;
cf. André's poem in Mem., p. 95, f.—On Ferdinand's attitude, see
the accounts of Marsin and his companions : Mem., p. 271; Berg.,
p. 364; also Ferdinand to Fuensalida, about July, 1508; Berg.,
p. 459, Aug. 7; ibid., 461–464; Col. de Doc., xxxix. 437–445,
Katharine to Ferdinand, March 9, 1509; Berg., p. 469; cf. ibid.,
ii. p. 3.

9 (*to page* 226).—Maximilian's and Charles's ratifications of the
treaty of Dec. 21, 1507, see in Rym., xiii. 188, 200, 212; Du Mont,
iv. 1, pp. 102, 108, f.; cf. Maximilian to Margaret : Le Glay, Corr., i.
39–41, 45, Berg., No. 580, f.; see also Rym., x. 212–215, Berg.
No. 583; cf. 11th, Rep. of the Dep. Keeper, Part iii., p. 113, f.—
On Henry's illness : Letter of Henry's printed in the Chronicle of
Calais, p. 52, f.; also Berg., pp. 408, 457, 460; Brown, No. 906; Lett.
and Pap., i. 362; André, Ann., 108, 112, f.—On Maximilian's loan,
see the latter's letter to Margaret, July 23, 1508, Le Glay, p. 76, f.;
Van den Bergh, p. 135, f.; Berg., No. 587; cf. Le Glay, i. 110, f.;
Berg., No. 578; Lett. and Pap., i. 343; Berg., No. 584.—Maximilian
still hoped for a renewal of the plan of the French marriage, as is
seen by the wish he expressed, that it should be determined in the
treaty of Dec. 21, 1507, that for a year he should be free to draw
back if Louis again agreed to a marriage between Charles and
Claude : Maximilian to Margaret, Dec. 4, 1507; Le Glay, i. 20, f.;
Berg., No. 556; Lanz, in the introduction to the Monum. Hapsburg.

ii. 1, p. 92, gathers from this desire of Maximilian's the mistaken idea that such a clause was really included in the treaty. Maximilian's letter to Margaret of July 23, 1508, in Le Glay, i. 76–78; Van den Bergh, 135–137.

On Wolsey's missions we have no very exact information. Wolsey himself related to his subsequent biographer, Cavendish, Life of Wolsey, pp. 18–21, cf. 22, that he had accomplished a diplomatic mission to Maximilian with special rapidity in a few days. Now we possess correspondence on a mission of Wolsey's, which has been much damaged by fire, but deciphered with great care by Mr. Gairdner, and published in Lett. and Pap., i. 426–452. As, according to this, Wolsey remained in the Netherlands for a long period, from the beginning of October on into November, 1508, he can scarcely have alluded to this mission in his conversation with Cavendish. He was then specially commended to a person distinguished in the documents as A, whom Gairdner, ibid., Pref., p. lx., rightly makes out to be the Bishop of Gurk. The very first instruction begins: "... idem capellanus dicet, quod post reditum suum in Angliam, cum sacræ regiæ maiestati ea omnia per ordinem retulisset, quæ A sibi declaravit" (Lett. and Pap., 426); and further (p. 429): "cum idem A. promiserit dicto capellano," whence it is evident there had been a previous mission, and that in fact to the Bishop of Gurk. But Henry had addressed credentials to the latter on Aug. 23, 1508, from Berwick, in Essex (Lett. and Pap., p. 367), in which no name is mentioned of the messenger, and in which it is in no way hinted that he was a person already well known to the bishop. On this account, therefore, but more on account of the difference of time (the credentials are of Aug. 23, while Wolsey did not arrive in Mechlin till Oct. 4), these credentials will not have been intended for the second mission, but give us the date of the first, which had been so quickly accomplished. I consider this assumption more probable than the connection which Mr. Gairdner attempts to establish between Cavendish's narrative and a notice in André's Annals (Mem., p. 127): "Rediit etiam eo die (Aug. 8) Caletus nuncius ex Caligio, et quidem impigre;" this must rather have been a messenger to Dr. Young and Brandon (Mem., 125), who had gone to Maximilian in the middle of July. Neither Mr. Gairdner's nor my views agree, however, with the statement in Cavendish that Wolsey left the king at Richmond, for from the end of July to the end of Aug., Henry was not there (cf. André, Ann., 126–128), and further, to have carried out the mission in the manner reported would have been quite impossible, because Maximilian, at the beginning and end

of Aug., was staying in Dordrecht (see Stälin's itinerary in the
"Forschungen zur deutschen Geschichte," i. 369), and Wolsey
could not have made the journey from Calais there in less than a
day.   Wolsey related the circumstance after his downfall, in Mar.
or April, 1530 (Cavendish, p. 22, " in the great park of Richmond "
where the cardinal was staying during those months), therefore fully
twenty-one years after the event ; this easily explains mistakes in
details without obliging us to doubt in general the fact that he executed his commission very quickly.—We learn nothing at all as to
the purport of the first mission, but I believe I may hazard the supposition that Charles and Mary's marriage was discussed, for the
following reasons : (1) At the end of July, 1508, the ambassadors of
the emperor and the Netherlands wrote from England in great
anxiety about the effect upon Henry of Maximilian's procrastination
in this matter (Van den Bergh, 132, f. ; Lett. and Pap., i. 365).   (2)
About the same time Maximilian even expressed himself very firmly
against the conclusion of the treaty (van den Bergh, pp. 135-137) ;
and yet, in spite of this, this affair in which Henry was so keenly
interested, was on the occasion of Wolsey's second mission only
mentioned in the instruction, and incidentally in an accompanying
report (Lett. and Pap., i. 427, 433) ; and especially (3) even before
Wolsey's arrival, Margaret, on Oct. 1, concluded the marriage treaty.
From this we must infer that these difficulties had, in the interval,
been removed, which again points to Wolsey's first mission, occurring
about the same time.—For the treaties concluded on Oct. 1 and 11,
1508, see Rym., xiii. 219-227 ; Berg., Nos. 592, f., 596, f. ; cf. Rym.,
p. 229, f. ; Berg., No. 598, for Maximilian and Charles's instructions
of Oct. 11 and 27 : Rym., pp. 227-229, 230-232 ; Berg., No. 597
and 594 (Berg., without any obvious reason, places the instruction
of the 27th under date of Oct. 7).   On the English embassage, see
Lett. and Pap., i. 444-448 ; cf. van den Bergh, pp. 125-131 ;
Report of the imperial ambassadors, Dec. 7, 1508, Lett. and Pap.,
i. 372-374 ; the description of the ceremony of betrothal on the 17th
in Rym., pp. 236-239 ; Du Mont, iv. 1, pp. 119-120 ; short notice
in Berg., No. 602 ; on the pledging of the jewel : Rym., p. 234, f.,
239-242 ; cf. Lett. and Pap., i. 440 ; on the further payments, see
Pauli, p. 624, note 1.

    10 (*to page* 231).—Alexander VI.'s confirmatory bull of Oct. 7,
1494, was discovered by Pocock, see Hist. Rev., vol. ii. (1887), pp.
112-114, only Pocock attaches too great importance to the renewal.
On the papal gift of the consecrated hat and sword, see Brown, Nos.
548, 550 ; Leland's Coll., iv. 244, f. ; cf. Arnold, p. 38 ; Grey Friars'

Chronicle, p. 24 (André, Vita, p. 46, makes a mistake about the person who brought them over); Brown, No. 725; André, Ann., p. 85, f. On Morton's elevation to the cardinalate: P. V., 730; Brown, Nos. 537, 551, 553, 582; Morton is called cardinal for the first time in the programme for the ceremonial observed when Henry was created Duke of York, 1494.—On the first incident with regard to the alum trade, see the report to Innocent VIII., Feb. 19, 1486, Brown, No. 509; the legal decision in Year Book, 1 Hen. VII., fol. 10; on the later occurrences: Brown, No. 548 and 551, and the copious correspondence in Reg. Brev. Jul. II., tom. 1.—On the question of the canonization of Henry VI., we are in possession of the briefs, word for word the same, of Alexander VI., Oct. 7, 1494: Wilkins, iii. 640, and Julius II., May 20, 1504: Ware, p. 84 and 87, f.; following this, in Hearne, Script. Veteres, i. App. 100–103, partly reprinted in Trevelyan Pap., iii. 4, f., without knowledge of the older publications. As both refer to Innocent's previous action, we may suppose that the same brief was also issued by him. Possibly the opening, "Ordo canonisationis sanctorum," Wilkins, pp. 636–639, had already been destined in 1494 to be laid before the king; cf. Parker, De Antiquit. Ecclesiæ, 447, f.; Collectarium mansuetudinum et bonorum morum regis Henrici VI., printed in Hearne, as above, 285, ff. A writer in the *Gentleman's Magazine*, New Series, i. (1834), p. 358, ff., in a description of Henry VII.'s character, by no means a successful performance, upholds the erroneous idea that the canonization did not take place because it would have been too expensive for the king. The originator of this view is Bacon, p. 207.—On the removal of Henry VI.'s bones to Westminster: Wilkins, iii. 635, f.; Rym., xiii. 103, f.—On the visitations of the monasteries: 1 Hen. VII., c. 4, 1485, Stat., ii. 500, f. (cf. Reeves, ed. Finlason, History of the English Law, iii. 167); Wilkins, iii. 618–620, 630–634 (cf. Hook, Lives of the Archbishops of Canterbury, v. 453, ff.); Parker, De Antiquit. Ecclesiæ, p. 447, Visitations of Norwich, and Rym., xii. 574.—Bishoprics conferred on John and Silvester de Giglis: Rym., xii. 657, f., 670, 704, f., 710; cf. Lett. and Pap., i. 102, f.; on Hadrian: xiii. 108; cf. Lett. and Pap., ii. 373, the form of his oath, xiii. 108–110; numerous examples of the handing over of the "custodia temporalium," and of the "restitutio temporalium," in Rym., xii. and xiii.; for the king's *congé d'élire*: xii. 373, 505, 666, 771; recommendation to elect Warham: Ellis, iii. 1, p. 166, f.; handing over the temporalities: Rym., xiii. 90; account of the installation: Leland Coll., iv. 16–32; the formula of oath in Wilkins, iii. 647, f.; cf. Parker, as above, 456, ff.

11 (*to page* 235).—André, Vita, p. 54, tries somewhat to enhance
Gigli's success with Henry in regard to the crusade tax in 1487, but
Gigli's own account, Aug. 17, 1487, Brown, No. 520, contradicts this ;
the papal bull of Oct. 18, 1488 : Wilkins, iii. 626–629 ; also see on the
crusade tax of 1489, Brown, Nos. 548, 550, 551, 553, cf. Parker, De
Antiquit. Eccl., 447 ; on the intended proclamation of an indulgence,
1497 : Brown, No. 744, f. On the use to be made of the levy, cf.
Ferdinand and Isabella to Puebla, April 29, 1502, Mem., pp. 410–
412 ; Berg., No. 315, and Cardinal Hadrian to Henry, Jan. 4, 1504,
Lett. and Pap., ii. 116, f.—The news of the taking of Modon is also
recorded by the City Chronicle, fol. 182a.—Powers for Gigli and
Hadrian, Feb. 10, 1500 ; Rym., xii. 747, f. ; Henry to Ferdinand
and Isabella, June 16, 1500, Berg., p. 225, f. ; also p. 215 ; Brown,
No. 805.—On the mission of Gaspar Pons, see Lett. and Pap., ii.
93–100 ; before this, cf. City Chron., 182a ; papal brief to Henry,
Nov. 3, 1501, Ellis, i. 1, pp. 48–50.—On the rating of the English
clergy : Wilkins, iii. 646, f. ; the apportioning of the sum of £12,000
among the various dioceses is not without interest : Lincoln stands
highest, with £2759 ; then Norwich, with £1883 ; Sarum, with
£1228 ; Winchester, with £973 ; Canterbury, with £959 ; London,
with £871 ; then, lowest, St. Asaph, with £40 ; Bangor, with £15 ;
and Llandaff, with £13. On the whole amount collected from the
rate, see P. V., 772 ; Henry's contribution : Exc. Hist., 128 ; cf.
Parker, as above, 451, f. ; Henry's answer to the Pope : Ellis, i. 1,
pp. 48–59 ; Halliwell, i. 185–194.—The negotiations with Hungary
and Venice : Brown, Nos. 818, 820–822, 826, 835 ; Rym., xiii. 4–6.
On the negotiations with France concerning a crusade, 1505 ; Lett. and
Pap., ii. 127–132, 138, f., 146 ; cf. 169, and André, Ann., 83.—Henry
elected Protector of the Knights of Rhodes, May 27, 1506, Lett.
and Pap., i. 287, f. ; Henry to Julius, Greenwich, May 15, 1507 :
Berg., No. 519 ; from a copy to be found in Venice, Brown, No.
893, dated " from our Palace in London," May 20 ; cf. also Brown,
No. 894, f. ; Col. de Doc., xxxix. 428–430 ; Berg., No. 528 ; Julius to
Henry, July 9, 1507, printed first in Collier, Eccles. Hist., ii. 733, f. ;
then in Lett. and Pap., ii. 170–174 ; abstract in Berg., No. 525 ;
Aug. 4 : Berg., No. 531 ; Dec. 23, Reg. Brev. Jul. II., tom. vii. p.
598 ; Henry to Julius, Sept. 8 : Collier, 735, f. ; Lett. and Pap., ii.
174–179 ; cf., Puebla's report, Oct. 5, Berg., pp. 437, 438.—On the
new indulgence, see the papal letters of Mar. 18 and July 17, 1508 :
Reg. Brev., Jul. II., tom. vii. 158, f., 391 ; cf., before, ibid., i. 443,
and on the last negotiations between Henry and Julius : Brown, No.
495.

To Chapter VII.

1 (*to page* 248).—The law against usury of 1487 : 3 Hen. VII.
c. 6, Stat., ii. 514, f.; of 1495 : 11 Hen. VII. c. 8, ibid., p. 574;
Morton's opening speech: Rot. Parl., vi. 458; Schanz, i. 560,
makes a mistake in one passage of the speech by transposing the
proportion between the sale and purchase.   More especially we find
ourselves unable to follow Schanz (i. 469, f.), when he speaks of
Henry's views as laid down in a regular "economic programme."
Schanz finds this programme in the long speech which Bacon (pp.
53–59) makes the chancellor, Morton, deliver before the Parliament
of 1487, and which Cunningham also accepts, p. 430, f. Schanz has
been misled as to the value of this speech, as Bacon gives it, by a
mistaken judgment of Pauli's, for, if compared with the only documentary record, Rot. Parl., vi. 385, Bacon's details prove to be
entirely arbitrary, though no doubt clever inventions to which he,
rather audaciously, tried to give an appearance of truth.

2 (*to page* 252).—The various laws on weights and measures : 7
Hen. VII. c. 3; 11 Hen. VII. c. 6; 12 Hen. VII. c. 5, Stat., ii.
551, f., 570–572, 637, f.—Schanz, i. 582, attributes the delay about
the measure passed in 1491 to a dislike on the part of Henry to
bear the cost assigned to him by the law, and says that therefore
the new law of 1495 was silent on this point.   But this law states the
fact that Henry had caused the measures to be made; the ground
for the delay was probably the wish for a better kind of distribution,
by means of the Commons themselves, which was in fact decided
upon in 1495.

3 (*to page* 257).—Anderson, Origin of Comm., i. 526, main-
tains that Henry had, like Edward III., promoted the manufacture of
cloth by introducing colonies of Flemish weavers, and that into Yorkshire, at Leeds, Wakefield, Halifax, cf. Schanz, i. 449; I am unable
to state how far this rests on good authority.—The prohibition of the
export of wool and undressed cloth under Edward IV., 7 Ed. IV.
c. 3: Stat., ii. 422, f., itself referred back to a statute of Edward
III.'s, 50 Ed. III. c. 7 : Stat., i. 398; Henry's law, 3 Hen. VII.
c. 12 : Stat., ii. 520, f.; cf. Schanz, ii., Urk. Beil., p. 529, i. 449, note
6.—The statute restricting the purchase of wool by foreigners, 4
Hen. VII. c. 11 : Stat., ii. 535, f.; cf. 4 Ed. IV. c. 4 : ibid., p. 410,
f., held good for eighteen counties in central and southern England;
the licence for the Venetians, May 1, 1506, was to last for five years :
45th Rep. of the Dep. Keep., App. i. 346.—The exceptional laws

for Norwich and Norfolk, 11 Hen. VII. c. 11 and 12 Hen. VII.
c. 1: Stat., ii. 577, 636; cf. André, Ann., p. 115, 119; the laws on
the importation of silk goods, 22 Ed. IV. c. 3; 1 Rich. III. c. 10;
1 Hen. VII. c. 9; 19 Hen. VII. c. 21: Stat., ii. 472, 493, f., 506,
664; cf Schanz, i. 456–459.

4 (*to page* 262).—For Henry's relations to agriculture, see
especially the excellent essay by Nasse, "Über die mittelalterliche
Feldgemeinschaft und die Einhegungen des 16 Jahrhunderts in
England."—The two laws of the third Parliament, 4 Hen. VII. c. 16
and 19: Stat., ii. 510, 542; see also the conclusions in Pauli's
Volkswirtschaftliche Denkschriften, p. 21, f.; cf. Nasse, p. 56.
On the prices of corn, see Rogers, Hist. of Agric. and Prices, iv.
217, and the table, p. 292. Nasse infers (p. 61) from the continuously low standard of prices of corn, that the production of it
could not have been replaced to any great extent by pasture, and
brings forward, besides, the statements of writers on agriculture in
the sixteenth century. All that, however, only proves, that *in spite*
of the conversion of arable land into pasture, the quantity of corn
cultivated was quite sufficient for the demand, and that this could be
the case, was probably due to the change in husbandry mentioned
in the writings cited, to the breaking up of the common field, to the
transition from the three-field system to that of convertible husbandry
—the more rational style of farming for England—whereby the pro-
ductiveness of the soil was increased. Contemporary accounts,
which all agree, and especially the statements in the laws themselves,
speak, in words too clear for us to doubt, of the change which had
already taken place to a very great extent; cf. also Ochenkowski,
p. 24, ff., 35, f., 42–44.—That the demand for wool had already
risen considerably under Edward IV., so that the former supply
began no longer to suffice is mentioned in the above cited article in
Pauli, p. 16; cf. p. 22. In spite of this the statistics of prices in
Rogers (see Table III., 328, containing the average for ten years)
show a fall in the price of wool for the time of Edward IV.; and
even the advances, which began under Henry VII., did not succeed
in again reaching the average of prices from 1400 to 1430, which
were not far exceeded till the general rise of prices in the middle of
the sixteenth century. This, too, only proves that the production
was able quickly again to keep pace with the demand, and, therefore,
fully agrees with the reports of extensive conversion into pasture.

With regard to the export of corn, Nasse is not quite accurate
when, p. 67, he speaks of the export of corn being as a rule forbidden. It had been forbidden earlier by the law 34 Ed. III.

c. 24, Stat., i. 368, but on the petition of the Commons this prohibition was removed by Richard II., 17 Rich. II. c. 7, ibid., ii.
88, f., and only the right reserved to the king's council to reimpose
it in necessary cases. The statute was confirmed by 4 Hen. VI. c.
5, ibid., 230, f., and by 15 Hen. VI. c. 2, ibid., 295, f., so far altered
that the export was to be allowed so long as the quarter of wheat
in the export market did not exceed 6s. 8d., and the quarter of
barley 3s. This law held good till the next Parliament, but was
not renewed till the next but one, and then for ten years, 20 Hen.
VI. c. 6, ibid., p. 319, f., and long before the expiration of the
term declared to be permanent by 23 Hen. VI. c. 5, ibid., 331, f.
A statute of Edward's, 3 Ed. IV. c. 2, ibid., p. 395, on the other
hand forbade the *import*, as long as in England the defined limits
of prices should not be exceeded. The statements in Rogers, iv.
147, are not quite accurate; cf. on the subject, Schanz, i. 639–641;
also Ochenkowski, p. 23, f. As Henry's last law had not been
repealed, the legal point was clear.—The king's prohibition to
export, dated Sept. 19, 1491: Lett. and Pap., ii. 372; on the rise
in prices at that time, see Rogers, iv. 286; cf. iii. 75, f. After this
prohibition, a licence to export was granted on April 4, 1492, Rym.,
xii. 475; besides this one, I only know of those mentioned in the
correspondence with the Pope, in 1504 and 1505: Reg. Brev. Julii
P. II. tom. i., 209, 228, 285, 403. We can therefore scarcely assert
that this licence continued to be necessary (cf. Schanz, i. 641),
especially as after the rise of 1491, prices again stood low: Rogers,
iv. 286, f. Also (for example, in the commercial treaty of 1496 with
the Netherlands), " victualia " were classed with other free export
and import commodities, and the right of prohibition only retained
that it might be enforced in the event of a scarcity at home: Rym.,
xii. 582.

On the export of horses: 11 Hen. VII. c. 13, Stat., ii. 578, f.; the
statement of its contents in Schanz, i. 461, is taken from the incorrect marginal notice, Stat., ii. 579; on the export of cattle, cf.
Schanz, ii., Urk. Beil., p. 530. The export of sheep was forbidden
by law, 3 Hen. VI. c. 2, Stat., ii. 227, f.; Edward's licence for
Margaret, Sept. 16, 1480, in Rym., xii. 137; on the consequences
of this exportation of sheep: Pauli, Volksw. Denkschr., p. 24 and
28. Henry's licence for William Tyll, April 8, 1489, in Campb., ii.
442. That the export of sheep took place under Henry VII. and
VIII. is confirmed by the customs table in Schanz, ii. 6.

5 (*to page* 270).—The name " Star Chamber " was taken from the
room where the Privy Council met in the Palace of Westminster, cf.

Palgrave, Origin. Author. of the Council, p. 38. Various theories exist as to the origin of the name ; it is usually supposed that the ceiling of the room was decorated with gilt stars, cf. also Pauli, p. 543. Another somewhat ingenious and not improbable explanation given by Blackstone, Commentaries, iv. 436, f., note, derives the name from the place where were deposited the contracts and obligations of the Jews, "starra" or "starrs" from the Hebrew "shetàr." When the origin had been forgotten, the word became connected with "star" and so we first find, 41 Ed. III., the title "la chambre des steilles." Another and somewhat poetical conjecture is offered by Hudson, in Collect. Jur., ii. 8, f.—The older law of the "Star Chamber," 31 Hen. VI. c. 2 : Stat., ii. 361–363 ; on the earlier jurisdiction of the council and chancellor, see Palgrave, as above ; Reeves, ed. Finlason, i. 95–99, ii. 293–296, 535, f., 600–602 ; cf. the earlier conclusions of Hudson, as above, ii. 9, ff. ; on the grievances of the Commons, Palgrave, as above, § 13, f.

The question whether the court of justice erected by the statute 3 Hen. VII. c. 1, Stat., ii. 509, f., and there designated by no special title, was the Star Chamber or not is a contested one. Hallam, Const. Hist., i. pp. 48–55, sees in the later Star Chamber, the Privy Council with its old, often contested, jurisdiction, and thinks its powers rested in no way on the authority of the statute 3 Hen. VII. c. 1, and that the court of justice erected by this statute, which only existed till the end of Henry VIII.'s reign, was not the Star Chamber. Palgrave, p. 99, sees in this law a transference of the jurisdiction of the entire Privy Council sitting at Whitehall or Greenwich, to a few members of the same assembled at Westminster, whereby he accepts a distinction between the Star Chamber and the Privy Council itself. Stephen, Criminal Law, i. 174, f., is of opinion that the statute was designed to confer legal authority upon that portion of the jurisdiction of the Star Chamber, which at the moment appeared the most important. Hallam goes much too far, whereas in the views of Palgrave and Stephen there is much that is decidedly correct ; only the idea of a distinction between the Council and the Star Chamber is to be rejected. Henry's statute legalised the jurisdiction—exercised hitherto arbitrarily by the Privy Council in the Star Chamber, in accordance with its original idea—over the most important causes which were not to be decided by the common law ; and conferred this jurisdiction, not on the whole Council, but on a committee of the Council, which, as a commission charged with its judicial powers, represented the Council itself. That in this, as in later statutes, the name of the

Star Chamber was not employed, only proves that this name was not yet so generally applied to the court as it was subsequently. This, however, need not prevent us from using it as the historical name which characterises the court in its special capacity. The statute 11 Hen. VII. c. 25, Stat., ii. 589, f., extended for a time the *legal* competence of the Star Chamber from dealing with the corruption of the jurors to hearing the appeal from the decision of the jury; it assigned as judges the Chancellor, the Lord Treasurer, the Chief Justices, and the Clerk of the Rolls. Of these the last was not named in 3 Hen. VII. c. 1, whilst in 11 Hen. VII. c. 25, the Lord Privy Seal, the bishop, and temporal lord of the council are omitted. Besides, the statute 3 Hen. VII. c. 1 does not pronounce very clearly on the relation of the persons named in it to one another; this is supplied by the Year Book, 8 Hen. VII. fol. 13, according to which the Chancellor, the Treasurer, and the Lord Privy Seal were the judges, the others only assessors co-opted by them. As, therefore, the judges could still be changed, a significant remnant of the old arbitrary jurisdiction of the council was left, the limits of competence determined by the law not being adhered to. The two laws only joined together particular persons and particular cases, outside these laws the old discretionary powers remained. This is proved by the case of the merchant adventurers and staplers, which also shows that we ought not, as Palgrave would have it, to divide the Star Chamber from the Privy Council, but that the Star Chamber is the Privy Council in its judicial capacity. The decree of the Star Chamber cited by Schanz, ii., Urk. Beil., p. 547, is introduced by the words: "Inspeximus tenorem cuiusdam decreti per nos et consilium nostrum apud Westminster in camera vocata 'le sterre chambre'. . . . redditi," and, in his later reference to this decree, the king speaks of "the deliberate advice of our counsell," ibid., p. 549. In Feb., 1494, a trial for high treason was held also in the Guildhall in London, before "diuerse lordes and Juges and other of the kyngis counsaill": City Chron., fol. 147*b*. Various cases are noted in the Calendar of Star Chamber Proceedings in the 49th Rep. of the Dep. Keeper, App. pp. 413, 418, 441, 446, 448, f. So much then is established—the Star Chamber is the Privy Council sitting as a court of justice either in its entirety or in committees; the statute 3 Hen. VII. c. 1 gave it a permanent legal basis as a definite committee and for definite causes, the statute 11 Hen. VII. c. 25 did the same, at least for a definite case, but not permanently. The supposed general bestowal of judicial powers on the whole Privy Council by 31 Hen. VI. c. 2 was also only for a time. We are quite justified in denominating all three statutes as "Star-Chamber" Statutes.

On the evils which previously prevailed, see Stephen, Crim. Law, i. 171, f. The laws on the official conduct of sheriffs and justices of the peace, 4 Hen. VII. c. 12 ; 11 Hen. VII. c. 15, c. 24, § 6, c. 25, § 2 ; 19 Hen. VII. c. 10, c. 13, § 2, Stat., ii. 536–538, 579, f., 589, 590, 654, f., 657, f. ; cf. 569, 656. Finlason, in his edition of Reeves, iii. 124, note, justly regards the statute on justices of the peace, when referring cases to king and chancellor, as referring them to the Star Chamber.—On the proceedings of juries in general and their organisation, see Biener, Das Englische Geschwor-Ger., ·i. ; Brunner, Die Entstehung der Schwurgerichte, and shorter in Holzen-dorff's Encyklopädie, ii. 2 ; Stephen, Crim. Law, i., Blackstone's and Stephen's Commentaries. On the earlier proceedings in regard to fresh trials, see the preamble to 11 Hen. VI. c. 4, Stat., ii. 280, and Reeves, ed. Finlason, iii. 145–147, note. Henry's laws, 11 Hen. VII. c. 24 (12 Hen. VII. c. 2 ; 19 Hen. VII. c. 3), and c. 25 : Stat., p. 588, f. (636, 649), and 589, f ; cf. 3 Hen. VII. c. 10 ; 11 Hen. VII. c. 21 and 26, ibid., p. 519, 584, f., 590, f. Cf. on the jurisdiction of the Star Chamber, the remarks and examples in Reeves, ed. Finlason, iii. 153–156, note, and Stephen, Crim. Law, i. 166–183, where are also given the views of Bacon, Hudson, Hallam, and Palgrave, also Blackstone, iv. 346, f. ; Stephen, Comment., iv. 292, f. Bacon's admiration for the Star Chamber is the result of a biased and incorrect view, because he has in his mind its action under James I.—On Henry's legislation, cf. Finlason's excellent appreciation in his edition of Reeves, iii. 119, note : "The great feature of this reign was not in novel or original legislation, but rather in measures to enforce the execution of existing laws, and all the new legislation of the reign will be found directed to that object, and designed to secure the maintenance of peace and the ascendancy of the royal power" (see also Finlason's subsequent remarks). And yet, although it is true that this legislation reconstructed rather than originated, Finlason here falls into the error of under-estimating its value (see especially the concluding statements, p. 192, ff.) ; he finally deter-mines that this legislation had only one end, that of extorting money for the king (cf. above, p. 279, note 2). Here, however, in opposition to his words quoted above, he forms a mistaken idea of its main object, and its paramount importance as a part of Henry's policy of personal government.

APPENDIX II.

ON THE ORIGINAL AUTHORITIES.

WE do not possess such a wealth of original authorities for the history of Henry VII. as for that of his son. The nature also of the original material handed down to us seems to mark his reign as the transition from medieval to modern times. It is quite possible to sketch in outline the picture of the reign from the original records, and from the documentary evidence of the actors themselves and of those contemporaries who stood in intimate relation to them, but at the same time we are obliged, more than in the ensuing period, to rely on historical narratives both contemporary and of a somewhat later date.

The existing records and original documents are to be found for the most part in print. Any still unprinted material I could collect, besides the London Chronicle in the British Museum, to be mentioned hereafter, served merely as a supplement to these, though, no doubt, often a welcome one. In the Record Office in London there are two boxes with papers, roughly, but on the whole correctly arranged, on the history of our period, and these are referred to in my notes as "in the Record Office;" I also found much in the manuscripts of the British Museum, but unfortunately my search for letters of Sir Reginald Bray's in the Westminster Archives was not attended with success. The copies from the Archives of the Vatican, which are in the Record Office, were also very useful to me.

The number both of early and of more recent printed collections is considerable : they are all given in the list of books of reference, in Appendix III. Such are the Statutes and Parliamentary rolls, Rymer's indispensable work, Leland's Collectanea, the collections made by Ellis, Halliwell, Campbell, and especially by Mr. James Gairdner, to whom we owe a large debt of gratitude. To these collections must be added the publications from Italian sources by Brown, and, above all, from the Spanish, by Bergenroth, and Zurita's work, compiled from original documents, from which I was able to obtain much additional matter, as well as isolated fragments in the Coleccion de Documentos Inéditos.

For the relations with the Burgundian Netherlands and Maximilian, we must refer to the collections of Le Glay, Chmel, Gachard, van den Bergh; for those with the Hansa, to the volumes of the Hanserecesse, edited by Schäfer; for the relations with France, to the Lettres de Louis XII., to Morice, Champollion, Le Glay, Bernier; for Scotland more especially to the Acts of Parliament, Ayloffe and Bain; also for Ireland to the Statutes, the Carew Papers, and so forth. We can gather much from the numerous publications of the Camden Society; they include, together with many chronicles, the very valuable "Relation of an unknown Italian," no doubt a Venetian, and the correspondence of the Plumpton family; these last are, however, surpassed in value by the Paston Letters, recently very carefully edited by Mr. James Gairdner.

The Spanish reports in Bergenroth's work are of special importance, for they throw quite a new light on the history of the time. The Spaniards were masters of the higher policy of their day, and their diplomatists, especially in the succeeding centuries, stand in statesmanlike insight and training far above the average of other statesmen of their time. In this respect, however, the reign of Ferdinand and Isabella was a time of beginnings. The despatches of such a man as Ayala are the best reports from an ambassador, on Henry VII. and his kingdom, which are at our command. Even the reports of the permanent Spanish representative Puebla are, in spite of Puebla's tiresome and self-satisfied loquacity and his lack of insight or judgment, an inexhaustible mine of reliable information. Nevertheless one must be careful not to be led astray by this conceited and gossiping personage.

The contemporary or somewhat later historical accounts are quite indispensable, and in order to appreciate their relative importance, a critical examination of them, which till now has not been attempted, would seem to be necessary. The object of these investigations is to make at least a first attempt towards a critical study and comparison of the original sources, not that I thereby claim to put forward a final opinion, but only intend to follow up various questions so far as seems necessary to form a sufficiently satisfactory judgment.

BERNARD ANDRÉ.

Bernard André, historiographer and "poeta laureatus" to Henry VII., was able to write from the most intimate contemporary knowledge, having been for four years tutor to Prince Arthur (Mem., p. 6 and 43). The notices on André's life have been collected by Mr. Gairdner in his preface to the Memorials (pp. viii.–xiii.). André was born at Toulouse, and appears to have come over to England with Henry, for he was not there at the time of the Wars of the Roses (Mem., p. 19), but formed part of the king's retinue, when he made his entry into London after the victory of Bosworth (ibid., p. 35). Bishop Fox, whom he calls his Mæcenas, was his special patron (ibid., p. 33). We find frequent mention of André as the recipient of a yearly salary, later of some small ecclesiastical benefices, of various presents of money, and from 1506–1521 of a formal New Year's gift (Rym., xii. 317 and 643 ; Gairdner, as above, p. ix., f., Exc. Hist., p. 109 and 143 ; Brewer, ii. 2, pp. 1444, 1449, 1454, iii. 2, p. 1533). On one special occasion he is mentioned, as a witness at the betrothal of his pupil Arthur, May 19, 1499 (Rym., xii. 759). Mr. Gairdner's supposition, as above, p. xiii., that he died in 1521 or shortly afterwards is, I find, confirmed by the way in which Erasmus speaks of him as already dead in a letter of Sept. 4, 1524 (Er. Epp., xviii. 46 ; Abstract in Brewer, iv. 1, No. 626).

André's principal function was to celebrate every special event in his French or Latin verses, of which he treats us to a considerable number in his chief historical work. He was still writing in Henry VIII.'s time, and celebrated the victories of the year 1513 over the French and Scotch (Brewer, i. No. 4443). His historical works which interest us are : De Vita atque gestis Henrici Septimi, Angliæ ac Franciæ regum potentissimi sapientissimique historia (quoted shortly as "Vita"), and Annales Henrici Septimi (quoted as "Ann."), of which only the Annus vicesimus (1504–1505) and the Annus vicesimus tertius (1507–1508) have been preserved, though he probably went on working through each successive year (cf. the way in which he expresses himself in his prefaces, p. 80 and 97). The Vita and Annals have been published by Mr. Gairdner in the Memorials of Henry VII.

André's chief work is the biography of Henry VII.; it breaks off with Perkin Warbeck's inroad into England, and his capture in 1497. André began to write in the year 1500 (Præf., p. 6, f.), and went on improving and amplifying even after April 2, 1502, as he mentions Arthur's death (p. 42 ; see before, p. 10, the words:

"Wallenses . . . quibus Arturus . . . cum haec scriberem, domi-
nabatur;" cf. p. 55 on Morton, who died in Oct., 1500: "piæ
memoriæ . . . cardinalis"). He characterises his book himself:
"Quum non tam historiam, quam vitam perscribere in animo sit"
(p. 5, cf. 19), and likewise the manner of his work (p. 7, f.), "statui ·
res gestas Regis Henrici septimi carptim, ut quæque memoriæ
mihi occurrentia, absque ullo instructore, digna mihi videbantur,
perscribere."

At first sight, therefore, the "Vita" does not appear as a complete
whole, but as a collection of fragments put together almost without
any regard to order, between which are everywhere greater or
smaller gaps. He himself often draws attention to his insufficient
knowledge of events; he was cut off from all personal intercourse
with the outside world by the sad lot of total blindness ; indeed, he
even somewhat coquets with this infirmity of his, to which he is
never tired of alluding (Vita, pp. 4, 6, 19, 32, 35). In his dedication
to Henry he lays stress on the fact of having been obliged to dictate
his work, and of having had no one to consult, and later on he
says he could only depend on oral information. And yet, living as
he did at court, mixed up in the life there, he might easily have
filled up the gaps in his knowledge, if he had set himself to do so
in earnest. But this he certainly did not do. He leaves out all
description of the battle of Bosworth : "donec plenius instructus
fuero" (p. 32). For that he might have had quite enough opportunity during the two years in which he was engaged in his work;
the same can be said about a similar remark on the ceremonial of
Henry's coronation (p. 36, f.) and on Warbeck's invasion, 1497
(p. 71). The main object with this courtly historian seems to have
been to adorn his writings with a superabundance of laudatory
phrases, with polished verses and imaginary speeches put into the
mouths of the actors in the principal events recorded. The
historical facts, which are comparatively but sparingly inserted in
his narrative, held with him obviously a secondary place. His
indifference with regard to these has of course had a serious effect
on the value of his writings to us.

I subjoin some examples of this : on page 12 André gives one
after another two different dates for Henry's birth (cf. Appendix i.
p. 319); on p. 24, f., he mixes up—adding also various incorrect
statements—those events which are connected with Henry's two
attempts at landing in 1483 and 1485 (cf. ibid., p. 321, f.); on
p. 32 the statements about Stanley's conduct are, to say the least,
inexact; on p. 46 his mention of the Bishop of Concordia is

wrong; on p. 47, ff., he places Northumberland's murder before
Simnel's insurrection; on p. 49 we find incorrect statements as to
Simnel's origin, and on p. 50 as to his coronation (cf. App. i. pp.
326 and 328); on p. 65, f., and 72, he weaves a perfect web of
myth round Warbeck's origin, and makes matters even worse by
asserting that he is giving the substance of Warbeck's confession—
thus we are left with a very meagre residuum of historical information,
reliable, after instances such as the above, only to a restricted degree.

To the dependence upon others of a blind man who can never
relate from his own personal observation must be added André's
extreme carelessness and want of judgment. Erasmus' unfavourable opinion of him (Ep. xviii. 46: "Bernardo . . . Arcturi
principis optimi non optimo duee ') is entirely confirmed by André's
works. Altogether his biography of the king has been productive
of far more confusion than enlightenment.

As André was a thoroughly honourable man, and was quite incapable of any desire to falsify information, he improves at once
when, as in his annals, he makes his notes, in diary fashion, keep
pace with the events. And yet his Annus vicesimus (1504–1505) is
very inadequate; he complains himself of having been only imper-
fectly informed, and, as with the Vita, this not very valuable work is
overladen with senseless rhetoric; thus, in spite of his flow of
words, he affords us but scant information on Henry's reform of the
coinage, and displays his slight comprehension of political events
by lauding Henry as the originator of the alliance between Ferdinand
the Catholic and Louis XII. in 1505 (p. 88).

Far the most useful material, which André as an historian has
left behind, is the Annus vicesimus tertius (1507, 1508). Here it
is obvious how easily he could obtain full information on outward
events. As he did not give himself time to work up the very
incomplete sketch in his own fashion, the contents of it are for us
all the more useful. The notes were evidently made concurrently
with the events; he began them on Oct. 31, 1507 (see p. 100).
Here only purely external events are treated of, but these are
recorded with the greatest fulness, and I can only join with Mr.
Gairdner—whose opinion of André is, to my mind, in other respects
too favourable—in regretting that we do not possess the same sort
of notes for the other years.

POLYDORUS VIRGILIUS.

The life in England of the Italian, Polydore Vergil of Urbino,
coincided, at least in part, with the reign of Henry VII., and his

Historiæ Anglicæ libri viginti septem, in the section on Henry VII.,
occupies, in the opinion of all students in research, the first rank
among historical authorities. Polydore Vergil came to England in
1502, for, according to a letter of Henry VIII.'s to Leo X. of Feb. 26,
1514, he had then been for twelve years in England (Brewer, i.
4819); his own first letters from England are dated June and
September, 1505 (Lett. and Pap., i. 248, f.). He was sub-collector
of the papal tax called Peter's pence.

His English history, in twenty-six books, extended down to the
death of Henry VII., and was, according to its dedication, dated
August, 1533, presented to his son, Henry VIII., and printed for the
first time in 1534, and for the second time in 1546. Polydore
Vergil himself gave to his work its enlarged form in twenty-seven
books, including also the time of Henry VIII.; and in this form it first
appeared in the year 1555, shortly after his death, which occurred in
extreme old age. (I quote from the edition of Thysius, Leiden, 1651.)

He wrote in Latin, in order to make a knowledge of English
history accessible to other nations; and for elegance of language,
easy narrative, firmness and independence of judgment, this cultured
humanist of Urbino far surpasses all the English historians of his
day. The book was not composed till the reign of Henry VIII.,
and it can be shown that he probably went on still working at it
between 1512 and 1524, particularly at the chapter on Henry VII.
(see pp. 744, 746, 760, cf. 527; also Pauli, v. 701).

The history of Henry VII. is by far the best and most original
part of the whole work. As in the case of the chronicler Hall, to
be mentioned hereafter, his history of Henry VII.'s time appears so
perfectly different in design and character from that of Henry VIII.,
that, when considering the two parts critically, we must be careful to
divide them. It is probable that, as soon as Polydore had conceived
the idea of his historical work, he commenced his notes in his diary
(see preface to the twenty-seventh book: "interrupta jam serie rerum
publicarum, quas in dies singulos annotare prius solebam "); but we
are unable to determine exactly the date when he did so. The earlier
period, compiled from English original authorities, does not concern
us. As Polydore was not living in England during the time of
Richard III., nor during the first fifteen years of Henry VII.'s reign,
he could only describe the events of those periods at second-hand.
The independent spirit which is displayed by Polydore in manipu-
lating his material, is in striking contrast to the English historians of
the day, and makes it specially difficult for us to discover the sources
from which he drew.

For Buckingham's insurrection, under Richard III., it is probable he had access to Thomas More's narrative (see on the subject App. i. p. 32 ɒ), he also, no doubt, made frequent use of documentary material; the short notices on the various Parliaments show some knowledge, though superficial, of the statutes then passed; his statements, p. 770, f., on the proceedings against criminal clerics correspond exactly with the articles in the statute 4 Hen. VII. c. 13, Stat., ii. 538. Evidently, for p. 771, f., he consulted the papal bull on the jubilee indulgence, and for p. 774, the papal bull (in Rym., xii. 541, f.) against the abuse of church asylums, and for p. 772, the Anglo-Scottish marriage treaty of Jan. 24, 1502. On other occasions he had at his disposal either diplomatic documents, or relied upon the subsequent narrative of persons who had taken an important part in the proceedings; his intercourse with the leading men must have given him altogether much information denied to others.

We will now examine into some of his statements. His account of Henry's journey in 1487, on p. 726, f., is confirmed by the dates of the decrees in Campbell, ii. 134–140 (cf. App. i., p. 326); his details of the Scotch invasion in Aug., 1497 (p. 726, f.), agree with the entries in the Treasury accounts (Lett. and Pap., ii. 332, ff.; cf. above, App. i., p. 347); so also the narrative of Warbeck's invasion (p. 765) with Henry's own report; his story of the border incident at Norham, p. 768, is also supported by contemporary evidence (see App. i. p. 355).

We stand, of course, on more firm ground for the last four to six years of the king's life, when Polydore was himself an eye-witness. The most brilliant portion of his work is his excellent appreciation of Henry's character, which concludes it. It may be noted that his general remarks on the king's beneficence are confirmed by the entries in his privy-purse account-book, and so also is, incidentally, an earlier and particularly striking remark on Henry's economic principles (p. 775) by the king's own words in the presence of the Spaniard Ayala (Berg., p. 177).

Though Polydore Vergil shows himself on the whole trustworthy as to actual facts, he often makes mistakes about the connection of those events which took place before he was living in the country, just as much as any other later historian. We must remember the erroneous statements, p. 746, about Warbeck's early history (see App. i., p. 335, f.); how he connects (p. 771) Henry's journey to Calais in May, 1500 (see App. i., p. 363), with the sweating sickness, which did not break out till after Henry's return (see App. i., p. 364);

and that with him originates the assertion that Curzon had acted as
a spy of Henry's (see App. i., p. 364). It also sometimes happens
that he presumably writes with a bias in Henry's favour, as in the
account of the marriage negotiations with Scotland (p. 769), when
against the evidence of fact he tries to ascribe the initiative to the
king of Scots (see App. i., p. 355). He blunders more seriously when
he makes Warbeck (p. 735) go back again from Kent to Flanders,
and especially in his often inexact chronology, for instance, of Parliaments and statutes ; thus, on p. 744, f., he joins Queen Elizabeth's
death with " non multo post," to the death of Arthur, which took
place the year before, and places immediately after it a notice on
the Parliament, which was not opened till the following year.   For
similar mistakes, see in App. i. pp. 323, 333, 341.

Thus Polydore Vergil is by no means an absolutely trustworthy
authority.   His chronological arrangement of events, and his reasons
for connecting them together, are especially to be regarded with mistrust.   But there is no doubt he has managed to get at good and
detailed original sources, and this knowledge is of importance for
us, since, for many sections, he is our only existing authority.   Thus,
our narrative down to the battle of Bosworth had to rely in a great
measure on him.   For some later events as well, for instance, for
the commencement of the Cornish rising, and James IV.'s invasion
in the year 1497, he is our only authority.   Certainly Polydore Vergil
is unable in such cases to console us for the lack of more original
information, but he can afford us some compensation, and for this
we must acknowledge our gratitude.

THE CHRONICLE OF EDWARD HALL.

Polydore Vergil had worked up for himself the information
he had collected into a complete historical work.   In quite a different
and for historical research, of course, much more satisfactory way,
do the original sources come to light which form the groundwork of
our information, and, moreover, are generally known to us in the
other narratives.   To these belongs, to begin with, the chronicle
of Edward Hall, who, born under Henry VII., passed his best years
during the reign of Henry VIII.   He had been educated at Cambridge,
at Gray's Inn in London, and at Oxford as a lawyer.   Became Common
Serjeant, then Under-Sheriff of the City of London, subsequently
himself a " Reader " at Gray's Inn, and in 1540, also a judge in the
Sheriffs' Court; he died in 1547 (cf. Wood, Athenæ Oxonienses,
edited by Bliss.   London, 1813, i. 164, f.).

His Chronicle includes the period of the Houses of York and
Lancaster, and culminates in a panegyric of Henry VIII. As Hall
made use of the first edition of Polydore Vergil's English History,
he cannot have begun to work up his materials before 1534; he
carried the work itself only as far as the twenty-fourth year of
Henry VIII.'s reign (1532–1533), the notes he left were collected
together after his death by Richard Grafton, without any further
addition, as he himself states, and the whole book dedicated to
King Edward VI.   In 1548 it was printed for the first time under
the title of, " The Union of the Two noble and illustre Famelies of
Lancaster and Yorke . . . beginnyng at the tyme of Kyng Henry
the Fowerth, the first aucthor of this deuision, and so successively
proceadyng to the Reigne of the High and Prudent Prince Kyng
Henry the Eight, the undubitate Flower and very Heire of both
the sayd Linages."   A second edition appeared in 1550; a reprint
was made in London in 1809.

For the period of Henry VIII., the Chronicle is an entirely
original authority; but, for the preceding epoch, only an account
at second-hand.   For the main facts Hall gives a free and sometimes even a literal translation of Polydore Vergil, adopting not only
his views, but also some of his statements which are in contradiction
to those made already by himself (for instance, Hall, p. 462, P. V.,
746 ; see also App. i. p. 335), he even goes so far as to copy down
word for word, without thought, a date given by P. V. for the
writing out of his own work (Hall, p. 478, P. V., 760).   It had long
been known that Hall's book was really an English transcript of
P. V.'s (see Pauli, v. 702; Gairdnėr in Early Chroniclers of England,
p. 304).   In spite of this Hall has, without exception, been made
use of as an original authority in those portions of his chronicle
which are nothing but an English translation of P. V.   We, however,
are prevented from doing the same, not only because we consider
it absolutely necessary to refer back to original sources, but also by
reason of the unreliability of Hall's transcript.   He does not exactly
invent, but he loves to embellish P. V.'s text in various ways, and
besides, often misunderstands him (cf., for instance, App. i., p. 323
and p. 363, f.).   It will be understood, therefore, that, in my narrative, wherever Hall relies on P. V. I have not troubled myself about
the Chronicle, but have only quoted it alongside as being derived
from P. V.'s work.

Hall, however, introduces into this history of his, which is
founded on P. V.'s, a great many items of information, such as
isolated events on the Continent, from French and Flemish sources

(pp. 441, 442, 444–447), and we further find in his work, some important, some unimportant, some short, or again detailed interpolations bearing strongly the impress of the city of London. This brings us to another important class of original authorities.

The London City Chronicles.

In the history of England the capital of the kingdom has always played a very prominent part. Within it, or in its neighbourhood were concentrated all the events that most affected the country ; it was bound up closely with the destinies of England, it formed the central point of the nation's commerce, and the riches of its merchants made its relations with the Crown always of special importance. It was therefore the object of particular attention from the Crown, and was endowed by it with special privileges. On great state occasions its Lord Mayor occupied a prominent position, while the sword-bearer of the city marched before him bearing the naked sword. Nowhere else could one be so well informed on the progress of public events as in this focus of public life, more especially as the monarch, when at a distance, never failed to send to the city authorities friendly information as to his actions.

There were many kinds of municipal records in England, such as the Chronicle of Calais and the Calendar of Ricart of Bristol, but they either gave only a small amount of information, or retained a merely local character, except on the rare occasions when the place happened to be the scene of more important events. This London always was. A history of London, therefore, almost always went in every respect beyond the limits of an ordinary city history, and became a civic history of the kingdom.

The names of the Lord Mayors and two sheriffs elected annually supplied the skeleton for these notes. As the year of the king's reign was also generally given, it was easy for chronological confusion to arise from these different starting-points. This is the case in the reign of Henry VII. with the events which occurred from the beginning of the first year of the reign at the end of August, till the close of October, the beginning of the new Lord Mayor's year, events which were usually reckoned as belonging to the preceding royal year ; we very frequently meet with mistakes arising from this in all these Chronicles.

For the period with which we are concerned, we have at our disposal two groups of records from the metropolis, differing very much from each other both as to bulk and value.

ARNOLD'S CHRONICLE AND AUTHORITIES BASED UPON IT.

Of the group of three chronicles—Arnold's, Wriothesley's, and the London Grey Friars' Chronicle—which are closely connected with each other, Arnold's is shown to be the predecessor of the others by the date at which it was written.

Richard Arnold was a citizen of London, born probably about 1450, dying about 1521 (cf. about him, Douce in the preface to his edition of Arnold). His work, sometimes entitled "The Customs of London," sometimes "Chronicle," is a collection, without arrangement, of charters, Acts of Parliament, papal bulls, ordinances, topographical notices, administrative customs, tariffs of prices and tolls, and various other things; even the Ballad of the Nut-Brown Maid is to be found amongst them. The first edition must have been printed at the beginning of the sixteenth century, the second in 1520, both without giving the name of the author; we find a passage from it quoted in the divorce trial of Henry VIII. (Brewer, iv. 3, p. 2587). A reprint followed, in 1811, the anonymous editor of which was F. Douce.

The list of city magistrates prefixed to this work is of value to us. It begins with Richard I., Cœur de Lion (Sept. 3, 1189), and is carried down to the end of the twelfth year of Henry VIII., January, 1521. In the first part this list of names is not often interrupted by records of events; it is not till Edward IV.'s time that these become frequent, at first scanty and meagre, with Henry VII. in greater detail. They mostly date from the period of Arnold's lifetime, and are altogether first-hand. The events cannot always have been noted at the time they occurred, otherwise such a mistake as placing the landing of King Philip two years too late would have been impossible (p. 43, Ann., 23 instead of 21). Most of Arnold's statements are to be relied upon, if the peculiarities before mentioned of the chronology of the city records be borne in mind.

The Chronicle of *Charles Wriothesley*, who was Windsor Herald from the year 1534, is nothing but an extract, in part a word for word transcript, of Arnold ("A Chronicle of England," edited by Douglas Hamilton for the Camden Society, New Ser., No. 11, 1875, from an anonymous copy of the time of James I.). Wriothesley carried his work on into the second year of Queen Elizabeth. The editor has pointed out that Wriothesley depended entirely upon Arnold, whose work he continued from 1522 on. With the exception of a few unimportant alterations, he follows his model closely, and, therefore, does not come under our consideration as an original authority.

2 D

The Chronicle of the Grey Friars of London is also based upon Arnold's Chronicle; it has been edited under that title by John Gough Nichols for the Camden Society, No. 53, 1852, omitting, unfortunately, the list of city magistrates given in the manuscript. It begins with the first year of Richard Cœur de Lion, as does Arnold, but adds to his scanty notices from other sources, and then relapses into entire dependence upon him for the time of Edward IV., continuing thus, except for a few meagre additions, till the sixteenth year of Henry VII. (1500–1501), inclusive. For this period the convent chronicle is of no more value as an original authority than Wriothesley; only in the thirteenth year (1497–1498) it gives some additional facts. These increase in number in the seventeenth year (1501–1502), and from that time the convent Chronicle altogether deserts its former guide, becomes independent, and gives notices of its own, which are valuable. However, they still continue scanty, until the close of Henry VIII.'s reign when, and for the two following reigns (till 1556), these contemporary notices become fuller and more general. It should be noted that the editor, Nichols (Pref. p. vii., f.), speaks of a resemblance between Arnold and the Chronicle down to 1502, without, however, arriving at the conclusion, which is inevitable, that the Chronicle is only a repetition of that of Arnold, abbreviating it in some parts and enlarging it in others.

From this group composed of Arnold's Chronicle, and those based upon it, we can only now and then extract a detail which our other sources do not supply, otherwise they for the most part merely confirm, by the statements in them, facts which have been recorded elsewhere. But there remains a second group of city records, also to be traced back to one common source, which is of incomparably greater value.

THE LONDON CHRONICLE OF ALDERMAN ROBERT FABIAN AND THE AUTHORITIES DERIVED FROM IT.

Robert Fabian's History of England and France, breaking off with the death of Richard III. in 1485, entitled, "The New Chronicles of England and France, in Two Parts; by Robert Fabian, named by himself the Concordance of Histories," has long been known, and widely diffused in print. Robert Fabian was a citizen of London, member of the Drapers' Guild, alderman, and, in 1493–1494, one of the sheriffs. We find his name mentioned on some special occasions; in 1502 he gave up his position as alderman, because, notwithstanding his easy circumstances, he wished to avoid being elected

Lord Mayor, on account of the expense of the office. He died in
1511 (cf. Ellis' statements in his edition of the Chronicle and Brit.
Mus. MS., Harl., 538, fol. 67*b*). Fabian's so-called " New Chronicle "
was first printed without a title in 1516, by Richard Pynson; in 1533
a reprint appeared under the title, " Fabian's cronycle newly prynted
wyth the cronycle, actes, and dedes done in the tyme of the reygne
of the moste excellent prynce kynge Henry the VII., father unto
our most drad souerayne lord kynge Henry VIII."

This supplement on Henry VII. (cited in the notes as " Fabian's
Abridgment ") differs essentially from the earlier portion of the
Chronicle; it consists of short but pithy notices, arranged in years,
dealing exclusively with English affairs; they bear indeed, as was to be
expected from Fabian's position, a specially local London character,
as do also the preceding portions of the Chronicle on English
History. For that this supplement in its present form is also the
work of Fabian, is proved by the words at the end of the edition of
1533: " Thus endeth Fabyan's cronycle." In 1542 and 1544 the
Chronicle appeared afresh, very much altered in parts and as we
note especially, carried on further; Ellis's edition, London, 1811, is
based upon the first edition, but compares and makes use of the
later, with a notice of the additions which belong to it. The Continuation of Fabian for Henry VII.'s reign, as it now lies before us,
was written, at least for the years down to 1502, probably in a connected form and as a supplement, for in Ann. 7 and 13, p. 684 and
686, we find Sheen spoken of as Richmond, which name was not
given to this palace of Henry's till after its rebuilding in 1501. The
great abundance and unusual accuracy of the historical details here
given us make it, however, impossible to believe that they were only
written down in that way at a subsequent period, and we are led to
regard this supplement as a later composition drawn from notes made
at the time the events occurred.

The key to the connection between these facts concerning the
city recorded here, and those introduced into Hall's Chronicle, was
supplied me by the Chronicle among the manuscripts in the British
Museum, of which much use has already been made, but which has
not yet been published: MS. Cotton Vitellius, A. XVI. (extracts
from the same, MS. Lansd., 949, fol. 40, ff.) : " Chronicum regum
Angliæ et Series maiorum et vice-comitum Civitatis London ab Anno
primo Henrici tertii ad Annum primum Hen. 8^n " (cited in the
notes as City Chronicle).

The Chronicle is divided into large sections, written in the
same clear hand, and apparently all at one time; the portion which

interests us begins with the death of Henry VI., and continues to the eleventh year of Henry VII., fol. 160*b*. Here a fresh hand begins; in the thirteenth year it changes twice, the last hand continues till the close of the eighteenth year; then another change sets in, the whole seems more carelessly put together, and the character of the contents becomes different. At first, and for the first years of Henry VII., the chronicle is scanty; with the sixth year (1490–1491) it becomes more detailed, especially from the ninth to the seventeenth year (1493–1502), but from the nineteenth year (1503) on, it gives only short notices which look like extracts.

The character of the records is purely local and municipal, all events of interest in the capital are noted, the political events in the same way in which they would be discussed in the leading London circles, and those which occurred at a distance from London as they were reported officially to the Lord Mayor. Official documents such as these were always at the disposal of the author; he often mentions letters from the king to the city authorities, and even gives an exact copy of them; he must, therefore, have been a man in an important position in the city, and this is the more likely, as events in which the Lord Mayor and aldermen bore a part are reported evidently on the very best authority.

One cursory glance into the City Chronicle was sufficient to settle the question of its relationship with Fabian's "Continuation," and to prove the latter an abridgment of the Chronicle. A comparison of the first sentences for the first and second years in the two Chronicles will explain the nature of this connection between them:

Year 1.

CITY CHRONICLE, fol. 141*b*.	FABIAN'S ABRIDGMENT, p. 683.
In this yere was a preest of ii. M. li. made to the kyng, whereof the ffelishippys of mercers grocers and drapers bare ix c. xxxviii li vi^s.	In thys yere a prest was made to the kynge of ii. M. li. of the whyche the mercers, grocers and drapers lent ix c. xxxvii li and vi^s.

Year 2.

Fol. 142*a*.	Ibid.
In this yere was kyng Henry the VIIth. maryed unto Dame Elizabeth theldest Doughter of kyng Edward the IIIIth. Also this yere was Stoke feelde, where by the kynges power was slayne therle of lyncolne, Marten Swart a Ducheman, and moche of the people that come w^i theym.	In thys yere the kynge maryed kyng Edwardes eldest doughter named Elizabeth. This yere was slayn at Stookfelde the erle of Lincolne.

As to the discrepancy in the numeral given in the first year, it may be noted that similar confusion between the numerals i., ii., iii.,

iiii. and their combinations occurs very often throughout the manuscripts.

The more detailed the City Chronicle becomes, the more is the effort to abbreviate visible in Fabian's Continuation, till finally it becomes hardly more than a mere abridgment of the fuller narrative of the Chronicle; it contains only notes where the other relates in detail, and it even omits various events altogether, which are recorded in the other. From the nineteenth year (1503) on, the resemblance between the two becomes closer again; they are practically identical, what discrepancies there are being not worth mentioning.

We should observe that in the list of mayors and sheriffs, some discrepancies exist between the City Chronicle and Arnold; for example, in the order in which the names of the two sheriffs stand in the list, also in their Christian names, whereas between Fabian and the Chronicle there is perfect agreement in this also.

The best evidence of this strikingly essential agreement is afforded by the list of minor essential differences, of course, also, only down to the nineteenth year. Similar differences in numbers to those in Ann. 1 occur in Ann. 3 and 14: City Chron., 142*b*, 174*b*, Fab., 683, 686; in Ann. 4 the leader of the rebels is called by the City Chronicle (143*a*) John a Chamber, and by Fab., 683, Chamberlayne, evidently from a confusion with "Syr Robert Chamberlayne," mentioned in Ann. 6, p. 684; Ann. 6, the City Chron. says, p. 144: "the more party of thaldermen;" Fab., 684: "every Alderman;" Ann. x., City Chron., 150*a*, correctly: "the lorde Edmonde Erle of Suffolk;" Fab., 685, wrongly, "Syr William de la Pool, then duke of Suffolk" (William was the name of a brother of Edmund's). These are discrepancies which are easily explained, if we take Fabian's Continuation for that period to be an abridgment of the other Chronicle, and written as a connected whole at a later date.

The otherwise close and constant agreement between the two cannot possibly be accidental. But the first idea that Fabian's Continuation is a mere abridgment of the City Chronicle cannot be maintained on closer examination. For, though they occur seldom, Fabian has some statements, which are not to be found in the City Chronicle: Ann. 1, the date of the coronation; Ann. 2, Arthur's birth; Ann. 3, the mention of an execution; Ann. 6, an additional record on the subject of a grant from the guilds; Ann. 8, another in the description of an execution; Ann. 9, the name of a Prior of Christ Church; the same again in Ann. 9, and also Ann. 13 and 15,—unimportant additions in themselves, but excluding the possibility of the entire dependence of Fabian's Continuation upon the City Chronicle.

The City Chronicle then, in its present form, is evidently not original. The original annotations, certainly, must have been in the main almost contemporaneous; this is proved by their accuracy and minuteness of detail; in Ann. 13, too, when mentioning Cabot's voyage in May, 1497, the remark is added, "but to this present moneth came nevir knowlege of their exployt." By Aug., 1497, Cabot had already returned. But that the Chronicle before us was written down connectedly in several long portions, is shown even by the character of the handwritings, and to this may be added some points which awaken at least a doubt whether we can regard the Chronicle as altogether original.

It is remarkable that the Chronicle, while seeming to attach great importance to the action of the Bishop of London with regard to the Prior of Christ Church, nowhere mentions the Prior's name (fol. 148*a* and 149*b*), which we only learn through Fabian. Probably it was mentioned in the first instance, but overlooked by the copyist. This is still more evident in the same year, at the mention of two condemned men, both of whose names are again supplied by Fabian; the Chronicle, fol. 149*a*, speaks in general only of "one John Norfolke," and after an account of his sentence and its execution, goes on, "and that other to stand upon the said pillory," which would be quite unintelligible, if we did not know through Fabian that two men were here in question. The copyist forgot that he had before quite overlooked the second. Further, on fol. 158*b*, the conclusion of the commercial treaty between England and the Netherlands is assigned to April, 1496, while immediately afterwards, fol. 159*a*, Feb. 24 is correctly given in the announcement of the same made by the Lord Mayor. The incomprehensible earlier statement can only be explained by the carelessness of a copyist, who, as Henry's ratification took place on March 26, probably found in the manuscript before him the mention of the public announcement of the treaty in April. At the beginning of the thirteenth year, fol. 168*b*, Henry's return after the victory over Warbeck is decidedly inexact (cf. above, App. i. 349, f.), and Warbeck's confession is here interpolated so abruptly that one has difficulty in seeing its connection with the events mentioned beside it. The whole passage gives the impression of being a hasty copy, or rather extract. When we think of the carelessness which a man like Hall displays with regard to the original before him, it cannot surprise us to find a later copyist, and that just after a new hand has begun to write, copying a passage incorrectly like the one quoted above on Cabot's voyage.

The supposition, that we have here to deal with a work written at second-hand, becomes a certainty when we think of the way in which it corresponds with Fabian's Continuation, and the extract-like character of that Continuation; according to this view both are independent and compressed reproductions—the City Chronicle, in most parts even a literal copy probably—of one and the same original—of a Chronicle of London written by a well-informed man, at the time when the events which he describes took place.

But let us pursue our examination a little further. At this point in our argument the London news in Hall's Chronicle may also be drawn in for comparison. As Hall interpolated his news of the city into the rest of his narrative, he was, of course, free to choose and arrange them as he wished; and yet, if we carefully collate these paragraphs of his with those in the City Chronicle, the same relation is apparent as between the latter and Fabian; that is, a full and indeed remarkable agreement in those events which are described by both, yet with such amplifications and additions on both sides as preclude the idea that the one is immediately derived from the other.

This sort of agreement between the two, with, at the same time, additions in both, is, for instance, to be noticed in the description of the storming of the Steelyard, Hall, p. 468, City Chron., 146*b*, ff.; of the battle of Blackheath (see above, App. i. 345); of Katharine's entry into London, Hall, 493, f., City Chron., 184*a*-195*a*; both agree entirely in their report of Warbeck's confession, even to clerical inaccuracies, though they insert it in a different place, Hall, p. 488, f., City Chron., 168*a*-170*b*. More conclusive is, of course, their similarity in errors. Both place Henry's crossing over to Calais incorrectly on Oct. 6, 1492, Hall, 457, City Chron., 145*b*; both give the incorrect date of the storming of the Steelyard in the same way, "the Tuesday before St. Edward's Day," Hall, 468, City Chron., 146*b* (see App. i. 340). On the other hand, there are errors and misinterpretations of Hall's which can at once be explained with the help of the Chronicle. Hall, 459, gives the date of Nov. 9 to the letter written by Henry to the Lord Mayor from France in 1492; according to the City Chronicle, 145*b*, it was read out that day in Guildhall. The City Chronicle, fol. 156*a*, in describing Perkin's attempt at landing in Kent, 1495, mentions besides four other leaders : "a Spanyard called Quyntyne, a ffrensheman called Capteyn Genyn," City Chron., 156*a*; from this Hall makes (472) one "quyntine or otherwise Genyn," and reckons therefore only five instead of six altogether

Hall also corrects the Chronicle for us. The latter, fol. 176*b*, places the sentence upon Warbeck on "Tuesday next ensuyng" after Saturday, Nov. 16, therefore the 19th. Hall, on the contrary, gives the right date—Nov. 21. In the original authority for both, "Thursday next ensuyng" probably were the words used.

Hall, on p. 481, f., gives a detailed description of Surrey's incursion into Scotland, and on p. 498 a short one of Margaret's journey thither and marriage, about which both Polydore Vergil and the Chronicle are silent; we find, however, both events recorded, though of course quite briefly, in Fabian's Continuation, so that here Hall and Fabian agree in news gathered from the same source, but which are omitted in the City Chronicle. How exactly this news came to be in the London Chronicle is not clear, probably through reports sent to the city authorities, such as those on the French war, Perkin's capture, and Henry's meeting with Philip at Calais.

On the whole it is easy, from the disjointed way in which events are recorded in Hall's Chronicle, to pick out those which have been taken by him from his city original. This City Chronicle forms, together with Polydore Vergil, the principal groundwork for Hall, and it is in those parts of his narrative which are derived from it, and not given in other works founded upon it, that Hall's value as an authority for Henry VII.'s reign mainly rests.

Now, we find in Hall, pp. 423, 483, 500, f., three pieces of information, probably originating in this city authority, which are not given in Fabian's "continuation" nor in the City Chronicle, but in that of John Stow (pp. 860, 872, 878).

John Stow (born 1525) was by trade a tailor, like his father, but abandoned his trade for love of his historical studies. We possess a petition from him, when a man of sixty, to the London magistrate, begging for a yearly pension on the strength of the chronicles he had written in honour of London (Brit. Mus. MS., Harl., 538, fol. 8; cf. 9). Stow's reward for his disinterested efforts, was that King James I. commended him to the generosity of his subjects—in fact, gave him permission to beg (ibid., fol. 9). Stow died in the greatest penury, in 1605.

In 1565, he first published "A Sumarie of Englyshe Chronicles," which is carried down to the year in which it appeared, and, in 1580, his most important and longest work, "The Chronicles of England, from Brute unto this present yeare of Christ, 1580." The arrangement is strictly chronological; he places the notices he has collected faithfully one after the other, without any attempt at linking them together or at adding to them any views of his own.

A cursory glance at the chapter on Henry VII. will suffice to show that this Chronicle is devoted exclusively to London affairs; it seems as if Stow had compiled his history for Londoners alone, and had wished to enlarge upon this history of the city only by the most indispensable additions from general history. If we place Stow and the other works derived from the London Chronicle side by side and compare them, here, too, we shall at once perceive what we have already pointed out—the general agreement between them, and at the same time the additional matter which they severally contain; the lists too of mayors and sheriffs in Stow coincide with those in the City Chronicle and Fabian, in those points wherein they differ from Arnold. With Hall, and also with Fabian's " continuation," Stow has points of agreement quite independent from the City Chronicle; thus, in a notice of prices, Ann. 2; City Chron., 861; Fab. 683; in the mention of the title of the Merchant Taylors, City Chron., 876; Fab., 688.

Of course Stow may himself also have made use of the second-hand Chronicles. Once, on page 863, he quotes Hall; but on looking closely, we find he makes use of him for those paragraphs on general history, which Hall interpolated into his record of city affairs, and where Hall in his turn depends upon Polydore Vergil (p. 859, 862–864, 868). It is interesting to note that the copy of the Chronicle in the British Museum contains remarks in Stow's handwriting. He also incidentally quotes the London Chronicle as his authority for Capell's first indictment, where he agrees entirely with the statements in the City Chronicle, fol. 154*a*. On pages 872, 874, 891, he occasionally consults other authorities, amongst them Arnold. It is possible that, in his eagerness to collect information, he may have taken this or that notice from city documents or other sources. Nevertheless, in the main, his groundwork seems to have been that original source common to the City Chronicle, to Hall, and to Fabian's Continuation—the unknown London Chronicle.

Stow makes also various statements which we do not find in any other of the derived Chronicles—statements which are distinguished by bearing specially on matters to do with London.

These particulars added by Stow to the other Chronicles are to be found, pp. 860, 866, 874, 875, 877, 879.

It is curious that Stow, in his description of the same events, only disagrees in two points with the other Chronicles. The date for the storming of the Steelyard, given by Hall, p. 468, and by the City Chronicle, 146*b*, as, " Tuesday before St. Edward's Day " is entered wrongly by Stow as the 9th instead of the 8th of October;

when houses in Westminster were demolished, in order to make room for building the chapel, according to Stow, 875, the tavern of the White Rose, according to the City Chronicle that of the Sun was pulled down—a difference which is not very material—probably there were two taverns.

We shall have later to deal specially with Bacon's "History of the Reign of Henry VII. ;" but we may as well mention here, that it is clear Bacon must also have made use, though not to any great extent, of the London Chronicle. On p. 39 (Lumby's edition), he makes mention, in common with the City Chronicle, fol. 142, of the rumour of Henry's defeat at Stoke; p. 98, f., he gives, with City Chron., 145*b*, and a shorter notice in Stow, p. 688, the description of a tournament, which ended disastrously, p. 185 with City Chron., 172, he gives the story of the converted heretic. But Bacon, in common with Stow, alone gives, p. 12, Stow, 860, the date for the outbreak of the sweating sickness ; p. 18, information about Henry's first loan ; p. 21, about Arthur's birth ; p. 154, the date of the battle of Black- heath. Obviously it is possible to refer these back to Stow, himself not an original authority, but, as elsewhere portions of Bacon's nar- rative are taken from the Chronicle, and are not to be found in Stow, it is more probable that Bacon made direct use of the Chronicle itself. In three other passages Bacon adds to stories, to be found also in the other derived Chronicles, small details which are wanting in these, and can only have come from the same original source : p. 99, lines 2–4 on the motive of a duel ; p. 152, ff., details about the battle of Blackheath, more than are supplied by the other- wise very minute Hall (p. 479), and p. 209, the motive for Capell's arrest. For paragraphs which are also to be referred directly or indirectly to the Chronicle, see pp. 128, 131, 162, 175, 188, 197, 209.

The general similarity of the information supplied by the City Chronicle and by Fabian's Continuation, and by the correspond- ing portions of Hall and of Stow, and finally also of Bacon; the striking agreement to be found in them, though these authorities are, for the most part at least, quite independent of one another ; the remarkable accuracy (also the same in all) of the facts recorded ; finally, the obviously extract-like character of the City Chronicle and of Fabian's Chronicle,—all combine to lead us irresistibly to the conclusion that a common source is to be found for them in a larger London Chronicle, the closest copy of which is the City Chronicle in manuscript.

But who was the author of this ? We know that he must have

II.]   *ROBERT FABIAN.*   411

occupied a prominent position in the city, as he drew from official municipal sources, and was also in possession of the most exact information about those matters in which the Mayor and his aldermen took part. All this would fit in well, if we take Fabian as the author, whose work too, the sequel to the Chronicle is stated to be, in the edition of 1533. Besides, Hall quotes Fabian as one of his authorities, and Stow gives Fabian the first place among his, at least, in his "Sumarie." It is clear that, for the history of Henry VII., Hall, at all events, cannot mean only the scanty abstract, which forms Fabian's "continuation."

In a volume of manuscripts, Brit. Mus. MS., Harl., 538, containing a detailed introduction of Stow's to his "A Survay of London," published in 1598, we find that when speaking of Baynard's Castle, fol. 19*a*, he gives an account of the reception of the ambassadors sent by the King of the Romans, and of the subsequent transactions, which harmonises exactly with a somewhat more detailed account in the City Chron., fol. 205*b*.; while the narrative in Hall, p. 497, supplies other particulars, and Fabian's Continuation (p. 688) omits it altogether. The notice in Stow is an interpolation into the text, made in rather darker ink; in the same hand are inserted on the margin the words "fabian writer" (word for word, but forming part of the text, the same passage is found without acknowledgment of the authority quoted, fol. 139*a*). Consequently, for one passage at least, and, indeed, exactly as we find it in our City Chronicle, and not in Fabian's Continuation, Fabian is named expressly as the author.

In the same manuscript, fol. 67*b*, Stow thus writes about Fabian himself: " Robert fabian draper, one of the shrives and alderman of London in the yere 1491 (!). He wrote a cronicle of london (the word has a line through it) england and of fraunce, begininge at the creation and endinge in the third A. henry the 8, which both (!) I have in writen hand, he deceased in anno 1511."

This statement contains, besides the mistake in the date of the year, an obvious contradiction. Fabian's history of England and France is one work ; when Stow, therefore, after naming it, speaks of it as two works, it is nonsense. The difficulty, however, is removed, if we take away the line through the word "London." Stow had two Chronicles in manuscript of Fabian's, and, probably, intended to write quite correctly, " of London and of England and France," but must have scratched through the name of the town, in order to avoid the tautology, without reflecting that he thereby quite contradicted what he had said before. He corrected this in his printed Survay of London, p. 81, and also in a statement in the Chronicle, p. 867, where he speaks only of the one Chronicle of England and France by Fabian, which had been carried down to the third year of Henry VIII.'s reign, but was not in print beyond the end of Richard III.'s. It can hardly be supposed that, when first writing his work, he should by mistake have remarked upon two Chronicles in his possession, and also have mentioned the name of Fabian's London Chronicle, if nothing of it was in existence. When Stow says of the manuscript in his possession of the printed Chronicle, that it was carried down to the third year of Henry VIII., he can only be alluding to the scanty continuation of Fabian's Chronicle, which does extend to that date. The supposition that in one of these two copies we have the City Chronicle, which had also been in his hands, cannot be accepted, because this manuscript breaks off with the first year of Henry VIII., and then subjoins an appendix containing different matter.

If we draw from this the conclusion that, besides the Chronicle printed at a later period, there was a special Chronicle of Fabian's which we do not now possess in the original, but which was made use of independently by the various aforenamed authors, all difficulties are smoothed away, and the problems satisfactorily solved.[1] In Fabian's Continuation we have, therefore, an abstract made at a later period by himself or some other person from his large Chronicle.

It should be noted that, with the nineteenth year (1503), the City Chronicle not only agrees word for word with this meagre abstract, but Hall also, from p. 498 on, becomes extraordinarily scanty in his information, and we only receive a few items of intelligence to do with the city from Stow; one cannot avoid the impression, that here too the original, as well as the copies, had become less full in detail. This coincides in a remarkable way with the fact that Fabian resigned his dignity as alderman in 1502. He probably did not therefore lose his interest in public affairs, nor yet his former connection with them, but he no longer occupied the same position at the centre of London life.

Though we thus find our supposition still further confirmed of the existence of a London Chronicle of Robert Fabian's, from which the other Chronicles are derived, there yet remains the important question, in what relation this unknown Chronicle of Fabian's, reaching back with its narrative to before the time of Henry VII., stood

---

[1] That some connection must exist between these authorities had already rightly been felt by Harrisse and Winsor, with regard to the portions of them dealing with the history of discovery. The latter even says, iii. 38 note, "Both Stow and Hackluyt must have used a genuine Fabian manuscript yet to be discovered."

with regard to the Chronicle we know, ending with the year 1485.
We must go back, at least so far as is absolutely necessary for the
solution of this question, to an earlier period than that with which
we are concerned. I shall here examine only the most important
secondary authority—the manuscript City Chronicle—and that only
for the two last decades before Henry's accession. For a comparative criticism of authorities a large and completely unworked field
here lies open before us, in which we must of necessity only venture
so far as is required for our purpose.

In Fabian's Anglo-French History, it is, of course, the English
portions alone that come under our consideration. The character
is again shown to be, throughout, the same; the events recorded
have almost exclusively to do with the Capital, and where they
come in contact with those in the manuscript they agree entirely, but
each one makes additions, though from the same group of materials.
A characteristic example may be shown from the twenty-first year of
Edward IV., City Chron., fol. 137a, £ ; Fabian, p. 667. It is on
the subject of a visit of the mayor and aldermen to the king whilst
hunting at Waltham.

FABIAN.	CITY CHRONICLE.
The kinge commaundyd his offycers to brynge the mayer and his company unto a pleasaunt lodge made all of grene bowys and garnisshed with tables and other thinges necessary, where they were set at dyner and seruyd . . . and caused them to be sette to dyner or he were seruyed of his owne . . .	Where when the mayr and his com-pany was comen there was ordeyned for theym a pleasaunt logge of grene bowhis and thedder was brought all thyngs necessarys for theym. And the kyng wold not go to dyner, tyll they were served. . . .

The agreement is, of course, not always so striking, but it is
always to be found in the accounts of those events which are given
by both. Fabian, as a rule, goes more into detail ; for instance, the
City Chronicle, fol. 141a, jumps suddenly, after announcing the death
of a sheriff, to the decisive battle of Bosworth, whereas Fabian relates
the events which led up to it.

A general confusion prevails among all these authorities with
regard to the dates for the first sweating sickness. Hall, p. 425,
places it at the beginning of the second year of Henry's reign;
according to the City Chron., fol. 141a, it began on Sept. 27 ;
according to Stow, on Sept. 21 ; according to Fabian's Abridgment,
on Oct. 11. Here the original must in some way or other have been
indistinct, and we have to try and reconcile, as well as we can, these
conflicting testimonies (see App. i. p. 323).

In other respects we arrive at exactly the same result, as to the relation between Fabian's larger Chronicle and the City Chronicle, as far the other known derivatives of the unknown London Chronicle; an undoubted close relation, and yet no possibility of a direct dependence of the one authority upon the other.[1] It appears, therefore, that Fabian's History of England and France is, in the English part, a later compilation from his own notes in the special London Chronicle.

For this also Stow's preface to the Survey of London, MS. Harl., 538, affords us a characteristic proof. Fol. 754, it is recorded, that "this house called the stocks market in London," was rebuilt in 1410, the eleventh year of Henry IV., and completed in the following year, and for this notice Fabian is given as the authority. There is nothing about it in the City Chronicle; and in the printed Fabian, p. 575, for the eleventh year of Henry IV., we only find that the building of "the market house called the Stocks," had been begun—of the completion in the following year, not a word. For this, therefore, Stow made use of a "Fabian," which does not exist for us in its original form, either in the printed, or in the manuscript Chronicle, and which, in this passage, at least, is more detailed than the other two.

Fabian's existing Chronicle not having been printed till after his death, it is probable that it was compiled during his latter years. It was also left uncompleted. An error on p. 668, where Lord Rivers is called "Sir Anthony Wydevile, called Lord Scalys," can be explained thus: Fabian, who was growing old, did his work less carefully; his selection of events to be recorded in his new work was incomplete. It is clear he intended to go on with it, and the short continuation with which we are acquainted was perhaps an abstract made by himself for the more general history; for, when we compare this abstract with the City Chronicle and Stow, we find the events which have specially to do with the city omitted. These abstracts included probably the first three years of Henry VIII., so that Stow, p. 867, was able to speak of a History of England and France by Fabian, extending down to that date, and printed as far as the death of Richard III. But this last remark is not correct as regards the edition of 1533.

We can very well assume, from the character of the printed

[1] Pauli, v. 655, has already pointed out the frequent word for word agreement of the two Chronicles, without, however, hazarding any supposition as to the connection between them. For instance, on p. 656, note 5, he cites the three authorities, the City Chronicle, Fabian, and Stow, for the drowning of Clarence in the butt of Malmsey. We now know that these three authorities represent the one derivative, Fabian.

1859, which does not really begin till 1501, is very meagre, and quite without value for the time of Henry VII.

Here the contemporary authorities—or those, which, like Stow and the portions about London in Hall, serve as contemporary authorities—come to an end. We must, however, go on to discuss two authors of the seventeenth century, who, whether rightly or wrongly, have always been considered important authorities for the history of Henry VII.—Bacon and Ware.

BACON.

By no author has the history, and especially the general estimate of the reign of Henry VII., been so influenced, and in fact dominated, as by Francis Bacon. The History of the Reign of King Henry the Seventh was written by Bacon during the months immediately following his downfall, from June to October, 1621. But he had ready to hand a considerable amount of material, prepared by himself in earlier years, which Speed had already been able to make use of in manuscript, for his History of Great Britain, published in 1611. These materials were probably considerable; but, even with these, the rapidity with which Bacon composed his history is surprising.

The Latin version was produced later, and founded on the English original. I quote the latter from Lumby's edition in the Pitt Press Series, Cambridge, 1889, as being easily accessible, but shall have sometimes to refer to Spedding's edition in The Works of Francis Bacon, vi., London, 1878.

A few isolated voices have, from time to time, been raised against Bacon. Mackintosh, in the second volume of his English History, combated in a general way Bacon's treatment, whereupon Spedding took up his defence in his preface; neither of them brought forward any circumstantial evidence in support of their views. Pauli, v. 702, f., shows himself clearly to be on Bacon's side, principally by the full use he makes of Bacon for his narrative. Schanz, i. 470, note i., also relies on Pauli's judgment, and so occasionally does Liebermann in Deutsche Zeitschrift für Gesch.-W. iv. (1890), p. 151. In reference to a special question, Madden, in Archæol., xxvii. p. 162, ff., draws attention to Bacon's superficial and faulty reproduction of original authorities, and so does Mr. Gairdner in Mem., Pref. p. xxx., ff.; cf., xvi., and with regard to another passage, ibid., p. xxv., f., and Henry VII., p. 33. In fact, Mr. Gairdner, in the last-named excellent little biography of the king, often takes the opportunity of criticising Bacon's statements, especially when they

have exercised a direct influence upon later historical views, see pp.
44, 106, f., 150, 174, 197, f., 214, f. On the other hand, Mr. Gairdner
himself accepts some information supplied to us on Bacon's authority
alone; thus, p. 151, the story of "Morton's Fork," pp. 147 and 195,
the names given to the treaties concluded with the Netherlands,
and, on p. 212, Mr. Gairdner quotes Bacon's opinion of Henry's
legislation as of one "who knew the traditions of those times."

It is certainly remarkable that an author, who wrote more than
a century after the events he describes, should have been given the
rank of an authoritative original writer, and yet that no examination
into the sources from which he drew his information should hitherto
have been attempted, which would have made it possible to form a
critical judgment of the value of his work. It seemed to me indispensable, before undertaking to write a history of Henry VII., to
examine closely into the worth of Bacon as an historical authority.

The result of a wearisome examination, sentence by sentence,
may thus be summed up: that in almost every case we can refer to
the original authorities, which formed the basis for Bacon's statements, and find that, with unimportant exceptions, we possess all
these authorities ourselves.

First we have only to make good what strikes us even at the first
glance, that the real original authority forming the ground-work of
Bacon's narrative, is Polydore Vergil, or to speak more accurately,
Polydore Vergil, as reproduced by Hall, whose additions and alterations are to be found throughout in Bacon's work (cf. Pauli, v. 703).
A casual extra detail about Tyrrel, p. 114, is also taken from Hall,
p. 337, f., not, as Lumby, p. 273, and Spedding, p. 141, note 4,
assert, directly from More's History of Richard III.; Hall served
as Bacon's intermedium. To this original stock Bacon contributed
much additional matter. We have already been able to show how
he availed himself of Fabian's London Chronicle; and he was
indebted to the collection of manuscripts belonging to his friend
Cotton, not only for this, but also for the Life of Henry by Bernard
André. Morton's negotiations with French ambassadors, in Bacon,
pp. 79–87, are to be traced to André's authority, p. 55; cf. Bacon, 88;
André, 56, f.; the name of "Juno" given to Margaret by Bacon, p.
104, to André, 65; the distorted story of Perkin Warbeck to André,
65, f., cf. 72 (here Bacon cites, "one that wrote in the same time");
cf. also Bacon, 124; André, 69; Bacon, 170; André, 73; Bacon,
220; André, 14.

On the subject of a passage of André's, p. 35, the misreading of
which by Bacon, p. 11, is pointed out by Mr. Gairdner in Mem.,

Pref., p. xxv. f., the question arises whether Bacon here availed himself of Speed's work, which agrees with him, and had already appeared, or whether the relation between them is reversed, as it is proved that Speed had lying before him the materials collected by Bacon. Mr. Gairdner traces the error back to Speed, just as Spedding in his edition of the works, p. 133, note 4, does errors about Warbeck's early history. In that case the two would each have borrowed the one from the other. To me it seems best to hold to Bacon as the more original authority; the question, however, is without importance for our purpose, as the documents, which are the foundation of both, are known to us, and it would not materially influence our general estimate of Bacon if these few errors could be ascribed to Speed.

Besides the two Chronicles, Cotton's collection, which Bacon in one place quotes, p. 140, yielded him also some material in documents; for instance, he could make use of the following : Perkin's proclamation, pp. 140-144, which for us is only preserved in one copy, Harl. MS., 283, fol. 123*b* (published from this by Spedding, as above, pp. 252-255); and, on p. 183, the letter from Cardinal Hadrian to Henry, dated Jan. 4, 1504, Cott., Cleop., E, iii., 162 (Lett. and Pap., ii. 116); pp. 198-202, the reports of an embassage sent to Spain in 1505, of which a copy exists, Cott., Vesp., C, vi. 338 (Mem., 223-281); p. 207, a brief of Julius II., of May 20, 1504, Cott., Cleop., E, 3 (Ware, pp. 84-87); p. 207, f., the pamphlets contained in MS. Cott., Galba., B, ii., on Wolsey's mission to the Netherlands. He quotes, on p. 210, at length a letter from the king to the London city authorities (Halliwell, i. pp. 194-196), and he shows some knowledge of the texts of treaties, pp. 187 and 189 ; cf. also pp. 109, 146, 160, 193.

For the history of the parliaments and for the laws passed by them, he made copious use of the Rolls of Parliament; p. 16, on Henry's attitude with regard to the previous attainders, he gives a somewhat free version of the legal decision from the Year Book, 1, Hen. VII., fol. 4*b* (cf. above, p. 27, note). We must not forget, in conclusion, that the history of the voyages to America, pp. 171-173, is to be traced back to Hackluyt.

This closes in the main the somewhat limited circle of Bacon's sources, and we have now to examine *how* he made use of them. His most important authority, Hall, he handles much more freely than Hall had handled his own authority, Polydore Vergil. It is, of course, natural that Bacon should have worked up his material, looking forward and back, and grouping it into a whole, according to his own views, and that he should form an independent judgment,

but beyond this he has throughout coloured his record of facts with
a very free imagination.

The report on the taking of Granada, p. 454, comes from Hall,
p. 454; what Bacon there asserts about letters from the Spanish
monarchs is an addition which rests on his own surmises. We
might also draw attention to the working-up of Perkin Warbeck's
story, pp. 106–131, from Hall, p. 461, ff.; here he inadvertently
adds to Warbeck's early history, "living much in English company, and having the English tongue perfect," whereas in Perkin's
confession, as recorded by Hall, it is expressly said that he only
learnt English afterwards. Hall's short, and indeed false, statement
about King Ferdinand's attitude with regard to Warwick's fate,
p. 491, is further freely enlarged upon by Bacon, p. 179, who
ascribes the initiative for Ferdinand's behaviour to Henry, and even
invents letters from Spain supposed to have been shown on this
occasion (cf. Gairdner, Henry VII., p. 174). He has also drawn
upon his imagination, pp. 136–139, for Perkin's address to James
of Scotland (Hall, 473, f., after P. V., 755, f.).

It is especially in the speeches that his imagination comes into play.
Thus Morton's speech, pp. 53–59, on the occasion of the opening of
Parliament, 1487, differs entirely from the documentary records in
the Rot. Parl. vi. 385, and yet, unfortunately, it has been regarded as
itself authentic (see above, p. 385). But here Bacon, who places this
Parliament a year too late, made the unlucky mistake of forming
the first part of his imaginary speech, pp. 53–57, on events which
took place in this later year, 1488. In the same way, pp. 89–91,
a speech put into the mouth of the king is pure invention, whilst
Hall, p. 451, cf. P. V., 739, only just mentions the fact that Henry
had spoken; it is the same with the negotiations between Morton
and the Frenchman Gaguin, pp. 79–87, which are imagined and
related in detail, from a short notice in André, p. 55.

What Bacon, pp. 140–144, gives as Perkin's proclamation only
partially agrees in a few passages with the genuine proclamation,
to which, however, he refers as his authority; it is evident here that
he worked from memory with the help of a few notes, and principally,
of his imagination. In the real text of the letter from Henry to the
Lord Mayor and aldermen (Halliwell, 194–196), reproduced in
substance by Bacon, p. 210, the saying he here ascribes to the king,
that he had built "a wall of brass" round his kingdom, is not to be
found.

There are two passages, however, in which Bacon—if we
regard him, and not Speed, as the real culprit—makes the greatest

confusion out of André's statements. According to Bacon, p. 17, Henry, after his victory at Bosworth, entered London "in a close chariot," whereon he hangs some observations; but Mr. Gairdner, Mem., Pref., p. xxvi., points out that the assertion has arisen from misreading "latenter" for André's word "laetanter," p. 35. André, p. 65, relates a wonderful story about Perkin Warbeck—that he had been brought up in England by a Jew named Edward, at whose subsequent baptism King Edward IV. had stood godfather, and further on, p. 72, he makes Perkin describe himself as, "Eduardi . . . Judæi . . . regis Eduardi filioli . . . servulus;" and again, "erat enim patronus meus regi Eduardo ac suis liberis familiarissimus."

Now, from this Bacon, p. 105, f., with special reference to the contemporary authority, makes out that King Edward had been Perkin's (!) godfather, and that Perkin "in being called King Edward's godson, or perhaps in sport King Edward's son," had imagined his foolish pretensions, and so Bacon makes Perkin's father a converted Jew, who lived in England in Edward IV.'s time, and was known at court. The absolute absurdity of this was first discovered by Madden, as above, p. 163, and its origin pointed out.

The statements, which are founded upon Fabian, prove to be, on the whole, correct; only Bacon, 180, f., asserts very positively that the negotiations which, according to the City Chron., fol. 180*b*, took place before the meeting of Henry and Philip at Calais, were made at the meeting itself and, indeed, in private between the two princes; we are, of course, justified in assuming this much—that at the meeting also the points to be discussed had been spoken of.

One example after another shows the superficial and arbitrary manner in which Bacon dealt with the information he culled from his authorities, while he gave the fullest play to his imagination. Thus, it is only from his own invention that he fills in the scanty account of Stanley's end, p. 122, f.; the same with the story of Perkin's attack on Kent, p. 129, and of Philip's arrival and sojourn in England in 1506, pp. 202–205.

This can only in part be excused by the hastiness of his work. The worst point about it is that Bacon tries to invest his own additions with an appearance of their being actually substantiated (cf. p. 57, and elsewhere), and in general always loves to give his own subjective opinion with the same preciseness as the objective matters of fact. And such a recorder as this have later writers of history accepted as a trustworthy voucher, and treated what he gave them as if it were original information! Thus the hitherto prevailing idea of Henry's conduct towards his wife Elizabeth has been founded on nothing but a self-conceived conjecture of this kind, put forward by Bacon (p. 19, cf. 22; see also Gairdner, Henry VII., p. 44); so it is with Bacon's assertion about the feeling in nation and Parliament urging the king on to war with France (p. 59, f.; cf. above, p. 329), and about Henry's putting on pressure for the conclusion of the marriage between Maximilian and Anne of Brittany (pp. 74, 77; cf. Ulmann, i. 121, f.; and above, p. 332). Even such an ardent defender of Bacon as Spedding (p. 155, note 1), calls attention to the fact that the prevailing idea about Henry's avarice rests on nothing beyond Bacon's casual observations; when, for instance (p. 207), Bacon states, adding the words, " the general opinion was," that the canonisation of Henry VI. had fallen through because Pope Julius II. had fixed the price too high for the king, it is a falsification of history due only to a desire to support this view of the king's character.

We must, therefore, regard every statement of Bacon's, for which no special original authority can be referred to, with a distrust which is only too well justified. Bacon alone (pp. 146 and 205) gives the names of *Intercursus, Magnus* and *Malus* to the commercial treaties of 1496 and 1506 between England and the Netherlands (see on the subject above: pp. 357, 373); he alone (p. 210) gives, " as by tradition it is reported," the amount of the money treasure left behind by Henry; he alone, the often-repeated anecdotes of " Morton's fork " (p. 93), of the attainder of the Earl of Oxford for an offence against the law of livery (p. 192), and of Henry's ape who tore up the account-book (p. 218).

These anecdotes, at best, rest only upon oral tradition, and happily, with one of them, we are able to show what was this tradition, and what Bacon made of it. The anecdote in question is about " Morton's fork." To the story of the levy of the benevolence of 1491, Bacon adds (p. 93), " There is a tradition of a dilemma, that Bishop Morton, the chancellor used, to raise up the benevolence to higher rates; and some called it his fork, and some his crutch. For he had couched an article in the instructions to the commissioners who were to levy the benevolence :—That if they met with any that were sparing, they should tell them that they must needs have, because they laid up; and if they were spenders, they must needs have, because it was seen in their port and manner of living. So neither kind came amiss."

Now Erasmus relates in " Ecclesiastæ sive de ratione concionandi libri iv." (Basle, 1535, p. 227), with an appeal to the testimony of Sir Thomas More, then still a youth: "Rex Henricus eius nominis Septimus proposuerat exactionem precariam, mutui nomine. Richardus

Episcopus Vintoniensis, cui cognomen vulpi, vir minime stupidus, apud clerum agebat principis sui negocium. Contra, sacerdotes hoc agebant, ut quam minimum darent. Idque ut efficerent, duplici uia captabant. Alii ueniebant, magnifice culti, ne uiderentur esse pecuniosi. Splendidus enim uictus exhaurit opes. Rursus alii veniebant sordide culti. Utrique se pariter excusabant. At Episcopus utrisque retorsit argumentum. Tibi, inquit, non deesse pecuniam declarat iste tuus amictus tam splendidus. Et te colligere pecuniam declarat, quod tam misere cultus es."

It is possible that in Erasmus's memory also the details of the story might have become somewhat effaced; anyhow it is he who records most faithfully the story, as it was current at the time. The answer was attributed, not to Morton, but to Bishop Fox, and, indeed, even he was not the originator of it, but the tax-paying clergy; he only turned the argument against them (cf. the article, Fox, in Nat. Biogr., xx. 152). We see by this that the other anecdotes in Bacon should be regarded with mistrust, until some other testimony is forthcoming to support them.

After these investigations we can now come to a general conclusion. Pauli, v. 703, after raising some objections to Bacon, thus closes his remarks: "These, however, are trifles, which do not diminish in the slightest the value of this excellent work." Spedding, who in his notes brings forward such overwhelming evidence of Bacon's untrustworthiness, endeavours at the same time in the oddest way to establish Bacon's excellence and reliability. But this is, in fact, only possible if, instead of judging Bacon by the standard of those qualities which the historian ought to require in his original authority, we take our standard from the work of a writer generally admired as perfect.

The fault hitherto has always been that admiration for his classical style, and for the perfection of his narrative, built though it was upon limited material, has been extended to Bacon's merits as an *original authority.* Yet no historian will or ought to pass over without notice a work so brilliantly written, so fascinating and inspiring in its insight and power of description; we learn from it how a great writer of the seventeenth century constructed his picture of the period from material of which almost all is equally accessible to us.

Our arguments, on the other hand, have only dealt with Bacon as the recorder of historical facts, and just because till now he has held the highest rank as such, and as we saw, has exercised a harmful influence, we ought the more decisively and plainly to insist that his

work (with the sole exception of the three little details which in
their connection seemed to be accurate, and which are traceable to
Fabian's Chronicle) ought to be expunged from the list of original
authorities for the history of Henry VII.   For, to sum up, we
possess almost all the direct and indirect sources of information from
which he drew, and he shows, in the use he made of them, such
indifference as regards simple historical truth, that he must, as a
voucher for facts, appear to us in a very doubtful light.   From this
point of view the cockney if limited honesty of a man like Stow is
for us of far greater value than the classical mind of a Bacon.

<h2 style="text-align:center">WARE.</h2>

A younger contemporary of Bacon's is the Irish historian Sir James
Ware (1594–1666).   When this writer in 1658 issued a second edition
of his " De Hibernia et Antiquitatibus eius Disquisitiones," he added
to it, " Rerum Hibernicarum Henrico VII. regnante Annales." We
are able not only to confirm his statements and, especially, often
his dates as correct (thus pp. 36, 45, 54, 60), but can also notice his
use of many sources known to us.   For instance, he was acquainted
with Polydore Vergil, whom he sometimes corrects (pp. 12, 28, 30–32,
36, f., 71, 97), he made use of Acts of Parliament, or remarks incidentally that he had hunted for them in vain (pp. 4, 41, f., 47, 66),
he relies upon the Book of Howth (pp. 7, 25, 26, 180), and once
upon Leland ("hactenus ineditus," p. 30).   He, like Bacon, is indebted
to Cotton for much of his information, for his notices from André
(pp. 13, 62, 97, f.), and many briefs and bulls (pp. 5, 16, 71, 72,
84–87).   Especially important for us is the use he makes of Irish
records, such as the report on Edgecombe's mission preserved at
Clogher (pp. 17–24, cf. Harris, Hibern., p. 29, f.), he quotes also,
" Author Annalium Ultoniensium, qui tum vixit," " Lucas Waddingus
Waterfordiensis, Annales Minores," "Librum Album Fisci (quem
Scaccarium appellamus) Dublini," the original of which he says was
burnt in 1610, but of which "notae . . . ex eo excerptæ" lay before
him, and the "Regestum" of the Archbishop of Armagh for a
Provincial Synod (pp. 27, 63, 64, 82).

Of course Ware, too, is not free from occasional errors, but his
endeavour to go back to original sources and to reproduce these
faithfully give him a value as an authority for the history of Ireland,
which should not be underrated, and I have been able to borrow
from him a number of important details.

APPENDIX III.

———◆◇◆———

LIST OF THE TITLES IN FULL OF ALL THE WORKS QUOTED.

ABRIDGMENT, Fabian's (see Appendix II. p. 402).

ACTES, Orders, and Decrees made by the King and his Counsell, remaining amongst the Records of the Court, now commonly called the Court of Requests, 1592.

ACTS OF THE PARLIAMENTS OF SCOTLAND, THE. Vol. ii. (1424–1557). London, 1814.

ALBÉRI, Le Relazioni degli Ambasciatori Veneti al Senato, raccolte ed illustrate da Eugenio Albéri. Series i., vol. iii. Florence, 1853.

ANDERSON, Adam, An Historical and Chronological Deduction of the Origin of Commerce, from the Earliest Accounts, etc., etc. 4 vols. London (1787–1789).

ANDRÉ, Bernardi Andreæ Tholosatis, poetæ laureati, regie historiographi, De Vita atque gestis Henrici Septimi in : Memorials, pp. 1–75 (see Appendix II. p. 393).

By the same, Annales Henrici Septimi, Annus vicesimus (1504–1505) and vicesimus tertius (1507–1508) in : Memor., pp. 77–130 (see the same, above).

D'ARGENTRÉ, Bertrand, L'histoire de Bretaigne . . . jusques au temps de Madame Anne, dernière duchesse, etc. Paris, 1588.

ARNOLD, Chronicle. Edition of 1811 (see Appendix II. p. 401).

AYLOFFE, Joseph, Calendars of the Ancient Charters, etc., etc. London, 1774.

BACON, Francis, The History of the Reign of King Henry the Seventh, edited by Lumby. Pitt Press Series. Cambridge, 1889.

By the same, Works, edited by Spedding, Ellis, Heath. Vol. vi.

Literary and Professional Works, i. New edition. London, 1878.

BAGA DE SECRETIS : The First Part of the Inventory and Calendar of the Contents of Baga de Secretis, heretofore kept in the Treasury of the Court of King's Bench, for the Reigns of Edw. IV., Hen. VII. and Henry VIII., printed as No. 6 in App. ii. of the 3rd Report of the Dep. Keeper of the Publ. Rec., pp. 263–268.

BAGWELL, Rich., Ireland under the Tudors. Vol. i. London, 1885.

BAIN, Joseph, Calendar of Documents relating to Scotland, preserved in H.M. Public Record Office. Vol. iv. (1357–1509 and Add.). Edinburgh, 1888.

BERGENROTH, G. A., Calendar of Letters, Despatches and State Papers, relating to the Negotiations between England and Spain, preserved in the Archives of Simancas and elsewhere. Vol. i. 1485–1509, ii. 1509–1525. London, 1862 and 1866.

BERGH, L. Ph.C., van den, Correspondance de Marguerite d'Antriche, Gouvernante des Pays-Bas, avec ses amis (1506–1528), 2 vols. Leyden, 1845, 1847.

BERNIER. See under PROCÈS-VERBAUX.

BIDDLE, Richard, Memoir of Sebastian Cabot with a review of the History of Maritime Discovery, illustrated by Docum. from the Rolls. London, 1831.

BIENER, Friedr. Aug., Das englische Geschworenengericht. 3 vols. Leipsic, 1852 and 1855.

BLACKSTONE, Sir William, Commentaries on the Laws of England. 23rd edition, edited by James Stewart. 4 vols. London, 1854.

BOOK OF HOWTH, printed in Carew Papers, which see.

BOURNE, Henry Fox, English Seamen under the Tudors. 2 vols. London, 1868.

BREWER, J. S., Letters and Papers, Foreign and Domestic, of the Reign of Henry VIII. Vol. i. ii., 2 ; iv. 2 and 3. London, 1862, 1864, 1872, 1876.

BROWN, Rawdon, Calendar of State Papers and Manuscripts, relating to English Affairs, existing in the Archives and Collections of Venice, and in other Libraries of Northern Italy. Vol. i. 1202–1509. London, 1864.

BRUNNER, Heinr., Die Entstehung der Schwurgerichte. Berlin, 1872.

By the same, Schwurgericht (geschichtlich) in Holzendorff, Encyklopädie der Rechtswissenschaft, ii. 1.

BUCK, George, History of the Life and Reigne of Richard the Third. London, 1646.

BURGESS, The Last Battle of the Roses. Leamington, 1872.

BUSCH, W., Der Ursprung der Ehescheidung Heinrichs VIII. von England: Der Sturz des Kardinals Wolsey im Scheidungshandel König Heinrichs VIII., in: Historisches Taschenbuch, vi. 8, p. 273, ff.; and 9, p. 41, ff. Leipsic, 1889 and 1890.

CAMBRIAN REGISTER, THE, for the year 1795. London, 1796.

CAMDEN MISCELLANY, THE, i. Camden Society, 1847.

CAMPBELL, Will., Materials for a History of the Reign of Henry VII., from Original Documents preserved in the Public Record Office. 2 vols. London, 1873 and 1877.

CAREW PAPERS, Calendar of the Carew Manuscripts, preserved in the Archiepiscopal Library at Lambeth, edited by J. S. Brewer and Will. Bullen. London, 1871.

CARVAJAL, Dr. D. Lorenzo Galindez, Anales Breves del reinado de los Reyes Católicos D. Fernando y Doña Isabel, de gloriosa memoria in: Col. de Doc. inéd. xviii. 227, ff.

CAVENDISH, George, The Life of Cardinal Wolsey, edited by Henry Morley. Second edition. London, 1887.

CHAMPOLLION-FIGEAC, Lettres des rois, reines et autres personnages des cours de France et de l'Angleterre, de Louis VII. à Henri IV. 2 vols. Paris, 1839–1842 (Coll. des Doc. inéd.).

CHMEL, Joseph, Urkunden, Briefe und Aktenstücke zur Geschichte Maximilians I., und seiner Zeit. Bibl. des Lit. Vereins., vol. x. Stuttgart, 1845.

CHRONICLE OF CALAIS, THE, in the reigns of Henry VII. and Henry VIII. to the year 1540, edited by John Gough Nichols. Camden Society, 1846.

CHRONICLERS OF EUROPE, EARLY, England, edited by James Gairdner, London, undated.

CITY CHRONICLE. See Appendix II., p. 403.

COLECCION DE DOCUMENTOS INÉDITOS para la historia de España. Vols. i., viii., xvi., xviii., xxxix. Madrid, 1842, 1846, 1851, 1861.

COLLIER, Jeremiah, An Ecclesiastical History of Great Britain, chiefly of England. 2 vols. 1708 and 1714.

CONT: CROYL: Historiæ Croylandensis Continuatio, in: Rerum Anglicarum Scriptorum Veterum, tom. i. (edit. by Gale). Oxford, 1684.

COOPER, Charles Henry, Memoir of Margaret, Countess of Richmond and Derby, edited by John E. B. Mayor. Cambridge, 1874.

Die alder excellenste cronyke von Brabant, Holland, Seelant, Vlaenderen. Antwerp, 1512.

CUNNINGHAM, W., The Growth of English Industry and Commerce during the Early and Middle Ages. Cambridge, 1890.

DIXON, William Hepworth, History of Two Queens, 1. Catherine of Aragon, 2. Anne Boleyn. 6 vols. Vol. i.–iii. Leipsic, 1873.

DU MONT, J., Corps universel diplomatique du droit des gens; contenant un recueil des traitez d'alliance, de paix, de treve, etc. Vol. iii. 2 and iv. 1. Amsterdam and the Hague, 1726.

DUPUY, Antoine, Histoire de la réunion de la Bretagne à la France. 2 vols. Paris, 1880.

ELLIS, Henry, Original Letters illustrative of English History, in three series. London, 1824, ff.

EPISTOLAE JACOBI IV., V., et Mariae Regum Scotorum, eorumque Tutorum et Regni Gubernatorum, edited by Ruddiman. 2 vols. Edinburgh, 1722 and 1724.

EXCERPTA HISTORICA, or Illustrations of English History, edited by Samuel Bentley. London, 1833.

FABIAN, Robert, The New Chronicles of England and France, etc. edited by Ellis. London, 1811. (See Appendix II., p. 402.)

By the same, London Chronicle. (See Appendix II., p. 403.)

FRASER, William, The Douglas Book. 4 vols. Edinburgh, 1885.

FRIEDMANN, Paul, Anne Boleyn—A Chapter of English History, 1527–1536. 2 vols. London, 1884.

GACHARD, M., Collection des Voyages des Souverains des Pays-Bas. Vol. i. Brussels, 1876.

GAIRDNER, James (see also Lett. and Pap., Mem., Past. Lett., and Early Chroniclers), History of the Life and Reign of King Richard III.; to which is added the Story of Perkin Warbeck from Original Documents. Second edition. London, 1879.

By the same, Henry the Seventh (in Twelve English Statesmen). London, 1889.

By the same, Did Henry VII. murder the Princes? in the English Histor. Review, vi. (1891) 444–464.

GAYANGOS, Pascual de (Supplement to Bergenroth's Col. of State Pap.). Vol. iii. 2, and iv. 1. London, 1877 and 1879.

GERIGK, Johannes, Das opus epistolarum des Petrus Martyr, ein Beitrag zur Kritik der Quellen des ausgehenden 15. und beginnenden 16. Jahrhunderts. Braunsberg, 1881.

GILBERT, John Thomas, History of the Viceroys of Ireland. London, 1865.

By the same, Calendar of Ancient Records of Dublin. Dublin, 1889.

GODEFROY, Histoire de Charles VIII., roy de France, par Guill. de Jaligny, André de la Vigne et autres historiens de ce temps-là, où sont decrites les choses les plus memorables arrivées pendant ce Regne, depuis 1483 jusques en 1498. Enrichie de plusieurs memoires, observations, contracts de mariage, traitez de paix et autres titres et pièces historiques non encore imprimées. Paris, 1636.

GOLDSMID, Edmund M., A Collection of Historical Documents illustrative of the reigns of the Tudor and Stuart Sovereigns. 2 vols. Edinburgh, 1886.

GREEN, John Richard, A Short History of the English People. Edit. 1888.

GREY FRIARS' CHRONICLE, Chronicle of the Grey Friars of London, edited by Nichols. Camden Society, 1852. (See Appendix II., p. 402.)

GROSS, Charles, The Gild Merchant. A contribution to British Municipal History. 2 vols. Oxford, 1890.

HÄBLER, Konrad, Der Streit Ferdinands des Katholischen und Philipps I. um die Regierung von Castilien, 1504–1506. Dresden, 1882.

HACKLUYT, Richard, The Voyages, Navigations, Traffiques and Discoveries of the English Nation, etc. Cited from the edition, London, 1600. New edition. 5 vols. London, 1810.

HAHN, S. F., Collectio monumentorum veterum et recentium ineditorum. 2 vols. Brunswick, 1724–1726.

HALL, Chronicle. New edition. London, 1809. (See Appendix II. p. 398.)

HALLAM, Henry, The Constitutional History of England from the Accession of Henry VII. to the Death of George II. 3 vols. Eighth edition. London, 1855.

HALLIWELL, Letters of the Kings of England. 2 vols. London, 1846.

HALSTED, Caroline A., Life of Margaret Beaufort, Countess of Richmond and Derby, mother of Henry the Seventh. Oxford, 1845.

HANSERECESSE, dritte Abteilung, bearb. von Dietrich Schäfer. Vol. i.–iv. (1477–1504). Leipsic, 1881–1890.

HARDWICKE PAPERS, P. Yorke, Earl of Hardwicke. Miscellaneous State Papers from 1501 to 1726. 2 vols. London, 1778.

HARRIS, Walter, Hibernica; or some Antient Pieces relating to Ireland. Dublin, 1757.

HARRISSE, Henri, Jean et Sébastien Cabot in: Schefer and Cordier, Recueil des Voyages, 1. Paris, 1882.

HEARNE, Thom., Duo rerum Anglicarum scriptores veteres, etc. 2 vols. Oxford, 1732.

HECKER, Die grossen Volkskrankheiten des Mittelalters, edited by Hirsch. Berlin, 1865.

HELLWALD, F. von, Sebastian Cabot (in: Samml. Gemeinverständl, wiss. Vorträge, vi. 123). Berlin, 1871.

HERBERT, Edward Lord, The Life and Reign of King Henry the Eighth, edition in the World Library of Standard Works. London. Without date.

HIRSCH, Handbuch der historisch-geographischen Pathologie. First part (second edition). Stuttgart, 1881.

HOOK, Walter Farquhar, Lives of the Archbishops of Canterbury. 12 vols. London, 1860–1876, v. 1867, vi. 1868.

HUDSON, William, A Treatise on the Court of Star Chamber, in Collectanea Juridica, ii. pp. 1–240. London, 1792.

HUME, David, The History of England. Vol. iii. London, 1822.

HUTTON, The Battle of Bosworth Field. Birmingham, 1788.

IVES, John, Select Papers, chiefly relating to English Antiquities. London, 1773.

KEILWEY, Robert, Reports d'ascuns Cases qui ont évenus aux Temps du Roy Henry VII. et du Roy Henry VIII. Third edition. London, 1688.

KRANTZ, Albert, Wandalia. Cologne, 1519.

KRAUS, Victor von, Maximilians I., oertraulicher Briefwechsel mit Sigmund Prüschenk, etc. Innspruck, 1875.

LAPPENBERG, Joh. Mart., Urkundliche Geschichte des Stahlhofs. Hamburg, 1851.

LETT. AND PAP. Letters and Papers illustrative of the Reigns of Richard III. and Henry VII., edited by James Gairdner. 2 vols. London, 1861 and 1863.

LEGGE, Alfred Owen, The Unpopular King: The Life and Times of Richard III. 2 vols. London, 1885.

LE GLAY, M., Correspondance de l'Empereur Maximilien I. et de Marguerite d'Autriche, de 1507 à 1519. 2 vols. Paris, 1839.

By the same, Négociations diplomatiques entre la France et l'Autriche (1501 to 1530). 2 vols. Paris, 1845. In Collect. des Docum. inéd.

LELAND, John, The Itinerary, edited by Hearne. Third edition. 9 vols. Oxford, 1768 and 1769.

By the same, De rebus Britannicis *Collectanea.* Edited by Hearne. Second edition. 6 vols. London, 1774.

LELAND, Thomas, History of Ireland. 3 vols. London, 1773.

LE ROUX DE LINCY, Vie de la reine Anne de Bretagne, femme des Rois de France, Charles VIII. et Louis XII. 4 vols. Paris, 1860.

LETTRES DU ROY LOUIS XII., et du Cardinal George d'Amboise. 2 vols. Brussels, 1712.

LICHNOWSKI, E. M., Fürst von, Geschichte des Hauses Habsburg bis zurn Tode Kaiser Maximilians I. 8 parts. Vienna, 1836–1844.

LINGARD, A History of England. Sixth edition. 10 vols. London, 1854–1855.

MADDEN, Sir Frederic, Documents relating to Perkin Warbeck, with remarks on his history in Archæologia : or Miscellaneous Tracts relating to Antiquity, xxvii., pp. 153–210. London, 1838.

MARKHAM, Clements R., Richard III., a Doubtful Verdict reviewed, in The Engl. Hist. Review. Vol. vi. (1891), 250–253.

MAULDE-LA-CLAVIÈRE, R., DE, Histoire de Louis XII., 1ᵉ partie : Louis d'Orléans. 2 vols. Paris, 1890.

MEMORIALS OF KING HENRY THE SEVENTH, edited by James Gairdner. London, 1858.

MICHEL, Francisque, Histoire du commerce et de la navigation à Bordeaux, principalement sous l'administration Anglaise. 2 vols. Bordeaux, 1867 and 1870.

MOLINET, Jean, Chroniques, 1476–1566, edited by Buchon. 5 vols. Paris, 1827, f.

MORE, Sir Thomas, Historie of Kyng Rycharde the Third, edited by Lumby. Pitt Press Series. Cambridge, 1883.

By the same, De optimo reipublicae statu deque nova insula *Utopia* libri duo. English translation by R. Robynson, edited by Lumby. Pitt Press Series.

MORICE, Mémoires pour servir de preuves à l'histoire ecclesiastique et civile de la Bretagne. 3 vols. Paris, 1742–1746.

NASSE, Erwin, Über die mittelalterliche Feldgemeinschaft und die Einhegungen des 16. Jahrhunderts in England. Bonn, 1869.

DICTIONARY OF NATIONAL BIOGRAPHY, edited by Leslie Stephen. London, 1885, ff.

NICOLAS, Sir Harris, Privy Purse Expenses of Elizabeth of York ; Wardrobe Accounts of Edward the Fourth, with a memoir of Elizabeth of York, and notes. London, 1830.

OCHENKOWSKI, W. von, Englands Wirtschaftliche Entwickelung bei Ausgang des Mittelalters. Jena, 1879.

P. V. (Polydore Vergil.), Historiæ Anglicæ Libri, xxvii., autore Polydoro Virgilio Urbinate. Ex nova Editione Antonii Thysii, J. C. Lugduni Batavorum, 1651.

PALGRAVE, Sir Francis, an Essay upon the Original Authority of the King's Council. London, 1834.

PARKER, Matthæi, Cantuariensis episcopi De Antiquitate Britannicæ Ecclesiæ et Privilegiis Ecclesiæ Cantuariensis, etc., rec. Sam. Drake. Londini, 1752.

PASTON LETTERS, THE, 1422–1509. New edition, by James Gairdner. VoL iii. Edward IV., Henry VII., 1471–1509. London, 1875.

PAULI, Reinhold, Geschichte von England (in Gesch. der europäischen Staaten). Vol. 5. Gotha, 1858.

By the same, Drei Volkswirtschaftliche Denkschriften aus der Zeit Heinrichs VIII. von England in : Abhandl. der Gött. Gesch. der Wiss. Vol. 23 (1878).

PÉLICIER, P., Essai sur le Gouvernement de la Dame de Beaujeu, 1483–1491. Chartres, 1882.

PESCHEL, Oskar, Geschichte des Zeitalters der Entdeckungen. Stuttgart and Augsburg, 1858. (The second edition, 1877, is an unaltered reprint of the first.)

PETRUS MARTYR, Opus epistolarum Petr. Mart. Anglerii Mediolanensis. Amsterdam, 1670.

PINKERTON, John, The History of Scotland from the Accession of the House of Stuart to that of Mary. 2 vols. London, 1797.

PLUMPTON CORRESPONDENCE, A Series of Letters, chiefly domestick, written in the reigns of Edward IV., Richard III., Henry VII., and Henry VIII., edited by Thomas Stapleton. Camden Society, 1839.

POCOCK, Records of the Reformation. 2 vols. Oxford, 1870.

PRESCOTT, Will. H., History of the Reign of Ferdinand and Isabella the Catholic of Spain.

PROCES-VERBAUX des séances du conseil de régence du roi Charles VIII. (Coll. des Doc. inéd.), edited by A. Bernier. Paris, 1836.

REEVES, History of the English Law from the Time of the Romans to the end of the Reign of Queen Elizabeth. A new edition in 3 vols., with numerous notes and an introductory dissertation, etc., edited by W. F. Finlason. London, 1869.

RELATION, Italian, A Relation of the Island of England about the year 1500, translated (giving the Italian text) by Charlotte Augusta Sneyd. Camden Society, 1847.

REPORTS of the Deputy Keeper of the Public Records. 50th Report, in 24 vols. 1840–1889.

REPORTS of the Deputy Keeper of the Public Records in Ireland. 20th Report. Dublin, 1888.

REPORTS of the Royal Commission of Historical Manuscripts. 11th Report. London, 1870–1887.

RICART, Rob., The Maire of Bristowe is Kalendar, edited by Lucy Toulmin Smith. Camden Society, 1872.

ROGERS, James E. Thorold, A History of Agriculture and Prices in

England from the year after the Oxford Parliament (1259) to the Commencement of the Continental War (1793). 6 vols. Vols. iii. and iv. (1401–1582). Oxford, 1882.

By the same, Six Centuries of Work and Wages: the History of English Labour. London, 1884.

ROPER, William, The Life of Sir Thomas More, edited by Singer, Chiswick, 1817.

ROTULI PARLIAMENTORUM, ut et Petitiones et Placita in Parliamento. Vol. vi. 12 Edw. IV. to 19 Hen. VII. (1472–1503).

ROTULI SCACCARII REGUM SCOTORUM, The Exchequer Rolls of Scotland, edited by George Burnett and Æ. J. G. Mackay. 13 vols. (to 1513). 1878–1891.

ROTULI SCOTLÆ, in Turri Londinensi et in Domo Capitulari Westmonasterii asservati. Vol. ii. (Rich. II. to Hen. VIII.) 1819.

RUGE, Sophus, Geschichte des Zeitalters der Entdeckungen, in Oncken : Allgem. Gesch. in Einzeldarstell, ii. 9. Berlin, 1881.

By the same, Christoph Columbus, in: Führende Geister, edited by Bettelheim. Vol. iv. Dresden, 1892.

RUTLAND PAPERS, Original Documents of the Courts and Times of Henry VII. and Henry VIII. Selected from the Private Archives of the Duke of Rutland, edited by Will. Jerdan. Camden Society, 1842.

RYLAND, R. H., The History, Topography, and Antiquities of the County and City of Waterford, etc. London, 1824.

RYMER, Thomas, Fœdera, Conventiones, Literæ et cuiuscunque generis Acta Publica inter Reges Angliæ et alios quosvis Imperatores, Reges, Pontifices, Principes vel communitates. Editio III. denuo collata studio Georgii Holmes. Vols. v. and vi. of the Hague edition, 1741. Qutoed from the London edition, vols. xii. and xiii.

SCHÄFER, Dietrich (see also Hanserecesse), Kritik von Schanz, Engl. Handels-politik, in Jahrbücher für Nationalökonomie und Statistik, edited by Conrad. Vol. xli., N. F. vii., pp. 88–126. Jena, 1883.

SCHANZ, Georg, Englische Handelspolitik gegen Ende des Mittelalters, mit besonderer Berücksichtigung des Zeitalters der beiden ersten Tudors Heinrich VII. and Heinrich VIII. Gekrönte Preisschrift. 2 Vols. Leipsic, 1881.

SCHMIDT, Richard, Staatsanwalt und Privatkläger. Leipsic, 1891.

SCRIPTORES Rerum Prussicarum, edited by Th. Hirsch, Max. Töppen, Ernst Strehlke. 5 vols. Leipsic, 1861–1874.

SEEBOHM, Frederic, The Oxford Reformers, John Colet, Erasmus, and Thomas More. Third edition. London, 1887.

SMITH, Charles, The Antient and Present State of the County and City of Waterford. Dublin, 1746.

By the same, The Antient and Present State of the County and City of Cork. 2 vols. Dublin, 1750.

SPEED, John, The History of Great Britaine. London, 1611.

STÄLIN, von, Aufenthaltsorte Kaiser Maximilians I., 1493–1519, in Forsch. zur deutsch. Gesch. i. 347–383.

STAT., The Statutes of the Realm, ii., 1816.

STATUTES, THE, at large, passed in the Parliaments held in Ireland, i. (1310–1612), Dublin, 1765.

IRISH STATUTES, THE. Revised edition. 3 Edw. II. to the Union, edited by W. F. Cullinan. London, 1885.

STEPHEN, Sir James Fitzjames, A History of the Criminal Law of England. 3 vols. London, 1883.

STEPHEN, H. J., New Commentaries on the Laws of England (partly founded on Blackstone). Eleventh Edition. 4 vols. London, 1890.

STOW, John, The Chronicles of England. London, 1580. (See Appendix II., p. 408.)

By the same, A Survay of London, contayning the originall, antiquity, increase, moderne estate and description of that citie, etc. London, 1598. New edition by Strype, ibid., 1720.

By the same, Memoranda : Three Fifteenth-Century Chronicles, with Historical Memoranda by John Stow, the Antiquary, etc., edited by James Gairdner. Camden Society, 1880.

STUBBS, Will, Seventeen Lectures on the Study of Mediæval and Modern History and Kindred Subjects. Oxford, 1886.

THOMAS, Will, The Pilgrim ; A Dialogue on the Life and Actions of King Henry the Eighth, edited by J. A. Froude. London, 1861.

TREVELYAN PAPERS, edited by Sir Walter C. Trevelyan and Sir Charles E. Trevelyan. Part III. Camden Society, 1872.

TYTLER, Patrick Fraser, History of Scotland. Fourth edition. 7 vols. Edinburgh, 1851.

ULMANN, Heinrich, Kaiser Maximilians I. 2 vols. Stuttgart, 1884 and 1891.

By the same, Kaiser Maximilians Absichten auf das Papsttum in den Jahren 1507–1511. Stuttgart, 1888.

VISITATIONS OF THE DIOCESE OF NORWICH, 1492–1532, edited by A. Jessopp. Camden Society, 1888.

W., S., The History of the two Impostors, Lambert Simnel and Perkin Warbeck, etc. London, 1745.

WARE, Annales : Jacobi Waraei De Hibernia et Antiquitatibus eius disquisitiones. Editio secunda. Accesserunt Rerum Hibernicarum Regnante Henrico VII. Annales nunc primum in lucem editi. London, 1658.

WEINREICH, Kaspar, Danziger Chronik, in Script. Rer. Pruss., IV., 725–800.

WILKINS, Concilia Magnæ Britanniæ et Hiberniæ. Vol. iii. London, 1737.

WILL, The, of Henry VII., edited by Thomas Astle. London, 1775.

WINSOR, Justine, Narrative and Critical History of America. Vol. iii. Boston and New York, undated. Chap. i. (the Voyages of the Cabots) written by Charles Deane.

WOOD, Athenæ Oxonienses, edited by Bliss. Vol. i. London, 1813.

WRIOTHESLEY, A Chronicle of England during the Reigns of the Tudors. 2 vols. Edited by Hamilton. Camden Society, 1875. (See Appendix II., p. 401.)

YEAR BOOK, In hoc volumine continentur omnes Anni Regis Henric. Septimi, ab anno primo usque ad annum vicesimum secundum eiusdem Regis, qui antea impressi fuerunt. London, 1580.

ZURITA, Anales de la corona de Aragon. 7 vols. Saragossa, 1610.

COMMENTS ON SPECIAL TOPICS.

BY JAMES GAIRDNER.

By the author's kind indulgence, I am permitted to add a few words on special topics touched upon in this volume, partly to elucidate certain points which may be more or less matters of opinion, and partly to supply additional information and corrections. As to the former, it will be seen that my own view differs occasionally from that of Dr. Busch, though I confess that in some things he has brought me over to his opinion; but while giving my reasons for occasional dissent, I have been even more anxious in these remarks to amplify, or state more clearly, those of his arguments with which I now concur, so as to prevent misconceptions on the part of others. For the rest, where I differ from the author, I do not wish to do more than indicate some grounds for questioning the judgment he has arrived at.

I.—THE TREATY OF MEDINA DEL CAMPO.
(*See pp.* 53, 54, *and Note* 6, *p.* 330.)

Dr. Busch modifies somewhat a criticism he originally made on what I have said in my little book on Henry VII., pp. 92, 93. But he considers that I have over magnified the practical importance to Henry of a clause in this treaty which he had originally overlooked; and on careful consideration I am disposed to agree with him. What I said, indeed, in reference to this clause, that it gave England the key of the position and not Spain, had a specious appearance of truth. It really did seem effectually to protect England (at least, for some time) from being obliged to go to war with France at the bidding of Ferdinand and Isabella; for it seemed to make that obligation altogether conditional. It expressly recognized an existing truce between England and France, and provided that for one year after the expiration of that truce, either Spain or England should be at liberty to make a new truce with France, including the other in it. So that unless war had actually broken out between

England and France (as the Spaniards evidently hoped it had) by the day that the treaty was signed, it looked as if either Spain or England could equally well put off going to war at the other's bidding, almost indefinitely.

Dr. Busch, however, considers the composition of this clause a very sophistical piece of business—"ein höchst sophistisches Machwerk," as he expressively calls it—drawn up to protect Spain from the demands of England, not England from the demands of Spain. And, strange as his reading of it struck me at first, I believe his view is the right one. Indeed, the express words of the clause are undoubtedly to that effect, nor had I overlooked their peculiar tenor ; but it seemed to me that the rights of England were saved in a general way in the latter part of the clause without any express bargain for reciprocity. For a literal translation of the clause (omitting verbiage) reads as follows :—

" Likewise it is agreed, as at present the King of England has a truce with the King of France till the 17th January next, that during the said truce the said King and Queen of Spain shall not be bound to make war on the said King of France at the request of the said King of England ; but when the said truce comes to an end, either of the said Princes, viz. of Spain or England, shall be at liberty for one year following to make a truce or abstain from war with the King of France without the consent of the other, provided that whoever makes the truce shall comprehend the other in it if he wish to be comprehended in the same ; and if he do not wish to be comprehended therein, the party which makes the truce may keep the same. But if war have really broken out this day between the Kings of England and France, then neither of the said princes (to wit, of Spain or England) shall be at liberty to enter a truce without express consent of the other."

The first section of this clause, it will be seen, only protects Spain from being bound to make war at the request of England, so long as the latter has a truce with France. But there are no express words (for none seemed necessary) to protect England against being called on to violate her truce with France at the bidding of Spain. While the truce lasted neither party could be expected to take the offensive against France at the bidding of the other; and when it ended either party was still free to remain at peace with France for one year longer. Thus the terms seemed tolerably equal on the face of things.

But it is quite clear that the Spanish diplomatists did not intend such perfect reciprocity of obligations, and as the treaty was negotiated on Spanish soil, it would have argued extraordinary diplomatic ability on the part of the English envoys, Savage and Nanfan, if they had been able to defeat the purposes of such sovereigns as Ferdinand and Isabella. For if the mutual liabilities of the two Powers had been only such as appeared upon the surface, the main object of the Spanish sovereigns might have been almost indefinitely postponed; Henry was not compelled to go to war with France for a period of nearly two years, and in the mean time the chapter of accidents might give'him great advantages.

Ferdinand, however, was evidently reckoning on the probability of England being involved in a war with France by the mere force of circumstances. Henry was already committed to the protection of Brittany against French aggression; and, moreover, though Ferdinand's ambassadors in England had in vain attempted to bind him by an express compact to make war on France at the bidding of Spain, he had been obliged, as the price of a Spanish alliance, to give them the most solemn assurance in private, attested by an oath of some of his councillors, that he was quite willing to do so, once the alliance was concluded. But at the very time he was giving this assurance to the Spanish ambassadors, he prolonged the truce with France for one year that he might not be called upon to begin hostilities till January, 1490. This truce, undoubtedly, Ferdinand was anxious that he should break or feel that he had some justification for breaking, and he evidently thought that it was not unlikely that it had been broken already, and that actual hostilities had been begun between England and France at the date that the treaty of Medina was signed.

As a matter of fact, Lord Willoughby de Broke with six thousand men was sent over immediately afterwards in aid of Brittany; so that from that day England was virtually a belligerent. And being so (that is, if he was so considered), Henry was bound not to desist from the war or make any new truce with France without the express consent of Spain. But if, contrary to expectation, Henry had succeeded in preserving the peace with France till January, 1490, he must not call upon Spain to begin hostilities during that period, nor even for a year after, if Spain were inclined at that date to make a truce with France herself. For Ferdinand and Isabella had quite enough on their hands while their war with the Moors lasted, and might not be able at that time conveniently to undertake a war with France also—at all events single-handed. This apparently was the object with which the clause was drawn up. But Henry had his own sophistries as well as Ferdinand, and does not seem to have considered himself a belligerent while he was merely aiding Brittany to protect herself, or standing on the defensive at Calais. But to avoid committing himself too deeply, he left the treaty unratified for about a year and a half—that is to say, until some months after the truce had actually expired, and all negotiations for its renewal, and even papal mediation between the two countries, had failed. Nay, the original treaty instrument ratified by Ferdinand and Isabella at Medina, the day after the treaty was concluded, which must have been sent to England to be exchanged for Henry's ratification, was returned into the archives of Spain, where it still remains, with the signatures of Ferdinand and Isabella cut off—a thing no doubt done at the time to make it null and void (see Bergenroth's Spanish Calendar, vol. i. p. 24, footnote).

II.—How Henry proposed to Supplement the Treaty.
(*See pp.* 59, *and Note* 7, *pp.* 330–332.)

Although Ferdinand and Isabella had thus, as we have seen, cancelled their own ratification of the treaty on not receiving Henry's in exchange, Henry himself merely kept the matter in suspense, and at length sent a ratification of his own to Spain, when it was important to him to obtain their active co-operation, in September, 1490. I have shown in my book ("Henry VII.," pp. 94, 95), that in doing so he also sent to Spain a supplementary treaty fully executed on his side, for the purpose of including not only England and Spain, but Maximilian also, in a threefold alliance against France on conditions more favourable to himself. Here I admit readily that my account of the diplomacy was imperfect, and therefore to some extent inaccurate, in taking no notice of an alternative proposal which the English ambassadors also took to Spain. Dr. Busch is quite right that what I have spoken of as a "new treaty conveyed to Spain along with the ratification of the other" (*i.e.* of that of Medina del Campo), was in effect only a proposal for a treaty, though in form a treaty fully executed on one side. But this I think is sufficiently apparent even in my own account of the matter. Ferdinand was in no way committed to the proposed treaty and he did not accept it. But I should have said also that there was another, which was clearly an alternative treaty, executed in like manner on one side, offered to Ferdinand at the same time; which he would not accept either. And this was really the simpler and more satisfactory of the two; for, after citing the terms of the old agreement, so unfavourable to England, it adds that whereas there should be among friends identity of purpose "et in rebus eorum gerendis æqualitas" (a most significant expression), it is concluded that after the commencement of the war neither shall withdraw from it or have any intelligence with France without the other's consent. Then follow provisions, contained also in the alternative treaty, about the sending of Katharine to England and about her dower. With this subject we are not here concerned, except that the identity of the provisions in the two treaties as regards Katharine, shows clearly that they were alternative treaty instruments as Dr. Busch himself points out. But this being so, I confess I cannot understand Dr. Busch's argument as to the treaty instrument referred to in my book, "that the conception is the same as in the treaty of Medina del Campo." Why, both the alternative treaty instruments had in view to modify the injustice of the treaty of Medina, and the difference between them was simply this : that the first forbade either party to make peace without the consent of the other, while the second forbade either to make peace until France had ceded *to both of them* all that they pretended to claim.

Dr. Busch, indeed, tells us (p. 331), that in the preamble to this second treaty, "the undue advantage conceded to Spain is adhered to in accordance with the treaty of Medina del Campo, and it is only further on that this is not again sufficiently expressed." The preamble does indeed *cite* the unequal terms laid down in the treaty of Medina, but it does so with these words premised : "quod *quamquam* in dictis literis inter eos ut præmittitur confectis . . . concordatum . . . fuerit;" and below we read, "*tamen*, quia in hujusmodi ipsis literis et capitulis," *i.e.*, "yet, because in the articles of the said treaty, certain points were not sufficiently clearly laid down about the war, it is agreed," etc. This surely does not mean retention of the undue advantage. It does look, no doubt, as if the old treaty was not to be superseded, but only supplemented in some points—that was Henry's insinuating way of putting it. But what he meant was expressed in definite language enough, and it seems extraordinary to me that Dr. Busch should think that the effect of the unequal arrangement was still continued, though "not again sufficiently clearly expressed." To me it seems quite "sufficiently clearly expressed," that that arrangement was to be altered, and Ferdinand, I am pretty sure, saw it clearly too. For the actual effect of the words of the treaty in this point is as follows : "*Although* it was provided by the treaty that," etc. . . . . "yet, as there are a good many points not therein sufficiently provided for, . . . it is agreed that neither prince shall desist from the war within two years without the other's consent, unless *not only* Normandy and Aquitaine be recovered by England, *but also* Roussillon and Cerdagne for Spain."

Of course it was no diplomatic triumph, because Ferdinand declined to accept either of the proposed modifications of the old treaty, and, most likely, Henry never expected him to do so. Ferdinand, in fact, ultimately got all he wanted when Henry made a mere demonstration of active hostility against France. But Henry got all he wanted by the mere demonstration also; and he was never again under any kind of obligation to make war for the sake of Spain.

III. KATHARINE GORDON.

(See page 118.)

It is not wonderful that Dr. Busch should have fallen into one slight error in which closer investigators have fallen as well. But it is a mistake that Sir Matthias, or, as he is more commonly called, Sir Matthew Cradock, was the second husband of Perkin Warbeck's wife. He was really the third; and, moreover, she was not buried by his side at Swansea, for she had yet a fourth husband after him, and found her grave ultimately in Berkshire, though either Sir Matthew, during their joint lives, or his executors just after his death, had erected a very fine tomb for himself and her, which still exists, with their effigies upon it, in Swansea church, in what is called the Herberts' Chapel. Of this monument an engraving will be found in Traherne's Historical Notices of Sir Matthew Cradock, a pamphlet published at Llanovery in 1840. Mr. Traherne also contributed to the Archæologia (vol. xxxii. p. 448) some further information about her and her last husband, Christopher Ashton, Esq., of Fyfield, near Abingdon, and an engraving of the tomb at Fyfield, in which her remains really rest. But Mr. Traherne himself is mistaken as to the order of her husbands. So it is desirable here to state the truth, I believe for the first time.

The first that she married after Perkin Warbeck's death appears to have been James Strangways, who was gentleman usher of the Chamber in the beginning of Henry VIII.'s reign, and apparently it was not till Henry VIII.'s time that she married him. Under Henry VII., when her first husband had come to such a disgraceful end, she resumed her maiden name of Gordon. As "lady Katherin Gourdon" she is mentioned as being present at the "fyancells" (or betrothal) of the Princess Margaret to James IV. of Scotland at Richmond, in January, 1502–3 (Leland's "Collectanea," iv. 260); and she seems to have been still a widow when, on the 2nd August, 1510 (2 Hen. VIII.), the king settled upon her some lands in Berkshire, once the property of the attainted earl of Lincoln, on condition that she should not go out of England, either to Scotland or to any other foreign country, without royal licence. On her marriage with Strangways she surrendered the patent of this grant, and a new grant of the lands was made to her husband and herself in survivorship. This new grant, which is dated February 13, 1512, is to "James Strangways, gentleman usher of the Chamber, and Katharine his wife, formerly Katharine Gordon" (Calendar of State Papers, Henry VIII., vol. i., No. 3005). In 1517 she was again a widow, and, on the 23rd June, received a further grant of lands in Berkshire out of those which had belonged to the Earl of Lincoln, again on the condition that she should not quit England for Scotland or any other foreign country (ib., vol. ii., No. 3391). A month later she had become the wife of Matthew Cradock, and as such she obtained, on the 24th July, 1517, a licence from the king to dwell with her husband in Wales, notwithstanding the restrictions previously placed upon her to remain in England (ib., vol. ii., No. 3512). Matthew Cradock was not yet knighted; but he was a gentleman of some importance in Glamorganshire, and had furnished for the French war of 1513 a ship of 240 tons (named after himself, *The Matthew Cradock*), and 195 men in her, he himself being captain (ib., vol. i., Nos. 3591, 3977, 5761). Sir Matthew died between June and August, 1531. Some time afterwards she married Christopher Ashton, another gentleman usher of the Chamber, who lived with her at Fyfield, one of the Berkshire manors granted to herself (ib., vol. xiii. pt. i., No. 190 (25) and p. 574). She made her will on the 12th Oct., 1537, in which she calls herself "some-time wife unto James Strangwis, late of Fyfelde aforesaid, esquire, deceased, and executrix of the testament and last will of the same James Strangwis; and also late wife unto my dear and well-beloved husband, Sir Matthew Cradock, of Cardiff in Wales, in the County of Glamorgan and Morgan, knight, deceased, and executrix of the testament and last will of the said Sir Matthew." She must have died very shortly after making her will, as it was proved on the 5th November following. Her tomb, on the north side of the chancel of Fyfield church, is called the "Lady Gordon's Monument" to this day.

IV. Sir Robert Curzon.

(*See pages* 168, 364.)

Dr. Busch has added so much to my account of the unfortunate Earl of Suffolk, and made it so much more lucid, that I quite regret that he has not corrected me a little further. In what I previously wrote on the subject, I had overlooked Molinet's testimony (cited above, pp. 362, 363) as to Suffolk's having gone as far as St. Omer. On the other hand, Dr. Busch fails to see that this materially affects my reason for believing that Curzon did not even from the first play the part of a spy on Suffolk, as stated by Polydore and Hall. Dr. Busch agrees with what I have said on this point, but I fear I must retract it. The chief reason I gave for so thinking (Lett. and Pap., i. pref. xl.) was that "Curzon was not sent after Suffolk, but went before him." And it is quite true that all the documents relating to this matter show that Curzon did go before him to the court of Maximilian, while of his going to St. Omer, or to any place in Flanders, they speak not a word. But it was only on his second flight that he went to Maximilian, of which Polydore Vergil and Hall take no notice, but say that he went to Flanders both on his first and on his second flight. Moreover, the instructions given to Guildford and Hatton in September, 1499, rather suggested that Suffolk, on his first flight, had got no further than Calais; whereas Molinet's evidence shows distinctly that he had gone as far as St. Omer. He did not, it is true, reach the court of his aunt, the Duchess Margaret, as Polydore Vergil and Hall assert; but he did make some little sojourn on the borders of Flanders, for St. Omer was in those days a Flemish town. And it was then, no doubt, that Curzon began to act as a spy upon him, for he obtained leave from the king to quit his post at Hammes on the 29th August, 1499, which was very shortly after Suffolk's *first* flight, the pretext on which this leave of absence was given being to enable him to go to Turkey and fight against the Infidels. True, it was a very convenient pretext; for there is no doubt that he actually went and gave his services in this cause to Maximilian, who created him a baron of the Holy Roman Empire. But it did not prevent his acting as a spy on Suffolk first.

Moreover, Polydore and Hall are not likely to be mistaken when they distinctly tell us that a belief in Curzon's double-dealing was generally entertained at the time, for reasons which are plainly stated, viz., first, that he had no apparent reason for disaffection; and secondly, that after all was over, he returned and was received into favour. To these reasons, manifest in his own day, we may add the fact that he had a pension of £400 a year given him by the Crown— an allowance worth fully ten times its nominal value now. Further, my attention has been called to the facts mentioned in Wodderspoon's Memorials of Ipswich, p. 256, that Curzon received King Henry VIII. in his house at Ipswich on the 8th October, 1522, and that Katharine of Arragon also honoured him with a visit in 1517. We know of no instance of men pardoned for real disloyalty receiving such favours from either the first or the second Tudor.

One argument, indeed, seems still to militate against the old view, and is certainly a weighty one. There is no doubt that it was owing to information sent by Curzon to Suffolk that the latter made his second escape from England; for we are told (Lett. and Pap. i. 134) that Curzon on his way to Turkey spoke to Maximilian of the "murders and tyrannies" of Henry VII. and of the purpose of Suffolk "to recover his right"; on which Maximilian declared his willingness, if he had "one of King Edward's blood in his hands," to help him to obtain the crown. It was this distinct assurance (although Maximilian afterwards denied having given it) that induced the unhappy earl to fly a second time; and if Curzon sent any such intimation to Suffolk privately, he was certainly a traitor to the king.

It is conceivable, no doubt, that playing the spy, he might have extracted this assurance from Maximilian, and sent it to the king as well as to Suffolk; in which case it was a shamefully wicked attempt to entangle Suffolk in a new conspiracy. But the fact that Suffolk was able to escape the king's vigilance—even though it may have been after the lapse of a year or more—makes this supposition rather improbable.

Nevertheless we ought, I think, to give some weight to the considerations above referred to, which, Polydore tells us, influenced the opinion of contemporaries, even if we should suppose that opinion itself to be mistaken. Curzon had suffered no wrong at the hands of Henry VII., and had no apparent cause för disaffection when he went over to Henry's enemies; neither was he in any way punished by the king for doing so, but after the whole conspiracy had been laid open and avenged he was freely taken into the king's favour. If these facts strongly suggested to contemporaries a suspicion that he had been acting secretly in the king's interest from the first, I cannot help thinking that the date of the licence given him by the king to quit his post (29 August, 1499) is not without significance. Nine days earlier, on the 20th August, a proclamation was issued to prevent any one leaving the Kingdom without a licence; and this was undoubtedly issued in consequence of Suffolk's first flight. It was not, however, according to P. V., until after the Earl's return, which very speedily followed, that Curzon fled to Flanders ("statim ut comes e Flandria reversus est, Robertus Cursonus . . . in Flandriam fugit"). And that he was supposed to go thither as a fugitive is itself suggestive. Why should he have done so? The document which gave him leave of absence to go and fight against the Infidels, commissioned him to surrender Hammes Castle to the keeping of Sir Sampson Norton, Sir Richard Lovelas and William Pawne; and this he surely must have done. His supposed flight then could not have been a real flight at all. He simply made Flanders the first stage of that journey into Turkey which he was fully permitted to undertake; and it would be easy when he was there to assume the character of a man turned out of office, and capable of sympathising with anybody else who had grudges against the king.

And here I must express my dissent from Professor Busch's new reading of the meaning of Polydore Vergil's words, where he thinks the pronoun "eum" in one place refers to Suffolk, and not, as Hall understood it, to Henry VII. The point has reference to the admission of Curzon into the order of knighthood, which surely was naturally owing to the king, as the throne is always the fountain of all honours. Grammatically, perhaps, Professor Busch is so far right that it *might* apply to Suffolk; but seeing that the very same pronoun *eum* in the preceding sentence undoubtedly applies to the king, and that the whole argument of Polydore suggests that Curzon was indebted to Henry, and was a very able instrument in his hands (*homo valens et meditatus*, Polydore calls him—"an able man who knew what he was about"), I think there can be very little doubt that even apart from his allegiance Curzon felt himself under greater obligations to Henry VII. than he did to Suffolk. At least this is what Polydore wishes us to believe, and we ought surely in fairness to try whether it will do. So far, at all events, there is no difficulty. Late in the autumn, probably, of the year 1499—just after Guildford and Hatton have succeeded in getting the fugitive earl to return from St. Omer—Curzon makes his pretended flight as a disaffected person to Flanders, to discover what more he can about Yorkist conspiracies, by winning the confidence of other Yorkist fugitives, and to inform Henry of the results of his inquiries.

There is always this penalty upon double dealing, that an agent cannot be wholly trusted by his employers. Just after this occurred the great blot on Henry's reign—the judicial murder of the poor innocent Earl of Warwick; and we know from Molinet (what English contemporaries did not like to say) that the fact gave much displeasure to the English nobility in general (Molinet's Chroniques, iv. 121). Would it have been at all wonderful if at this time Curzon shared the general feeling of honest men, and felt himself among the really disaffected? Even as double dealer, no doubt, it suited the part he had to play to talk to Maximilian of the "murders and tyrannies" of King Henry VII., and of the purpose of Suffolk to recover his right; but might he not have spoken with some real feeling in the matter, and even wished Suffolk success? It looks not improbable. Taking the lowest estimate of such a man—as a time-server—he might possibly think Henry was going to be driven from his throne if Suffolk could have organized a conspiracy against him. In that case he had made Suffolk his friend by communicating to him the offer of Maximilian; and for himself he was going to Turkey to be out of the way, and compound matters with his own conscience, whatever occurred, by a pious work in fighting against the Infidels. Without thinking very badly of him, we may suppose that he was really perplexed about his true duty, and really wanted to be out of the way, as, very likely, he may have done for some time past. Only the decided success or failure of a cause settles all questions of political duty in the end; and however Suffolk might be an object of compassion, there could be no doubt that duty rallied all men ultimately to the side of Henry. Curzon could make his peace with the king all the better because he had done him service of real importance in Flanders; and if he had been for awhile even in thought disaffected, it suited both Henry's policy and his own to hush the matter up.

But when did Curzon cease to be treated externally as a conspirator against the king? As late as Easter, 1505, his friend Sir Matthew Browne, who had been one of his sureties for the keeping of Hammes Castle, actually forfeited his recognisance of £500 by judgment of the Lord Chancellor. Suffolk was then in the hands of the Duke of Gueldres, and desperate as his fortunes were, it was not clear even yet that he might not become dangerous to Henry. Next year he was Henry's prisoner, and all danger was over. Curzon made his peace with the king, and ultimately even received the pension above mentioned (though this, I think, must have been given him by Henry VIII., for I find no record of it under Henry VII.), and the forfeiture of Browne's recognisance was ultimately annulled in the second year of Henry VIII. (Calendar of Henry VIII., vol. i. No. 1155).

END OF VOL. I.

PRINTED BY WILLIAM CLOWES AND SONS, LIMITED,
LONDON AND BECCLES.

By Lieut.-Gen. McLEOD INNES, R.E., V.C.

LUCKNOW AND OUDE IN THE MUTINY.

A NARRATIVE AND A STUDY.

With numerous Maps, Plans, etc.   Demy 8vo, cloth, 12*s.* net.

The Times says : "A most valuable contribution to the history of the great crisis."

The Army and Navy Gazette says : "Recent literature concerning the Indian Mutiny has brought us nothing so valuable. . . . His knowledge of India and her people is accurate and profound. . . . The facts are marshalled with consummation and skill. In this book General Innes has rendered invaluable service in regard to the military history of the Mutiny and of the Indian Empire."

The Athenæum says : "We rise from its perusal with clearer and better defined knowledge than we before possessed of the origin and spread of the Sepoy Mutiny."

The Speaker says : "No previous account approaches that of General Innes in charm of style, fulness of detail, and sound military judgment. . . . The first five chapters are devoted to an admirable *resumé* of the great Mutiny as a whole, in which the various stages are separately treated, and the strategic considerations presented with a clearness attained by no previous writer. A keen but never unkindly critic, General Innes has made a notable contribution to military literature from a standpoint higher than that of the mere soldier."

The Broad Arrow says : "A more truthful, instructive, and interesting contribution to the history of the great Indian convulsion of 1857 than the work before us has never before been made. Only authenticated facts are used as the basis of all criticism : the different springs of action are carefully weighed and examined ; theories are subjected to closer examination ; and finally the kernel of the work, namely, the defence of the Residency, is here dealt with by one who played a conspicuous part in that defence."

The Scotsman says : "The story has never been told with the same fulness and accuracy, or with equal clearness and precision. . . . Far and away the completest and most satisfactory book on its subject."

The Pall Mall Gazette says : "A book full of most interesting and valuable matter—a book the only fault of which is the over-modesty which has betrayed its author into ignoring almost entirely his own gallant personality. The book comes nearer a comprehensive yet succinct history of the Mutiny than do treatises of much greater detail. The General Sketch of the Mutiny is a masterpiece of lucid and pregnant condensation."

The Manchester Guardian says : "We have had many previous accounts of the defence, but none so full, clear, and intelligible."

The Review of Reviews says : "A contribution to our knowledge of the inner history of the rebellion whose value cannot be over-estimated."

LONDON : A. D. INNES & CO., 31 & 32, BEDFORD STREET, STRAND.

By ROBERT K. DOUGLAS.

New and cheaper Edition.

SOCIETY IN CHINA.

An Account of the Every-day Life of the Chinese People. Social, Political, and Religious. Crown 8vo, cloth, 6s. Library Edition, with 22 Illustrations. Demy 8vo, cloth, 16s.

Mr. Henry Norman, in "Peoples and Politics of the Far East," says: "Professor Douglas's book tells the truth about China in so indisputable and entertaining a manner, and he speaks with so much authority, that there is very little left for any one else to say. I have omitted from this volume much of my material about China, and my experiences there, simply because Professor Douglas's work has covered the ground finally."

The Times says: "Not only does Mr. Douglas's book supply a complete conspectus of the polity, institutions, manners, and sentiments of this petrified race, but it reviews clearly the history of foreign relations with China, and points a moral which British diplomatists would do well to lay to heart in future difficulties with China."

The Scotsman says: "It is an excellent book, perhaps the best and most trustworthy on its subject. . . . So easily accessible in its popular form, it ought to have a wide circulation."

The Admiralty and Horse Guards Gazette says: "From beginning to end 'Society in China' is the most complete and intelligent work on China and her people which has yet been published."

The Daily Telegraph says: "Every page of this admirable book teems with interesting information."

The Daily Graphic says: "This book is one of the best that has ever been written on China. In addition to being a storehouse of knowledge, it is one of the most entertaining works published for a long time."

By the Rev. Canon I. GREGORY SMITH, M.A., LL.D.

CHRISTIAN MONASTICISM FROM THE FOURTH TO THE NINTH CENTURIES OF THE CHRISTIAN ERA.

Large crown 8vo, cloth, 14s.

The Spectator says: "The authorities are exactly what they ought to be . . . the best English text-book on the general subject of early monasticism. . . . It will be long before another more exhaustive is required."

The School Guardian says: "As a book of reference the work cannot be too highly praised "

The Manchester Guardian says: "A good outline of the early history of a remarkable movement."

The Morning Post says: "The book is evidently the result of much research and its literary style is admirable."

The Church Quarterly says: "A contribution of real value to the literature of its subject."

The Speaker says: "An excellent book."

LONDON: A. D. INNES & CO., 31 & 32, BEDFORD STREET, STRAND.

www.ingramcontent.com/pod-product-compliance
Lightning Source LLC
Chambersburg PA
CBHW022013110726
47901CB00006B/1501